SRA
Reading Mastery
Signature Edition

Presentation Book B
Grade 3

Siegfried Engelmann
Susan Hanner

 **SRA**

Columbus, OH

SRAonline.com

 SRA

Send all inquiries to this address:
SRA/McGraw-Hill
4400 Easton Commons
Columbus, OH 43219

ISBN: 978-0-07-612577-7
MHID: 0-07-612577-7

10 11 12 13 LMN 21 20 19 18 17

Table of Contents

Curriculum Map *following final lesson*

Lessons 71–75 • Planning Page   *Looking Ahead*

	Lesson 71	**Lesson 72**	**Lesson 73**	**Lesson 74**	**Lesson 75**
LESSON EVENTS	Vocabulary Sentence **Vocabulary Sentence** Reading Words Story Background Story Reading Paired Practice Independent Work Workcheck Spelling	Vocabulary Sentence Reading Words Story Reading Paired Practice Independent Work Workcheck Spelling	Vocabulary Sentences Reading Words Story Reading Paired Practice Independent Work Workcheck Spelling	Vocabulary Sentence **Vocabulary Sentence** Reading Words Paired Practice Study Items Independent Work Workcheck Spelling	Vocabulary Sentence Reading Words Story Reading Crossword Puzzle Fluency: Rate/ Accuracy Independent Work Workcheck Spelling
VOCABULARY SENTENCE	#17: The <u>boring</u> speaker <u>disturbed</u> the <u>audience</u>. **#18: A lot of <u>folks</u> <u>mobbed</u> the <u>cute</u> singer.**	#18: A lot of <u>folks</u> <u>mobbed</u> the <u>cute</u> singer.	sentence #16 sentence #17 sentence #18	#18: A lot of <u>folks</u> <u>mobbed</u> the <u>cute</u> singer. **#19: The <u>tour</u> to the islands was a <u>fantastic</u> experience.**	#19: The <u>tour</u> to the islands was a <u>fantastic</u> <u>experience</u>.
READING WORDS: WORD TYPES	modeled words mixed words	modeled words multi-syllable words 2-syllable words	modeled words mixed words	mixed words multi-syllable words	mixed words
NEW VOCABULARY	deserve	library somersault o'clock yucky	admission tightrope	tune beak	chant flop jammed
STORY BACKGROUND	*Teaching Animals a Hard Trick*				
STORY	*The Pet Shop*	*Maria and Waldo Make A Deal*	*Waldo Starts Training Animals*	*The Animal Show*	*A Big Crowd*
SKILL ITEMS	Vocabulary sentences		Vocabulary sentence	Vocabulary sentences	Sequencing Crossword puzzle
SPECIAL MATERIALS				2 identical glass glasses, water	Thermometer charts
SPECIAL PROJECTS/ ACTIVITIES				Activity after lesson 74	

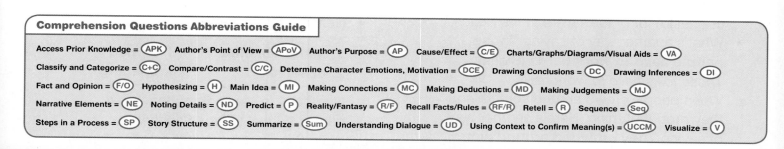

Comprehension Questions Abbreviations Guide

Access Prior Knowledge = APK   Author's Point of View = APoV   Author's Purpose = AP   Cause/Effect = C/E   Charts/Graphs/Diagrams/Visual Aids = VA

Classify and Categorize = C+C   Compare/Contrast = C/C   Determine Character Emotions, Motivation = DCE   Drawing Conclusions = DC   Drawing Inferences = DI

Fact and Opinion = F/O   Hypothesizing = H   Main Idea = MI   Making Connections = MC   Making Deductions = MD   Making Judgements = MJ

Narrative Elements = NE   Noting Details = ND   Predict = P   Reality/Fantasy = R/F   Recall Facts/Rules = RF/R   Retell = R   Sequence = Seq

Steps in a Process = SP   Story Structure = SS   Summarize = Sum   Understanding Dialogue = UD   Using Context to Confirm Meaning(s) = UCCM   Visualize = V

LESSON 71

EXERCISE 1

Vocabulary Review

a. You learned a sentence that tells what the speaker did.
- Everybody, say the sentence. Get ready. (Signal.) *The boring speaker disturbed the audience.*
- (Repeat until firm.)

b. I'll say part of the sentence. When I stop, you say the next word. Listen: The boring speaker … Everybody, what's the next word? (Signal.) *Disturbed.*

c. Listen: The … Everybody, what's the next word? (Signal.) *Boring.*
- Say the whole sentence. Get ready. (Signal.) *The boring speaker disturbed the audience.*

d. Listen: The boring speaker disturbed the … Everybody, what's the next word? (Signal.) *Audience.*

EXERCISE 2

Vocabulary

a. **Find page 367 in your textbook.** ✔
- Touch sentence 18. ✔
- This is a new vocabulary sentence. It says: A lot of folks mobbed the cute singer. Everybody, read that sentence. Get ready. (Signal.) *A lot of folks mobbed the cute singer.*
- Close your eyes and say the sentence. Get ready. (Signal.) *A lot of folks mobbed the cute singer.*
- (Repeat until firm.)

b. The sentence tells about a lot of **folks**. **Folks** is another word for **people**. Everybody, what's another way of saying **A lot of people were at the beach?** (Signal.) *A lot of folks were at the beach.*
- What's another way of saying **Those people have to work hard?** (Signal.) *Those folks have to work hard.*

c. When people crowd around something, they **mob** that thing. Here's another way of saying **They crowded around him: They mobbed him.**

- Your turn. What's another way of saying **A thousand people crowded into the building?** (Signal.) *A thousand people mobbed the building.*
- What's another way of saying **They crowded around the science exhibit?** (Signal.) *They mobbed the science exhibit.*

d. The sentence says that a lot of folks mobbed the **cute** singer. Something that is good-looking and charming is cute.
- Everybody, what's another word for **good-looking and charming?** (Signal.) *Cute.*
- What's another way of saying **The little girl was very good-looking and charming?** (Signal.) *The little girl was cute.*
- What's another way of saying **He thinks that he is good-looking and charming?** (Signal.) *He thinks that he is cute.*

e. Listen to the sentence again: A lot of folks mobbed the cute singer.
- Everybody, say the sentence. Get ready. (Signal.) *A lot of folks mobbed the cute singer.*

f. Everybody, what's another word for **crowded around?** (Signal.) *Mobbed.*
- What's another word for **good-looking and charming?** (Signal.) *Cute.*
- What's another word for **people?** (Signal.) *Folks.*
- (Repeat step f until firm.)

EXERCISE 3

Reading Words

Column 1

a. Find lesson 71 in your textbook. ✔
- Touch column 1. ✔
- (Teacher reference:)

| 1. Maria Sanchez | 3. dipped |
| 2. deserve | 4. opening |

b. Number 1 is **Maria Sanchez.** What name? (Signal.) *Maria Sanchez.*

c. Word 2 is **deserve.** What word? (Signal.) *Deserve.*

- Spell **deserve.** Get ready. (Tap for each letter.) *D-E-S-E-R-V-E.*
- Something you **deserve** is something you should receive. Here's another way of saying **That criminal should receive punishment: That criminal deserves punishment.**
- Everybody, what's another way of saying **I should receive more money?** (Signal.) *I deserve more money.*
- What's another way of saying **She should receive more thanks for what she does?** (Signal.) *She deserves more thanks for what she does.*

d. Word 3. What word? (Signal.) *Dipped.*
- Spell **dipped.** Get ready. (Tap for each letter.) *D-I-P-P-E-D.*

e. Word 4. What word? (Signal.) *Opening.*
- Spell **opening.** Get ready. (Tap for each letter.) *O-P-E-N-I-N-G.*

f. Let's read those words again, the fast way.
- Number 1. What name? (Signal.) *Maria Sanchez.*
- Word 2. What word? (Signal.) *Deserve.*
- (Repeat for: **3. dipped, 4. opening.**)

g. (Repeat step f until firm.)

Column 2

h. Find column 2. ✔
- *(Teacher reference:)*

1. unusually	4. purred
2. spoon	5. meowed
3. rice	6. hamsters

i. Word 1. What word? (Signal.) *Unusually.*
- (Repeat for words 2–6.)

j. Let's read those words again.
- Word 1. What word? (Signal.) *Unusually.*
- (Repeat for words 2–6.)

k. (Repeat step j until firm.)

Individual Turns

(For columns 1 and 2: Call on individual students, each to read one to three words per turn.)

EXERCISE 4

Story Background

a. Find part B in your textbook. ✔

- You're going to read the next story about Waldo. First you'll read the information passage. It gives some facts about teaching animals a hard trick.

b. Everybody, touch the title. ✔
- (Call on a student to read the title.) *[Teaching Animals a Hard Trick.]*
- Everybody, what's the title? (Signal.) *Teaching Animals a Hard Trick.* (ND)
- You already learned the basic rule for teaching tricks to animals. Now you're going to learn about how to teach a trick that is very hard.

c. (Call on individual students to read the passage, each student reading two or three sentences at a time. Ask the specified questions as the students read.)

Teaching Animals a Hard Trick

In the last lesson, you learned the main rule for training an animal to do a trick. Sometimes you reward the animal.

- When do you reward the animal? (Call on a student. Idea: *When the animal does the trick; when the animal does what you tell it to do.*) (RF/R)

Sometimes you don't reward the animal.

- When don't you reward the animal? (Call on a student. Ideas: *When the animal doesn't do what you tell it to do; when the animal doesn't do the trick.*) (RF/R)

The animal learns that the only way to get the reward is to do the trick. The animal wants the reward, so the animal does the trick.

Sometimes, the animal is not able to do the trick that you want it to do. Maybe you want the animal to jump up in the air and do a somersault before it lands on its feet.

- Everybody, look at the pictures. They show a dog jumping up in the air and doing a backward somersault before it lands. Touch picture 1. ✔ (VA)

- What's the dog doing in that picture? (Call on a student. Idea: *Jumping into the air.*) (VA)
- Everybody, touch picture 2. ✔ (VA)
- What's the dog doing in that picture? (Call on a student. Ideas: *Turning a somersault; flipping backwards.*) (VA)
- Everybody, touch picture 3. ✔ (VA)
- What's the dog doing in that picture? (Call on a student. Idea: *Landing on its feet.*) (VA)
- Everybody, would a dog be able to do that trick the first time it tried? (Signal.) *No.* (MJ)
- I wonder how you train the dog to do that trick. We'll find out.

When you teach a hard trick, you don't follow the rule for teaching simple tricks.

- What is the rule for simple tricks? (Call on a student. Idea: *Reward the animal when it does what you tell it to do.*) (RF/R)
- We can't use that rule for hard tricks.

Here's why: The animal can't do the trick at first. So the animal will not receive any rewards for doing the trick. If the animal doesn't receive any rewards, the animal will stop trying to learn the trick.

- That's a big problem. The animal can't possibly do the trick at first, so, if we reward the animal only for doing the trick, we won't reward the animal at all. The animal gets no rewards. So the animal will stop trying to do the trick.
- Everybody, if the trick is very hard, will the animal be able to do it at first? (Signal.) *No.* (RF/R)
- So will the animal get a reward for doing the trick? (Signal.) *No.* (RF/R)
- So will the animal keep trying to do the trick? (Signal.) *No.* (RF/R)
- Why not? (Call on a student. Idea: *Because it's not getting any rewards.*) (DC)

Here is what you do when you're teaching the animal a trick it can't do at first: You help the animal do the trick. And you reward the animal for <u>trying</u> to do it.

- You help the animal. And what do you reward the animal for doing? (Call on a student. Idea: *Trying to do the trick.*) (RF/R)

You keep rewarding the animal for getting closer to doing the trick.

- That's the secret for teaching hard tricks. You keep rewarding the animal for getting closer and closer to doing the trick.

To teach the animal how to somersault in the air, you put a belt around the animal so the animal won't fall on its back. Then you reward the animal each time the animal <u>tries</u> to do the trick. At first, you may give the animal a reward if the animal just jumps up in the air.

- Everybody, touch the picture below that shows the dog with a belt around it. ✔ (VA)
- That dog is learning the trick. In the picture the dog is just jumping into the air. Everybody, will the dog receive a reward for doing that at first? (Signal.) *Yes.* (RF/R)

After a while, you may reward the animal for jumping up in the air and trying to lean backward. If the animal just jumps in the air, you don't reward it anymore.

- Listen to that part again: After a while, you may reward the animal for jumping up in the air and trying to lean backward. If the animal just jumps in the air, you don't reward it anymore.
- Everybody, if the animal just jumps up in the air now, do you reward it? (Signal.) *No.* (RF/R)
- What does the animal have to do now to get a reward? (Call on a student. Idea: *Jump in the air and lean backward.*) (RF/R)

Later, you may reward the animal if the animal turns upside down in the air.

- Everybody, when the animal can turn upside down, would you reward the animal for just jumping in the air? (Signal.) *No.* (RF/R)

- Would you reward the animal for jumping up and leaning back? (Signal.) *No.* (RF/R)
- What would you reward the animal for? (Call on a student. Idea: *Turning upside down.*) (RF/R)
- What keeps the animal from landing on its head? (Call on a student. Idea: *The belt.*) (ND)
- I don't think the animal would keep trying to do the trick if it landed on its head each time it tried. That's not a very good reward.

Later, you may reward the animal if the animal turns almost all the way around in the air.

- Everybody, when the animal can do this, would you reward the animal for turning upside down in the air? (Signal.) *No.* (RF/R)
- What would you reward the animal for? (Call on a student. Idea: *Turning almost all the way around in the air.*) (RF/R)

Later, you may reward the animal for turning all the way around in the air. At last, you reward the animal if the animal does the trick without the belt around it.

- Now the animal is doing the trick without any help at all.

Remember, if the animal can't do the trick at first, you reward the animal for <u>trying</u> to do the trick. When the animal gets better, you don't reward the animal unless the animal comes closer to doing the trick.

By rewarding animals for trying, you can teach an animal amazing things. You can teach a dog to ride a bicycle. You can teach a dog to turn a doorknob and to open a door. You can teach a dog to get the newspaper and bring it to you.

- Name some other hard tricks you might teach a dog. (Call on individual students. Ideas: *Jumping through a hoop, climbing a ladder, etc.*) (DC)

Story Reading

a. Find part C in your textbook. ✔
- The error limit for group reading is 11 errors.
b. Everybody, touch the title. ✔
- (Call on a student to read the title.) *[The Pet Shop.]*
- Everybody, what's the title? (Signal.) *The Pet Shop.* (ND)
c. (Call on individual students to read the story, each student reading two or three sentences at a time. Ask the specified questions as the students read.)

- (**Correct errors:** Tell the word. Direct the student to reread the sentence.)
- (If the group makes more than 11 errors, direct the students to reread the story.)

The Pet Shop

The owner of the pet shop was named Maria Sanchez.

- Everybody, what was her name? (Signal.) *Maria Sanchez.* (ND)

She loved the pet shop, but it was not making money.

- What does that mean, it wasn't making money? (Call on a student. Ideas: *People weren't buying things; business was bad.*) (UCCM)

Each month she had less money. She knew that if things didn't change, she would have to close the shop very soon. She had tried different ways to interest more people in buying pets. She put ads in the newspaper, and she did a lot of other things.

- What other things could she do? (Call on individual students. Ideas: *Send flyers to people; put ads on the radio; etc.*) (DI)

Maria Sanchez usually spent a lot of time thinking about how to make her pet shop more interesting and about how she could make the pet shop earn more money.

- Name the two things she spent a lot of time thinking about. (Call on a student. Idea: *How to make her pet shop more interesting and how the pet shop could earn more money.*) (ND)

But she had never thought of cooking up the kind of food that Waldo made. She stood there in the kitchen of her pet shop, watching Waldo pour different things that he had cooked into a big bowl. She couldn't believe what was happening. Birds and squirrels were looking in the window. Dogs and cats were running around outside the window. The animals in the pet shop were howling and screeching and jumping around.

"What makes the animals act that way?" she asked Waldo.

He smiled and looked up from his cooking. "My food," he said. "They love it."

She picked up a large spoon. "Do you mind if I try some?" she asked.

"No," he said. "It's very good food."

- Everybody, is she going to like it? (Signal.) *No.* (P)

She dipped her spoon into the bowl, filled it with food, and put it in her mouth. She tried not to make a sour face, but the food tasted bad— very bad. "My," she said, trying to smile, "that certainly has an unusual taste."

- Everybody, is that true? (Signal.) *Yes.* (DC)
- Why do you think she doesn't just tell Waldo that it tastes bad? (Call on a student. Idea: *Because she doesn't want to hurt his feelings.*) (DI)

She wasn't really lying. The food did have an unusual taste—unusually bad.

Waldo finished cooking some corn and rice. He dumped the corn and rice into the bowl with the other things he had cooked. Then he began to whistle. He walked into the pet shop with his food. Maria followed.

Waldo began opening the bird cages. "No," Maria shouted. "We'll never be able to catch them."

"They won't fly away," Waldo said. And he was right. They landed on his shoulders and on his head. Two of them tried to get into the ✹ bowl of food, but he brushed them away with his hand.

- Everybody, show me how he did that. ✔ (V)

Those two birds landed on his shoulder and sat there.

Next, Waldo went to the cages with the cats. He opened all the cages. "No," Maria shouted. "They'll go after the birds."

- Everybody, will they? (Signal.) *No.* (MJ)
- What will they do? (Call on a student. Idea: *Try to get Waldo's food.*) (P)

"No, they won't," Waldo said. And he was right again. The cats rubbed against Waldo's legs. They put their tails high in the air. They meowed and purred loudly.

- Show me how a cat purrs loudly. (Call on a student.) ✔ (V)

Next, Waldo opened the cages for the dogs.

- What is Maria going to say now? (Call on a student. Idea: *No, they'll chase the cats.*) (P)

"No," Maria started to say. Then she stopped and said, "I know. They won't chase the cats."

"Right," Waldo said. The dogs didn't pay any attention to the cats. They barked and wagged their tails and jumped up to get the food from the bowl. Waldo held the bowl high so they couldn't reach it.

Then Waldo opened all the other cages. Rabbits and hamsters and other animals came out and tried to get close to Waldo.

Maria couldn't believe what she saw. Here was Waldo holding a bowl of food above his head. More than fifty animals were around him and on him.

- Look at the picture and see if you can name some of the animals that are sitting on him. (Call on a student. Ideas: *Parrots, other birds; etc.*) (VA)
- What are some of the other animals that you see in the picture? (Call on a student. Ideas: *Monkey, squirrel, mouse; etc.*) (VA)
- Read the rest of the story to yourself and be ready to answer some questions. Raise your hand when you're done.

Waldo said, "Now we can show people the pets that you have for sale." Waldo walked to the front window of the pet shop. He sat down with his back to the window. The animals crowded close to him and tried to reach the bowl, but he held it above his head.

Maria looked outside the window. People who were passing by the pet shop stopped and looked. They smiled and pointed to the different animals. At first there were only four or five people standing in front of the window. But soon there was a large crowd of more than thirty people.

Waldo was now feeding the animals. He held a little bit of food high in the air. The birds flew from

his shoulders and his head. They flew around and took the food from his hand. Maria watched. The other animals watched. The people outside the window watched. The birds went back to Waldo's shoulders and head. Then Waldo fed the dogs and cats and rabbits and hamsters and all the other animals. The people outside were laughing and pointing.

- (After all students have raised their hand:)
- Where did Waldo sit? (Call on a student. Idea: *In the window of the pet shop.*) (ND)
- Everybody, which animals did he feed first? (Signal.) *Birds.* (ND)
- How did they get the food? (Call on a student. Idea: *They flew around and took it from Waldo's hand.*) (ND)
- Then what did the birds do? (Call on a student. Idea: *Flew back to Waldo's head and shoulders.*) (ND)
- Name some of the animals that he fed after he fed the birds. (Call on a student. Ideas: *Dogs, cats, rabbits; etc.*) (ND)
- What was happening outside the window? (Call on a student. Idea: *A crowd was gathering.*) (ND)
- Do you think that some of these people will buy pets? (Call on a student. Student preference.) (MJ)

EXERCISE 6

Paired Practice

You're going to read aloud to your partner. Today the **B** members will read first. Then the **A** members will read from the star to the end of the story. (Observe students and give feedback.)

End-of-lesson activities

INDEPENDENT WORK

Now finish the independent work for lesson 71. Raise your hand when you're finished. (Observe students and give feedback.)

WORKCHECK

a. (Direct students to take out their marking pencils.)

- We're going to check your independent work. Remember, if you got an item wrong, make an **X** next to the item.

b. (For each item: Read the item. Call on a student to answer it. If the answer is wrong, say the correct answer. Refer to the Answer Key for the correct answers.)

c. Now use your marking pencil to fix up any items you got wrong. Remember, all mistakes must be fixed up before you hand in your independent work.

SPELLING

(Present Spelling lesson 71 after completing Reading lesson 71. See *Spelling Presentation Book.*)

EXERCISE 1

Vocabulary Review

a. Here's the new vocabulary sentence: A lot of folks mobbed the cute singer.
   - Everybody, say the sentence. Get ready. (Signal.) *A lot of folks mobbed the cute singer.*
   - (Repeat until firm.)
b. Everybody, what's another word for **good-looking and charming?** (Signal.) *Cute.*
   - What's another word for **people?** (Signal.) *Folks.*
   - What's another word for **crowded around?** (Signal.) *Mobbed.*

EXERCISE 2

Reading Words

Column 1

a. **Find lesson 72 in your textbook.** ✔
   - Touch column 1. ✔
   - (Teacher reference:)

1. library	**3. music**
2. taught	**4. somersault**

b. Word 1 is **library.** What word? (Signal.) *Library.*
   - Spell **library.** Get ready. (Tap for each letter.) L-I-B-R-A-R-Y.
   - Who knows what a library is? (Call on a student. Idea: *A place with lots of books.*)
c. Word 2 is **taught.** What word? (Signal.) *Taught.*
   - Spell **taught.** Get ready. (Tap for each letter.) T-A-U-G-H-T.
d. Word 3 is **music.** What word? (Signal.) *Music.*
   - Spell **music.** Get ready. (Tap for each letter.) M-U-S-I-C.
e. Word 4 is **somersault.** What word? (Signal.) *Somersault.*
   - Who can tell me how to do a somersault? (Call on a student. Idea: *You squat down, bend over, and roll over.*)

f. Let's read those words again, the fast way.
   - Word 1. What word? (Signal.) *Library.*
   - (Repeat for words 2–4.)
g. (Repeat step f until firm.)

Column 2

h. Find column 2. ✔
   - (Teacher reference:)

1. <u>seven</u>teen	**3. <u>pupp</u>ies**
2. <u>is</u>n't	**4. <u>re</u>ward**

i. These words have more than one part. The first part of each word is underlined.
j. Word 1. What's the underlined part? (Signal.) *seven.*
   - What's the whole word? (Signal.) *Seventeen.*
   - Word 2. What's the underlined part? (Signal.) *is.*
   - What's the whole word? (Signal.) *Isn't.*
   - Word 3. What's the underlined part? (Signal.) *pupp.*
   - What's the whole word? (Signal.) *Puppies.*
   - Word 4. What's the underlined part? (Signal.) *re.*
   - What's the whole word? (Signal.) *Reward.*
k. Let's read those words again, the fast way.
   - Word 1. What word? (Signal.) *Seventeen.*
   - (Repeat for words 2–4.)
l. (Repeat step k until firm.)

Column 3

m. Find column 3. ✔
   - (Teacher reference:)

1. o'clock	**3. mommy**
2. yucky	**4. deserves**

n. Word 1. What word? (Signal.) *O'clock.*
   - O'clock tells about the hour of the day. If the hour is five, the time is five o'clock.
   - Everybody, what's the time if the hour is seven? (Signal.) *Seven o'clock.*
   - What's the time if the hour is eleven? (Signal.) *Eleven o'clock.*
o. Word 2. What word? (Signal.) *Yucky.*

- Things that are unpleasant or foul or slimy are **yucky.**
- Everybody, what's another way of saying **That mud feels slimy?** (Signal.) *That mud feels yucky.*
- What's another way of saying **That garbage smells foul?** (Signal.) *That garbage smells yucky.*
- What's another way of saying **That food tastes unpleasant?** (Signal.) *That food tastes yucky.*

p. Word 3. What word? (Signal.) *Mommy.*
q. Word 4. What word? (Signal.) *Deserves.*
r. Let's read those words again.
- Word 1. What word? (Signal.) *O'clock.*
- (Repeat for: **2. yucky, 3. mommy, 4. deserves.**)
s. (Repeat step r until firm.)

Individual Turns

(For columns 1–3: Call on individual students, each to read one to three words per turn.)

EXERCISE 3

Fact Review

a. Let's review some facts you have learned. First we'll go over the facts together. Then I'll call on individual students to do some facts.
b. Everybody, tell me which is **bigger** than Earth—**Jupiter** or **Io.** (Pause.) Get ready. (Signal.) *Jupiter.* APK
- Tell me what color lava is after it's cooled **a little bit.** (Pause.) Get ready. (Signal.) *Brown.* APK
- Tell me what color lava is after it's **completely cooled.** (Pause.) Get ready. (Signal.) *Gray.* APK
- If you drop something on Earth, it falls to the ground. Tell me what makes it fall. (Pause.) Get ready. (Signal.) *Gravity.* APK
- (Repeat step b until firm.)
c. Tell me which has **more** gravity—**Jupiter** or **Earth.** (Pause.) Get ready. (Signal.) *Jupiter.* APK
- So tell me where you would feel **heavier—on Jupiter** or **on Earth.** (Pause.) Get ready. (Signal.) *On Jupiter.* APK
- Tell me how long it takes Io to go all the way around Jupiter. Less than (Pause.) Get ready. (Signal.) *Two days.* APK
- (Repeat step c until firm.)

d. Tell me how much oxygen is on Io. (Pause.) Get ready. (Signal.) *None.* APK
- If you are **very heavy** on a planet, that planet has lots of (Pause.) Get ready. (Signal.) *Gravity.* RF/R
- Tell me where you can jump three meters high—**on Io** or **on Jupiter.** (Pause.) Get ready. (Signal.) *On Io.* APK
- (Repeat step d until firm.)
e. Let's say an object weighed 20 pounds on Earth. Tell me if that object would weigh **more** than 20 pounds on Jupiter. (Pause.) Get ready. (Signal.) *Yes.* RF/R
- Tell me which has **less** gravity—**Jupiter** or **Io.** (Pause.) Get ready. (Signal.) *Io.* APK
- Tell me if you would feel **heavy** or **light** on Io. (Pause.) Get ready. (Signal.) *Light.* APK
- (Repeat step e until firm.)

Individual Turns

Now I'm going to call on individual students to do some facts.

(Call on individual students to do the set of facts in step b, step c, step d, or step e.)

EXERCISE 4

Story Reading

a. Find part B in your textbook. ✔
- The error limit for group reading is 13 errors.
b. Everybody, touch the title. ✔
- (Call on a student to read the title.) *[Maria and Waldo Make a Deal.]*
- Everybody, what's the title? (Signal.) *Maria and Waldo Make a Deal.* ND
- What kind of deal do you think they'll make? (Call on a student. Idea: *Waldo will train animals and Maria will give him money.*) P
c. (Call on individual students to read the story, each student reading two or three sentences at a time. Ask the specified questions as the students read.)

- (**Correct errors:** Tell the word. Direct the student to reread the sentence.)
- (If the group makes more than 13 errors, direct the students to reread the story.)

Maria and Waldo Make a Deal

Usually, Maria Sanchez sold eight pets a week. On the first day that Waldo cooked, she sold seventeen pets.

- Everybody, how many pets did she usually sell in a week? (Signal.) *8.* (ND)
- How many did she sell in just one day when Waldo cooked? (Signal.) *17.* (ND)
- Why do you think she sold so many more pets when Waldo cooked? (Call on a student. Idea: *Because the animals looked so cute.*) (DI)

And all those animals were sold in less than one hour. By the time Waldo had finished cooking, it was already four o'clock. The pet shop closed at five o'clock. But during that time, Maria had sold more pets than she usually sold in two weeks.

As Waldo sat in the window of the pet shop with birds, and dogs, and cats, and other animals, people gathered to watch. They pointed and laughed and said things like, "Oh, look at that striped kitten. Isn't it cute?"

Some of the children watching the show said things like, "Mommy, can we get that little dog with the long ears? Please?"

- Say that the way a little kid would say it to a mother. (Call on a student. Student should speak in a pleading tone of voice.) (V)

The mothers and fathers were saying things like, "Well, I don't know if we should have a pet," but the children kept saying, "Please. Can we just go inside and look at it?"

- What's going to happen if they go inside and look at it? (Call on a student. Idea: *They'll buy it.*) (P)

So the parents and the children would go inside the pet shop. And once they picked up one of the animals and petted it, they usually bought the animal. Parents and children were holding cats that were purring and puppies that were licking faces and wagging tails. They were giving little bits of Waldo's food to parrots and rabbits. And Maria was very busy.

- What do you think she was doing? (Call on a student. Ideas: *Selling animals; collecting money.*) (DI)

When the pet shop closed at five o'clock, she turned to Waldo and said, "If you want a job here, you've got it. In fact, I'll make a deal with you. I'll give you 20¢ for every dollar that I make when I sell a pet."

- What's the deal she wants to make with Waldo? (Call on a student. Idea: *She'll give him twenty cents for every dollar she makes from selling pets.*) (ND)

Waldo jumped up and down.

- Everybody, did he like that deal? (Signal.) *Yes.* (DC)

"All right!" he shouted. "This is great!" After he and Maria talked some more, Waldo ran home. On the way, he thought about how he would change his plans about cooking in the garage.

- What were his plans about cooking in the garage? (Call on a student. Idea: *He'd fix up the garage so he could cook and sleep there.*) (APK)
- Why would he want to change those plans now? (Call on a student. Idea: *He can cook at the pet shop so he doesn't need the garage.*) (DI)

Waldo was out of breath when he got home. His mother said, "Waldo, what happened to you? You're nearly an hour late."

Waldo said, "I've got a new job. I'm going to work in a pet shop."

Waldo's father said, "That sounds fine. What are you going to do at the pet shop?"

Waldo said, "I'm going to train the animals and show them off so that people will want to buy them."

Waldo's mother said, "How are you going to do that?"

Before Waldo could answer, his sister Fran said, "I know what ⭐ he's going to do. He's going to cook up some of that yucky food. Don't let him do it."

Waldo's brother said, "Yeah, make him stop cooking."

Waldo's sister said, "Yeah, and make him answer the phone."

"Wait a minute," Waldo's father said. "Let Waldo talk."

Waldo said, "I'm going to cook, but I won't cook around here. I'll cook at the pet shop."

Waldo's brother said, "That place will stink so much that nobody will come in it."

Waldo started to get angry. "I'm a good cook," he said. "I can't help it if the only people who like my food are not people."

- Listen to what Waldo said again: "I can't help it if the only people who like my food are not people!" What does that mean, the only people who like his food aren't people? (Call on a student. Idea: *Only animals like his food.*) UCCM
- The next sentence has an underlined word. Remember how to read it.

Waldo's sister laughed and said, "Oh, that makes a <u>lot</u> of sense. The only people are not people. Make him stop cooking."

- She's not being serious when she says, "That makes a lot of sense." She's making fun of Waldo. Listen to how she said that: "Oh, that makes a **lot** of sense. The only people are not people."

Waldo's father said to Fran, "Just be quiet and give Waldo a chance to tell us about his job."

Waldo explained, "I'll cook at the pet shop and I'll make a lot of money. The owner of the pet shop told me that she would give me 20¢ for every dollar that she made from selling a pet. I'll be rich."

- What does that mean, I'll be rich? (Call on a student. Idea: *He'll have a lot of money.*) UCCM

"Yeah," his brother said. "But how are people going to buy pets if they're holding their noses all the time?"

- Why does Waldo's brother think they'll be holding their noses? (Call on a student. Idea: *Because Waldo's food smells so bad.*) DI

"Be quiet," Waldo's mother said. "I think Waldo deserves a chance to cook again if he cooks at the pet shop."

- Everybody, is his mother going to let him cook at the pet shop? (Signal.) *Yes.* DC
- Read the rest of the story to yourself and be ready to answer some questions. Raise your hand when you're done.

Waldo said, "There's a kitchen in the back of the pet shop and I can cook everything I need there. And I did it today." Waldo went on to explain how he had cooked the food, let the animals out of their cages, and sat in the window with them. "The pet shop was mobbed," he concluded. "And people were buying pets like crazy."

"I think that's very nice," his mother said.

"I think it stinks," his sister said. "You should make him …" "That's enough," Waldo's father said.

Waldo said, "I think I'm going to start training some of the animals to do tricks. I don't know much about training animals, but I'll get some books and read them. I know that the animals will do anything to get my food. So I'll use the food as a reward. And I think I can train the animals to do some really good tricks."

Waldo's father said, "As long as you don't cook around the house, I think your plan sounds very good. You may work in the pet shop."

- (After all students have raised their hand:)
- Everybody, did Waldo know a lot about training animals? (Signal.) *No.* ⓃⒹ
- How did he plan to find out how to train animals? (Call on a student. Idea: *Get books and study.*) ⓃⒹ
- Everybody, did Waldo's parents like the plan? (Signal.) *Yes.* ⓃⒹ

EXERCISE 5

Paired Practice

You're going to read aloud to your partner. Today the **A** members will read first. Then the **B** members will read from the star to the end of the story. (Observe students and give feedback.)

End-of-lesson Activities

INDEPENDENT WORK

Now finish the independent work for lesson 72. Raise your hand when you're finished. (Observe students and give feedback.)

WORKCHECK

a. (Direct students to take out their marking pencils.)
- We're going to check your independent work. Remember, if you got an item wrong, make an **X** next to the item.
b. (For each item: Read the item. Call on a student to answer it. If the answer is wrong, say the correct answer. Refer to the Answer Key for the correct answers.)
c. Now use your marking pencil to fix up any items you got wrong. Remember, all mistakes must be fixed up before you hand in your independent work.

SPELLING

(Present Spelling lesson 72 after completing Reading lesson 72. See *Spelling Presentation Book.*)

EXERCISE 1

Vocabulary Review

a. You learned a sentence that tells what made them anxious.
- Everybody, say that sentence. Get ready. (Signal.) *The incredible whales made them anxious.*
- (Repeat until firm.)

b. You learned a sentence that tells what the boring speaker did.
- Say that sentence. Get ready. (Signal.) *The boring speaker disturbed the audience.*
- (Repeat until firm.)

c. Here's the last sentence you learned: A lot of folks mobbed the cute singer.
- Everybody, say that sentence. Get ready. (Signal.) *A lot of folks mobbed the cute singer.*
- (Repeat until firm.)

d. Everybody, what's another word for **people?** (Signal.) *Folks.*
- What's another word for **good-looking and charming?** (Signal.) *Cute.*
- What's another word for **crowded around?** (Signal.) *Mobbed.*

e. Once more. Say the sentence that tells what a lot of folks did. Get ready. (Signal.) *A lot of folks mobbed the cute singer.*

EXERCISE 2

Reading Words

Column 1

a. **Find lesson 73 in your textbook.** ✔
- Touch column 1. ✔
- (Teacher reference:)

1. admission	4. tour
2. fantastic	5. music
3. experience	

b. Word 1 is **admission.** What word? (Signal.) *Admission.*
- The amount you pay to get into a show is the **admission** for that show. If the amount you pay is a dollar, the admission is a dollar.

- Everybody, what's another way of saying **The amount you pay to get in is five dollars?** (Signal.) *The admission is five dollars.*
- What's another way of saying **The show is free?** (Signal.) *The admission is free.*

c. Word 2 is **fantastic.** What word? (Signal.) *Fantastic.*

d. Word 3 is **experience.** What word? (Signal.) *Experience.*

e. Word 4 is **tour.** What word? (Signal.) *Tour.*
- Spell **tour.** Get ready. (Tap for each letter.) *T-O-U-R.*

f. Word 5. What word? (Signal.) *Music.*
- Spell **music.** Get ready. (Tap for each letter.) *M-U-S-I-C.*

g. Let's read those words again, the fast way.
- Word 1. What word? (Signal.) *Admission.*
- (Repeat for words 2–5.)

h. (Repeat step g until firm.)

Column 2

i. Find column 2. ✔
- (Teacher reference:)

1. tightrope	4. somersaults
2. library	5. peppy
3. taught	6. rewarded

j. Word 1. What word? (Signal.) *Tightrope.*
- A tightrope is a rope high above the ground that circus people walk on.

k. Word 2. What word? (Signal.) *Library.*
- Spell **library.** Get ready. (Tap for each letter.) *L-I-B-R-A-R-Y.*

l. Word 3. What word? (Signal.) *Taught.*
- Spell **taught.** Get ready. (Tap for each letter.) *T-A-U-G-H-T.*

m. Word 4. What word? (Signal.) *Somersaults.*
- (Repeat for words 5 and 6.)

n. Let's read those words again.
- Word 1. What word? (Signal.) *Tightrope.*
- (Repeat for words 2–6.)

o. (Repeat step n until firm.)

Individual Turns

(For columns 1 and 2: Call on individual students, each to read one to three words per turn.)

EXERCISE 3

Story Reading

a. Find part B in your textbook. ✔
- The error limit for group reading is 13 errors.

b. Everybody, touch the title. ✔
- (Call on a student to read the title.) [Waldo Starts Training Animals.]
- Everybody, what's the title? (Signal.) Waldo Starts Training Animals. (ND)

c. (Call on individual students to read the story, each student reading two or three sentences at a time. Ask the specified questions as the students read.)

- (**Correct errors:** Tell the word. Direct the student to reread the sentence.)
- (If the group makes more than 13 errors, direct the students to reread the story.)

Waldo Starts Training Animals

The man at the library looked at the stack of books that Waldo had and he said, "What are you going to do with all those books on animal training?" Waldo explained.

- Everybody, where is Waldo now? (Signal.) At the library. (DC)
- What is he doing at the library? (Call on a student. Idea: Getting books about animal training.) (DC)
- What do you think he said when he explained what the books were for? (Call on a student. Idea: I'm going to start training animals.) (P)

He had so many books that he was tired of carrying them by the time he got home. He took them to his room, and he started to read. And he kept on reading during every spare minute he had.

- When would you have a spare minute? (Call on a student. Ideas: Before dinner, after school.) (DC)

Some books told about training your pet dog. Others told about training horses. Others told about training birds. Others told about training monkeys.

Within a month, Waldo had read all the books. But he didn't wait to finish the books before he started to train animals at the pet shop. At first he taught the animals easy tricks. He found out that the easiest animals to teach are birds.

- That's strange. Everybody, which are the easiest animals to train? (Signal.) Birds. (ND)

The day after he read a book on how to train pigeons, he trained three pigeons to tap dance.

Here's what he did. He took one pigeon from a cage. He put the pigeon on a table. He waited for the pigeon to turn its head to one side. When it turned its head, he gave it a tiny bit of food.

- Everybody, when did he reward the pigeon? (Signal.) When it turned its head. (ND)
- So what do you think the pigeon will keep on doing to get another reward? (Signal.) Turning its head. (DC)

Then he waited for the pigeon to turn its head and move its feet. Again, he gave the pigeon a bit of food.

- He changed his rule for rewarding the pigeon. What does the pigeon have to do now to get a reward? (Call on a student. Idea: Turn its head and move its feet.) (ND)

Then Waldo waited until the pigeon turned its head, moved its feet and flapped its wings.

- What does the pigeon have to do now to get a reward? (Call on a student. Idea: Turn its head, move its feet, and flap its wings.) (ND)

Lesson 73 **15**

Within a few minutes, the pigeon was doing a dance with its wings out to the sides. Now Waldo attached little buttons to the pigeon's feet.

- What are the buttons going to do each time the pigeon takes a step? (Call on a student. Idea: *Make a tapping noise.*) Ⓓ

Each time the pigeon took a step, the buttons on its feet made tapping sounds. Now Waldo turned on a CD player. The music he played was very peppy.

- What kind of music is peppy? (Call on a student. Ideas: *Lively; jazzy; etc.*) Ⓓ
- Make some peppy music. (Call on a student.) ✔ Ⓥ

Whenever the pigeon moved its feet in time with the music, Waldo gave it a little bit of food.

- What does that mean, in time with the music? (Call on a student. Idea: *It tapped with the beat of the music.*) ⓊⒸⒸⓂ
- Do you know how to clap in time with music? (Call on individual students. Student preference.) Ⓜ
- The pigeon had to move its feet so that the buttons tapped in time with the music.

Within half an hour, the pigeon was tap dancing in time with the music. The training for the second pigeon was a little different.

- Everybody, did Waldo train the second pigeon the same way he trained the first pigeon? (Signal.) *No.* Ⓝ
- Do you have any idea why he would train the second pigeon in a different way? (Call on a student. Student preference.) Ⓜ

Waldo left the music on and let the first pigeon keep dancing. From time to time, Waldo gave the first pigeon a bit of food. Waldo rewarded the second pigeon each time it did something the first pigeon did.

- When did he reward the second pigeon? (Call on a student. Idea: *Each time it did something the first pigeon did.*) Ⓝ

Within a few minutes, the second pigeon was holding its wings out to the sides and dancing in time with the music.

- How long did it take the second pigeon to learn to dance? (Call on a student. Idea: *A few minutes.*) Ⓝ
- How long did it take the first pigeon? (Call on a student. Idea: *Half an hour.*) Ⓝ

Waldo kept the music playing and brought out the third pigeon.

- How is he going to train this pigeon? (Call on a student. Idea: *The same way he trained the second pigeon.*) Ⓟ

When Maria came out of the back room and saw what the pigeons were doing, her eyes became very large.

- Why? (Call on a student. Idea: *Because she couldn't believe what she saw.*) Ⓜ

"I've never seen ⭐ anything like this in my life," she said. The three pigeons were dancing in time with the music.

Waldo moved the table to the front window and turned the music on very loud. Within a few minutes, a large crowd gathered. They were clapping in time with the music and smiling at the animals.

- Look at the picture. Everybody, what are the pigeons doing? (Signal.) *Dancing.* Ⓥ

- What are the people doing? (Signal.) *Clapping.* (VA)
- Why is that question mark above the pigeon on the sidewalk? (Call on a student. Idea: *He doesn't understand why the pigeons are dancing.*) (VA)

Within a few more minutes, people were coming into the pet shop and trying to talk to Maria over the loud music. "Are those pigeons for sale?" they asked.

Maria answered, "No, they're not. But if you want a dancing pigeon, we can train one for you."

- Why didn't she want to sell those pigeons? (Call on a student. Idea: *Because she wanted to use them for advertising.*) (DI)

That day, she took orders for eight dancing pigeons.

- What does that mean, she took orders for pigeons? (Call on a student. Idea: *People wanted pigeons and paid for them.*) (UCCM)
- Everybody, do you think these dancing pigeons cost the same as regular pigeons? (Signal.) *No.* (MJ)
- Why would the dancing pigeons cost more? (Call on a student. Idea: *Because they had to be trained.*) (DC)

After the shop closed, Maria said to Waldo, "If you can train animals to do things like that, we should put on some shows. People would pay to see tap-dancing birds."

Waldo smiled. "That's a great idea," he said. "But let's not just have tap-dancing birds. Let's have cats that ride bicycles, and dogs that do somersaults in the air, and rabbits that walk tightropes."

"Do you know how to train animals to do those tricks?" she asked.

Waldo explained that he had books that told how to teach hard tricks and that he would study those books and learn how to train the animals.

- Read the rest of the story to yourself and be ready to answer some questions. When you read this part of the story, read it carefully and look at each picture the story tells you to look at. The pictures show some of the things that Waldo did. Raise your hand when you're done.

So Waldo read during all his spare time. And when he went to the pet shop, he worked with the animals. The first thing he did was train a rabbit to walk on a tightrope. Actually, he had two tightropes side by side. First he stretched two thick ropes out on a table. Each time the rabbit stood with all four feet on the ropes, he gave the rabbit a bit of food. (Look at picture 1.) When the rabbit got good at doing this part of the trick, Waldo changed the rule for rewarding the rabbit. Now he gave a reward if the rabbit kept all four feet on the ropes while walking forward. Then Waldo stretched the ropes out a few centimeters above the table. He put a little belt around the rabbit and held on to the belt so that the rabbit wouldn't fall if it missed the ropes. (Look at picture 2.) Waldo rewarded the rabbit for trying to walk on the ropes. Soon the rabbit could walk without any help from Waldo. Then Waldo put up thin ropes instead of thick ones. (Look at picture 3.) When Waldo finished training the animal to walk on the thin ropes, he decided to make a super trick. So he trained four mice to sit on the back of the rabbit as the rabbit walked along the tightropes. (Look at picture 4.)

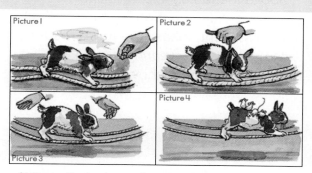

- (After all students have raised their hand:)

- Everybody, when he trained the rabbit to walk on the tightrope, where did he put the ropes at first? (Signal.) *On the table.* (ND)
- Everybody, were those thin ropes or thick ropes? (Signal.) *Thick ropes.* (ND)
- At first, what did he reward the rabbit for doing? (Call on a student. Idea: *Standing with all four paws on the ropes.*) (ND)
- When Waldo put the ropes a few centimeters above the table, how did he help the rabbit so it wouldn't fall? (Call on a student. Idea: *He put a belt around it.*) (ND)
- What did he reward the rabbit for doing? (Call on a student. Idea: *For trying to walk on the ropes.*) (ND)
- What did Waldo do after the rabbit could walk on the thick ropes without any help? (Call on a student. Idea: *He used thin ropes.*) (ND)
- After the rabbit could walk on the thin ropes without any help, what did Waldo do to make a super trick? (Call on a student. Idea: *He trained four mice to sit on the rabbit's back as the rabbit walked the tight ropes.*) (ND)
- How do you think he rewarded the mice for sitting on the rabbit's back? (Call on a student. Idea: *He gave them some food he had cooked.*) (P)
- The pictures show the way Waldo trained the rabbit. Everybody, where are the ropes in the first picture? (Signal.) *On the table.* (VA)
- What is the rabbit trying to do? (Call on a student. Idea: *Walk on the ropes.*) (VA)
- What is Waldo holding? (Call on a student. Idea: *Some of his food.*) (VA)
- Where are the ropes in picture 2? (Call on a student. Idea: *A few centimeters above the table.*) (VA)
- What is different about picture 3? (Call on a student. Ideas: *The ropes are thin; the rabbit's not wearing a belt.*) (VA)
- The super trick is shown in picture 4.

Paired Practice

You're going to read aloud to your partner. Today the **B** members will read first. Then the **A** members will read from the star to the end of the story. (Observe students and give feedback.)

End-of-lesson Activities

INDEPENDENT WORK

Now finish the independent work for lesson 73. Raise your hand when you're finished. (Observe students and give feedback.)

WORKCHECK

a. (Direct students to take out their marking pencils.)
- We're going to check your independent work. Remember, if you got an item wrong, make an **X** next to the item.
b. (For each item: Read the item. Call on a student to answer it. If the answer is wrong, say the correct answer. Refer to the Answer Key for the correct answers.)
c. Now use your marking pencil to fix up any items you got wrong. Remember, all mistakes must be fixed up before you hand in your independent work.

SPELLING

(Present Spelling lesson 73 after completing Reading lesson 73. See *Spelling Presentation Book.*)

> *Note:* You will need some special materials for some study items in lesson 74. See page 23 for details.

EXERCISE 1

Vocabulary Review

a. You learned a sentence that tells what a lot of folks did.
- Everybody, say the sentence. Get ready. (Signal.) *A lot of folks mobbed the cute singer.*
- (Repeat until firm.)

b. I'll say part of the sentence. When I stop, you say the next word. Listen: A lot of folks mobbed the … Everybody, what's the next word? (Signal.) *Cute.*

c. Listen: A lot of … Everybody, what's the next word? (Signal.) *Folks.*
- Say the whole sentence. Get ready. (Signal.) *A lot of folks mobbed the cute singer.*

d. Listen: A lot of folks … Everybody, what's the next word? (Signal.) *Mobbed.*

EXERCISE 2

Vocabulary

a. **Find page 367 in your textbook.** ✔
- Touch sentence 19. ✔
- This is a new vocabulary sentence. It says: The tour to the islands was a fantastic experience. Everybody, read that sentence. Get ready. (Signal.) *The tour to the islands was a fantastic experience.*
- Close your eyes and say the sentence. Get ready. (Signal.) *The tour to the islands was a fantastic experience.*
- (Repeat until firm.)

b. When you go on a tour, you take a trip to several places. A trip to four islands is called a tour to four islands.
- Everybody, what's a trip to three castles called? (Signal.) *A tour to three castles.*
- What's a trip to seven cities called? (Signal.) *A tour to seven cities.*

c. The sentence says the tour was a fantastic experience. Another word for **fantastic** is **wonderful.**
- Everybody, what's another way of saying **They had a wonderful time?** (Signal.) *They had a fantastic time.*

- What's another way of saying **The food was wonderful?** (Signal.) *The food was fantastic.*

d. Each thing you do is an **experience.** If you go to the store, your experience is going to the store. If you tour seven cities, your experience is touring seven cities.

e. Listen to the sentence again: The tour to the islands was a fantastic experience. Everybody, say the sentence. Get ready. (Signal.) *The tour to the islands was a fantastic experience.*

f. Everybody, what word describes each thing you do? (Signal.) *Experience.*
- What's another word for **wonderful?** (Signal.) *Fantastic.*
- What's another word for **a trip to several places?** (Signal.) *Tour.*
- (Repeat step f until firm.)

EXERCISE 3

Reading Words

Column 1

a. Find lesson 74 in your textbook. ✔
- Touch column 1. ✔
- (Teacher reference:)

1. tune	3. beak
2. lamb	4. experience

b. Word 1. What word? (Signal.) *Tune.*
- Spell **tune.** Get ready. (Tap for each letter.) *T-U-N-E.*
- A tune is a song. Everybody, what's another way of saying **She sang a simple song?** (Signal.) *She sang a simple tune.*
- What's another way of saying **That song reminds me of the beach?** (Signal.) *That tune reminds me of the beach.*

c. Word 2. What word? (Signal.) *Lamb.*
- Spell **lamb.** Get ready. (Tap for each letter.) *L-A-M-B.*

d. Word 3. What word? (Signal.) *Beak.*
- Spell beak. Get ready. (Tap for each letter.) *B-E-A-K.*

- The bill of a bird is called a **beak.** The bird's nose and mouth are in the beak.
- Everybody, what do we call the bill of a bird? (Signal.) *Beak.*

e. Word 4. What word? (Signal.) *Experience.*

f. Let's read those words again, the fast way.
- Word 1. What word? (Signal.) *Tune.*
- (Repeat for: **2. lamb, 3. beak, 4. experience.**)

g. (Repeat step f until firm.)

Column 2

h. Find column 2. ✔
- (Teacher reference:)

1. <u>applaud</u>ed	4. <u>you</u>'d
2. <u>Home</u>r	5. <u>fan</u>tastic
3. <u>side</u>walk	

i. These words have more than one part. The first part of each word is underlined.

j. Word 1. What's the underlined part? (Signal.) *applaud.*
- What's the whole word? (Signal.) *Applauded.*
- Word 2. What's the underlined part? (Signal.) *home.*
- What's the whole word? (Signal.) *Homer.*
- Word 3. What's the underlined part? (Signal.) *side.*
- What's the whole word? (Signal.) *Sidewalk.*
- Word 4. What's the underlined part? (Signal.) *you.*
- What's the whole word? (Signal.) *You'd.*
- Word 5. What's the underlined part? (Signal.) *fan.*
- What's the whole word? (Signal.) *Fantastic.*

k. Let's read those words again.
- Word 1. What word? (Signal.) *Applauded.*
- (Repeat for words 2–5.)

l. (Repeat step k until firm.)

Column 3

m. Find column 3. ✔
- (Teacher reference:)

1. song	4. stove
2. admission	5. tour
3. reminded	

n. Word 1. What word? (Signal.) *Song.*
- (Repeat for words 2–5.)

o. Let's read those words again.
- Word 1. What word? (Signal.) *Song.*
- (Repeat for words 2–5.)

p. (Repeat step o until firm.)

Individual Turns

(For columns 1–3: Call on individual students, each to read one to three words per turn.)

EXERCISE 4

Story Reading

a. Find part B in your textbook. ✔
- The error limit for group reading is 10 errors.

b. Everybody, touch the title. ✔
- (Call on a student to read the title.) *[The Animal Show.]*
- Everybody, what's the title? (Signal.) *The Animal Show.*

c. (Call on individual students to read the story, each student reading two or three sentences at a time. Ask the specified questions as the students read.)

- (**Correct errors:** Tell the word. Direct the student to reread the sentence.)
- (If the group makes more than 10 errors, direct the students to reread the story.)

The Animal Show

During the third week that Waldo worked at the pet shop, Maria put this sign in the window of the pet shop:

- Let's read what the sign says.

Super Animal Show

Friday, April 4 at 7 o'clock in the evening at Samson High School.
SEE Gormer the rabbit walk the tight rope!
SEE Henry the cat ride a bicycle!
SEE five trick dogs!
SEE Dino—the smartest pony in the world!
Admission $1.00.

- Name some of the acts that Waldo and Maria will put on in this show. (Call on a student. Ideas: *A rabbit walking a tightrope; tap dancing pigeons; etc.*) (ND)
- When is the show going to take place? (Call on a student. Ideas: *Friday at 7 in the evening; April 4.*) (ND)
- Everybody, where will it take place? (Signal.) *Samson High School.* (ND)
- What is the admission? (Signal.) *One dollar.* (ND)
- What does that mean, the admission is one dollar? (Call on a student. Idea: *It costs one dollar to get into the show.*) (UCCM)

Every day that week, a large crowd gathered in front of the pet shop after school. Maria would walk outside and say, "Today we'll show you some of the things that you'll see in the show this Friday night." Then she would introduce Waldo to the crowd. She would say, "This is Waldo Greem. He's the person who trained these animals."

Waldo would wave to the crowd and feel embarrassed as they applauded.

- Everybody, what would the crowd do when Waldo was introduced? (Signal.) *Applaud.* (ND)
- How would Waldo feel? (Signal.) *Embarrassed.* (ND)

Then Waldo would bring some animals outside, and the animals would put on one of the tricks. One day, he brought out one of the trained dogs. This dog held a little hammer in its mouth. Waldo put a row of glasses in front of the dog. Each glass had some water in it, but no two glasses had the same amount of water.

- Listen to that part again.
  Then Waldo would bring some animals outside, and the animals would put on one of the tricks. One day, he brought out one of the trained dogs. This dog held a little hammer in its mouth. Waldo put a row of glasses in front of the dog. Each glass had some water in it, but no two glasses had the same amount of water.

- Everybody, if no two glasses had the same amount of water in them, was the water just as high in any two glasses? (Signal.) *No.* (DC)

When the dog tapped a glass with the hammer, the glass made a ringing sound.

- Did you ever tap a glass with water in it? (Call on a student. Student preference.) (MC)
- Some glasses make a pretty ringing sound, just like a bell.

Here's the rule about the sound each glass made: The more water the glass has, the lower the sound it makes.

- Listen to that rule again and get ready to say it: The more water the glass has, the lower the sound it makes. Everybody, say the rule. Get ready. (Signal.) *The more water the glass has, the lower the sound it makes.* (RF/R)
- (Repeat until firm.)
- Which glass makes a higher sound, one that's almost filled up or one that's almost empty? (Signal.) *One that's almost empty.* (RF/R)
- What kind of sound does the glass that's almost empty make? (Signal.) *A high sound.* (RF/R)

If the glass is almost empty, it makes a high ring. If the glass is almost filled with water, it makes a very low ring.

- Everybody, look at the picture. It shows the dog with the hammer in front of the row of glasses. Touch the glass that would make the **highest** ring when the dog taps it. ✔ (RF/R)
- Touch the glass that would make the lowest ring when the dog taps it. ✔ (RF/R)

Maria told the crowd, "This dog is named Homer. And Homer is going to play 'Mary Had a Little Lamb' on these glasses." Waldo patted the dog on the head and said, "Play the tune." The dog started to tap different glasses. The crowd recognized the song and started to sing as the dog tapped: "Mary had a little lamb, little lamb, little lamb …"

When the dog finished playing the song, it stood up on its hind legs and tossed the hammer high into the air. Waldo caught the hammer and threw a little bit of food high into the air. The dog caught the food. The crowd clapped and cheered. "Do it again," some people said. Then other people joined in. "Yes, do it again. Do it again. Do it again."

"Okay," Waldo said. "We'll do it one more time." Waldo gave the hammer back to Homer, patted Homer on the head, and said, "Play the tune."

And the dog played the tune again, without making one mistake.

The crowd clapped. Maria held up her hands to quiet the crowd. "Remember," she said, "this is just one of the acts that you ⭐ may see this Friday night at Samson High School. Bring your friends and your family."

- Do you think some of the people will go to Samson High School to see the whole show? (Call on a student. Idea: *Yes.*) Ⓟ

❀ On the following afternoon, Waldo had two parrots do tricks on a little swing. The parrots did some amazing things. They held on to the swing with their beaks. They did somersaults on the swing. One parrot stood on the head of the other parrot, and both parrots did a giant somersault. Then one parrot held on to the tail feathers of the other parrot and they spun around and around as the swing went back and forth.

- The picture shows the parrots spinning around while one parrot holds on to the tail feathers of the other parrot.

From time to time, Waldo would toss a little bit of food to the parrots. They would catch the food with their beaks.

- Everybody, touch the parrots' beaks in the picture. ✔ ⓋⒶ
- Touch their tail feathers. ✔ ⓋⒶ

Again the crowd went wild. Again Maria reminded the crowd that the pet shop would put on a full show that Friday night at ❀ Samson High School. She reminded the people to bring their friends and family. "Remember," she said, "The admission is only $1.00."

• • •

- There are three dots in the story. What does that mean? (Call on a student. Idea: *Part of the story is missing.*) ⓈⓈ

Waldo looked at the people who were lined up outside Samson High School.

- Everybody, where is Waldo now? (Signal.) *Samson High School.* ⒹⒸ
- So you can figure out what day of the week it is now. Everybody, what day? (Signal.) *Friday.* ⒹⒾ
- The show hasn't started yet. The people are lined up to get inside.
- Read the rest of the story to yourself and be ready to answer some questions. Raise your hand when you're done.

"Wow," he said. "I think they all brought their friends and their families." There was a line of people that went all the way out to the sidewalk and halfway around the block.

Maria said to Waldo, "The show will start in less than an hour. So you'd better go inside and start cooking your food."

"Right," Waldo said. He had brought all the things that he needed to cook. There was a large kitchen in the high school. So he and Maria had decided to do the cooking in the high school. They thought that plan would be better than cooking in the pet shop and then bringing the food over in a car. Maria had pointed out, "If you cook at the high school, we won't have a thousand animals following the car over to the high school."

So Waldo went to the kitchen of the high school. He laid out the things that he wanted to cook. Then he turned on the stove and waited for it to get hot. He waited and waited. Suddenly, he realized that the stove was not working. He ran from the kitchen and found Maria. "I can't cook," he said. "The stove doesn't work."

Maria didn't say anything for a moment. Then she said, "I'll go back to the pet shop and get some pet food that is supposed to be really good. I just hope the animals will work for that food."

"Me, too," Waldo said.

- (After all students have raised their hand:)
- Everybody, were a lot of people going to watch the show? (Signal.) *Yes.* ⓃⒹ
- Why did Waldo and Maria decide to cook the food at the high school rather than cooking it at the pet shop and then bringing it over in a car? (Call on a student. Idea: *So animals wouldn't follow them.*) ⓃⒹ
- Why would animals follow the car? (Call on a student. Idea: *Because they'd want some of Waldo's food.*) ⒹⒸ
- Why wasn't Waldo able to cook his food in the high school kitchen? (Call on a student. Idea: *Because the stove wouldn't work.*) ⓃⒹ
- What kind of food did Maria decide to use for rewards? (Call on a student. Idea: *Pet food that she had at the pet shop.*) ⓃⒹ
- Do you think the animals will work for that food? (Call on individual students. Student preference.) Ⓟ

Paired Practice

You're going to read aloud to your partner. Today the **A** members will read first. Then the **B** members will read from the star to the end of the story. (Observe students and give feedback.)

Study Items

a. There are some study items on page 22 of the textbook. Everybody, touch the directions at the top of the page. ✔

b. Follow along while I read the directions: Get two glasses that look the same. The glasses must be made of glass, not plastic or paper. Fill one glass half full of water. Tap the glass and listen to the sound it makes. Now fix up the second glass so that it makes the same sound as the first glass. Write the answers to these items.

c. Now let's read the items. (Call on a student to read item 18.) *How much water is in the second glass when both glasses make the same sound?*

d. Let's figure out the answer to that item. (Fill one glass half full.)

- Listen to the sound this glass makes when I tap it. (Tap the first glass. Ask the students:) How much water will be in the second glass when it makes the same sound as the first glass? (Ideas: *Half a glass; the same amount as the first glass.*) ⓇⒻ/Ⓡ

e. (Put a little bit of water in the second glass and tap it. Add more water and tap both glasses to show the similarity in sound. Continue adding water to the second glass and tapping both glasses until the students identify the sounds as being the same.)

f. (Tell the students to write their answer to item 18.)

g. (Call on a student to read item 19.) *Change the amount of water in the second glass so it makes a sound that is lower than the sound of the first glass. Did you add water to the second glass or take water away?* ⓇⒻ/Ⓡ

- (Have students predict if you need to add water or take water away to make a lower sound.)
- (Take water away from second glass. Tap both glasses.)
- (Direct students to write the answer to item 19.)

h. (Call on a student to read item 20.) *Find out how a xylophone works and tell how its keys are like glasses of water.*

- (Assist students in finding information about how a xylophone works; then direct students to write the answer to item 20.)

End-of-lesson Activities

INDEPENDENT WORK

Now finish the independent work for lesson 74. Raise your hand when you're finished. (Observe students and give feedback.)

WORKCHECK

a. (Direct students to take out their marking pencils.)

- We're going to check your independent work. Remember, if you got an item wrong, make an **X** next to the item.

b. (For each item: Read the item. Call on a student to answer it. If the answer is wrong, say the correct answer. Refer to the Answer Key for the correct answers.)

c. Now use your marking pencil to fix up any items you got wrong. Remember, all mistakes must be fixed up before you hand in your independent work.

SPELLING

(Present Spelling lesson 74 after completing Reading lesson 74. See *Spelling Presentation Book.*)

ACTIVITIES

(Present Activity 15 after completing Reading lesson 74. See *Activities across the Curriculum.*)

EXERCISE 1

Vocabulary Review

a. Here's the new vocabulary sentence: The tour to the islands was a fantastic experience.
- Everybody, say the sentence. Get ready. (Signal.) *The tour to the islands was a fantastic experience.*
- (Repeat until firm.)

b. Everybody, what's another word for **wonderful?** (Signal.) *Fantastic.*
- What word describes each thing you do? (Signal.) *Experience.*
- What's another word for **a trip to several places?** (Signal.) *Tour.*

EXERCISE 2

Reading Words

Column 1

a. **Find lesson 75 in your textbook.** ✔
- Touch column 1. ✔
- (Teacher reference:)

1. chant	**5. Gormer**
2. flop	**6. lowest**
3. jammed	**7. pecked**
4. carrot	

b. Word 1. What word? (Signal.) *Chant.*
- Spell **chant.** Get ready. (Tap for each letter.) *C-H-A-N-T.*
- When you chant, you say the same thing over and over. Here's a chant: We want to eat. We want to eat. We want to eat.

c. Word 2. What word? (Signal.) *Flop.*
- Spell **flop.** Get ready. (Tap for each letter.) *F-L-O-P.*
- If something is a **flop,** that thing did not work well. If his invention didn't work well, his invention was a flop.
- Everybody, what would we say if a show did not work well? (Signal.) *The show was a flop.*
- What would we say if his song did not sound very good? (Signal.) *His song was a flop.*

d. Word 3. What word? (Signal.) *Jammed.*
- Spell **jammed.** Get ready. (Tap for each letter.) *J-A-M-M-E-D.*
- **Jammed** is another word for **crowded.** Here's another way of saying **The house was crowded: The house was jammed.**
- Everybody, what's another way of saying **The street was crowded?** (Signal.) *The street was jammed.*

e. Word 4. What word? (Signal.) *Carrot.*
- Spell **carrot.** Get ready. (Tap for each letter.) *C-A-R-R-O-T.*

f. Word 5. What word? (Signal.) *Gormer.*
- (Repeat for words 6 and 7.)

g. Let's read those words again, the fast way.
- Word 1. What word? (Signal.) *Chant.*
- (Repeat for words 2–7.)

h. (Repeat step g until firm.)

EXERCISE 3

Story Reading

a. Find part B in your textbook. ✔
- The error limit for group reading is 12 errors.

b. Everybody, touch the title. ✔
- (Call on a student to read the title.) *[A Big Crowd.]*
- Everybody, what's the title? (Signal.) *A Big Crowd.* (ND)
- Where do you think that big crowd is? (Call on a student. Ideas: *At the high school.*) (P)

c. (Call on individual students to read the story, each student reading two or three sentences at a time. Ask the specified questions as the students read.)

- (**Correct errors:** Tell the word. Direct the student to reread the sentence.)
- (If the group makes more than 12 errors, direct the students to reread the story.)

A Big Crowd

The large hall in Samson High School was jammed.

- What does that mean, the hall was jammed? (Call on a student. Idea: *It was full of people.*) (UCCM)

Maria told Waldo that there were nearly two thousand people in the hall.

- Everybody, how many people were in the hall? (Signal.) *Nearly two thousand.* (ND)
- Were there **less than two thousand** or **more than two thousand?** (Signal.) *Less than two thousand.* (UCCM)

Some people had come from over thirty miles away to see the show. And when Maria walked out on the stage to announce the first act, the crowd cheered and applauded.

But the show was a complete flop.

- Everybody, was the show a good one? (Signal.) *No.* (DC)
- What do you think went wrong? (Call on a student. Ideas: *The animals didn't do their tricks; the food didn't work.*) (P)

Each trick started out pretty well, but then the animals stopped performing.

- Why do you think the animals stopped performing? (Call on a student. Idea: *Because they didn't get any of Waldo's special food.*) (DC)

The first act was Homer. He played "Mary Had a Little Lamb" without making one mistake. Then he tossed the hammer into the air. Waldo caught it and tossed an ordinary dog treat into the air.

- Everybody, is that the kind of reward that Homer works for? (Signal.) *No.* (APK)
- How do you think Homer will respond to a dog treat? (Call on a student. Idea: *He won't like it.*) (MJ)

The dog caught it, took one bite of it, and spit it out.

- What did Homer think of that dog treat? (Call on a student. Idea: *He didn't like it.*) (DC)
- Everybody, do you think he'll keep working for dog treats? (Signal.) *No.* (P)

The crowd began to chant, "Do it again. Do it again."

"All right," Maria said. "Here is 'Mary Had a Little Lamb' one more time." Waldo handed the hammer to Homer. Waldo patted Homer on the head and said, "Play the tune." Homer looked at Waldo, hit the glass that made the lowest sound three times, and dropped the hammer on the floor.

- Everybody, did he play the tune? (Signal.) *No.* (DC)
- How do you think the audience will respond to that? (Call on a student: Idea: *They won't like it.*) (P)

Waldo tried again. He gave the hammer to Homer, patted him on the head, and said, "Play the tune," one more time. This time, Homer just dropped the hammer on the floor and looked down.

Maria came out on the stage smiling. "He's just a little tired, folks. But don't worry, we have other acts."

The other acts were even worse. Gormer the rabbit was next. Here's how Waldo usually rewarded Gormer and the four mice for doing the trick. First, Gormer would stand on the table with his front legs on the tightrope, waiting for the four mice to get on his back. Waldo always gave Gormer a little bit of special food for waiting without moving. As the mice climbed onto Gormer's back, Waldo gave each mouse a little bit of food. Then after the rabbit had walked all the way across the tightrope, Waldo would reward all the animals again with a little bit of food.

- That's how Waldo usually rewarded the animals. But he doesn't have any special food now.

This time, Waldo rewarded the rabbit with little pieces of carrot, and he rewarded the mice with little bits of cheese. Here's what happened: Gormer got in place with his front feet on the tightrope. Waldo gave Gormer a little piece of carrot. The rabbit sniffed the carrot and then started to look around.

- What was it looking for? (Call on a student. Idea: *Its special food.*) (DI)

The four mice climbed onto Gormer's back. As each mouse got in place, Waldo gave the mouse a ⭐ bit of cheese. Not one of the mice ate the cheese. The first three mice just sniffed it and looked away. The fourth mouse sniffed the cheese and then took a bite out of Waldo's finger. Waldo jumped back very suddenly. The rabbit jumped. The mice jumped and started fighting. The rabbit leaped into the air and ran off the stage. One mouse was still hanging on to Gormer. The others were on the table, still fighting.

- Everybody, listen to that part again and get a picture of how bad that act was.

  The four mice climbed onto Gormer's back. As each mouse got in place, Waldo gave the mouse a bit of cheese. Not one of the mice ate the cheese. The first three mice just sniffed it and looked away. The fourth mouse sniffed the cheese and then took a bite out of Waldo's finger. Waldo jumped back very suddenly. The rabbit jumped. The mice jumped and started fighting. The rabbit leaped into the air and ran off the stage. One mouse was still hanging on to Gormer. The others were on the table, still fighting.

- Look at the picture. It shows the end of the act. Why are those lines coming out of Waldo's fingers? (Call on a student. Idea: *Because Waldo's finger hurts.*) (VA)

- What's the rabbit doing? (Call on a student. Idea: *Jumping off the table.*) (VA)
- What are the mice doing? (Call on a student. Ideas: *One is hanging on to the rabbit; three are fighting.*) (VA)

The people in the audience started talking to each other. "What's going on?" some of them were saying. "This isn't a very good show at all."

Maria came onto the stage again. "Sorry about that, folks," she said. She was trying to smile. "But you know how animals are. Let's hope our next act will do a little better. This act is one of the most amazing acts you will ever see. If you've never seen pigeons tap dance, this act will be a real treat for you. And here they are, ladies and gentlemen, the tap-dancing pigeons."

The crowd applauded. Some people were saying, "I've seen this act and it is great."

- Read the rest of the story to yourself and be ready to answer some questions. Raise your hand when you're done.

The tap-dancing pigeons weren't very great this time. Waldo brought out the pigeons, turned on the peppy music, and gave the birds the signal to start dancing. And they danced quite well, at least for a while. Usually, Waldo would toss them little bits of special food as they danced. This time, he tossed them little bits of bird seed. The birds blinked and spit out the seeds. Before the song was half over, one of them stopped dancing and started to peck at the buttons that were attached to its feet. Then one of the other birds started dancing out of time with the music. Soon that pigeon stopped dancing. It pecked at the third bird. The third bird pecked the first bird. The first bird flew to the back of the hall and landed on top of a picture.

"This is a bad act," somebody shouted from the back of the audience. Again, the people in the

> audience began to talk to each other. Maria came out on the stage and smiled. She tried to talk, but the people in the audience did not listen. They were busy talking to each other. They were saying things like, "Who said this was a good show?" and "These animals aren't even trained well."
>
> Waldo was thinking, "I hope this show will be over soon."

- (After all students have raised their hand:)
- How did Waldo usually reward the pigeons as they danced? (Call on a student. Idea: *With special food.*) (ND)
- What did he use to reward them this time? (Call on a student. Idea: *Bird seed.*) (ND)
- Name some things that happened after he gave the pigeons the bird seed. (Call on individual students. Ideas: *The birds spit out the seeds; two birds pecked each other; two birds stopped dancing; one bird danced very slowly; etc.*) (ND)
- How did Waldo feel? (Call on a student. Ideas: *Embarrassed; he wanted the show to be over soon.*) (DCE)

EXERCISE 4

Crossword Puzzle

a. **Everybody, find part A in your workbook.** ✔
- This is a crossword puzzle. To work it, you read each item and write the word that is described in the item.
b. I'll do item 2 with you. Item 2 is under a heading that says **across.** That means word 2 goes from side to side. It's item 2, so it's marked with a little 2 on the puzzle.
- Everybody, touch the **2** on the puzzle and run your finger **across** to show where word 2-across will go. ✔
c. Here's item 2-across: A planet that is close to the sun is <u>blank</u>. What could the answer be? (Call on individual students. Ideas: *Mercury, Venus.*)

- Everybody, count the number of spaces on the puzzle for word 2-across and tell me how many letters the word must have. (Wait.)
- Everybody, how many letters? (Signal.) *Seven.*
- So what word is it? (Signal.) *Mercury.*
- You know that the word cannot be **Venus** because the word **Venus** does not have enough letters.
d. Find the word **Mercury** in the box and get ready to spell that word. ✔
- Everybody, spell **Mercury.** Get ready. (Tap for each letter.) *M-E-R-C-U-R-Y.*
- Check the word Mercury to make sure that it has seven letters. (Wait.)
- Now write **Mercury** as word 2-across in the puzzle. Write one letter in each space. (Observe students and give feedback.)
e. You work the other items that go across the same way we worked word 2. You read the item and figure out the possible words. Then you check the number of letters the word must be. If you don't know how to spell the word, look for the word in the box.
f. I'll do one more item with you. It's the first item in the **down** list. Everybody, touch item 1 in the **down** list. ✔
- It's a **down** item, which means that the word goes from top to bottom. Touch the **1** in the puzzle. Run your finger all the way down from the **1** to show where the item goes. ✔
- I'll read item 1-down. The amount you pay to get into a show is called the <u>blank</u>. What word could that be? (Call on individual students. Ideas: *Cost, admission.*)
- It could be **cost** or **admission.** If you check the number of letters for item 1-down, you'll know which word it is. Check the spelling. Then write the word for item 1-down. ✔
g. Finish the rest of the puzzle now. Work the other items that go across before you do the **down** items.
(Observe students and give feedback.)

Fluency: Rate/Accuracy

Note: There is a fluency checkout in this lesson; therefore, there is no paired practice.

a. Today is a reading checkout day. While you're doing your independent work, I'm going to call on you one at a time to read part of the story from lesson 74.

• Remember, you pass the checkout by reading the passage in less than a minute without making more than 2 mistakes. And when you pass the checkout, you'll color the space for lesson 75 on your thermometer chart.

b. (Call on individual students to read the portion of story 74 marked with ✿.)

• (Time the student. Note words that are missed and total number of words read.)

• (Teacher reference:)

> ✿ On the following afternoon, Waldo had two parrots do tricks on a little swing. The parrots did some amazing things. They held on to the swing with their beaks. They did somersaults on the swing. One parrot stood on the head of the other parrot, and both parrots did a [50] giant somersault. Then one parrot held on to the tail feathers of the other parrot and they spun around and around as the swing went [75] back and forth. From time to time, Waldo would toss a little bit of food to the parrots. They would catch the food with their [100] beaks.
>
> Again the crowd went wild. Again Maria reminded the crowd that the pet shop would put on a full show that Friday night at ✿ [125] Samson High School.

• (If the student reads the passage in one minute or less and makes no more than 2 errors, direct the student to color in the space for lesson 75 on the new thermometer chart.)

• (If the student makes any mistakes, point to each word that was misread and identify it.)

• (If the student does not meet the rate-error criterion for the passage, direct the student to practice reading the story with the assigned partner.)

End-of-lesson Activities

INDEPENDENT WORK

Now finish the independent work for lesson 75. Raise your hand when you're finished. (Observe students and give feedback.)

WORKCHECK

a. (Direct students to take out their marking pencils.)

• We're going to check your independent work. Remember, if you got an item wrong, make an **X** next to the item.

b. (For each item: Read the item. Call on a student to answer it. If the answer is wrong, say the correct answer. Refer to the Answer Key for the correct answers.)

c. Now use your marking pencil to fix up any items you got wrong. Remember, all mistakes must be fixed up before you hand in your independent work.

SPELLING

(Present Spelling lesson 75 after completing Reading lesson 75. See *Spelling Presentation Book.*)

Lessons 76-80 • Planning Page

Looking Ahead

	Lesson 76	Lesson 77	Lesson 78	Lesson 79	Lesson 80
LESSON EVENTS	Vocabulary Sentences Reading Words Story Reading Paired Practice Crossword Puzzle Independent Work Workcheck Spelling	Vocabulary Sentence Reading Words Story Reading Paired Practice Crossword Puzzle Independent Work Workcheck Spelling	**Vocabulary Sentence** Reading Words Story Reading Paired Practice Independent Work Workcheck Spelling	Vocabulary Sentence Reading Words Story Background Story Reading Paired Practice Independent Work Workcheck Spelling	Fact Game Fluency: Rate/ Accuracy Test Marking the Test Test Remedies Spelling
VOCABULARY SENTENCE	sentence #17 sentence #18 sentence #19	#19: The <u>tour</u> to the islands was a <u>fantastic</u> <u>experience</u>.	**#20: She will <u>contact</u> the person we want to <u>hire</u>.**	#20: She will <u>contact</u> the person we want to <u>hire</u>.	
READING WORD: WORD TYPES	mixed words	compound words mixed words	r-e words multi-syllable words	mixed words	
NEW VOCABULARY	shortly	waste		*Greeley*	
STORY BACKGROUND	*Teaching Animals a Hard Trick*			*Colorado and Utah*	
STORY	*Problems at the Pet Shop*	*Changing the Rewards*	*New Rewards and a New Super Trick*	*A Great Show*	
SKILL ITEMS	Vocabulary sentence Crossword puzzle	Vocabulary sentences Crossword puzzle	Crossword puzzle	Sequencing	Test: Vocabulary sentences #18, 19
SPECIAL MATERIALS					Thermometer charts, dice, Fact Game 80, Fact Game Answer Key, scorecard sheets
SPECIAL PROJECTS/ ACTIVITIES					

Comprehension Questions Abbreviations Guide

Access Prior Knowledge = (APK)   Author's Point of View = (APoV)   Author's Purpose = (AP)   Cause/Effect = (C/E)   Charts/Graphs/Diagrams/Visual Aids = (VA)

Classify and Categorize = (C+C)   Compare/Contrast = (C/C)   Determine Character Emotions, Motivation = (DCE)   Drawing Conclusions = (DC)   Drawing Inferences = (DI)

Fact and Opinion = (F/O)   Hypothesizing = (H)   Main Idea = (MI)   Making Connections = (MC)   Making Deductions = (MD)   Making Judgements = (MJ)

Narrative Elements = (NE)   Noting Details = (ND)   Predict = (P)   Reality/Fantasy = (R/F)   Recall Facts/Rules = (RF/R)   Retell = (R)   Sequence = (Seq)

Steps in a Process = (SP)   Story Structure = (SS)   Summarize = (Sum)   Understanding Dialogue = (UD)   Using Context to Confirm Meaning(s) = (UCCM)   Visualize = (V)

EXERCISE 1

Vocabulary Review

a. You learned a sentence that tells what the boring speaker did.
- Everybody, say that sentence. Get ready. (Signal.) *The boring speaker disturbed the audience.*
- (Repeat until firm.)

b. You learned a sentence that tells what a lot of folks did.
- Say that sentence. Get ready. (Signal.) *A lot of folks mobbed the cute singer.*
- (Repeat until firm.)

c. Here's the last sentence you learned: The tour to the islands was a fantastic experience.
- Everybody, say that sentence. Get ready. (Signal.) *The tour to the islands was a fantastic experience.*
- (Repeat until firm.)

d. Everybody, what's another word for **a trip to several places?** (Signal.) *Tour.*
- What word describes each thing you do? (Signal.) *Experience.*
- What's another word for **wonderful?** (Signal.) *Fantastic.*

e. Once more. Say the sentence about the tour to the islands. Get ready. (Signal.) *The tour to the islands was a fantastic experience.*

EXERCISE 2

Reading Words

Column 1

a. **Find lesson 76 in your textbook.** ✔
- Touch column 1. ✔
- (Teacher reference:)

1. **shortly**	4. **softly**
2. **refund**	5. **growl**
3. **angrily**	6. **upstairs**

b. Word 1. What word? (Signal.) *Shortly.*
- Spell **shortly.** Get ready. (Tap for each letter.) *S-H-O-R-T-L-Y.*

- Another word for **soon** is **shortly.** Everybody, what's another way of saying **I will be there soon?** (Signal.) *I will be there shortly.*
- What's another way of saying **We'll be leaving soon?** (Signal.) *We'll be leaving shortly.*

c. Word 2. What word? (Signal.) *Refund.*
- Spell **refund.** Get ready. (Tap for each letter.) *R-E-F-U-N-D.*

d. Word 3. What word? (Signal.) *Angrily.*
- Spell **angrily.** Get ready. (Tap for each letter.) *A-N-G-R-I-L-Y.*

e. Word 4. What word? (Signal.) *Softly.*
- Spell **softly.** Get ready. (Tap for each letter.) *S-O-F-T-L-Y.*

f. Word 5. What word? (Signal.) *Growl.*

g. Word 6. What word? (Signal.) *Upstairs.*

h. Let's read those words again, the fast way.
- Word 1. What word? (Signal.) *Shortly.*
- (Repeat for words 2–6.)

i. (Repeat step h until firm.)

EXERCISE 3

Story Reading

a. Find part B in your textbook. ✔
- The error limit for group reading is 11 errors.

b. Everybody, touch the title. ✔
- (Call on a student to read the title.) [*Problems at the Pet Shop.*]
- Everybody, what's the title? (Signal.) *Problems at the Pet Shop.* (ND)

c. (Call on individual students to read the story, each student reading two or three sentences at a time. Ask the specified questions as the students read.)

- (**Correct errors:** Tell the word. Direct the student to reread the sentence.)
- (If the group makes more than 11 errors, direct the students to reread the story.)

Problems at the Pet Shop

Half the people left before the show was over.

- Why? (Call on a student. Ideas: *Because the animals weren't doing their tricks; because it was a bad show.*) (APK)

Some of them made comments as they walked out of the large hall. Some said, "This show stinks." Others said things like, "I drove twenty miles to see this show. I should have stayed home."

Maria tried to smile and pretend that everything was going well, but the people in the audience made a lot of noise when she tried to talk. When the show was finished, only a few people clapped. The others just stood up and left.

When the hall was empty, Maria and Waldo went around trying to find the birds and other animals that were hiding. It took them over an hour to find the last animal, Gormer. Then they had to break up a cat fight and another fight between two pigeons.

Waldo felt terrible. "Those people paid money to see this show and it was a terrible flop," he said.

"Well," Maria said and patted him on the back. "I think we've learned something from this experience."

- What could they learn from this experience? (Call on a student. Idea: *That they needed Waldo's special food.*) Ⓓ

Maria continued, "We must make sure that we have the food that you cook. Other food will not work."

"I know," Waldo said and shook his head. "I just feel sorry for all the people who had to sit through our show tonight."

The next day, Waldo had more problems. When he arrived at the pet shop after school, he saw a line of people outside. Each person was carrying one of the trained animals that Maria had sold. The people did not look very happy. Waldo asked a young woman who was holding a trained pigeon, "Is anything wrong?"

"A lot is wrong," she said angrily. "I bought a pigeon that was supposed to dance. It won't dance for me. It danced the first couple of times I turned on the music, but now it just looks at me and blinks. If I try to put buttons on its feet, it pecks me." The

woman held out her hand. It had little red marks on it.

- What made those little red marks? (Call on a student. Idea: *The pigeon's pecks.*) Ⓓ

She said, "See what that bird did to me? I want my money back."

- Everybody, does she want to keep the pigeon? (Signal.) *No.* Ⓓⓒ
- What does she want instead? (Call on a student. Ideas: *A refund; money.*) ⓃⒹ

The man who was in front of her said, "I want my money back, too. My rabbit is supposed to walk a tightrope, but the only thing it wants to do is bite me if I try to pick it up."

"We all want our money back," a man near the end of the line said. "Who wants a dog that does nothing but growl ⭐ at you if you tell it to do a somersault?"

- Why won't any of these animals do their tricks? (Call on a student. Idea: *Because they aren't getting Waldo's special food for rewards.*) Ⓓ

Waldo went inside the pet shop. Maria was busy giving people their money back and putting animals back in cages. She looked up at Waldo and shook her head. She didn't have to say anything. Waldo knew how she felt.

- How did she feel? (Call on a student. Ideas: *Sad; upset.*) ⒹⓒⒺ

Waldo didn't put on a show that night. He helped Maria refund money to the people. Shortly before the store closed, they took care of the last person. After that person left, Maria said, "Well, there goes all the money we've made during the last month."

- Where did all the money go? (Call on a student. Idea: *Back to the people who bought the pets.*) Ⓓⓒ

She walked to the front window and stared outside for a long time. Then she turned around and said, "Waldo, I don't think our deal is going to work."

- What deal is she talking about? (Call on a student. Idea: *That Waldo would get twenty cents for every dollar she made.*) (APK)

"I understand," Waldo said softly. He felt very, very bad. "I understand," he repeated. Then he said, "But I really want to thank you for giving me a chance. I …" He couldn't seem to find any more words to say. So he put his head down and walked from the pet shop. He walked home very slowly.

- Read the rest of the story to yourself and be ready to answer some questions. Raise your hand when you're done.

He explained his problem to his parents. His mother said, "Oh, that is too bad."

His father said, "You seem to have a problem, but maybe you can solve it."

"How?" Waldo asked.

"I don't know much about training animals," his father said. "But I think you have a training problem. Your animals will work when you reward them with your special food. But they won't work for any other rewards. Isn't there some way you can train them to work for other rewards?"

"I'm not sure," Waldo said. "But I have a lot of books in my room. I'll read them and find out."

During dinner, Waldo wasn't sad. He could hardly wait to go upstairs and start reading his books. If there was a way to teach the animals to work for other rewards, he would just train the animals that people had returned to the pet shop. Then those animals would not need Waldo's special cooking anymore. During dinner, he kept saying to himself, "I just hope there is a way to train those animals to work for other rewards."

"Waldo," his mother said, "you're hardly eating anything."

His sister said, "He doesn't like any cooking unless it's <u>his</u> cooking."

"That's not true," Waldo said. "I just . . ."

That's enough," Waldo's father said. "Let's not argue while we're eating."

When dinner was finished, Waldo ran to his room and started looking through his books. "I just hope there is a way," he said to himself.

- (After all students have raised their hand:)
- Everybody, did Waldo feel sad during dinner? (Signal.) *No.* (DC)
- What was he thinking about during dinner? (Call on a student. Ideas: *Reading his books on training; retraining the animals.*) (ND)
- Everybody, did he eat a lot during dinner? (Signal.) *No.* (ND)
- What did he do right after dinner? (Call on a student. Idea: *Ran to his room and started looking through his books.*) (ND)

EXERCISE 4

Paired Practice

You're going to read aloud to your partner. Today the **B** members will read first. Then the **A** members will read from the star to the end of the story. (Observe students and give feedback.)

EXERCISE 5

Crossword Puzzle

a. **Everybody, find part A in your workbook.** ✔
- We'll do item 4-across together. Touch the place it starts on the puzzle. ✔
- Here's item 4-across: Things that you see all the time in different places are <u>blank</u> things. What could the answer be? (Call on individual students. Ideas: *Usual, ordinary, common.*)
- Everybody, check the number of spaces on the puzzle and see which word will fit. If you don't know how to spell a word, check the word in the box. Then write the word for 4-across. (Observe students and give feedback.)

b. Here's item 1-down: You may get a <u>blank</u> on your foot if your shoe doesn't fit well. What could the answer be? (Call on individual students. Ideas: *Blister, sore.*)

• Everybody, check the number of spaces on the puzzle and see which word will fit. Then write the correct word for 1-down. (Observe students and give feedback.)

c. Finish the rest of the puzzle now. Remember to do all the **across** items before you do the **down** items. (Observe students and give feedback.)

End-of-lesson Activities

Now finish the independent work for lesson 76. Raise your hand when you're finished. (Observe students and give feedback.)

a. (Direct students to take out their marking pencils.)

• We're going to check your independent work. Remember, if you got an item wrong, make an **X** next to the item.

b. (For each item: Read the item. Call on a student to answer it. If the answer is wrong, say the correct answer. Refer to the Answer Key for the correct answers.)

c. Now use your marking pencil to fix up any items you got wrong. Remember, all mistakes must be fixed up before you hand in your independent work.

(Present Spelling lesson 76 after completing Reading lesson 76. See *Spelling Presentation Book.*)

EXERCISE 1

Vocabulary Review

a. You learned a sentence that tells about the tour to the islands.
- Everybody, say that sentence. Get ready. (Signal.) *The tour to the islands was a fantastic experience.*
- (Repeat until firm.)

b. I'll say part of the sentence. When I stop, you say the next word. Listen: The … Everybody, what's the next word? (Signal.) *Tour.*

c. Listen: The tour to the islands was a fantastic. … Everybody, what's the next word? (Signal.) *Experience.*
- Say the whole sentence. Get ready. (Signal.) *The tour to the islands was a fantastic experience.*

d. Listen: The tour to the islands was a … Everybody, what's the next word? (Signal.) *Fantastic.*

EXERCISE 2

Reading Words

Column 1

a. **Find lesson 77 in your textbook.** ✔
- Touch column 1. ✔
- (Teacher reference:)

1. upstairs	3. tightrope
2. backyard	4. sidewalk

b. All these words are compound words. The first part of each word is underlined.

c. Word 1. What's the underlined part? (Signal.) *up.*
- What's the whole word? (Signal.) *Upstairs.*
- Word 2. What's the underlined part? (Signal.) *back.*
- What's the whole word? (Signal.) *Backyard.*
- Word 3. What's the underlined part? (Signal.) *tight.*
- What's the whole word? (Signal.) *Tightrope.*
- Word 4. What's the underlined part? (Signal.) *side.*

- What's the whole word? (Signal.) *Sidewalk.*

d. Let's read those words again, the fast way.
- Word 1. What word? (Signal.) *Upstairs.*
- (Repeat for words 2–4.)

e. (Repeat step d until firm.)

Column 2

f. Find column 2. ✔
- (Teacher reference:)

1. waste	3. pyramid
2. changing	4. demonstrated

g. Word 1. What word? (Signal.) *Waste.*
- When we **waste** something, we use it the wrong way.
- Everybody, what are we doing when we use **water** the wrong way? (Signal.) *Wasting water.*
- What are we doing when we use **energy** the wrong way? (Signal.) *Wasting energy.*

h. Word 2. What word? (Signal.) *Changing.*
- (Repeat for words 3 and 4.)

i. Let's read those words again.
- Word 1. What word? (Signal.) *Waste.*
- (Repeat for words 2–4.)

j. (Repeat step i until firm.)

Individual Turns
(For columns 1 and 2: Call on individual students, each to read one to three words per turn.)

EXERCISE 3

Story Reading

a. Find part B in your textbook. ✔
- The error limit for group reading is 13 errors.

b. Everybody, touch the title. ✔
- (Call on a student to read the title.) *[Changing the Rewards.]*
- Everybody, what's the title? (Signal.) *Changing the Rewards.* ⓝⒹ

c. (Call on individual students to read the story, each student reading two or three sentences at a time. Ask the specified questions as the students read.)

- **(Correct errors:** Tell the word. Direct the student to reread the sentence.)
- (If the group makes more than 13 errors, direct the students to reread the story.)

Changing the Rewards

The first book that Waldo looked through did not tell about how to train animals to work for new rewards. The second book didn't, either. But there was a big part in the third book. The title of that part was: "Training an Animal to Work for New Rewards."

- What was the title? (Call on a student.) *Training an Animal to Work for New Rewards.* ⓃⒹ
- Why did Waldo want to train the animals to work for new rewards? (Call on a student. Idea: *So other people could get the animals to do their tricks.*) ⒶⓅⓀ
- What new rewards would he want them to work for? (Call on a student. Ideas: *Regular food; pats on the head; etc.*) ⒹⒾ

"Wow," Waldo said, and started to laugh. "I found it! I found it!"

Then he started to read. He kept reading until his mother came into his room and told him that it was very late and that he had to go to bed.

- When did he start reading? (Call on a student. Idea: *After dinner.*) ⒶⓅⓀ
- When did he stop reading? (Call on a student. Ideas: *When his mother told him to go to bed; when it was very late.*) ⓃⒹ
- So he must have read all evening long.

He didn't go to sleep right away.

- What do you think he was thinking about? (Call on a student. Ideas: *What he'd read; training animals with new rewards.*) ⒹⒾ

After the lights were turned off, he kept thinking about the things that he had read. In his mind, he began to make up a plan about how he would train the animals to work for new rewards.

He kept remembering the rule that the book gave for teaching animals

to like new rewards. Here is that rule: You slowly change the reward.

- Everybody, say that rule. Get ready. (Signal.) *You slowly change the reward.* ⓇⒻ/Ⓡ
- (Repeat until firm.)
- Do you change the reward fast? (Signal.) *No.* ⓇⒻ/Ⓡ

The book explained how to change the reward. "You start with the reward the animal will work for. Then you start to change it a little bit at a time. You keep changing it until it is the new reward."

- Listen to that part again. It's very important.

    The book explained how to change the reward. "You start with the reward the animal will work for. Then you start to change it a little bit at a time. You keep changing it until it is the new reward."
- What kind of reward do you start with? (Call on a student. Idea: *One the animal will work for.*) ⓇⒻ/Ⓡ
- Then what do you do to the reward the animal will work for? (Call on a student. Idea: *Change it a little bit at a time.*) ⓇⒻ/Ⓡ
- When do you stop changing it? (Call on a student. Idea: *When it becomes the new reward.*) ⓇⒻ/Ⓡ
- What reward do Waldo's animals work for? (Call on a student. Idea: *His special food.*) ⒶⓅⓀ
- So what reward will he start with? (Call on a student. Idea: *His special food.*) ⓇⒻ/Ⓡ
- Then what will he do to that reward? (Call on a student. Idea: *Change it a little bit at a time.*) ⓇⒻ/Ⓡ
- I wonder how he can change the reward a little bit at a time.

The book told about how to teach a dog to work for a pat on the head. At first the dog will do the trick for a food reward. But the trainer wants the dog to work for a pat on the head.

- Everybody, what reward will the trainer start with? (Signal.) *Food.* ⓃⒹ
- What's the reward he wants the dog to work for? (Signal.) *A pat on the head.* ⓃⒹ

The trainer starts slowly changing the food reward. At first, the trainer gives the dog the food reward, and at the same time, the trainer pats the dog on the head.

- So he has to start by rewarding the dog with food. The trainer first changed the food reward by giving the food reward and also doing something else. What is the other thing the trainer does? (Call on a student. Idea: *Pats the dog on the head.*) (ND)

Later, the trainer starts giving the dog less food each time the dog does the trick and gives the dog more pats on the head.

- How is the trainer changing the reward now? (Call on a student. Idea: *Giving less food and more pats on the head.*) (ND)

After a while, the trainer does not give the dog a food reward each time the dog does the trick. Sometimes, the trainer gives the food reward. But <u>every</u> <u>time</u> the dog does the trick, the trainer gives it pats on the head.

- Everybody, does the trainer now give a food reward every time the dog does the trick? (Signal.) *No.* (ND)
- But what reward does the trainer give each time? (Signal.) *A pat on the head.* (ND)

After a while, the dog works for just the pats on the head. The trainer does not have to give the dog the food reward.

The next morning, Waldo got up very early and went to the pet shop before going to school. The shop wasn't open yet. He knocked and knocked on the front door until Maria answered. "I was in the back," she said. "I guess I didn't hear you knocking." ⭐

Waldo said, "I think I've worked out a solution to our problem. I think I can train the animals to work for regular food. Or maybe I can train them to work for no food at all."

"Do you really think you can do that?" Maria asked.

"I think I can," Waldo replied. "At least I've read part of a book that explains how to do it."

Maria smiled and then shook her head no. "Maybe we'd better not try," she said. "We've had two very bad experiences with your special food rewards."

- Who can name the two very bad experiences? (Call on a student. Ideas: *The animals in the show wouldn't do tricks without special food; people returning their pets.*) (APK)

"Please," Waldo said. "Please, give me one more chance. If it doesn't work, you won't have to pay me. But I really want to try to train those animals so that other people can get them to do their tricks."

Maria smiled again. Then she said very slowly, "Well … all right. Let's try to do that."

"Okay," Waldo said, and laughed. "Wow. I can hardly wait until school is over today." Waldo was going to use the rules that he had read about for teaching animals to work for new rewards. The book told which reward you start with.

- Which reward is that? (Call on a student. Idea: *One the animal will work for.*) (RF/R)

The book then told what you do to that reward.

- What do you do to that reward? (Call on a student. Idea: *Change it slowly.*) (RF/R)

And the book told when you stop changing that reward.

- When do you stop changing it? (Call on a student. Idea: *When it becomes the new reward.*) (RF/R)
- Read the rest of the story to yourself and be ready to answer some questions. Raise your hand when you're done.

Waldo was going to use these rules. He was going to start with the reward that the animals would work for. Then he was going to slowly change that reward. He was going to keep changing the reward until the animals were working for regular food.

The school day seemed to drag on and on. Waldo looked at his watch every five or ten minutes. Each time, he said to himself, "Will this school day ever be over?"

It seemed as if a whole year passed before the last bell of the school day rang. The kids rushed from their classroom. Waldo was one of the first outside. He ran to the pet shop. When he arrived there, he was out of breath. But he didn't waste a second. He went into the kitchen and fixed some food. He didn't pay much attention to the three dogs and the goat that were looking in the kitchen window. Then he took his food inside the pet shop. The animals were jumping around and making a lot of noise.

Maria looked at him, and he looked at her. With a smile, he said, "Well, I sure hope it works."

Maria said, "We'll soon find out." And they did.

- (After all students have raised their hand:)
- How long did the school day seem to Waldo? (Call on a student. Ideas: *Very long; as if a whole year had passed.*) (ND)
- What did he do right after school? (Call on a student. Idea: *Went to the pet shop.*) (ND)
- What was the first thing he did inside the pet shop? (Call on a student. Idea: *Fixed some food.*) (ND)
- What was he hoping to do with the special food? (Call on a student. Ideas: *Train the animals to work for regular food or no food; retrain the animals.*) (DI)
- I wonder how it will work out.
- How could he slowly change the special food into regular food? (Call on a student. Idea: *Mix lots of special food with a little regular food and then use less and less special food and more and more regular food.*) (P)

Paired Practice

You're going to read aloud to your partner. Today the **A** members will read first. Then the **B** members will read from the star to the end of the story. (Observe students and give feedback.)

Crossword Puzzle

a. **Everybody, find part A in your workbook.** ✔
- We'll do item 4-across together. Touch the place it starts on the puzzle. ✔
- Here's item 4-across: Another word for **amazing** is <u>blank</u>. Everybody, what word? (Signal.) *Incredible.*
- Check the number of spaces on the puzzle and see if that word will fit. If you don't know how to spell it, check the list of words in the box. Then write the correct word for 4-across.
(Observe students and give feedback.)

b. Here's item 1-down: The people who watch an event are called the <u>blank</u>. Everybody, what word? (Signal.) *Audience.*
- Check the spelling for **audience.** Then write it for 1-down.
(Observe students and give feedback.)

c. Finish the rest of the puzzle now. Remember to do all the **across** items before you do the **down** items.
(Observe students and give feedback.)

End-of-lesson Activities

Now finish the independent work for lesson 77. Raise your hand when you're finished. (Observe students and give feedback.)

a. (Direct students to take out their marking pencils.)

- We're going to check your independent work. Remember, if you got an item wrong, make an **X** next to the item.

b. (For each item: Read the item. Call on a student to answer it. If the answer is wrong, say the correct answer. Refer to the Answer Key for the correct answers.)

c. Now use your marking pencil to fix up any items you got wrong. Remember, all mistakes must be fixed up before you hand in your independent work.

SPELLING

(Present Spelling lesson 77 after completing Reading lesson 77. See *Spelling Presentation Book.*)

LESSON 78

EXERCISE 1

Vocabulary Sentence

a. **Find page 367 in your textbook.** ✔
- Touch sentence 20. ✔
- This is a new vocabulary sentence. It says: She will contact the person we want to hire. Everybody, say the sentence. Get ready. (Signal.) *She will contact the person we want to hire.*
- Close your eyes and say the sentence. Get ready. (Signal.) *She will contact the person we want to hire.*
- (Repeat until firm.)

b. When you **contact** somebody, you get in touch with that person. Everybody, what's another way of saying **We got in touch with her over the internet?** (Signal.) *We contacted her over the internet.*
- What's another way of saying **They got in touch with me by phone?** (Signal.) *They contacted me by phone.*

c. The sentence says: She will contact the person we want to **hire.** When you hire somebody, you give the person a job.
- Here's another way of saying **She hoped they would give her a job: She hoped they would hire her.**
- Your turn. What's another way of saying **They will give jobs to a hundred people?** (Signal.) *They will hire a hundred people.*
- What's another way of saying **I don't think we should give a job to that person?** (Signal.) *I don't think we should hire that person.*

d. Listen to the sentence again: She will contact the person we want to hire. Everybody, say that sentence. Get ready. (Signal.) *She will contact the person we want to hire.*

e. Everybody, what word tells about giving somebody a job? (Signal.) *Hire.*
- What word tells about getting in touch with somebody? (Signal.) *Contact.*
- (Repeat step e until firm.)

EXERCISE 2

Reading Words

Column 1

a. Find lesson 78 in your textbook.
- Touch column 1. ✔
- (Teacher reference:)

1. retrained	4. remind
2. resold	5. refund
3. returned	

- All these words begin with the letters **R-E.**
b. Word 1. What word? (Signal.) *Retrained.*
- (Repeat for words 2–5.)
c. Let's read those words again.
- Word 1. What word? (Signal.) *Retrained.*
- (Repeat for words 2–5.)
d. (Repeat step c until firm.)

Column 2

e. Find column 2. ✔
- (Teacher reference:)

1. regular	3. couple
2. hungry	4. contacted

f. Word 1. What word? (Signal.) *Regular.*
- (Repeat for words 2–4.)
g. Let's read those words again.
- Word 1. What word? (Signal.) *Regular.*
- (Repeat for words 2–4.)
h. (Repeat step g until firm.)

Individual Turns

(For columns 1 and 2: Call on individual students, each to read one to three words per turn.)

EXERCISE 3

Story Reading

a. Find part B in your textbook. ✔
- The error limit for group reading is 15 errors.
b. Everybody, touch the title. ✔
- (Call on a student to read the title.) *[New Rewards and a New Super Trick.]*
- Everybody, what's the title? (Signal.) *New Rewards and a New Super Trick.* (ND)

- What is the new reward that Waldo wants the animals to work for? (Call on a student. Idea: *Regular food.*) (APK)
- What reward is he going to start with when he trains the animals to work for the new reward? (Call on a student. Idea: *His special food.*) (RF/R)
- And what's he going to do to the special food? (Call on a student. Idea: *Slowly change it.*) (RF/R)
- c. (Call on individual students to read the story, each student reading two or three sentences at a time. Ask the specified questions as the students read.)

- **(Correct errors:** Tell the word. Direct the student to reread the sentence.)
- (If the group makes more than 15 errors, direct the students to reread the story.)

New Rewards and a New Super Trick

Waldo took one of the tap-dancing pigeons from its cage. He put the pigeon on the table and gave it a little bit of special food. Then Waldo turned on the peppy music. The pigeon danced and Waldo rewarded it with another tiny bit of special food.

- The rule that Waldo read about said that you should start with the reward that the animal likes. That's what Waldo is doing. Now he'll start changing the reward.

Then Waldo put his hands in the bowl of special food and rubbed the food all over the palms of his hands.

- Everybody, show me the palms of your hands. ✔ (VA)
- Show me how you'd rub your hands with food so that you would get your palms covered with food. ✔ (V)

"What are you doing?" Maria asked.

"I'm going to fix up the regular birdseed so that it is more like my special food."

Waldo picked up a handful of birdseed and rubbed until each seed was coated with a little tiny bit of special food. "Let's see if the pigeon likes this birdseed," he said. He tossed one seed in front of the

pigeon. Before the seed hit the table, the pigeon caught it in the air with a snap.

- What's that snap? (Call on a student. Idea: *The bird eating the seed.*) (DC)

Waldo turned on the CD player, and the bird held its wings out and danced in time with the music. When the song was finished, Waldo dropped a couple of coated seeds in front of the pigeon. "Snap, snap." The seeds were gone in an instant.

- Waldo changed the reward a little bit and it worked.

The bird worked for the new reward. Again Waldo played the tune, and again the pigeon danced. After the song was finished, Waldo gave the bird two coated seeds and one seed that was not coated with special food. "Snap, snap, snap."

- He changed the reward again. How did he change it this time? (Call on a student. Idea: *He gave one regular seed along with two coated ones.*) (ND)
- Everybody, did the bird eat all the seeds? (Signal.) *Yes.* (DC)
- How do you know? (Call on a student. Idea: *There were three snaps.*) (ND)

Waldo gave that pigeon a rest while he worked with the second pigeon. That pigeon also liked the coated seeds. After it danced, he gave it two coated seeds and one seed that was not coated. "Snap, snap, snap."

- Everybody, how many seeds did he give that pigeon? (Signal.) *Three.* (ND)
- How many did the pigeon eat? (Signal.) *Three.* (DC)

Waldo went back to the first pigeon. This time he gave the pigeon one coated seed and two regular seeds. "Snap, snap, snap."

- How did he change the reward this time? (Call on a student. Idea: *He gave one coated seed and two regular ones.*) (ND)

- Everybody, did it work? (Signal.) *Yes.* (DC)
- How do you know? (Call on a student. Idea: *There were three snaps.*) (ND)

Before Waldo went home that night, all three pigeons were working for three regular seeds.

- How had he changed the reward after the pigeons worked for two regular seeds and one coated seed? (Call on a student. Idea: *He gave them three regular seeds.*) (P)

Waldo trained the other animals the same way he trained the pigeons. To train the rabbit to work for regular food, he rubbed his hands over bits of carrots. When the rabbit first did the trick on the tightropes, he gave it a tiny bit of his special food. Next, he gave it two pieces of coated carrots. "GULP, GULP."

- What's making that gulp, gulp? (Call on a student. Idea: *The rabbit eating the carrots.*) (DI)
- Everybody, show me how you would swallow something with a gulping sound. ✔
- Everybody, how many pieces of carrot did he give the rabbit? (Signal.) *Two.* (V)
- How many did the rabbit eat? (Signal.) *Two.* (DC)
- How do you know? (Call on a student. Idea: *There were two gulps.*) (ND)

The next time the rabbit did the trick, he gave it two pieces of coated carrots and a tiny piece of carrot that was not coated. "GULP, GULP, gulp."

- Everybody, how many pieces did the rabbit eat? (Signal.) *Three.* (DC)
- Which of those gulps is for the uncoated carrot? (Call on a student. Idea: *The third one.*) (DC)
- How do you know? (Call on a student. Idea: *It's the smallest gulp.*) (ND)

By the end of the day, the rabbit was walking the tightrope for three pieces of regular carrot.
"I think it's going to work," Waldo announced.
"I think you're right," Maria said.
Before Waldo and Maria left the pet

shop that night, Maria called the people who had returned the trained pigeons and the trained rabbit. "I think we've fixed the problem," she told them. "Why don't you stop by and we'll show you how that animal performs now. You don't have to buy it back if you don't want to. But that animal ⭐ will do the trick now.

- Who did Maria call? (Call on a student. Idea: *The people who had returned the trained pigeons and the trained rabbit.*) (ND)
- What did she tell them about the animal they had bought? (Call on a student. Idea: *That the animal would do the tricks now.*) (ND)

The next day, all the people who had returned pets came back to the pet shop. Maria demonstrated how the retrained pets would work for regular food. All the people bought their pets back.

- How many of the people who returned their pets came back to the pet shop? (Call on a student. Idea: *All of them.*) (ND)
- How many of those people bought their pets back? (Call on a student. *Idea: All of them.*) (ND)

As soon as Waldo got to the pet shop after school, he started to train some animals to do a super trick.

- What was Waldo doing? (Call on a student. Idea: *Started to train some animals to do a super trick.*) (ND)
- Raise your hand if you can name all three big things that happened. (Call on a student. Idea: *Maria resold the pets that were retrained, Waldo retrained some of the other animals, Waldo started training on a super trick.*) (ND)

Waldo got the idea for the super trick from working with the mice that sat on Gormer's back. Waldo said to himself, "Why not make a super trick with many, many animals piled up?" His first idea was to make a regular pyramid of animals. For a regular pyramid there would be a row of animals standing on the floor.

- Get a picture of that—a row of animals lined up on the floor. (V)

On top of the bottom row would be another smaller row of animals.

- Picture that, a smaller row of animals standing on top of the first row of animals. (V)

On top of the smaller row would be a row that was even smaller. At the top of the pyramid would be one animal.
This picture shows a regular pyramid of animals:

- Everybody, look at the picture. The pyramid starts with a row of animals lined up on the floor. Touch that row. ✔ (VA)
- Everybody, what kind of animals are those? (Signal.) *Horses.* (VA)
- Touch the smaller row on top of the horses. ✔ (VA)
- What kind of animals are those? (Signal.) *Dogs.* (VA)
- Touch the animal on the very top of the pyramid. ✔
- What kind of animal is that? (Signal.) *Pigeon.* (VA)
- Does this picture look like the picture you got in your head when we read about the pyramid of animals? (Call on a student. Student preference.) (MC)

The more Waldo thought about the regular pyramid, the less he liked the idea. The trick seemed too easy.

- Why didn't he like the regular pyramid? (Call on a student. Idea: *It seemed too easy.*) (ND)

So Waldo started to think of a better trick. After a few moments, he got the idea for a pyramid that was upside-down.

- Everybody, show me with your hands what that pyramid would look like. (Check for a V-shape.) (V)

This pyramid wouldn't have one animal at the <u>top</u> of the pyramid. It would have one animal at the <u>bottom</u>. Two animals would stand on that animal. Four animals would stand on top of the two animals. And eight animals would stand on top of the four animals.
This picture shows that upside-down pyramid:

- What kind of animal is at the bottom of the pyramid? (Call on a student. Ideas: *A huge dog; a St. Bernard.*) (VA)
- That animal must be very strong to hold all those other animals.
- Everybody, what kind of animals are at the top of the pyramid? (Signal.) *Pigeons.* (VA)
- Count the pigeons and see how many there are. (Wait.) How many? (Signal.) *Sixteen.* (VA)
- Teaching the animals to do this trick is going to involve a lot of work.
- Read the rest of the story to yourself and be ready to answer some questions. Raise your hand when you're done.

It was after four o'clock when Waldo got the idea for the upside-down pyramid, so he didn't have much time to work on it before the shop closed. He started with the animal that would stand at the bottom of the pyramid. That animal was a great big dog, strong enough to hold many, many animals. He took the dog from its cage and trained it to stand still in the middle of the floor. The training took only a few minutes and a little bit of Waldo's special food.

Now Waldo brought out two smaller dogs. First he put them on the back of the huge dog. When all the dogs stood still, he rewarded all of them with a bit of special food. Next, Waldo trained the smaller dogs to jump onto the back of the larger dog. He trained the black dog to stand with its paws on the huge dog's head. He trained the spotted dog to stand on the huge dog's rear end.

After the three dogs were trained, Waldo started to work on the harder part of the trick. He had to train four animals to stand on the dogs. He decided to train cats to do this part of the trick. Dogs don't usually like to have cats standing on their backs, and cats don't usually like to stand on dogs. But Waldo used his special food to reward the animals. So before the shop closed, Waldo had trained three dogs and four cats for the first part of the super trick.

- (After all students have raised their hand:)
- Each dog had to jump to a special place on the big dog's back. Where did the black dog put its front paws? (Call on a student. Idea: *On the huge dog's head.*) (ND)
- Where did the spotted dog put its front paws? (Call on a student. Idea: *On the huge dog's rear end.*) (ND)
- Everybody, how many animals did Waldo have to train to stand on the two smaller dogs? (Signal.) *Four.* (ND)
- What kind of animals did he train to stand on these dogs? (Signal.) *Cats.* (ND)
- Did the dogs and cats fight when Waldo trained them? (Signal.) *No.* (ND)

- Why not? (Call on a student. Idea: *Because Waldo used his special food to reward them.*) (ND)
- Everybody, before the shop closed, how many dogs had Waldo trained for the pyramid? (Signal.) *Three.* (ND)
- How many cats had he trained? (Signal.) *Four.* (ND)
- He is a very fast trainer.

Paired Practice

You're going to read aloud to your partner. Today the **B** members will read first. Then the **A** members will read from the star to the end of the story. (Observe students and give feedback.)

End-of-lesson Activities

INDEPENDENT WORK

Now finish the independent work for lesson 78. Raise your hand when you're finished. (Observe students and give feedback.)

WORKCHECK

a. (Direct students to take out their marking pencils.)
- We're going to check your independent work. Remember, if you got an item wrong, make an **X** next to the item.
b. (For each item: Read the item. Call on a student to answer it. If the answer is wrong, say the correct answer. Refer to the Answer Key for the correct answers.)
c. Now use your marking pencil to fix up any items you got wrong. Remember, all mistakes must be fixed up before you hand in your independent work.

SPELLING

(Present Spelling lesson 78 after completing Reading lesson 78. See *Spelling Presentation Book.*)

EXERCISE 1

Vocabulary Review

a. Here's the new vocabulary sentence: She will contact the person we want to hire.
- Everybody, say the sentence. Get ready. (Signal.) *She will contact the person we want to hire.*
- (Repeat until firm.)

b. Everybody, what word tells about giving somebody a job? (Signal.) *Hire.*
- What word tells about getting in touch with somebody? (Signal.) *Contact.*

EXERCISE 2

Reading Words

Column 1

a. **Find lesson 79 in your textbook.** ✔
- Touch column 1. ✔
- (Teacher reference:)

1. **Greeley**	5. **perfectly**
2. **upside-down**	6. **whistled**
3. **spoke**	7. **information**
4. **shown**	

b. Word 1. What word? (Signal.) *Greeley.*
- Greeley is the name of a city in Colorado.

c. Word 2. What word? (Signal.) *Upside-down.*
- (Repeat for words 3–7.)

d. Let's read those words again.
- Word 1. What word? (Signal.) *Greeley.*
- (Repeat for words 2–7.)

e. (Repeat step d until firm.)

EXERCISE 3

Story Background

a. Find part B in your textbook. ✔
- You're going to read the next story about Waldo. First you'll read the information passage. It gives some facts about Colorado and Utah.

b. Everybody, touch the title. ✔
- (Call on a student to read the title.) *[Colorado and Utah.]*
- Everybody, what's the title? (Signal.) *Colorado and Utah.* ⓝⒹ

c. (Call on individual students to read the passage, each student reading two or three sentences at a time. Ask the specified questions as the students read.)

Colorado and Utah

In a later lesson, Waldo and Maria go to two states in the United States—Colorado and Utah.

- Everybody, what are the two states they go to? (Signal.) *Colorado and Utah.* ⓝⒹ

First they go to two cities in Colorado—Denver, Colorado, and Greeley, Colorado.

- Name the two cities in Colorado. (Call on a student.) *Denver and Greeley.* ⓇⒻ/Ⓡ
- Everybody, what state are these cities in? (Signal.) *Colorado.* ⓇⒻ/Ⓡ

Then they go to the state of Utah.

- Everybody, which state do they go to after Colorado? (Signal.) *Utah.* ⓇⒻ/Ⓡ

The map shows these places. The map also shows the great mountains that Waldo and Maria drive over when they go from Colorado to Utah. These mountains are called the Rocky Mountains.

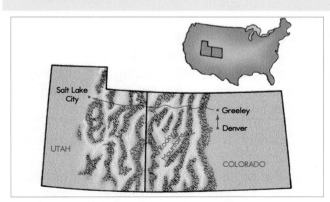

- Everybody, what's the name of those mountains? (Signal.) *Rocky Mountains.* ⓝⒹ
- Touch the small map of the United States in the corner of the picture. ✔ ⓥⒶ

- The part that is brown is the part that is shown in the big map. That part is made up of the state of Colorado and the state of Utah. Everybody, touch the brown part of the little map. ✔ (VA)
- Now look at the big map. Use your finger and make a line around the whole state of Colorado. ✔ (VA)
- Use your finger and make a line around the whole state of Utah. ✔ (VA)
- Run your finger along the Rocky Mountains. ✔ (VA)
- Tell me the direction that Waldo and Maria must travel to go from Colorado to Utah. Get ready. (Signal.) *West.* (VA)
- The arrows show the trip Waldo and Maria planned. Everybody, touch the first city they go to in Colorado. ✔ (VA)
- What's the name of the city? (Signal.) *Denver.* (VA)
- Touch the next city in Colorado. ✔
- What's the name of that city? (Signal.) *Greeley.* (VA)
- What's the name of the mountains they must cross after leaving Greeley, Colorado? (Signal.) *Rocky Mountains.* (VA)
- The road must go over those mountains.
- What's the name of the city they go to in Utah? (Signal.) *Salt Lake City.* (VA)

EXERCISE 4

Story Reading

a. Find part C in your textbook. ✔
- The error limit for group reading is 12 errors.
b. Everybody, touch the title. ✔
- (Call on a student to read the title.) *[A Great Show.]*
- Everybody, what's the title? (Signal.) *A Great Show.* (ND)
c. (Call on individual students to read the story, each student reading two or three sentences at a time. Ask the specified questions as the students read.)

- **(Correct errors:** Tell the word. Direct the student to reread the sentence.)
- (If the group makes more than 12 errors, direct the students to reread the story.)

A Great Show

Just before the pet shop closed, Waldo showed Maria the animals he had just trained. "Watch this," he

said. He used his hand to give the large dog a signal.

- Everybody, show me how he would do that. ✔ (V)

The large dog walked to the middle of the floor and stood still. Waldo then signaled the black dog and the spotted dog. They ran up to the huge dog and jumped on its back. Then Waldo signaled the four cats. Two of them jumped on the back of the black dog and two of them jumped on the back of the spotted dog.

Maria said, "That's amazing."

"Yeah," Waldo said. "And that's just the first part of the trick. But watch this."

Waldo turned to the animals and said, "Speak!"

All the animals spoke. The huge dog spoke with a very deep "Woof."

- Make the woof sound of a great huge dog. (Call on a student.) ✔ (V)

The dogs on top spoke with sharp barks: "Ruf, ruf."

- Make those sounds. (Call on a student.) ✔ (V)
- Make both sounds—the one for the huge dog and the one for the smaller dogs. (Call on a student. Check for "woof" sounds for the huge dog and "ruf" sounds for the smaller dogs.)

The cats on top of the dogs spoke with loud meows.

- Make those sounds. (Call on a student.) ✔ (V)

Maria laughed. "Oh, that's a great trick," she said.

Waldo said, "Just wait until I train the rest of the animals for that upside-down pyramid. We'll have a super trick."

🌸 Waldo went on to explain how he planned to complete the pyramid. He told her that he planned to train eight squirrels to stand on the four cats and sixteen pigeons to stand on the eight squirrels.

- Everybody, what kind of animals will Waldo train to stand on the cats? (Signal.) *Squirrels.* ⓃⒹ
- What kind of animals will stand on the squirrels? (Signal.) *Pigeons.* ⓃⒹ
- How many pigeons? (Signal.) *Sixteen.* ⓃⒹ

Waldo concluded by saying, "The next time we put on a show, it will be the greatest animal show that anybody ever saw."

Maria said, "I hope so. Every time I think of the first show we put on, I feel like dying."

Waldo said, "It will be different next time."

And he was right.

•　　•　　•

- What do the dots in the story mean? (Call on a student. Idea: *Part of the story is missing.*) ⓈⓈ

The hall at Samson High School was packed again.

- Where is the story taking place now? (Call on a student. Idea: *Samson High School.*) ⒹⒸ
- When we left Waldo and Maria, Waldo was in the middle of training animals. Now the story is telling about the crowd at Samson High School. Name some things that must have happened so that Waldo was ready for another show. (Call on a student. Ideas: *He finished training the animals for the upside-down pyramid; trained other animals for other tricks; finished retraining animals to work for regular food.*) ⒹⒾ

For a week before the show, Maria and Waldo had shown some of the acts that would be in the show. Each day, outside ✿ the pet shop, they showed a different act. There was one that they didn't show—the upside-down pyramid.

- Why do you think they didn't show that act? (Call on a student. Idea: *So it would be a surprise.*) ⒹⒾ

Waldo didn't want anybody to see this act before the show.

Just like the first show at Samson High School, some people had come from thirty miles away to see the show. But Waldo didn't worry about cooking his special food this time, because all the animals had been trained to work for regular food. When Waldo trained animals for a new ✦ trick, he used his special food because the animals would do anything to get that food. So the animals that made the upside-down pyramid had started out with special food, but now they worked for regular food. So did all the other animals in Waldo's acts.

- Why did Waldo start training animals with the special food? (Call on a student. Ideas: *Because the animals would do anything to get that food; so the animals would work hard.*) ⓃⒹ
- What did he do as soon as they learned their new tricks? (Call on a student. Ideas: *He started to change the reward; he taught them to work for regular food.*) ⓃⒹ
- So he doesn't have to worry about having special food for them.

Maria walked onto the stage at Samson High School and the audience applauded. She bowed and waved. Then she announced the first act, the dancing pigeons. They danced in time with the music. The audience went wild. "Again," they shouted. And Waldo gave the pigeons the signal to dance again. They did it without making a mistake.

The next act was Homer the dog. He played "Mary Had a Little Lamb" without a mistake. People in the audience clapped in time with the music. "Again," they shouted after the act was finished. So Waldo gave Homer the signal to do the trick again and Homer performed without a mistake.

After each animal performed, Waldo rewarded it with some bits of regular food.

The next act was Gormer the rabbit, who walked the tightropes with four mice on his back. They performed perfectly.

- Everybody, did they make any mistakes? (Signal.) *No.* ⓓⓒ

"Again," the crowd shouted, and the animals did the trick again.

- Read the rest of the story to yourself and be ready to answer some questions. Raise your hand when you're done.

> Then Waldo brought out a new act. This act had been shown in front of the pet shop. It was a very good act, but not a super act. Three striped cats howled and meowed in time with the music. Waldo put on a CD. As soon as the music started, the cats sang. As they sang, they sat up with their front paws under their chin. The audience laughed and wanted the cats to perform again. So Waldo played the CD again, and again the cats howled and meowed in time with the music.
> Next was the dog that did backward somersaults in the air. First Waldo held out a stick and signaled the dog to jump over the stick. Then Waldo signaled the dog to roll over, to sit up, to speak, and to walk on its hind legs. Then Waldo signaled the dog to do the backward somersaults. When the dog started to do the somersaults, the people in the audience counted together, "One … two … three … four … five … six." Then the people applauded, as Waldo tossed some dog treats to the dog.
> Now came the super act.

- (After all students have raised their hand:)
- Everybody, show me how the cats held their paws as they sang. ✔ ⓥ
- Everybody, how many somersaults did the dog do? (Signal.) *Six.* ⓓⓒ
- Which act comes after the somersaulting dog? (Call on a student. Idea: *The upside-down pyramid.*) ⓓⓒ

Paired Practice

You're going to read aloud to your partner. Today the **A** members will read first. Then the **B** members will read from the star to the end of the story. (Observe students and give feedback.)

End-of-lesson Activities

INDEPENDENT WORK

Now finish the independent work for lesson 79. Raise your hand when you're finished. (Observe students and give feedback.)

WORKCHECK

a. (Direct students to take out their marking pencils.)
- We're going to check your independent work. Remember, if you got an item wrong, make an **X** next to the item.
b. (For each item: Read the item. Call on a student to answer it. If the answer is wrong, say the correct answer. Refer to the Answer Key for the correct answers.)
c. Now use your marking pencil to fix up any items you got wrong. Remember, all mistakes must be fixed up before you hand in your independent work.

SPELLING

(Present Spelling lesson 79 after completing Reading lesson 79. See *Spelling Presentation Book.*)

> *Note:* You will need to reproduce blackline masters for the Fact Game in lesson 80 (Appendix G in Teacher's Guide).

EXERCISE 1

Fact Game

a. You're going to play the game that uses the facts you have learned. Remember the rules. The player rolls the number cubes, figures out the number of the question, reads that question out loud, and answers it. The monitor tells the player if the answer is right or wrong. If it's wrong, the monitor tells the right answer. If it's right, the monitor gives the player one point. Don't argue with the monitor. The number cubes go to the left and the next player has a turn. You'll play the game for 10 minutes.

b. (Divide students into groups of four or five. Assign monitors. Circulate as students play the game. Comment on groups that are playing well.)

c. (At the end of 10 minutes, have all students who earned more than 10 points stand up.)

- (Tell the monitor of each game that ran smoothly:) Your group did a good job.

EXERCISE 2

Fluency: Rate/Accuracy

a. Today is a test day and a reading checkout day. While you're writing answers, I'm going to call on you one at a time to read part of the story we read in lesson 79. When I call you to come and do your checkout, bring your thermometer chart.

- Remember, you pass the checkout by reading the passage in less than a minute without making more than 2 mistakes. And when you pass the checkout, you color the space for lesson 80 on your thermometer chart.

b. (Call on individual students to read the portion of story 79 marked with ✿.)

- (Time the student. Note words that are missed and number of words read.)

- (Teacher reference:)

✿ Waldo went on to explain how he planned to complete the pyramid. He told her that he planned to train eight squirrels to stand on the four cats and sixteen pigeons to stand on the eight squirrels. Waldo concluded by saying, "The next time we put on a show, it [50] will be the greatest animal show that anybody ever saw."

Maria said, "I hope so. Every time I think of the first show we put [75] on, I feel like dying."

Waldo said, "It will be different next time."

And he was right.

• • •

The hall at Samson High School was packed [100] again. For a week before the show, Maria and Waldo had shown some of the acts that would be in the show. Each day, outside ✿ [125] the pet shop, they showed a different act.

- (If the student reads the passage in one minute or less and makes no more than 2 errors, direct the student to color in the space for lesson 80 on the thermometer chart.)

- (If the student makes any mistakes, point to each word that was misread and identify it.)
- (If the student does not meet the rate-error criterion for the passage, direct the student to practice reading the story with the assigned partner.)

EXERCISE 3

Test

a. **Find page 47 in your textbook.** ✔
- This is a test. You'll work items you've done before.
b. Work carefully. Raise your hand when you've completed all the items. (Observe students but do not give feedback on errors.)

EXERCISE 4

Marking the Test

a. (Check students' work before beginning lesson 81. Refer to the Answer Key for the correct answers.)
b. (Record all test 8 results on the Test Summary Sheet and the Group Summary Sheet. Reproducible Summary Sheets are at the back of the the *Teacher's Guide*.)

EXERCISE 5

Test Remedies

(Provide any necessary remedies for test 8 before presenting lesson 81. Test remedies are discussed in the *Teacher's Guide*.)

Test 8 Firming Table

Test Item	Introduced in lesson		Test Item	Introduced in lesson
1	71		14	78
2	71		15	79
3	71		16	79
4	71		17	79
5	71		18	79
6	74		19	79
7	74		20	79
8	74		21	79
9	77		22	74
10	77		23	71
11	77		24	74
12	77		25	71
13	78		26	71

SPELLING

(Present Spelling lesson 80 after completing Reading lesson 80. See *Spelling Presentation Book*.)

Lessons 81–85 • Planning Page *Looking Ahead*

	Lesson 81	Lesson 82	Lesson 83	Lesson 84	Lesson 85
LESSON EVENTS	Vocabulary Sentences Reading Words Story Reading Paired Practice Independent Work Workcheck Spelling	Vocabulary Sentence Reading Words Story Reading Paired Practice Independent Work Workcheck Spelling	**Vocabulary Sentence** Reading Words Fact Review Story Reading Paired Practice Independent Work Workcheck Spelling	Vocabulary Sentence Reading Words Story Background Story Reading Paired Practice Independent Work Workcheck Spelling	Vocabulary Sentences Reading Words Story Reading Fluency: Rate/ Accuracy Independent Work Workcheck Spelling
VOCABULARY SENTENCE	sentence #18 sentence #19 sentence #20	#20: She will <u>contact</u> the person we want to <u>hire</u>.	**#21: I have <u>confidence</u> we can <u>avoid</u> a long <u>conversation</u>.**	#21: I have <u>confidence</u> we can <u>avoid</u> a long <u>conversation</u>.	sentence #19 sentence #20 sentence #21
READING WORDS: WORD TYPES	modeled words words with underlined parts	modeled words multi-syllable words mixed words	compound words multi-syllable words	mixed words multi-syllable words	modeled words mixed words
NEW VOCABULARY	success woman's	emergency brake bare gear platform		instructor deathly	guide deadly fear panic
STORY BACKGROUND				*Facts About Coral*	
STORY	*Plans for a Trip*	*On the Tour*	*The Pyramid*	*The Animals' Greatest Show*	*Darla's Fear*
SKILL ITEMS	Vocabulary sentence Crossword puzzle	Vocabulary sentence		Sequencing	Vocabulary sentence
SPECIAL MATERIALS					Thermometer charts
SPECIAL PROJECTS/ ACTIVITIES		Activity after lesson 82		Project after lesson 84	

Comprehension Questions Abbreviations Guide

Access Prior Knowledge = (APK) Author's Point of View = (APoV) Author's Purpose = (AP) Cause/Effect = (C/E) Charts/Graphs/Diagrams/Visual Aids = (VA)

Classify and Categorize = (C+C) Compare/Contrast = (C/C) Determine Character Emotions, Motivation = (DCE) Drawing Conclusions = (DC) Drawing Inferences = (DI)

Fact and Opinion = (F/O) Hypothesizing = (H) Main Idea = (MI) Making Connections = (MC) Making Deductions = (MD) Making Judgements = (MJ)

Narrative Elements = (NE) Noting Details = (ND) Predict = (P) Reality/Fantasy = (R/F) Recall Facts/Rules = (RF/R) Retell = (R) Sequence = (Seq)

Steps in a Process = (SP) Story Structure = (SS) Summarize = (Sum) Understanding Dialogue = (UD) Using Context to Confirm Meaning(s) = (UCCM) Visualize = (V)

LESSON 81

EXERCISE 1

Vocabulary Review

a. You learned a sentence that tells what a lot of folks did.
- Everybody, say that sentence. Get ready. (Signal.) *A lot of folks mobbed the cute singer.*
- (Repeat until firm.)

b. You learned a sentence about the tour to the islands.
- Say that sentence. Get ready. (Signal.) *The tour to the islands was a fantastic experience.*
- (Repeat until firm.)

c. Here's the last sentence you learned: She will contact the person we want to hire.
- Everybody, say that sentence. Get ready. (Signal.) *She will contact the person we want to hire.*
- (Repeat until firm.)

d. Everybody, what word tells about getting in touch with somebody? (Signal.) *Contact.*
- What word tells about giving somebody a job? (Signal.) *Hire.*

e. Once more. Say the sentence that tells who she will contact. Get ready. (Signal.) *She will contact the person we want to hire.*

EXERCISE 2

Reading Words

Column 1

a. **Find lesson 81 in your textbook.** ✔
- Touch column 1. ✔
- (Teacher reference:)

1. success	4. hire
2. Christmas	5. officer
3. fantastic	

b. Word 1 is **success.** What word? (Signal.) *Success.*
- Spell **success.** Get ready. (Tap for each letter.) *S-U-C-C-E-S-S.*

- When you have success, you do very well at something. If somebody has success in school, the person does very well in school. Tell me about a person who has success in business. (Call on a student. Idea. *The person does very well in business.*)

c. Word 2. What word? (Signal.) *Christmas.*
- (Repeat for words 3–5.)

d. Let's read those words again, the fast way.
- Word 1. What word? (Signal.) *Success.*
- (Repeat for words 2–5.)

e. (Repeat step d until firm.)

Column 2

f. Find column 2. ✔
- (Teacher reference:)

1. **woman's**	4. **schoolwork**
2. **trailer**	5. **contacted**
3. **tours**	

g. These words have more than one part. The first part of each word is underlined.

h. Word 1. What's the underlined part? (Signal.) *woman.*
- What's the whole word? (Signal.) *Woman's.*
- Something that belongs to a woman is the **woman's.** A coat that belongs to the woman is the woman's coat.
- Word 2. What's the underlined part? (Signal.) *trail.*
- What's the whole word? (Signal.) *Trailer.*
- Spell **trailer.** Get ready. (Tap for each letter.) *T-R-A-I-L-E-R.*
- Word 3. What's the underlined part? (Signal.) *tour.*
- What's the whole word? (Signal.) *Tours.*
- Spell **tours.** Get ready. (Tap for each letter.) *T-O-U-R-S.*
- Word 4. What's the underlined part? (Signal.) *school.*
- What's the whole word? (Signal.) *Schoolwork.*
- Word 5. What's the underlined part? (Signal.) *contact.*
- What's the whole word? (Signal.) *Contacted.*

i. Let's read those words again, the fast way.
- Word 1. What word? (Signal.) *Woman's.*
- (Repeat for: **2. trailer, 3 tours, 4. schoolwork, 5. contacted.**)
j. (Repeat step i until firm.)

Individual Turns

(For columns 1 and 2: Call on individual students, each to read one to three words per turn.)

Story Reading

a. Find part B in your textbook. ✔
- The error limit for group reading is 15 errors.
b. Everybody, touch the title. ✔
- (Call on a student to read the title.) *[Plans for a Trip.]*
- Everybody, what's the title? (Signal.) *Plans for a Trip.* (ND)
- What trick did an animal do at the end of the last story? (Call on a student. Ideas: *Somersaults.*) What was the next act going to be? (Call on a student. Ideas: *The upside-down pyramid; the super trick.*) (APK)
c. (Call on individual students to read the story, each student reading two or three sentences at a time. Ask the specified questions as the students read.)

- (Correct errors: Tell the word. Direct the student to reread the sentence.)
- (If the group makes more than 15 errors, direct the students to reread the story.)

Plans for a Trip

Maria walked out to the middle of the stage. "Ladies and gentlemen," she said. "You know that dogs don't like cats and cats don't like squirrels and squirrels don't get along well with birds. You're going to love this next act because it involves dogs, cats, squirrels and birds. All these animals will work together to form an upside-down pyramid. So welcome all these animals and watch them work together." The audience welcomed the animals by clapping very loudly.

All the animals came onto the stage and faced the audience. First the large dog walked out and stood in the middle of the stage.

Then the two smaller dogs walked out and took their places, one on each side of the huge dog. Then the four cats came out. Two went on one side of the stage and two went on the other. The squirrels came out next. The audience laughed as the squirrels took their places with their long tails held high in the air.

The last animals to come out on the stage were the birds—sixteen pigeons. When all the animals were lined up facing the audience, Waldo gave them a signal and all of them bowed. The animals with four legs bowed by lifting one front paw and then bending forward. The birds crossed their legs and bent forward.

- Everybody, show me how the four-legged animals held their front paws and bent forward. ✔ (V)

People in the audience laughed and shouted.

Then Waldo gave a signal to the two smaller dogs. They jumped onto the back of the huge dog. Next, Waldo signaled the cats. They took their place. People in the audience were pointing and laughing and talking. Waldo felt very good.

Next, Waldo signaled the squirrels. When they took their place, the audience applauded so loudly that it sounded like thunder. Maria walked to the middle of the stage and said, "And now for the top of the pyramid, sixteen pigeons."

Waldo signaled the pigeons. They took off and flew over the audience. They circled the hall three times. Everybody watched them. Then Waldo whistled loudly and all the birds landed on top of the squirrels. At first the audience didn't clap. Everybody just went "Ohhh," and "Oooo," and "Wow." Then the people

clapped and cheered and stood up and cheered louder.
Waldo said to himself, "That's a good trick."

• • •

- Tell me what the birds did before they landed on the squirrels. (Call on a student. Idea: *Circled the hall three times.*) ⓃⒹ
- Everybody, how did Waldo signal the birds to land on the squirrels? (Signal.) *He whistled.* ⓃⒹ
- How did the audience first respond when the birds landed? (Call on a student. Idea: *They said, "Ohhh," "Oooo," and "Wow."*) ⓃⒹ
- What do those three dots in the story mean? (Call on a student. Idea: *Part of the story is missing.*) ⓈⓈ

For a few days after the big show at Samson High School, Waldo felt very excited. People stopped him on the street and said things like, "We saw your show. It was fantastic." Waldo always thanked the people, but he felt a little embarrassed.

- Why would he feel embarrassed? (Call on a student. Idea: *Because he felt funny about people making a big deal about the animals.*) ⒹⒸⒺ

Things were very busy at the pet shop.

- Why? (Call on a student. Idea: *Because lots of pets were being sold.*) ⒹⒾ

Maria didn't have enough pets to fill the orders for trained dogs, trained pigeons, and trained cats. Some people put in special orders.

- What does that mean, special orders? (Call on a student. Idea: *People wanted special animals to do special tricks.*) ⓊⒸⒸⓂ ⒹⒸ

One man wanted a cat that would ring a bell when it wanted to go ✦ outside.

- That's a special order.

An old woman wanted a dog that would keep rabbits and birds out of her garden.
A truck driver wanted a trained cat that would ride in the truck with her and honk the truck horn when the woman gave it a signal.
So Maria was on the phone most of the time taking orders, and Waldo was busy training animals. One day, Maria told Waldo, "We've never had this much business, not even at Christmas time."

- Everybody, what time of year is normally the busiest for the pet shop? (Signal.) *Christmas time.* ⒹⒸ
- How much business does Maria have now? (Call on a student. Idea: *More than at Christmas time.*) ⓃⒹ

Five days after the big show at Samson High School, Maria asked Waldo, "How would you like to go on a tour?"
"What's that?" Waldo asked.
"A tour is a traveling show."

- Everybody, what's a tour? (Signal.) *A traveling show.* ⓃⒹ

She continued, "We go to one city and put on a show. Then we go to the next city and put on a show. The tour that I'm thinking about would take about a month. We'd put on shows in over thirty cities."

- Everybody, how long will the tour last? (Signal.) *About a month.* ⓃⒹ
- How many shows is Maria planning for the tour? (Signal.) *Over thirty.* ⓃⒹ

"Wow," Waldo said. "That's great." Then he hesitated. "But . . ."
Before he could tell Maria what the problem was, she said, "I know what you're thinking. You're wondering how you'll do your schoolwork if you're on this trip."

- What did she think Waldo was worried about? (Call on a student. Idea: *How he could do his schoolwork while on the tour.*) ⓃⒹ

"That's right," Waldo said. "If I'm out of school for a month, I'll be far behind in my schoolwork."

"I've already taken care of that," Maria said. "I've called your school and told them about the tour. They're going to tell me what work will be covered in the classes that you're taking. On the tour, I'll go over that work with you. I'll be your teacher."

- How would Waldo keep up with his schoolwork? (Call on a student. Idea: *Maria would be his teacher.*) (ND)
- Read the rest of the story to yourself and be ready to answer some questions. Raise your hand when you're done.
- There are three dots in the middle of the part you'll read. So figure out where Waldo is after the three dots.

Waldo smiled. "Do you mean we'll study on the tour?"

"Sure," she said. "We're going to take a small truck and a big trailer. The animals will be in the trailer. You and I will be in the truck. We'll hire a driver to drive the truck. So you and I can study as we go from city to city."

Maria went on to explain that a person who put on tours for good shows contacted her and set up the places they would go. "And we'll make a lot of money," Maria said. "All we need now is permission from your parents."

• • •

"Waldo, you're hardly eating," Waldo's mother said. "What's the matter?"

Waldo's sister said, "Oh, he doesn't eat any food unless he . . ."
"That's enough," Waldo's father said. Then he turned to Waldo and said, "I feel that you're trying to tell us something. What is it?"

"Well," Waldo said slowly. "Can I go on a tour and put on shows in over thirty cities with the animals?"

Waldo's mother sat up very straight and put her fork down. "What are you talking about?" she said. "What tour? Which cities?"

So Waldo explained the tour. Then he added, "I'll get my schoolwork done. The school has given permission. Everything is all set if you give me permission. Can I go?"

- (After all students have raised their hand:)
- Everybody, what will Waldo and Maria be in when they travel from city to city? (Signal.) *A truck.* (ND)
- What will be behind the truck? (Signal.) *A trailer.* (ND)
- What will the trailer hold? (Signal.) *The animals.* (ND)
- Who will drive the truck? (Signal.) *A driver.* (ND)
- Where was Waldo after the three dots in the story? (Call on a student. Idea: *At his house.*) (DC)
- Everybody, which member of the family was not eating? (Signal.) *Waldo.* (ND)
- What did Waldo ask his parents at the end of the story? (Call on a student. Idea: *If he could go on the tour with Maria.*) (ND)
- Listen to what Waldo said when he tried to convince his parents that he should go on the trip.

    "I'll get my schoolwork done. The school has given permission. Everything is all set if you give me permission. Can I go?"

If you were Waldo's parents, would you be persuaded by what Waldo said?

- A person like Grandmother Esther could persuade people that the trip was even more important than it really was. Pretend that Waldo is Grandmother Esther and say some of the persuasive things that she might say about the trip. (Call on individual students. Praise attempts to use superlatives, for example the most important, the greatest, the last chance; a presentation that was loud and emphatic.) (APK)

EXERCISE 4

Paired Practice

You're going to read aloud to your partner. Today the **B** members will read first. Then the **A** members will read from the star to the end of the story. (Observe students and give feedback.)

End-of-Lesson Activities

INDEPENDENT WORK

Now finish the independent work for lesson 81. Raise your hand when you're finished. (Observe students and give feedback.)

WORKCHECK

a. (Direct students to take out their marking pencils.)
- We're going to check your independent work. Remember, if you got an item wrong, make an **X** next to the item.
b. (For each item: Read the item. Call on a student to answer it. If the answer is wrong, say the correct answer. Refer to the Answer Key for the correct answers.)
c. Now use your marking pencil to fix up any items you got wrong. Remember, all mistakes must be fixed up before you hand in your independent work.

SPELLING

(Present Spelling lesson 81 after completing Reading lesson 81. See *Spelling Presentation Book*.)

EXERCISE 1

Vocabulary Review

a. You learned a sentence that tells who she will contact.
- Everybody, say that sentence. Get ready. (Signal.) *She will contact the person we want to hire.*
- (Repeat until firm.)

b. I'll say part of the sentence. When I stop, you say the next word. Listen: She will . . . Everybody, what's the next word? (Signal.) *Contact.*

c. Listen: She will contact the person we want to . . . Everybody, what's the next word? (Signal.) *Hire.*
- Say the whole sentence. Get ready. (Signal.) *She will contact the person we want to hire.*

EXERCISE 2

Reading Words

Column 1

a. **Find lesson 82 in your textbook.** ✔
- Touch column 1. ✔
- (Teacher reference:)

1. emergency brake	4. avoid
2. confidence	5. bare
3. conversation	6. gear

b. Number 1 is **emergency brake.** What words? (Signal.) *Emergency brake.*
- An emergency brake is a brake you use if the regular brake does not work.

c. Word 2 is **confidence.** What word? (Signal.) *Confidence.*

d. Word 3 is **conversation.** What word? (Signal.) *Conversation.*

e. Word 4 is **avoid.** What word? (Signal.) *Avoid.*
- Spell avoid. Get ready. (Tap for each letter.) *A-V-O-I-D.*

f. Word 5. What word? (Signal.) *Bare.*
- Spell **bare.** Get ready. (Tap for each letter.) *B-A-R-E.*
- When something is bare, it has no coverings. Everybody, what would you call roots that have no covering? (Signal.) *Bare roots.*

- What would you call wood that has no covering? (Signal.) *Bare wood.*

g. Word 6. What word? (Signal.) *Gear.*
- Spell **gear.** Get ready. (Tap for each letter.) *G-E-A-R.*
- The supplies and equipment that you take with you are called your gear. A person with a lot of gear has a lot of supplies and equipment. If you took camping gear with you, what kind of things would you take? (Call on individual students. Ideas: *Tent, sleeping bags, camp stove, sleeping pads; etc.*)

h. Let's read those words again, the fast way.
- Number 1. What words? (Signal.) *Emergency brake.*
- Word 2. What word? (Signal.) *Confidence.*
- (Repeat for words 3–6.)

i. (Repeat step h until firm.)

Column 2

j. Find column 2. ✔
- (Teacher reference:)

1. platform	4. pickup
2. haven't	5. steering
3. understood	

k. These words have more than one part. The first part of each word is underlined.

l. Word 1. What's the underlined part? (Signal.) *plat.*
- What's the whole word? (Signal.) *Platform.*
- A platform is a level place that is above the places around it.
- Word 2. What's the underlined part? (Signal.) *have.*
- What's the whole word? (Signal.) *Haven't.*
- Word 3. What's the underlined part? (Signal.) *under.*
- What's the whole word? (Signal.) *Understood.*
- Word 4. What's the underlined part? (Signal.) *pick.*
- What's the whole word? (Signal.) *Pickup.*
- Word 5. What's the underlined part? (Signal.) *steer.*

- What's the whole word? (Signal.) *Steering.*
- m. Let's read those words again, the fast way.
  - Word 1. What word? (Signal.) *Platform.*
  - (Repeat for: **2. haven't, 3. understood, 4. pickup, 5. steering.**)
- n. (Repeat step m until firm.)

Column 3

o. Find column 3. ✔
- (Teacher reference:)

1. success	4. pressed
2. hooked	5. winding
3. tires	

p. Word 1. What word? (Signal.) *Success.*
- (Repeat for words 2–5.)
q. Let's read those words again.
- Word 1. What word? (Signal.) *Success.*
- (Repeat for words 2–5.)
r. (Repeat step q until firm.)

Individual Turns

(For columns 1–3: Call on individual students, each to read one to three words per turn.)

EXERCISE 3

Story Reading

a. Find part B in your textbook. ✔
- The error limit for group reading is 16 errors.
b. Everybody, touch the title. ✔
- (Call on a student to read the title.) *[On the Tour.]*
- Everybody, what's the title? (Signal.) *On the Tour.* ⓃⒹ
c. (Call on individual students to read the story, each student reading two or three sentences at a time. Ask the specified questions as the students read.)

- (**Correct errors:** Tell the word. Direct the student to reread the sentence.)
- (If the group makes more than 16 errors, direct the students to reread the story.)

On the Tour

Waldo had just asked his parents an important question.

- What question? (Call on a student. Idea: *Can I go [on the trip]?*) ⒶⓅⓀ

Waldo's father said, "I'd like to talk to Maria and get a little more information about this trip. But if the tour is like you say it is, I don't see any problem."

- What does Waldo's father want to do before he gives permission? (Call on a student. Ideas: *Talk to Maria; get more information about the trip.*) ⓃⒹ
- Why does he want to do that? (Call on a student. Ideas: *So he'll know all about the trip; to make sure Waldo will get his schoolwork done.*) ⒹⒾ

Waldo's father stood up. "I'll call her right now." He walked toward the phone. Before he could pick it up, it rang. He answered, "Hello." Then there was a long pause. "No," he said. "We haven't seen any goats around here for days. If I see one with a red collar, I'll be sure to let you know." He hung up the phone.

- Somebody called Waldo's house. What did the person want to know? (Call on a student. Idea: *If Waldo's father had seen a goat with a red collar.*) ⒹⒾ
- Why do you think that person called Waldo's house? (Call on a student. Idea: *Because lots of animals used to go to Waldo's house.*) ⒹⒸ

Then Waldo's father called Maria. "Tell me about this tour," he said. He talked on the phone for about five minutes. He didn't say much except, "Yes, yes," and "Well, that sounds fine," and "Oh, I see."

After he hung up, he went into the other room with Waldo's mother. He came back and called Maria again. "That sounds like a very good tour," he said. "We'll let Waldo go on it."

- Everybody, when Waldo's father talked on the phone to Maria, did he become persuaded that Waldo could go on the trip? (Signal.) *Yes.* ⓂⒸ
- We don't know what Maria said, but she must have been more persuasive than Waldo was. What are some of the things she could have said to persuade Waldo's father? (Call on individual students. Ideas: *The trip was very important; not many people have the chance to take such a trip; Waldo would be safe because Maria would keep an eye on him; she could help him with his schoolwork and make sure that he worked on it every day; the trip could make Waldo very famous and rich.*) ⓂⒸ

Waldo jumped up from his chair. "I'm going!" he said. "I'm going on a tour! Oh, boy!"

- How did Waldo feel? (Call on a student. Ideas: *Excited; he could hardly wait*.) DCE

Waldo's brother said, "I'll bet Waldo will want to make a lot of food before he goes. Don't let him cook here."

Waldo's mother said, "Don't worry, dear. Waldo can do all his cooking at the pet shop. And you should try to be nice to your brother, because he's going to be gone for a month."

• • •

The tour was a fantastic success. The halls in all the cities were sold out.

- What does that mean, they were sold out? (Call on a student. Idea: *All the tickets had been bought*.) UCCM

People were lined up for blocks outside some of the halls. There were posters and ads in the newspapers. At the top of the posters and ads were the words: "The most incredible animal show on Earth."

The tour took Waldo and Maria to Denver, Colorado. That was their sixth show.

- Everybody, how many shows had they done **before** they got to Denver? (Signal.) *Five.* DC

From Denver, they went to another city in Colorado—Greeley. Then they started the long drive over the Rocky Mountains. Their next stop was in the state of Utah, on the other side of the Rocky Mountains.

After leaving Greeley, Waldo and Maria were trying to study in the truck as the driver took them up the winding mountain roads. Waldo had

trouble keeping his mind on the work, because the view outside was incredible. Waldo had never seen mountains like these before. Their tops were covered with snow, and they were so big and steep that he could hardly believe what he was seeing. From time to time, the truck would go near the edge of the road and Waldo could look down. Each time he looked down, he would get an uneasy feeling.

- Why? (Call on a student. Idea: *Because he was up so high*.) DC
- What would he feel uneasy about? (Call on a student. Ideas: *How close he was to the edge; the truck going over the edge; falling*.) DI

The mountains seemed to go almost straight down, down, down. Every now and then he caught himself thinking, "If the truck ever went over the edge . . ."

- What would happen? (Call on a student. Idea: *Everyone would die*.) P

Then he would stop himself and try to think about how beautiful the mountains were.

After a while, Maria said, "I'll tell you what. Let's stop trying to study for a while. Let's just look at the mountains."

An hour later, the truck was still winding its way through the mountains. Now the truck was near the top of the highest ⭐ mountains. Deep banks of snow were on either side of the road. A mountain goat was standing on some bare rocks that were sticking out of the snow.

Then the truck came to a sign that said, "Check your brakes—long downgrade."

- Everybody, look at the picture. It shows the truck going through the mountains. What is inside the trailer? (Signal.) *The animals.* (APK)
- Touch the sign that says "Check your brakes." ✔ (VA)
- Touch the mountain goat. ✔ (VA)
- Touch the bank of snow on either side of the road. ✔ (VA)

"What does that sign mean?" Waldo asked.

The driver said, "We're going to start going down the other side of the mountain now, and we'll be going down for a long, long time. You don't want to go down this part of the road unless you have good brakes."

The pickup truck started down the winding road. At first it moved slowly. Then Waldo noticed that the truck was gaining speed.

- What does gaining speed mean? (Call on a student. Idea: *Going faster.*) (UCCM)

Waldo looked over at the driver. The driver's face had a serious expression, and Waldo noticed that he was holding the steering wheel so hard that parts of his hands were white.

- Something is wrong. Everybody, show me how the driver looked when he had a serious expression. ✔ (V)
- Make a fist so hard that parts of your hand turn lighter. ✔ (V)

Maria asked, "Aren't you going a little fast for this road?"

The driver said, "The trailer brakes aren't working."

- What's wrong? (Call on a student. Idea: *The trailer brakes weren't working.*) (ND)
- That truck can't go down a steep grade if the trailer brakes aren't working. The trailer will push the truck so hard that the truck won't be able to slow down.

The driver continued, "The truck brakes are all right. But they're working very hard, and they'll start to fade out soon."

- What does that mean, the brakes will fade out? (Call on a student. Idea: *They'll keep getting weaker until they don't work at all.*) (UCCM)

Waldo remembered back to the time when they were getting ready to leave on the trip. The driver hooked up a line from the trailer to the truck. He had explained to Waldo that the line was connected to the brakes on the trailer. When the driver put on the truck brakes, the trailer brakes would also work. The driver had told Waldo that the trailer was so heavy that it needed its own brakes. Without those brakes, the pickup truck would have a hard time stopping.

- Read the rest of the story to yourself and be ready to answer some questions. Raise your hand when you're done.

Now the truck was going very fast down the mountain. The tires screeched as the truck went around a sharp curve. For a moment, it seemed as if the truck would go over the edge. In fact, the truck went through some stones on the side of the road. Then it came back on the road and continued to gain speed.

The driver said, "The trailer is pushing us, and the truck brakes are gone now."

The truck seemed to be flying down the road. It came up behind a car that was loaded with camping gear. The driver of the pickup truck honked the horn and went around the car like it was standing still. Faster, faster, faster. The truck was now on a long, straight part of the road, but the grade was very steep and the truck was going so fast that the engine sounded as if it was ready to fly apart. Waldo could smell the burnt-out brakes.

Waldo was almost afraid to look outside, so he watched the driver. The driver had his foot pressed down hard on the brake pedal, but the pickup truck continued to speed down the long, straight part of the road. The driver turned on the truck lights and pressed his hand against the horn. Waldo understood what the driver was trying to do. He was trying to warn the other cars on the road that the truck was in trouble. The sounds were terrible—the engine screaming, the horn blasting, the air rushing outside the truck. And the smell of the burnt-out brakes was strong. Waldo felt sick. He tried not to think about what was happening. He tried not to think about his animals in the trailer and what might happen to them.

- (After all students have raised their hand:)
- How close to the edge did the truck come when it went around one curve? (Call on a student. Ideas: *Very close; close enough to go on the stones next to the road.*) ⓝⓓ
- What happened to the truck brakes? (Call on a student. Idea: *They stopped working.*) ⓝⓓ
- What did the truck do when it came up behind the car that was loaded with camping gear? (Call on a student. Ideas: *Honked its horn; passed the car.*) ⓝⓓ
- How did the truck engine sound? (Call on a student. Idea: *As if it was ready to fly apart.*) ⓝⓓ
- Why? (Call on a student. Ideas: *Because the truck was going so fast; the engine was working so hard.*) ⓓⒸ

- Everybody, what could Waldo smell? (Signal.) *Burnt-out brakes.* ⓝⓓ
- When the truck brakes are used, they get hot. The driver had used them so much that they burned out completely. Waldo smelled those burnt-out brakes.
- What two things did the driver do to warn the other cars that the truck was in trouble? (Call on a student. Idea: *Turned on the truck lights and honked the horn.*) ⓝⓓ

Paired Practice

You're going to read aloud to your partner. Today the **A** members will read first. Then the **B** members will read from the star to the end of the story. (Observe students and give feedback.)

End-of-Lesson Activities

INDEPENDENT WORK

Now finish the independent work for lesson 82. Raise your hand when you're finished. (Observe students and give feedback.)

WORKCHECK

a. (Direct students to take out their marking pencils.)
- We're going to check your independent work. Remember, if you got an item wrong, make an **X** next to the item.
b. (For each item: Read the item. Call on a student to answer it. If the answer is wrong, say the correct answer. Refer to the Answer Key for the correct answers.)
c. Now use your marking pencil to fix up any items you got wrong. Remember, all mistakes must be fixed up before you hand in your independent work.

SPELLING

(Present Spelling lesson 82 after completing Reading lesson 82. See *Spelling Presentation Book.*)

ACTIVITIES

(Present Activity 16 after completing Reading lesson 82. See *Activities across the Curriculum.*)

EXERCISE 1

Vocabulary

a. **Find page 367 in your textbook.** ✔
- Touch sentence 21. ✔
- This is a new vocabulary sentence. It says: I have confidence that we can avoid a long conversation. Everybody, read that sentence. Get ready. (Signal.) *I have confidence that we can avoid a long conversation.*
- Close your eyes and say the sentence. Get ready. (Signal.) *I have confidence that we can avoid a long conversation.*
- (Repeat until firm.)

b. When you have **confidence** about something, you are **sure** about it. Here's another way of saying **She was sure that her answer was right: She had confidence that her answer was right.** Everybody, what's another way of saying **She was sure that her answer was right?** (Signal.) *She had confidence that her answer was right.*
- What's another way of saying **They were sure that they could get home in time?** (Signal.) *They had confidence that they could get home in time.*

c. When people talk to each other about something, they have a **conversation** about that thing. Here's another way of saying **Two people talked about school: Two people had a conversation about school.**
- Everybody, what's another way of saying **They talked about the movie for hours?** (Signal.) *They had a conversation about the movie for hours.*

d. The sentence talks about avoiding a long conversation. When you **avoid** something, you **stay away from** that thing. When you avoid Milly, you stay away from Milly. Everybody, what do you do if you avoid a long conversation? (Signal.) *Stay away from a long conversation.*
- What do you do if you stay away from ice cream? (Signal.) *Avoid ice cream.*

e. Listen to the sentence again: I have confidence that we can avoid a long conversation. Everybody, say the sentence. Get ready. (Signal.) *I have confidence that we can avoid a long conversation.*

f. Everybody, what word tells what you do when you stay away from something? (Signal.) *Avoid.*
- What word tells that you are sure about something? (Signal.) *Confidence.*
- What word describes people talking to each other about something? (Signal.) *Conversation.*
- (Repeat step f until firm.)

EXERCISE 2

Reading Words

Column 1

a. Find lesson 83 in your textbook. ✔
- Touch column 1. ✔
- (Teacher reference:)

1. schoolwork	3. pickup
2. understood	4. policemen

b. These words are compound words. The first part of each word is underlined.

c. Word 1. What's the underlined part? (Signal.) *school.*
- What's the whole word? (Signal.) *Schoolwork.*
- Word 2. What's the underlined part? (Signal.) *under.*
- What's the whole word? (Signal.) *Understood.*
- Word 3. What's the underlined part? (Signal.) *pick.*
- What's the whole word? (Signal.) *Pickup.*
- Word 4. What's the underlined part? (Signal.) *police.*
- What's the whole word? (Signal.) *Policemen.*

d. Let's read those words again, the fast way.
- Word 1. What word? (Signal.) *Schoolwork.*
- (Repeat for words 2–4.)

e. (Repeat step d until firm.)

Column 2

f. Find column 2. ✔
- (Teacher reference:)

> 1. platform   4. conversation
> 2. avoid   5. emergency
> 3. sharply   6. confidence

g. Word 1. What word? (Signal.) *Platform.*
- Spell **platform.** Get ready. (Tap for each letter.) *P-L-A-T-F-O-R-M.*

h. Word 2. What word? (Signal.) *Avoid.*
- Spell **avoid.** Get ready. (Tap for each letter.) *A-V-O-I-D.*

i. Word 3. What word? (Signal.) *Sharply.*
- Spell **sharply.** Get ready. (Tap for each letter.) *S-H-A-R-P-L-Y.*

j. Word 4. What word? (Signal.) *Conversation.*
- (Repeat for words 5 and 6.)

k. Let's read those words again, the fast way.
- Word 1. What word? (Signal.) *Platform.*
- (Repeat for words 2–6.)

l. (Repeat step k until firm.)

Individual Turns

(For columns 1 and 2: Call on individual students, each to read one to three words per turn.)

EXERCISE 3

Fact Review

a. Let's review some facts you have learned. First we'll go over the facts together. Then I'll call on individual students to do some facts.

b. Everybody, tell me how fast Traveler Four travels. (Pause.) Get ready. (Signal.) *1,000 miles per second.* (RF/R)
- Name the planets, starting with Mercury. Get ready. (Signal.) *Mercury, Venus, Earth, Mars, Jupiter, Saturn, Uranus, Neptune, Pluto.* (RF/R)
- Tell me how far it is from Earth to Jupiter. (Pause.) Get ready. (Signal.) *400 million miles.* (RF/R)
- Name the mountains you drive over to get from Colorado to Utah. (Pause.) Get ready. (Signal.) *Rocky Mountains.* (RF/R)
- (Repeat step b until firm.)

c. When lava is very hot, it's orange. Everybody, tell me what color lava is after it cools a little bit. (Pause.) Get ready. (Signal.) *Brown.* (RF/R)
- Tell me what color lava is after it's completely cooled. (Pause.) Get ready. (Signal.) *Gray.* (RF/R)
- Name the country that the states of Colorado and Utah are in. (Pause.) Get ready. (Signal.) *United States.* (RF/R)
- Tell me which direction you go to get from Colorado to Utah. (Pause.) Get ready. (Signal.) *West.* (RF/R)
- (Repeat step c until firm.)

Individual Turns

Now I'm going to call on individual students to do some facts. (Call on individual students to do the set of facts in step b or step c.)

EXERCISE 4

Story Reading

a. Find part B in your textbook. ✔
- The error limit for group reading is 12 errors.

b. Everybody, touch the title. ✔
- (Call on a student to read the title.) *[The Pyramid.]*
- Everybody, what's the title? (Signal.) *The Pyramid.* (ND)
- Where did we leave Waldo and Maria? (Call on a student. Idea: *Speeding down a mountain.*) (APK)
- What was the problem? (Call on a student: Idea: *The truck brakes and the trailer brakes were not working.*) (APK)

c. (Call on individual students to read the story, each student reading two or three sentences at a time. Ask the specified questions as the students read.)

- (**Correct errors:** Tell the word. Direct the student to reread the sentence.)
- (If the group makes more than 12 errors, direct the students to reread the story.)

The Pyramid

"Isn't there anything we can do?" Maria shouted.

"There's an emergency brake in the trailer," the driver said. "But I don't know how we can get back there to push down on it."

Waldo turned around and looked at the trailer. It was like a big box with a little window facing the truck. The window was too small for anybody to climb through.

Waldo asked, "How does the emergency brake work and where is it?"

The driver explained, "The brake is on the left side of the trailer. It's on a little platform. But you have to push down on it with a lot of weight to make it work. You have to press down on it with the weight of at least 80 pounds."

- Everybody, how much weight do you have to push down with to make the emergency brake work? (Signal.) *80 pounds.* (ND)

The truck was speeding toward another curve. It wasn't a very sharp curve, but the truck and trailer almost tipped over when it went around the curve. The truck started to slide and the tires screeched. The rear wheels of the truck started to slide off the road. Waldo looked down. For a moment he didn't breathe. Then the truck came back onto the road. A car coming the other way was right in front of the truck. The truck driver kept honking the horn. The car turned sharply. The truck just missed the car and continued to fly down the road.

"I'm going to work that emergency brake," Waldo yelled.

He opened the back window of the truck and climbed through it into the pickup bed.

- Everybody, look at the picture. It shows Waldo in the pickup bed.

Just then, the truck went around another curve. The curve was not very sharp, but the truck was going so fast that Waldo almost fell out of the truck bed. His heart was pounding and he had trouble breathing, because the wind was blowing so hard.

He crawled to the back of the truck bed, stood up, and leaned against the front of the trailer. The little window was open. Inside, he could see the animals. They looked frightened. They were either lying down or standing with their legs far apart so that they wouldn't fall down. The dogs and cats were panting.

Waldo called the huge dog that stood at the bottom of the pyramid.

- What do you think Waldo is going to try to get that dog to do? (Call on a student. Ideas: *Push on the brake; make a pyramid.*) (P)

The dog was lying in the middle of the floor. When Waldo called, the dog stopped panting and looked at Waldo, but the dog did not move. Waldo stuck his hand through the open window and gave the dog a signal to walk to ☆ the left side of the trailer. Waldo called the dog three times and gave the signal three times before the dog slowly stood up and followed the signal.

- What's on the left side of the trailer? (Call on a student. Idea: *The emergency brake.*) (ND)

When the dog got near the platform with the emergency brake on it, Waldo gave the dog a signal to put its front paws on the platform. "Up," Waldo shouted. "Get up." The dog looked at Waldo. Then, as the truck trembled and rocked from side to side, the huge dog put one paw on the platform and then the other paw on the platform. The emergency brake was right in front of the dog's paws. "Forward!" Waldo shouted. The huge dog moved its paws forward. Now the dog's two front paws were on the brake pedal, pushing down.

- Everybody, how many paws did the huge dog have on the brake pedal? (Signal.) *Two.* (ND)
- Look at the picture on page 60. Touch the platform the emergency brake is on. ✔ (VA)
- Touch the brake pedal that the dog's paws are pushing down on. ✔ (VA)
- Is the dog pushing down on that pedal with all its weight? (Signal.) *No.* (DC)
- Yes, the dog is pushing down with two paws, not all four paws, so it's not pushing down with all its weight.
- Do you think the dog has enough weight on the pedal to make the emergency brake work? (Call on a student. Student preference.) (MJ)

"Good," Waldo shouted. "Good boy."
But the trailer did not slow down.

- Everybody, was there enough weight on the emergency brake to make it work? (Signal.) *No.* (DC)
- How much weight has to push down on the brake before it works? (Signal.) *80 pounds.* (ND)

Although the dog weighed more than 100 pounds, the dog did not have all its weight on the brake pedal. Only the dog's front paws were on the brake. So only part of the dog's weight was pushing down on the brake.

- Listen to that part again.
  Although the dog weighed more than 100 pounds, the dog did not have all its weight on the brake pedal. Only the dog's front paws were on the brake. So only part of the dog's weight was pushing down on the brake.
- Everybody, if the dog had all its weight on the brake, would the brake work? (Signal.) *Yes.* (DC)
- Why? (Call on a student. Idea: *Because the dog weighed more than 100 pounds.*) (ND)
- Why wasn't all the dog's weight on the brake? (Call on a student. Idea: *Because only its front paws were on it.*) (ND)
- Read the rest of the story to yourself and be ready to answer some questions. Raise your hand when you're done.

"I need more weight on that brake," Waldo said to himself. Waldo turned around to see where the truck was going. Far ahead down the road was a curve—a sharp one. If the truck went into that curve at high speed, the truck would go off the mountain.
Waldo signaled the two smaller dogs. "Make a pyramid," he said, and gave the dogs a hand signal.

The two smaller dogs seemed afraid to try to jump on the huge dog. The spotted dog tried, but fell off. The black dog tried and managed to stay on the huge dog's back. Then the spotted dog tried again. This time, that dog stayed on the huge dog's back.

The truck was starting to slow down. It was moving at a terrible speed, but Waldo could feel it start to slow down. Waldo turned around and looked at the sharp curve ahead of the truck. It wasn't far away now, and it was getting closer by the second. The dogs were not putting enough weight on the brake to make the truck stop fast.

"Cats," Waldo yelled. "Cats, get on the pyramid." He signaled the cats. For a moment, they stood without moving. Then, with one great leap, the first cat jumped onto the back of the spotted dog. Then another cat, and another. Finally, the last cat got on the pyramid.

The truck was almost to the curve.

- (After all students have raised their hand:)
- Everybody, did both the smaller dogs get on the huge dog the first time they tried? (Signal.) *No.* ⓝⒹ
- What happened? (Call on a student. Idea: *The spotted dog fell off.*) ⓝⒹ
- Everybody, was the weight of the three dogs enough to make the brake work? (Signal.) *Yes.* ⓝⒹ
- Was there enough weight to make the brake stop the trailer very fast? (Signal.) *No.* ⓝⒹ
- Why was it important for the trailer to stop fast? (Call on a student. Idea: *Because they were getting close to a sharp curve.*) ⒹⒸ
- So what did Waldo do to get more weight on the brake? (Call on a student. Idea: *Signaled the cats to get on the pyramid.*) ⓝⒹ

- Do you think there will be enough weight with the cats on the pyramid? (Call on individual students. Student preference.) Ⓟ

Paired Practice

You're going to read aloud to your partner. Today the **B** members will read first. Then the **A** members will read from the star to the end of the story. (Observe students and give feedback.)

End-of-Lesson Activities

INDEPENDENT WORK

Now finish the independent work for lesson 83. Raise your hand when you're finished. (Observe students and give feedback.)

WORKCHECK

a. (Direct students to take out their marking pencils.)
- We're going to check your independent work. Remember, if you got an item wrong, make an **X** next to the item.
b. (For each item: Read the item. Call on a student to answer it. If the answer is wrong, say the correct answer. Refer to the Answer Key for the correct answers.)
c. Now use your marking pencil to fix up any items you got wrong. Remember, all mistakes must be fixed up before you hand in your independent work.

SPELLING

(Present Spelling lesson 83 after completing Reading lesson 83. See *Spelling Presentation Book.*)

Note: A special project occurs after lesson 84. No special materials are required.

EXERCISE 1

Vocabulary Review

a. Here's the new vocabulary sentence: I have confidence that we can avoid a long conversation.
- Everybody, say the sentence. Get ready. (Signal.) *I have confidence that we can avoid a long conversation.*
- (Repeat until firm.)

b. Everybody, what word describes people talking to each other about something? (Signal.) *Conversation.*
- What word tells that you are sure about something? (Signal.) *Confidence.*
- What word tells what you do when you stay away from something? (Signal.) *Avoid.*

EXERCISE 2

Reading Words

Column 1

a. **Find lesson 84 in your textbook.** ✔
- Touch column 1. ✔
- (Teacher reference:)

1. police officer	4. screw
2. instructor	5. unhappy
3. claws	6. jewelry

b. Number 1. What words? (Signal.) *Police officer.*

c. Word 2. What word? (Signal.) *Instructor.*
- Another word for **teacher** is **instructor.**
- Everybody, what's another way of saying **a new teacher?** (Signal.) *A new instructor.*
- What's another way of saying **a math teacher?** (Signal.) *A math instructor.*

d. Word 3. What word? (Signal.) *Claws.*
- Spell **claws.** Get ready. (Tap for each letter.) *C-L-A-W-S.*

e. Word 4. What word? (Signal.) *Screw.*
- Spell **screw.** Get ready. (Tap for each letter.) *S-C-R-E-W.*

f. Word 5. What word? (Signal.) *Unhappy.*
- Spell **unhappy.** Get ready. (Tap for each letter.) *U-N-H-A-P-P-Y.*

g. Word 6. What word? (Signal.) *Jewelry.*

h. Let's read those words again, the fast way.
- Number 1. What words? (Signal.) *Police officer.*
- (Repeat for words 2–6.)
i. (Repeat step h until firm.)

Column 2

j. Find column 2. ✔
- (Teacher reference:)

1. <u>death</u>ly	4. <u>direct</u>ing
2. <u>brave</u>ry	5. <u>ear</u>rings
3. <u>high</u>way	

k. These words have more than one part. The first part of each word is underlined.

l. Word 1. What's the underlined part? (Signal.) *death.*
- What's the whole word? (Signal.) *Deathly.*
- If something reminds you of death, that thing is **deathly.** A stillness that reminds you of death is a deathly stillness. Everybody, what would you call a face that reminds you of death? (Signal.) *A deathly face.*
- Word 2. What's the underlined part? (Signal.) *brave.*
- What's the whole word? (Signal.) *Bravery.*
- Word 3. What's the underlined part? (Signal.) *high.*
- What's the whole word? (Signal.) *Highway.*
- Word 4. What's the underlined part? (Signal.) *direct.*
- What's the whole word? (Signal.) *Directing.*
- Word 5. What's the underlined part? (Signal.) *ear.*
- What's the whole word? (Signal.) *Earrings.*

m. Let's read those words again, the fast way.
- Word 1. What word? (Signal.) *Deathly.*
- (Repeat for words 2–5.)
n. (Repeat step m until firm.)

Individual Turns

(For columns 1 and 2: Call on individual students, each to read one to three words per turn.)

Story Background

a. Find part B in your textbook. ✔
• You're going to read the last story about Waldo. First you'll read the information passage. It gives some facts about coral.
b. Everybody, touch the title. ✔
• (Call on a student to read the title.) *[Facts About Coral.]*
• Everybody, what's the title? (Signal.) *Facts About Coral.* ⓃⒹ
c. (Call on individual students to read the passage, each student reading two or three sentences at a time. Ask the specified questions as the students read.)

Facts About Coral
When you are underwater in a warm ocean, you may see more than 20 different kinds of coral.

• Where do you see lots of different kinds of coral? (Call on a student. Idea: *Underwater in a warm ocean.*) ⓇⒻ/Ⓡ

The picture shows three kinds of coral.

• The first picture shows staghorn coral. That coral looks like the antlers of a deer. That's where its name comes from.
• Everybody, what's the name of the next coral? (Signal.) *Brain coral.* ⓃⒹ
• Why is it called brain coral? (Call on a student. Idea: *Because it looks like a brain.*) ⒹⒾ
• Everybody, what's the name of the last coral? (Signal.) *Red coral.* ⓃⒹ

In some places, you'll see underwater hills that are covered with coral. These places are called coral reefs.
Here are some facts about coral reefs:
• The coral is made up of the skeletons of tiny animals.

• Everybody, say the fact. Get ready. (Signal.) *The coral is made up of the skeletons of tiny animals.* ⓇⒻ/Ⓡ
• Touch the picture of the coral reef. ✔ Ⓥ Ⓐ

• That looks like a garden of different plants, but all that coral is made up of skeletons of tiny animals.

• Those animals do not swim around. They live and die in one place.

• Everybody, do those animals swim around? (Signal.) *No.* ⓇⒻ/Ⓡ
• That's right. They stay in one place their whole life.

• The coral is easy to destroy but takes years and years to grow back.

• Everybody, say that fact. Get ready. (Signal.) *The coral is easy to destroy but takes years and years to grow back.* ⓇⒻ/Ⓡ
• If divers wanted to, they could break up all the coral in that picture of the reef. It wouldn't take long, but it might take a hundred years for the coral to grow back.

• Some kinds of coral, like red coral, are very valuable because they are now very rare. They are used to make jewelry. Here's a picture of earrings made of red coral.

• Those earrings are very pretty, but they are not cheap.

Story Reading

a. Find part C in your textbook. ✔
• The error limit for group reading is 10 errors.
b. Everybody, touch the title. ✔
• (Call on a student to read the title.) *[The Animals' Greatest Show.]*
• Everybody, what's the title? (Signal.) *The Animals' Greatest Show.* ⓃⒹ
c. (Call on individual students to read the story, each student reading two or three sentences at a time. Ask the specified questions as the students read.)

• (**Correct errors:** Tell the word. Direct the student to reread the sentence.)
• (If the group makes more than 10 errors, direct the students to reread the story.)

The Animals' Greatest Show

Inside the trailer, four cats were standing on two dogs. One of the dogs started to howl because the cat was digging into the dog with its claws. But the dog kept its place and the cats kept their place on the pyramid. And the truck was stopping very fast now. In fact, it was stopping so fast that the animals almost fell over. Slower, slower, slower.

- Why was the truck stopping so fast? (Call on a student. Ideas: *Because there was lots of weight on the brake; because four cats and three dogs were standing on the brake.*) (DC)

The truck was at the curve now, but it was hardly moving. Then it came to a stop right in the middle of the curve. The driver jumped out of the truck and opened the back door of the trailer. He ran over to the emergency brake and turned a screw that kept the brake locked in place.

- How did he keep the brake locked in place? (Call on a student. Idea: *By turning a screw.*) (ND)
- Everybody, show me with your hand how you would turn a screw. ✔ (V)

Waldo was right behind the driver. The pyramid was still standing. All the animals were panting. The spotted dog looked very unhappy. One of the cats on that dog's back was the one that was hanging on with its claws.

"Can they move now?" Waldo asked.

"Yeah," the driver said. "The brake is locked."

Cars were stopping in back of the trailer. Two of them were police cars. People were starting to gather around the trailer.

- Why were the people stopping and gathering around the trailer? (Call on a student. Idea: *To find out what happened.*) (DC)

"Okay," Waldo said to the animals. "Get down." The cats jumped from the smaller dogs and the smaller dogs jumped from the back of the huge dog. Waldo hugged the huge dog. "You saved our lives," he said. Then he hugged the other dogs and he petted the cats. He thanked each animal. The animals started to calm down.

A police officer was now looking inside the door of the trailer. "What happened?" he asked. Maria was standing next to him. She explained.

- What would she say to explain what happened? (Call on a student. Idea: *The brakes went out and the animals saved them.*) (P)

As Maria talked to the police officer, Waldo looked at the animals in the trailer and said, "I'm going to give all of you a special treat." He went to the front of the trailer and opened a pot that was filled with his special food. He gave each animal a treat. Now they were very calm and very happy.

He asked Maria, "Do you ★ think it would be all right if I let them out of the trailer for a couple of minutes?"

"Sure," Maria said.

By now a large crowd had gathered around the truck and trailer. When the dogs, cats, squirrels and rabbits jumped from the trailer, somebody in the crowd said, "I saw this act in Denver. It was great."

"Me, too," some of the other people said.

Now the pigeons were flying from the trailer and starting to circle over it. One police officer said, "Are all these animals trained to do tricks?"

"They sure are," Waldo said.

The driver was talking to two police officers. Two other police officers were directing traffic around the truck and trailer. But nearly all the cars that came by stopped, and the people got out to join the crowd.

Then somebody from the crowd said, "Could you do one trick for us?"

Waldo looked at Maria. She smiled. "I'll show you the trick that I like best," Waldo said.

- Everybody, which trick is that? (Signal.) *The upside-down pyramid.* ⓓⓘ
- Read the rest of the story to yourself and be ready to answer some questions. Raise your hand when you're done.

Waldo signaled the huge dog to stand next to the road. Then he signaled the two smaller dogs. They jumped onto the back of the huge dog. Then came the cats. Then came the squirrels. Finally, Waldo whistled and sixteen pigeons landed on the squirrels. For a moment, the crowd was silent. Then people began to clap and cheer. "That's amazing," some of them shouted.

✿ "Yes," Waldo said. "That's the best trick in the world." It was the best trick in the world because it saved so many lives.

Waldo signaled the pigeons and they flew from the pyramid. The squirrels jumped down, the cats jumped down, followed by the two smaller dogs.

Within an hour, the brakes on the trailer and the truck were fixed, and the truck continued on its way to Utah. A long line of cars followed the trailer.

The show in Utah was a great success. The newspapers carried stories about the experience that Waldo and Maria had in the Rocky Mountains.

Waldo was very pleased with the show. But the show that he remembered as the greatest one his animals ever did took ✿ place in a trailer that was speeding down a mountain road.

- (After all students have raised their hand:)
- Why does Waldo think that the pyramid is the best trick in the world? (Call on a student. Idea: *Because it saved their lives.*) ⓓⓒ
- How long did it take to get the brakes fixed on the truck and the trailer? (Call on a student. Idea: *Less than an hour.*) ⓝⓓ
- Where did the truck and trailer go then? (Call on a student. Ideas: *Utah; Salt Lake City.*) ⓝⓓ
- What followed the truck and trailer? (Call on a student. Idea: *A long line of cars.*) ⓝⓓ
- How did the show in Utah go? (Call on a student. Idea: *Very well.*) ⓝⓓ
- Which show did Waldo remember as the greatest show his animals ever did? (Call on a student. Idea: *The one in the trailer that sped down a mountain road.*) ⓝⓓ

EXERCISE 5

Paired Practice

You're going to read aloud to your partner Today the **A** members will read first. Then the **B** members will read from the star to the end of the story. (Observe students and give feedback.)

End-of-Lesson Activities

Now finish the independent work for lesson 84. Raise your hand when you're finished. (Observe students and give feedback.)

a. (Direct students to take out their marking pencils.)

• We're going to check your independent work. Remember, if you got an item wrong, make an **X** next to the item.

b. (For each item: Read the item. Call on a student to answer it. If the answer is wrong, say the correct answer. Refer to the Answer Key for the correct answers.)

c. Now use your marking pencil to fix up any items you got wrong. Remember, all mistakes must be fixed up before you hand in your independent work.

(Present Spelling lesson 84 after completing Reading lesson 84. See *Spelling Presentation Book.*)

Special Project

Note: After completing lesson 84, do this special project with the students. You may do the project during another part of the school day.

a. Everybody, find page 69 in your textbook
- (Call on individual students to read the project, each student reading two or three sentences.)
- (Teacher reference:)

Special Project

For this project, your group may either decide to train an animal to do a new trick or write a report that tells how you would train an animal.

If the group decides to train an animal, think about training a pigeon to do a dance. Pigeons learn to dance quite fast. If you train a hamster or a white rat, the training will take more time because these animals will not learn the trick as fast as a pigeon learns to dance. But you may teach a rat to walk a rope or teach a hamster to climb to the top of a tower that you make.

If you train an animal, write a report that tells how you did it. Tell about the rewards that you used to train the animal and tell about the steps that you used in training the animal.

If you do not train an animal, write a report that tells which rewards you would use and how you would use them. Tell all the things you would do to train the animal. Remember, the animal will not be able to do the trick the first time it tries, so you have to reward the animal for trying.

---

b. (Divide the class into groups of four or five.)
- (Arrange a time when the group members can meet and work out the plans for either telling how the group would train an animal or for training one. Possibly the entire class could train an animal, with several class members assigned to perform the actual training and each group responsible for observing and writing up the outcomes. Before the actual training begins, make sure that the class has arrived at a plan that seems manageable. Also, if the steps in this plan are apparently too difficult for the animal, help the class reorganize the steps so that the animal is able to achieve the initial steps of the training.)
c. (Direct the students to write up their plan or report according to this outline:)
- Type of animal
- Describe the trick
- Describe the first steps in training
- Describe what the animal must do before the next step is presented
- Describe the rewards

EXERCISE 1

Vocabulary Review

a. You learned a sentence that tells about the tour to the islands.

- Everybody, say that sentence. Get ready. (Signal.) *The tour to the islands was a fantastic experience.*
- (Repeat until firm.)

b. You learned a sentence that tells who she will contact.

- Say that sentence. Get ready. (Signal.) *She will contact the person we want to hire.*
- (Repeat until firm.)

c. Here's the last sentence you learned: I have confidence that we can avoid a long conversation.

- Everybody, say that sentence. Get ready. (Signal.) *I have confidence that we can avoid a long conversation.*
- (Repeat until firm.)

d. Everybody, what word tells that you are sure about something? (Signal.) *Confidence.*

- What word describes people talking to each other about something? (Signal.) *Conversation.*
- What word tells what you do when you stay away from something? (Signal.) *Avoid.*

e. Once more. Say the sentence that starts with the words **I have confidence.** Get ready. (Signal.) *I have confidence that we can avoid a long conversation.*

EXERCISE 2

Reading Words

Column 1

a. **Find lesson 85 in your textbook.** ✔
- Touch column 1. ✔
- (Teacher reference:)

1. scuba	4. badly
2. guide	5. instructor
3. Darla	6. partner

b. Word 1 is **scuba.** What word? (Signal.) *Scuba.*

- Spell **scuba.** Get ready. (Tap for each letter.) *S-C-U-B-A.*

c. Word 2 is **guide.** What word? (Signal.) *Guide.*

- Spell **guide.** Get ready. (Tap for each letter.) *G-U-I-D-E.*
- A tour guide is a person who shows the way on a tour. Everybody, what do we call a person who shows the way on a **tour?** (Signal.) *Tour guide.*
- What do we call a person who shows the way when people go fishing? (Signal.) *Fishing guide.*

d. Word 3. What word? (Signal.) *Darla.*

- Spell **Darla.** Get ready. (Tap for each letter.) *D-A-R-L-A.*

e. Word 4. What word? (Signal.) *Badly.*

- Spell **badly.** Get ready. (Tap for each letter.) *B-A-D-L-Y.*

f. Word 5. What word? (Signal.) *Instructor.*

g. Word 6. What word? (Signal.) *Partner.*

h. Let's read those words again, the fast way.
- Word 1. What word? (Signal.) *Scuba.*
- (Repeat for words 2–6.)

i. (Repeat step h until firm.)

Column 2

j. Find column 2. ✔
- (Teacher reference:)

1. deadly fear	4. child
2. Mrs. Wilson	5. bravery
3. highway	6. surfaced

k. Number 1. What words? (Signal.) *Deadly fear.*

- A **deadly fear** is a **great fear.** Everybody, what's another way of saying **He had a great fear of high places?** (Signal.) *He had a deadly fear of high places.*
- What's another way of saying **She had a great fear of water?** (Signal.) *She had a deadly fear of water.*

l. Number 2. What name? (Signal.) *Mrs. Wilson.*

m. Word 3. What word? (Signal.) *Highway.*
- (Repeat for words 4–6.)

n. Let's read those words again.
- Number 1. What words? (Signal.) *Deadly fear.*
- Number 2. What name? (Signal.) *Mrs. Wilson.*
- Word 3. What word? (Signal.) *Highway.*
- (Repeat for words: **4. child, 5. bravery, 6. surfaced.**)
o. (Repeat step n until firm.)

Column 3

p. Find column 3. ✔
- (Teacher reference:)

1. panic	**4.** sissy
2. deathly	**5.** reef
3. Julie	**6.** fought

q. Word 1. What word? (Signal.) *Panic.*
- When you panic, you become so afraid that your mind doesn't work well. Everybody, what word describes what a boy does when a boy is so afraid that his mind doesn't work? (Signal.) *Panic.*
r. Word 2. What word? (Signal.) *Deathly.*
- (Repeat for words 3–6.)
s. Let's read those words again.
- Word 1. What word? (Signal.) *Panic.*
- (Repeat for words 2–6.)
t. (Repeat step s until firm.)

Individual Turns

(For columns 1–3: Call on individual students, each to read one to three words per turn.)

EXERCISE 3

Story Reading

a. Find part B in your textbook. ✔
- This is the first part of a new story. The error limit for group reading is 13 errors.
b. Everybody, touch the title. ✔
- (Call on a student to read the title.) [Darla's Fear.]
- Everybody, what's the title? (Signal.) *Darla's Fear.* (ND)
c. (Call on individual students to read the story, each student reading two or three sentences at a time. Ask the specified questions as the students read.)

- (**Correct errors:** Tell the word. Direct the student to reread the sentence.)
- (If the group makes more than 13 errors, direct the students to reread the story.)

Darla's Fear

Darla Jackson was good at so many things that you wouldn't think she was afraid of anything. But she had one deadly fear. She wasn't afraid of high places. In fact, she loved to go mountain climbing with her older sister, Julie. Together, they climbed some of the highest mountains in California. Darla wasn't afraid of animals. She raised pet mice and for a while she had three pet snakes. She wasn't afraid of beetles or spiders. And Darla wasn't afraid of the dark. She and her sister camped out in places that were so dark at night that they couldn't see anything, although they could hear the sounds of animals that came near the camp.

And Darla wasn't afraid of work. She did very well in school and she worked hard around the house—mowing the lawn, helping paint the house, keeping her room clean.

But Darla had a deadly fear of water.

- Name some things that Darla was not afraid of. (Call on a student. Ideas: *High places; animals; the dark; work.*) (ND)
- Everybody, in what state did she and her sister climb mountains? (Signal.) *California.* (ND)
- Everybody, what was Darla deathly afraid of? (Signal.) *Water.* (ND)

She was so afraid of water that she couldn't even put her face underwater for a second without feeling as if the water was going to choke her. Her sister Julie was a good swimmer. "Come on, Darla," she used to holler from the deep water. "Don't be a sissy. Jump in and get wet." But the closest Darla ever came to swimming was to wade around in water that came up to her chest. When the water got up to her neck, she started to panic.

- What does that mean, she started to panic? (Call on a student. Idea: *She was so afraid that her mind wouldn't work well.*) (UCCM)

When the water reached her neck, something inside her said, "Get out of here. Get out now." Then she'd become afraid that a wave would come along and splash her in the face.

Several times, she managed to get into neck-deep water, and she fought her fear. But just about the time that she thought she might learn to get used to deep water, a kid would come by and splash her in the face. She would panic, cough and get out of the water as fast as she could. The kids would laugh at her. She would become angry with them, but they would go into deeper water and call to her, "Come and get us."

- Everybody, would she be able to get them? (Signal.) *No.* (DC)
- Why not? (Call on a student. Idea: *Because she was afraid of deep water.*) (ND)

One day when she went to school, her class was studying bravery and what it means to be brave. Her teacher, Mrs. Wilson, explained, "Somebody might go into a burning building to save a child. That is an act of bravery."

- What was the act of bravery you just read about? (Call on a student. Idea: *Saving a child from a burning building.*) (ND)
- What's another act of bravery? (Call on individual students. Ideas: *Saving a drowning person; pulling someone up from a cliff; etc.*) (DI)

Mrs. Wilson continued, "But for the person who goes into a burning building, the act might not take much bravery at all. That person might not be afraid of being close to fire. And that person might have confidence that she will not get hurt."

- Everybody, does the act of bravery always mean that the person is being brave? (Signal.) *No.* (ND)
- Why wouldn't the act of going into a burning building be a great act of bravery for some people? (Call on a student. Idea: *Because they may not be afraid to be close to fire.*) (ND)

Mrs. Wilson hesitated for a moment. Then she continued, "To be brave, ⭐ you must do things that are hard for you to do."

- Listen to that rule again. To be brave you must do things that are hard for you to do. Everybody, say that rule. Get ready. (Signal.) *To be brave you must do things that are hard for you to do.* (RF/R)
- (Repeat until firm.)

Mrs. Wilson went on to say, "Sometimes the greatest acts of bravery may not seem very brave to other people. If a person is deathly afraid of high places, climbing a ladder may be a great act of bravery. If a person is deathly afraid of snakes, holding a snake may take an incredible amount of bravery."

- When would climbing a ladder be a great act of bravery? (Call on a student. Idea: *When the person was very afraid of heights.*) (ND)
- When would holding a snake be a great act of bravery? (Call on a student. Idea: *When the person was afraid of snakes.*) (ND)
- What would be a great act of bravery for Darla? (Call on a student. Idea: *Going into deep water.*) (DC)

Darla almost felt that Mrs. Wilson was talking to her. For Darla, mountain climbing didn't take much bravery. Darla had confidence that she wouldn't fall. She was a very good climber. She figured that climbing a mountain was as safe as driving down a highway in a car. If you make a stupid mistake, you could become badly hurt, but it's not too difficult to avoid these mistakes. Darla felt the same way about the other things that she did. She was very good at them, and other people commented about how amazing and brave she was. But doing these things did not require much bravery for Darla.

- Everybody, were mountain climbing and camping at night and holding snakes acts of bravery for Darla? (Signal.) *No.* (ND)
- Why not? (Call on a student. Idea: *Because she wasn't afraid of heights and snakes and the dark.*) (ND)

After school that day, Darla walked home with Julie. Julie kept trying to start a conversation, but Darla couldn't stop thinking about bravery. Finally, she asked her sister, "Am I brave?"

Her sister laughed and then shrugged. "I never thought about it."

- Laugh and shrug and say that the way Julie said it. (Call on a student.) ✔ (V)
- Read the rest of the story to yourself and be ready to answer some questions. Raise your hand when you're done.

Then Julie continued, "Yeah, I guess you are brave—at least in most things. But you sure are a sissy about going in the water."

"I know," Darla said. Then Darla added, "I'm not really very brave at all, because the things I do are pretty easy for me. Going in the water is sure different, though. If I just start thinking about it, I get scared."

"So you're a sissy about the water," her sister commented. "You'll probably get over it some day."

Darla said, "If I were brave, I'd get over my fear of water right now."

Julie looked at Darla, and the two girls fell into silence as they walked along the sidewalk. The sunshine was bright and warm. The girls walked for about a minute without saying anything. Suddenly, Darla stopped and said, "Julie, I've got to learn how to swim. I've got to be brave."

Julie smiled. "It's easy, Darla. The water won't bite you."

Darla said, "It's not easy for me. It's going to be the hardest thing I've ever done in my life. But I've decided that I won't like myself very much unless I'm brave."

Julie said, "I think they're going to give swimming lessons at the high school. I hear that the instructor is very good."

Darla made a face. "Every time I think about it, I get scared. Feel the palms of my hands." The palms were sweaty. Darla said, "I'm scared. But I'll do it."

- (After all students have raised their hand:)
- What did Darla decide to do? (Call on a student. Idea: *Learn how to swim.*) (ND)
- Everybody, where were the swimming lessons to be held? (Signal.) *At the high school.* (ND)
- What sign did Darla have to show that she became frightened when she thought about swimming? (Call on a student. Idea: *Her palms got sweaty.*) (ND)
- Everybody, show me your palm. ✔ (V)
- Do you think Darla will overcome her fear? (Call on individual student. Student preference.) (MJ)

Fluency: Rate/Accuracy

> *Note:* There is a fluency checkout in this lesson; therefore, there is no paired practice.

a. Today is a reading checkout day. While you're doing your independent work, I'm going to call on you one at a time to read part of the story from lesson 84.

• Remember, you pass the checkout by reading the passage in less than a minute without making more than 2 mistakes. And when you pass the checkout, you'll color the space for lesson 85 on your thermometer chart.

b. (Call on individual students to read the portion of story 84 marked with ❀.)

• (Time the student. Note words that are missed and total number of words read.)

• (Teacher reference:)

> ❀ "Yes," Waldo said. "That's the best trick in the world." It was the best trick in the world because it saved so many lives.
>
> Waldo signaled the pigeons and they flew from the pyramid. The squirrels jumped down, the cats jumped down, followed by the two smaller dogs.
>
> Within an [50] hour, the brakes on the trailer and the truck were fixed, and the truck continued on its way to Utah. A long line of cars [75] followed the trailer.
>
> The show in Utah was a great success. The newspapers carried stories about the experience that Waldo and Maria had in the [100] Rocky Mountains.
>
> Waldo was very pleased with the show. But the show that he remembered as the greatest one his animals ever did took place ❀ [125] in a trailer that was speeding down a mountain road.

• (If the student reads the passage in one minute or less and makes no more than 2 errors, direct the student to color in the space for lesson 85 on the thermometer chart.)

• (If the student makes any mistakes, point to each word that was misread and identify it.)

• (If the student does not meet the rate-error criterion for the passage, direct the student to practice reading the story with the assigned partner.)

End-of-Lesson Activities

INDEPENDENT WORK

Now finish the independent work for lesson 85. Raise your hand when you're finished. (Observe students and give feedback.)

WORKCHECK

a. (Direct students to take out their marking pencils.)

• We're going to check your independent work. Remember, if you got an item wrong, make an **X** next to the item.

b. (For each item: Read the item. Call on a student to answer it. If the answer is wrong, say the correct answer. Refer to the Answer Key for the correct answers.)

c. Now use your marking pencil to fix up any items you got wrong. Remember, all mistakes must be fixed up before you hand in your independent work.

SPELLING

(Present Spelling lesson 85 after completing Reading lesson 85. See *Spelling Presentation Book.*)

Lessons 86–90 • Planning Page

Looking Ahead

	Lesson 86	**Lesson 87**	**Lesson 88**	**Lesson 89**	**Lesson 90**
LESSON EVENTS	**Vocabulary Sentence** Reading Words Story Background Story Reading Paired Practice Independent Work Workcheck Spelling	Vocabulary Sentence Reading Words Fact Review Story Reading Paired Practice Independent Work Workcheck Spelling	Vocabulary Sentence Reading Words Story Reading Paired Practice Independent Work Workcheck Spelling	Vocabulary Sentences Reading Words Fact Review Story Background Story Reading Paired Practice Independent Work Workcheck Spelling	Fact Game Fluency: Rate/ Accuracy Test Marking the Test Test Remedies Spelling
VOCABULARY SENTENCE	#22: The scuba diver and her partner surfaced near the reef.	#22: The scuba diver and her partner surfaced near the reef.	sentence #21 sentence #22	#22: The scuba diver and her partner surfaced near the reef.	
READING WORDS: WORD TYPES	modeled words words with underlined parts	modeled words -ed words mixed words	modeled words mixed words	modeled words words with an ending words with underlined parts	
NEW VOCABULARY	anchored separated scene flailed rapidly	buoyant buoyancy device barracuda mass especially twilight trailed darting	Iditarod Anchorage grasp	Denali Knik musher overcome white-capped	
STORY BACKGROUND	*Facts About Pressure*			*Facts About the Iditarod*	
STORY	*Getting Ready to Dive*	*An Underwater World*	*An Emergency*	*The Trip to the Water's Surface*	
SKILL ITEMS	Vocabulary sentences		Vocabulary sentence Sequencing	Vocabulary sentences Crossword puzzle	Test: Vocabulary sentences
SPECIAL MATERIALS					Thermometer charts, dice, Fact Game 90, Fact Game Answer Key, scorecard sheets
SPECIAL PROJECTS/ ACTIVITIES	Activity after lesson 86	Activity after lesson 87	Activity after lesson 88	Activity after lesson 89	

Comprehension Questions Abbreviations Guide

Access Prior Knowledge = (APK)   Author's Point of View = (APoV)   Author's Purpose = (AP)   Cause/Effect = (C/E)   Charts/Graphs/Diagrams/Visual Aids = (VA)

Classify and Categorize = (C+C)   Compare/Contrast = (C/C)   Determine Character Emotions, Motivation = (DCE)   Drawing Conclusions = (DC)   Drawing Inferences = (DI)

Fact and Opinion = (F/O)   Hypothesizing = (H)   Main Idea = (MI)   Making Connections = (MC)   Making Deductions = (MD)   Making Judgements = (MJ)

Narrative Elements = (NE)   Noting Details = (ND)   Predict = (P)   Reality/Fantasy = (R/F)   Recall Facts/Rules = (RF/R)   Retell = (R)   Sequence = (Seq)

Steps in a Process = (SP)   Story Structure = (SS)   Summarize = (Sum)   Understanding Dialogue = (UD)   Using Context to Confirm Meaning(s) = (UCCM)   Visualize = (V)

EXERCISE 1

Vocabulary Review

a. You learned a sentence that starts with the words **I have confidence.**
 • Everybody, say that sentence. Get ready. (Signal.) *I have confidence that we can avoid a long conversation.*
 • (Repeat until firm.)

b. I'll say part of the sentence. When I stop, you say the next word. Listen: I have . . . Everybody, what's the next word? (Signal.) *Confidence.*

c. Listen: I have confidence that we can . . . Everybody, what's the next word? (Signal.) *Avoid.*
 • Say the whole sentence. Get ready. (Signal.) *I have confidence that we can avoid a long conversation.*

d. Listen: I have confidence that we can avoid a long . . . Everybody, what's the next word? (Signal.) *Conversation.*

EXERCISE 2

Vocabulary

a. **Find page 367 in your textbook.** ✔
 • Touch sentence 22. ✔
 • This is a new vocabulary sentence. It says: The scuba diver and her partner surfaced near the reef. Everybody, read that sentence. Get ready. (Signal.) *The scuba diver and her partner surfaced near the reef.*
 • Close your eyes and say the sentence. Get ready. (Signal.) *The scuba diver and her partner surfaced near the reef.*
 • (Repeat until firm.)

b. A scuba diver goes underwater wearing a mask and a tank of air. The diver breathes the air. The mask allows the diver to see things clearly underwater.

c. The sentence tells about the scuba diver and her **partner.** A partner is somebody you do something with. If you have a diving partner, you dive with that person. What would you do with somebody who was a running partner? (Call on a student. Idea: *Run with the person.*)

d. When a diver **surfaces,** the diver swims up to the surface of the water. Everybody, what's another way of saying **They swam up to the surface near the boat?** (Signal.) *They surfaced near the boat.*

e. A **reef** is a ridge that forms underwater.

f. Listen to the sentence again: The scuba diver and her partner surfaced near the reef. Everybody, say the sentence. Get ready. (Signal.) *The scuba diver and her partner surfaced near the reef.*

g. Everybody, what word describes a person you do something with? (Signal.) *Partner.*
 • What words tell about someone who goes underwater with a mask and a tank of air? (Signal.) *Scuba diver.*
 • What word tells about a ridge that forms underwater? (Signal.) *Reef.*
 • What word tells that people swam to the surface? (Signal.) *Surfaced.*
 • (Repeat step g until firm.)

EXERCISE 3

Reading Words

Column 1

a. Find lesson 86 in your textbook. ✔
 • Touch column 1. ✔
 • (Teacher reference:)

| 1. anchored | 3. scene |
| 2. separated | 4. partner |

b. Word 1 is **anchored.** What word? (Signal.) *Anchored.*
 • Spell **anchored.** Get ready. (Tap for each letter.) *A-N-C-H-O-R-E-D.*
 • An anchor is a weight that is attached to a boat. When you want the boat to stay in one place, you drop the anchor to the bottom of the water. Everybody, what do we call a weight that keeps a boat in one place? (Signal.) *Anchor.*
 • If a boat is anchored, it has an anchor on the bottom of the water.

c. Word 2 is **separated.** What word? (Signal.) *Separated.*
 • Spell **separated.** Get ready. (Tap for each letter.) *S-E-P-A-R-A-T-E-D.*

- Things that are separated are no longer together. If two sisters are separated, they are no longer together.
- Everybody, if the seeds and the shells are no longer together, what do you know about them? (Signal.) *They're separated.*

d. Word 3 is **scene.** What word? (Signal.) *Scene.*
- Spell **scene.** Get ready. (Tap for each letter.) *S-C-E-N-E.*
- If you look at something with many things or parts in it, you're looking at a scene. A picture of a farm with many things in it is a farm scene. What do we call a picture of a **city** with many things in it? (Signal.) *A city scene.*

e. Word 4. What word? (Signal.) *Partner.*
- Spell **partner.** Get ready. (Tap for each letter.) *P-A-R-T-N-E-R.*

f. Let's read those words again, the fast way.
- Word 1. What word? (Signal.) *Anchored.*
- (Repeat for words: 2. **separated,** 3. **scene,** 4. **partner.**)
g. (Repeat step f until firm.)

Column 2
h. Find column 2. ✔
- (Teacher reference:)

1. flailed	3. panicked
2. rapidly	4. mouthpiece

- Those words have more than one part. The first part of each word is underlined.
i. Word 1. What's the underlined part? (Signal.) *flail.*
- What's the whole word? (Signal.) *Flailed.*
- When you flail your arms, you swing them around in all directions. Everybody, what are people doing when they swing their arms around in all directions? (Signal.) *Flailing.*
- Word 2. What's the underlined part? (Signal.) *rapid.*
- What's the whole word? (Signal.) *Rapidly.*
- Another word for **quickly** is **rapidly.** What's another way of saying **She talked quickly?** (Signal.) *She talked rapidly.*
- What's another way of saying **We went down the mountain quickly?** (Signal.) *We went down the mountain rapidly.*

- Word 3. What's the underlined part? (Signal.) *panick.*
- What's the whole word? (Signal.) *Panicked.*
- Word 4. What's the underlined part? (Signal.) *mouth.*
- What's the whole word? (Signal.) *Mouthpiece.*

j. Let's read those words again, the fast way.
- Word 1. What word? (Signal.) *Flailed.*
- (Repeat for words 2–4.)
k. (Repeat step j until firm.)

Column 3
l. Find column 3. ✔
- (Teacher reference:)

1. guide	3. scuba
2. hose	4. quit

m. Word 1. What word? (Signal.) *Guide.*
- (Repeat for words 2–4.)
n. Let's read those words again.
- Word 1. What word? (Signal.) *Guide.*
- (Repeat for words 2–4.)
o. (Repeat step n until firm.)

Individual Turns
(For columns 1–3: Call on individual students, each to read one to three words per turn.)

EXERCISE 4

Story Background
a. Find part B in your textbook. ✔
- You're going to read the next story about Darla. First you'll read the information passage. It gives some facts about pressure.
b. Everybody, touch the title. ✔
- (Call on a student to read the title.) *[Facts About Pressure.]*
- Everybody, what's the title? (Signal.) *Facts About Pressure.* (ND)
c. (Call on individual students to read the passage, each student reading two or three sentences at a time. Ask the specified questions as the students read.)

Facts About Pressure

If you hold a balloon as you go underwater, the balloon gets smaller and smaller the deeper you go.

Here's a balloon when it is 10 feet underwater.

Here's the same balloon when it is 90 feet underwater.

- Which balloon is smaller? (Call on a student. Idea: *The balloon that is 90 feet underwater.*) C/C
- If we take that balloon down another 90 feet deeper, what would happen to its size? (Call on a student. Idea: *It would get smaller.*) RF/R

Here are facts about pressure:
When you are at the surface of the water, there is some pressure on your body.

- Everybody, is there any pressure on your body when you are at the surface of the water? (Signal.) *Yes.* RF/R

When you go 33 feet underwater, the pressure is two times as great as it is at the surface.

- Everybody, how far down do you have to go to have two times as much pressure on your body? (Signal.) *33 feet.* RF/R

When you go down another 33 feet, the pressure is three times as great as it is at the surface.

- Everybody, when you go down 33 feet and then another 33 feet, how many times greater is the pressure? (Signal.) *Three.* RF/R
- If you went down another 33 feet, how many times greater would the pressure be than it is at the surface? (Signal.) *Four.* RF/R

EXERCISE 5

Story Reading

a. Find part C in your textbook. ✔
- The error limit for group reading is 12 errors.
b. Everybody, touch the title. ✔
- (Call on a student to read the title.) *[Getting Ready to Dive.]*
- Everybody, what's the title? (Signal.) *Getting Ready to Dive.* ND
- The picture on the next page shows somebody wearing a scuba diving outfit. Later you can study the picture. Make sure you know the parts that are labeled so you'll be able to do the items in your workbook.
c. (Call on individual students to read the story, each student reading two or three sentences at a time. Ask the specified questions as the students read.)

- (Correct errors: Tell the word. Direct the student to reread the sentence.)
- (If the group makes more than 12 errors, direct the students to reread the story.)

Getting Ready to Dive

The small boat rolled slowly over the waves. Below the boat, the color of the water changed from dark blue to light green. Places that were light green were shallow. Places that were dark, dark blue were deep.

- Where is this scene taking place? (Call on a student. Ideas: *On water; below the boat.*) DI
- What's the rule about the color of the water? (Call on a student. Idea: *The water is darker the deeper it is.*) RF/R

"Okay," the diving guide said to Darla and Julie and the other five divers who were on the boat. "Check your scuba gear and get ready to dive. This is the place we're going down."

- What are Darla and the others going to do? (Call on a student. Idea: *Go scuba diving.*) (DC)
- When we left Darla, how did she feel about the water? (Call on a student. Idea: *She was very afraid of it.*) (APK)
- If she's scuba diving now, what must have happened since we left her? (Call on a student. Ideas: *She must have gotten less afraid of the water; she learned how to swim and scuba dive.*) (DI)

A shot of panic went through Darla, and for a moment she almost said, "No, I'm not going to do it." But then she talked to herself. "There's nothing to be afraid of. You can do it. You can do it."

- Everybody, has Darla completely overcome her fear of water? (Signal.) *No.* (DC)

Darla's hand was trembling as she grabbed the dial that was attached to her air hose.

- Why was her hand trembling? (Call on a student. Idea: *Because she was afraid.*) (DI)

The dial showed how much air was in her tank. The tank was full. Darla checked the rest of her equipment and tried to ignore her fear.

She looked at her sister and smiled, but she was not smiling inside. She was thinking back to the first day she went to the swimming class. She was the oldest person in that class, and the most frightened. She remembered how some of the little kids had laughed at her because she was so afraid to put her face in the water. But she had learned.

She had learned how to float with her face down in the water. She had learned to turn her face out of the

water and take a breath while she floated face down. She had learned to kick her feet and to pull with her arms. She had become a fair swimmer by the time she had finished her swimming lessons.

- Everybody, who was the oldest person in Darla's swimming class? (Signal.) *Darla.* (ND)
- Listen to that part again and get ready to answer some questions.
  She had learned how to float with her face down in the water. She had learned to turn her face out of the water and take a breath while she floated face down. She had learned to kick her feet and to pull with her arms. She had become a fair swimmer by the time she had finished her swimming lessons.
- When she learned to swim, what was the first thing she had learned? (Call on a student. Idea: *How to float face down in the water.*) (ND)
- Then what had she learned? (Call on a student. Idea: *To turn her face out of the water and take a breath.*) (ND)
- The story says that at the end of the class, she was a fair swimmer. What does that mean? (Call on a student. Idea: *She swam pretty well.*) (UCCM)

Then Darla had taken scuba diving lessons. For Darla, these lessons were more frightening than the swimming lessons. The first time she had tried to wear a scuba mask, she was in a swimming pool. Water leaked inside the mask. She breathed water through her nose and panicked. As she stood on the deck of the diving boat in the hot sun, she remembered how she had panicked.

- Where is Darla when she is thinking about her scuba lessons? (Call on a student. Idea: *On the deck of the diving boat.*) (ND)
- And what is she thinking about as she stands on the deck of the diving boat? (Call on a student. Ideas: *How she had panicked at one of her scuba lessons; how water had leaked into her mask.*) (ND)

Again her mind went back to the first time she wore a scuba mask. She remembered how she flailed with her arms and legs, got a mouth full of water, ✦ and came out of the swimming pool coughing. She almost quit her scuba lessons after that experience. She had panicked a second time when she first tried to use the mouthpiece for the scuba gear. The instructor had told her how to hold the mouthpiece in her mouth so that she would be able to breathe through it. But when Darla went underwater and tried to breathe, water came into her mouth and again, she came out of the pool coughing.

Darla had kept working. She had studied her scuba books very carefully. She had felt that she wouldn't be as afraid of the water if she knew more about it. And she had learned a great deal. She learned about the different animals that live in the oceans, which animals are dangerous and which aren't. She learned all about how to use her scuba gear—how to use the feet fins, the dials and the mask. But the most amazing things she learned about had to do with water pressure.

- Name some things that she learned about. (Call on individual students. Ideas: *Animals that live in the ocean; her scuba gear; water pressure.*) Ⓝ

- Everybody, what was the most amazing thing she learned about? (Signal.) *Water pressure.* Ⓝ

She had never thought much about the pressure of water before she had taken the scuba lessons.

"Are you almost ready?" Julie asked.

- Everybody, who asked that question? (Signal.) *Julie.* Ⓝ

- Is this part of what Darla remembers or something that is happening on the deck of the diving boat? (Signal.) *Something that is happening on the deck of the diving boat.* Ⓓ

- Read the rest of the story to yourself and be ready to answer some questions. Raise your hand when you're done.

"I'm almost ready," Darla said, checking her mask.
Darla's mind went back to the time she had learned about pressure. Darla remembered that there is some pressure on a diver's body when the diver is at the surface. She remembered how deep a diver had to go to have two times as much pressure on the body.

Darla remembered some of the problems a diver may have if the diver comes up too fast. If a diver goes too deep and comes up too fast, the diver can die.

Darla's mind drifted back to the diving boat. Darla shook her head and smiled. She wondered why she was thinking about pressure and about her first scuba lessons. The diving boat rolled from side to side. The diving guide was standing behind Darla now, checking her air tanks. "You're all set," he said.

The diving guide said to the divers, "Remember, we're going down about 100 feet here. So don't try to come up too fast."

A shot of fear ran through Darla again. Her hand trembled as she put her mask in place. The deepest she had ever gone before was fifty feet.

- (After all students have raised their hand:)

- Everybody, how deep would a diver have to go to have two times as much pressure as there is at the surface? (Signal.) *33 feet.* ⓇⒻ/Ⓡ

- Everybody, about how deep was Darla going to dive? (Signal.) *100 feet.* Ⓝ

- So she would have four times the pressure on her body that she would have on land. I can understand why she is frightened. If anything goes wrong down there, she's in real trouble.

- Everybody, what's the deepest Darla had ever dived? (Signal.) *50 feet.* Ⓝ

- At 33 feet, she'd have 2 times the surface pressure; at 66 feet she'd have 3 times the surface pressure. At 99 feet, she'd have 4 times the pressure.

Paired Practice

You're going to read aloud to your partner. Today the **B** members will read first. Then the **A** members will read from the star to the end of the story. (Observe students and give feedback.)

End-of-Lesson Activities

INDEPENDENT WORK

Now finish the independent work for lesson 86. Raise your hand when you're finished. (Observe students and give feedback.)

WORKCHECK

a. (Direct students to take out their marking pencils.)
- We're going to check your independent work. Remember, if you got an item wrong, make an **X** next to the item.
b. (For each item: Read the item. Call on a student to answer it. If the answer is wrong, say the correct answer. Refer to the Answer Key for the correct answers.)
c. Now use your marking pencil to fix up any items you got wrong. Remember, all mistakes must be fixed up before you hand in your independent work.

SPELLING

(Present Spelling lesson 86 after completing Reading lesson 86. See *Spelling Presentation Book.*)

ACTIVITIES

(Present Activity 17 after completing Reading lesson 86. See *Activities across the Curriculum.*)

EXERCISE 1

Vocabulary Review

a. Here's the new vocabulary sentence: The scuba diver and her partner surfaced near the reef.

- Everybody, say the sentence. Get ready. (Signal.) *The scuba diver and her partner surfaced near the reef.*
- (Repeat until firm.)

b. Everybody, what word tells that people swam to the surface? (Signal.) *Surfaced.*

- What word tells about a ridge that forms underwater? (Signal.) *Reef.*
- What word describes a person you do something with? (Signal.) *Partner.*
- What words tell about a person who goes underwater with a mask and a tank of air? (Signal.) *Scuba diver.*

EXERCISE 2

Reading Words

Column 1

a. **Find lesson 87 in your textbook.** ✔

- Touch column 1. ✔
- (Teacher reference:)

1. **buoyant**	3. **barracuda**
2. **buoyancy device**	4. **especially**

b. Word 1 is **buoyant.** What word? (Signal.) *Buoyant.*

- Things that are buoyant float. Everybody, if a cork is very buoyant, what do you know about it? (Signal.) *It floats.*
- If something is the **opposite** of buoyant, what does it do? (Call on a student. Idea: *Sinks.*)

c. Number 2 is **buoyancy device.** What words? (Signal.) *Buoyancy device.*

- A buoyancy device is something a diver wears to control how buoyant the diver is underwater.

d. Word 3 is **barracuda.** What word? (Signal.) *Barracuda.*

- A barracuda is a large arrow-shaped fish with sharp teeth.

e. Word 4 is **especially.** What word? (Signal.) *Especially.*

- **Especially** is another word for **really.** Everybody, what's another way of saying **It's really cold out today?** (Signal.) *It's especially cold out today.*

f. Let's read those words again, the fast way.

- Word 1. What word? (Signal.) *Buoyant.*
- Number 2. What words? (Signal.) *Buoyancy device.*
- Word 3. What word? (Signal.) *Barracuda.*
- Word 4. What word? (Signal.) *Especially.*

g. (Repeat step f until firm.)

Column 2

h. Find column 2. ✔

- (Teacher reference:)

1. **trailed**	4. **separated**
2. **entered**	5. **branched**
3. **tilted**	6. **anchored**

- All these words end with the letters **E-D.**

i. Word 1. What word? (Signal.) *Trailed.*

- Spell **trailed.** Get ready. (Tap for each letter.) *T-R-A-I-L-E-D.*
- If something trails, it follows behind something else. If the puppy follows her mother, the puppy trails her mother. Everybody, what is a shark doing when it follows a boat? (Signal.) *Trailing the boat.*

j. Word 2. What word? (Signal.) *Entered.*

- Spell **entered.** Get ready. (Tap for each letter.) *E-N-T-E-R-E-D.*

k. Word 3. What word? (Signal.) *Tilted.*

- Spell **tilted.** Get ready. (Tap for each letter.) *T-I-L-T-E-D.*

l. Word 4. What word? (Signal.) *Separated.*

- Spell **separated.** Get ready. (Tap for each letter.) *S-E-P-A-R-A-T-E-D.*

m. Word 5. What word? (Signal.) *Branched.*

n. Word 6. What word? (Signal.) *Anchored.*

o. Let's read those words again.

- Word 1. What word? (Signal.) *Trailed.*
- (Repeat for words 2–6.)

p. (Repeat step o until firm.)

Column 3

q. Find column 3. ✔
- (Teacher reference:)

1. mass	4. scene
2. pair	5. coral
3. hissing	6. brain

r. Word 1. What word? (Signal.) *Mass.*
- A **mass** of things is a large number of those things crowded together. A mass of rocks and stones is a large number of rocks and stones crowded together. Everybody, what do we call a large number of bubbles crowded together. (Signal.) *A mass of bubbles.*

s. Word 2. What word? (Signal.) *Pair.*
- (Repeat for words 3–6.)

t. Let's read those words again.
- Word 1. What word? (Signal.) *Mass.*
- (Repeat for words 2–6.)

u. (Repeat step t until firm.)

Column 4

v. Find column 4. ✔
- (Teacher reference:)

1. twilight	4. stiff
2. darting	5. rapidly
3. soda	

w. Word 1. What word? (Signal.) *Twilight.*
- Twilight is the time just after the sun goes down. There is still some light, but it is pretty dark. Everybody, what do we call the time just after the sun goes down? (Signal.) *Twilight.*

x. Word 2. What word? (Signal.) *Darting.*
- When things move very fast, they dart. Everybody, if birds dart around us, what are the birds doing? (Signal.) *Moving very fast.*

y. Word 3. What word? (Signal.) *Soda.*
- (Repeat for words 4 and 5.)

z. Let's read those words again.
- Word 1. What word? (Signal.) *Twilight.*
- (Repeat for words 2–5.)

a. (Repeat step z until firm.)

Individual Turns

(For columns 1–4: Call on individual students, each to read one to three words per turn.)

Fact Review

a. Let's review some facts you have learned. First we'll go over the facts together. Then I'll call on some of you to do some facts.

b. Everybody, tell me which direction you go to get from Colorado to Utah. (Pause.) Get ready. (Signal.) *West.*
- Name the country that the states of Colorado and Utah are in. (Pause.) Get ready. (Signal.) *United States.*
- Name the mountains you go over to get from Colorado to Utah. (Pause.) Get ready. (Signal.) *Rocky Mountains.*
- (Repeat step b until firm.)

c. Tell me how many feet underwater you would be when the pressure is **two** times as great as it is on land. (Pause.) Get ready. (Signal.) *33.*
- Tell me how many feet underwater you would be when the pressure is **three** times as great as it is on land. (Pause.) Get ready. (Signal.) *66.*
- Tell me how long it takes Jupiter to spin around one time. (Pause.) Get ready. (Signal.) *10 hours.*
- (Repeat step c until firm.)

Individual Turns

Now I'm going to call on individual students to do some facts. (Call on individual students to do the set of facts in step b or step c.)

Story Reading

a. Find part B in your textbook. ✔
- The error limit for group reading is 14 errors.

b. Everybody, touch the title. ✔
- (Call on a student to read the title.) *[An Underwater World.]*
- Everybody, what's the title? (Signal.) *An Underwater World.* ⓃⒹ

c. (Call on individual students to read the story, each student reading two or three sentences at a time. Ask the specified questions as the students read.)

- (**Correct errors:** Tell the word. Direct the student to reread the sentence.)
- (If the group makes more than 14 errors, direct the students to reread the story.)

An Underwater World

The diving boat was anchored in a place where the water changed from light green to dark, dark blue.

- What do those colors tell you about how deep the water is? (Call on a student. Idea: *That it changes from shallow to deep*.) (RF/R)

One by one, the divers went down the ladder on the side of the boat and entered the warm water. The boat was about one thousand miles east of the United States, just south of the Bermuda Islands.

ATLANTIC OCEAN

Bermuda Islands
X

Florida

- Everybody, look at the map.
- Touch the X. That's the place they were diving. ✔ (VA)
- About how far east of the United States is that **X**? (Signal.) *1,000 miles.* (VA)
- Everybody, what's the name of the islands that are near the place they are diving? (Signal.) *The Bermuda Islands.* (VA)
- In which direction would the divers have to go from the X to reach the Bermuda Islands? (Signal.) *North.* (VA)
- What's the name of the ocean they're diving in? (Signal.) *The Atlantic Ocean.* (VA)

Darla was the last diver to go down the ladder and enter the warm water.

"Now stick together," the guide said as he floated with his mask tilted back on his forehead. "You've got your partners. Stay with your partner. If you see something you want to look at, signal me. If one person stops, we all stop or somebody's going to get lost."

The guide continued, "If you get separated, go to the surface of the water. Don't try to look for the rest of us. Just go to the surface. And remember, don't go up too fast. Take at least two minutes to go up, or you may get the bends."

- Who should each diver stay with? (Call on a student. Idea: *A partner*.) (ND)
- What should a diver do if the diver gets separated from the others? (Call on a student. Idea: *Go to the surface*.) (ND)
- Everybody, can the diver go up to the surface fast? (Signal.) *No.* (ND)
- Why not? (Call on a student. Idea: *Because the diver might get the bends*.) (ND)
- We'll find out what the bends are.

The bends. Darla had read about the bends. She knew that a person gets them because of the great pressure of water. When a person goes 100 feet underwater, the pressure of the water is pushing against the person's body with four times the pressure that would be on a person standing in air.

- Everybody, how deep are Darla and the others going down? (Signal.) *100 feet.* (ND)
- How many times greater is the pressure at 100 feet under the water than it is on land? (Signal.) *Four times.* (ND)

When you're 100 feet down, four times the normal pressure pushes against your body. When a person comes up very fast, the pressure on the body goes down very fast. It goes down so fast that bubbles start to form in the blood, the same way bubbles form in a bottle of soda pop when you open the bottle. There is great pressure inside the bottle when it is capped. When you open the bottle, the pressure inside goes down very fast, and the bubbles form. That's just what happens to the blood when the pressure goes down very fast.

- Listen to that part again.

  When you're 100 feet down, four times the normal pressure pushes against your body. When a person comes up very fast, the pressure on the body goes down very fast. It goes down so fast that bubbles start to form in the blood, the same way bubbles form in a bottle of soda pop when you open the bottle. There is great pressure inside the bottle when it is capped. When you open the bottle, the pressure inside goes down very fast, and the bubbles form. That's just what happens to the blood when the pressure goes down very fast.

- What happens to the pressure on soda pop when you open a bottle? (Call on a student. Idea: *The pressure goes down very fast.*) ⓃⒹ
- Everybody, so what forms in the soda pop? (Signal.) *Bubbles.* ⓃⒹ
- What does the pressure on the body do when you come up very fast? (Call on a student. Idea: *It goes down very fast.*) ⓃⒹ
- Everybody, so what forms in the blood? (Signal.) *Bubbles.* ⓃⒹ
- Those bubbles can kill you or seriously hurt you.

Bubbles won't form in the blood if the pressure changes slowly. That's why the divers should take at least two minutes to go up to the surface.

As the diving guide floated on his back, he pulled his mask over his face and held his arm up. Then he pointed down and disappeared below the surface. The other divers followed. Darla's partner was Julie. They swam side by side and they were the last pair of divers to go down.

For Darla, going underwater was like going into a different world. She did not feel comfortable in this world. The sounds were different. She could hear herself breathe. With each breath that she took, the air hose made a loud, hissing sound.

- Everybody, make the sound that the air hose made each time she breathed. ✔ Ⓥ

Each breath that she let out made the sound of bubbles—blub, blubble, blub. She could hear her heart pounding. Aside from these sounds, everything was silent except for the occasional squeaking or clicking of a sea animal.

In this strange underwater world, Darla floated. She didn't feel the weight of the heavy tanks on her back or the weight of anything. ⭐ But even though she floated slowly down through the green water, she did not escape from the pressure of the water. When she had gone down only fifteen feet, her ears started to hurt because of the great pressure that was pushing against her body.

- Everybody, how deep was she when her ears started to hurt? (Signal.) *Fifteen feet.* ⓃⒹ
- What made them hurt? (Call on a student. Idea: *The great pressure pushing against her.*) ⓃⒹ

She could feel the pressure squeeze her mask tightly against her face. She held her nose, closed her mouth, and pushed air out very hard. Her ears felt better now.

When Darla and Julie were about 50 feet below the surface, Darla noticed that Julie was saying something and pointing down. Darla couldn't understand what Julie was saying. It sounded something like "Blulululu Blulululu." Darla looked down to see what Julie was trying to point out. Below the sisters was an incredible scene. They were right above a great reef that was covered with plants. Some plants had huge leaves that seemed to wave in the water currents. Some coral looked like small trees that branched in all directions, other coral looked like round domes. Darla knew that these were large brain coral.

- Everybody, look at the picture. It shows Darla and the other divers. Touch the pair of divers that are Darla and her sister. Remember, they're the last ones. ✔ (VA)
- Touch a coral that looks like a tree branching in all directions. ✔ (VA)
- Touch a coral that looks like a round dome. ✔ (VA)
- Read the rest of the story to yourself and be ready to answer some questions. Raise your hand when you're done.

A school of silver fish was swimming through the coral—darting one way and then another. Next to them were three yellow fish. Above them was a huge black fish, swimming slowly in the other direction.

Darla smiled to herself. Her face felt stiff because the mask was pushing against her face with great pressure.

Darla and Julie hesitated above the reef and looked at the coral and the

fish. The other divers were about fifty feet ahead of Darla and Julie, so Darla pointed at them and signaled her sister that they should catch up.

The divers followed the reef for about six hundred feet. Then they started down into a valley between two reefs. The water at the bottom of this valley was dark purple, almost black. Darla looked down at the other divers and realized that they looked like insects who were slowly gliding through a purple sky. The only difference was the trail of bubbles that followed each diver. Each time a diver breathed, out came a boiling mass of bubbles that broke into tiny bubbles and trailed up to the surface. The divers were now going down rapidly. Darla had to clear her ears again. Her mask was starting to hurt her face.

The diving guide pointed to the right. Darla searched the ocean to see what he was pointing at. For a moment she couldn't see anything unusual. Then she saw a giant ray fish, slowly flapping its fins as it glided through the valley. Darla thought, "That ray really looks like it is flying in the air."

Again, the diving guide pointed down and again the group of divers followed him. Darla was no longer afraid, but she didn't feel very comfortable. She told herself that she should enjoy the things around her. She told herself, "Not many people get to see the things that are around me right now. So enjoy them." But this experience was new for Darla.

The group was now down 66 feet. The pressure on Darla was three times the pressure on land.

- (After all students have raised their hand:)
- When Darla looked at the other divers below her, what did she think they looked like? (Call on a student. Idea: *Insects.*)
- What did the diving guide point out to the group? (Call on a student. Idea: *A giant ray fish.*)
- Look at the picture. You can see a giant ray fish.
- Everybody, how deep was Darla at the end of the story? (Signal.) *66 feet.*
- How many times greater was the water pressure than it is on land? (Signal.) *Three times.*
- Did Darla feel comfortable? (Signal.) *No.*
- Why not? (Call on a student. Ideas: *Because she was down so deep; because the pressure was so great; because diving was a new experience for her.*)
- Those big fins on each side of the ray fish are called wings. Why do you think they're called wings? (Call on a student. Ideas: *Because they look like wings; because they help the ray move through the water like a bird's wings help it move through air.*)

Paired Practice

You're going to read aloud to your partner. Today the **A** members will read first. Then the **B** members will read from the star to the end of the story. (Observe students and give feedback.)

End of Lesson Activities

INDEPENDENT WORK

Now finish the independent work for lesson 87. Raise your hand when you're finished. (Observe students and give feedback.)

WORKCHECK

a. (Direct students to take out their marking pencils.)
- We're going to check your independent work. Remember, if you got an item wrong, make an **X** next to the item.
b. (For each item: Read the item. Call on a student to answer it. If the answer is wrong, say the correct answer. Refer to the Answer Key for the correct answers.)
c. Now use your marking pencil to fix up any items you got wrong. Remember, all mistakes must be fixed up before you hand in your independent work.

SPELLING

(Present Spelling lesson 87 after completing Reading lesson 87. See *Spelling Presentation Book.*)

ACTIVITIES

(Present Activity 18 after completing Reading lesson 87. See *Activities across the Curriculum.*)

EXERCISE 1

Vocabulary Review

a. You learned a sentence that tells who she will contact.

- Everybody, say that sentence. Get ready. (Signal.) *She will contact the person we want to hire.*
- (Repeat until firm.)

b. You learned a sentence that starts with the words **I have confidence.**

- Say that sentence. Get ready. (Signal.) *I have confidence that we can avoid a long conversation.*
- (Repeat until firm.)

c. Here's the last sentence you learned: The scuba diver and her partner surfaced near the reef.

- Everybody, say that sentence. Get ready. (Signal.) *The scuba diver and her partner surfaced near the reef.*
- (Repeat until firm.)

d. Everybody, what word tells about a ridge that forms underwater? (Signal.) *Reef.*

- What word tells that people swam to the surface? (Signal.) *Surfaced.*
- What words tell about a person who goes underwater with a mask and a tank of air? (Signal.) *Scuba diver.*
- What word describes a person you do something with? (Signal.) *Partner.*

e. Once more. Say the sentence that tells where people surfaced. Get ready. (Signal.) *The scuba diver and her partner surfaced near the reef.*

EXERCISE 2

Reading Words

Column 1

a. **Find lesson 88 in your textbook.** ✔

- Touch column 1. ✔
- (Teacher reference:)

1. Iditarod	4. buoyant
2. Anchorage	5. barracuda
3. twilight	6. teasing

b. Word 1 is **Iditarod (Eye-dit'-uh-rod).** What word? (Signal.) *Iditarod.*

- Spell **Iditarod.** Get ready. (Tap for each letter.) *I-D-I-T-A-R-O-D.*
- The Iditarod is a sled-dog race that is run every year in Alaska.

c. Word 2 is **Anchorage.** What word? (Signal.) *Anchorage.*

- Spell **Anchorage.** Get ready. (Tap for each letter.) *A-N-C-H-O-R-A-G-E.*
- Anchorage is the name of a city in Alaska.

d. Word 3. What word? (Signal.) *Twilight.*

- Spell **twilight.** Get ready. (Tap for each letter.) *T-W-I-L-I-G-H-T.*

e. Word 4. What word? (Signal.) *Buoyant.*

- Spell **buoyant.** Get ready. (Tap for each letter.) *B-U-O-Y-A-N-T.*

f. Word 5. What word? (Signal.) *Barracuda.*

g. Word 6. What word? (Signal.) *Teasing.*

h. Let's read those words again, the fast way.

- Word 1. What word? (Signal.) *Iditarod.*
- (Repeat for words 2–6.)

i. (Repeat step h until firm.)

Column 2

j. Find column 2. ✔

- (Teacher reference:)

1. grasp	4. upwards
2. especially	5. struggling
3. buoyancy	6. suffer

k. Word 1. What word? (Signal.) *Grasp.*

- If you **grasp** something, you grab it and hold onto it. Here's another way of saying I **grabbed the branch and held onto it: I grasped the branch.**
- Your turn. What's another way of saying I **grabbed the saddle and held onto it?** (Signal.) *I grasped the saddle.*

l. Word 2. What word? (Signal.) *Especially.*

- (Repeat for words 3–6.)

m. Let's read those words again.

- Word 1. What word? (Signal.) *Grasp.*
- (Repeat for words 2–6.)

n. (Repeat step m until firm.)

Individual Turns

(For columns 1 and 2: Call on individual students, each to read one to three words per turn.)

Story Reading

a. Find part B in your textbook. ✔
- The error limit for group reading is 15 errors.

b. Everybody, touch the title. ✔
- (Call on a student to read the title.) [An Emergency.]
- Everybody, what's the title? (Signal.) An Emergency. ⓃⒹ

c. (Call on individual students to read the story, each student reading two or three sentences at a time. Ask the specified questions as the students read.)

- (**Correct errors:** Tell the word. Direct the student to reread the sentence.)
- (If the group makes more than 15 errors, direct the students to reread the story.)

An Emergency

About ten minutes after the dive began, the group of divers had reached the bottom of the valley between two long reefs. The bottom was 100 feet below the surface.

- Everybody, about how long did it take the divers to get 100 feet below the surface? (Signal.) Ten minutes. ⓃⒹ

Here the pressure was four times as great as it was on land. Darla's mask pressed against her face with great pressure. Her ears seemed to ring. Her mouth was dry and she had trouble swallowing.

- Name some things that the great water pressure was doing to Darla. (Call on a student. Ideas: Her mask pressed against her face; her ears rang; her mouth was dry; she had trouble swallowing.) ⓃⒹ

And things looked different. There weren't as many plants as there were above on the reefs. And things were not as bright. When Darla looked up, she could see the sun shining above the surface of the water, but it looked like a light gray circle.

- Everybody, when the sun is shining brightly, can you just look right into the sun? (Signal.) No. ⒶⓅⓀ
- Don't try. You'll burn your eyes. What does the sun look like to you? (Call on a student. Idea: A very bright circle.) ⓂⒸ
- Everybody, could Darla look at the sun when she was 100 feet under the water? (Signal.) Yes. ⓃⒹ
- What did the sun look like to Darla? (Call on a student. Idea: A light gray circle.) ⓃⒹ
- Everybody, did things look **darker** or **lighter** 100 feet below the surface? (Signal.) Darker. ⓃⒹ
- How many plants were down there? (Call on a student. Idea: Not as many as there were higher up.) ⓃⒹ
- The plants need sunlight. There isn't as much sunlight down there, so only very special plants can live deep underwater.

The other divers seemed to be swimming through twilight. A slow stream of dark gray bubbles followed each diver.

- What color are bubbles that you see in a swimming pool or a lake? (Call on a student. Idea: White.) ⒶⓅⓀ
- Everybody, did the bubbles look white to Darla? (Signal.) No. ⓃⒹ
- What color did they look? (Signal.) Gray. ⓃⒹ
- Why did they look gray instead of white? (Call on a student. Idea: Because it was so dark around her.) ⒹⒸ

Darla and her sister stayed close to each other and tried to stay close to the other divers. However, as they moved through the valley, Darla saw a school of fish above her. They were not tiny silver fish, but large, arrow-shaped fish. She pointed up and said the name of these fish to her sister. "Barracuda," she said. But it sounded like "bububuda."

- Everybody, what kind of fish did she see? (Signal.) *Barracuda.* (ND)
- Look at the picture. You can see the barracudas swimming above Darla and Julie. They look like black cutouts because it is so dark where Darla is.

Darla had read about barracudas. They were dangerous, perhaps more dangerous than sharks or killer whales. Barracudas swim in large schools and they grow to a length of almost two meters. A barracuda's mouth is filled with sharp teeth, and barracudas have been known to attack swimmers and kill them.

The barracudas above Darla and her sister swam swiftly through the water, moving in almost a straight line. Darla and her sister watched them until they disappeared into the darkness of the water above them. When Darla turned around, she did not see the other divers. She signaled her sister that they should catch up to the others. The sisters began to swim fast along the floor of the valley. Darla could not swim as fast as her sister. As Julie moved ahead of Darla, Julie turned around and motioned for Darla to catch up. Darla could see that Julie was smiling. She was teasing Darla.

- Everybody, who was a better swimmer, Darla or Julie? (Signal.) *Julie.* (ND)
- Who had been swimming for a longer time? (Signal.) *Julie.* (ND)
- How did Darla know that Julie was teasing her? (Call on a student. Idea: *Because Julie was smiling.*) (ND)

Darla kicked harder and pulled harder with her arms, but she couldn't catch up to Julie, who stayed just ahead of Darla. The girls swam rapidly along the bottom for about a minute, but still they could not see the other divers. Darla was starting to feel a little nervous, especially as she moved through a current of very cool water. The water at 100 feet down is cooler than it is at the surface, but every now and then there is a current of water that is very cool. The one that Darla and Julie were going through now gave Darla a chill.

- Everybody, where is the water cooler, **at the surface,** or **100 feet below the surface?** (Signal.) *100 feet below the surface.* (ND)
- Is all the water the same temperature at 100 feet below the surface? (Signal.) *No.* (ND)
- What does it mean, the current gave her a chill? (Call on a student. Idea: *It made her colder.*) (UCCM)

"Where are the other divers?" Darla asked herself.
Darla remembered what their guide had told them to do if they were separated from the group.

- What should they do? (Call on a student. Idea: *Go to the surface.*) (APK)

Darla was just about ready to signal Julie that they should ⭐ go to the surface. Suddenly, Julie turned around and pointed to the air hose. Darla noticed that Julie had a frightened expression. Then Darla noticed that Julie was not letting out large masses of bubbles. Only a small trail of bubbles was coming out of her mouth.

- What **should** the bubbles look like when you breathe out underwater? (Call on a student. Idea: *Large masses*.) (ND)
- What did Julie's bubbles look like? (Call on a student. Idea: *A small trail*.) (ND)
- Why do you think not many bubbles were coming out? (Call on a student. Idea: *She's not getting enough air*.) (DI)
- Yes, for some reason Julie is not getting air from her tank, so she can't breathe.

Julie was excited. She kept pointing at her air hose. Her eyes were wide. Before Darla could think about what was happening, Julie pointed up toward the surface and began to swim toward the surface very fast.

- What's going to happen to her if she goes up very fast? (Call on a student. Idea: *She'll get the bends*.) (DI)

"No!" Darla shouted as loudly as she could. "No!"

But Julie was already about five feet above her and moving very fast.

"I must catch her," Darla thought to herself.

- Everybody, who swims faster, Darla or Julie? (Signal.) *Julie.* (ND)
- So do you think Darla can catch her? (Call on a student. Idea: *No*.) (MJ)

Darla used every bit of strength she had. She kicked with all her might and she pulled hard with her arms. Then she remembered her buoyancy device. The device is a little air bag above the air tanks. The diver can fill the buoyancy device with air or let air out of it. When it is filled with air, the diver is very buoyant, which means that the diver floats to the surface very fast.

- Everybody, what can the diver let in or out of the buoyancy device? (Signal.) *Air.* (ND)
- When the device is filled with air, what does the diver do? (Call on a student. Idea: *Floats to the surface very fast*.) (ND)

When there is no air in the buoyancy device, the diver is not very buoyant and the diver sinks to the bottom.

Darla pressed the button that filled her buoyancy device with air and she shot upwards very fast. Within a couple of seconds, she caught up to her sister. She grabbed Julie around the waist with one arm. With the other, she pressed the button that lets the air out of her buoyancy device.

- Why did she press the button that lets air out of her buoyancy device? (Call on a student. Idea: *Because she didn't want to go to the surface too fast*.) (DC)
- Yes, she caught up to Julie so she could keep her from going to the surface too fast. But Julie needs air right now. I wonder how Darla will solve that problem.
- Read the rest of the story to yourself and be ready to answer some questions. Raise your hand when you're done.

Julie was struggling to get free. Her face was turning red. Her eyes were now very wide and she was flailing her arms and legs. Darla knew that if Julie went up too fast, she would suffer from the bends.

Now Darla was faced with one of the most difficult decisions she had ever made in her life. She could share her air hose with her sister. To do that, Darla would take a deep breath, remove the air hose from her mouth and give it to her sister. Her sister would then take a deep breath from the hose and return it to Darla. The decision was difficult for Darla because she started to feel a great panic when she thought about removing the air hose from her mouth, 100 feet below the surface. "I can't do it," she said to herself as she struggled with her sister. "You must do it," she told herself. "If you don't, Julie will die."

Darla gathered all her bravery, took a deep breath, and removed her air hose. Julie grabbed it with both hands and shoved the mouthpiece into her mouth. A few seconds later, she let out a huge cloud of bubbles, and then another, and then another. Darla signaled her sister to give the air hose back, but Julie was holding the hose with both hands and not paying any attention to Darla. Julie was in a state of panic.

- (After all students have raised their hand:)
- Darla had to make a decision. What was that? (Call on a student. Idea: *Whether to share her air hose with her sister.*) (ND)
- What would she do to share her air hose? (Call on a student. Idea: *Take a deep breath, remove the air hose from her mouth, and give the hose to her sister.*) (ND)
- When Julie took the air hose, great clouds of bubbles came out of her mouth. What did that mean? (Call on a student. Idea: *She had breathed a lot of air.*) (DC)
- What did Julie do when Darla signaled that she should give the air hose back to Darla? (Call on a student. Idea: *Held the hose with both hands and ignored Darla.*) (ND)
- Why didn't Julie pay any attention to Darla? (Call on a student. Idea: *Because she was in a state of panic.*) (ND)
- Everybody, did Julie know what she was doing? (Signal.) *No.* (ND)

EXERCISE 4

Paired Practice

You're going to read aloud to your partner. Today the **B** members will read first. Then the **A** members will read from the star to the end of the story. (Observe students and give feedback.)

End-of-Lesson Activities

INDEPENDENT WORK

Now finish the independent work for lesson 88. Raise your hand when you're finished. (Observe students and give feedback.)

WORKCHECK

a. (Direct students to take out their marking pencils.)
- We're going to check your independent work. Remember, if you got an item wrong, make an **X** next to the item.
b. (For each item: Read the item. Call on a student to answer it. If the answer is wrong, say the correct answer. Refer to the Answer Key for the correct answers.)
c. Now use your marking pencil to fix up any items you got wrong. Remember, all mistakes must be fixed up before you hand in your independent work.

SPELLING

(Present Spelling lesson 88 after completing Reading lesson 88. See *Spelling Presentation Book.*)

ACTIVITIES

(Present Activity 19 after completing Reading lesson 88. See *Activities across the Curriculum.*)

EXERCISE 1

Vocabulary Review

a. You learned a sentence that tells where people surfaced.
- Everybody, say that sentence. Get ready. (Signal.) *The scuba diver and her partner surfaced near the reef.*
- (Repeat until firm.)

b. I'll say part of the sentence. When I stop, you say the next word. Listen: The scuba diver and her . . . Everybody, what's the next word? (Signal.) *Partner.*

c. Listen: The scuba diver and her partner surfaced near the . . . Everybody, what's the next word? (Signal.) *Reef.*
- Say the whole sentence. Get ready. (Signal.) *The scuba diver and her partner surfaced near the reef.*

d. Listen: The scuba diver and her partner . . . Everybody, what's the next word? (Signal.) *Surfaced.*

e. Listen: The . . . Everybody, what's the next word? (Signal.) *Scuba.*

EXERCISE 2

Reading Words

Column 1

a. **Find lesson 89 in your textbook.** ✔
- Touch column 1. ✔
- (Teacher reference:)

1. **Denali**	4. **command**
2. **Knik**	5. **veterinarian**
3. **honor**	6. **thorough**

b. Word 1 is **Denali.** What word? (Signal.) *Denali.*
- Spell **Denali.** Get ready. (Tap for each letter.) *D-E-N-A-L-I.*
- Denali is the name of a huge mountain in Alaska. It's also the name of a character you'll read about.

c. Word 2 is **Knik.** What word? (Signal.) *Knik.*
- Spell Knik. Get ready. (Tap for each letter.) *K-N-I-K.*
- Knik is the name of a town in Alaska.

d. Word 3 is **honor.** What word? (Signal.) *Honor.*
- Spell **honor.** Get ready. (Tap for each letter.) *H-O-N-O-R.*

e. Word 4 is **command.** What word? (Signal.) *Command.*
- Spell **command.** Get ready. (Tap for each letter.) *C-O-M-M-A-N-D.*

f. Word 5 is **veterinarian.** What word? (Signal.) *Veterinarian.*

g. Word 6 is thorough. What word? (Signal.) *Thorough.*

h. Let's read those words again, the fast way.
- Word 1. What word? (Signal.) *Denali.*
- (Repeat for words 2–6.)

i. (Repeat step h until firm.)

Column 2

j. Find column 2. ✔
- (Teacher reference:)

1. **musher**	4. **bodies**
2. **argument**	5. **married**
3. **grasping**	

- All these words have an ending.

k. Word 1. What word? (Signal.) *Musher.*
- A musher is a person who drives a sled-dog team.

l. Word 2. What word? (Signal.) *Argument.*
- (Repeat for words 3–5.)

m. Let's read those words again.
- Word 1. What word? (Signal.) *Musher.*
- (Repeat for words 2–5.)

n. (Repeat step m until firm.)

Column 3

o. Find column 3. ✔
- (Teacher reference:)

1. <u>over</u>come	4. <u>pin</u>ched
2. <u>Anchor</u>age	5. <u>exam</u>ination
3. <u>four</u>teen	

- These words have more than one part. The first part of each word is underlined.

p. Word 1. What's the underlined part? (Signal.) *over.*
- What's the whole word? (Signal.) *Overcome.*

- When you **overcome** a problem, you **solve** it. Everybody, what's another way of saying **She solved her fear of water?** (Signal.) *She overcame her fear of water.*
- What's another way of saying **She solved her money problems?** (Signal.) *She overcame her money problems.*
- Word 2. What's the underlined part? (Signal.) *Anchor.*
- What's the whole word? (Signal.) *Anchorage.*
- Word 3. What's the underlined part? (Signal.) *four.*
- What's the whole word? (Signal.) *Fourteen.*
- Word 4. What's the underlined part? (Signal.) *pinch.*
- What's the whole word? (Signal.) *Pinched.*
- Word 5. What's the underlined part? (Signal.) *examin.*
- What's the whole word? (Signal.) *Examination.*

q. Let's read those words again, the fast way.
- Word 1. What word? (Signal.) *Overcome.*
- (Repeat for: **2. Anchorage, 3. fourteen, 4. pinched, 5. examination.**)

r. (Repeat step q until firm.)

Column 4

s. Find column 4. ✔
- (Teacher reference:)

1. Nome	4. Iditarod
2. white-capped	5. fresh
3. traded	6. locker

t. Word 1. What word? (Signal.) *Nome.*
- Nome is a very small city in Alaska. Everybody, where is Nome? (Signal.) *In Alaska.*

u. Word 2. What word? (Signal.) *White-capped.*
- A white-capped wave is a wave with white foam on top of it.

v. Word 3. What word? (Signal.) *Traded.*
- (Repeat for words 4–6.)

w. Let's read those words again.
- Word 1. What word? (Signal.) *Nome.*
- (Repeat for words 2–6.)

x. (Repeat step w until firm.)

Individual Turns
(For columns 1–4: Call on individual students, each to read one to three words per turn.)

Fact Review

a. Let's review some facts you have learned. First we'll go over the facts together. Then I'll call on some of you to do some facts.

b. Everybody, name the ocean the Bermuda Islands are in. (Pause.) Get ready. (Signal.) *Atlantic Ocean.* (RF/R)
- Name the ocean you go through when you go **west** from the United States. (Pause.) Get ready. (Signal.) *Pacific Ocean.* (RF/R)
- Tell me if things look **light** or **dark** when you're scuba diving 100 feet deep. (Pause.) Get ready. (Signal.) *Dark.* (RF/R)
- (Repeat step b until firm.)

c. Let's say you open a bottle of soda pop. Tell me if the pressure inside the bottle goes **up** or **down.** (Pause.) Get ready. (Signal.) *Down.* (RF/R)
- Tell me what forms in the soda pop. (Pause.) Get ready. (Signal.) *Bubbles.* (RF/R)
- Name the arrow-shaped fish that live in the ocean. (Pause.) Get ready. (Signal.) *Barracudas.* (RF/R)
- (Repeat step c until firm.)

d. Tell me if the water in the ocean is warmer **at 100 feet down** or **at the surface.** (Pause.) Get ready. (Signal.) *At the surface.* (RF/R)
- Tell me if all the water at 100 feet down is the same temperature. (Pause.) Get ready. (Signal.) *No.* (RF/R)
- Tell me what a buoyancy device is filled with. (Pause.) Get ready. (Signal.) *Air.* (RF/R)
- (Repeat step d until firm.)

Individual Turns
Now I'm going to call on individual students to do some facts. (Call on individual students to do the set of facts in step b, step c, or step d.)

Story Background

a. Find part B in your textbook. ✔

- You're going to read the last story about Darla. First you'll read the information passage. It gives some facts about the Iditarod.

b. Everybody, touch the title. ✔

- (Call on a student to read the title.) *[Facts About the Iditarod.]*
- Everybody, what's the title? (Signal.) *Facts About the Iditarod.* ⓃⒹ

c. (Call on individual students to read the passage, each student reading two or three sentences at a time. Ask the specified questions as the students read.)

Facts About the Iditarod

Every year, in early March, a great sled-dog race starts in Anchorage, Alaska, and ends in Nome, Alaska. That's a distance of more than 11 hundred miles. The map shows the route of the Iditarod.

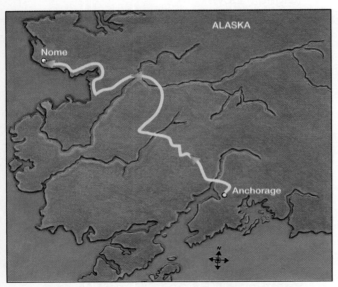

- Everybody, in what state is the Iditarod? (Signal.) *Alaska.* ⓇⒻ/Ⓡ
- In what city does it begin? (Signal.) *Anchorage.* ⓇⒻ/Ⓡ
- Anchorage is a big city with thousands of people.

- Everybody, in what city does it end? (Signal.) *Nome.* ⓇⒻ/Ⓡ
- Nome is not a big city. It's a pretty small town that is far away from any large city.

The people who enter the Iditarod race are called mushers. A musher is a person who drives a team of sled dogs. The musher usually stands at the back of the sled and shouts commands to the dogs.

- Everybody, what do we call the person who drives the sled? (Signal.) *A musher.* ⓇⒻ/Ⓡ
- Where does the musher usually stand? (Call on a student. Idea: *At the back of the sled.*) ⓇⒻ/Ⓡ
- How does the musher let the dogs know what they are supposed to do? (Call on a student. Idea: *He shouts commands to them.*) ⓇⒻ/Ⓡ

The dogs pull the sled. Some sleds have as many as sixteen dogs pulling it. Some sleds have only twelve or fourteen dogs.

The picture shows a sled in action.

- Everybody, touch the musher. ✔ ⓋⒶ
- Touch the sled. ✔ ⓋⒶ
- Raise your hand when you know how many dogs are pulling this sled. (Wait.)
- Everybody, how many dogs? (Signal.) *Fourteen.* ⓋⒶ

The race from Anchorage to Nome takes about 10 days. Sometimes it takes longer. If the weather is very bad, the musher who wins the race may be on the Iditarod trail for eleven days. Even if the winning sled gets to Nome in eleven days, the sled travels about 100 miles per day.

EXERCISE 5

Story Reading

a. Find part C in your textbook. ✔
- The error limit for group reading is 12 errors.
b. Everybody, touch the title. ✔
- (Call on a student to read the title.) *[The Trip to the Water's Surface.]*
- Everybody, what's the title? (Signal.) *The Trip to the Water's Surface.* ⓃⒹ
c. (Call on individual students to read the story, each student reading two or three sentences at a time. Ask the specified questions as the students read.)

- (**Correct errors:** Tell the word. Direct the student to reread the sentence.)
- (If the group makes more than 12 errors, direct the students to reread the story.)

The Trip to the Water's Surface

Three times Darla signaled her sister to let go of the air hose, but Julie was grasping the air hose with both hands and breathing. Darla was starting to panic now.

- Why? (Call on a student. Idea: *Because she was almost out of air.*) ⒹⒾ
- Everybody, did Julie know what she was doing? (Signal.) *No.* ⒹⒸ

Darla was running out of air. She pinched Julie's hand and pointed to the air hose.

- That hurts. Why did she do that? (Call on a student. Idea: *To get Julie's attention.*) ⒹⒾ

Suddenly, Julie's eyes changed. They had been wide and wild. Now they moved toward Darla. Julie took a deep breath and then handed the air hose to Darla just in time.

- Just in time for what? (Call on a student. Idea: *For Darla to get some air.*) ⒹⒸ
- Everybody, does Julie know what is happening now? (Signal.) *Yes.* ⒹⒸ

Darla took a couple of breaths of fresh air, took another deep breath and handed the hose back to Julie.
    Darla and Julie traded the air hose back and forth a couple of times. Julie seemed all right now. As she was taking a couple of deep breaths, Darla pointed up.

- What do you think she's trying to signal to her sister? (Call on a student. Idea: *That they should go up.*) ⒹⒾ

Together, the girls moved up slowly. Darla could feel the difference in pressure as she moved up.

- They were moving up. Everybody, so what happens to the pressure—does it get **greater** or **less**? (Signal.) *Less.* ⓇⒻ/Ⓡ

Darla's mask was not pressing against her face as hard, and her ears did not have the ringing sound they had when she had been 100 feet down.

- Why not? (Call on a student. Idea: *Because the water pressure was not as great.*) ⓇⒻ/Ⓡ

The girls continued to move up until they were ten feet below the surface. Then they stopped. They would have to stay here for one minute, until their bodies got used to the lower pressure.

- Everybody, how far from the surface are they? (Signal.) *Ten feet.* ⓃⒹ
- How long must they stay there? (Signal.) *One minute.* ⓃⒹ

- What would happen if they just kept going up? (Call on a student. Idea: *They would get the bends.*) (RF/R)

Darla kept looking at her watch as she and Julie took turns using the air hose. The one minute seemed to take one hour.

- Why? (Call on a student. Idea: *She was so anxious to get to the top.*) (DI)

At last, Darla's watch told her that they could move up again.

⚙ She signaled her sister that they could go the rest of the way to the surface. Up, up, through the clouds of bubbles. Up, all the way to the surface.

As soon as Darla surfaced, she noticed the sounds of birds and the splashing of water. Julie came up right beside her. Julie pushed her mask back onto her forehead. "Wow!" she shouted. "We made it!"

Darla smiled as she pushed her mask back. "Yeah," she said. "Yeah."

Julie swam over and kissed Darla on the cheek. "Thanks," she said. Darla hugged her sister.

In the distance, the diving boat was moving toward them, making a row of white-capped waves. The girls waved and shouted, "Over here!" Before the boat reached the girls, Julie said, ⚙ "Well, I guess you're the brave one. When I lost my air, I couldn't think. I just panicked."

"I would have done the same thing," Darla said. "I was scared to death."

Julie replied, "I'm sure glad you stopped ✦ me. I guess I didn't know what I was doing. I just had to have air."

- Where was Julie trying to go when Darla stopped her? (Call on a student. Idea: *To the surface.*) (APK)
- Why? (Call on a student. Idea: *To get some air.*) (APK)

Suddenly, Darla realized that she was brave. She remembered how she had felt when she and her sister were slowly returning to the surface. The wait had seemed like a long, long time, but Darla hadn't felt panic.

She looked at her sister and said, "Yeah, I guess I overcame my fear of water."

•　　•　　•

- What do the dots that follow this part tell you? (Call on a student. Idea: *Part of the story is missing.*) (SS)
- See if you can figure out what is happening in the next part.

Darla walked into the locker room next to the swimming pool. She changed into her swimming suit. Then she walked through the hallway to the swimming pool. A group of people was gathered at the shallow end of the pool. Darla walked to the other end of the pool, where the scuba gear was laid out. She picked up a pair of fins and a mask. Then she checked one of the air tanks to make sure that it was filled.

She carried the fins and the mask as she walked toward the group of people at the shallow end of the pool. As she approached the group she said, "Hello, I'm Darla Jackson, and I'm going to be your scuba diving instructor."

- Everybody, do you think this scene took place right after the girls finished their dive? (Signal.) *No.* (DC)
- Name some things that must have happened after Julie and Darla dived. (Call on a student. Ideas: *Darla must have learned how to be a scuba instructor; Julie and Darla went back home; etc.*) (DI)
- Read the rest of the story to yourself and be ready to answer some questions. Raise your hand when you're done.

The students told Darla their names. Then Darla said, "To understand scuba diving you must understand water pressure. The pressure on your body becomes very great when you dive. When you go down 33 feet in water, the pressure on your body is two times as great as it is when you're standing on land. When you go down 66 feet, the pressure on your body is three times as great as it is on land."

As Darla talked, her mind went back to the first time she had gone down 100 feet. Since that dive, she had gone down much farther. She had already taken ten dives below 130 feet and thirty dives below 100 feet. She had gone diving with her sister in the Pacific Ocean and the Atlantic Ocean. She had been swimming with seals, whales and even sharks. She no longer had fear of the water, but she remembered how she had felt on her first deep dive.

"Oh, yes," she said to the group. "Some of you may be afraid of the water. You can overcome that fear if you train yourself to think about the things you must do. I know that you can overcome the fear because when I started out, I was as afraid of the water as anybody that ever lived."

The people in the group smiled, and Darla went on with the instruction.

- (After all students have raised their hand:)
- As Darla talked to the group, what did she remember? (Call on a student. Idea: *The first time she dove 100 feet.*) (ND)
- Everybody, was that the last time she had gone that deep? (Signal.) *No.* (ND)
- How deep had she gone since then? (Signal.) *130 feet.* (ND)
- Name two oceans that she and her sister had been diving in. (Call on a student.) *Atlantic and the Pacific.* (ND)
- What did she tell the students who had great fear of the water? (Call on a student. Idea: *You can overcome the fear.*) (ND)

- Everybody, did Darla know what she was talking about? (Signal.) *Yes.* (DC)

EXERCISE 6

Paired Practice

You're going to read aloud to your partner. Today the **A** members will read first. Then the **B** members will read from the star to the end of the story. (Observe students and give feedback.)

End-of-Lesson Activities

INDEPENDENT WORK

Now finish the independent work for lesson 89. Raise your hand when you're finished. (Observe students and give feedback.)

WORKCHECK

a. (Direct students to take out their marking pencils.)
- We're going to check your independent work. Remember, if you got an item wrong, make an **X** next to the item.
b. (For each item: Read the item. Call on a student to answer it. If the answer is wrong, say the correct answer. Refer to the Answer Key for the correct answers.)
c. Now use your marking pencil to fix up any items you got wrong. Remember, all mistakes must be fixed up before you hand in your independent work.

SPELLING

(Present Spelling lesson 89 after completing Reading lesson 89. See *Spelling Presentation Book*.)

ACTIVITIES

(Present Activity 20 after completing Reading lesson 89. See *Activities across the Curriculum*.)

Note: You will need to reproduce blackline masters for the Fact Game in lesson 90 (Appendix G in *Teacher's Guide*).

Materials for Lesson 90

Fact Game

For each team (4 or 5 students):
- pair of number cubes (or dice)
- copy of Fact Game 90 (Reproducible blackline masters are in Appendix G of the *Teacher's Guide*.)

For each student:
- their copy of the scorecard sheet (at end of workbook B)

For each monitor:
- a pencil
- Fact Game 90 answer key (at end of textbook B)

Fluency: Rate/Accuracy

Each student needs their thermometer chart.

EXERCISE 1

Fact Game

a. You're going to play the game that uses the facts you have learned. Remember the rules. The player rolls the number cubes, figures out the number of the question, reads that question out loud, and answers it. The monitor tells the player if the answer is right or wrong. If it's wrong, the monitor tells the right answer. If it's right, the monitor gives the player one point. Don't argue with the monitor. The number cubes go to the left and the next player has a turn. You'll play the game for 10 minutes.

b. (Divide students into groups of four or five. Assign monitors. Circulate as students play the game. Comment on groups that are playing well.)

c. (At the end of 10 minutes, have all students who earned more than 10 points stand up.)

- (Tell the monitor of each game that ran smoothly:) Your group did a good job.

EXERCISE 2

Fluency: Rate/Accuracy

a. Today is a test day and a reading checkout day. While you're writing answers, I'm going to call on you one at a time to read part of the story we read in lesson 89.

- Remember, you pass the checkout by reading the passage in less than a minute without making more than 2 mistakes. And when you pass the checkout, you color the space for lesson 90 on your thermometer chart.

b. (Call on individual students to read the portion of story 89 marked with ✿.)

- (Time the student. Note words that are missed and number of words read.)

- (Teacher reference:)

✿ She signaled her sister that they could go the rest of the way to the surface. Up, up, through the clouds of bubbles. Up, all the way to the surface.

As soon as Darla surfaced, she noticed the sounds of birds and the splashing of water. Julie came up right [50] beside her. Julie pushed her mask back onto her forehead. "Wow!" she shouted. "We made it!"

Darla smiled as she pushed her mask back. "Yeah," [75] she said. "Yeah."

Julie swam over and kissed Darla on the cheek. "Thanks," she said. Darla hugged her sister.

In the distance, the diving boat [100] was moving toward them, making a row of white-capped waves. The girls waved and shouted, "Over here!" Before the boat reached the girls, Julie said, ✿ [125] "Well, I guess you're the brave one."

- (If the student reads the passage in one minute or less and makes no more than 2 errors, direct the student to color in the space for lesson 90 on the thermometer chart.)

- (If the student makes any mistakes, point to each word that was misread and identify it.)
- (If the student does not meet the rate-error criterion for the passage, direct the student to practice reading the story with the assigned partner.)

EXERCISE 3

Test

a. **Find page 97 in your textbook.** ✔
- This is a test. You'll work items you've done before.
- Work carefully. Raise your hand when you've completed all the items. (Observe students but do not give feedback on errors.)

EXERCISE 4

Marking The Test

a. (Check students' work before beginning lesson 91. Refer to the *Answer Key* for the correct answers.)
b. (Record all test 9 results on the Test Summary Sheet and the Group Summary Sheet. Reproducible Summary Sheets are at the back of the *Teacher's Guide.*)

EXERCISE 5

Test Remedies

(Provide any necessary remedies for test 9 before presenting lesson 91. Test remedies are discussed in the *Teacher's Guide.*)

Test 9 Firming Table

Test Item	Introduced in lesson	Test Item	Introduced in lesson	Test Item	Introduced in lesson
1	84	13	86	25	88
2	84	14	87	26	89
3	86	15	87	27	89
4	86	16	87	28	89
5	86	17	87	29	89
6	87	18	87	30	89
7	87	19	88	31	83
8	88	20	88	32	86
9	88	21	88	33	86
10	88	22	88	34	83
11	86	23	88	35	83
12	86	24	88	36	86

SPELLING

(Present Spelling lesson 90 after completing Reading lesson 90. See *Spelling Presentation Book.*)

Lessons 91–95 • Planning Page

	Lesson 91	Lesson 92	Lesson 93	Lesson 94	Lesson 95
LESSON EVENTS	**Vocabulary Sentence** Reading Words Story Background Story Reading Paired Practice Independent Work Workcheck Spelling	Vocabulary Sentence Reading Words Story Background Story Reading Paired Practice Independent Work Workcheck Spelling	Vocabulary Sentences Reading Words Story Reading Paired Practice Independent Work Workcheck Spelling	Vocabulary Sentence Reading Words Story Reading Paired Practice Independent Work Workcheck Spelling	**Vocabulary Sentence** Reading Words Story Background Story Reading Fluency: Rate/ Accuracy Independent Work Workcheck Spelling
VOCABULARY SENTENCE	#23: The <u>veterinarian</u> gave the dogs a <u>thorough</u> <u>examination</u>.	#23: The <u>veterinarian</u> gave the dogs a <u>thorough</u> <u>examination</u>.	sentence #21 sentence #22 sentence #23	#23: The <u>veterinarian</u> gave the dogs a <u>thorough</u> <u>examination</u>.	**#24: Visibility was <u>miserable</u> in the <u>fierce</u> <u>blizzard</u>.**

READING WORDS: WORD TYPES	modeled words
	words with an
	  ending
	mixed words
		modeled words
		words with an
		  ending
		mixed words
			modeled words
			words with
			  underlined parts
			mixed words
				modeled words
				words with an
				  ending
				2-syllable words
				mixed words
					modeled words
					–ed words
					mixed words
					multi-syllable words

NEW VOCABULARY	reins kennel purpose strain harnessed Nome parka husky	include official	assistant exchange certificate injure health according endurance nightmare	courage challenging dedicated hip joint limp x-ray	volunteer weary Sweden competed amused feat
STORY BACKGROUND	Sled-Dog Teams	Booties			Supplies for the Race
STORY	Susie and Denali	Getting Ready for a Practice Run	A Practice Run	Examination Day	The Big Race
SKILL ITEMS		Vocabulary	Vocabulary sentence Crossword puzzle	Vocabulary sentences Vocabulary	
SPECIAL MATERIALS					Thermometer charts
SPECIAL PROJECTS/ ACTIVITIES				Activity after lessons 94-97	

Comprehension Questions Abbreviations Guide

Access Prior Knowledge = (APK)   Author's Point of View = (APoV)   Author's Purpose = (AP)   Cause/Effect = (C/E)   Charts/Graphs/Diagrams/Visual Aids = (VA)

Classify and Categorize = (C+C)   Compare/Contrast = (C/C)   Determine Character Emotions, Motivation = (DCE)   Drawing Conclusions = (DC)   Drawing Inferences = (DI)

Fact and Opinion = (F/O)   Hypothesizing = (H)   Main Idea = (MI)   Making Connections = (MC)   Making Deductions = (MD)   Making Judgements = (MJ)

Narrative Elements = (NE)   Noting Details = (ND)   Predict = (P)   Reality/Fantasy = (R/F)   Recall Facts/Rules = (RF/R)   Retell = (R)   Sequence = (Seq)

Steps in a Process = (SP)   Story Structure = (SS)   Summarize = (Sum)   Understanding Dialogue = (UD)   Using Context to Confirm Meaning(s) = (UCCM)   Visualize = (V)

104   Lessons 91—95 • Planning Page

EXERCISE 1

Vocabulary

a. **Find page 367 in your textbook.** ✔
- Touch sentence 23. ✔
- This is a new vocabulary sentence. It says: The veterinarian gave the dogs a thorough examination. Everybody, read that sentence. Get ready. (Signal.) *The veterinarian gave the dogs a thorough examination.*
- Close your eyes and say the sentence. Get ready. (Signal.) *The veterinarian gave the dogs a thorough examination.*
- (Repeat until firm.)

b. A veterinarian is an animal doctor. Everybody, what's another way of saying **The animal doctor operated on a horse?** (Signal.) *The veterinarian operated on a horse.*

c. Something is **thorough** if it doesn't overlook anything. Everybody, what do we call a **checkup** that does not overlook anything? (Signal.) *A thorough checkup.*
- What do we call a **cleaning job** that doesn't overlook anything? (Signal.) *A thorough cleaning job.*

d. An examination is a checkup. If a doctor gives you a checkup, the doctor gives you an examination. Everybody, what's another way of saying **His teeth need a checkup?** (Signal.) *His teeth need an examination.*
- What's another way of saying **The checkup went quickly?** (Signal.) *The examination went quickly.*

e. Listen to the sentence again: The veterinarian gave the dogs a thorough examination. Everybody, say the sentence. Get ready. (Signal.) *The veterinarian gave the dogs a thorough examination.*

f. Everybody, what word means **animal doctor?** (Signal.) *Veterinarian.*
- What word means **checkup?** (Signal.) *Examination.*
- What word means that nothing is overlooked? (Signal.) *Thorough.*
- (Repeat step f until firm.)

EXERCISE 2

Reading Words

Column 1

a. Find lesson 91 in your textbook. ✔
- Touch column 1. ✔
- (Teacher reference:)

1. reins	3. gee
2. Butch	4. purpose

b. Word 1 is **reins.** What word? (Signal.) *Reins.*
- Spell **reins.** Get ready. (Tap for each letter.) *R-E-I-N-S.*
- Reins are the straps that are attached to horses. The rider holds the other end of the reins and uses them to steer the horse. Everybody, what do we call the straps that are used to steer horses? (Signal.) *Reins.*

c. Word 2 is **Butch.** What word? (Signal.) *Butch.*
- Spell **Butch.** Get ready. (Tap for each letter.) *B-U-T-C-H.*

d. Word 3 is **gee.** What word? (Signal.) *Gee.*
- Spell **gee.** Get ready. (Tap for each letter.) *G-E-E.*

e. Word 4 is **purpose.** What word? (Signal.) *Purpose.*
- Spell **purpose.** Get ready. (Tap for each letter.) *P-U-R-P-O-S-E.*
- If you do something **on purpose,** you do something the way you planned to do it. Everybody, what's another way of saying **She didn't say that the way she planned?** (Signal.) *She didn't say that on purpose.*

f. Let's read those words again, the fast way.
- Word 1. What word? (Signal.) *Reins.*
- (Repeat for words 2–4.)

g. (Repeat step f until firm.)

Column 2

h. Find column 2. ✔

- (Teacher reference:)

1. harnessed	**4. yapping**
2. referring	**5. commands**
3. toughness	

- All these words have an ending.
i. Word 1. What word? (Signal.) *Harnessed.*
- When a sled-dog team is attached to a sled, the team is **harnessed** to the sled.
j. Word 2. What word? (Signal.) *Referring.*
- (Repeat for words 3–5.)
k. Let's read those words again.
- Word 1. What word? (Signal.) *Harnessed.*
- (Repeat for words 2–5.)
l. (Repeat step k until firm.)

Column 3

m. Find column 3. ✔
- (Teacher reference:)

1. Uncle Chad	**4. goal**
2. parka	**5. leash**
3. husky	**6. Denali**

n. Number 1. What name? (Signal.) *Uncle Chad.*
o. Word 2. What word? (Signal.) *Parka.*
- A parka is a warm winter jacket with a hood. Everybody, what do we call a warm winter jacket with a hood? (Signal.) *Parka.*
p. Word 3. What word? (Signal.) *Husky.*
- A husky is a strong sled dog that survives well in very cold weather.
q. Word 4. What word? (Signal.) *Goal.*
r. (Repeat for words 5 and 6.)
s. Let's read those words again.
- Number 1. What name? (Signal.) *Uncle Chad.*
- Word 2. What word? (Signal.) *Parka.*
- (Repeat for words 3–6.)
t. (Repeat step s until firm.)

Column 4

u. Find column 4. ✔
- (Teacher reference:)

1. kennel	**4. crisp**
2. strain	**5. Knik**
3. Susie	**6. honor**

v. Word 1. What word? (Signal.) *Kennel.*
- A kennel is a place where dogs are kept. Everybody, what do we call a place where dogs are kept? (Signal.) *Kennel.*
w. Word 2. What word? (Signal.) *Strain.*
- When somebody pulls or pushes as hard as possible, the person is **straining.** Everybody, what's another way of saying **The horses pulled as hard as they could?** (Signal.) *The horses strained.*
- What's another way of saying **They were exhausted from pushing and pulling so hard?** (Signal.) *They were exhausted from straining so hard.*
x. Word 3. What word? (Signal.) *Susie.*
- (Repeat for words 4–6.)
y. Let's read those words again.
- Word 1. What word? (Signal.) *Kennel.*
- (Repeat for words 2–6.)
z. (Repeat step y until firm.)

Column 5

a. Find column 5. ✔
- (Teacher reference:)

1. Nome	**4. whoa**
2. alongside	**5. zero**
3. wool	

b. Word 1. What word? (Signal.) *Nome.*
c. Word 2. What word? (Signal.) *Alongside.*
- (Repeat for words 3–5.)
d. Let's read those words again.
- Word 1. What word? (Signal.) *Nome.*
- (Repeat for words 2–5.)
e. (Repeat step d until firm.)

Individual Turns

(For columns 1–5: Call on individual students, each to read one to three words per turn.)

EXERCISE 3

Story Background

a. Find part B in your textbook. ✔
- You're going to start a new story today. First you'll read the information passage. It gives some facts about sled-dog teams.
b. Everybody, touch the title. ✔
- (Call on a student to read the title.) *[Sled-Dog Teams.]*

- Everybody, what's the title? (Signal.) *Sled-Dog Teams.* (ND)

c. (Call on individual students to read the passage, each student reading two or three sentences at a time. Ask the specified questions as the students read.)

Sled-Dog Teams

Most sled-dog teams have an even number of dogs—twelve, fourteen or sixteen. In the Iditarod, a musher can't have more than sixteen dogs.

- If the team has an even number of dogs, they are in pairs. You can see a team in the picture. Raise your hand when you know how many are in that team. (Wait.)
- Everybody, how many dogs? (Signal.) *10.* (VA)
- Yes, ten. Is ten an even number? (Signal.) *Yes.* (APK)

The first pair of dogs in the team are the lead dogs. Lead dogs must be very smart and they must be leaders, so the other dogs will follow them.

- Everybody, what's the name of the first pair of dogs in the team? (Signal.) *Lead dogs.* (RF/R)
- What kind of dogs are selected to be lead dogs? (Call on a student. Idea: *They must be smart and must be good leaders.*) (RF/R)

The pair of dogs just behind the lead dogs are called swing dogs. They are the best dogs at following and they are very fast. When the lead dogs swing to the left, the swing dogs follow closely to make sure the other dogs follow the same path.

- Everybody, what's the name of the pair of dogs just behind the lead dogs? (Signal.) *Swing dogs.* (RF/R)
- What kind of dogs are selected to be swing dogs? (Call on a student. Idea: *They're fast and they're best at following.*) (RF/R)

The pair of dogs closest to the sled are called wheel dogs. Wheel dogs must be very strong because when the sled gets stuck, the wheel dogs are the ones who have to pull it out or turn it so it is free.

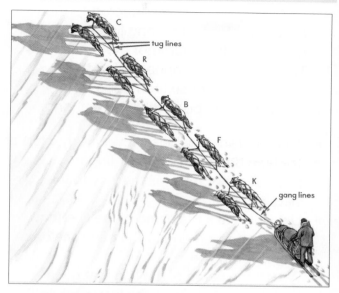

- Everybody, what's the name of the dogs closest to the sled? (Signal.) *Wheel dogs.* (RF/R)
- What kind of dogs are selected to be wheel dogs? (Call on a student. Idea: *They're very strong.*) (RF/R)
- Everybody, look at the picture and raise your hand when you know what letter shows the lead dogs. (Wait.)
- Everybody, what letter shows the lead dogs? (Signal.) *C.* (RF/R)
- Raise your hand when you know the letter that shows the wheel dogs. (Wait.)
- Everybody, what letter for the wheel dogs? (Signal.) *K.* (RF/R)
- Raise your hand when you know the letter that shows the swing dogs. (Wait.)
- Everybody, what letter for the swing dogs? (Signal.) *R.* (RF/R)
- (Repeat until firm.)

The dogs are harnessed together with nylon straps. Each dog wears a criss-cross harness.

- Everybody, touch one of the harnesses in the picture. ✔ (VA)
- You can see how the straps cross back and forth.

Each harness is attached to a tug line.

- The tug lines for the lead dogs are labeled in the picture. Everybody, touch one of the tug lines. ✔ (VA)

All the tug lines are connected to the gang line. That's the long line that runs down the middle of the team. The gang line is connected to the sled. If there are sixteen dogs, the gang line may be over sixty feet long.

- The gang line is labeled. Everybody, start at the lead dogs and run your finger along the gang line, all the way to the sled. ✔ (VA)
- Listen: What's the name of the line that goes from each dog to the gang line? (Signal.) *Tug line.* (RF/R)
- What's the name of the line that goes from the lead dogs all the way back to the sled? (Signal.) *Gang line.* (RF/R)
- (Repeat until firm.)

EXERCISE 4

Story Reading

a. Find part C in your textbook. ✔
- The error limit for group reading is 11 errors.
b. Everybody, touch the title. ✔
- (Call on a student to read the title.) *[Susie and Denali.]*
- Everybody, what's the title? (Signal.) *Susie and Denali.* (ND)
c. (Call on individual students to read the story, each student reading two or three sentences at a time. Ask the specified questions as the students read.)

- **(Correct errors:** Tell the word. Direct the student to reread the sentence.)
- (If the group makes more than 11 errors, direct the students to reread the story.)

Susie and Denali

Susie put on her parka and mittens. It was warmer today, about 4 degrees below zero.

Susie went outside and called, "Denali." A large Alaskan husky came running through the crisp snow, stopped in front of her, sat down, and wagged his tail. "It will happen in a little more than two weeks," Susie said. Denali licked his chops and looked as if he understood her.

Susie was referring to the Iditarod. This year it would begin on March 15. Susie's Uncle Chad was going to be a musher in this year's race. He lived less than a mile from Susie's place in Knik, Alaska, and Susie had been working with him for almost a year, getting ready for the race.

- Who was going to be a musher in the race? (Call on a student. Idea: *Susie's Uncle Chad.*) (ND)
- Everybody, who helped Chad train his team? (Signal.) *Susie.* (ND)
- In what state did they live? (Signal.) *Alaska.* (ND)
- What was the date for the beginning of the race? (Signal.) *March 15.* (ND)
- The race was a little more than two weeks away. Raise your hand if you know about what date it was now? (Call on a student. Idea: *March 1.*) (DI)
- What was the temperature? (Call on a student. Idea: *About 4 degrees below zero.*) (ND)
- That's very cold for March.

Susie harnessed Denali to a practice sled. She stood next to the sled and called out, "Mush."

Denali pulled hard and the sled jumped forward. Susie ran alongside the sled, then jumped on the back. Denali knew that he was going to Uncle Chad's place, and he was eager to get there. The snow squeaked and crunched as Denali pulled the sled along, next to the road.

Susie imagined that she was in the great Iditarod race. She tried to imagine what it was like with fourteen or even sixteen dogs in front of her, as they pulled a sled through country that was so wild that there were no roads in many places, just the Iditarod trail. Susie had heard stories about the Iditarod and the dangers mushers had to face—getting lost, being attacked by animals and, the most feared problem of all, freezing.

"Whoa," she called to Denali. Uncle Chad's place was on the other side of the road. A large truck went by. The driver waved to Susie. She waved back and then called out, "Mush." Denali pulled the sled across the road. Some of Chad's dogs were looking at Denali from their kennel. Two of them were barking.

Uncle Chad came out, wearing a wool shirt, gloves and earmuffs, but no coat. He was handsome and, for an instant, Susie wondered why he had never married. She also wondered how he could dress like that in cold weather. He called to her, "Susie, bring Denali around back. Today, we're going to run with a loaded sled."

"Can Denali be one of your wheel dogs?" ⭐

"Maybe later." He smiled. She didn't.

"Oh, come on," she said. "He's a good wheel dog. He knows all the commands, and . . ."

"Susie," Chad said. "I need to find out how the regular team of fourteen dogs is going to do in really rough country."

- Everybody, what was the name of Susie's dog? (Signal.) *Denali.* (ND)
- Was he one of Chad's regular dogs? (Signal.) *No.* (DI)
- How was Chad dressed? (Call on a student. Idea: *He was wearing a shirt, gloves, and earmuffs, but no coat.*) (ND)

- Why didn't Chad want Denali to be one of the wheel dogs? (Call on a student. Idea: *He needs to work the regular team in rough country.*) (ND)
- Where are wheel dogs in the team? (Call on a student. Idea: *Right in front of the sled.*) (RF/R)

Chad walked to the kennel, opened the kennel gate and said, "Into the truck, you guys." The dogs ran around, jumped up on Chad and Susie, and then jumped in the back of Chad's truck. Three dogs got into arguments about who would sit closest to the sled, which was already in the truck bed. They growled and snapped.

"Stop that," Chad said, and the dogs settled down. Most of them were a lot smaller than Denali, but they were all very strong, and they were all tough. They would need that toughness when they ran the Iditarod because then they would have to pull the sled all day long—sometimes for more than fourteen hours a day.

- Read the rest of the story to yourself and be ready to answer some questions. Raise your hand when you're done.

Susie had gone on more than a hundred practice runs with Chad, and she knew every dog that he owned—all fifteen of them. Although she knew a lot about mushing, she was always amazed at how much more Chad knew about it. He had been in the Iditarod once before, but he didn't do very well. The sled broke down about 200 miles from Nome, and he didn't finish the race. His goal for this year was to finish. He wasn't thinking about being in first or second place, just finishing. Susie had once told him, "You know so much about mushing, you could win first place!"

He had laughed and said, "Some mushers in that race know more about mushing than I'll ever learn. It's just an honor to be in the same race they are in."

> The truck pulled off the road. Down below was Eagle River Valley. It looked very steep. Chad said, "We'll take the sled down into the valley and around the rocky parts."
>
> Chad jumped out of the truck and told the dogs, "Everybody out of the truck." The dogs were glad to obey that command. Some of them looked like they were flying as they jumped out of the truck bed. Through the snow they raced, yapping and running in circles. Then Chad whistled, and they all crowded around him with their tails wagging.

- (After all students have raised their hand:)
- How many practice runs had Susie gone on with Chad? (Call on a student. *Idea: Over a hundred.*) ⓃⒹ
- Everybody, how many times had Chad been in the Iditarod? (Signal.) *One.* ⓃⒹ
- How many times did he finish the race? (Call on a student. Idea: *None.*) ⓃⒹ
- Why didn't he finish that race? (Call on a student. Idea: *His sled broke down.*) ⓃⒹ
- Where was the truck at the end of the story? (Call on a student. Idea: *Above Eagle River Valley.*) ⓃⒹ

EXERCISE 5

Paired Practice

You're going to read aloud to your partner. Today the **B** members will read first. Then the **A** members will read from the star to the end of the story. (Observe students and give feedback.)

End-of-Lesson Activities

INDEPENDENT WORK

Now finish the independent work for lesson 91. Raise your hand when you're finished. (Observe students and give feedback.)

WORKCHECK

a. (Direct students to take out their marking pencils.)
- We're going to check your independent work. Remember, if you got an item wrong, make an **X** next to the item.
b. (For each item: Read the item. Call on a student to answer it. If the answer is wrong, say the correct answer. Refer to the Answer Key for the correct answers.)
c. Now use your marking pencil to fix up any items you got wrong. Remember, all mistakes must be fixed up before you hand in your independent work.

SPELLING

(Present Spelling lesson 91 after completing Reading lesson 91. See *Spelling Presentation Book.*)

EXERCISE 1
Vocabulary Review

a. Here's the new vocabulary sentence: The veterinarian gave the dogs a thorough examination.
* Everybody, say the sentence. Get ready. (Signal.) *The veterinarian gave the dogs a thorough examination.*
* (Repeat until firm.)
b. Everybody, what word means that nothing is overlooked? (Signal.) *Thorough.*
* What word means **checkup?** (Signal.) *Examination.*
* What word means **animal doctor?** (Signal.) *Veterinarian.*

EXERCISE 2
Reading Words
Column 1
a. **Find lesson 92 in your textbook.** ✔
* Touch column 1. ✔
* (Teacher reference:)

1. include	3. purpose
2. official	4. leashes

b. Word 1 is **include.** What word? (Signal.) *Include.*
* Spell **include.** Get ready. (Tap for each letter.) *I-N-C-L-U-D-E.*
* When you include something, you let it inside something else. If you let Marge in a group, you include Marge in the group. Everybody, what are you doing if you let Bill into a group? (Signal.) *Including Bill in the group.*
c. Word 2 is **official.** What word? (Signal.) *Official.*
* Spell **official.** Get ready. (Tap for each letter.) *O-F-F-I-C-I-A-L.*
* An official is somebody who can judge if things are done as they are supposed to be done. An official for a race would judge whether all the things are done as they are supposed to be done. Everybody, what do we call a person who can judge if things are done as they're supposed to be done? (Signal.) *An official.*
d. Word 3. What word? (Signal.) *Purpose.*
* Spell **purpose.** Get ready. (Tap for each letter.) *P-U-R-P-O-S-E.*
e. Word 4. What word? (Signal.) *Leashes.*
* Spell **leashes.** Get ready. (Tap for each letter.) *L-E-A-S-H-E-S.*
f. Let's read those words again, the fast way.
* Word 1. What word? (Signal.) *Include.*
* (Repeat for words 2–4.)
g. (Repeat step f until firm.)

Column 2
h. Find column 2. ✔
* (Teacher reference:)

1. booties	3. strained
2. stiffen	4. huffed

* All these words have an ending.
i. Word 1. What word? (Signal.) *Booties.*
* (Repeat for words 2–4.)
j. Let's read those words again.
* Word 1. What word? (Signal.) *Booties.*
* (Repeat for words 2–4.)
k. (Repeat step j until firm.)

Column 3
l. Find column 3. ✔
* (Teacher reference:)

1. gang	4. haw
2. reins	5. canvas
3. gee	6. Velcro

m. Word 1. What word? (Signal.) *Gang.*
* (Repeat for words 2–6.)
n. Let's read those words again.
* Word 1. What word? (Signal.) *Gang.*
* (Repeat for words 2–6.)
o. (Repeat step n until firm.)

Individual Turns
(For columns 1–3: Call on individual students, each to read one to three words per turn.)

Story Background

a. Find part B in your textbook. ✔
- You're going to read the next story about the Iditarod. First you'll read the information passage. It gives some facts about booties.

b. Everybody, touch the title. ✔
- (Call on a student to read the title.) *[Booties.]*
- Everybody, what's the title? (Signal.) *Booties.* (ND)

c. (Call on individual students to read the passage, each student reading two or three sentences at a time. Ask the specified questions as the students read.)

Booties

The rules of the Iditarod require every dog to wear booties on its feet, and the musher must have a spare set of booties for each dog. Most mushers take along more than 1,000 booties and change them every two days.

- Everybody, what do dogs in the Iditarod have to wear? (Signal.) *Booties.* (RF/R)

The booties are designed to protect the dogs' feet. In some places, the dogs go over ice. Without booties, they may get serious ice cuts on their paws. Even if they cut one of their paws while wearing a bootie, the bootie will protect the cut.

- How do booties help a dog's feet? (Call on a student. Idea: *The booties protect the dog's paws.*) (RF/R)
- Is it better for a dog with a cut paw to wear booties or not to wear them? (Call on a student. Idea: *To wear them.*) (RF/R)

Also, dogs without booties get balls of snow packed between the pads on their paws. This is uncomfortable for the dogs. When it happens, a dog would like to stop, sit down, and chew the snow from between the pads. But there's no time for this kind of stopping during the race. So

dogs without booties would suffer. They would also slip around a lot more than dogs with booties.

Not all booties are made of the same material. The booties that Chad preferred are made of canvas. These booties have Velcro flaps.

- Look at the picture. That shows the kind of booties that Chad preferred. Everybody, what's that strap made of? (Signal.) *Velcro.* (ND)
- What's the rest of the bootie made of? (Signal.) *Canvas.* (ND)
- Canvas is a heavy cloth that protects things well.

Putting booties on the dogs is tricky. If booties are too tight, the dog's blood cannot circulate around the paws, so the dog's ankles swell up. If the booties are too loose, they fall off.

- What can happen if the booties are too tight? (Call on a student. Ideas: *Blood cannot circulate; the dog's ankles can swell.*) (RF/R)
- What can happen if they are too loose? (Call on a student. Idea: *They can fall off.*) (RF/R)

Before putting on the booties, the musher sometimes rubs a special cream on a dog's pads. The cream keeps the pads soft, so they won't crack.

EXERCISE 4

Story Reading

a. Find part C in your textbook. ✔
- The error limit for group reading is 6 errors.

b. Everybody, touch the title. ✔
- (Call on a student to read the title.) *[Getting Ready for a Run.]*
- Everybody, what's the title? (Signal.) *Getting Ready for a Run.* ⓝⒹ

c. (Call on individual students to read the story, each student reading two or three sentences at a time. Ask the specified questions as the students read.)

> - (**Correct errors:** Tell the word. Direct the student to reread the sentence.)
> - (If the group makes more than 6 errors, direct the students to reread the story.)

Getting Ready for a Run

"Let's harness up," Chad said. As he hooked up the dogs to their tug lines, Susie began to put booties on the dogs. Susie and Chad didn't put booties on the dogs for ordinary practice runs in open fields. But the dogs needed booties for a tough run like the one they would do today. Also, Chad wanted to make sure that none of the dogs would have problems with the booties.

Before putting on the booties, Susie rubbed a special cream on each dog's pads. Susie and Chad worked fast, but it took more than 30 minutes to get everything ready. At last, the dogs were lined up in pairs—seven pairs. Each dog's harness was attached to a tug line and each tug line was attached to the gang line. A neck line connected each pair of dogs together. When all fourteen dogs were in place and ready to go, the lead dogs were over fifty feet from the sled.

- Everybody, how many dogs did Chad plan to run in the Iditarod? (Signal.) *14.* ⒶⓅⓀ
- How many dogs was he practicing with at Eagle River Valley? (Signal.) *14.* ⓝⒹ
- Yes, he wanted to work with the team that he would use in the race.

- What did Susie and Chad do that was different than what they did for other practice runs? (Call on a student. Idea: *They put booties on the dogs.*) ⓝⒹ
- Why did they put booties on this time? (Call on a student. Ideas: *Because they were going to do a tough run; they wanted to be sure no dogs would have problems with the booties.*) ⓝⒹ
- Everybody, how far was it from the sled to the lead dogs? (Signal.) *Over 50 feet.* ⓝⒹ
- That's a long distance. If the front end of a sled was just coming into one end of a large classroom, the lead dog would be in the next classroom.

Steering dogs is tricky. It's not like steering horses because horses have reins. If you move the reins to the left, the horse turns left. Sled dogs don't have reins. The only thing mushers use to steer the dogs is their voice. They shout out commands that the dogs follow. Some of the commands are for only some dogs. So the dogs have to know which commands they are to obey and which commands are for other dogs.

- Steering a team of horses is different from steering a team of dogs. How does the driver let horses know which way to turn or what to do? (Call on a student. Idea: *The driver moves the reins.*) ⓝⒹ
- How does a musher let dogs know which way to turn or what to do? (Call on a student. Idea: *The musher gives the dogs commands.*) ⓝⒹ

After all the dogs were harnessed, Chad loaded four large sacks of dirt on the sled. He said, "This dirt weighs over ★ 300 pounds, so the dogs will be pulling more weight than they'll have to pull during the race, but I want to see what the team can do in tough places."

- Everybody, how much weight did Chad put on the sled? (Signal.) *Over 300 pounds.* ⓝⒹ

Then he jumped on the back of the sled and shouted out, "Muuush, you sled dogs. Muuush."

- Would the sled have **less than 300 pounds** or **more than 300 pounds** in the Iditarod? (Signal.) *Less than 300 pounds.* (ND)
- Why did Chad want the dogs to work with a lot of weight? (Call on a student. Idea: *To see how they'd do.*) (ND)
- Everybody, look at the picture. What's Chad doing? (Call on a student. Idea: *Loading bags on the sled.*) (VA)

- What's Susie doing? (Call on a student. Idea: *Holding some of the dogs.*) (VA)
- Those are the two dogs that are not going to be part of the team.
- Read the rest of the story to yourself and be ready to answer some questions. Raise your hand when you're done.

The dogs put their heads down and their shoulders up. They pulled and strained and wagged their tails. They panted and huffed and pulled harder. At first, the sled moved slowly, but then the dogs began to run—faster and faster. Susie had two dogs on leashes—Denali and Butch, the other dog that was not on the gang line. They ran behind the sled, but they could not keep up with the sled.

Down the slope the sled went. As it approached the bottom, Chad shouted, "Come gee," and the lead dogs made a circle to the right and headed back up the hill. They slowed down quickly and soon were almost standing still. Chad jumped off and got behind the sled. He pushed while the dogs pulled, and up the hill they went.

"Haw," Chad shouted, and the team turned a little to the left where there were large snow-covered rocks. A moment later, the sled was stuck against a rock. Susie wondered why Chad had led the dogs here when he could have easily directed them to the left or right to avoid the rocks. Then Susie figured out that Chad had done it on purpose. He wanted to get stuck so he could see if the team would have problems getting the sled free.

- (After all students have raised their hand:)
- Everybody, what command did Chad use to make the sled turn left? (Signal.) *Haw.* (ND)
- What command did he use to make the sled turn right? (Signal.) *Come gee.* (ND)
- What command did he use to make the team go forward? (Signal.) *Mush.* (ND)
- Look at the picture on the next page. Why did Chad get the sled stuck like that? (Call on a student. Idea: *To give the dogs practice in getting it unstuck.*) (ND)
- What do you think the team will have to do to get the sled free? (Call on individual students. Student preference.) (P)

Paired Practice

You're going to read aloud to your partner. Today the **A** members will read first. Then the **B** members will read from the star to the end of the story. (Observe students and give feedback.)

End-of-Lesson Activities

INDEPENDENT WORK

Now finish the independent work for lesson 92. Raise your hand when you're finished. (Observe students and give feedback.)

WORKCHECK

a. (Direct students to take out their marking pencils.)

• We're going to check your independent work. Remember, if you got an item wrong, make an **X** next to the item.

b. (For each item: Read the item. Call on a student to answer it. If the answer is wrong, say the correct answer. Refer to the Answer Key for the correct answers.)

c. Now use your marking pencil to fix up any items you got wrong. Remember, all mistakes must be fixed up before you hand in your independent work.

SPELLING

(Present Spelling lesson 92 after completing Reading lesson 92. See *Spelling Presentation Book.*)

EXERCISE 1

Vocabulary Review

a. You learned a sentence that starts with the words **I have confidence.**

- Everybody, say that sentence. Get ready. (Signal.) *I have confidence that we can avoid a long conversation.*
- (Repeat until firm.)

b. You learned a sentence that tells about the scuba diver.

- Say that sentence. Get ready. (Signal.) *The scuba diver and her partner surfaced near the reef.*
- (Repeat until firm.)

c. Here's the last sentence you learned: The veterinarian gave the dogs a thorough examination.

- Everybody, say that sentence. Get ready. (Signal.) *The veterinarian gave the dogs a thorough examination.*
- (Repeat until firm.)

d. Everybody, what word means **animal doctor?** (Signal.) *Veterinarian.*

- What word means that nothing is overlooked? (Signal.) *Thorough.*
- What word means **checkup?** (Signal.) *Examination.*

e. Once more. Say the sentence that tells what the veterinarian did. Get ready. (Signal.) *The veterinarian gave the dogs a thorough examination.*

EXERCISE 2

Reading Words

Column 1

a. **Find lesson 93 in your textbook.** ✔

- Touch column 1. ✔
- (Teacher reference:)

1. assistant	4. according
2. certificate	5. endurance
3. health	

b. Word 1 is **assistant.** What word? (Signal.) *Assistant.*

- An assistant is somebody who helps the person who is in charge. A teacher's assistant is a person who helps the teacher. Everybody, what would you call someone who helps a doctor? (Signal.) *Doctor's assistant.*

c. Word 2 is **certificate.** What word? (Signal.) *Certificate.*

- A certificate is a paper that proves something. If you have a birth certificate, it proves where and when you were born. A graduation certificate proves where you graduated and when you graduated.

d. Word 3 is **health.** What word? (Signal.) *Health.*

- Your health refers to how well your body is. If you are in good health, your body is well. You're healthy. What word refers to how well your body is? (Signal.) *Health.*

e. Word 4 is **according.** What word? (Signal.) *According.*

- If you do something that follows the rules, you do things **according to** the rules. If you do something that follows what somebody said, you do that thing according to what somebody said. Everybody, what's another way of saying **She was doing things that follow the rules?** (Signal.) *She was doing things according to the rules.*
- What's another way of saying **I'm doing things that follow their directions?** (Signal.) *I'm doing things according to their directions.*

f. Word 5 is **endurance.** What word? (Signal.) *Endurance.*

- Endurance tells how long you can keep doing something. If you have great endurance, you can do it for a long time. What do you know about someone who can run for a long time? (Call on a student: Idea: *The person has great endurance.*)

g. Let's read those words again, the fast way.

- Word 1. What word? (Signal.) *Assistant.*
- (Repeat for words 2–5.)

h. (Repeat step g until firm.)

Column 2

i. Find column 2. ✔

- (Teacher reference:)

1. nightmare	4. backwards
2. exchange	5. inched
3. stiffened	6. examined

- The first part of each word is underlined.
- j. Word 1. What's the underlined part? (Signal.) *night.*
- What's the whole word? (Signal.) *Nightmare.*
- A nightmare is a bad, bad dream. Everybody, what word means **a bad, bad dream?** (Signal.) *Nightmare.*
- Word 2. What's the underlined part? (Signal.) *ex.*
- What's the whole word? (Signal.) *Exchange.*
- **Exchange** is another word for **trade.** When you trade a shirt for a hat, you exchange a shirt for a hat. Everybody, what's another way of saying **I'll trade this hat for a larger hat?** (Signal.) *I'll exchange this hat for a larger hat.*
- What's another way of saying **He is always trading his presents for other things?** (Signal.) *He is always exchanging his presents for other things.*
- Word 3. What's the underlined part? (Signal.) *stiffen.*
- What's the whole word? (Signal.) *Stiffened.*
- Word 4. What's the underlined part? (Signal.) *back.*
- What's the whole word? (Signal.) *Backwards.*
- Word 5. What's the underlined part? (Signal.) *inch.*
- What's the whole word? (Signal.) *Inched.*
- Word 6. What's the underlined part? (Signal.) *exam.*
- What's the whole word? (Signal.) *Examined.*
- k. Let's read those words again, the fast way.
- Word 1. What word? (Signal.) *Nightmare.*
- (Repeat for words 2–6.)
- l. (Repeat step k until firm.)

Column 3
m. Find column 3. ✔

- (Teacher reference:)

1. injure	4. included
2. pest	5. officials
3. thorough	6. veterinarian

- n. Word 1. What word? (Signal.) *Injure.*
- Spell **injure.** Get ready. (Tap for each letter.) *I-N-J-U-R-E.*
- **Injured** is another word for **hurt.** If your leg is hurt, your leg is injured. Everybody, what's another way of saying **Her arm was hurt?** (Signal.) *Her arm was injured.*
- What's another way of saying **They were hurt in the accident?** (Signal.) *They were injured in the accident.*
- o. Word 2. What word? (Signal.) *Pest.*
- Spell **pest.** Get ready. (Tap for each letter.) *P-E-S-T.*
- p. Word 3. What word? (Signal.) *Thorough.*
- Spell **thorough.** Get ready. (Tap for each letter.) *T-H-O-R-O-U-G-H.*
- q. Word 4. What word? (Signal.) *Included.*
- Spell **included.** Get ready. (Tap for each letter.) *I-N-C-L-U-D-E-D.*
- r. Word 5. What word? (Signal.) *Officials.*
- s. Word 6. What word? (Signal.) *Veterinarian.*
- t. Let's read those words again.
- Word 1. What word? (Signal.) *Injure.*
- (Repeat for words 2–6.)
- u. (Repeat step t until firm.)

Individual Turns
(For columns 1–3: Call on individual students, each to read one to three words per turn.)

EXERCISE 3

Story Reading

- a. Find part B in your textbook. ✔
- The error limit for group reading is 13 errors.
- b. Everybody, touch the title. ✔
- (Call on a student to read the title.) *[A Practice Run.]*
- Everybody, what's the title? (Signal.) *A Practice Run.* ⓃⒹ
- c. (Call on individual students to read the story, each student reading two or three sentences at a time. Ask the specified questions as the students read.)

A Practice Run

The sled was stuck against a rock on the slope. Susie patted Denali's head and said, "Watch carefully so you'll know what to do." Denali stiffened up as he tried to figure out what he was to watch.

Chad said, "Wheel dogs, haw." Denali jumped. At the same time, the pair of dogs just in front of the sled pulled hard to their right. The other dogs backed up a little bit. The pulling turned the sled so that it was now facing almost uphill. It was no longer up against a rock.

Now Chad shouted two more commands. "Haw," he called out and the lead dogs moved left. Then he shouted, "Mush," and all of the dogs pulled the sled uphill, away from the rocks.

After the sled had gone a little ways, Chad shouted, "Whoa," stepped on the brake and got off the sled. He ran up to the left lead dog and patted her on the head. Then he patted the wheel dogs and said, "Good job." He smiled at Susie and said, "Not one pair of dogs got tangled up. That was great."

- Chad used the wheel dogs to turn the sled. Then the rest of the dogs circled around and pulled the sled uphill.

- Look at the picture. What's happening in the picture? (Call on a student. Idea: *The wheel dogs are pulling the sled free.*) VA
- What do you think will happen next? (Call on a student. Idea: *They'll keep practicing.*) P

For the next three hours, Chad did everything he could do to get the sled stuck. One time the sled was going across a steep bank when the sled tipped over and Chad went tumbling down the side of the hill. When he stopped rolling, he sat up, spit out some snow and began to laugh. As Susie watched, she forgot that she was supposed to hold the leashes of the two dogs. When they saw Chad rolling down the hill, they thought Chad was playing, so they raced down the hill. Before Chad could get up, the dogs were all over him, licking his face, growling and pretending to bite his boots and mittens. Some of the dogs on the gang line wanted to join in, but the lead dogs did not move, so the team had to stay where it was.

- Everybody, look at the picture. What's happening in the picture? (Call on a student. Idea: *Butch and Denali are jumping all over Chad.*) (VA)
- What made those dogs think that Chad was playing? (Call on a student. Ideas: *He rolled down the hill because he was laughing.*) (DC)
- Why don't those dogs in the team join in the fun? (Call on a student. Idea: *Because the lead dogs didn't move.*) (ND)

A few minutes later, the sled was upright and the team was again pulling the sled across the slope. It turned down to the river where he again got it stuck between a rock and a tree. This time, Chad could not free the sled, so he unharnessed the team, unloaded the sled and pulled the sled backwards until it was free.

Before hitching the team to the sled again, Chad said, "Let's try a run with sixteen dogs."

Susie felt a big smile form on her face. When Chad ran sixteen dogs, they included Denali and Butch. Both Denali and Butch were wheel dogs.

With sixteen dogs, the sled went a little faster and could get up the hills with a little less trouble. Chad got the sled stuck against a tree on the slope. Chad gave the dogs the order to wheel. The four wheel dogs pulled and strained and snorted, but the sled didn't turn uphill. "Come on, wheel dogs," Chad called. "Let's see you dig in. Haw, haw." This time the

sled inched to the side as the dogs tugged. Then it turned a little more. After four more tugs, the sled was free.

Chad ran the sixteen dogs up, down, and across the slopes of Eagle River Valley. Things went well, except one time, he turned the dogs uphill and some of the dogs got on the wrong side of their partners. They were all tangled up. Finally, the team headed back to the truck. Susie was waiting. She said, "The team looked strong with sixteen dogs." Chad shook his head and made a face. "The team is stronger, all right," he said. "But it's a lot easier for them to get tangled up on the turns."

- What was better about using 16 dogs instead of 14 dogs? (Call on a student. Ideas: *The team was stronger; the sled went faster.*) (ND)
- What was worse about using 16 dogs? (Call on a student. Idea: *It's easier for them to get tangled up.*) (ND)
- Read the rest of the story to yourself and be ready to answer some questions. Raise your hand when you're done.

Just before Chad dropped off Susie and Denali, Susie said, "Are you thinking about running sixteen dogs in the Iditarod?"

"I've thought about it," he said, "but I think a team of fourteen would be a lot easier to handle, and it would be less work."

Susie really wanted Denali to be in the race. She didn't want to be a pest, but it didn't seem fair for Denali not to go.

As Susie walked around the back of the truck to get Denali, Chad called to her. "Remember, tomorrow is examination day."

"I know," she said.

"I'll pick you up at seven in the morning."

That evening, Susie thought about examination day. Before a team can run in the Iditarod, all the dogs must pass a thorough examination. A veterinarian must check them over carefully—their heart, their eyes and ears, their temperature, their legs, their back and their blood. If they don't pass the examination, they don't run in the Iditarod. The officials who run the race set the day for the dogs to be examined. Tomorrow was that day. It would take about twenty minutes for each dog to be examined. Susie figured that examining fourteen dogs would take at least four hours if only one vet examined all the dogs.

- (After all students have raised their hand:)
- Why did Susie keep asking questions about Denali being in the race? (Call on a student. Idea: *Because she really wants him to be in the race.*) ⓓⓒ
- What was going to happen tomorrow? (Call on a student. Idea: *The dogs would be examined by a vet.*) ⓝⓓ
- What happens if a dog does not pass the examination? (Call on a student. Idea: *That dog can't be in the race.*) ⓝⓓ
- How long did Susie figure it would take for one vet to examine all the dogs? (Call on a student. Idea: *At least 4 hours.*) ⓝⓓ
- How could the race officials make it so that the examination would not take that long? (Call on a student. Idea: *Have more than one vet.*) ⓓⓒ
- It would be a problem if a dog didn't pass the examination. Who thinks all of Chad's dogs will pass the examination? (Student preference.) ⓟ
- We'll find out next time.

Paired Practice

You're going to read aloud to your partner. Today the **B** members will read first. Then the **A** members will read from the star to the end of the story. (Observe students and give feedback.)

End-of-Lesson Activities

INDEPENDENT WORK

Now finish the independent work for lesson 93. Raise your hand when you're finished. (Observe students and give feedback.)

WORKCHECK

a. (Direct students to take out their marking pencils.)
- We're going to check your independent work. Remember, if you got an item wrong, make an **X** next to the item.
b. (For each item: Read the item. Call on a student to answer it. If the answer is wrong, say the correct answer. Refer to the Answer Key for the correct answers.)
c. Now use your marking pencil to fix up any items you got wrong. Remember, all mistakes must be fixed up before you hand in your independent work.

SPELLING

(Present Spelling lesson 93 after completing Reading lesson 93. See *Spelling Presentation Book.*)

EXERCISE 1

Vocabulary Review

a. You learned a sentence that tells what the veterinarian did.
- Everybody, say that sentence. Get ready. (Signal.) *The veterinarian gave the dogs a thorough examination.*
- (Repeat until firm.)

b. I'll say part of the sentence. When I stop, you say the next word. Listen: The veterinarian gave the dogs a . . . Everybody, what's the next word? (Signal.) *Thorough.*

c. Listen: The . . . Everybody, what's the next word? (Signal.) *Veterinarian.*
- Say the whole sentence. Get ready. (Signal.) *The veterinarian gave the dogs a thorough examination.*

d. Listen: The veterinarian gave the dogs a thorough . . . Everybody, what's the next word? (Signal.) *Examination.*

EXERCISE 2

Reading Words

Column 1

a. **Find lesson 94 in your textbook.** ✔
- Touch column 1. ✔
- (Teacher reference:)

1. visibility	4. courage
2. fierce	5. challenging
3. miserable	6. dedicated

b. Word 1 is **visibility.** What word? (Signal.) *Visibility.*

c. Word 2 is **fierce.** What word? (Signal.) *Fierce.*

d. Word 3 is **miserable.** What word? (Signal.) *Miserable.*

e. Word 4 is **courage.** What word? (Signal.) *Courage.*
- Another word for **bravery** is **courage.** Everybody, what's another way of saying **He lacked bravery?** (Signal.) *He lacked courage.*
- What's another way of saying **She performed an act of bravery?** (Signal.) *She performed an act of courage.*

f. Word 5 is **challenging.** What word? (Signal.) *Challenging.*
- Another word for **very difficult** is **challenging.** If an event is very difficult, that event is challenging. Everybody, what's another way of saying **The trail was very difficult?** (Signal.) *The trail was challenging.*

g. Word 6 is **dedicated.** What word? (Signal.) *Dedicated.*
- If something is **dedicated** to a person, it is done out of respect to that person. If a race is dedicated to Jimmy, the race is done out of respect to Jimmy. Everybody, what word indicates that something is done out of respect to a person? (Signal.) *Dedicated.*

h. Let's read those words again, the fast way.
- Word 1. What word? (Signal.) *Visibility.*
- (Repeat for words 2–6.)

i. (Repeat step h until firm.)

Column 2

j. Find column 2. ✔
- (Teacher reference:)

1. assistants	4. healthy
2. injured	5. certificates
3. according	

- All these words have an ending.

k. Word 1. What word? (Signal.) *Assistants.*
- (Repeat for words 2–5.)

l. Let's read those words again.
- Word 1. What word? (Signal.) *Assistants.*
- (Repeat for words 2–5.)

m. (Repeat step l until firm.)

Column 3

n. Find column 3. ✔
- (Teacher reference:)

1. alarm	4. nightmare
2. blizzard	5. checkpoint
3. exchange	

o. Word 1. What word? (Signal.) *Alarm.*
- Spell **alarm.** Get ready. (Tap for each letter.) *A-L-A-R-M.*

p. Word 2. What word? (Signal.) *Blizzard.*

- Spell **blizzard.** Get ready. (Tap for each letter.) *B-L-I-Z-Z-A-R-D.*
q. Word 3. What word? (Signal.) *Exchange.*
- Spell **exchange.** Get ready. (Tap for each letter.) *E-X-C-H-A-N-G-E.*
r. Word 4. What word? (Signal.) *Nightmare.*
s. Word 5. What word? (Signal.) *Checkpoint.*
t. Let's read those words again.
- Word 1. What word? (Signal.) *Alarm.*
- (Repeat for: **2. blizzard, 3. exchange, 4. nightmare, 5. checkpoint.**)
u. (Repeat step t until firm.)

Column 4
v. Find column 4. ✔
- (Teacher reference:)

1. hip joint	**4. replace**
2. limp	**5. Chugger**
3. x-ray	

w. Number 1. What words? (Signal.) *Hip joint.*
- The place where the leg joins the hip is the hip joint. Everybody, see if you can find your hip joint. ✔
x. Word 2. What word? (Signal.) *Limp.*
- The opposite of **stiff** is **limp.** Everybody, what's the opposite of a stiff rag? (Signal.) *A limp rag.*
y. Word 3. What word? (Signal.) *X-ray.*
- An x-ray is a photograph that shows someone's bones. Everybody, what's the name of a photograph that shows someone's bones? (Signal.) *X-ray.*
z. Word 4. What word? (Signal.) *Replace.*
a. Word 5. What word? (Signal.) *Chugger.*
b. Let's read those words again.
- Number 1. What words? (Signal.) *Hip joint.*
- Word 2. What word? (Signal.) *Limp.*
- (Repeat for words 3–5.)
c. (Repeat step b until firm.)

Individual Turns
(For columns 1–4: Call on individual students, each to read one to three words.)

EXERCISE 3

Story Reading
a. Find part B in your textbook. ✔
- The error limit for group reading is 9 errors.

b. Everybody, touch the title. ✔
- (Call on a student to read the title.) *[Examination Day.]*
- Everybody, what's the title? (Signal.) *Examination Day.* ⓃⒹ
- What's going to happen in this part of the story? (Call on a student. Idea: *Chad's team will be examined by a vet.*) Ⓟ
- What was the main thing that Chad and Susie did in the last part of the story? (Call on a student. Idea: *They did a practice run.*) ⒶⓅⓀ
c. (Call on individual students to read the story, each student reading two or three sentences at a time. Ask the specified questions as the students read.)

- (**Correct errors:** Tell the word. Direct the student to reread the sentence.)
- (If the group makes more than 9 errors, direct the students to reread the story.)

Examination Day

Susie didn't like getting up early, so she set her alarm clock for 6:40. That gave her only twenty minutes before Chad would pick her up. She dressed quickly, ran downstairs and started gulping down her breakfast. Her mother said, "You're eating faster than Denali. Slow down."

"Mmkay," she said.

- What time did Susie get up? (Call on a student. Idea: *Twenty to seven.*) ⓃⒹ
- Everybody, how much time did that leave her to get dressed and eat breakfast? (Signal.) *20 minutes.* ⓃⒹ
- At what time would Chad come over? (Signal.) *7 o'clock.* ⒹⒸ
- Her mother said that she was eating faster than Denali. When dogs eat, do they usually spend much time chewing their food? (Signal.) *No.* ⒶⓅⓀ
- They just get a mouthful and swallow it.

The weather reporter on the radio was saying, "Looks as if the Iditarod will be run in winter weather this year. A large mass of cold, cold air is moving in from the north." The report gave Susie a nervous feeling. Bad weather can make the Iditarod a nightmare for the mushers and the dogs.

Five minutes later Susie was standing outside, dressed in her parka. It was seven o'clock. The wind was sharp and ugly, and Chad was late. When Chad's truck finally pulled up at 7:10, Susie noticed something very strange.

- Everybody, what time was Chad supposed to be there? (Signal.) *7 o'clock.* (APK)
- How many minutes late was he? (Signal.) *Ten.* (ND)

Butch was in the back of the truck. He wasn't one of Chad's regular wheel dogs, so why would he be going for an examination?

"Hey, Uncle Chad," she said. "Why is Butch in the truck?"

Chad replied, "For the same reason that Denali's going to be in the truck."

"What's that reason?"

"I decided to run sixteen dogs."

"Sixteen?"

Susie understood what Chad said as soon as he spoke the words. But it took her a few seconds to realize what she was about to shout. "Denali's going to run in the Iditarod!"

She jumped up and down three times before she ran over to Denali's kennel. She opened the gate and told Denali to get on the truck. Then she opened the truck door, leaned over, and gave Chad a great hug. "Yes, yes!" she shouted.

He said, "You're yelling in my ear."

- Everybody, when Chad talked about the race on the day before, how many dogs did he intend to run? (Signal.) *14.* (APK)
- How many dogs did he intend to run today? (Signal.) *16.* (ND)
- What are the names of the two dogs that will be added to the team? (Call on a student.) *Butch, Denali.* (ND)

She hugged Chad a few more times, and then her thoughts suddenly changed. She wondered if Denali was really ready for the race. What if he got injured? What if the weather got so bad that the sled got lost? What if . . .

✿ Susie didn't ask Chad these questions. But she had a lot of others, and she asked them—one after another as the truck drove to the examination station. She was still asking questions as she and Chad waited at the station while the dogs were being examined. A veterinarian ✦ and three assistants were checking Chad's team. The inside of the station was pretty cold because the dogs were more comfortable in cold than they were in heated places. At last Susie asked Chad her last question. "Why did you decide to run with sixteen dogs?"

"Well," Chad said. "It was a tough decision. A team of sixteen dogs is a headache even if they work well together. But I figured that I would be better ✿ off with more dogs. In case something happens, we'll still probably have enough dogs to finish the race."

- Read the rest of the story to yourself and be ready to answer some questions. Raise your hand when you're done.

Susie knew what Chad was referring to. According to the rules of the Iditarod, a musher cannot exchange dogs. If a dog gets injured, the musher must carry it in the sled to the next checkpoint on the trail and leave the dog there. The musher can't replace it with another dog. If too many dogs are injured, the musher can't continue in the race. The rules state that a musher must have at least five dogs on the gang line at the end of the race.

Chad said, "If the team of sixteen is too much trouble to handle, I'll just leave some of them at a checkpoint and go on with either fourteen or maybe twelve dogs. We'll just have to see how well the team of sixteen does on the trail."

The veterinarian and one of her assistants approached Chad and Susie. The assistant was carrying a pile of certificates. The veterinarian handed them to Chad and said, "Fifteen of your dogs check out fine. But the dog named Chugger may have a hip problem. I can't be sure. She doesn't limp, and the x-rays don't show any serious problem, but I'm not sure her hip joint is healthy." She shook her head. Then she added, "But I won't keep her out of the race if you want to keep her on your team."

Now Chad shook his head. Chugger was one of his wheel dogs. She was strong and smart. She was almost nine years old, but she had never had any serious health problems.

The vet said, "I'm telling you about this because I want you to understand that she may have a problem. I'm not sure I would take her if she were my dog."

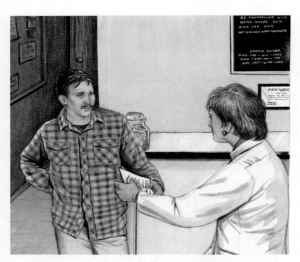

- (After all students have raised their hand:)

- Why did Chad think he would be better off with 16 dogs instead of 14 dogs? (Call on a student. Idea: *If something happens to some dogs, he'll still have enough dogs to finish the race.*) ND
- How many dogs can a musher exchange during the race? (Call on a student. Idea: *None.*) ND
- What happens to an injured dog? (Call on a student. Idea: *The musher takes it to the next checkpoint and leaves it there.*) ND
- Everybody, according to the rules, a musher must have at least how many dogs on the gang line at the end of the race? (Signal.) *Five.* ND
- What did Chad plan to do if the team of 16 turned out to be too much trouble? (Call on a student. Idea: *Leave some dogs at a checkpoint.*) ND
- Everybody, how many dogs had a problem at the examination? (Signal.) *One.* ND
- What's the name of that dog? (Signal.) *Chugger.* ND
- What kind of problem did the vet think she might have? (Call on a student. Idea: *A problem with a hip.*) ND
- What was Chugger's job on Chad's team? (Call on a student. Idea: *She's a wheel dog.*) ND
- Everybody, was the vet going to keep Chugger out of the race? (Signal.) *No.* ND
- But she warned Chad that Chugger may have a problem. What do you think Chad is going to do about Chugger? (Call on individual students. Student preference.) MJ
- We'll find out next time.
- Everybody, look at the picture. What are those papers that the vet is handing to Chad? (Call on a student. Idea: *Certificates.*) VA
- Do you think this picture took place **before** she told him about Chugger or **after** she told him? (Call on a student. Idea: *After.*) MJ
- What clues in the picture make you think it happened after she told him? (Call on a student. Idea: *Chad looks worried.*) VA

Paired Practice

You're going to read aloud to your partner. Today the **A** members will read first. Then the **B** members will read from the star to the end of the story. (Observe students and give feedback.)

End-of-Lesson Activities

INDEPENDENT WORK

Now finish the independent work for lesson 94. Raise your hand when you're finished. (Observe students and give feedback.)

WORKCHECK

a. (Direct students to take out their marking pencils.)

• We're going to check your independent work. Remember, if you got an item wrong, make an **X** next to the item.

b. (For each item: Read the item. Call on a student to answer it. If the answer is wrong, say the correct answer. Refer to the Answer Key for the correct answers.)

c. Now use your marking pencil to fix up any items you got wrong. Remember, all mistakes must be fixed up before you hand in your independent work.

SPELLING

(Present Spelling lesson 94 after completing Reading lesson 94. See *Spelling Presentation Book.*)

ACTIVITIES

(Present Activity 21 after completing Reading lesson 94-97. See *Activities across the Curriculum.*)

LESSON 95

Vocabulary

a. **Find page 367 in your textbook.** ✔
  - Touch sentence 24. ✔
  - This is a new vocabulary sentence. It says: Visibility was miserable in the fierce blizzard. Everybody, read that sentence. Get ready. (Signal.) *Visibility was miserable in the fierce blizzard.*
  - Close your eyes and say the sentence. Get ready. (Signal.) *Visibility was miserable in the fierce blizzard.*
  - (Repeat until firm.)
b. Visibility is how well you can see things. If the visibility is good, you can see well. If the visibility is poor, you can't see well.
  - Everybody, what's the visibility like if you can see well? (Signal.) *Good.*
c. Something that is **very wild** is **fierce.** Everybody, what do we call **a very wild animal?** (Signal.) *A fierce animal.*
  - What do we call **a very wild ocean?** (Signal.) *A fierce ocean.*
  - What do we call **a very wild storm?** (Signal.) *A fierce storm.*
d. **Miserable** is another word for **terrible.** Everybody, what's another way of saying **a terrible vacation?** (Signal.) *A miserable vacation.*
  - What's another way of saying **She felt terrible?** (Signal.) *She felt miserable.*
e. A blizzard is a snowstorm that is windy and very cold. Everybody, what do we call a snowstorm that is windy and very cold? (Signal.) *Blizzard.*
f. Listen to the sentence again: Visibility was miserable in the fierce blizzard. Everybody, say the sentence. Get ready. (Signal.) *Visibility was miserable in the fierce blizzard.*
g. Everybody, what's another word for **terrible?** (Signal.) *Miserable.*
  - What word means **very wild?** (Signal.) *Fierce.*
  - What word refers to how well you can see things? (Signal.) *Visibility.*
  - What word names a snowstorm that is windy and very cold? (Signal.) *Blizzard.*
  - (Repeat step g until firm.)

Reading Words

Column 1

a. Find lesson 95 in your textbook. ✔
  - Touch column 1. ✔
  - (Teacher reference:)

1. volunteer	4. photo
2. blizzard	5. Sweden
3. weary	

b. Word 1 is **volunteer.** What word? (Signal.) *Volunteer.*
  - A volunteer is a person who does a job without pay. A fireman who works without pay is a volunteer fireman. Everybody, what do we call an assistant who works without pay? (Signal.) *A volunteer assistant.*
c. Word 2. What word? (Signal.) *Blizzard.*
  - Spell **blizzard.** Get ready. (Tap for each letter.) *B-L-I-Z-Z-A-R-D.*
d. Word 3. What word? (Signal.) *Weary.*
  - Spell **weary.** Get ready. (Tap for each letter.) *W-E-A-R-Y.*
  - Another word for **very tired** is **weary.** Everybody, what's another way of saying **She was very tired after chopping wood?** (Signal.) *She was weary after chopping wood.*
  - What's another way of saying **That work made them very tired?** (Signal.) *That work made them weary.*
e. Word 4. What word? (Signal.) *Photo.*
  - Spell **photo.** Get ready. (Tap for each letter.) *P-H-O-T-O.*
f. Word 5. What word? (Signal.) *Sweden.*
  - Spell **Sweden.** Get ready. (Tap for each letter.) *S-W-E-D-E-N.*
  - Sweden is a country that's part of the land the Vikings once ruled. Everybody, what's a country that's part of the land the Vikings once ruled? (Signal.) *Sweden.*
g. Let's read those words again, the fast way.
  - Word 1. What word? (Signal.) *Volunteer.*
  - (Repeat for words 2–5.)
h. (Repeat step g until firm.)

Column 2

i. Find column 2. ✔
- (Teacher reference:)

1. competed	3. mushed
2. amused	4. dedicated

- All these words end with the letters **E-D**. But be careful, because **E-D** makes different sounds in the words.

j. Word 1. What word? (Signal.) *Competed.*
- Things that compete with each other are in a contest with each other. If plants compete for more sunlight, they are in a contest to see which plant gets the most sunlight. If two men are competing in a race, they are in a contest to see who will win the race.

k. Word 2. What word? (Signal.) *Amused.*
- When something amuses a person, it makes the person laugh. Here's another way of saying **The clown made the crowd laugh: The clown amused the crowd.**
- Everybody, what's another way of saying **The dog made me laugh?** (Signal.) *The dog amused me.*

l. Word 3. What word? (Signal.) *Mushed.*
m. Word 4. What word? (Signal.) *Dedicated.*
n. Let's read those words again.
- Word 1. What word? (Signal.) *Competed.*
- (Repeat for words 2–4.)
o. (Repeat step n until firm.)

Column 3

p. Find column 3. ✔
- (Teacher reference:)

1. Mr. Martin	4. courage
2. feat	5. unties
3. events	

q. Number 1. What name? (Signal.) *Mr. Martin.*
r. Word 2. What word? (Signal.) *Feat.*
- Amazing things that people do are **feats**. Walking a tightrope is a difficult feat.
s. Word 3. What word? (Signal.) *Events.*
- (Repeat for words 4 and 5.)

t. Let's read those words again.
- Number 1. What name? (Signal.) *Mr. Martin.*
- Word 2. What word? (Signal.) *Feat.*
- (Repeat for words 3–5.)
u. (Repeat step t until firm.)

Column 4

v. Find column 4. ✔
- (Teacher reference:)

1. endurance	3. Hoover
2. challenging	4. demanding

w. Word 1. What word? (Signal.) *Endurance.*
- (Repeat for words 2–4.)
x. Let's read those words again.
- Word 1. What word? (Signal.) *Endurance.*
- (Repeat for words 2–4.)
y. (Repeat step x until firm.)

Individual Turns

(For columns 1–4: Call on individual students, each to read one to three words per turn.)

EXERCISE 3

Story Background

a. Find part B in your textbook. ✔
- You're going to read the next story about the Iditarod. First you'll read the information passage. It gives some facts about the race.
b. Everybody, touch the title. ✔
- (Call on a student to read the title.) *[Supplies for the Race.]*
- Everybody, what's the title? (Signal.) *Supplies for the Race.* ⓃⒹ
c. (Call on individual students to read the passage, each student reading two or three sentences at a time. Ask the specified questions as the students read.)

Supplies for the Race

The rules of the Iditarod require each musher to bring along supplies that are needed for the musher and the dogs to survive under severe conditions. The rules require the musher to have an ax, a good sleeping bag, snowshoes and enough food for one day.

- Listen to that part again.
  The rules require the musher to have an ax, a good sleeping bag, snowshoes and enough food for one day.
- Who can name all the things a musher needs? (Call on a student. Idea: *Snowshoes, enough food for one day, an ax, a good sleeping bag.*) (RF/R)

The sled must have at least two pounds of food for each dog and one day's worth of food for the musher. The rules also require the sled to have enough room to carry at least one injured dog.

- How much food does each dog need every day? (Call on a student. Idea: *At least 2 pounds.*) (RF/R)
- The sled must also have room for something else. What's that? (Call on a student. Idea: *An injured dog.*) (RF/R)

EXERCISE 4

Story Reading

a. Find part C in your textbook. ✔
- The error limit for group reading is 11 errors.
b. Everybody, touch the title. ✔
- (Call on a student to read the title.) [*The Big Race.*]
- Everybody, what's the title? (Signal.) *The Big Race.* (ND)
c. (Call on individual students to read the story, each student reading two or three sentences at a time. Ask the specified questions as the students read.)

- (**Correct errors:** Tell the word. Direct the student to reread the sentence.)
- (If the group makes more than 11 errors, direct the students to reread the story.)

The Big Race

- What important thing did the vet tell Chad and Susie last time? (Call on a student. Idea: *That one dog may have a problem with her hip.*) (APK)

Chad didn't talk much in the truck as he drove back to Susie's place. Susie could see that he was thinking

about what to do with Chugger. She didn't say anything. She knew that Chad had to make his own decision because he would be the one who would have to live with it. The only dogs that are more important than the wheel dogs are the lead dogs. Susie knew that Chad did not want to replace either of his regular wheel dogs because they worked well together. As Chad drove, he said, "She hasn't had any problems on the practice runs." A few minutes later he said, "Neither of her parents had hip problems." When the truck was about a mile from Susie's place, he said, "I'll make a decision tomorrow."

When he dropped Susie off, he said, "I've made up my mind about Chugger. I'm going to keep her on the team. I think she'll be fine."

- Everybody, did Chad think Chugger would have any problems in the race? (Signal.) *No.* (ND)
- He gave a couple of reasons why he didn't think she'd have problems. What are those reasons? (Call on a student. Idea: *She hadn't had any problems on the practice runs and neither of her parents had hip problems.*) (ND)

Later that evening, Susie thought about the adventure that Chad was going to have. As she thought about the Iditarod, she looked at a photo on the wall that showed a smiling woman surrounded by sled dogs. The woman was Susan Butcher. She had entered the Iditarod seventeen times, and she actually finished it sixteen times.

- Everybody, what's the name of the woman in the picture? (Signal.) *Susan Butcher.* (ND)
- How many times had she entered the Iditarod? (Signal.) *17.* (ND)
- How many times had she finished? (Signal.) *16.* (ND)
- That's amazing.

Not only did she finish the race, but one time, she came in third place. Four times she came in second place. This was an amazing feat for a woman who competed against the greatest mushers in the world in an event that required courage, strength and incredible endurance. Even more amazing than her four second-place finishes was her first-place finish in 1986. And she also finished first in 1987, 1988 and 1990.

Susie wondered how she had done it—four first-place finishes in what has to be one of the most challenging events a person could enter.

- Everybody, how many times had she finished in third place? (Signal.) *One.* ⓃⒹ
- How many times had she finished in second place? (Signal.) *4.* ⓃⒹ
- How many times did she come in first? (Signal.) *4.* ⓃⒹ

• • •

More than 75 teams were ready to start the Iditarod. The weather was miserable. The temperature was near freezing and a thick wet snow was falling. The dogs were panting. They knew that they were going to start something that was very demanding.

The race had started at 10 A.M., but it hadn't started for all the mushers. One musher started at a time. In fact, the first musher who was called ⭐ to the starting line had died earlier that year. After calling his name, the announcer explained to the crowd that the race was dedicated to him. Two minutes later the first musher left. Everybody cheered. Some of the dogs barked and howled. Others just looked around panting. Two minutes after that musher had left, another musher started.

- What was the temperature at the time the race began? (Call on a student. Ideas: *About 32 degrees; near freezing.*) ⓃⒹ
- How many mushers left at the same time? (Signal.) *One.* ⓃⒹ

- How much time passed before the next musher started? (Signal.) *Two minutes.* ⓃⒹ
- So if a musher was the twentieth one in line, how long would it be before that musher would start the race? (Call on a student. Idea: *Forty minutes.*) ⒹⒸ

Musher number 16 amused the crowd, but he didn't do it on purpose. He had tied the back of his sled to a pickup truck. When the announcer called his number, he mushed, the team pulled hard, and as they crossed the start line, the dogs were pulling the pickup truck along behind them. The announcer said, "Now there's a team with some real power. Think of how well they're going to do when Mr. Martin unties them from his truck." Everybody laughed.

- Read the rest of the story to yourself and be ready to answer some questions. Raise your hand when you're done.

It was now after 11 A.M., but Chad hadn't started yet. He was the 61st musher in the race. Just ahead of him was a musher from Sweden. Behind Chad was a musher from Michigan. That musher had run the Iditarod six times.

Chad and Susie were busy getting ready. They were putting booties on the dogs' feet. Chad brought along more than a thousand booties. He figured that he would change booties about every two days and more often if the snow was hard and frozen.

"Number 59," the announcer called from the start line. "Terry North from Colorado. It's your turn, Terry. Good luck." Terry tipped his hat and shouted, "Mush," so loudly that some of the dogs that were not in his team tried to run. One of them was Hoover, a dog in Chad's team.

Chad said, "Take it easy, Hoover. It won't be long now."

Chad and Susie checked the supplies one last time. They had already done it three times earlier, and if something was missing now, there wasn't much they could do about it because of the most important rule of the Iditarod. Once the race starts, all mushers are on their own. They can't try to get help from anybody who is not in the race. They can't use a phone, a radio, or any other device that would allow others to help them. When they are on the trail, they must do the best they can without help from anybody.

- (After all students have raised their hand:) Everybody, what number was Chad? (Signal.) *61.* (ND)
- From which country was the musher who was in front of Chad? (Signal.) *Sweden.* (ND)
- When the mushers are on the trail, what can't they do? (Call on a student. Ideas: *Ask for help; use a phone; use a radio.*) (ND)

EXERCISE 5

Fluency: Rate/Accuracy

Note: There is a fluency checkout in this lesson; therefore, there is no paired practice.

a. Today is a reading checkout day. While you're doing your independent work, I'm going to call on you one at a time to read part of the story from lesson 94.
- Remember, you pass the checkout by reading the passage in less than a minute without making more than 2 mistakes. And when you pass the checkout, you'll color the space for lesson 95 on your thermometer chart.
b. (Call on individual students to read the portion of the story 94 marked with ✿.)
- (Time the student. Note words that are missed and total number of words read.)
- (Teacher reference:)

✿ Susie didn't ask Chad these questions. But she had a lot of others, and she asked them—one after another as the truck drove to the examination station. She was still asking questions as she and Chad waited at the station while the dogs were being examined. A veterinarian [50] and three assistants were checking Chad's team. The inside of

the station was pretty cold because the dogs were more comfortable in cold than they [75] were in heated places. At last Susie asked Chad her last question. "Why did you decide to run with sixteen dogs?"
"Well," Chad said. "It was [100] a tough decision. A team of sixteen dogs is a headache even if they work well together. But I figured that I would be better ✿ [125] off with more dogs.

- (If the student reads the passage in one minute or less and makes no more than 2 errors, direct the student to color in the space for lesson 95 on the thermometer chart.)

- (If the student makes any mistakes, point to each word that was misread and identify it.)
- (If the student does not meet the rate-error criterion for the passage, direct the student to practice reading the story with the assigned partner.)

End-of-Lesson Activities

INDEPENDENT WORK

Now finish the independent work for lesson 95. Raise your hand when you're finished. (Observe students and give feedback.)

WORKCHECK

a. (Direct students to take out their marking pencils.)
- We're going to check your independent work. Remember, if you got an item wrong, make an **X** next to the item.
b. (For each item: Read the item. Call on a student to answer it. If the answer is wrong, say the correct answer. Refer to the Answer Key for the correct answers.)
c. Now use your marking pencil to fix up any items you got wrong. Remember, all mistakes must be fixed up before you hand in your independent work.

SPELLING

(Present Spelling lesson 95 after completing Reading lesson 95. See *Spelling Presentation Book.*)

	Lesson 96	**Lesson 97**	**Lesson 98**	**Lesson 99**	**Lesson 100**
LESSON EVENTS	Vocabulary Sentence Reading Words Story Background Story Reading Paired Practice Independent Work Workcheck Spelling	Vocabulary Sentences Reading Words Story Reading Paired Practice Independent Work Workcheck Spelling	Vocabulary Sentence Reading Words Story Background Story Reading Paired Practice Independent Work Workcheck Spelling	Reading Words Story Reading Paired Practice Independent Work Workcheck Spelling	Fact Game Fluency: Rate/ Accuracy Test Marking the Test Test Remedies Spelling
VOCABULARY SENTENCE	#24: <u>Visibility</u> was <u>miserable</u> in the <u>fierce</u> <u>blizzard</u>.	sentence #22 sentence #23 sentence #24	#24: <u>Visibility</u> was <u>miserable</u> in the <u>fierce</u> <u>blizzard</u>.		

READING WORDS: WORD TYPES	modeled words
	words with an
	  ending
	mixed words
		compound words
		mixed words
			modeled words
			words with an
			  ending
				modeled words
				multi-syllable words	

NEW VOCABULARY	recently gust scent cruel tempted trudged	compass peered beware plunge	arrangements congratulate sheltered tarps	curious victory demand award insist hero aimlessly lantern	
STORY BACKGROUND	*Checkpoints*		*Rest Periods*		
STORY	*On the Trail*	*Lost*	*Beware of Streams*	*End of the Race*	

SKILL ITEMS		Vocabulary
		  sentence
		Crossword puzzle
			Vocabulary
			  sentences
				Vocabulary	Test: Vocabulary
					  sentences

SPECIAL MATERIALS					Thermometer charts,
					  dice, Fact Game
					  100, Fact Game
					  Answer Key,
					  scorecard sheets,
					  *materials for
					  project

SPECIAL PROJECTS/ ACTIVITIES					Project after lesson 100

*Iditarod website, magazines, newspapers, books on Iditarod.

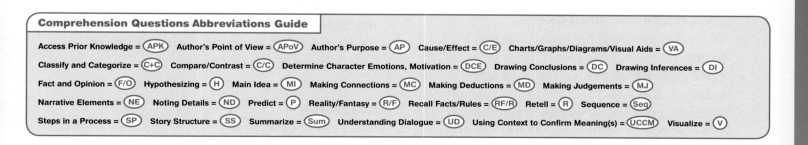

Comprehension Questions Abbreviations Guide

Access Prior Knowledge = APK   Author's Point of View = APoV   Author's Purpose = AP   Cause/Effect = C/E   Charts/Graphs/Diagrams/Visual Aids = VA

Classify and Categorize = C+C   Compare/Contrast = C/C   Determine Character Emotions, Motivation = DCE   Drawing Conclusions = DC   Drawing Inferences = DI

Fact and Opinion = F/O   Hypothesizing = H   Main Idea = MI   Making Connections = MC   Making Deductions = MD   Making Judgements = MJ

Narrative Elements = NE   Noting Details = ND   Predict = P   Reality/Fantasy = R/F   Recall Facts/Rules = RF/R   Retell = R   Sequence = Seq

Steps in a Process = SP   Story Structure = SS   Summarize = Sum   Understanding Dialogue = UD   Using Context to Confirm Meaning(s) = UCCM   Visualize = V

EXERCISE 1

Vocabulary Review

a. Here's the new vocabulary sentence: Visibility was miserable in the fierce blizzard.

- Everybody, say the sentence. Get ready. (Signal.) *Visibility was miserable in the fierce blizzard.*
- (Repeat until firm.)

b. Everybody, what word names a snowstorm that is windy and very cold? (Signal.) *Blizzard.*

- What word refers to how well you can see things? (Signal.) *Visibility.*
- What word means **very wild?** (Signal.) *Fierce.*
- What's another word for **terrible?** (Signal.) *Miserable.*

EXERCISE 2

Reading Words

Column 1

a. **Find lesson 96 in your textbook.** ✔

- Touch column 1. ✔
- (Teacher reference:)

1. recently	4. tempted
2. scent	5. checkpoint
3. cruel	6. handlebar

b. Word 1 is **recently.** What word? (Signal.) *Recently.*

- Spell **recently**. Get ready. (Tap for each letter.) R-E-C-E-N-T-L-Y.
- If something happened not long ago, that thing happened **recently.** Everybody, what's another way of saying **The circus was in town not long ago?** (Signal.) *The circus was in town recently.*

c. Word 2 is **scent.** What word? (Signal.) *Scent.*

- Spell **scent**. Get ready. (Tap for each letter.) S-C-E-N-T.
- Another word for the **smell** of something is the **scent** of something. The smell of a rose is the scent of the rose. Everybody, what's the smell of a deer? (Signal.) *The scent of a deer.*

d. Word 3. What word? (Signal.) *Cruel.*

- Spell **cruel.** Get ready. (Tap for each letter.) C-R-U-E-L.
- Cruel is another word for **very mean.** A very mean act is a cruel act. Everybody, what word means **very mean?** (Signal.) *Cruel.*

e. Word 4. What word? (Signal.) *Tempted.*

- Spell **tempted.** Get ready. (Tap for each letter.) T-E-M-P-T-E-D.
- If you are **tempted** to do something, part of you wants to do it but another part doesn't. If a person is tempted to eat more ice cream, how does the person feel? (Call on a student. Idea: *Part of the person wants to do it and another part doesn't.*)

f. Word 5. What word? (Signal.) *Checkpoint.*

g. Word 6. What word? (Signal.) *Handlebar.*

h. Let's read those words again, the fast way.

- Word 1. What word? (Signal.) *Recently.*
- (Repeat for words 2–6.)

i. (Repeat step h until firm.)

Column 2

j. Find column 2. ✔

- (Teacher reference:)

1. trudged	3. stinging
2. rainy	4. volunteers

- All these words have an ending.

k. Word 1. What word? (Signal.) *Trudged.*

- When you trudge, you walk along slowly. Everybody, what word means **to walk along slowly?** (Signal.) *Trudge.*

l. Word 2. What word? (Signal.) *Rainy.*

- (Repeat for words 3 and 4.)

m. Let's read those words again.

- Word 1. What word? (Signal.) *Trudged.*
- (Repeat for words 2–4.)

n. (Repeat step m until firm.)

Column 3

o. Find column 3. ✔

- (Teacher reference:)

1. **Ms. Siri Carlson**	4. **evergreen**
2. **Libby Riddles**	5. **struck**
3. **Bowman**	

p. Number 1. What name? (Signal.) *Ms. Siri Carlson.*

q. Number 2. What name? (Signal.) *Libby Riddles.*

r. Word 3. What word? (Signal.) *Bowman.*
- (Repeat for words 4 and 5.)

s. Let's read those words again.
- Number 1. What name? (Signal.) *Ms. Siri Carlson.*
- Number 2. What name? (Signal.) *Libby Riddles.*
- Word 3. What word? (Signal.) *Bowman.*
- (Repeat for words 4 and 5.)

t. (Repeat step s until firm.)

Column 4

u. Find column 4. ✔
- (Teacher reference:)

1. **gust**	4. **blizzard**
2. **weary**	5. **birthday**
3. **sleeve**	6. **snowmobile**

v. Word 1. What word? (Signal.) *Gust.*
- A gust of wind is a strong wind that starts suddenly and doesn't last long.

w. Word 2. What word? (Signal.) *Weary.*
- (Repeat for words 3–6.)

x. Let's read those words again.
- Word 1. What word? (Signal.) *Gust.*
- (Repeat for words 2–6.)

y. (Repeat step x until firm.)

Individual Turns

(For columns 1–4: Call on individual students, each to read one to three words per turn.)

<hr>

EXERCISE 3

Story Background

a. Find part B in your textbook. ✔
- You're going to read the next story about the Iditarod. First you'll read the information passage. It gives some facts about checkpoints.

b. Everybody, touch the title. ✔
- (Call on a student to read the title.) [*Checkpoints.*]

- Everybody, what's the title? (Signal.) *Checkpoints.* ⓃⒹ

c. (Call on individual students to read the passage, each student reading two or three sentences at a time. Ask the specified questions as the students read.)

Checkpoints

Checkpoints are places along the Iditarod trail where mushers can rest their teams, make repairs, and feed their dogs. The places are called checkpoints because race officials check to make sure that all the mushers pass through each checkpoint. If mushers don't get to a checkpoint, the officials send out planes or snowmobiles to find them.

- Why are checkpoints called checkpoints? (Call on a student. Idea: *Because officials check that all the mushers go through each checkpoint.*) ⓇⒻ/Ⓡ
- What are some of the things that mushers do at checkpoints? (Call on a student. Ideas: *Repair sleds; repair equipment; feed and water dogs; let dogs rest.*) ⓇⒻ/Ⓡ

Checkpoints are about 50 miles apart, so there are usually 24 checkpoints from the beginning of the Iditarod trail to Nome. A lot of things happen at these checkpoints. A musher can drop off an injured or sick dog at a checkpoint. Airplanes deliver food for dogs and mushers to most of the checkpoints. Some of the checkpoints have veterinarians and assistants who check the dogs.

- How does food get to the checkpoints? (Call on a student. Idea: *By plane.*) ⓇⒻ/Ⓡ
- A musher usually carries only enough food for about one day. But there's food at some of the checkpoints.
- How far apart are the checkpoints? (Call on a student. Idea: *About 50 miles.*) ⓇⒻ/Ⓡ
- About how many checkpoints are there from Anchorage to Nome? (Call on a student. Idea: *Usually 24.*) ⓇⒻ/Ⓡ

Story Reading

a. Find part C in your textbook. ✔

- The error limit for group reading is 13 errors.

b. Everybody, touch the title. ✔

- (Call on a student to read the title.) *[On the Trail.]*
- Everybody, what's the title? (Signal.) *On the Trail.* ⓃⒹ

c. (Call on individual students to read the story, each student reading two or three sentences at a time. Ask the specified questions as the students read.)

- (**Correct errors:** Tell the word. Direct the student to reread the sentence.)
- (If the group makes more than 13 errors, direct the students to reread the story.)

On the Trail

"Number 60," the announcer called. "From Sweden, in her third Iditarod, Siri Carlson." Susie had talked with Ms. Carlson before the race. "Good luck," Susie called and Ms. Carlson waved to her.

The moment she left, Susie's heart started to pound. This was it. In two minutes, Chad would be off and on his own. He would be challenging cruel weather and fierce winds. And Denali would be out there with him. For a moment, Susie was tempted to grab Chad's sleeve and say, "Don't do it, Chad. It's too dangerous." But instead, she smiled.

- How did Susie feel? (Call on a student. Ideas: *Nervous, afraid, excited, worried.*) ⒹⒸⒺ
- Why didn't she let Chad know how she felt? (Call on a student. Idea: *She didn't want him to worry about her.*) ⒹⒾ
- Do you think Susie was worried about something happening to Denali? (Call on a student. Idea: *Yes.*) ⒹⒸ
- What was the name of the woman who left just before Chad? (Call on a student.) *Siri Carlson.* ⓃⒹ

Chad looked at Susie, smiled nervously and shook his head. "I'm nervous now," he said. "I always feel that way before a race starts."

A few moments later the announcer said, "Number 61, from the town of Knik, which is just outside the great city of Anchorage, in the great state of Alaska, Chad Bowman. Last time he tried, he didn't have very good luck. This time, I hope his luck will be better. See you in Nome, Chad."

Chad waved, and his sled went down the well-used trail. Then Susie watched it get smaller and smaller as the snow continued to fall. Then Susie could hardly see it.

Then . . .

• • •

- The last sentence is not finished. What should it say? (Call on a student. Idea: *Then it was gone.*) ⒹⒸ
- How do you think Susie felt after the sled disappeared? (Call on a student. Ideas: *Worried, nervous, afraid.*) ⒹⒸⒺ

Hundreds of volunteer workers are needed to make the Iditarod successful. These volunteers do everything from helping injured dogs to flying planes that deliver food to checkpoints. Mushers carry only enough food for about one day on the trail. They get the rest of the food they need at the checkpoints.

Mushers have to do a lot of things and they must do them without help from anybody at the checkpoint. The first thing mushers do at a checkpoint is feed their dogs, then they set up a place for the dogs to rest.

- What are the first two things that mushers do at a checkpoint? (Call on a student. Ideas: *Feed their dogs and make beds for them.*) ⓃⒹ
- Do you think they do it that way even if they are hungry themselves? (Call on a student. Idea: *Yes.*) ⒹⒸ

- Yes, those dogs work very hard and they need food if they are to keep from getting weak.

Mushers often cut branches from evergreen trees and make beds for their dogs. They must also get water for the dogs. They either heat snow to melt it or haul water from a stream.

- How do mushers get water? (Call on a student. Idea: *By melting snow or hauling water from a stream.*) (ND)
- What do mushers use to make beds for their dogs? (Call on a student. Idea: *Evergreen branches.*) (ND)

They check the dogs' paws, booties and harnesses. Then the mushers take a little time to eat, and maybe they'll even take a nap before continuing. After they leave the checkpoint, they usually don't see anything but the trail, the snow and their dogs until they reach the next checkpoint. Sometimes they will catch up to another sled. That sled moves over and lets them pass.

• • •

It was now the third day of the race and Chad's team was in the mountains. On the day before the race had started, the weather reports warned about a great storm moving from the north. That storm had arrived. Chad was trying to make his way through ★ very rough country. He wasn't riding on the back of the sled. He was walking behind the sled as he held the handlebar, but he wasn't walking very fast. The wind blasted the snow with stinging force and the temperature was around 10 degrees below zero. The snow was hard and icy. The dogs were weary, and so was Chad. He could not see past the wheel dogs.

- Everybody, how many days into the race was it now? (Signal.) *3.* (ND)
- What kind of country was Chad in? (Call on a student. Ideas: *The mountains; rough country.*) (ND)
- How cold was it? (Call on a student. Idea: *About 10 degrees below zero.*) (ND)
- What was the wind like? (Call on a student. Ideas: *Blasting; blowing very hard.*) (ND)
- How far could Chad see? (Call on a student. Ideas: *Not very far; not past the wheel dogs.*) (ND)
- Why couldn't he see further? (Call on a student. Idea: *Because it was snowing so hard.*) (ND)
- Everybody, look at the picture on the next page. Would you recognize that person as Chad? (Signal.) *No.* (VA)
- He looks very cold and uncomfortable.

As a stinging gust of wind struck him, he shook his head and laughed to himself. He shouted above the wind, "Why do they call this place Rainy Pass? It's always frozen and cold."

- Everybody, what was the name of the pass? (Signal.) *Rainy Pass.* (ND)
- Why did that name seem strangely funny to Chad? (Call on a student. Idea: *Because it's always frozen and cold.*) (DC)

As Chad trudged through the blizzard, he remembered the story of the first woman to win the Iditarod. Her name is Libby Riddles. She won the race in 1985. That was one of the longest races ever because the weather was so bad. The race was stopped twice because the planes could not get to the checkpoints and drop off food. Most of the mushers were at Rainy Pass the first time the race was stopped.

- Everybody, what's the name of the first woman to win the Iditarod? (Signal.) *Libby Riddles.* (ND)
- In what year did she win it? (Signal.) *1985.* (ND)
- Where were she and most of the other mushers when the race was stopped the first time? (Signal.) *Rainy Pass.* (ND)
- That's where Chad is right now. Do you think they'll have to stop the race? (Call on individual students. Student preference.) (P)
- Read the rest of the story to yourself and be ready to answer some questions. Raise your hand when you're done.

At that moment, Susie was in her warm living room, writing Chad a letter as her mother watched TV. Susie wrote a letter every day. She sent all of them to Nome. She wanted to make sure that when Chad finally arrived there, he would have a lot of mail from Susie. Here's part of the letter she was writing now:

Do you know that in two days, it will be Denali's birthday? He'll be three years old.

Suddenly, the TV program stopped and an announcer said, "Here's a special report on the Iditarod from Rainy Pass." The picture on the TV showed snow blowing and a reporter who was yelling over the wind. He told about the high winds at Rainy Pass. He said, "The winds are blowing so hard that some of the mushers are lost because they can't see the trail. The race officials may have to send out search parties if some of the teams don't show up at the checkpoint pretty soon."

Susie didn't finish the letter she had started. Denali's birthday didn't seem very important any more. Instead, she wrote another letter.

Dear Uncle Chad,
    The weather report from Rainy Pass is scary. I hope you are not one of those mushers who got lost. I hope they found all the mushers who got lost. And I hope their dogs are okay. I hope that your team is doing well.
      With love,
      Susie

What she really wanted to say in her letter was, "Oh please make sure that Denali is all right. Oh please don't get lost. And if you do get lost, please find your way to the next checkpoint."

- (After all students have raised their hand:)
- Why did Susie write a different letter after she heard the TV report? (Call on a student. Idea: *Because Denali's birthday didn't seem very important anymore.*) (DC)
- What did the race officials at Rainy Pass think they might have to do if the blizzard continues? (Call on a student. Idea: *Stop the race.*) (ND)

EXERCISE 5

Paired Practice

You're going to read aloud to your partner. Today the **B** members will read first. Then the **A** members will read from the star to the end of the story. (Observe students and give feedback.)

End-of-Lesson Activities

INDEPENDENT WORK

Now finish the independent work for lesson 96. Raise your hand when you're finished. (Observe students and give feedback.)

WORKCHECK

a. (Direct students to take out their marking pencils.)

• We're going to check your independent work. Remember, if you got an item wrong, make an **X** next to the item.

b. (For each item: Read the item. Call on a student to answer it. If the answer is wrong, say the correct answer. Refer to the Answer Key for the correct answers.)

c. Now use your marking pencil to fix up any items you got wrong. Remember, all mistakes must be fixed up before you hand in your independent work.

SPELLING

(Present Spelling lesson 96 after completing Reading lesson 96. See *Spelling Presentation Book.*)

EXERCISE 1

Vocabulary Review

a. You learned a sentence that tells about the scuba diver.
  • Everybody, say that sentence. Get ready. (Signal.) *The scuba diver and her partner surfaced near the reef.*
  • (Repeat until firm.)

b. You learned a sentence that tells what the veterinarian did.
  • Say that sentence. Get ready. (Signal.) *The veterinarian gave the dogs a thorough examination.*
  • (Repeat until firm.)

c. Here's the last sentence you learned: Visibility was miserable in the fierce blizzard.
  • Everybody, say that sentence. Get ready. (Signal.) *Visibility was miserable in the fierce blizzard.*
  • (Repeat until firm.)

d. Everybody, what word means **very wild?** (Signal.) *Fierce.*
  • What word names a snowstorm that is windy and very cold? (Signal.) *Blizzard.*
  • What word refers to how well you can see things? (Signal.) *Visibility.*
  • What's another word for **terrible?** (Signal.) *Miserable.*

e. Once more. Say the sentence that tells about visibility. Get ready. (Signal.) *Visibility was miserable in the fierce blizzard.*

EXERCISE 2

Reading Words

Column 1

a. **Find lesson 97 in your textbook.** ✔
  • Touch column 1. ✔
  • (Teacher reference:)

1. **snowmobile**	4. **checkpoint**
2. **evergreen**	5. **nightmare**
3. **birthday**	6. **handlebar**

b. All these words are compound words. The first part of each word is underlined.

c. Word 1. What's the underlined part? (Signal.) *snow.*
  • What's the whole word? (Signal.) *Snowmobile.*
  • Word 2. What's the underlined part? (Signal.) *ever.*
  • What's the whole word? (Signal.) *Evergreen.*
  • Word 3. What's the underlined part? (Signal.) *birth.*
  • What's the whole word? (Signal.) *Birthday.*
  • Word 4. What's the underlined part? (Signal.) *check.*
  • What's the whole word? (Signal.) *Checkpoint.*
  • Word 5. What's the underlined part? (Signal.) *night.*
  • What's the whole word? (Signal.) *Nightmare.*
  • Word 6. What's the underlined part? (Signal.) *handle.*
  • What's the whole word? (Signal.) *Handlebar.*

d. Let's read those words again, the fast way.
  • Word 1. What word? (Signal.) *Snowmobile.*
  • (Repeat for words 2–6.)

e. (Repeat step d until firm.)

Column 2

f. Find column 2. ✔
  • (Teacher reference:)

1. **compass**	3. **recently**
2. **peered**	4. **total**

g. Word 1. What word? (Signal.) *Compass.*
  • Spell **compass.** Get ready. (Tap for each letter.) *C-O-M-P-A-S-S.*
  • A compass is a tool that shows the directions north, south, east and west. Some compasses have a needle. That needle always points north. Everybody, what do we call a tool that shows the directions? (Signal.) *Compass.*

h. Word 2. What word? (Signal.) *Peered.*
  • Spell **peered.** Get ready. (Tap for each letter.) *P-E-E-R-E-D.*

- When you look at something as hard as you can, you peer at that thing. Everybody, what's another way of saying **He looked as hard as he could at the mountain?** (Signal.) *He peered at the mountain.*
  i. Word 3. What word? (Signal.) *Recently.*
- Spell **recently.** Get ready. (Tap for each letter.) *R-E-C-E-N-T-L-Y.*
  j. Word 4. What word? (Signal.) *Total.*
- Spell **total.** Get ready. (Tap for each letter.) *T-O-T-A-L.*
  k. Let's read those words again.
- Word 1. What word? (Signal.) *Compass.*
- (Repeat for: **2. peered, 3. recently, 4. total.**)
  l. (Repeat step k until firm.)

Column 3
  m. Find column 3. ✔
- (Teacher reference:)

| 1. beware | 3. visibility |
| 2. plunge | 4. scent |

  n. Word 1. What word? (Signal.) *Beware.*
- Here's another way of saying **Watch out for the dog: Beware of the dog.**
- Everybody, what's another way of saying **Watch out for loose gravel?** (Signal.) *Beware of loose gravel.*
  o. Word 2. What word? (Signal.) *Plunge.*
- If something **plunges** into the water, it dives into the water. Everybody, what's another way of saying **He dove into the water?** (Signal.) *He plunged into the water.*
  p. Word 3. What word? (Signal.) *Visibility.*
  q. Word 4. What word? (Signal.) *Scent.*
  r. Let's read those words again.
- Word 1. What word? (Signal.) *Beware.*
- (Repeat for words 2–4.)
  s. (Repeat step r until firm.)

Individual Turns
(For columns 1–3: Call on individual students, each to read one to three words per turn.)

EXERCISE 3

Story Reading
  a. Find part B in your textbook. ✔
- The error limit for group reading is 11 errors.

  b. Everybody, touch the title. ✔
- (Call on a student to read the title.) *[Lost.]*
- Everybody, what's the title? (Signal.) *Lost.* (ND)
  c. (Call on individual students to read the story, each student reading two or three sentences at a time. Ask the specified questions as the students read.)

- (**Correct errors:** Tell the word. Direct the student to reread the sentence.)
- (If the group makes more than 11 errors, direct the students to reread the story.)

Lost
Chad was lost. The snow had been blowing so hard that he had lost the trail to Rainy Pass. He had an idea of which direction that he should be going and he noticed that the snow was deep. That meant that nobody had been over the snow recently.

- Everybody, if Chad was on the trail, would the snow be very deep? (Signal.) *No.* (DC)
- Why not? (Call on a student. Idea: *Because the teams ahead of Chad would have trampled the snow down.*) (ND)

The dogs were very tired from plowing through the deep snow. And it was getting dark out. In about half an hour, it would be completely dark. Chad didn't know if he was left of the trail or right of the trail. So he wasn't sure which way he should head to find the trail. He decided that the best thing to do was not to find the trail but to find the checkpoint. He turned on the light that was on his hat. He took out his compass and looked at the direction his sled was heading. It was going too far to the north. Chad knew that this part of the trail went almost straight west on its way to Rainy Pass. He also noticed that the slopes he was going over were too steep. Both those clues told him that he should just turn left and head straight west. That's what he did.

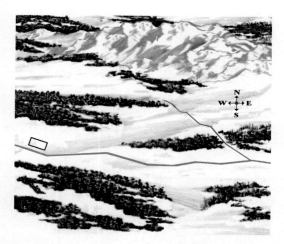

- Everybody, listen to that part again. Chad didn't know if he was left of the trail or right of the trail. So he wasn't sure which way he should head to find the trail. He decided that the best thing to do was not to find the trail but to find the checkpoint. He turned on the light that was on his hat. He took out his compass and looked at the direction his sled was heading. It was going too far to the north. Chad knew that this part of the trail went almost straight west on its way to Rainy Pass. He also noticed that the slopes he was going over were too steep. Both those clues told him that he should just turn left and head straight west. That's what he did.
- Everybody, which way should he be heading? (Signal.) *West.* (ND)
- But he was heading too far to which direction? (Signal.) *North.* (ND)
- Touch the place on the map where Chad is now. His trail is that blue line. (Observe students and give feedback.) (VA)
- Touch the trail he should be on. That trail is the red line. (Observe students and give feedback.) (VA)
- Chad used a compass to figure out which direction is west. Will he have to turn **left** or **right** to go west? (Signal.) *Left.* (ND)

A half hour later, in almost total darkness, the wind died down. The blowing snow settled from the air. Chad peered to the north to see where the mountains were.

"Yes," he said. The mountains were where they should be. That meant

that Chad was going in the right direction. A moment later, he looked ahead and he could see the lights from the lodge at Rainy Pass. "Yes," he repeated. "Yes." He could also see the trail. It was just a little bit to his right.

The dogs seemed to pep up. They could see the lights and smell the food from the checkpoint. "Mush," Chad yelled and the dogs pulled hard. "You guys are lucky," he said to his team. "If you had just an ordinary musher, you might have to spend all night on the trail. Tonight, you'll have a real treat."

- What's the treat? (Call on a student. Idea: *They'll spend the night at the checkpoint, not on the trail.*) (DC)
- Everybody, did Chad think he was better than an ordinary musher? (Signal.) *Yes.* (DC)
- If the dogs had an ordinary musher, why might they have had to spend all night on the trail? (Call on a student. Idea: *Because an ordinary musher might not be able to find the checkpoint.*) (DC)

The wind started up again, blowing swirls of snow and making it impossible for Chad to see anything but snow. "Come on, you guys," he said to his team. "The sooner you reach those lights, the sooner we'll be able to rest in real comfort."

About twenty minutes later, Chad entered the checkpoint at Rainy Pass. A lot of people were there, and most of them looked worried. One of the first questions that the officials asked Chad was "Did you see any other teams?"

"No," Chad said.

"Well, two teams are missing, number 58 and number 60."

Chad explained how he may have passed them without knowing it. "I lost the trail for a while. I went too far north, so I cut back and went west."

"How was the visibility out there?"

"Most of the time I couldn't see my lead dogs."

As Chad was unpacking, unhitching his dogs, and feeding them, the officials continued to ask questions. Then they said, "We're going to take some snowmobiles back along the trail and see if we can find 58 and 60. We're thinking of going down the regular trail and also going back along the route that you took. If their dogs pick up the scent of your dogs, they may try to take the same route you took."

- Everybody, how many mushers were missing? (Signal.) *2.* ⓃⒹ
- How did the officials plan to search for them? (Call on a student. Idea: *With snowmobiles.*) ⓃⒹ
- Why did they want to go back along Chad's trail as well as the regular trail? (Call on a student. Idea: *Because other teams might smell Chad's team and follow the smell.*) ⓃⒹ
- Read the rest of the story to yourself and be ready to answer some questions. Raise your hand when you're done.

Chad tried to describe his route, but he could see that the officials were not able to understand all the things he explained. At last, Chad said, "If you can drive me down the trail a mile or so, I can show you where to go."

A few minutes later, three snowmobiles set out down the trail. Chad was driving one of them. The wind had stopped. When the snowmobiles came to the place where Chad had joined the trail, he pointed out the route he had taken. The other two snowmobiles went back along Chad's trail and the regular trail. Chad drove his snowmobile back to the checkpoint.

As Chad checked the equipment and took care of his dogs, he kept thinking about the lost teams, especially number 60, Siri Carlson from Sweden. What was she doing now? Was she okay? Would they find her?

Chad didn't find out until the next morning. He slept in the lodge that night, on a real bed. What a treat. When he was leaving the lodge in the morning to check on his dogs, he saw her. "Hi," he said and asked about her adventure. She told him that she had lost the trail and the sled had tumbled down a slope. Two of her dogs were injured and a runner on her sled was broken. Chad wanted to help her fix the sled, but that was against the rules. So he wished her good luck. Then he said, "I hope I see you on the trail tomorrow."

She smiled and said, "I'll be there, don't worry."

- (After all students have raised their hand:)
- When did Chad finally see Siri Carlson? (Call on a student. Idea: *In the morning.*) ⓃⒹ
- What had happened to her? (Call on individual students. Ideas: *She got lost; her sled rolled down a hill and broke a runner; two of her dogs were hurt.*) ⓃⒹ
- Everybody, did she plan to continue the race? (Signal.) *Yes.* ⓃⒹ
- She must be pretty brave. Do you think Chad will see her again on the trail? (Call on individual students. Student preference.) ⓂⒿ
- Who is in the picture? (Call on a student. Idea: *Chad and Siri.*) ⓋⒶ
- Where are they? (Call on a student. Idea: *Outside the lodge at Rainy Pass.*) ⓋⒶ
- Everybody, what time of day is it? (Signal.) *Morning.* ⓃⒹ
- What does Siri have to do before she can leave the checkpoint? (Call on individual students. Ideas: *Fix her sled; arrange for her injured dogs to be flown somewhere.*) ⒹⒾ

EXERCISE 4

Paired Practice

You're going to read aloud to your partner. Today the **A** members will read first. Then the **B** members will read from the star to the end of the story. (Observe students and give feedback.)

End-of-Lesson Activities

INDEPENDENT WORK

Now finish the independent work for lesson 97. Raise your hand when you're finished. (Observe students and give feedback.)

WORKCHECK

a. (Direct students to take out their marking pencils.)

• We're going to check your independent work. Remember, if you got an item wrong, make an **X** next to the item.

b. (For each item: Read the item. Call on a student to answer it. If the answer is wrong, say the correct answer. Refer to the Answer Key for the correct answers.)

c. Now use your marking pencil to fix up any items you got wrong. Remember, all mistakes must be fixed up before you hand in your independent work.

SPELLING

(Present Spelling lesson 97 after completing Reading lesson 97. See *Spelling Presentation Book.*)

Vocabulary Review

a. You learned a sentence that tells about visibility.

- Everybody, say that sentence. Get ready. (Signal.) *Visibility was miserable in the fierce blizzard.*
- (Repeat until firm.)

b. Tell me the **first** word of the sentence. Get ready. (Signal.) *Visibility.*

c. I'll say part of the sentence. When I stop, you say the next word. Listen: Visibility was . . . Everybody, what's the next word? (Signal.) *Miserable.*

- Say the whole sentence. Get ready. (Signal.) *Visibility was miserable in the fierce blizzard.*

d. Listen: Visibility was miserable in the . . . Everybody, what's the next word? (Signal.) *Fierce.*

e. Listen: Visibility was miserable in the fierce . . . Everybody, what's the next word? (Signal.) *Blizzard.*

- Say the whole sentence. Get ready. (Signal.) *Visibility was miserable in the fierce blizzard.*

Reading Words

Column 1

a. **Find lesson 98 in your textbook.** ✔
- Touch column 1. ✔
- (Teacher reference:)

1. arrangements	4. crust
2. congratulate	5. dried
3. beware	

b. Word 1 is **arrangements.** What word? (Signal.) *Arrangements.*

- When you make **arrangements** to do something, you make a plan to do that thing. Everybody, what's another way of saying **She made a plan to take a trip?** (Signal.) *She made arrangements to take a trip.*

c. Word 2 is **congratulate.** What word? (Signal.) *Congratulate.*

- When you congratulate somebody, you praise the person for something the person did well.

d. Word 3. What word? (Signal.) *Beware.*

- Spell **beware.** Get ready. (Tap for each letter.) *B-E-W-A-R-E.*

e. Word 4. What word? (Signal.) *Crust.*

- Spell **crust.** Get ready. (Tap for each letter.) *C-R-U-S-T.*

f. Word 5. What word? (Signal.) *Dried.*

- Spell **dried.** Get ready. (Tap for each letter.) *D-R-I-E-D.*

g. Let's read those words again, the fast way.

- Word 1. What word? (Signal.) *Arrangements.*
- (Repeat for words 2–5.)

h. (Repeat step g until firm.)

Column 2

i. Find column 2. ✔
- (Teacher reference:)

1. sheltered	3. plunged
2. tarps	4. tucking

- All these words have an ending.

j. Word 1. What word? (Signal.) *Sheltered.*

- Things that are **sheltered** are protected. If something is sheltered from the wind, it is protected from the wind. Everybody, what's another way of saying **They were protected from the snow?** (Signal.) *They were sheltered from the snow.*

k. Word 2. What word? (Signal.) *Tarps.*

- A tarp is a large covering made of canvas or plastic. Tarps are used to cover things like boats or sleds. Everybody, what's the name of a large covering made of canvas or plastic? (Signal.) *Tarp.*

l. Word 3. What word? (Signal.) *Plunged.*

m. Word 4. What word? (Signal.) *Tucking.*

n. Let's read those words again.
- Word 1. What word? (Signal.) *Sheltered.*
- (Repeat for words 2–4.)

o. (Repeat step n until firm.)

EXERCISE 3

Story Backgroud

a. Find part B in your textbook. ✔
- You're going to read the next story about the Iditarod. First you'll read the information passage. It gives some facts about rest periods.

b. Everybody, touch the title. ✔
- (Call on a student to read the title.) [Rest Periods.]
- Everybody, what's the title? (Signal.) *Rest Periods.* ⓝⒹ

c. (Call on individual students to read the passage, each student reading two or three sentences at a time. Ask the specified questions as the students read.)

Rest Periods

One rule of the Iditarod is that every musher must take a 24-hour rest at one of the checkpoints and an eight-hour rest at two of the other checkpoints. This rule was put in so that the dogs would not have to work so hard that they collapsed on the trail.

- Everybody, how many long stops must every musher take? (Signal.) *One.* ⓇⒻ/Ⓡ
- How long is the longest stop? (Signal.) *24 hours.* ⓇⒻ/Ⓡ
- How long are the other two stops? (Signal.) *8 hours.* ⓇⒻ/Ⓡ
- Why did they make this rule about resting? (Call on a student. Idea: *So the dogs wouldn't collapse on the trail.*) ⓝⒹ
- Chad stayed overnight at the Rainy Pass checkpoint. Was that his 24-hour rest or one of the 8-hour rests? (Call on a student. Idea: *8-hour rest.*) ⒹⒸ

During the first years of the race, a lot of dogs died from injury, starvation, and working too hard. During the first year of the race, 1973, thirty dogs died during the race. Even today, with all the care that the mushers take to make sure the dogs are treated well, two or three dogs die during every race. That's not a large number if you remember that there may be 800

dogs entered in a race, but it's still more dogs than anybody wants to die.

- Everybody, when was the first race? (Signal.) *1973.* ⓇⒻ/Ⓡ
- How many dogs died in that race? (Signal.) *30.* ⓇⒻ/Ⓡ
- How many dogs die in races that they run now? (Call on a student. Idea: *Two or three.*) ⓇⒻ/Ⓡ

Chad had not lost any dogs when he tried running the Iditarod before, but one of Chad's best friends lost two dogs in 1998.

- That must have been terrible.

EXERCISE 4

Story Reading

a. Find part C in your textbook. ✔
- The error limit for group reading is 9 errors.

b. Everybody, touch the title. ✔
- (Call on a student to read the title.) [Beware of Streams.]
- Everybody, what's the title? (Signal.) *Beware of Streams.* ⓝⒹ

c. (Call on individual students to read the story, each student reading two or three sentences at a time. Ask the specified questions as the students read.)

- (**Correct errors:** Tell the word. Direct the student to reread the sentence.)
- (If the group makes more than 9 errors, direct the students to reread the story.)

Beware of Streams

It was day nine of the race, and Chad was lost again.

- Everybody, what day was it when he reached Rainy Pass? (Signal.) *Day 3.* ⒶⓅⓀ
- What day is it now? (Signal.) *Day 9.* ⓝⒹ
- Everybody, look at the map. The map shows where Chad was on the different days. Touch the place he was at the end of day 3. ✔ ⓋⒶ

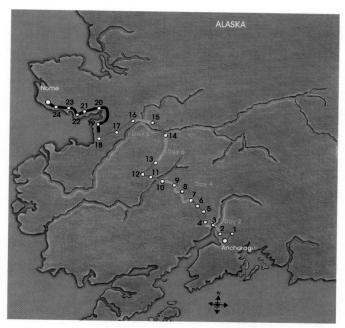

ALASKA

- What's the number of the checkpoint for the end of day 3? (Signal.) *6.* (VA)
- Now touch where Chad was on day 9. ✔ (VA)
- He's getting close to Nome. What checkpoint is he at? (Signal.) *16.* (VA)
- What was his problem on day 9? (Call on a student. Idea: *He was lost again.*) (ND)

After he left Rainy Pass, things went pretty smoothly for three days. Then the weather turned bad again. Chad's team went only about fifty miles one day and fifty miles the next day. The winds and weather were so bad that he didn't feel it was safe to try to go any farther. Today started out a lot better, but about halfway between checkpoint 18 and 19, a terrible storm moved in. Chad could not see the lead dogs and sometimes he couldn't see the wheel dogs. He found a sheltered place and stayed there for more than two hours. Then he tried to move on. Within an hour he had lost the trail. He headed north along the ocean, hoping that he would find the trail again, but as the team was slowly crossing a low area, one of the worst possible things happened. The sled was going over a thick crust of frozen snow. Below that snow was a fast-moving stream. Chad didn't know that until the back of the sled suddenly broke through the crust of ice and fell into the water below.

- Everybody, look at the picture. The sled is falling into that hole. The wheel dogs look like they're being pulled backwards into the hole.

The air temperature was around zero. If a person gets wet at that temperature, that person could easily die by freezing. Chad got wet. The rear end of the sled plunged into the water. The front end of the sled was pointing up. As Chad was trying to climb up to the front of the sled, the snow cracked again and the wheel dogs fell into the water. Chugger let out a cry.

The team stopped. Denali and Butch looked back. Chad was up to his chest in the water. He had to get the sled out of the water quickly. Denali and Butch were the dogs that had to pull the sled out. "Mush," Chad shouted. "Mush, Denali. Mush, Butch. Mush, . . ." They did. They got low and strained as they pulled forward. "Mush."

Slowly, the team dragged Chugger and Buck out of the water. Then the sled came out—with streams of water flowing from it.

- How deep was the water? (Call on a student. Idea: *Chest deep.*) (ND)
- Which dogs had to do most of the pulling to get the sled out of the water? (Call on a student.) *Denali and Butch.* (ND)

Chad was soaked. He knew that he had only minutes to get warm or he would freeze. He drove the team to a grove of trees. He noticed that Chugger was not able to pull. Then Chad quickly removed some tarps from the ⭐ sled and hung them from the trees so they made a tent. He quickly unpacked dry clothes from the sled and some emergency wood. This wood was treated and it would burn even if it were wet.

- Everybody, look at the picture. Where's Chad going in the picture? (Call on a student. Idea: *To the tent*.) Ⓥ
- What's he going to do with the wood? (Call on a student. Idea: *Build a fire*.) Ⓝ
- What's he going to do with the clothes? (Call on a student. Idea: *Put them on*.) Ⓓ
- How much time does he have to light a fire, dry off, and change his clothes? (Call on a student. Idea: *Minutes*.) Ⓝ
- Read the rest of the story to yourself and be ready to answer some questions. Raise your hand when you're done.

As the wind howled and the snow blew, Chad built a fire inside the tent. It took Chad only about two minutes to start the fire, but he could feel that his legs were starting to get numb. A minute later the fire was putting out good heat. By now, Chad had taken off his wet clothes, dried himself as fast as he could and started putting on dry clothes.

He stayed inside the tent until the feeling had returned to his legs. Then he went out to check on the dogs. Chugger could not walk on all four legs. Her back left leg did not work because her hip had failed.

Chad took Chugger off the gang line and carried her into the tent. He dried her off and then put a blanket around her. She licked his face as he was tucking her in. Then he took Buck, the other regular wheel dog, off the gang line. Buck would walk behind the sled until the team reached the next checkpoint. Denali and Butch would be the wheel dogs for the rest of the race.

Chad stayed at the grove for three hours, until the weather cleared. Then he climbed a nearby hill so he could look in all directions for the trail. He didn't have much hope of seeing it, but he thought it was worth trying. To his surprise, he saw a dog sled as soon as he got to the top of the hill. It was a few hundred yards to the east. When he took a closer look, he said, "I know who that is." It was Siri Carlson. Chad whistled and waved.

She waved back and shouted something, but he couldn't hear what she said. He signaled that he would catch up with her. Then he ran back to his team and hitched them to the gang line. He put Chugger in the sled. When Chad told the team to mush, Chugger tried to stand up. Chad patted her and said, "Not you, Chugger. You just take it easy." The team went east over the hills until it reached the trail. Chad could see Siri's team about half a mile ahead of him.

- (After all students have raised their hand:)
- What are the things that Chad did inside the tent? (Call on a student. Idea: *Built a fire, changed clothes, dried off Chugger and wrapped her in a blanket.*) (ND)
- Why didn't he just do those things outside the tent? (Call on a student. Idea: *Because it was too cold.*) (DI)
- Everybody, which dog failed? (Signal.) *Chugger.* (ND)
- Did the vet warn Chad that something might go wrong with Chugger's hip? (Signal.) *Yes.* (APK)
- Why do you think Chad didn't leave Buck on the gang line and just replace Chugger with Denali or Butch? (Call on a student. Ideas: *Buck is used to working with Chugger; Denali and Butch are used to working together.*) (DC)
- Everybody, did Chad have a lot of trouble finding the trail? (Signal.) *No.* (ND)
- Whose sled did he see? (Call on a student. Idea: *Siri Carlson's.*) (ND)
- Which dogs were now the wheel dogs? (Call on a student.) *Denali and Butch.* (ND)
- Where was Chugger? (Call on a student. Idea: *In the sled.*) (ND)
- Where was Buck? (Call on a student. Idea: *Behind the sled.*) (ND)

EXERCISE 5

Paired Practice

You're going to read aloud to your partner. Today the **B** members will read first. Then the **A** members will read from the star to the end of the story. (Observe students and give feedback.)

End-of-Lesson Activities

INDEPENDENT WORK

Now finish the independent work for lesson 98. Raise your hand when you're finished. (Observe students and give feedback.)

WORKCHECK

a. (Direct students to take out their marking pencils.)
- We're going to check your independent work. Remember, if you got an item wrong, make an **X** next to the item.

b. (For each item: Read the item. Call on a student to answer it. If the answer is wrong, say the correct answer. Refer to the Answer Key for the correct answers.)

c. Now use your marking pencil to fix up any items you got wrong. Remember, all mistakes must be fixed up before you hand in your independent work.

SPELLING

(Present Spelling lesson 98 after completing Reading lesson 98. See *Spelling Presentation Book.*)

EXERCISE 1

Reading Words

Column 1

a. **Find lesson 99 in your textbook.** ✔
- Touch column 1. ✔
- (Teacher reference:)

> | 1. anxious | 4. insist |
> |---|---|
> | 2. Angela | 5. demand |
> | 3. curious | |

b. Word 1 is **anxious.** What word? (Signal.) *Anxious.*
- Spell **anxious.** Get ready. (Tap for each letter.) *A-N-X-I-O-U-S.*

c. Word 2 is **Angela.** What word? (Signal.) *Angela.*
- Spell **Angela.** Get ready. (Tap for each letter.) *A-N-G-E-L-A.*

d. Word 3 is **curious.** What word? (Signal.) *Curious.*
- Spell **curious.** Get ready. (Tap for each letter.) *C-U-R-I-O-U-S.*
- When you are curious about something, you want to know about that thing. Here's another way of saying **She wanted to know about rockets: She was curious about rockets.** Everybody, what's another way of saying **She wanted to know about her new teacher?** (Signal.) *She was curious about her new teacher.*

e. Word 4 is **insist.** What word? (Signal.) *Insist.*
- Spell **insist.** Get ready. (Tap for each letter.) *I-N-S-I-S-T.*
- When you keep arguing that you must have something, you **insist** on that thing. Here's another way of saying **He kept arguing about going to the mountain: He insisted on going to the mountain.** Everyone, what's another way of saying **He kept arguing about going to the mountain?** (Signal.) *He insisted on going to the mountain.*
- What's another way of saying **He kept arguing about wearing his red jacket?** (Signal.) *He insisted on wearing his red jacket.*

f. Word 5 is **demand.** What word? (Signal.) *Demand.*
- When you **demand** something, you **insist** on that thing. If a baby demands more food, the baby insists on having more food. How do babies show that they are demanding more food? (Call on a student. Ideas: *Cry; pound on the table; etc.*)

g. Let's read those words again, the fast way.
- Word 1. What word? (Signal.) *Anxious.*
- (Repeat for words 2–5.)

h. (Repeat step g until firm.)

Column 2

i. Find column 2. ✔
- (Teacher reference:)

> | 1. aimlessly | 4. surprise |
> |---|---|
> | 2. lantern | 5. finisher |
> | 3. arrangements | 6. congratulated |

j. These words have more than one part. The first part of each word is underlined.

k. Word 1. What's the underlined part? (Signal.) *aim.*
- What's the whole word? (Signal.) *Aimlessly.*
- When you do things **aimlessly,** you don't have a plan about what you're doing. When you walk aimlessly, you don't have a plan about where you're going. Everybody, what word describes how you're working when you don't have a plan? (Signal.) *Aimlessly.*
- Word 2. What's the underlined part? (Signal.) *lan.*
- What's the whole word? (Signal.) *Lantern.*
- A lamp that sends out light in all directions is a **lantern.** Everybody, what's a lamp that sends out light in all directions? (Signal.) *Lantern.*
- Word 3. What's the underlined part? (Signal.) *arrange.*
- What's the whole word? (Signal.) *Arrangements.*
- Word 4. What's the underlined part? (Signal.) *sur.*

- What's the whole word? (Signal.) *Surprise.*
- Word 5. What's the underlined part? (Signal.) *finish.*
- What's the whole word? (Signal.) *Finisher.*
- Word 6. What's the underlined part? (Signal.) *congratulate.*
- What's the whole word? (Signal.) *Congratulated.*

l. Let's read those words again, the fast way.
- Word 1. What word? (Signal.) *Aimlessly.*
- (Repeat for: **2. lantern, 3. arrangements, 4. surprise, 5. finisher, 6. congratulated.**)
m. (Repeat step l until firm.)

Column 3

n. Find column 3. ✔
- (Teacher reference:)

1. victory	4. buddies
2. award	5. miserable
3. hero	6. fierce

o. Word 1. What word? (Signal.) *Victory.*
- Another word for a **win** is a **victory.** If you have a win over a team, you have a victory over the team. What's another way of saying **Our team had three wins this year?** (Signal.) *Our team had three victories this year.*
p. Word 2. What word? (Signal.) *Award.*
- An award is something you receive for doing something special. If you do well in math, you may receive an award. If you win a race, you'll receive an award.
q. Word 3. What word? (Signal.) *Hero.*
- A hero is somebody we admire for having great courage or doing great things.
r. Word 4. What word? (Signal.) *Buddies.*
- (Repeat for words 5 and 6.)
s. Let's read those words again.
- Word 1. What word? (Signal.) *Victory.*
- (Repeat for words 2–6.)
t. (Repeat step s until firm.)

Individual Turns

(For columns 1–3: Call on individual students, each to read one to three words per turn.)

Story Reading

a. Find part B in your textbook. ✔
- The error limit for group reading is 12 errors.
b. Everybody, touch the title. ✔
- (Call on a student to read the title.) *[End of the Race.]*
- Everybody, what's the title? (Signal.) *End of the Race.* (ND)
c. (Call on individual students to read the story, each student reading two or three sentences at a time. Ask the specified questions as the students read.)

- (**Correct errors:** Tell the word. Direct the student to reread the sentence.)
- (If the group makes more than 12 errors, direct the students to reread the story.)

End of the Race

Chad's team was on the trail again. Siri Carlson was about half a mile ahead of Chad.

"Come on, you guys," Chad said to his team. "If you want some company, we'll have to go faster than this. Mush, you sled dogs. Mush." Chad pedaled with one foot to help make the sled go faster. The team had only fourteen dogs in it, but they pulled hard. And before long, they caught up to Siri's team.

Chad told her what had happened and how the dogs were able to pull the sled out of the water. She said, "You must have strong wheel dogs."

"I do," Chad said. "Although I don't think Chugger will be pulling sleds from now on." Chad and Siri reached checkpoint 19 about an hour later. They stayed there for eight hours. Chad made arrangements for a plane to take Chugger back to Anchorage. He changed the gang line so that there was one dog in front of Butch and Denali. That dog was Buck.

- Everybody, how many dogs were now on the gang line? (Signal.) *15.* (DC)

- One dog did not have a partner. Which dog was that? (Signal.) *Buck.* (DC)
- Where was Buck? (Call on a student. Idea: *Right in front of Butch and Denali.*) (ND)
- The picture shows how Chad changed the gang line.

After eight hours of resting, Chad and his team went on the trail again. The weather was cold, but the air was clear and the dogs wanted to run. They made good time. So did Siri's team. Chad was in front of them for most of the trip to Nome.

Chad saw the first signs of the town just after the sun had set the next day. Chad could hardly believe that he had been on the trail for eleven days. In some ways, it didn't seem that long. In other ways, it seemed as if he had been on the Iditarod trail for as long as he could remember.

Siri finished ahead of Chad—in the same order they started. She finished in 34th place. He finished in 35th place. He gave her a big hug. "You're a good musher," he said.

"Thank you!" she said. "It was a wonderful experience, and I hate to see it end."

The words seemed strange. Chad thought how the cruel winds, the fierce weather and the dangers make your days miserable. But when you cross that finish line, you know that you and your dogs worked as a team that battled the cold, the snow, the winds, and you won. You went over 11 hundred miles in only 11 days. This victory was even sweeter to Chad when the race officials told him that the weather for this race had been worse than it had been since 1985.

• • •

- Everybody, in what place did Chad finish? (Signal.) *35th.* (ND)
- In what place did Siri Carlson finish? (Signal.) *34th.* (ND)
- Do you think Chad was disappointed because he didn't finish in first or second place? (Call on a student. Idea: *No.*) (MJ)
- What was his main goal for the race? (Call on a student. Idea: *To finish the race.*) (APK)
- Everybody, did he meet that goal? (Signal.) *Yes.* (DC)
- Look at the picture. It shows the finish line in Nome. Going under that arch is what the mushers dream about when they are on the trail.

The plane from Nome landed in Anchorage the next day at about the same time the last finisher of the Iditarod was crossing the finish line. Every year, the last-place team receives the red-lantern award. This year, the red-lantern winner finished in 12 days, 4 hours.

Chad had taken two showers since finishing the race, and he had slept until after eight in the morning. His clothes were clean, but he hadn't shaved.

The plane was met by a cheering crowd—friends and relatives of the mushers who were flying back with Chad. Susie was there. The day before, she had gone to the airport to pick up Chugger. The vet had told her that there wasn't much she could do to fix Chugger's hip, but that her hip would probably be okay as long as she didn't try to pull sleds or do heavy work.

The first thing Susie did was find Denali and give him a whole lot of hugs and kisses. She whispered to him, "You're a hero. I knew you would be. You're wonderful."

- How did Chad get from Nome to Anchorage? (Call on a student. Idea: *By plane.*) (ND)

- Everybody, was Chad the only musher on the plane? (Signal.) *No.* (ND)
- Who met Chad at the airport? (Signal.) *Susie.* (ND)
- What had she done the day before? (Call on a student. Idea: *Gone to the airport to pick up Chugger.*) (ND)
- What did the vet say about Chugger? (Call on a student. Ideas: *There wasn't much she could do to fix her hip; her hip would probably be okay as long as she didn't do heavy work.*) (ND)
- Read the rest of the story to yourself and be ready to answer some questions. Raise your hand when you're done.

Of course, after Chad loaded his team into his truck, Susie had lots of questions. First she asked whether Chad had received all her mail and read it. He told her that he had received it and had read all of it. Then most of Susie's questions were about Denali. She was most interested in what Denali did when the sled broke through the crust and fell into the water. "Was he the one who helped most to pull you out?"

"Well, you could probably say that," Chad replied. "He didn't slip backwards, and when I told the dogs to pull, he pulled hard."

"He was a hero, wasn't he?" she said.

❁ "Well, I guess you could say that," Chad replied. "I was proud of all the dogs, and Denali certainly did his share, maybe even more than his share."

"He did as well as the older dogs, didn't he?"

"Yes, he did," Chad said. "And if it's all right with you, I'll want him to be a regular wheel dog for next year's Iditarod."

"Well, sure," she said. "I wouldn't want you to go out there without him. You need Denali."

So even before everybody had congratulated Chad on finishing the race, he was making plans about next year's race. Part of the plans included working with Siri Carlson. She planned to do summer training with Chad and his team. And Susie got the idea that ❁ Chad and Siri seemed to like each other more than they would if they were just mushing buddies.

She was right. Two years later, Chad and Siri got married. And Denali ran in six more Iditarods. The musher for the first five races was Chad. The musher for the sixth race was Susie.

- (After all students have raised their hand:)
- What did Chad tell Susie he wanted to do with Denali? (Call on a student. Idea: *Make him a regular wheel dog for the next Iditarod.*) (ND)
- Who did Chad plan to practice with the next summer? (Call on a student. Idea: *Siri Carlson.*) (ND)
- What did Siri and Chad do later on? (Call on a student. Idea: *Get married.*) (ND)
- Everybody, how many more Iditarods did Denali run in? (Signal.) *6.* (ND)
- Who was the musher for the last of those races? (Signal.) *Susie.* (ND)
- Look at the box at the end of the story. There's supposed to be a picture that shows the end of the story, but that picture is missing. I'm not sure what it should show. Maybe it should show just Susie and Denali. Maybe it should show Siri and Chad after they crossed the finish line. Maybe it should show something that happened after the race.
- (Ask the group for ideas about what should be in the picture.)
- We could either draw pictures that show the end of the story, or find some pictures that we could cut out to make a collage showing the ending of the story.
- (Assign students in groups of 3 or 4. Each group is to figure out a plan for a picture and then make the picture.)

Paired Practice

You're going to read aloud to your partner. Today the **A** members will read first. Then the **B** members will read from the star to the end of the story. (Observe students and give feedback.)

End-of-Lesson Activities

INDEPENDENT WORK

Now finish the independent work for lesson 99. Raise your hand when you're finished. (Observe students and give feedback.)

WORKCHECK

a. (Direct students to take out their marking pencils.)

• We're going to check your independent work. Remember, if you got an item wrong, make an **X** next to the item.

b. (For each item: Read the item. Call on a student to answer it. If the answer is wrong, say the correct answer. Refer to the Answer Key for the correct answers.)

c. Now use your marking pencil to fix up any items you got wrong. Remember, all mistakes must be fixed up before you hand in your independent work.

SPELLING

(Present Spelling lesson 99 after completing Reading lesson 99. See *Spelling Presentation Book.*)

Note: You will need to reproduce blackline masters for the Fact Game in lesson 100 (Appendix G in the *Teacher's Guide*).
A special project occurs after lesson 100. See page 154 for the materials you'll need.

Materials for Lesson 100

Fact Game

For each team (4 or 5 students):
- pair of number cubes (or dice)
- copy of Fact Game 100 (Reproducible blackline masters are in Appendix G of the *Teacher's Guide.*)

For each student:
- their copy of the scorecard sheet

For each monitor:
- a pencil
- Fact Game 100 answer key

Fluency: Rate/Accuracy

Each student needs their thermometer chart.

EXERCISE 1

Fact Game

a. You're going to play the game that uses the facts you have learned. Remember the rules. The player rolls the number cubes, figures out the number of the question, reads that question out loud, and answers it. The monitor tells the player if the answer is right or wrong. If it's wrong, the monitor tells the right answer. If it's right, the monitor gives the player one point. Don't argue with the monitor. The number cubes go to the left and the next player has a turn. You'll play the game for 10 minutes.

b. (Divide students into groups of four or five. Assign monitors. Circulate as students play the game. Comment on groups that are playing well.)

c. (At the end of 10 minutes, have all students who earned more than 10 points stand up.)

- (Tell the monitor of each game that ran smoothly:) Your group did a good job.

EXERCISE 2

Fluency: Rate/Accuracy

a. Today is a test day and a reading checkout day. While you're writing answers, I'm going to call on you one at a time to read part of the story we read in lesson 99. When I call you to come and do your checkout, bring your thermometer chart.

- Remember, you pass the checkout by reading the passage in less than a minute without making more than 2 mistakes. And when you pass the checkout, you color the space for lesson 100 on your thermometer chart.

b. (Call on individual students to read the portion of story 99 marked with ✿.)

- (Time the student. Note words that are missed and the number of words read.)

- (Teacher reference:)

✿ "Well, I guess you could say that," Chad replied. "I was proud of all the dogs, and Denali certainly did his share, maybe even more than his share."

"He did as well as the older dogs, didn't he?"

"Yes, he did," Chad said. "And if it's all right with you, [50] I'll want him to be a regular wheel dog for next year's Iditarod."

"Well, sure," she said. "I wouldn't want you to go out there [75] without him. You need Denali."

So even before everybody had congratulated Chad on finishing the race, he was making plans about next year's race. Part [100] of the plans included working with Siri Carlson.

She planned to do summer training with Chad and his team. And Susie got the idea that ✿ [125] Chad and Siri seemed to like each other more than they would if they were just mushing buddies.

- (If the student reads the passage in one minute or less and makes no more than 2 errors, direct the student to color in the space for lesson 100 on the thermometer chart.)

- (If the student makes any mistakes, point to each word that was misread and identify it.)

- (If the student does not meet the rate-error criterion for the passage, direct the student to practice reading the story with the assigned partner.)

Test

a. **Find page 148 in your textbook.** ✔
- This is a test. You'll work items you've done before.

b. Work carefully. Raise your hand when you've completed all the items. (Observe students but do not give feedback.)

Marking The Test

a. (Check students' work before beginning lesson 101. Refer to the Answer Key for the correct answers.)

b. (Record all test 10 results on the Test Summary Sheet and the Group Summary Sheet. Reproducible Summary Sheets are at the back of the *Teacher's Guide*.)

Test Remedies

(Provide any necessary remedies for test 10 before presenting lesson 101. Test remedies are discussed in the *Teacher's Guide*.)

Test 10 Firming Table

Test Item	Introduced in lesson	Test Item	Introduced in lesson	Test Item	Introduced in lesson
1	91	12	94	22	96
2	91	13	94	23	96
3	91	14	95	24	96
4	91	15	95	25	98
5	91	16	95	26	98
6	92	17	95	27	95
7	92	18	95	28	95
8	92	19	95	29	91
9	92	20	95	30	91
10	92	21	96	31	95
11	93				

SPELLING

(Present Spelling lesson 100 after completing Reading lesson 100. See *Spelling Presentation Book*.)

Special Projects

Note: After completing lesson 100, do these special projects with the students. You may do the projects during another part of the school day.

Project 1

a. (Divide the group into teams of three.)

b. (Explain the rules of the scavenger hunt: Each team will have the same list of things to find about the Iditarod. Some of the things may be found on a computer. Some things may be found in magazines or newspapers.)

Special Project

Things to be found:
- A photograph of the finish line in Nome.
- A map that shows the Iditarod trail and all the checkpoints.
- A magazine article that tells something about the Iditarod.
- A chart that shows how long it took all the mushers in the last Iditarod to finish the race.
- An article that explains who the dog Balto was and how he was related to the Iditarod.

c. (Go over the list of items each team is to find. Answer questions about where or how to locate some information. You may want to alert librarians and/or computer labs to be prepared to assist students. Tell teams that they can ask parents or anyone else for help in finding the items. To receive credit for an item, they must bring it, or a copy, to the classroom.)
- (Arrange for a librarian or volunteer to show students how to find some of the items using the internet. Tell teams that if they get stuck they should ask questions to help them.)

Project 2
- (Direct students to ask questions about the Iditarod that were not covered in the story. Show them how to use the Iditarod Web site (www.Iditarod.com) to find answers to their questions.)

Lessons 101–105 • Planning Page *Looking Ahead*

	Lesson 101	Lesson 102	Lesson 103	Lesson 104	Lesson 105
LESSON EVENTS	Reading Words Story Reading Paired Practice Independent Work Workcheck Spelling	**Vocabulary Sentence** Reading Words Fact Review Story Background Story Reading Paired Practice Independent Work Workcheck Spelling	Vocabulary Sentence Reading Words Story Reading Paired Practice Independent Work Workcheck Spelling	Fact Review Vocabulary Sentences Reading Words Story Reading Paired Practice Independent Work Workcheck Spelling	Vocabulary Sentence Reading Words Story Reading Fact Review Fluency: Rate/ Accuracy Independent Work Workcheck Spelling
VOCABULARY SENTENCE		**#25: At <u>midnight</u>, he saw a <u>familiar</u> <u>galaxy</u>.**	#25: At <u>midnight</u>, he saw a <u>familiar</u> <u>galaxy</u>.	sentence #23 sentence #24 sentence #25	#25: At <u>midnight</u>, he saw a <u>familiar</u> <u>galaxy</u>.
READING WORDS: WORD TYPES	modeled words mixed words words with an ending multi-syllable words	modeled words 2-syllable words	modeled word mixed words	mixed words	modeled words
NEW VOCABULARY	chilly	science swooping	level		
STORY BACKGROUND		*The Speed of Light*			
STORY	*Go Anywhere—See Anything*	*The First Trip*	*Al Learns More About Speed*	*Al Takes a Test About Speed*	*Al Learns About Matter*
SKILL ITEMS	Vocabulary Crossword puzzle		Vocabulary	Vocabulary sentence	Vocabulary sentences
SPECIAL MATERIALS					Thermometer charts
SPECIAL PROJECTS/ ACTIVITIES					Activity after lesson 105

Comprehension Questions Abbreviations Guide

Access Prior Knowledge = (APK)　Author's Point of View = (APoV)　Author's Purpose = (AP)　Cause/Effect = (C/E)　Charts/Graphs/Diagrams/Visual Aids = (VA)

Classify and Categorize = (C+C)　Compare/Contrast = (C/C)　Determine Character Emotions, Motivation = (DCE)　Drawing Conclusions = (DC)　Drawing Inferences = (DI)

Fact and Opinion = (F/O)　Hypothesizing = (H)　Main Idea = (MI)　Making Connections = (MC)　Making Deductions = (MD)　Making Judgements = (MJ)

Narrative Elements = (NE)　Noting Details = (ND)　Predict = (P)　Reality/Fantasy = (R/F)　Recall Facts/Rules = (RF/R)　Retell = (R)　Sequence = (Seq)

Steps in a Process = (SP)　Story Structure = (SS)　Summarize = (Sum)　Understanding Dialogue = (UD)　Using Context to Confirm Meaning(s) = (UCCM)　Visualize = (V)

LESSON 101

EXERCISE 1

Reading Words

Column 1

a. **Find lesson 101 in your textbook.** ✔
- Touch column 1. ✔
- (Teacher reference:)

1. familiar	4. Angela
2. galaxy	5. stir
3. anxious	6. curious

b. Word 1 is **familiar.** What word? (Signal.) *Familiar.*
- Spell **familiar.** Get ready. (Tap for each letter.) *F-A-M-I-L-I-A-R.*
c. Word 2 is **galaxy.** What word? (Signal.) *Galaxy.*
- Spell **galaxy.** Get ready. (Tap for each letter.) *G-A-L-A-X-Y.*
d. Word 3. What word? (Signal.) *Anxious.*
- Spell **anxious.** Get ready. (Tap for each letter.) *A-N-X-I-O-U-S.*
e. Word 4. What word? (Signal.) *Angela.*
- Spell **Angela.** Get ready. (Tap for each letter.) *A-N-G-E-L-A.*
f. Word 5. What word? (Signal.) *Stir.*
g. Word 6. What word? (Signal.) *Curious.*
h. Let's read those words again.
- Word 1. What word? (Signal.) *Familiar.*
- (Repeat for words 2–6.)
i. (Repeat step h until firm.)

Column 2

j. Find column 2. ✔
- (Teacher reference:)

1. aimlessly	3. creepy
2. demanded	4. surprised

- All these words have an ending.
k. Word 1. What word? (Signal.) *Aimlessly.*
l. (Repeat for words 2–4.)
m. Let's read those words again.
- Word 1. What word? (Signal.) *Aimlessly.*
- (Repeat for words 2–4.)
n. (Repeat step m until firm.)

Column 3

o. Find column 3. ✔
- (Teacher reference:)

1. chilly	4. agreeing
2. insisted	5. midnight
3. anywhere	

- All these words have more than one syllable. The first part of each word is underlined.
p. Word 1. What's the underlined part? (Signal.) *chill.*
- What's the whole word? (Signal.) *Chilly.*
- **Chilly** means **sort of cold.** If the weather is chilly, it is sort of cold.
q. Word 2. What's the underlined part? (Signal.) *in.*
- What's the whole word? (Signal.) *Insisted.*
r. Word 3. What's the underlined part? (Signal.) *any.*
- What's the whole word? (Signal.) *Anywhere.*
s. Word 4. What's the underlined part? (Signal.) *agree.*
- What's the whole word? (Signal.) *Agreeing.*
t. Word 5. What's the underlined part? (Signal.) *mid.*
- What's the whole word? (Signal.) *Midnight.*
u. Let's read those words again.
- Word 1. What word? (Signal.) *Chilly.*
- (Repeat for words 2–5.)
v. (Repeat step u until firm.)

Individual Turns
(For columns 1–3: Call on individual students, each to read one to three words per turn.)

EXERCISE 2

Story Reading

a. Find part B in your textbook. ✔
- The error limit for group reading is 13 errors. Read carefully.
b. Everybody, touch the title. ✔
- (Call on a student to read the title.) *[Go Anywhere—See Anything.]*
- Everybody, what's the title? (Signal.) *Go Anywhere—See Anything.* ⓝⓓ

- (Call on individual students to read the story, each student reading two or three sentences at a time. Ask the specified questions as the students read.)

- **(Correct errors:** Tell the word. Direct the student to reread the sentence.)
- (If the group makes more than 13 errors, direct the students to reread the story.)

Go Anywhere—See Anything

Al hadn't done well on the test that he had taken in school that day, but Al was not really very disappointed. Al didn't like school very much, so he wasn't anxious about doing well on tests. He didn't care much about the test, and he didn't feel good about school or about himself.

- Everybody, was Al a good student? (Signal.) *No.* (ND)
- Did he like school very much? (Signal.) *No.* (ND)
- Did he feel very good about himself? (Signal.) *No.* (ND)

Al walked from school with his older sister Angela, she was trying to talk Al into playing baseball.

"No," Al replied. "You play. I'm going to walk around for a while."

- Everybody, what did Angela want Al to do? (Signal.) *Play baseball.* (ND)
- What did Al want to do instead? (Call on a student. Idea: *Walk around for a while.*) (ND)

That's just what Al did.

He walked aimlessly down one street and then down another. Now and then a very cold wind would swirl between the buildings and stir up the scraps of paper in the streets. From time to time Al felt chilly, and he thought about the colder weather that was on its way. In two weeks it would be Christmas.

- Everybody, in which month does Christmas come? (Signal.) *December.* (APK)
- So if this story takes place two weeks before Christmas, what month is it in? (Signal.) *December.* (DC)

Al wasn't paying much attention to where he was going, but he wasn't worried about getting lost. He knew that he'd be able to find his way home from just about anyplace in the city.

Al wasn't sure how he got to that strange street with the strange store, but suddenly he noticed a sign in a dirty window of an old store. The sign said, "GO ANYWHERE. SEE ANYTHING."

- Everybody, what did the sign say? (Signal.) *Go anywhere. See anything.* (ND)
- I wonder what kind of store would have a sign like that in the window.

For some reason, that sign caught Al's attention. "What does that mean?" he asked himself. He pressed his nose against the dirty window and looked inside. He saw nothing but darkness.

- Everybody, could he see things inside the store? (Signal.) *No.* (ND)

Suddenly a voice asked, "Would you like to go anywhere or see anything?"

Al turned around quickly and saw a very tall old man next to him. The old man was smiling. Al shrugged and looked away. "I don't have any money," Al said softly.

The old man laughed and then replied, "Money? You don't need money." He spoke very loudly. Al glanced around to see who was watching him, but he was surprised to see that the street was empty—no people, no cars. The old man continued, "This is my store. And you don't need money in my store."

- Everybody, does this store seem like stores you've gone to? (Signal.) *No.* (MJ)
- The store is strange and the street is strange. What's strange about the street? (Call on a student. Ideas: *It was empty; there were no people and no cars.*) (DC)

The old man motioned to Al. "Come in," he said in a loud voice as he opened the door. A strange little bell rang—ding, ding. The old man held the door open and repeated, "Come in, my friend. Come in."

Al shook his head no and said, "I've got to go home. I . . ."

- How do you think Al feels? (Call on a student. Idea: *Nervous.*) (DCE)

"Come in," the old man insisted. "You know that you are curious about what's inside and how you could go anywhere and see anything."

The old ⭐ man was right. Al looked in both directions down the street. Then he slowly followed the old man inside. The inside of the store was dark, quiet and creepy.

The door closed behind Al and the bell rang again—ding, ding. The old man said, "Where do you want to go?"

Al said, "Well, I—I don't know."

The old man laughed. Suddenly, he stopped and bent over so that his face was right in front of Al's. Al could see all the lines in the old man's face. The old man said, "My friend, would you like to go inside a volcano? Would you like to visit another planet? Would you like to swim with whales? Just name anything that you want to see and you will see it. What do you want to see? Where do you want to go?"

Al said, "I would like to see a movie."

"No!" the old man shouted. "I don't show movies. You can see a movie anywhere. I can show you things that movies can't show. I can take you inside the brain of a person. I can take you to the bottom of the ocean."

- Name some places the old man says that he can take Al. (Call on individual students. Ideas: *Inside the brain of a person; to the bottom of the ocean; inside a volcano; to another planet; to swim with whales.*) (ND)

- I wonder if the old man can really do that.
- Read the rest of the story to yourself and be ready to answer some questions. Raise your hand when you're finished.

Al said, "But I told you I can't pay you anything."

The old man smiled. "You don't pay with money. You pay by passing a test."

"A test?" Al asked.

"Yes," the old man replied. "I will take you anywhere. I will show you anything. And then I will give you a test on what you saw. If you do not pass the test, I will never take you to another place or show you another thing. If you do pass the test, then you may go on another trip with me."

The store became silent. Al thought the old man was crazy, and part of Al's mind was telling him to get out of the store. Al kept looking around the inside of the store, but he couldn't see anything because it was too dark.

"Where do you want to go? What do you want to see?" the old man repeated.

Al responded, "I would like to go in a racing car."

"Why?" the old man demanded. Al answered, "I like to go fast."

The old man smiled. "Speed. That's what you want to see. Speed. You want speed, and I will show you speed. But you must remember everything you will see so that you can pass the test."

"Okay," Al said, but he wasn't sure what he was agreeing to or why he agreed. Maybe he was curious to find out how the old man could show speed.

- (After all students have raised their hand:) What's the rule about what happens if Al doesn't pass the test? (Call on a student. Idea: *He doesn't get to go on another trip.*) (RF/R)
- Everybody, at the end of the story, what did Al say he wanted to go in? (Signal.) *A racing car.* (ND)

- The old man asked him why he wanted to go in a racing car. What did Al say? (Call on a student. Idea: *He liked to go fast.*) (ND)
- Everybody, did Al agree to let the old man show him about speed? (Signal.) *Yes.* (ND)
- Was Al sure why he agreed to do that? (Signal.) *No.* (ND)
- The old man told Al that he would have to remember everything he learned about speed. Why? (Call on a student. Idea: *So he could pass a test.*) (ND)

EXERCISE 3

Paired Practice

You're going to read aloud to your partner. The **B** members will read first. Then the **A** members will read from the star to the end of the story. (Observe students and give feedback.)

End-of-Lesson Activities

INDEPENDENT WORK

Now finish your independent work for lesson 101. Raise your hand when you're finished. (Observe students and give feedback.)

WORKCHECK

a. (Direct students to take out their marking pencils.)
- We're going to check your workbook and textbook items. Remember, if you got an item wrong, make an **X** next to the item.

b. (For each item: Read the item. Call on a student to answer it. If the answer is wrong, say the correct answer. Refer to the Answer Key for the correct answers.)

c. Now use your marking pencil to fix up any items you got wrong. Remember, all mistakes must be fixed up before you hand in your work.

SPELLING

(Present Spelling lesson 101 after completing Reading lesson 101. See *Spelling Presentation Book.*)

LESSON 102

Vocabulary

a. **Find page 367 in your textbook.** ✔
- Touch sentence 25. ✔
- This is a new vocabulary sentence. It says: At midnight, he saw a familiar galaxy. Everybody, read that sentence. Get ready. (Signal.) *At midnight, he saw a familiar galaxy.*
- Close your eyes and say the sentence. Get ready. (Signal.) *At midnight, he saw a familiar galaxy.*
- (Repeat until firm.)

b. Midnight is the middle of the night. It is 12 o'clock at night. Everybody, what's another way of saying **They went to bed at 12 o'clock at night?** (Signal.) *They went to bed at midnight.*

c. The sentence says he saw a **familiar** galaxy. Things that are **well-known** to you are **familiar** to you. Everybody, what's another way of saying **The road was well-known to her?** (Signal.) *The road was familiar to her.*
- What's another way of saying **She looked at a picture that was well-known to her family?** (Signal.) *She looked at a picture that was familiar to her family.*

d. A galaxy is a group of millions and millions of stars. Everybody, what's the name of a group of millions and millions of stars? (Signal.) *Galaxy.*

e. Listen to the sentence again: At midnight, he saw a familiar galaxy. Everybody, say the sentence. Get ready. (Signal.) *At midnight, he saw a familiar galaxy.*

f. What word refers to something that is well-known to you? (Signal.) *Familiar.*
- What word means **12 o'clock at night?** (Signal.) *Midnight.*
- What word names a group of millions and millions of stars? (Signal.) *Galaxy.*
- (Repeat step f until firm.)

Reading Words

Column 1

a. Find lesson 102 in your textbook. ✔
- Touch column 1. ✔
- (Teacher reference:)

1. science	4. galaxy
2. confused	5. familiar
3. observed	6. speedometer

b. Word 1 is **science.** What word? (Signal.) *Science.*
- Spell **science.** Get ready. (Tap for each letter.) *S-C-I-E-N-C-E.*
- The careful study of anything in the world is a science. The study of water is a science. The study of butterflies is another science. The study of words is another science. The study of stars is another science.

c. Word 2 is **confused.** What word? (Signal.) *Confused.*
- Spell **confused.** Get ready. (Tap for each letter.) *C-O-N-F-U-S-E-D.*

d. Word 3 is **observed.** What word? (Signal.) *Observed.*
- Spell **observed.** Get ready. (Tap for each letter.) *O-B-S-E-R-V-E-D.*

e. Word 4. What word? (Signal.) *Galaxy.*
- Spell **galaxy.** Get ready. (Tap for each letter.) *G-A-L-A-X-Y.*

f. Word 5. What word? (Signal.) *Familiar.*
- Spell **familiar.** Get ready. (Tap for each letter.) *F-A-M-I-L-I-A-R.*

g. Word 6. What word? (Signal.) *Speedometer.*

h. Let's read those words again.
- Word 1. What word? (Signal.) *Science.*
- (Repeat for words 2–6.)

i. (Repeat step h until firm.)

Column 2

j. Find column 2. ✔
- (Teacher reference:)

1. <u>swoop</u>ing	4. <u>speed</u>ed
2. <u>rac</u>er	5. <u>crack</u>ling
3. <u>race</u>track	6. <u>mid</u>night

- All these words have more than one syllable. The first syllable of each word is underlined.

k. Word 1. What's the first syllable? (Signal.) *swoop.*
- What's the whole word? (Signal.) *Swooping.*
- When birds dip down and glide back up, they are swooping. Everybody, what do we call it when birds dip down and then glide back up? (Signal.) *Swooping.*

l. Word 2. What's the first syllable? (Signal.) *race.*
- What's the whole word? (Signal.) *Racer.*

m. Word 3. What's the first syllable? (Signal.) *race.*
- What's the whole word? (Signal.) *Racetrack.*

n. Word 4. What's the first syllable? (Signal.) *speed.*
- What's the whole word? (Signal.) *Speeded.*

o. Word 5. What's the first syllable? (Signal.) *crack.*
- What's the whole word? (Signal.) *Crackling.*

p. Word 6. What's the first syllable? (Signal.) *mid.*
- What's the whole word? (Signal.) *Midnight.*

q. Let's read those words again.
- Word 1. What word? (Signal.) *Swooping.*
- (Repeat for words 2–6.)

r. (Repeat step q until firm.)

Individual Turns

(For columns 1 and 2: Call on individual students, each to read one to three words per turn.)

EXERCISE 3

Fact Review

a. Let's review some facts you have learned.

b. Everybody, tell me how many planets are in the solar system. (Pause.) Get ready. (Signal.) *9.* RF/R
- Name the planets, starting with the planet closest to the sun. (Pause.) Get ready. (Tap for each name.) *Mercury, Venus, Earth, Mars, Jupiter, Saturn, Uranus, Neptune, Pluto.* RF/R
- Name the biggest planet. (Pause.) Get ready. (Signal.) *Jupiter.* RF/R
- (Repeat step b until firm.)

EXERCISE 4

Story Background

a. Find part B in your textbook. ✔
- You're going to read the next story about Al. First you'll read the information passage. It gives some facts about light.

b. Everybody, touch the title. ✔
- (Call on a student to read the title.) *[The Speed of Light.]*
- Everybody, what's the title? (Signal.) *The Speed of Light.* ND

c. (Call on individual students to read the passage, each student reading two or three sentences at a time. Ask the specified questions as the students read.)

The Speed of Light

Here are facts about light:
- Light is the fastest thing there is. Light travels millions of miles in an hour. In only one second, light travels 186 thousand miles.

- Listen again. In only one second, light travels 186 thousand miles.
- Everybody, how many miles does light go in only one second? (Signal.) *186 thousand.* RF/R
- (Repeat until firm.)

- If you could travel at the speed of light, you would go around Earth almost eight times in one second.

- Everybody, how many times could light go around Earth in one second? (Signal.) *Eight.* RF/R

- The sun is 93 million miles from Earth.

- Everybody, say that fact. Get ready. (Signal.) *The sun is 93 million miles from Earth.* (RF/R)
- How far is the sun from the Earth? (Signal.) *93 million miles.* (RF/R)

But light from the sun reaches Earth in only eight minutes.

- Everybody, how long does it take light to go from the sun to Earth? (Signal.) *Eight minutes.* (RF/R)

Remember, nothing goes faster than light, and light travels at the speed of 186 thousand miles per second.

- Everybody, how fast does light travel? (Signal.) *186 thousand miles per second.* (RF/R)
- (Repeat until firm.)

EXERCISE 5

Story Reading

a. Find part C in your textbook. ✔
- The error limit for group reading is 11 errors. Read carefully.
b. Everybody, touch the title. ✔
- (Call on a student to read the title.) [*The First Trip.*]
- Everybody, what's the title? (Signal.) *The First Trip.* (APK)
- (Call on individual students to read the story, each student reading two or three sentences at a time. Ask the specified questions as the students read.)

- (**Correct errors:** Tell the word. Direct the student to reread the sentence.)
- (If the group makes more than 11 errors, direct the students to reread the story.)

The First Trip

Al was inside a strange dark store on a strange street, but he wasn't sure why he was inside that store.

- The story says that it was a strange store on a strange street. What was strange about the street? (Call on a student. Idea: *There were no cars or people.*) (APK)

- Everybody, what did the sign in the window of that store say? (Signal.) *Go anywhere. See anything.* (APK)
- How much light was in that store? (Call on a student. Idea: *Not much.*) (APK)

And Al wasn't sure whether the old man who owned the store was crazy. That old man had just told Al that he would show Al about speed, and that Al would have to pass a test on everything the old man showed him. Al agreed, but he wasn't sure what he agreed to or why.

Suddenly, Al noticed that the inside of the store was getting light. It got lighter and lighter and lighter. Then suddenly the walls seemed to melt. He could hardly believe what was happening.

Al was no longer standing inside the store, but next to a racetrack. There was a big red racing car right in front of him. The sun was shining and everything was bright.

Al said, "Where—where are we?"

- Where is Al now? (Call on a student. Idea: *At a racetrack.*) (ND)
- How do you think he feels? (Call on a student. Ideas: *Surprised; confused.*) (DCE)
- I can understand why he didn't believe what was happening.

The old man replied, "You are safe when you're with me. Don't worry. You will be home in time for supper."

"How did we get here?" Al asked. "I don't know what happened."

The old man said, "I told you that I would take you anywhere and show you anything. You want to know about speed. This is where we start. Get in the racer."

Al got in the racing car. The old man got behind the wheel and started the engine. "Rrrrrrrooooaaaarrrrr."

The old man said, "Put on your helmet and your safety belt. And get ready for speed."

"Rrrrrrrooooooaaaarr," went the engine.

"Squeeeee," went the tires, and the car jumped forward. The car sped down the racetrack. The sound of the wind became very loud as the car went faster and faster.

"Now we are going 100 miles per hour," the old man shouted above the wind. "If we kept going at this speed, we would go 100 miles every hour."

- Everybody, how fast are they going? (Signal.) *100 miles per hour.* ⓃⒹ
- If you go 100 miles per hour, how far will you go every hour? (Signal.) *100 miles.* ⓃⒹ

Suddenly, the car speeded up.

Things were racing by Al so fast that he could hardly see them. The old man hollered above the roar of the wind and the screaming ✦ of the engine, "Look at the speedometer. Tell me how fast we are going now."

Al yelled, "One hundred and thirty miles per hour."

"Right," the old man yelled. "What does that mean?"

Al answered without taking his eyes off the road. "We would go one hundred and thirty miles in an hour."

"Good," the old man shouted. "Now let's go really fast."

The car went faster and faster. It went so fast that Al could hardly breathe. The engine was screaming. Al glanced at the speedometer. It read 200, which meant that the car was going two hundred miles per hour.

- Everybody, how fast is the racer going? (Signal.) *200 miles per hour.* ⓃⒹ
- Why did the old man and Al have to shout? (Call on a student. Ideas: *Because the car's engine was so loud; because of the wind*.) ⒹⒸ

"Slow down," Al shouted.

"Slow down?" the old man yelled. Then he laughed above the roaring wind. "You wanted to find out about speed. And we are still not going very fast. In fact, we're hardly moving at all."

Al sat back in the seat and closed his eyes. He did not want to see what would happen next.

- What did Al tell the old man to do when they were going 200 miles per hour? (Call on a student. Idea: *To slow down*.) ⓃⒹ
- What was the old man's reply? (Call on a student. Idea: *We're hardly moving*.) ⓃⒹ
- Why did Al close his eyes? (Call on a student. Idea: *Because he didn't want to see what would happen next*.) ⓃⒹ

Suddenly, there was a crackling sound over the racetrack. Al looked up. A jet plane was swooping over the racing car. In only a few seconds, the plane sped past the racing car and was a mile in front of the car.

- Everybody, how fast were Al and the old man going? (Signal.) *200 miles per hour.* ⓃⒹ
- Which vehicle was moving faster, the racing car or the jet plane? (Signal.) *The jet plane.* ⓃⒹ
- How do you know that the jet plane was moving much faster than the racing car? (Call on a student. Idea: *Because the plane passed up the car in only a few seconds*.) ⒹⒸ
- Read the rest of the story to yourself and be ready to answer some questions. Raise your hand when you're finished.

"Wow!" Al shouted. "That plane passed us up like we were standing still."

"Yes," the old man hollered. "This car is really very slow. Let's get into something that has some more speed."

"I think I better go home," Al yelled. "It's getting late and . . ."

Suddenly, Al was no longer in the racing car. He was in the front seat of a jet plane. Everything was quiet inside the plane. There was no howling wind or screaming engine noise. There was just some soft humming sound.

Al looked out the window. He could see the racing car below. He could see the track.

Al shook his head. "How did we get here?"

> The old man said, "Never mind that. Look at the speedometer and tell me how fast we are going."
>
> Al looked. He couldn't believe it. "Five hundred miles per hour," he said.

- (After all students have raised their hand:) Everybody, at the end of the story, were Al and the old man still in the racing car? (Signal.) *No.* (ND)
- Where were they? (Signal.) *In a jet plane.* (ND)
- Did they have to shout to be heard? (Signal.) *No.* (ND)
- Why not? (Call on a student. Idea: *Because it was quiet in the plane.*) (ND)
- Everybody, how fast was the jet plane going? (Signal.) *500 miles per hour.* (ND)
- Everybody, look at the picture. Where are Al and the old man in that picture? (Call on a student. Idea: *In the race car.*) (VA)
- You can see the jet plane swooping past them. What's going to happen a few seconds after this picture? (Call on a student. Idea: *They'll be in the plane.*) (ND)
- Everybody, how fast are they going in the picture? (Signal.) *200 miles per hour.* (ND)
- How fast will they be going a few seconds from now? (Signal.) *500 miles per hour.* (ND)

EXERCISE 6

Paired Practice

You're going to read aloud to your partner. The **A** members will read first. Then the **B** members will read from the star to the end of the story. (Observe students and give feedback.)

End-of-Lesson Activities

INDEPENDENT WORK

Now finish your independent work for lesson 102. Raise your hand when you're finished. (Observe students and give feedback.)

WORKCHECK

a. (Direct students to take out their marking pencils.)
- We're going to check your workbook and textbook items. Remember, if you got an item wrong, make an **X** next to the item.

b. (For each item: Read the item. Call on a student to answer it. If the answer is wrong, say the correct answer. Refer to the Answer Key for the correct answers.)

c. Now use your marking pencil to fix up any items you got wrong. Remember, all mistakes must be fixed up before you hand in your work.

SPELLING

(Present Spelling lesson 102 after completing Reading lesson 102. See *Spelling Presentation Book.*)

EXERCISE 1

Vocabulary Review

a. Here's the new vocabulary sentence: At midnight, he saw a familiar galaxy.
- Everybody, say the sentence. Get ready. (Signal.) *At midnight, he saw a familiar galaxy.*
- (Repeat until firm.)

b. What word names a group of millions and millions of stars? (Signal.) *Galaxy.*
- What word refers to something that is well known to you? (Signal.) *Familiar.*
- What word means **12 o'clock at night?** (Signal.) *Midnight.*

EXERCISE 2

Reading Words

Column 1

a. **Find lesson 103 in your textbook.** ✔
- Touch column 1. ✔
- (Teacher reference:)

1. narrow	3. puddle
2. level	4. rocket

b. Word 1 is **narrow.** What word? (Signal.) *Narrow.*
- Spell **narrow.** Get ready. (Tap for each letter.) *N-A-R-R-O-W.*

c. Word 2. What word? (Signal.) *Level.*
- Spell **level.** Get ready. (Tap for each letter.) *L-E-V-E-L.*
- When something is level, it is flat. It doesn't go up and it doesn't go down. Everybody, what do we call something that doesn't go up or down? (Signal.) *Level.*

d. Word 3. What word? (Signal.) *Puddle.*
- Spell **puddle.** Get ready. (Tap for each letter.) *P-U-D-D-L-E.*

e. Word 4. What word? (Signal.) *Rocket.*
- Spell **rocket.** Get ready. (Tap for each letter.) *R-O-C-K-E-T.*

f. Let's read those words again.
- Word 1. What word? (Signal.) *Narrow.*
- (Repeat for words 2–4.)

g. (Repeat step f until firm.)

EXERCISE 3

Story Reading

a. Find part B in your textbook. ✔
- The error limit for group reading is 12 errors. Read carefully.

b. Everybody, touch the title. ✔
- (Call on a student to read the title.) *[Al Learns More About Speed.]*
- Everybody, what's the title? (Signal.) *Al Learns More About Speed.* ⓃⒹ
- (Call on individual students to read the story, each student reading two or three sentences at a time. Ask the specified questions as the students read.)

- (**Correct errors:** Tell the word. Direct the student to reread the sentence.)
- (If the group makes more than 12 errors, direct the students to reread the story.)

Al Learns More About Speed

Al and the old man were in a jet plane speeding above the racetrack at 500 miles per hour.

"Five hundred miles per hour," Al repeated to himself.

The plane turned and then swooped down. It streaked along above the racetrack and then sped past the end of the track. Then it suddenly swooped almost straight up before leveling off.

Al could see a town below. He said, "It doesn't feel like we're going fast. It felt like we were going faster in the racer. It's so quiet inside this plane."

The old man laughed and pulled the handle that made the plane go faster. After a few moments, things became very, very quiet. Al could no longer hear the humming sounds of the engine. The old man said, "Now we are going faster than the speed of sound."

- Everybody, how fast are they going? (Signal.) *Faster than the speed of sound.* ⓃⒹ
- Where did it feel faster to Al, inside the racer or inside the jet plane? (Signal.) *Inside the racer.* ⓃⒹ

- Why did it feel faster in the racer? (Call on a student. Ideas: *Because it was noisier; because the wind was blowing on them in the racer.*) (DC)

The old man continued, "We are going 900 miles per hour. It's very quiet now because the jet engines of the plane are behind us. The sound from the engines cannot catch up with us. The sound from the engines travels one mile in five seconds. But we are traveling one mile in less than five seconds."

- Listen to that part again:

  The old man continued, "We are going 900 miles per hour. It's very quiet now because the jet engines of the plane are behind us. The sound from the engines cannot catch up with us. The sound from the engines travels one mile in five seconds. But we are traveling one mile in less than five seconds."

- Everybody, how long does it take sound to travel one mile? (Signal.) *Five seconds.* (ND)
- How long does it take the **plane** to travel one mile? (Signal.) *Less than five seconds.* (ND)
- Where are the jet engines of the plane? (Call on a student. Ideas: *Behind Al and the old man; at the back of the plane.*) (ND)
- Everybody, which is going faster, the plane or the sound from the engines? (Signal.) *The plane.* (DC)
- So can the engine sound catch up to the front of the plane? (Signal.) *No.* (ND)

The old man smiled and said, "And now we are going to make this plane go just as fast as it can go."

The old man pulled the handle as far as it would go, and Al watched the speedometer move. Now the plane was going 1,000 miles per hour. Now the plane was going 1,200 miles per hour. Now it was going 1,500 miles per hour.

The old man said, "Think of it. If we keep going at this speed for one hour, we will travel 1,500 miles. We will travel nearly halfway across the United States in one hour."

- Everybody, how fast could the plane go? (Signal.) *1,500 miles per hour.* (ND)
- So how many miles could it travel in one hour? (Signal.) *1,500.* (ND)

"Wow!" Al said. "And it doesn't even feel like we're moving fast."

Al watched the towns move by below the plane. He watched the fields and the clouds. Suddenly, something sped past the plane. It was a long, silver rocket ship.

Al said, "That rocket went by us like we were standing still."

"Yes," the old man said. "A rocket is a lot faster than a jet plane. So . . ."

- What do you think is going to happen now? (Call on a student. Idea: *Al and the old man will be in the rocket.*) (P)

When the old man stopped talking, Al noticed that things had changed. He looked around. He was no longer inside a jet plane. He was sitting in a deep seat. Al and the old man were inside a rocket.

The old man pointed to one of the dials. "Look how fast we're going now."

Al looked at the dial. "Nine thousand miles per hour!"

- Everybody, how fast are they going now? (Signal.) *9,000 miles per hour.* (ND)

"Yes," the old man said. "We're not going 100 miles per hour. We're not going 900 miles per hour. We're going 9,000 miles per hour."

The old man continued, "But we are really not going very fast at all." The old man pointed to the sun and continued, "If we kept going at this speed, it would take us over one year to reach the sun."

- Everybody, how long would it take them to reach the sun at this speed? (Signal.) *Over one year.* (ND)

"Wow!" Al said. "That's a long time."

"Yes," the old man said. "We're still moving very slowly." He laughed and then continued. "If you want to move fast, you have to travel at the speed of light."

Al started to say, "How can we go that fast?" Before he could say the first word of that question, he realized that he was floating in space. The rocket ship was gone. The old man was next to Al. "We're now traveling as fast as light," the old man explained. "And we're going toward the sun."

- Read the rest of the story to yourself and be ready to answer some questions. Raise your hand when you're finished.

Al didn't reply. He just stared at the huge burning ball that was getting bigger and bigger.

The old man said, "Light travels 186 thousand miles every <u>second</u>. At this speed it will take us about eight minutes to reach the sun."

Al said, "It doesn't even feel like we're moving. It feels like we're standing still."

The old man said, "That's because there is no air up here. You can't feel air rush by you."

The sun looked very, very big and very bright. Al could see great flames shooting up from the surface of the sun. He could see a bright star near the sun. He asked, "How long would it take us to reach that star if we kept moving at the speed of light?"

The old man laughed. "Seventy years," he said.

"Wow!" Al said. "I'd be an old man by the time we got there."

Al looked around. In back of him he saw a large cloud of stars. "How long would it take to reach those stars?" he asked.

The old man smiled. "You're looking at a galaxy. It would take 200 million years to reach that galaxy."

"I can't believe it," Al said.

The sun was now very close. It was a mass of burning gas so bright that Al couldn't stand it. He closed his eyes. Suddenly, he felt something under his feet.

When he opened his eyes, he noticed that everything was dark. He was back in the dark store. The old man was standing in front of him. "Come back tomorrow," the old man said. "Come back tomorrow and pay for the trip by passing the test. If you pass the test, I will take you on another trip. Go anywhere. See anything."

- (After all students have raised their hand:) When Al and the old man moved out of the rocket ship, they were moving toward a huge burning ball. Everybody, what was that burning ball? (Signal.) *The sun.* (ND)
- How far does light travel in one second? (Signal.) *186,000 miles.* (ND)
- How long does it take light to travel from the sun to Earth? (Signal.) *8 minutes.* (ND)
- Why doesn't it feel like you're moving when you're in space? (Call on a student. Idea: *Because there's no air rushing by you.*) (DC)
- Al saw a cloud of stars. Everybody, what is a cloud of stars called? (Signal.) *A galaxy.* (ND)
- How long did the old man say it would take to reach the galaxy that Al saw? (Signal.) *200 million years.* (ND)
- Why did Al close his eyes when he was close to the sun? (Call on a student. Idea: *Because it was so bright.*) (DI)
- Where was he when he opened his eyes? (Call on a student. Idea: *In the old man's store.*) (ND)
- What did the old man tell him to do? (Call on a student. Idea: *Come back tomorrow and take the test.*) (ND)
- What happens if Al passes the test? (Call on a student. Idea: *The old man will take him on another trip.*) (ND)
- What happens if he doesn't pass the test? (Call on a student. Idea: *He won't go on another trip.*) (DC)

- Do you think he'll pass it? (Call on individual students. Student preference.) (MJ)

Paired Practice

You're going to read aloud to your partner. The **B** members will read first. Then the **A** members will read from the star to the end of the story. (Observe students and give feedback.)

End-of-Lesson Activities

Now finish your independent work for lesson 103. Raise your hand when you're finished. (Observe students and give feedback.)

a. (Direct students to take out their marking pencils.)

- We're going to check your workbook and textbook items. Remember, if you got an item wrong, make an **X** next to the item.

b. (For each item: Read the item. Call on a student to answer it. If the answer is wrong, say the correct answer. Refer to the Answer Key for the correct answers.)

c. Now use your marking pencil to fix up any items you got wrong. Remember, all mistakes must be fixed up before you hand in your work.

(Present Spelling lesson 103 after completing Reading lesson 103. See *Spelling Presentation Book*.)

EXERCISE 1

Fact Review

a. Let's review some facts you have learned. First we'll go over the facts together. Then I'll call on individual students to do some facts.

b. Everybody, tell me how long it takes **sound** to travel one mile. (Pause.) Get ready. (Signal.) *5 seconds.* (RF/R)

• Tell me if it took Al's jet plane **more than** 5 seconds or **less than** 5 seconds to go one mile. (Pause.) Get ready. (Signal.) *Less than 5 seconds.* (APK)

• Tell me how many miles **light** travels in one second. (Pause.) Get ready. (Signal.) *186 thousand.* (RF/R)

• Tell me about how long it takes light to travel from the sun to Earth. (Pause.) Get ready. (Signal.) *8 minutes.* (RF/R)

• (Repeat step b until firm.)

c. Name the dial that tells how **fast** a vehicle is going. (Pause.) Get ready. (Signal.) *Speedometer.* (RF/R)

• Let's say the speedometer needle in the red racer is pointing to sixty. Tell me how fast the racer is going. (Pause.) Get ready. (Signal.) *60 miles per hour.* (RF/R)

• Tell me how **far** the racer will go in one hour. (Pause.) Get ready. (Signal.) *60 miles.* (RF/R)

• (Repeat step c until firm.)

d. Tell me what a cloud of stars is called. (Pause.) Get ready. (Signal.) *A galaxy.* (RF/R)

• Tell me which goes faster, a racing car or a bicycle. (Pause.) Get ready. (Signal.) *A racing car.* (RF/R)

• Tell me which goes faster, a racing car or light. (Pause.) Get ready. (Signal.) *Light.* (RF/R)

• (Repeat step d until firm.)

Individual Turns

• Now I'm going to call on individual students to do some facts.

• (Call on individual students to do the set of facts in step b, c, or d.)

EXERCISE 2

Vocabulary Review

a. You learned a sentence that tells what the veterinarian did.

• Everybody, say that sentence. Get ready. (Signal.) *The veterinarian gave the dogs a thorough examination.*

• (Repeat until firm.)

b. You learned a sentence that tells about visibility.

• Say that sentence. Get ready. (Signal.) *Visibility was miserable in the fierce blizzard.*

• (Repeat until firm.)

c. Here's the last sentence you learned: At midnight, he saw a familiar galaxy.

• Everybody, say that sentence. Get ready. (Signal.) *At midnight, he saw a familiar galaxy.*

• (Repeat until firm.)

d. What word means **12 o'clock at night?** (Signal.) *Midnight.*

• What word refers to something that is well-known to you? (Signal.) *Familiar.*

• What word names a group of millions and millions of stars? (Signal.) *Galaxy.*

e. Once more. Say the sentence that tells what he saw at midnight. Get ready. (Signal.) *At midnight, he saw a familiar galaxy.*

EXERCISE 3

Reading Words

a. **Find lesson 104 in your textbook.** ✔

• Touch word 1. ✔

• (Teacher reference:)

1. narrow	4. science
2. confused	5. observed
3. simply	6. staring

b. Word 1. What word? (Signal.) *Narrow.*

• Spell **narrow.** Get ready. (Tap for each letter.) *N-A-R-R-O-W.*

c. Word 2. What word? (Signal.) *Confused.*

• Spell **confused.** Get ready. (Tap for each letter.) *C-O-N-F-U-S-E-D.*

d. Word 3. What word? (Signal.) *Simply.*

• Spell **simply.** Get ready. (Tap for each letter.) *S-I-M-P-L-Y.*

e. Word 4. What word? (Signal.) *Science.*

• Spell **science.** Get ready. (Tap for each letter.) *S-C-I-E-N-C-E.*

f. Word 5. What word? (Signal.) *Observed.*

• Word 6. What word? (Signal.) *Staring.*

g. Let's read those words again.

• Word 1. What word? (Signal.) *Narrow.*

• (Repeat for: **2. confused, 3. simply, 4. science, 5. observed, 6. staring.**)

h. (Repeat step g until firm.)

Story Reading

a. Find part B in your textbook. ✔

• The error limit for group reading is 11 errors. Read carefully.

b. Everybody, touch the title. ✔

• (Call on a student to read the title.) *[Al Takes a Test About Speed.]*

• Everybody, what's the title? (Signal.) *Al Takes a Test About Speed.* ⓝⒹ

• What happens if he passes the test? (Call on a student. Idea: *He gets to go on another trip.*) ⒶⓅⓀ

• What happens if he doesn't pass it? (Call on a student. Idea: *He doesn't get to go on another trip.*) ⒶⓅⓀ

• (Call on individual students to read the story, each student reading two or three sentences at a time. Ask the specified questions as the students read.)

• (**Correct errors:** Tell the word. Direct the student to reread the sentence.)

• (If the group makes more than 11 errors, direct the students to reread the story.)

Al Takes a Test About Speed

Al left the store feeling confused. He walked down the strange, empty street until he came to a corner that seemed familiar. Then he began to run. He continued to run all the way home. His experience with the old man was so incredible that he couldn't believe it. He kept thinking about the race car, the rocket, the galaxy and the speed of light.

When he got home, his mother said, "Where have you been?"

Al wanted to tell her, but he didn't say anything because he didn't think that she would believe him.

• Everybody, would you believe him if you were his mother and he told you where he had been? (Signal.) *No.* ⓜⒸ

Al simply shrugged and said, "I was out."

• Do you ever answer like that when your mother asks you where you've been? (Call on a student. Student preference.) ⓜⒸ

"How did your test go in school?" his mother asked.

"I don't know," he said, looking down.

"That test was in science, wasn't it?" his mother asked.

"Yeah, science," Al said. "I don't like science."

❀ Al ate dinner with Angela and his mother. He watched television after dinner. Then he went to bed, but he had trouble going to sleep. He kept thinking about that strange store and that old man.

The next morning, Al left for school very early. He wanted to see what his science book said about speed. He wanted to make sure that he would pass the test and go on another trip with the old man.

When Al read about the speed of light, a funny thing happened. Al had read about the speed of light before. And he had found it very dull. But when he read about it now, it was very interesting.

• Why was it interesting now? (Call on a student. Ideas: *Because he had experienced it; he had traveled as fast as the speed of light.*) ⒹⒾ

Another funny thing happened later in the day. The teacher ❀ was talking about sound. She asked the class, "Why do you think it is quiet in a jet plane that is traveling 900 miles per hour?"

• What's the answer? (Call on a student. Idea: *Because the engines are behind the people on the plane and the jet is traveling faster than the sound of the engines.*) ⒶⓅⓀ

Al raised his hand to answer the question. Everybody looked at him because Al never raised his hand in school and never answered questions. The teacher called on Al. He said, "It's quiet in a jet because the engines are behind the people in the plane. And the jet is going faster than the sound of the engines. The sound of the engines is traveling a mile every five seconds. But the jet is traveling faster than that."

The teacher looked at Al and blinked. Then she smiled and nodded her head. "That's right, Al," she said.

The other kids were staring at Al with open mouths. For some reason, Al didn't feel embarrassed. He smiled and felt pretty good.

- Why did he feel pretty good? (Call on a student. Ideas: *Because he knew the answer so well; because he was smart.*) DCE

After school Al started to look for the old man's store. He went down one street and then down another. He didn't remember where the store was. ⭐ Al walked and walked. But he didn't see the store with the sign in the window that said, GO ANYWHERE. SEE ANYTHING.

He was just about ready to go home when he turned down a very narrow street. Al looked at the street sign on the corner. The name of the street was Anywhere Street.

Al walked down the street. Then he saw the sign in the window—GO ANYWHERE. SEE ANYTHING. He ran up to the store. He hesitated and then opened the door. A little bell rang—ding, ding. Al closed the door behind him and stood there in the dark. Everything was very quiet. Then he heard a voice. "I see you have come back to pay for your trip."

- Everybody, whose voice is that? (Signal.) *The old man's.* ND
- Read the rest of the story to yourself and be ready to answer some questions. Raise your hand when you're finished.

Suddenly, the old man's face moved out of the darkness. The old man said, "I will ask you one question. If you answer it, you pass the test. And by passing the test, you pay for your last trip."

Al said, "I'm ready."

The old man said, "Here is the question. What does it mean to go fast?"

Al thought and thought. Then he said, "Maybe I won't give you the right answer. But I don't know what fast means. When we were going in the racing car, it felt like we were going so fast I couldn't stand it. But when we were traveling in space, it didn't feel like we were going fast at all." Al looked at the old man's face. The old man's expression was serious. Maybe Al's answer was wrong.

Al decided to explain what he meant. He continued, "Light travels 186 thousand miles every second. But at the speed of light it would take us millions of years to reach the galaxy we saw. So light isn't very fast at all. And so I don't know what it means to say that something is fast."

The old man's face looked very cold. Then the old man smiled and said, "You are a smart boy. You are a thinking boy. You have passed your test. You have paid for your trip."

The old man bent over so that his face was very close to Al's face. "And where do you want to go for your next trip? Go anywhere. See anything."

Al thought back to the things that his class had been studying. One thing was matter. His teacher had told the class that all things are made of matter and that there are three forms of matter. But Al didn't understand the three forms of matter.

Al looked at the old man and said, "I would like to find out about matter."

- (After all students have raised their hand:) Everybody, did Al pass the test? (Signal.) *Yes.* ND

- For the test, the old man asked one question. What was the question? (Call on a student.) *What does it mean to go fast?* (ND)
- Everybody, did Al say he knew what it meant to go fast? (Signal.) *No.* (ND)
- What did he want to find out about for his next trip? (Signal.) *Matter.* (ND)
- His teacher had told him that all things are made up of matter and that there are different forms of matter. Everybody, how many forms are there? (Signal.) *Three.* (ND)
- Did Al understand the three forms of matter? (Signal.) *No.* (ND)

EXERCISE 5

Paired Practice

You're going to read aloud to your partner. The **A** members will read first. Then the **B** members will read from the star to the end of the story. (Observe students and give feedback.)

End-of-Lesson Activities

INDEPENDENT WORK

Now finish your independent work for lesson 104. Raise your hand when you're finished. (Observe students and give feedback.)

WORKCHECK

a. (Direct students to take out their marking pencils.)
- We're going to check your workbook and textbook items. Remember, if you got an item wrong, make an **X** next to the item.
b. (For each item: Read the item. Call on a student to answer it. If the answer is wrong, say the correct answer. Refer to the Answer Key for the correct answers.)
c. Now use your marking pencil to fix up any items you got wrong. Remember, all mistakes must be fixed up before you hand in your work.

SPELLING

(Present Spelling lesson 104 after completing Reading lesson 104. See *Spelling Presentation Book.*)

EXERCISE 1

Vocabulary Review

a. You learned a sentence that tells what he saw at midnight.
- Everybody, say that sentence. Get ready. (Signal.) *At midnight, he saw a familiar galaxy.*
- (Repeat until firm.)

b. I'll say part of the sentence. When I stop, you say the next word. Listen: At midnight, he saw a . . . Everybody, what's the next word? (Signal.) *Familiar.*

c. Listen: At . . . Everybody, what's the next word? (Signal.) *Midnight.*
- Say the whole sentence. Get ready. (Signal.) *At midnight, he saw a familiar galaxy.*

d. Listen: At midnight he saw a familiar . . . Everybody, what's the next word? (Signal.) *Galaxy.*

EXERCISE 2

Reading Words

a. **Find lesson 105 in your textbook.** ✔
- Touch word 1. ✔
- (Teacher reference:)

1. molecule	4. billion
2. crystal	5. frying
3. burner	

b. Word 1 is **molecule.** What word? (Signal.) *Molecule.*
- Spell **molecule.** Get ready. (Tap for each letter.) M-O-L-E-C-U-L-E.

c. Word 2 is **crystal.** What word? (Signal.) *Crystal.*
- Spell **crystal.** Get ready. (Tap for each letter.) C-R-Y-S-T-A-L.

d. Word 3. What word? (Signal.) *Burner.*
- Spell **burner.** Get ready. (Tap for each letter.) B-U-R-N-E-R.

e. Word 4. What word? (Signal.) *Billion.*
- Spell **billion.** Get ready. (Tap for each letter.) B-I-L-L-I-O-N.

f. Word 5. What word? (Signal.) *Frying.*

g. Lets read those words again.
- Word 1. What word? (Signal.) *Molecule.*
- (Repeat for words 2–5.)
h. (Repeat step g until firm.)

EXERCISE 3

Story Reading

a. Find part B in your textbook. ✔
- The error limit for group reading is 11 errors. Read carefully.
b. Everybody, touch the title. ✔
- (Call on a student to read the title.) *[Al Learns About Matter.]*
- Everybody, what's the title? (Signal.) *Al Learns About Matter.* ⓃⒹ
- (Call on individual students to read the story, each student reading two or three sentences at a time. Ask the specified questions as the students read.)

- (**Correct errors:** Tell the word. Direct the student to reread the sentence.)
- (If the group makes more than 11 errors, direct the students to reread the story.)

Al Learns About Matter

Al had just told the old man that he would like to find out about matter.

"Matter?" the old man asked. "It is all around you. I am matter. You are matter. The air is matter. Everything is matter."

Suddenly, Al noticed a large frying pan in the middle of the floor. The old man said, "Here's the rule about the three forms of matter. When an object is hard, it is matter in the solid form. When the object gets hot enough, it changes into the liquid form of matter. When it gets much hotter, it changes into the gas form of matter. Remember: solid, liquid and gas."

- I'll read that part again and then ask some questions.

  The old man said, "Here's the rule about the three forms of matter. When an object is hard, it is matter in the solid form. When the object gets hot enough, it changes into the liquid form of matter. When it gets much hotter, it changes into the gas form of matter. Remember: solid, liquid, and gas."

- Everybody, how many forms of matter are there? (Signal.) *Three.* (ND)
- When things are hard, they are matter in which form? (Signal.) *Solid.* (ND)
- When they get hotter, which form of matter do they change into next? (Signal.) *Liquid.* (ND)
- When they get still hotter, which form of matter do they change into? (Signal.) *Gas.* (ND)
- Listen: Solid, liquid, gas.
- Everybody, say the three forms. Get Ready. (Signal.) *Solid, liquid, gas.* (RF/R)
- (Repeat until firm.)

  The old man pointed to the frying pan. "What form of matter is that frying pan?"

  "It's solid," Al replied.

  "Watch what happens to it when it gets hotter," the old man said.

- Everybody, what form of matter was the frying pan? (Signal.) *Solid.* (ND)
- What's going to happen first to that pan when it gets hotter? (Call on a student. Idea: *It will change to liquid.*) (P)
- Then what's going to happen to it when it gets even hotter? (Call on a student. Idea: *It will change to gas.*) (P)

  Al watched. He noticed that the frying pan was starting to glow. He could feel the heat from it.

  At first the glow was a very dull red color. Then the color became brighter and brighter. Soon the frying pan was glowing like the burner on a hot, hot stove.

- What is the color of a burner on a hot stove when it glows? (Call on a student. Ideas: *Red; orange.*)

  "It's still getting hotter," the old man said.

  The frying pan started to turn bright orange. Then bright yellow. Soon it was brighter than a light bulb and the whole room was bright with the light from the frying pan. As Al observed the frying pan, he noticed that it was starting to melt. Al could hardly believe what he saw. He said, "It's melting."

- Everybody, so what form of matter is it changing into now? (Signal.) *Liquid.* (ND)

  The old man said, "That frying pan is matter. And it's changing from the solid form of matter to the liquid form."

  The bright glowing liquid melted into a puddle that was now turning white hot. Suddenly, Al noticed that the puddle was getting smaller and smaller. And Al could see a bright cloud forming in the air.

- It's changing into another form of matter. Everybody, what form is that? (Signal.) *Gas.* (ND)
- Why is the puddle getting smaller? (Call on a student. Ideas: *Because the liquid is turning into gas; it's going into the air.*) (DC)
- What's the bright cloud that is forming in the air? (Call on a student. Idea: *The gas form of the frying pan.*) (DI)

  The old man said, "You have seen the solid form of the frying pan and the liquid form. Now the matter is changing into the hottest form—gas. The gas is going into the air around us. The gas is that cloud that you see."

  Soon, the puddle had disappeared, and the room was filled with an amazingly bright light.

  The old man said, "The metal is now as hot as the outside of the sun. The metal turned into a gas."

  The gas was so bright that Al could hardly look at it. He remembered the great ⭐ flames that he had seen shooting up from the surface of the sun. Then he realized that those great flames were matter in the gas form.

Al started to say, "The sun is . . ." Before he could finish, he noticed that he was no longer in the store. He was floating in space. The sky all around him was black. In front of him was the sun.

The old man said, "Yes, the sun is matter in the gas form. We are going to fly inside the sun this time."

They flew through the great flames on the surface of the sun. Soon they were inside the sun. Bright gas was all around them. The whole inside of the sun was nothing but bright, bright gas.

- The old man must have magic powers because Al and the old man would become so hot inside the sun that they would disappear and turn into gas.

The old man held up a rock. "What form of matter is this rock?" he asked.

Al replied.

- Everybody, what did Al say? (Signal.) *Solid.* (DC)
- Read the rest of the story to yourself and be ready to answer some questions. Raise your hand when you're finished.

The old man said, "I will show you how hot it is inside the sun. Watch what happens to this rock when I let go of it."

The old man let go of the rock. In an instant, the rock disappeared. It did not burn or melt. It simply disappeared.

"What happened to it?" Al asked.

The old man said, "It turned into gas. The inside of the sun is so hot that it would turn anything into the gas form of matter."

The old man told Al, "You have seen matter change from solid, to liquid, to gas. Now you will see matter going the other way."

Suddenly, Al and the old man were no longer inside the sun. They were standing in a field on Earth. The old man was holding a huge bottle that had no cap on it.

"What's inside this bottle?" the old man asked.

"Nothing," Al replied.

"Wrong," the old man said. "There is air inside this bottle. And air is matter in its hottest form."

"But it's not hot here," Al said.

"For air, it's hot," the old man replied. "Air is matter in the gas form. If we make this air cooler, it will change. First it will go into the liquid form of matter. Then it will go into the solid form."

The old man put a cap on the huge bottle.

"But it's not hot here," Al said. "And . . ."

Before Al could continue, he noticed that he and the old man were in space again. Ahead of them was a large planet that had huge rings around it. The old man was holding the bottle.

- (After all students have raised their hand:) Where did Al and the old man go right after they left the sun? (Call on a student. Idea: *To a field on Earth.*) (ND)
- What was the old man holding? (Call on a student. Idea: *A huge bottle.*) (ND)
- Everybody, Al didn't think that anything was inside the bottle. But what was in the bottle? (Signal.) *Air.* (ND)
- In which form of matter is air? (Signal.) *Gas.* (ND)
- What first happens to air if you make it cold enough? (Call on a student. Idea: *It turns into liquid.*) (ND)
- And what would happen to the liquid air if you made it still colder? (Call on a student. Idea: *It would turn into solid air.*) (ND)
- Why didn't Al think that the air was in its hottest form? (Call on a student. Idea: *Because it wasn't hot.*) (ND)
- Before Al could ask any more questions, where were Al and the old man? (Call on a student. Idea: *In space.*) (ND)

- Does anyone know the name of the planet they were approaching? (Call on a student.) *Saturn.* Ⓓⓘ

EXERCISE 4
Fact Review

a. Let's review some facts you have learned. First we'll go over the facts together. Then I'll call on individual students to do some facts.

b. Everyone, tell me how long it takes light to travel from the sun to Earth. (Pause.) Get ready. (Signal.) *8 minutes.* ⓇⒻ/Ⓡ
- Tell me how far light travels in one second. (Pause.) Get ready. (Signal.) *186 thousand miles.* ⓇⒻ/Ⓡ
- Tell me how long it takes sound to travel one mile. (Pause.) Get ready. (Signal.) *5 seconds.* ⓇⒻ/Ⓡ
- (Repeat step b until firm.)

c. Tell me how many forms of matter there are. (Pause.) Get ready. (Signal.) *Three.* ⓇⒻ/Ⓡ
- Name the coldest form of matter. (Pause.) Get ready. (Signal.) *Solid.* ⓇⒻ/Ⓡ
- Name the hottest form. (Pause.) Get ready. (Signal.) *Gas.* ⓇⒻ/Ⓡ
- (Repeat step c until firm.)

Individual Turns
- Now I'm going to call on individual students to do some facts.
- (Call on individual students to do the set of facts in step b or step c.)

EXERCISE 5
Fluency: Rate/Accuracy

Note: There is a fluency checkout in this lesson; therefore, there is no paired practice.

a. Today is a reading checkout day. While you're doing your independent work, I'm going to call on you one at a time to read part of the story from lesson 104.
- Remember, you pass the checkout by reading the passage in less than a minute without making more than 2 mistakes. And when you pass the checkout, you'll color the space for lesson 105 on your thermometer chart.

b. (Call on individual students to read the portion of story 104 with ✿.)
- (Time the student. Note words that are missed and number of words read.)
- (Teacher reference:)

> ✿ Al ate dinner with Angela and his mother. He watched television after dinner. Then he went to bed, but he had trouble going to sleep. He kept thinking about that strange store and that old man.
>
> The next morning, Al left for school very early. He wanted to see what [50] his science book said about speed. He wanted to make sure that he would pass the test and go on another trip with the old [75] man.
>
> When Al read about the speed of light, a funny thing happened. Al had read about the speed of light before. And he had [100] found it very dull. But when he read about it now, it was very interesting.
>
> Another funny thing happened later in the day. The teacher ✿ [125] was talking about sound.

- (If the student reads the passage in one minute or less and makes no more than 2 errors, direct the student to color in the space for lesson 105 on the thermometer chart.)

- (If the student makes any mistakes, point to each word that was misread and identify it.)
- (If the student does not meet the rate-error criterion for the passage, direct the student to practice reading the story with the assigned partner.)

End-of-Lesson Activities

INDEPENDENT WORK

Now finish your independent work for lesson 105. Raise your hand when you're finished. (Observe students and give feedback.)

WORKCHECK

a. (Direct students to take out their marking pencils.)

• We're going to check your workbook and textbook items. Remember, if you got an item wrong, make an **X** next to the item.

b. (For each item: Read the item. Call on a student to answer it. If the answer is wrong, say the correct answer. Refer to the Answer Key for the correct answers.)

c. Now use your marking pencil to fix up any items you got wrong. Remember, all mistakes must be fixed up before you hand in your work.

Note: A special project occurs after lesson 106. See page 182 for the materials you'll need.

SPELLING

(Present Spelling lesson 105 after completing Reading lesson 105. See *Spelling Presentation Book.*)

ACTIVITIES

(Present Activity 22 after completing Reading lesson 105. See *Activities across the Curriculum*.)

Lessons 106–110 • Planning Page   *Looking Ahead*

	Lesson 106	Lesson 107	Lesson 108	Lesson 109	Lesson 110
LESSON EVENTS	**Vocabulary Sentence** Reading Words Story Reading Paired Practice Independent Work Workcheck Spelling	Fact Review Vocabulary Sentence Reading Words Story Reading Paired Practice Independent Work Workcheck Spelling	Vocabulary Sentences Reading Words Story Reading Paired Practice Independent Work Workcheck Spelling	Vocabulary Sentences Reading Words Story Reading Paired Practice Independent Work Workcheck Spelling	Fact Game Fluency: Rate/ Accuracy Test Marking the Test Test Remedies Spelling
VOCABULARY SENTENCE	**#26: The crystal contained more than a billion molecules.**	#26: The crystal contained more than a billion molecules.	sentence #24 sentence #25 sentence #26	#26: The crystal contained more than a billion molecules.	
READING WORDS: WORD TYPES	modeled words	words with parts	modeled words	multi-syllable words	
NEW VOCABULARY	iron	relax		vibrate	
STORY BACKGROUND					
STORY	*Al Visits Saturn and Pluto*	*Al Takes a Test on Matter*	*Al Takes Another Test*	*Al Learns About Molecules*	
SKILL ITEMS	Sequencing		Vocabulary sentence Crossword puzzle	Vocabulary sentences	Test: Vocabulary sentences
SPECIAL MATERIALS	*materials for project				Thermometer charts, dice, Fact Game 110, Fact Game Answer Key, scorecard sheets
SPECIAL PROJECTS/ ACTIVITIES	Project after lesson 106				

*Reference materials (books on the solar system, encyclopedias, CD-ROMs) and poster-making supplies (butcher paper or poster board, markers, crayons, paints, scissors, paste, magazines for pictures).

Comprehension Questions Abbreviations Guide

Access Prior Knowledge = (APK)   Author's Point of View = (APoV)   Author's Purpose = (AP)   Cause/Effect = (C/E)   Charts/Graphs/Diagrams/Visual Aids = (VA)

Classify and Categorize = (C+C)   Compare/Contrast = (C/C)   Determine Character Emotions, Motivation = (DCE)   Drawing Conclusions = (DC)   Drawing Inferences = (DI)

Fact and Opinion = (F/O)   Hypothesizing = (H)   Main Idea = (MI)   Making Connections = (MC)   Making Deductions = (MD)   Making Judgements = (MJ)

Narrative Elements = (NE)   Noting Details = (ND)   Predict = (P)   Reality/Fantasy = (R/F)   Recall Facts/Rules = (RF/R)   Retell = (R)   Sequence = (Seq)

Steps in a Process = (SP)   Story Structure = (SS)   Summarize = (Sum)   Understanding Dialogue = (UD)   Using Context to Confirm Meaning(s) = (UCCM)   Visualize = (V)

EXERCISE 1

Vocabulary

a. **Find page 367 in your textbook.** ✔
- Touch sentence 26. ✔
- This is a new vocabulary sentence. It says: The crystal contained more than a billion molecules. Everybody, read that sentence. Get ready. (Signal.) *The crystal contained more than a billion molecules.*
- Close your eyes and say the sentence. Get ready. (Signal.) *The crystal contained more than a billion molecules.*
- (Repeat until firm.)

b. A crystal is a shiny material that has flat sides and sharp edges. Some rocks form crystals. Everybody, what's the name for a shiny material that has flat sides and sharp edges? (Signal.) *Crystal.*

c. The sentence says the crystal contained more than a **billion** molecules. A billion is a thousand millions. That's a lot of millions. Everybody, what word means **a thousand millions?** (Signal.) *Billion.*

d. Molecules are the smallest parts of a material. The smallest part of salt is a salt molecule. Molecules are so small that there are millions of salt molecules in a grain of salt. Everybody, what word means **the smallest parts of a material?** (Signal.) *Molecules.*

e. Listen to the sentence again: The crystal contained more than a billion molecules. Everybody, say the sentence. Get ready. (Signal.) *The crystal contained more than a billion molecules.*

f. Everybody, what word means **a thousand millions?** (Signal.) *Billion.*
- What word names a shiny material that has flat sides and sharp edges? (Signal.) *Crystal.*
- What word means **the smallest parts of a material?** (Signal.) *Molecules.*
- (Repeat step f until firm.)

EXERCISE 2

Reading Words

a. Find lesson 106 in your textbook. ✔
- Touch word 1. ✔
- (Teacher reference:)

1. iron	**4. billion**
2. control	**5. crystals**
3. molecule	**6. relax**

b. Word 1 is **iron.** What word? (Signal.) *Iron.*
- Spell **iron.** Get ready. (Tap for each letter.) *I-R-O-N.*
- Iron is a heavy metal that magnets stick to.

c. Word 2 is **control.** What word? (Signal.) *Control.*
- Spell **control.** Get ready. (Tap for each letter.) *C-O-N-T-R-O-L.*

d. Word 3. What word? (Signal.) *Molecule.*
- Spell **molecule.** Get ready. (Tap for each letter.) *M-O-L-E-C-U-L-E.*

e. Word 4. What word? (Signal.) *Billion.*
- Spell **billion.** Get ready. (Tap for each letter.) *B-I-L-L-I-O-N.*

f. Word 5. What word? (Signal.) *Crystals.*

g. Word 6. What word? (Signal.) *Relax.*

h. Let's read those words again.
- Word 1. What word? (Signal.) *Iron.*
- (Repeat for words 2–6.)

i. (Repeat step h until firm.)

EXERCISE 3

Story Reading

a. Find part B in your textbook. ✔
- The error limit for group reading is 11 errors. Read carefully.

b. Everybody, touch the title. ✔
- (Call on a student to read the title.) *[Al Visits Saturn and Pluto.]*
- Everybody, what's the title? (Signal.) *Al Visits Saturn and Pluto.* (ND)
- (Call on individual students to read the story, each student reading two or three sentences at a time. Ask the specified questions as the students read.)

- (**Correct errors:** Tell the word. Direct the student to reread the sentence.)
- (If the group makes more than 11 errors, direct the students to reread the story.)

Al Visits Saturn and Pluto

The old man and Al were approaching the planet Saturn. The old man was carrying a bottle of air.

- Everybody, what planet were they approaching? (Signal.) *Saturn.* (ND)
- Where did they get the air that's inside the bottle? (Call on a student. Idea: *From Earth.*) (APK)

The old man said, "Saturn is very far from the sun. So this planet is very cold. We'll go to the side of the planet that is not facing the sun. There it is over 200 degrees below zero."

- How cold is it on that side of Saturn? (Call on a student. Idea: *Over 200 degrees below zero.*) (ND)

The old man held up the bottle. "Watch," he said. "The air inside this bottle will now become the same temperature as the surface of Saturn."

A puddle started to form in the bottom of the bottle. The puddle was clear, like water. "What's that?" Al asked.

The old man said, "Part of the air has turned into a liquid. Air is made up of different gases. One of those gases is now a liquid."

Al said, "Would that liquid turn into a solid if it got colder?"

- Everybody, what's the answer? (Signal.) *Yes.* (RF/R)

"Yes," the old man said. "If we took this liquid to the planet Pluto, the liquid would turn into a solid."

"Can we go there?" Al asked.

The old man smiled, and suddenly Al noticed that he and the old man were flying toward a small planet. "That's Pluto," the old man said. "It is much farther from the sun than Saturn. From Pluto the sun doesn't give off any more light or heat than a very large star would."

Al and the old man landed on Pluto. Al watched the liquid in the bottle, which slowly began to freeze. It turned into a hard lump that looked like ice.

- Everybody, where is it colder, on Saturn or on Pluto? (Signal.) *On Pluto.* (ND)
- Why is it colder on Pluto than it is on Saturn? (Call on a student. Idea: *Because Pluto is farther from the sun.*) (ND)
- Everybody, what form of matter did the air become on Saturn? (Signal.) *Liquid.* (ND)
- What form of matter did it become on Pluto? (Signal.) *Solid.* (ND)

"Now the air is a solid," the old man said.

He opened the bottle, turned it over, and the lump of solid air fell to the surface of Pluto. Al looked at that surface. It looked just like the solid air. It was shiny and hard, like ice. "What is this stuff we're standing on?" Al asked.

The old man said, "Frozen gases. All of the gases on Pluto are frozen. They cover the surface of this planet."

"Wow!" Al said. As he studied the surface, things seemed to get darker and darker. Al suddenly realized that he was standing on a floor, not on the planet Pluto. He looked around and noticed that he was back in the old man's store.

The old man was saying, ⭐ "You have learned a lot about matter. Remember everything you have seen. Remember that everything is made up of matter. And matter comes in three forms. You can change matter from one form to another form by making the matter hotter or colder."

Al said, "We saw a lot of things. I just hope I can remember everything."

The old man said, "If you want to understand matter, think about water. Water is a liquid. But what happens to the liquid when you make it cold enough?"

Al said, "It turns into ice."

"Yes," the old man said. "It turns into a solid. And what happens to water if you get it hot enough?"

Al said, "It turns into steam."

"That's right," the old man said. "That steam is water in the gas form. All matter is like water. It changes from a solid to a liquid to a gas. Even the gases in the sun will turn into solid matter if you make them cold enough."

- Everybody, what do we call the coldest form of water? (Signal.) *Ice.* ⓝⓓ
- What do we call the hottest form of water? (Signal.) *Steam.* ⓝⓓ
- When water turns to ice, which form of matter is it? (Signal.) *Solid.* ⓓⒸ
- When it is water, which form of matter is it? (Signal.) *Liquid.* ⓓⒸ
- When it turns into steam, which form of matter is it? (Signal.) *Gas.* ⓓⒸ
- Read the rest of the story to yourself and be ready to answer some questions. Raise your hand when you're finished.

The old man bent over so that his face was close to Al's face. "Think about what you have seen on this trip. Think about the sun. Think about Saturn. Think about Pluto. And think about matter. Remember—you must pass a test on what you have seen. If you fail the test, I will never take you on another trip."

Suddenly, the old man was gone.

Al was standing alone in the dark store. He opened the door and went outside. The bell went ding, ding. There were no cars and no other people on Anywhere Street.

As Al walked slowly down the street, he thought about what he had just seen. He looked at the sidewalk and he thought, "That sidewalk would turn into liquid if it got hot enough. And that sidewalk would turn into gas if it got even hotter."

Al turned the corner and left Anywhere Street. He looked at cars and at buildings, and he realized that everything he looked at was matter. For the first time, Al knew what matter was. And he knew what the teacher meant when she had said that all matter has three forms.

Suddenly Al realized that he was very smart. That made him feel excited. "Wow!" he said, and laughed out loud. Then he started to run home.

- (After all students have raised their hand:) What was strange about Anywhere Street? (Call on a student. Idea: *There were no people or cars.*) ⒶⓅⓀ
- As Al walked home, he looked at the sidewalk and realized something about it. What did he realize? (Call on a student. Idea: *The sidewalk could turn into liquid and then gas if it got hot enough.*) ⓝⓓ
- Name some other things that Al recognized as matter in the solid form. (Call on a student. Idea: *Cars and buildings.*) ⓝⓓ
- How did Al feel about himself when he realized that he understood matter? (Call on a student. Idea: *He felt very smart.*) ⓝⓓ

EXERCISE 4

Paired Practice

You're going to read aloud to your partner. The **B** members will read first. Then the **A** members will read from the star to the end of the story. (Observe students and give feedback.)

End-of-Lesson Activities

INDEPENDENT WORK

Now finish your independent work for lesson 106. Raise your hand when you're finished. (Observe students and give feedback.)

a. (Direct students to take out their marking pencils.)

• We're going to check your workbook and textbook items. Remember, if you got an item wrong, make an **X** next to the item.

b. (For each item: Read the item. Call on a student to answer it. If the answer is wrong, say the correct answer. Refer to the Answer Key for the correct answers.)

c. Now use your marking pencil to fix up any items you got wrong. Remember, all mistakes must be fixed up before you hand in your work.

SPELLING

(Present Spelling lesson 106 after completing Reading lesson 106. See *Spelling Presentation Book.*)

Special Project

Note: After completing lesson 106, do this special project with the students. You may do this project during another part of the school day.

Materials: Reference materials (books on the solar system, encyclopedias, CD-ROMs) and poster-making supplies (butcher paper or poster board, markers, crayons, paints, scissors, paste, magazines for pictures)

a. Find page 180 in your textbook. ✔
• (Call on individual students to read two or three sentences.)
• (Teacher reference:)

Special Project

The story you have read tells about Saturn and Pluto. You have made a chart that shows the planets from Mercury through Jupiter. Add Saturn, Pluto, and the other two planets—Uranus and Neptune—to your chart. Find out the facts about these planets and write them on the chart.

b. (Divide the group into subgroups, each of which is responsible for finding out information about one or two planets. Use encyclopedias [such as *World Book*] to get information that answers the five questions about each planet: Saturn, Uranus, Neptune, Pluto. Write the five questions from textbook A page 331 on the board:)
• How big is the planet?
• How many hours does it take to turn around? (How long is a day on that planet?)
• How long does it take to circle the sun?
• How many moons does it have?
• How far from the sun is it?
c. (Help each group find the information needed for the chart. Then direct the groups to add the information to the chart.)

EXERCISE 1

Fact Review

a. Let's review some facts you have learned.

b. Everybody, tell me which form of matter air is on Earth. (Pause.) Get ready. (Signal.) *Gas.* (RF/R)

- Tell me which form of matter air is on Pluto. (Pause.) Get ready. (Signal.) *Solid.* (RF/R)
- Tell me which form of matter air is on Saturn. (Pause.) Get ready. (Signal.) *Liquid.* (RF/R)
- (Repeat step b until firm.)

c. Tell me what form of matter ice is. (Pause.) Get ready. (Signal.) *Solid.* (RF/R)

- Tell me what form of matter ice becomes when it melts. (Pause.) Get ready. (Signal.) *Liquid.* (RF/R)
- Tell me what form of matter water becomes when it's heated enough. (Pause.) Get ready. (Signal.) *Gas.* (RF/R)
- Tell me what we call water in the gas form. (Pause.) Get ready. (Signal.) *Steam.* (RF/R)
- (Repeat step c until firm.)

d. Tell me which has stronger gravity, Jupiter or Io. (Pause.) Get ready. (Signal.) *Jupiter.* (RF/R)

- Tell me which place is smaller than Earth, Jupiter or Io? (Pause.) Get ready. (Signal.) *Io.* (RF/R)
- Tell me where you could jump 8 feet high, on Jupiter or Io. (Pause.) Get ready. (Signal.) *Io.* (RF/R)
- Tell me about how long it takes Io to go all the way around Jupiter. (Pause.) Get ready. (Signal.) *2 days.* (RF/R)
- (Repeat step d until firm.)

e. Tell me how long it takes light to travel from the sun to Earth. (Pause.) Get ready. (Signal.) *8 minutes.* (RF/R)

- Tell me how far light travels in one second. (Pause.) Get ready. (Signal.) *186 thousand miles.* (RF/R)
- Tell me what a cloud of stars is called. (Pause.) Get ready. (Signal.) *Galaxy.* (RF/R)
- Tell me how many planets are in the solar system. (Pause.) Get ready. (Signal.) *9.* (RF/R)
- (Repeat step e until firm.)

f. Name the planets in the solar system, starting with the planet closest to the sun. Get ready. (Tap for each name.) *Mercury, Venus, Earth, Mars, Jupiter, Saturn, Uranus, Neptune, Pluto.* (RF/R)

- (Repeat step f until firm.)

Individual Turns

- Now I'm going to call on individual students to do some facts.
- (Call on individual students to do the facts in step b, c, d, e, or f.)

EXERCISE 2

Vocabulary Review

a. Here's the new vocabulary sentence: The crystal contained billions of molecules.

- Everybody, say the sentence. Get ready. (Signal.) *The crystal contained billions of molecules.*
- (Repeat until firm.)

b. What word means **the smallest parts of a material?** (Signal.) *Molecules.*

- What word names a shiny material that has flat sides and sharp edges? (Signal.) *Crystal.*
- What word means **a thousand millions?** (Signal.) *Billion.*

EXERCISE 3

Reading Words

Column 1

a. **Find lesson 107 in your textbook.** ✔

- Touch column 1. ✔
- (Teacher reference:)

1. **re**lax	4. **start**ed
2. **pop**corn	5. **star**ed
3. **door**knob	6. **con**trol

- All these words have more than one part. The first part of each word is underlined.

b. Word 1. What's the underlined part? (Signal.) *re.*

- What's the whole word? (Signal.) *Relax.*
- Spell **relax.** Get ready. (Tap for each letter.) *R-E-L-A-X.*

- When you relax, you take it easy. Everybody, what's another way of saying **They took it easy in the backyard?** (Signal.) *They relaxed in the backyard.*
- What's another way of saying **I will take it easy this weekend?** (Signal.) *I will relax this weekend.*
  c. Word 2. What's the underlined part? (Signal.) *pop.*
- What's the whole word? (Signal.) *Popcorn.*
- Spell **popcorn.** Get ready. (Tap for each letter.) P-O-P-C-O-R-N.
  d. Word 3. What's the underlined part? (Signal.) *door.*
- What's the whole word? (Signal.) *Doorknob.*
- Spell **doorknob.** Get ready. (Tap for each letter.) D-O-O-R-K-N-O-B.
  e. Word 4. What's the underlined part? (Signal.) *start.*
- What's the whole word? (Signal.) *Started.*
  f. Word 5. What's the underlined part? (Signal.) *stare.*
- What's the whole word? (Signal.) *Stared.*
  g. Word 6. What's the underlined part? (Signal.) *con.*
- What's the whole word? (Signal.) *Control.*
  h. Let's read those words again.
- Word 1. What word? (Signal.) *Relax.*
- (Repeat for: **2. popcorn, 3. doorknob, 4. started, 5. stared, 6. control.**)
  i. (Repeat step h until firm.)

Story Reading

a. Find part B in your textbook. ✔
- The error limit for group reading is 12 errors. Read carefully.
b. Everybody, touch the title. ✔
- (Call on a student to read the title.) *[Al Takes a Test on Matter.]*
- Everybody, what's the title? (Signal.) *Al Takes a Test on Matter.* (ND)
- (Call on individual students to read the story, each student reading two or three sentences at a time. Ask specified questions as the students read.)

- (**Correct errors:** Tell the word. Direct the student to reread the sentence.)
- (If the group makes more than 12 errors, direct the students to reread the story.)

Al Takes a Test on Matter

When Al got home, it was supper time. Al's mother asked him where he'd been, but he was embarrassed about telling her. She wouldn't have believed that he'd gone to Saturn and Pluto.

After supper, Al played ball with his sister on the sidewalk. After they had played for about an hour, they went inside. Angela said, "There's a good movie on TV, about World War Two. Why don't we watch it?"

Al hesitated. Angela continued, "I'll fix some popcorn and we'll relax and watch the movie."

Al agreed. The movie was very good, but it lasted until nearly midnight.

When the movie was over, Al was so tired that he didn't spend any time thinking about the things he had seen on his trip with the old man.

- What's going to happen to Al if he's not careful? (Call on a student. Ideas: *He won't pass the old man's test; he won't be able to go on any more trips.*) Ⓟ

The next morning, Al was still so tired that he couldn't think about his trip. Shortly before lunch, he became so tired that he fell asleep in school.

After school Al went back to Anywhere Street, walked up to the old man's store and opened the door. Ding, ding, went the bell. The inside of the store was very quiet and very dark. Al stood in the dark for a long time.

Suddenly, the old man appeared and said, "Now you must pay for the trip by taking a test. Are you ready?"

"Yes," Al said.

- Everybody, is he really ready? (Signal.) *No.* (MJ)

- What would he have had to do to be ready for the test? (Call on a student. Ideas: *Thought about what he had learned; gone to bed early.*) (DI)
- Name some things he did the night before instead of getting ready for the test. (Call on a student. Ideas: *He stayed up too late; he played ball with Angela; he watched a movie.*) (ND)

"Remember," the old man said, "if you don't pass the test, I will not take you on any more trips."

Al nodded and tried to make his mind start to work.

The old man said, "Which form of matter is the hottest form? Which form of matter is the coldest form?"

- What are the answers to those questions? (Call on a student. Idea: *The hottest form is gas and the coldest form is solid.*) (RF/R)

Al thought, but he couldn't seem to control his mind. Finally he said, "I don't know." Al looked down for a moment. When he looked up, the old man was gone, and Al was all alone in the dark store.

Al spoke to the dark store. "I'm— I'm sorry. I don't know the answer. But . . ."

Nobody replied. Al listened, but he did not hear anything. He stared into the darkness but there was no sign of the old man. Finally, Al walked outside. Ding, ding, the bell went, and the door closed behind him. As Al started down Anywhere Street, he glanced back at the window of the store. There was no sign that said, GO ANYWHERE. SEE ANYTHING. Instead there was another sign in the window, which said, STORE FOR SALE.

"What's happening?" Al asked aloud. He walked back to the door and tried to open it, but the door was locked.

Al walked home very slowly, realizing that he would never be able to go on another trip with the old

man. He started to think of the places the ⭐ old man could have taken him. Al wanted to swim in the ocean with whales and go inside a volcano and learn how plants grow. But he had not passed the test, so he had not paid for his last trip.

As Al approached his house, he started to get an idea. After dinner, Al asked his mother, "Do we have a science book that tells about matter?"

- What do you think Al's plan is? (Call on a student. Idea: *To study about matter.*) (DI)

His mother said, "What would we do with a book about matter?"

Al said, "I've got to get a book that tells about matter. Do you have any idea where I can get one?"

"I don't know," his mother said. Then she added, "Wait a minute. Go to the library."

"Where's that?" Al asked.

Angela was sitting across the room from Al. She stood up and said, "Come on. I'll show you."

- Read the rest of the story to yourself and be ready to answer some questions. Raise your hand when you're finished.

Al and his sister walked to the library, went inside and walked up to a woman behind a large counter. Angela said, "My brother wants a book that tells about matter. He wants a science book."

"Come with me," the woman said, and led the way to a wall of the library that was covered with books—rows and rows of books. She pointed to one of the rows. "These are all science books. Any one of these books will tell you about matter."

Al took one of the books and sat down at a large table where he started reading.

Angela said, "I think I'm going home. Can you find your way back?"

"Sure," Al said without looking up from the book.

When Al had finished reading the part of the book that told about matter, everything was clear to him. He knew the answer to the old man's questions. He knew that the gas form is the hottest form of matter and that the coldest form is the solid form. He knew that air turns into a solid on Pluto.

Al put the book back on the shelf and ran from the library. He ran down street after street until he came to Anywhere Street. He ran up to the old store. The sign in the window still said, STORE FOR SALE.

Al banged on the door. "Let me in," he yelled. "Let me in and I will pay for my trip."

He stopped banging and listened. No sounds came from inside the dark store. Al started to feel anxious. Again he pounded on the door. "Give me another chance," he shouted. "I'll pass any test you want to give me."

After pounding and shouting for several minutes, Al was ready to give up. Almost without thinking, he grabbed the doorknob and turned it. The door opened and the bell went ding, ding.

- (After all students have raised their hand:) Where did Al go after leaving the library? (Call on a student. Idea: *To the old man's store.*) ND
- What did Al do to try to catch the old man's attention? (Call on a student. Idea: *He banged on the door and shouted.*) ND
- Do you think the old man heard him? (Call on a student. Idea: *Yes.*) MJ
- What happened when Al turned the doorknob? (Call on a student. Idea: *The door opened and the bell went ding, ding.*) ND

- What does that mean if the store is open again? (Call on a student. Ideas: *The old man is there; Al will get to take another test.*) DI
- Everybody, was Al ready for the test now? (Signal.) *Yes.* MJ

Paired Practice

You're going to read aloud to your partner. The **A** members will read first. Then the **B** members will read from the star to the end of the story. (Observe students and give feedback.)

End-of-Lesson Activities

INDEPENDENT WORK

Now finish your independent work for lesson 107. Raise your hand when you're finished. (Observe students and give feedback.)

WORKCHECK

a. (Direct students to take out their marking pencils.)
- We're going to check your workbook and textbook items. Remember, if you got an item wrong, make an **X** next to the item.
b. (For each item: Read the item. Call on a student to answer it. If the answer is wrong, say the correct answer. Refer to the Answer Key for the correct answers.)
c. Now use your marking pencil to fix up any items you got wrong. Remember, all mistakes must be fixed up before you hand in your work.

SPELLING

(Present Spelling lesson 107 after completing Reading lesson 107. See *Spelling Presentation Book.*)

EXERCISE 1

Vocabulary Review

a. You learned a sentence that tells about visibility.

- Everybody, say that sentence. Get ready. (Signal.) *Visibility was miserable in the fierce blizzard.*
- (Repeat until firm.)

b. You learned a sentence that tells what he saw at midnight.

- Everybody, say that sentence. Get ready. (Signal.) *At midnight, he saw a familiar galaxy.*
- (Repeat until firm.)

c. Here's the last sentence you learned: The crystal contained more than a billion molecules.

- Everybody, say that sentence. Get ready. (Signal.) *The crystal contained more than a billion molecules.*
- (Repeat until firm.)

d. What word names a shiny material that has flat sides and sharp edges? (Signal.) *Crystal.*

- What word means **the smallest parts of a material?** (Signal.) *Molecules.*
- What word means **a thousand millions?** (Signal.) *Billion.*

e. Once more. Say the sentence that tells about the crystal. Get ready. (Signal.) *The crystal contained more than a billion molecules.*

EXERCISE 2

Reading Words

a. **Find lesson 108 in your textbook.** ✔

- Touch word 1. ✔
- (Teacher reference:)

1. vibrate	5. incredible
2. create	6. incredibly
3. iron	7. temperature
4. blush	

b. Word 1 is **vibrate.** What word? (Signal.) *Vibrate.*

- Spell **vibrate.** Get ready. (Tap for each letter.) *V-I-B-R-A-T-E.*

c. Word 2 is **create.** What word? (Signal.) *Create.*

- Spell **create.** Get ready. (Tap for each letter.) *C-R-E-A-T-E.*

d. Word 3. What word? (Signal.) *Iron.*

- Spell **iron.** Get ready. (Tap for each letter.) *I-R-O-N.*

e. Word 4. What word? (Signal.) *Blush.*

- Spell **blush.** Get ready. (Tap for each letter.) *B-L-U-S-H.*

f. Word 5. What word? (Signal.) *Incredible.*

- (Repeat for words 6 and 7.)

g. Let's read those words again.

- Word 1. What word? (Signal.) *Vibrate.*
- (Repeat for words 2–7.)

h. (Repeat step g until firm.)

EXERCISE 3

Story Reading

a. Find part B in your textbook. ✔

- The error limit for group reading is 13 errors. Read carefully.

b. Everybody, touch the title. ✔

- (Call on a student to read the title.) *[Al Takes Another Test.]*
- Everybody, what's the title? (Signal.) *Al Takes Another Test.* ⓃⒹ
- (Call on individual students to read the story, each student reading two or three sentences at a time. Ask the specified questions as the students read.)

- (**Correct errors:** Tell the word. Direct the student to reread the sentence.)
- (If the group makes more than 13 errors, direct the students to reread the story.)

Al Takes Another Test

Al stood inside the dark store. He said, "I want to pay for my trip."

There was no answer.

Al said, "You don't have to take me on any more trips. I just want to pay for my last trip. You took me on a trip, and I want to pay for it."

"All right," a voice said. Suddenly the old man was standing in front of Al. "I will have to give you a harder test, because you did not pay for the trip the first time."

"I'm ready," Al said. "Ask me anything about matter."

The old man said, "Here is the first question: Which is the hottest form of matter and which is the coldest form of matter?"

Al smiled and answered the question.

- What's the answer? (Call on a student. Idea: *The hottest form is gas and the coldest form is solid.*) (RF/R)

"That is right," the old man said without smiling. "Here is the next question: Do all things turn into gas at the same temperature?"

- Everybody, what's the answer? (Signal.) *No.* (RF/R)
- Name something that turns into gas only when it becomes very, very hot. (Call on a student. Ideas: *Iron; water; rocks.*) (APK)
- Name something that turns into gas at a pretty low temperature. (Call on a student. Idea: *Air.*) (APK)

Al said, "Not all things turn into gas at the same temperature. Look at this room. There is air in the room and there is glass in the window. Glass is solid but the air is gas. Yet the glass and the air are the same temperature."

The old man asked what a rock would do inside the sun. Al told him.

- What did Al say? (Call on a student. Idea: *It would turn into gas.*) (APK)

The old man asked many other questions. Al answered each question.

Finally the old man put a hand on Al's shoulder and smiled. "You have passed the test," he said. "You have paid for your trip. So I will give you another chance and take you on another trip. Where would you like to go now?"

Al said, "I had better go home right now. But can I come back tomorrow and go on a trip with you?"

- Why did Al think he should go home now? (Call on a student. Ideas: *Because it was late; so he could get enough sleep.*) (DI)
- What had Al done right after supper? (Call on a student. Idea: *Gone to the library.*) (APK)
- It took him some time to read about matter and then go to Anywhere Street, so it must be pretty late now.

"Come back tomorrow," the old man said. "We can go anywhere and see anything. And you pay for your trip by passing a test."

Al went outside. "Ding, ding," the bell sounded. Al looked at the window of the store. The sign that said STORE FOR SALE was gone and another sign was in its place.

- Everybody, what did the sign that was there now say? (Signal.) *Go anywhere. See anything.* (DI)

Al ran all the way home. Angela was sitting in the living room watching TV. She said, "Hey, they're going to have a good movie on TV. Do you want to watch it with me?"

- Everybody, what do you think Al will say? (Signal.) *No.* (P)

"No thanks," Al said. "I want to get to bed. I'm tired. And I've got a lot to do tomorrow."

The next day Al surprised the class again. The teacher was giving the class a lesson on ★ science. She said, "How do you know that air is matter? You can't see air, so how could you show that air is actually matter?"

Al raised his hand. He was the only one to raise a hand. The teacher looked surprised as she asked, "What do you think, Al?"

Al said, "Here's one way to show that air is matter. You could take a bottle of air. You put a lid on the bottle so nothing can get in the bottle and nothing can get out of the bottle. Then you start cooling the bottle. When it gets really cold, you'll see a puddle in the bottom of the bottle. That puddle is the air. That air was in the bottle all the time. It was in the gas form when you put it in the bottle. Now it is in liquid form."

- Everybody, was that a pretty good answer? (Signal.) *Yes.* (MJ)
- How did Al know all that information about air? (Call on a student. Ideas: *From his trip; from the books he read.*) (DC)

Al stopped talking. Everyone was quiet. The teacher and the other kids stared at Al without saying anything. They just stared. Al felt embarrassed.

Finally, one of the kids said, "Wow! Where did Al learn all of that stuff?"

Another kid said, "Who said Al isn't smart?"

As some of the kids began to applaud, Al could feel himself blush.

- Read the rest of the story to yourself and be ready to answer some questions. Read it carefully, because it tells about molecules. You may have to read it twice. Raise your hand when you're finished.

After school, Al went back to Anywhere Street. He opened the door to the old man's store. "Ding, ding," the bell sounded. "I'm ready to go on a trip," Al said. He didn't see anybody inside the store, but he knew the old man was there.

The old man stepped out of the darkness, smiling. "Go anywhere. See anything. Go to the center of Earth. Swim to the bottom of an ocean. Where do you want to go?"

Al thought for a moment. When Al had studied matter in the library, he had learned that all matter is made up of tiny parts called molecules. Al knew that air molecules were

different from wood molecules or glass molecules. He knew that a sugar molecule didn't look like an iron molecule or a molecule from a rock. Al wanted to know more about molecules. So he said, "Can I see molecules?"

The old man laughed. "Molecules? Look around you, my friend. You see billions and billions of molecules. Everything you see is made up of molecules. All matter is made up of molecules."

"But I can't see them," Al said. "When I look at a table, I don't see molecules. I see wood. When I look at a window, I don't see molecules. I see glass. I want to see molecules."

- (After all students have raised their hand:) Everybody, what did the old man say that all matter is made of? (Signal.) *Molecules.* (ND)
- Could Al actually see the billions of molecules that were around him? (Signal.) *No.* (ND)
- Why not? (Call on a student. Idea: *Because molecules are too small.*) (DI)
- Everybody, do sugar molecules look like iron molecules? (Signal.) *No.* (ND)
- Do you think that all sugar molecules look like each other? (Call on individual students. Student preference.) (MJ)
- All sugar molecules **do** look like each other.

EXERCISE 4

Paired Practice

You're going to read aloud to your partner. The **B** members will read first. Then the **A** members will read from the star to the end of the story. (Observe students and give feedback.)

End-of-Lesson Activities

Now finish your independent work for lesson 108. Raise your hand when you're finished. (Observe students and give feedback.)

a. (Direct students to take out their marking pencils.)

• We're going to check your workbook and textbook items. Remember, if you got an item wrong, make an **X** next to the item.

b. (For each item: Read the item. Call on a student to answer it. If the answer is wrong, say the correct answer. Refer to the Answer Key for the correct answers.)

c. Now use your marking pencil to fix up any items you got wrong. Remember, all mistakes must be fixed up before you hand in your work.

(Present Spelling lesson 108 after completing Reading lesson 108. See *Spelling Presentation Book.*)

Vocabulary Review

a. You learned a sentence that tells about the crystal.
  - Everybody, say that sentence. Get ready. (Signal.) *The crystal contained more than a billion molecules.*
  - (Repeat until firm.)
b. I'll say part of the sentence. When I stop, you say the next word. Listen: The . . . Everybody, what's the next word? (Signal.) *Crystal.*
c. Listen: The crystal contained more than a . . . Everybody, what's the next word? (Signal.) *Billion.*
  - Say the whole sentence. Get ready. (Signal.) *The crystal contained more than a billion molecules.*
d. Listen: The crystal contained more than a billion . . . Everybody, what's the next word? (Signal.) *Molecules.*

Reading Words

a. **Find lesson 109 in your textbook.** ✔
  - Touch word 1. ✔
  - (Teacher reference:)

1. vibrating	3. carefully
2. temperature	4. realized

  - All these words have more than one part. The first part of each word is underlined.
b. Word 1. What's the underlined part? (Signal.) *vi.*
  - What's the whole word? (Signal.) *Vibrating.*
  - Spell **vibrating.** Get ready. (Tap for each letter.) V-I-B-R-A-T-I-N-G.
  - When something vibrates, it moves back and forth so fast you can hardly see it move. Everybody, what are things doing when they move back and forth so fast you can hardly see them move? (Signal.) *Vibrating.*
c. Word 2. What's the underlined part? (Signal.) *temp.*
  - What's the whole word? (Signal.) *Temperature.*

d. Word 3. What's the underlined part? (Signal.) *careful.*
  - What's the whole word? (Signal.) *Carefully.*
e. Word 4. What's the underlined part? (Signal.) *real.*
  - What's the whole word? (Signal.) *Realized.*
  - Spell **realized.** Get ready. (Tap for each letter.) R-E-A-L-I-Z-E-D.
f. Let's read those words again.
  - Word 1. What word? (Signal.) *Vibrating.*
  - (Repeat for words 2–4.)
g. (Repeat step f until firm.)

Story Reading

a. Find part B in your textbook. ✔
  - The error limit for group reading is 11 errors. Read carefully.
b. Everybody, touch the title. ✔
  - (Call on a student to read the title.) *[Al Learns About Molecules.]*
  - Everybody, what's the title? (Signal.) *Al Learns About Molecules.* (ND)
  - (Call on individual students to read the story, each student reading two or three sentences at a time. Ask the specified questions as the students read.)

  - (**Correct errors:** Tell the word. Direct the student to reread the sentence.)
  - (If the group makes more than 11 errors, direct the students to reread the story.)

Al Learns About Molecules

Al had told the old man that he wanted to see molecules. The old man held out his hand. In his hand was a tiny pile of sand. The old man said, "Watch very carefully. I will put one grain of sand on the floor. We will go on a trip inside that grain of sand. Then you will be able to get a good look at molecules of sand."

The old man took a tiny grain of sand from the pile and put it on the floor. He placed the grain of sand right in front of Al's shoe.

As Al watched the grain of sand, he noticed that something strange was happening. Al realized that he was getting smaller and smaller and smaller. The old man was getting smaller, too.

Al looked up. The room had become bright. The ceiling seemed to be a mile above him. Al looked at the grain of sand in front of him. It appeared to be as big as a car.

"This way, my friend," the old man called, as he climbed to the top of the grain of sand.

Al ran toward the grain of sand. He ran past an ant, which looked as big as an elephant.

- Everybody, show me how big Al and the old man must have been if an ant looked as big as an elephant to them. ✔ Ⓥ
- Yes, they must be so small that we could hardly see them without a magnifying glass.

Al climbed up on the grain of sand. The grain was very rough, and it was covered with big pieces of shiny rocks.

Al asked, "Are those shiny pieces molecules?"

The old man replied, "No, no, my friend. Those shiny parts are crystals."

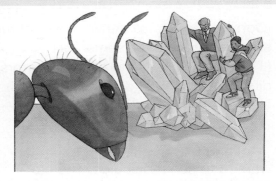

- Everybody, what are the shiny parts? (Signal.) *Crystals.* ⓃⒹ
- Touch a crystal in the picture on the next page. ✔ ⓋⒶ

The old man continued, "We've got to get a thousand times smaller than we are now before you can see a molecule. Here we go."

Suddenly, the grain of sand seemed to get bigger and bigger. It got so big that it seemed bigger than the biggest building Al had ever seen. It got bigger than a mountain. Soon it was so big that Al couldn't see anything but huge crystals all around him. Some crystals looked bigger than a school building.

The crystals continued to grow until they were as big as mountains. Then Al noticed that there were large holes inside the crystals. Al was starting to float into one of the holes. The floating reminded him of ◀ the way he had felt when he had floated in outer space.

- As Al got smaller and smaller, how big did the crystals seem to him? (Call on a student. Idea: *As big as mountains.*) ⓃⒹ
- Everybody, what did he notice inside the crystals? (Signal.) *Holes.* ⓃⒹ
- How did he get inside one of the holes? (Call on a student. Idea: *By floating.*) ⓃⒹ
- As he floated, he had the same feeling he had experienced in another place. Where was that? (Call on a student. Idea: *In space.*) ⓃⒹ

The old man said, "In a minute you will be small enough to see molecules."

Al continued to float into a hole inside one of the crystals. The hole was so large that Al couldn't see anything solid.

"Where are we?" Al asked.

The old man laughed. "We are inside the grain of sand."

"We can't be," Al said. "I don't see any sand."

The old man replied, "A grain of sand is made up of space and molecules."

- Everybody, what is the inside of a grain of sand made up of? (Signal.) *Space and molecules.* ⓃⒹ
- Has Al seen any molecules yet? (Signal.) *No.* ⓃⒹ
- What is he seeing now? (Call on a student. Idea: *Empty space.*) ⓃⒹ

The old man pointed and said, "Look—way over there."

Al looked in the direction the old man pointed. He saw something that looked like a big blob, vibrating very fast.

- What was the blob doing? (Call on a student. Idea: *Vibrating very fast.*) (ND)
- What do you think that blob is? (Call on a student. Idea: *A molecule.*) (DI)

The old man said, "That's a molecule."

"Wow!" Al said.

The old man pointed in another direction. "Look over there and you'll see another molecule."

Al looked. "I see it," he said. Then Al saw another molecule and another molecule. The molecules seemed to be in a row. Now Al could see another row of molecules above the first row. Every molecule was vibrating very fast.

- How are the molecules arranged as they vibrate? (Call on a student. Idea: *In rows.*) (DC)
- Everybody, use two fingers to show me how two molecules would be lined up as they vibrate very fast. Remember to keep them lined up in a row. ✔ (V)
- Read the rest of the story to yourself and be ready to answer some questions. Raise your hand when you're finished.

Al said, "The molecules are all lined up in rows."

The old man said, "These molecules are in the solid form of matter. That is why they are lined up. Remember this rule: When molecules are in the solid form, they are lined up and they stay in place."

❀ "That's really interesting," Al said, looking at the top row of vibrating molecules.

The old man continued, "These molecules are the same temperature as the room. If we make the grain of sand colder and colder, you will see a change in the molecules."

"I don't understand," Al said. "These molecules are in the solid form of matter. The solid form of matter is the coldest form. So how could the molecules change if the matter gets colder? The molecules will still be in the solid form."

The old man smiled. "I see that you are using the information you have learned. Good for you, my friend. And you are right. The molecules will remain in the solid form of matter, but watch what happens ❀ to them when the temperature gets lower than the temperature on Pluto."

- (After all students have raised their hand:) Name the two things about molecules that are in the solid form of matter. (Call on a student. Idea: *They are lined up and they stay in place.*) (RF/R)
- Everybody, are the molecules in the grain of sand the **same temperature** or a **different temperature** compared to the temperature of the room? (Signal.) *Same temperature.* (DC)
- What did the old man say would happen if the molecule becomes colder and colder? (Call on a student. Idea: *It would change.*) (ND)
- Al argued that it couldn't change. Why did he think that was true? (Call on a student. Idea: *It's already in the solid form of matter. That's the coldest form. So no matter how cold it got, it would still be in the solid form.*) (ND)
- How cold did the old man plan to make the grain of sand? (Call on a student. Idea: *Colder than Pluto.*) (ND)
- I'll read the part that tells what Al said. Listen to his argument:

  "These molecules are in the solid form of matter. The solid form of matter is the coldest form. So how could the molecules change if the matter gets colder? The molecules will still be in the solid form."

- Everybody, is Al right? (Signal.) *Yes.* (ND)
- Is Al using information that he has learned? (Signal.) *Yes.* (ND)

- But the old man insisted that something would change. What do you think might happen? (Call on a student. Praise students who suggest that the vibrations may change in some way.) (P)

Paired Practice

You're going to read aloud to your partner. The **A** members will read first. Then the **B** members will read from the star to the end of the story. (Observe students and give feedback.)

End-of-Lesson Activities

Now finish your independent work for lesson 109. Raise your hand when you're finished. (Observe students and give feedback.)

a. (Direct students to take out their marking pencils.)
- We're going to check your workbook and textbook items. Remember, if you got an item wrong, make an **X** next to the item.
b. (For each item: Read the item. Call on a student to answer it. If the answer is wrong, say the correct answer. Refer to the Answer Key for the correct answers.)
c. Now use your marking pencil to fix up any items you got wrong. Remember, all mistakes must be fixed up before you hand in your work.

(Present Spelling lesson 109 after completing Reading lesson 109. See *Spelling Presentation Book*.)

> *Note:* You will need to reproduce blackline masters for the Fact Game in lesson 110 (Appendix G in the *Teacher's Guide*).

Test 11

LESSON **110**

Materials for Lesson 110
Fact Game
For each team (4 or 5 students):
- pair of number cubes (or dice)
- copy of Fact Game 110 (Reproducible blackline masters are in Appendix G of the *Teacher's Guide.*)

For each student:
- their copy of the scorecard sheet (at end of workbook B)

For each monitor:
- a pencil
- Fact Game 110 answer key (at end of textbook B)

Fluency: Rate/Accuracy
Each student needs their thermometer chart.

EXERCISE 1

Fact Game

a. (Divide students into groups of four or five. Assign monitors.)
b. You'll play the game for 10 minutes. (Circulate as students play the game. Comment on groups that are playing well.)
c. (At the end of 10 minutes, have all students who earned more than 10 points stand up.)
- (Tell the monitor of each game that ran smoothly:) Your group did a good job.

EXERCISE 2

Fluency: Rate/Accuracy

a. Today is a test day and a reading checkout day. While you're writing answers, I'm going to call on you one at a time to read part of the story we read in lesson 109.
- Remember, you pass the checkout by reading the passage in less than a minute without making more than 2 mistakes. And when you pass the checkout, you color the space for lesson 110 on your thermometer chart.

b. (Call on individual students to read the portion of story 109 marked with ✿.)
- (Time the student. Note words that are missed and number of words read.)
- (Teacher reference:)

✿ "That's really interesting," Al said, looking at the top row of vibrating molecules.

The old man continued, "These molecules are the same temperature as the room. If we make the grain of sand colder and colder, you will see a change in the molecules."

"I don't understand," Al said. "These [50] molecules are in the solid form of matter. The solid form of matter is the coldest form. So how could the molecules change if the [75] matter gets colder? The molecules will still be in the solid form."

The old man smiled. "I see that you are using the information you [100] have learned. Good for you, my friend. And you are right. The molecules will remain in the solid form of matter, but watch what happens ✿ [125] to them when the temperature gets lower than the temperature on Pluto."

- (If the student reads the passage in one minute or less and makes no more than 2 errors, direct the student to color in the space for lesson 110 on the thermometer chart.)

- (If the student makes any mistakes, point to each word that was misread and identify it.)
- (If the student does not meet the rate-error criterion for the passage, direct the student to practice reading the story with the assigned partner.)

Lesson 110 **195**

EXERCISE 3

Test

a. **Find page 196 in your textbook.** ✔
- This is a test. You'll work items you've done before.

b. Work carefully. Raise your hand when you've completed all the items. (Observe students but do not give feedback on errors.)

EXERCISE 4

Marking the Test

a. (Check students' work before beginning lesson 111. Refer to the Answer Key for the correct answers.)

b. (Record all test 11 results on the Test Summary Sheet and the Group Summary Sheet. Reproducible Summary Sheets are at the back of the *Teacher's Guide*.)

EXERCISE 5

Test Remedies

(Provide any necessary remedies for test 11 before presenting lesson 111. Test remedies are discussed in the *Teacher's Guide*.)

Test 11 Firming Table

Test Item	Introduced in lesson	Test Item	Introduced in lesson	Test Item	Introduced in lesson
1	102	13	105	25	107
2	102	14	105	26	107
3	102	15	105	27	107
4	103	16	105	28	108
5	103	17	105	29	108
6	103	18	105	30	108
7	103	19	106	31	108
8	104	20	106	32	106
9	105	21	106	33	102
10	105	22	106	34	102
11	105	23	106	35	106
12	105	24	106	36	102

SPELLING

(Present Spelling lesson 110 after completing Reading lesson 110. See *Spelling Presentation Book*.)

Note: A special project occurs after lesson 111. See page 202 for the materials you'll need.

Lessons 111–115 • Planning Page   *Looking Ahead*

	Lesson 111	Lesson 112	Lesson 113	Lesson 114	Lesson 115
LESSON EVENTS	**Vocabulary Sentence** Reading Words Story Reading Paired Practice Independent Work Workcheck Spelling	Vocabulary Sentence Reading Words Story Reading Paired Practice Independent Work Workcheck Spelling	Fact Review Vocabulary Sentences Reading Words Story Reading Paired Practice Independent Work Workcheck Spelling	**Vocabulary Sentence** Vocabulary Sentence Reading Words Story Reading Paired Practice Independent Work Workcheck Spelling	Vocabulary Sentence Reading Words Story Reading Fluency: Rate/ Accuracy Independent Work Workcheck Spelling
VOCABULARY SENTENCE	**#27: The poem they <u>created</u> was <u>nonsense</u>.**	#27: The poem they <u>created</u> was <u>nonsense</u>.	sentence #25 sentence #26 sentence #27	**#28: The <u>squid</u> <u>wriggled</u> <u>its</u> <u>tentacles</u>.** #27: The poem they <u>created</u> was <u>nonsense</u>.	#28: The <u>squid</u> <u>wriggled</u> <u>its</u> <u>tentacles</u>.
READING WORDS: WORD TYPES	modeled words words with endings	mixed words multi-syllable words	modeled words	multi-syllable words mixed words	modeled words 2-syllable words
NEW VOCABULARY	prove usual		unbearable	wriggled disk	transparent addressed exclaimed indeed
STORY BACKGROUND					
STORY	*Al Learns More About Molecules*	*Al Takes a Test About Molecules*	*Angela Meets the Old Man*	*Angela and Al Learn About Water Pressure*	*Al and Angela See Strange Sea Animals*
SKILL ITEMS	Crossword puzzle	Crossword puzzle	Vocabulary sentence	Vocabulary Vocabulary sentence	
SPECIAL MATERIALS	*materials for project				Thermometer charts
SPECIAL PROJECTS/ ACTIVITIES	Project after lesson 111				

*Reference materials: (books on matter and molecules, encyclopedias, CD-ROMs); poster-making supplies (butcher paper or poster board, markers, crayons, paints, scissors, paste, magazines for pictures); model-making supplies (styrofoam balls, toothpicks, paints).

Comprehension Questions Abbreviations Guide

Access Prior Knowledge = (APK)   Author's Point of View = (APoV)   Author's Purpose = (AP)   Cause/Effect = (C/E)   Charts/Graphs/Diagrams/Visual Aids = (VA)

Classify and Categorize = (C+C)   Compare/Contrast = (C/C)   Determine Character Emotions, Motivation = (DCE)   Drawing Conclusions = (DC)   Drawing Inferences = (DI)

Fact and Opinion = (F/O)   Hypothesizing = (H)   Main Idea = (MI)   Making Connections = (MC)   Making Deductions = (MD)   Making Judgements = (MJ)

Narrative Elements = (NE)   Noting Details = (ND)   Predict = (P)   Reality/Fantasy = (R/F)   Recall Facts/Rules = (RF/R)   Retell = (R)   Sequence = (Seq)

Steps in a Process = (SP)   Story Structure = (SS)   Summarize = (Sum)   Understanding Dialogue = (UD)   Using Context to Confirm Meaning(s) = (UCCM)   Visualize = (V)

EXERCISE 1

Vocabulary

a. **Find page 367 in your textbook.** ✔
- Touch sentence 27. ✔
- This is a new vocabulary sentence. It says: The poem they created was nonsense. Everybody, say that sentence. Get ready. (Signal.) *The poem they created was nonsense.*
- Close your eyes and say the sentence. Get ready. (Signal.) *The poem they created was nonsense.*
- (Repeat until firm.)

b. **Create** is another word for **make.** Everybody, what's another way of saying **They made a poem?** (Signal.) *They created a poem.*

c. The sentence says that the poem was **nonsense. Nonsense** means **no sense at all.** The poem didn't make any sense. Everybody, what word means **no sense at all?** (Signal.) *Nonsense.*

d. Listen to the sentence again: The poem they created was nonsense. Everybody, say the sentence. Get ready. (Signal.) *The poem they created was nonsense.*

e. What word means **made?** (Signal.) *Created.*
- What word means **no sense at all?** (Signal.) *Nonsense.*

EXERCISE 2

Reading Words

Column 1

a. Find lesson 111 in your textbook. ✔
- Touch column 1. ✔
- (Teacher reference:)

1. prove	3. usual
2. broadly	4. created

b. Word 1 is **prove.** What word? (Signal.) *Prove.*
- Spell **prove.** Get ready. (Tap for each letter.) *P-R-O-V-E.*

- When you prove something, you show that it has to be true. Everybody, what do you do when you show that something has to be true? (Signal.) *Prove that it is true.*

c. Word 2 is **broadly.** What word? (Signal.) *Broadly.*
- Spell **broadly.** Get ready. (Tap for each letter.) *B-R-O-A-D-L-Y.*
- He smiled **broadly.**

d. Word 3 is **usual.** What word? (Signal.) *Usual.*
- Spell **usual.** Get ready. (Tap for each letter.) *U-S-U-A-L.*
- Things that are usual are things that happen most of the time. If the usual time for lunch is 12 o'clock, that means that most of the time lunch is at 12 o'clock.

e. Word 4. What word? (Signal.) *Created.*
- Spell **created.** Get ready. (Tap for each letter.) *C-R-E-A-T-E-D.*

f. Let's read those words again.
- Word 1. What word? (Signal.) *Prove.*
- (Repeat for words 2–4.)

g. (Repeat step f until firm.)

Column 2

h. Find column 2. ✔
- (Teacher reference:)

1. globes	3. observer
2. incredibly	4. nonsense

i. All these words have an ending.
- Word 1. What word? (Signal.) *Globes.*
- (Repeat for words 2–4.)

j. (Repeat step i until firm.)

k. Let's read those words again.
- Word 1. What word? (Signal.) *Globes.*
- (Repeat for words 2–4.)

l. (Repeat step k until firm.)

Individual Turns

(For columns 1 and 2: Call on individual students, each to read one to three words per turn.)

Story Reading

a. Find part B in your textbook. ✔
- The error limit for group reading is 11 errors. Read carefully.

b. Everybody, touch the title. ✔
- (Call on a student to read the title.) *[Al Learns More About Molecules.]*
- Everybody, what's the title? (Signal.) *Al Learns More About Molecules.* (ND)
- (Call on individual students to read the story, each student reading two or three sentences at a time. Ask the specified questions as the students read.)

> - (**Correct errors:** Tell the word. Direct the student to reread the sentence.)
> - (If the group makes more than 11 errors, direct the students to reread the story.)

Al Learns More About Molecules

The molecules were getting colder. As Al watched, he noticed that they were not vibrating as fast. They stayed in rows but they were moving slower and slower and slower.

- Everybody, when the temperature goes down, do the molecules stay in rows? (Signal.) *Yes.* (ND)
- How do they change when the temperature goes down? (Call on a student. Idea: *They vibrate slower.*) (ND)

The old man said, "The grain of sand is now as cold as the surface of Pluto. And it's getting colder and colder."

Suddenly, Al noticed that the molecules were standing still, lined up in perfect rows. The old man said, "Now the grain of sand is as cold as it can get. At this temperature, nothing moves."

- How cold is the grain of sand now? (Call on a student. Idea: *As cold as it can get.*) (ND)
- What are the molecules doing? (Call on a student. Idea: *Standing still.*) (ND)

As Al and the old man floated toward one of the molecules, Al observed that the molecule was made up of many little parts that seemed to be floating in space.

- Everybody, was the molecule made up of one piece? (Signal.) *No.* (ND)
- It was made up of many parts.

These parts formed three large globes. The middle globe was the biggest. There was a large ball in the center of this globe. Fourteen tiny balls moved around the ball in the center.

- Everybody, listen to that part again: These parts formed three large globes. The middle globe was the biggest. There was a large ball in the center of this globe. Fourteen tiny balls moved around the ball in the center.
- Which globe was the biggest? (Call on a student. Idea: *The middle one.*) (ND)
- That globe had tiny balls moving around the center ball. Everybody, how many tiny balls were there? (Signal.) *Fourteen.* (ND)
- Everybody, look at the picture on the next page. Touch the middle globe. ✔ (VA)
- Count the little balls around the center ball and see if there are 14. ✔ (VA)
- Everybody, how many little balls are there? (Signal.) *14.* (ND)

As Al looked at the middle globe, he noticed that the tiny balls weren't touching the center ball, but were arranged in space around the center ball. Some tiny balls were far away from the center ball. Other tiny balls were closer to the center ball. Al said, "Those little balls in the center globe look like planets around the sun."

- What did Al think the little balls looked like? (Call on a student. Idea: *The planets around the sun.*) (ND)

"You are a very good observer," the old man said as he pointed to the other sand molecules. "And look over there," he continued. "All the sand molecules look exactly the same. All have three globes. Each middle globe has fourteen tiny balls."

- What things are the same about all molecules from the grain of sand? (Call on a student. Idea: *They all have three globes and each middle globe has fourteen tiny balls.*) (ND)

"This is amazing," Al said. He counted the tiny balls around one of the other middle globes and then repeated, "This is amazing."

- How many tiny balls do you think he counted? (Call on a student.) *14.* (DI)

Then the old man said, "Now watch a molecule as it starts to get hotter."

- What will the molecule do as it gets hotter? (Call on a student. Idea: *It will start to vibrate.*) (DC)

The molecule started to tremble. Then it started to vibrate faster and faster and faster. The old man said, "Now the molecule is the same temperature as this room again. But watch what happens when the molecule gets so hot that the sand turns into a liquid."

The old man continued, "When the molecules are in the liquid form, they will not be in rows and they will move very, very fast."

The molecule ✦ started to vibrate fast, so fast that Al could hardly follow it with his eyes. Suddenly the molecule shot past Al and the old man and disappeared. Al noticed that the rows of molecules had disappeared. The molecules were flying this way and that way, in all directions—very fast. One of them almost hit Al and the old man.

- Name two ways the molecules change when the matter turns into the liquid form. (Call on a student. Idea: *They move very fast and they aren't in rows.*) (ND)

The old man said, "The liquid form of the sand is still getting hotter."

- Everybody, if it gets hotter, what form of matter will it turn into? (Signal.) *Gas.* (RF/R)
- And what do you think the molecules will do? (Call on a student. Idea: *Move much faster.*) (P)

The old man continued, "In a moment that liquid will turn into a gas. You'll have to look very carefully to see the molecules."

The molecules now looked as if they were moving over a thousand miles an hour. "Wiiish." One went flying by Al like a shot. He waited and waited for another molecule to fly by, but none came by for a few minutes. Then—"wiiish"—another molecule flew by at an incredible speed.

- What does that mean, an incredible speed? (Call on a student. Idea: *Super fast.*) (UCCM)

"I don't see many molecules now," Al said.

The old man said, "When matter is in the solid form, the molecules are close together. When matter is in the liquid form, the molecules are much farther apart. But when matter is in the gas form, the molecules are farther apart than they are in the liquid form. And they move incredibly fast. They are not in rows. They fly in all directions."

- Everybody, in which form of matter are the molecules closest together? (Signal.) *Solid.* (ND)
- In which form of matter are they farthest apart? (Signal.) *Gas.* (ND)
- In which form of matter are the molecules in rows? (Signal.) *Solid.* (ND)
- Do they move at all when the solid matter is at room temperature? (Signal.) *Yes.* (ND)
- In which form of matter do the molecules move the fastest? (Signal.) *Gas.* (ND)
- Read the rest of the story to yourself and be ready to answer some questions. Raise your hand when you're finished.

"Wiiish." Another molecule flew past Al and the old man. As Al floated, he tried to make sure that he would remember the things he had seen. He remembered how the molecules looked when they were as cold as they could get. He remembered how they looked in the solid form at room temperature. He remembered how they changed when they got hot enough to go into the liquid form. And he remembered how they looked in the gas form.

Suddenly Al noticed that everything was getting darker and darker. Now Al could see that he was no longer small. He was standing inside the old man's store.

The old man said, "You wanted molecules. You got molecules. Remember everything that you have seen. Pass the test and pay for your trip. Then you can go on another trip. Go anywhere. See anything."

Al said, "Don't worry. I'll pass the test."

- (After all students have raised their hand:) Name some things that Al tried to remember as he floated inside the gas. (Call on individual students. Ideas: *How the molecules looked when they were cold; how the molecules looked in the solid form; how the molecules changed in the liquid form; etc.*) Ⓝ⒟
- How did the molecules look when the sand was as cold as it could get? (Call on a student. Idea: *They were standing still in rows.*) Ⓝ⒟
- How did the molecules look when they were at room temperature? (Call on a student. Idea: *They moved back and forth quickly in rows.*) Ⓝ⒟
- How did they look when the sand was in the liquid form? (Call on a student. Idea: *They moved faster and not in rows.*) Ⓝ⒟
- How did they look when the sand was in the gas form? (Call on a student. Idea: *They moved very, very fast in all directions and they were far apart.*) Ⓝ⒟
- Everybody, in which form are the molecules farthest apart? (Signal.) *Gas.* Ⓓ⒞
- In which form are they closest together? (Signal.) *Solid.* Ⓓ⒞

Paired Practice

You're going to read aloud to your partner. The **B** members will read first. Then the **A** members will read from the star to the end of the story. (Observe students and give feedback.)

End-of-Lesson Activities

INDEPENDENT WORK

Now finish your independent work for lesson 111. Raise your hand when you're finished. (Observe students and give feedback.)

WORKCHECK

a. (Direct students to take out their marking pencils.)
- We're going to check your workbook and textbook items. Remember, if you got an item wrong, make an **X** next to the item.

b. (For each item: Read the item. Call on a student to answer it. If the answer is wrong, say the correct answer. Refer to the Answer Key for the correct answers.)

c. Now use your marking pencil to fix up any items you got wrong. Remember, all mistakes must be fixed up before you hand in your work.

SPELLING

(Present Spelling lesson 111 after completing Reading lesson 111. See *Spelling Presentation Book*.)

Special Project

Note: After completing lesson 111, do this special project with the students. You may do this project during another part of the school day.

Materials: Reference materials (books on matter and molecules, encyclopedias, CD-ROMs)

Optional Materials: Poster-making supplies (butcher paper or poster board, markers, crayons, paints, scissors, paste, magazines for pictures); model-making supplies (styrofoam balls, toothpicks, paints)

a. Find page 202 in your textbook. ✔
- (Call on individual students to read two or three sentences.)
- (Teacher reference:)

> ### Special Project
>
> You have read about molecules. One thing that you have learned is that molecules from different materials look different. Make a chart that shows molecules from different materials. Look up **molecules** in an encyclopedia, a science book, or on the computer. Find pictures of different molecules. See if you can find pictures of water molecules and oxygen molecules.
>
> Make pictures of some of the molecules that these books show. Label each type of molecule. You may want to make an impressive wall chart or models of some molecules.

b. (Help the students find pictures of molecules in an encyclopedia or in a science book or on the computer. Direct them to draw and label some of the molecules they find illustrated. You may also direct them to make a chart for the molecule pictures.)

EXERCISE 1

Vocabulary Review

a. Here's the new vocabulary sentence: The poem they created was nonsense.
- Everybody, say that sentence. Get ready. (Signal.) *The poem they created was nonsense.*
- (Repeat until firm.)

b. Everybody, what word means **no sense at all?** (Signal.) *Nonsense.*
- What word means **made?** (Signal.) *Created.*

EXERCISE 2

Reading Words

Column 1

a. **Find lesson 112 in your textbook.** ✔
- Touch column 1. ✔
- (Teacher reference:)

1. broadly	4. spelling
2. prove	5. studied
3. usual	6. unbearable

b. Word 1. What word? (Signal.) *Broadly.*
- Spell **broadly.** Get ready. (Tap for each letter.) *B-R-O-A-D-L-Y.*

c. Word 2. What word? (Signal.) *Prove.*
- Spell **prove.** Get ready. (Tap for each letter.) *P-R-O-V-E.*

d. Word 3. What word? (Signal.) *Usual.*
- Spell **usual.** Get ready. (Tap for each letter.) *U-S-U-A-L.*

e. Word 4. What word? (Signal.) *Spelling.*
- Spell **spelling.** Get ready. (Tap for each letter.) *S-P-E-L-L-I-N-G.*

f. Word 5. What word? (Signal.) *Studied.*
- Word 6. What word? (Signal.) *Unbearable.*

g. Let's read those words again.
- Word 1. What word? (Signal.) *Broadly.*
- (Repeat for words 2–6.)

h. (Repeat step g until firm.)

Column 2

i. Find column 2. ✔

- (Teacher reference:)

1. however	3. concluded
2. indeed	4. demonstrated

j. Word 1. What word? (Signal.) *However.*
- (Repeat for words 2–4.)

k. I'll say sentences one way. You'll say them using one of the synonyms in column 2.

l. Listen: Certainly, she was happy now. Everybody, say that sentence. Get ready. (Signal.) *Certainly, she was happy now.*
- One of the words in column 2 means the same thing as **certainly.** That word is **indeed.** Say the sentence with that word. Get ready. (Signal.) *Indeed, she was happy now.*

m. Listen: They showed how to make a kite. Say that sentence. Get ready. (Signal.) *They showed how to make a kite.*
- Now say that sentence with the word in column 2 that means the same thing as **showed.** Get ready. (Signal.) *They demonstrated how to make a kite.*

n. Listen: He finished his speech. Say that sentence. Get ready. (Signal.) *He finished his speech.*
- Now say that sentence with the word that means the same thing as **finished.** Get ready. (Signal.) *He concluded his speech.*

o. Listen: She was tired, but she kept walking. Say that sentence. Get ready. (Signal.) *She was tired, but she kept walking.*
- Now say that sentence with the word that means **but.** Get ready. (Signal.) *She was tired; however, she kept walking.*
- (Repeat steps l through o until firm.)

Individual Turns

(For columns 1 and 2: Call on individual students, each to read one to three words per turn.)

EXERCISE 3

Story Reading

a. Find part B in your textbook. ✔
- The error limit for group reading is 15 errors. Read carefully.

b. Everybody, touch the title. ✔
- (Call on a student to read the title.) [*Al Takes a Test About Molecules.*]
- Everybody, what's the title? (Signal.) *Al Takes a Test About Molecules.* ⓝⓓ
- What's going to happen in this story?
- (Call on individual students to read the story, each student reading two or three sentences at a time. Ask the specified questions as the students read.) Ⓟ

- **(Correct errors:** Tell the word. Direct the student to reread the sentence.)
- (If the group makes more than 15 errors, direct the students to reread the story.)

Al Takes a Test About Molecules

The next morning, Al walked to school with Angela. Al couldn't keep his secret any longer.

- What secret is that? (Call on a student. Ideas: *The secret about the old man's store; the secret about going anywhere and seeing anything.*) ⒶⓅⓀ

Part of his mind told him that Angela wouldn't believe him. Another part just had to tell somebody about his experience on Anywhere Street. The air was very cold and Al could see his breath. As he breathed out and observed the little cloud, he thought to himself, "That cloud is made up of molecules."

"What did you say about molecules?" his sister asked.

Al didn't realize that he had talked out loud.

- What did he say out loud? (Call on a student.) [*"That cloud is made up of molecules."*] ⓝⓓ

"Oh, I was just thinking about molecules," he said. By now part of him was saying, "Go ahead, tell her about Anywhere Street."

Another part responded, "No, Al. She'll think you're crazy."

Suddenly Al said, "Molecules are really interesting. Do you know that the molecules from a grain of sand all look the same?"

"Yeah," his sister replied. "We studied molecules in school."

"But did you know that all sand molecules are made up of three globes? The middle globe is the biggest. And it has fourteen tiny balls that float around a ball in the center."

His sister looked at him and made a sour face. "How do you know that?"

- How does he know that? (Call on a student. Idea: *He saw them.*) ⒶⓅⓀ

"You're not going to believe this," Al said. "But I saw those molecules."

"Where?" his sister asked.

For a moment Al couldn't bring himself to tell her where he had seen them. But then he took a deep breath and said, "I went inside a grain of sand."

- How do you think his sister is going to respond to what Al just said? (Call on a student. Idea: *She won't believe him.*) Ⓜⓙ

"Oh, I see," his sister said smiling. "You went inside a grain of sand. It must have been one big grain."

- Everybody, does she believe him? (Signal.) *No.* ⒹⒸ

"I'm not kidding," Al said. He tried to sound serious, but he couldn't seem to look Angela in the eyes. He knew how crazy he must have sounded. "I got so small that I went inside a little tiny grain of sand."

"I see," his sister said. "You went inside a grain of sand and counted the number of balls that are in the molecules. And while you were doing that, I rode a horse to the moon and back."

- Everybody, is she being serious? (Signal.) *No.* Ⓜⓙ
- Why did she say she rode a horse to the moon and back? (Call on a student. Idea: *Doing that is as ridiculous as going inside a grain of sand.*) ⒹⒸ

"I'm serious, Angela," Al insisted. "I'm telling you what happened. It really, really happened."

"Get out of here," she said, and started to walk ahead of Al. He caught up and grabbed her arm. "Now, listen to me. I want to tell you what happened." He felt angry now, and he didn't have any trouble looking her in the eyes—straight in the eyes.

Al explained about the old man and about the trip inside the grain of sand. Then Al said, "I can prove it. I can tell you about things that I wouldn't know about if I hadn't gone inside a grain of sand."

"What can you tell me?" his sister asked.

"I can tell you how the molecules move." Al and his sister were standing near an empty lot. Al picked up a stick and drew ⭐ three rows of dots in the dirt. He explained, "That's how the molecules are lined up in solid matter. They're all in rows and they keep their place. But they vibrate at room temperature." Al held the end of the stick against one of the molecules that he had drawn in the dirt and said, "When the matter turns into a liquid, the molecules start moving around like this." Al drew a fast line across the dirt with the end of the stick. "They start flying in all directions."

He drew lines from another molecule in a different direction. "And when the liquid turns into a gas, the molecules move even faster, much faster. And they're very far apart. Sometimes more than a minute would pass before I'd see one. Then suddenly one would flash past me."

"Well, I'll say this," Angela said after Al had finished. "You sure know a lot about molecules. I'll give you that much. But that doesn't prove that you were inside a grain of sand."

Al stared at his sister for a moment. Then he turned away and shook his head. He knew that he wouldn't believe her if she told him she'd been inside a grain of sand. So he didn't say anything more about his trip.

Al and Angela went to school. Al did well in school. He worked hard in reading and arithmetic. The class had a spelling test, and Al missed only one word. One of the words that he got right was **molecule.** Only three other kids got that word right.

- Read the rest of the story to yourself and be ready to answer some questions. Raise your hand when you're finished.

After school Al went back to Anywhere Street. As usual, there were no people or cars on the street. Al opened the door to the store, and the bell went ding, ding.

Inside the dark and quiet store, a voice said, "Are you ready to pay for your trip to the molecules?"

Al said, "Yes, I'm ready."

The old man bent over so that his face was close to Al's. The old man said, "Here is the first question: How can we make molecules stand still?"

Al said, "Make the matter as cold as it can get. When matter gets cold enough, the molecules stop moving."

The old man looked at Al. He smiled broadly and then asked, "How can you make the molecules go very, very fast?"

Al explained.

"You have passed the test," the old man said. "You are a good thinker."

The old man straightened up and waved his hand. "Now where do you want to go? Remember—go anywhere. See anything."

Al asked, "Could I take my sister with me on the next trip? She's smart and she'd really love to go on these trips."

The old man smiled. He said, "Bring her with you. But remember—she'll have to pass a test on what she sees."

"She'll pass the test," Al said.

Al ran from the store. The bell went ding, ding. Al could hardly wait to tell Angela.

- (After all students have raised their hand:) The old man asked Al, "How can we make molecules stand still? What's the answer? (Call on a student. Idea: *Cool them.*) (RF/R)
- Then Al explained how you can make the molecules go very, very fast. What did he say when he explained? (Call on a student. Idea: *Heat them.*) (ND)
- What did Al ask the old man after he passed the test? (Call on a student. Idea: *If Angela could go on the next trip.*) (ND)
- What did the old man say? (Call on a student. Idea: *That Angela could go but she'll have to pass a test.*) (ND)
- Do you think Al will have trouble convincing Angela to go on the trip? (Call on individual students. Student preference.) (MJ)
- Do you think the trip would be more fun if you could go with somebody else? (Call on a student. Idea: *Yes.*) (MC)

EXERCISE 4

Paired Practice

You're going to read aloud to your partner. The **A** members will read first. Then the **B** members will read from the star to the end of the story. (Observe students and give feedback.)

End-of-Lesson Activities

INDEPENDENT WORK

Now finish your independent work for lesson 112. Raise your hand when you're finished. (Observe students and give feedback.)

WORKCHECK

a. (Direct students to take out their marking pencils.)
- We're going to check your workbook and textbook items. Remember, if you got an item wrong, make an **X** next to the item.
b. (For each item: Read the item. Call on a student to answer it. If the answer is wrong, say the correct answer. Refer to the Answer Key for the correct answers.)
c. Now use your marking pencil to fix up any items you got wrong. Remember, all mistakes must be fixed up before you hand in your work.

SPELLING

(Present Spelling lesson 112 after completing Reading lesson 112. See *Spelling Presentation Book.*)

EXERCISE 1

Fact Review

a. Let's review some facts you have learned. First we'll go over the facts together. Then I'll call on individual students to do some facts.

b. Tell me which form of matter is the coldest. (Pause.) Get ready. (Signal.) *Solid.* (RF/R)

- Tell me which form of matter is the hottest. (Pause.) Get ready. (Signal.) *Gas.* (APK)

- Tell me in which form of matter molecules move the slowest. (Pause.) Get ready. (Signal.) *Solid.* (RF/R)

- Tell me in which form of matter molecules move the fastest. (Pause.) Get ready. (Signal.) *Gas.* (APK)

- (Repeat step b until firm.)

c. If something is matter in the liquid form, would you make it **hotter** or **colder** to change it into a gas? (Signal.) *Hotter.* (RF/R)

- If something is matter in the liquid form, would you make it **hotter** or **colder** to change it into a solid? (Signal.) *Colder.* (APK)

- Tell me what we call water in the gas form. (Pause.) Get ready. (Signal.) *Steam.* (RF/R)

- Tell me what we call water in the solid form. (Pause.) Get ready. (Signal.) *Ice.* (APK)

- (Repeat step c until firm.)

d. Tell me in which form of matter air is on Pluto. (Pause.) Get ready. (Signal.) *Solid.* (RF/R)

- Tell me in which form of matter air is on Earth. (Pause.) Get ready. (Signal.) *Gas.* (APK)

- Tell me in which form of matter air is on Saturn. (Pause.) Get ready. (Signal.) *Liquid.* (RF/R)

- (Repeat step d until firm.)

e. Tell me in which form of matter molecules are in rows. (Pause.) Get ready. (Signal.) *Solid.* (APK)

- Tell me in which form of matter molecules are farthest apart. (Pause.) Get ready. (Signal.) *Gas.* (RF/R)

- Tell me in which form of matter molecules are closest together. (Pause.) Get ready. (Signal.) *Solid.* (APK)

- (Repeat step e until firm.)

Individual Turns

- Now I'm going to call on individual students to do some facts.

- (Call on individual students to do the set of facts in step b, c, d, or e.)

EXERCISE 2

Vocabulary Review

a. You learned a sentence that tells what he saw at midnight.

- Everybody, say that sentence. Get ready. (Signal.) *At midnight, he saw a familiar galaxy.*

- (Repeat until firm.)

b. You learned a sentence that tells about the crystal.

- Everybody, say that sentence. Get ready. (Signal.) *The crystal contained more than a billion molecules.*

- (Repeat until firm.)

c. Here's the last sentence you learned. The poem they created was nonsense.

- Everybody, say that sentence. Get ready. (Signal.) *The poem they created was nonsense.*

- (Repeat until firm.)

d. What word means **no sense at all?** (Signal.) *Nonsense.*

- What word means **made?** (Signal.) *Created.*

e. Once more. Say the sentence that tells about the poem they created. Get ready. (Signal.) *The poem they created was nonsense.*

EXERCISE 3

Reading Words

a. **Find lesson 113 in your textbook.** ✔

- Touch word 1. ✔

- (Teacher reference:)

1. tentacles	4. wriggled
2. unbearable	5. nonsense
3. squid	

b. Word 1 is **tentacles.** What word? (Signal.) *Tentacles.*

c. Word 2. What word? (Signal.) *Unbearable.*

- If you can't stand something, that thing is **unbearable.** Everybody, what do you call pain that you can't stand? (Signal.) *Unbearable pain.*

- What do you call a person you can't stand? (Signal.) *An unbearable person.*

d. Word 3. What word? (Signal.) *Squid.*

- Spell **squid.** Get ready. (Tap for each letter.) *S-Q-U-I-D.*

e. Word 4. What word? (Signal.) *Wriggled.*

- Spell **wriggled.** Get ready. (Tap for each letter.) *W-R-I-G-G-L-E-D.*

f. Word 5. What word? (Signal.) *Nonsense.*

- Spell **nonsense.** Get ready. (Tap for each letter.) *N-O-N-S-E-N-S-E.*

g. Let's read those words again.

- Word 1. What word? (Signal.) *Tentacles.*
- (Repeat for: **2. unbearable, 3. squid, 4. wriggled, 5. nonsense.**)

h. (Repeat step g until firm.)

EXERCISE 4

Story Reading

a. Find part B in your textbook. ✔

- The error limit for group reading is 16 errors. Read carefully.

b. Everybody, touch the title. ✔

- (Call on a student to read the title.) *[Angela Meets the Old Man.]*
- Everybody, what's the title? (Signal.) *Angela Meets the Old Man.* (ND)
- (Call on individual students to read the story, each student reading two or three sentences at a time. Ask the specified questions as the students read.)

- (**Correct errors:** Tell the word. Direct the student to reread the sentence.)
- (If the group makes more than 16 errors, direct the students to reread the story.)

Angela Meets the Old Man

After supper Al said to Angela, "Let's go for a walk. I want to tell you something."

- What's he going to tell her? (Call on a student. Idea: *That she can go on a trip with Al and the old man.*) (DI)

Al didn't want his mother to hear what he was going to tell Angela.

- Why not? (Call on a student. Ideas: *Because their mother wouldn't believe it; she'd think Al was crazy.*) (DI)

The air outside felt very cold. As they walked along, Al said, "I asked the old man if I could take you with me on one of the trips. He said it was okay. So after school tomorrow, you come to the store with me and we can go anywhere you want to go and we can see anything in the whole solar system."

"Al, stop this nonsense," Angela said. "You had your joke about the molecules. Now stop kidding around."

"Angela, I'm not kidding. I'm as serious as I can be. Come on, just go to the store with me."

"Do you really expect me to believe that there's an old man that can take people inside a grain of sand?"

"That's right," Al insisted. "And that's not all. He can take us to the stars. He can take us inside the sun or to the bottom of the ocean. He can take us anywhere."

"I'm not going to listen to any more of this nonsense," Angela said.

Al grabbed his sister by the shoulders and faced her. The light from a streetlight was shining on her face. "Please," Al said. "Please go with me, just one time. It's not a joke. You don't have to believe me. Go with me to the store tomorrow. Would you do that much?"

She sighed and pushed Al away. "All right," she said. "I don't know why, but I'll do it."

Al said, "You won't be sorry. You'll see."

The next day seemed to drag for Al. His mind kept making up pictures of how Angela would respond when she found out that Al had been telling the truth. He could almost see her face. Her mouth would fall open and her eyes would become wide. Then she would say, "Wow, you were telling me the truth."

- Everybody, show me how Al thinks Angela's face will look when she finds out that he's telling the truth. ✔ (V)

Al's mind must have created that picture of Angela's face twenty times during the school day.

After school, Al and his sister walked down street after street. Finally, Angela stopped and said, "There is no Anywhere Street."

"No, honest," Al said. "We'll be there in a couple of blocks."

Angela sighed and started walking again. At last they came to the corner of Anywhere Street. Al pointed to the street sign. "See?" he said. "What did I tell you?"

"Well, you were telling the truth about one thing," she said.

"Right," Al said. "And look down the street. Do you see any cars or any people?"

"Wow," his sister said. "That's amazing." Then she added, "But that doesn't mean I believe you about the old man."

They walked to the store. Al pointed to the sign in the window. "See?" he said. "What did I tell you?"

"Wow," she said. Then she shook her head. "This is too ✦ much."

Al opened the door. The bell sounded. "This is Angela," Al said into the darkness. "She wants to go on a trip with me."

Silence.

- Everybody, can they see the old man? (Signal.) *No.* ⓓⓒ
- How do you think Angela feels now? (Call on a student. Idea: *It's a joke.*) ⓓⓒⓔ

Angela said, "Oh, I get it. I'm supposed to think that you're talking to somebody. There's no old man in here. There's just a dark . . ."

"Go anywhere, see anything," the old man said loudly, and seemed to pop out of the darkness.

Al looked at his sister's face in the dim light. It was just like the picture that he had imagined. Her mouth was open and her eyes were wide. She didn't say anything as she took several steps backward, toward the door.

- Why is she moving backward toward the door? (Call on a student. Ideas: *She is surprised; she is afraid.*) ⓓⓒ

"Go to the stars," the old man said in a booming voice. "Or travel with kangaroos across Australia. See the moons of Jupiter or swim with whales. Where do you want to go?"

Angela's expression had not changed. She stared at the old man. The old man pointed his finger at her. "Tell me where you want to go and we'll go there."

Angela spoke very softly as she said, "I—I just came here with Al. I don't want to go anywhere."

"Of course you want to go somewhere, perhaps inside a volcano."

"No," she said softly. "I just want to go home." She moved closer to the door.

"Come on," Al said. "Tell him something you'd like to learn about, and he'll show it to you."

Suddenly Angela's expression changed. "This has gone far enough," she said. "I just want to get out of here."

- How does she feel now? (Call on a student. Ideas: *Afraid; angry.*) ⓓⓒⓔ

"Oh, you would like to be far away from here?" The old man asked.

"Very far away," Angela said. "I don't know what kind of joke this is, but I'm going to get . . ."

- Read the rest of the story to yourself and be ready to answer some questions. Raise your hand when you're finished.

Suddenly the store became brighter and the walls seemed to melt and change into other forms. Al looked around and realized that he and his sister were standing in the middle of a hot field. Next to them was a jungle. Cries of birds came from the jungle, and the sun beat down on them. The old man was sitting on a large rock a few meters away, fanning himself with a large leaf. Angela's expression was once more like the one that Al had imagined.

"You wanted to get far away," the old man said. "You are far away. You are in Africa."

The heat from the sun was almost unbearable. Al took off his jacket and opened his shirt, but his sister just stood there, slowly turning around with wide eyes and open mouth.

The old man said to Angela, "Is there anything special that you would like to see here?"

She slowly shook her head no.

The old man said, "Well, I would like to see an elephant."

As soon as the words came from the old man's mouth, a great elephant charged from the jungle, holding its trunk high in the air. It was charging toward Al and Angela. Angela mumbled something and then started to run away very fast.

- (After all students have raised their hand:) Everybody, what's the name of the place where Al and Angela were? (Signal.) *Africa.* ⓃⒹ
- Did Angela say that she wanted to see anything? (Signal.) *No.* ⓃⒹ
- What did the old man say that he wanted to see? (Signal.) *An elephant.* ⓃⒹ
- What did the elephant do? (Call on a student. Ideas: *Charged out of the jungle; charged toward Al and Angela.*) ⓃⒹ
- What did Angela do? (Call on a student. Idea: *Started running away.*) ⓃⒹ

Paired Practice

You're going to read aloud to your partner. The **B** members will read first. Then the **A** members will read from the star to the end of the story. (Observe students and give feedback.)

End-of-Lesson Activities

INDEPENDENT WORK

Now finish your independent work for lesson 113. Raise your hand when you're finished. (Observe students and give feedback.)

WORKCHECK

a. (Direct students to take out their marking pencils.)
- We're going to check your workbook and textbook items. Remember, if you got an item wrong, make an **X** next to the item.

b. (For each item: Read the item. Call on a student to answer it. If the answer is wrong, say the correct answer. Refer to the Answer Key for the correct answers.)

c. Now use your marking pencil to fix up any items you got wrong. Remember, all mistakes must be fixed up before you hand in your work.

SPELLING

(Present Spelling lesson 113 after completing Reading lesson 113. See *Spelling Presentation Book.*)

EXERCISE 1

Vocabulary

a. **Find page 367 in your textbook.** ✔
- Touch sentence 28. ✔
- This is a new vocabulary sentence. It says: The squid wriggled its tentacles. Everybody, say that sentence. Get ready. (Signal.) *The squid wriggled its tentacles.*
- Close your eyes and say the sentence. Get ready. (Signal.) *The squid wriggled its tentacles.*
- (Repeat until firm.)

b. The sentence refers to a squid. A squid is a sea animal that looks like an octopus that has ten tentacles. Some squids are much longer than an elephant.

c. The sentence says that the squid **wriggled** its tentacles. When something wriggles, it squirms and moves in all directions.

d. The squid's **tentacles** are its ten arms. These arms are like huge snakes that can grab and hold on to things. Everybody, what are the long arms of a squid called? (Signal.) *Tentacles.*
- How many tentacles does a squid have? (Signal.) *10.*

e. Listen to the sentence again: The squid wriggled its tentacles. Everybody, say that sentence. Get ready. (Signal.) *The squid wriggled its tentacles.*

f. Everybody, what word means **squirmed around in all directions?** (Signal.) *Wriggled.*
- What word names a sea animal? (Signal.) *Squid.*
- What word refers to arms that are like huge snakes? (Signal.) *Tentacles.*
- (Repeat step f until firm.)

EXERCISE 2

Vocabulary Review

a. You learned a sentence that tells about the poem they created.
- Everybody, say that sentence. Get ready. (Signal.) *The poem they created was nonsense.*
- (Repeat until firm.)

b. I'll say part of the sentence. When I stop, you say the next word. Listen: The poem they . . . Everybody, what's the next word? (Signal.) *Created.*

c. Listen: The poem they created was . . . Everybody, what's the next word? (Signal.) *Nonsense.*
- Say the whole sentence. Get ready. (Signal.) *The poem they created was nonsense.*

EXERCISE 3

Reading Words

Column 1

a. Find lesson 114 in your textbook. ✔
- Touch column 1. ✔
- (Teacher reference:)

1. <u>wriggle</u>d	4. <u>lump</u>y
2. <u>anxious</u>ly	5. <u>grape</u>fruit
3. <u>water</u>melon	6. <u>dimm</u>er

b. All these words have more than one syllable. The first part of each word is underlined.

c. Word 1. What's the underlined part? (Signal.) *wriggle.*
- What's the whole word? (Signal.) *Wriggled.*

d. Word 2. What's the underlined part? (Signal.) *anxious.*
- What's the whole word? (Signal.) *Anxiously.*

e. Word 3. What's the underlined part? (Signal.) *water.*
- What's the whole word? (Signal.) *Watermelon.*

f. Word 4. What's the underlined part? (Signal.) *lump.*
- What's the whole word? (Signal.) *Lumpy.*

g. Word 5. What's the underlined part? (Signal.) *grape.*
- What's the whole word? (Signal.) *Grapefruit.*

h. Word 6. What's the underlined part? (Signal.) *dimm.*
- What's the whole word? (Signal.) *Dimmer.*

i. Let's read those words again.
* Word 1. What word? (Signal.) *Wriggled.*
* (Repeat for: **2. anxiously,**
  3. watermelon, 4. lumpy, 5. grapefruit,
  6. dimmer.)
j. (Repeat step i until firm.)

Column 2

k. Find column 2. ✔
* (Teacher reference:)

1. tentacles	4. shocked
2. exclaimed	5. grown
3. disk	

l. Word 1. What word? (Signal.) *Tentacles.*
m. Word 2. What word? (Signal.) *Exclaimed.*
n. Word 3. What word? (Signal.) *Disk.*
* Spell **disk.** Get ready. (Tap for each letter.) *D-I-S-K.*
* A flat circle is a disk. A ball is not a disk, because a ball is not flat. Everybody, what do we call a flat circle? (Signal.) *Disk.*
o. Word 4. What word? (Signal.) *Shocked.*
* Spell **shocked.** Get ready. (Tap for each letter.) *S-H-O-C-K-E-D.*
p. Word 5. What word? (Signal.) *Grown.*
* Spell **grown.** Get ready. (Tap for each letter.) *G-R-O-W-N.*
* You've grown a lot this year.
q. Let's read those words again.
* Word 1. What word? (Signal.) *Tentacles.*
* (Repeat for words 2–5.)
r. (Repeat step q until firm.)

Individual Turns

(For columns 1 and 2: Call on individual students, each to read one to three words per turn.)

EXERCISE 4

Story Reading

a. Find part B in your textbook. ✔
* The error limit for group reading is 15 errors. Read carefully.
b. Everybody, touch the title. ✔
* (Call on a student to read the title.) *[Angela and Al Learn About Water Pressure.]*
* Everybody, what's the title? (Signal.) *Angela and Al Learn About Water Pressure.* ⓃⒹ

* What's going to happen in this story? (Call on a student. Idea: *Angela and Al will learn about water pressure.*) Ⓟ
* (Call on individual students to read the story, each student reading two or three sentences at a time. Ask the specified questions as the students read.)

* (**Correct errors:** Tell the word. Direct the student to reread the sentence.)
* (If the group makes more than 15 errors, direct the students to reread the story.)

Angela and Al Learn About Water Pressure

As the huge elephant ran after Angela, Al ran over to the old man. "Stop that," he demanded. "Don't scare my sister like that."

The old man smiled.

"I mean it," Al said. "Get rid of that elephant."

"What elephant?" the old man asked.

* Do you think the elephant is still running after Angela? (Call on a student. Idea: *No.*) Ⓓ Ⓘ

Angela was standing about thirty meters from Al and the old man. She was slowly turning around. The elephant was not in sight.

"It's okay, Angela," Al said. Slowly Angela walked back toward Al, glancing over her shoulder every few steps.

* What do you think she was looking for? (Call on a student.) *[The elephant.]* Ⓓ Ⓘ

She still had a shocked expression on her face. "It just disappeared," she said softly. "That elephant just disappeared." Then she asked, "Can we get out of here?"

"Certainly," the old man replied. "But you'll have to tell me where you want to go and what you want to see."

Angela didn't say anything. She just shook her head.

Al said, "I've got an idea. Let's go to the bottom of the ocean. We could see all kinds of interesting things down there."

Angela said, "No. I don't think that . . ."

- What do you think she was going to say? (Call on a student. Idea: *I don't think that I'd like to go there.*) Ⓟ

The jungle and the sky seemed to melt into a deep green. "What's happening?" Angela asked anxiously.

Al and the others were no longer standing on ground. They were floating through the green water of an ocean.

"We'll drown," Angela said. "We're underwater."

"Don't worry, my friend," the old man said. "You are with me on a very special trip. You'll be able to breathe and to talk. The water pressure will not bother you. But you will be able to see things that most people only read about."

Al could see the sun above the surface of the water. It was a light green disk. Below them, the green water turned to blue and deep purple. A school of red fish was swimming next to Al and the others. The old man said, "I will show you water pressure."

"It's impossible to see pressure," Al said. "It's just an invisible force, like the wind."

"Come with me to the bottom of this ocean and I will show you pressure." The old man pointed down. "We are only about 30 feet deep now. The bottom of the ocean below us is 200 feet from the surface, so we have a long way to go."

- Everybody, about how deep were they? (Signal.) *30 feet deep.* ⓝⒹ
- How deep was the bottom of the ocean where they were? (Signal.) *200 feet deep.* ⓝⒹ
- They have to go down 170 feet to reach the bottom.

Al and Angela followed the old man, deeper and deeper. Occasionally, Al looked up at the sun. It became dimmer and dimmer as the water changed from green to dark blue. Now Al swam past strange lumpy rocks.

The old man said, "Those rocks are covered with coral."

- Everybody, what are the rocks covered with? (Signal.) *Coral.* ⓝⒹ

The old man continued, "Coral is made of millions and millions of small sea animals. When the animals die, their shells stay on the rock. After hundreds and hundreds of years, you cannot see the rock anymore because it is covered with a thick layer of coral."

- What is coral made of? (Call on a student. Idea: *The shells of sea animals.*) ⓝⒹ
- Why can't you see the rock after it has been in the ocean for years and years? (Call on a student. Idea: *Because there's so much coral on it.*) ⓝⒹ

When they reached the bottom, the old man said, "Now I will show you pressure." He took out a balloon and blew it up until it was about as big as an apple.

- Everybody, show me how big it was. ✔ Ⓥ

The old man said, "This balloon will change as we move up toward the surface. You watch it and see how it changes. While you're watching it, remember this rule: The deeper something is, the more pressure there is on that thing." The old man repeated the rule.

- Everybody, what's the rule? (Signal.) *The deeper something is, the more pressure there is on that thing.* ⓇⒻ/Ⓡ
- (Repeat until firm.)
- Where would a balloon have more pressure on it, at 200 feet below the surface or at 100 feet below the surface? (Signal.) *At 200 feet.* ⒹⒸ

- If a balloon had more pressure pushing on it, would it be **bigger** or **smaller**? (Signal.) *Smaller.* (DI)
- So where would a balloon be smaller, at 200 feet below the surface or at 100 feet below the surface? (Signal.) *At 200 feet.* (DC)

> "I don't understand why the pressure is greater when you're deeper," Al said.
>
> The old man pointed up. He said, "The pressure is greater because the water above you weighs more. The weight of all that water pushes against you. So if you are very deep, there is a lot of weight pushing against you."

- Why is the pressure greater when you go deeper? (Call on a student. Idea: *Because there's more water pushing down on you.*) (ND)

> Al said, "I get it. And if you're not as deep, there isn't as much weight pushing down on you."
>
> "Correct," the old man said. Then he began to swim up toward the surface. "Watch what happens to the balloon," he said.

- Everybody, are they very deep now? (Signal.) *Yes.* (ND)
- So is there a lot of pressure on the balloon now? (Signal.) *Yes.* (DC)
- When they go up, will there be **more pressure** on the balloon or **less pressure?** (Signal.) *Less pressure.* (RF/R)
- So the size of the balloon will change if there is not as much pressure pushing on it. Will the balloon get bigger or smaller? (Signal.) *Bigger.* (DC)

> Angela pointed to the balloon and said, "It's getting bigger." Now the balloon was as big as a grapefruit.
>
> The old man said, "Can you tell me why it is getting bigger?"
>
> "I think so," Angela replied. "When we go up, the water above us doesn't weigh as much. So the water doesn't push against the balloon as hard."

> "A very smart young lady," the old man said as he continued toward the surface. Now the balloon had grown to the size of a watermelon.

- Everybody, show me how big it is now. ✔ (V)
- Read the rest of the story to yourself and be ready to answer some questions. Raise your hand when you're finished.

> The old man stopped 30 feet below the surface. "If we go any higher, the balloon will burst. Tell me why."
>
> Al answered, "Because there will be less pressure, and the balloon will keep getting bigger until it breaks."
>
> The old man moved up about three feet and "BLOOM, bubble, bubble," the balloon burst and sent a huge blob of bubbles to the surface. The old man held the broken balloon and said, "You have just seen pressure."
>
> "That's amazing," Angela said.
>
> The old man said, "There is more to the ocean than pressure. So let's go back down and see some of the other wonders of the ocean. But before we do, I want you to think about what you have just seen. I want you to remember how the balloon changed. And I want you to understand why it changed." The old man stopped talking.
>
> Al thought very hard. He remembered the rule: The deeper something is, the more pressure there is on that thing. He remembered how the balloon got bigger and bigger when there was less pressure on it. After a few moments, Al said, "I'll remember everything."
>
> "Me too," his sister said.
>
> "Good," the old man said. "Now let's go back down and see some of the wonders of the sea."
>
> Al was ready to see them. Angela said, "That sounds great."

- (After all students have raised their hand:) The old man stopped 30 feet below the surface. Everybody, as he went up, did the balloon have **more pressure** or **less pressure on it?** (Signal.) *Less pressure.* (RF/R)

- So did the balloon get **bigger** or **smaller?** (Signal.) *Bigger.* (DC)
- Then what happened to the balloon? (Call on a student. Idea: *It broke.*) (ND)
- What did the old man say that they would see next? (Call on a student. Idea: *Wonders of the sea.*) (ND)
- How did Angela feel about seeing the wonders of the sea? (Call on a student. Idea: *She wanted to see them.*) (ND)
- Do you think she's enjoying herself now? (Call on a student.) *[Yes.]* (MJ)

EXERCISE 5

Paired Practice

You're going to read aloud to your partner. The **A** members will read first. Then the **B** members will read from the star to the end of the story. (Observe students and give feedback.)

End-of-Lesson Activities

INDEPENDENT WORK

Now finish your independent work for lesson 114. Raise your hand when you're finished. (Observe students and give feedback.)

WORKCHECK

a. (Direct students to take out their marking pencils.)
- We're going to check your workbook and textbook items. Remember, if you got an item wrong, make an **X** next to the item.
b. (For each item: Read the item. Call on a student to answer it. If the answer is wrong, say the correct answer. Refer to the Answer Key for the correct answers.)
c. Now use your marking pencil to fix up any items you got wrong. Remember, all mistakes must be fixed up before you hand in your work.

SPELLING

(Present Spelling lesson 114 after completing Reading lesson 114. See *Spelling Presentation Book.*)

EXERCISE 1

Vocabulary Review

a. Here's the new vocabulary sentence: The squid wriggled its tentacles.

- Everybody, say that sentence. Get ready. (Signal.) *The squid wriggled its tentacles.*
- (Repeat until firm.)

b. Everybody, what word names a sea animal? (Signal.) *Squid.*

- What word refers to arms that are like huge snakes? (Signal.) *Tentacles.*
- What word means **squirmed around in all directions?** (Signal.) *Wriggled.*
- (Repeat step b until firm.)

EXERCISE 2

Reading Words

Column 1

a. **Find lesson 115 in your textbook.** ✔

- Touch column 1. ✔
- (Teacher reference:)

1. transparent	4. triceps
2. addressed	5. muscle
3. expensive	

b. Word 1 is transparent. What word? (Signal.) *Transparent.*

- If something is transparent, you can see things clearly through it. A window is transparent. Water is transparent. A magnifying glass is transparent.
- Everybody, what do we call things that you can see through clearly? (Signal.) *Transparent.*

c. Word 2 is **addressed.** What word? (Signal.) *Addressed.*

- Spell **addressed.** Get ready. (Tap for each letter.) *A-D-D-R-E-S-S-E-D.*
- When letters are addressed to you, they have your name and address on them.

d. Word 3 is **expensive.** What word? (Signal.) *Expensive.*

- Spell **expensive.** Get ready. (Tap for each letter.) *E-X-P-E-N-S-I-V-E.*

e. Word 4 is **triceps.** What word? (Signal.) *Triceps.*

- Spell **triceps.** Get ready. (Tap for each letter.) *T-R-I-C-E-P-S.*

f. Word 5 is **muscle.** What word? (Signal.) *Muscle.*

- Spell **muscle.** Get ready. (Tap for each letter.) *M-U-S-C-L-E.*

g. Let's read those words again.

- Word 1. What word? (Signal.) *Transparent.*
- (Repeat for words 2–5.)

h. (Repeat step g until firm.)

Column 2

i. Find column 2. ✔

- (Teacher reference:)

1. exclaimed	3. squirting
2. indeed	4. headfirst

- All these words have more than one syllable. The first syllable of each word is underlined.

j. Word 1. What's the first syllable? (Signal.) *ex.*

- What's the whole word? (Signal.) *Exclaimed.*
- When you exclaim, you say something as if it is very important. Here's a sentence: "Stop, stop!" he exclaimed. Everybody, what are you doing when you say something as if it is very important? (Signal.) *Exclaiming.*

k. Word 2. What's the first syllable? (Signal.) *in.*

- What's the whole word? (Signal.) *Indeed.*
- **Indeed** is another word for **certainly.**
- Everybody, what's another way of saying **Certainly I will go with you?** (Signal.) *Indeed I will go with you.*
- What's another way of saying **She was certainly tired?** (Signal.) *She was indeed tired.*

l. Word 3. What's the first syllable? (Signal.) *squirt.*

- What's the whole word? (Signal.) *Squirting.*

m. Word 4. What's the first syllable? (Signal.) *head.*

- What's the whole word? (Signal.) *Headfirst.*

n. Let's read those words again.
- Word 1. What word? (Signal.) *Exclaimed.*
- (Repeat for: **2. indeed, 3. squirting, 4. headfirst.**)

o. (Repeat step n until firm.)

Individual Turns

(For columns 1 and 2: Call on individual students, each to read one to three words per turn.)

EXERCISE 3

Story Reading

a. Find part B in your textbook. ✔
- The error limit for group reading is 14 errors. Read carefully.

b. Everybody, touch the title. ✔
- (Call on a student to read the title.) *[Al and Angela See Strange Sea Animals.]*
- Everybody, what's the title? (Signal.) *Al and Angela See Strange Sea Animals.* (ND)
- (Call on individual students to read the story, each student reading two or three sentences at a time. Ask the specified questions as the students read.)

- (**Correct errors:** Tell the word. Direct the student to reread the sentence.)
- (If the group makes more than 14 errors, direct the students to reread the story.)

Al and Angela See Strange Sea Animals

The old man said, "We're going to go deeper in the water again and observe some of the animals that live in the ocean. Before we go down, I want you to tell me what will happen to this balloon."

Suddenly a very large balloon appeared in the old man's hand. It was the size of a watermelon.

- What's going to happen to it when they go down in the water? (Call on a student. Idea: *It will get smaller.*) (DC)
- Why? (Call on a student. Idea: *Because the water pressure will get greater.*) (RF/R)

Angela said, "The balloon will get smaller and smaller."

"Correct," the old man said. "But can you tell me why?"

"I can," Al said. "As we go deeper, the water above us will weigh more and more. The weight of that water will press against the balloon and make it smaller and smaller."

The old man smiled broadly and said, "You learn well from the things you have seen."

Al smiled back at the old man, feeling very smart.

Then Al and Angela followed the old man down. The balloon that the old man held did just what Angela had said it would do.

- What's that? (Call on a student. Idea: *It got smaller.*) (DC)

The water turned from light blue to dark blue as they went down deeper and deeper. When they were 200 feet deep, the balloon was about the size of an apple.

Suddenly the old man let go of the balloon. It went up toward the surface. As it went up, it got bigger and bigger and bigger.

The old man said, "Follow me and we'll go to a place where the ocean is very deep."

Down they went. The water was very dark now—deep purple. Al could no longer see the sun above him.

- Why is it so dark now? (Call on a student. Idea: *Because they're so deep.*) (DC)

The old man held up a giant flashlight and turned it on. Then he said, "We are now 300 feet below the surface. The pressure down here is amazing. But there are animals that live down here. Let me show you one of them." The old man directed the beam of the giant flashlight to one side. For a moment Al could not believe what he saw in the beam of light. It was an incredible monster that had a tube on one end and many arms on the other end.

Al jumped back when he saw the monster. "What is that?" he asked.

The old man replied, "That is a giant squid. These squid will grow to the size of a big tree. The one you are looking at now is about fifty feet long."

- Everybody, look at the picture. Touch the part of the squid that looks like a tube. ✔ (VA)
- About how long is that squid? (Signal.) *50 feet.* (ND)
- That's longer than a classroom.

"Fifty feet!" Al exclaimed. "That's longer than our house."

"Correct," the old man said.

Al was about to ask what that huge squid ate when suddenly a dark form moved into the flashlight beam. It was another animal, even bigger than the squid.

"A whale!" Angela exclaimed.

"Correct again," the old man replied.

"Is that a killer whale?" Al asked.

"No," the old man said. "This whale is called a blue whale. It is much longer than a killer whale."

- Everybody, look at the first picture on the next page. ✔ (VA)
- It shows a killer whale above a blue whale. The killer whale is much, much smaller than the blue whale.
- Turn back to page 219.

"Wow!" Al exclaimed. "Will that whale eat the squid?"

"No," the old man replied. "Watch what the squid does."

Suddenly, the squid moved very fast. It moved headfirst, with its arms trailing its body. The old man said, "The squid moves by squirting out water, the same way a jet plane moves by pushing out air."

- How does the squid make itself move? (Call on a student. Idea: *By squirting out water.*) (ND)

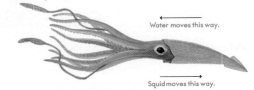

Water moves this way.

Squid moves this way.

- The bottom picture shows how a squid moves. Touch the arrow that shows which way the water squirts out. ✔ (VA) The squid moves in the opposite direction. Touch the arrow that shows which way the squid moves. ✔ (VA)

In an instant the squid caught up to the huge whale. In another instant, the squid's long arms reached out and began to wrap around the whale. The whale was bigger than the squid, but the squid had a good hold on the whale.

The old man said, "The arms of the squid are called tentacles."

- Everybody, what are the arms called? (Signal.) *Tentacles.* (ND)

The old man continued, "The squid can hang on because its tentacles have little cups that stick to the surface of the whale."

- Why can the squid hold on tightly with its tentacles? (Call on a student. Idea: *Because the tentacles have little cups on them.*) (ND)

Al watched the two giants fighting. The whale turned this way and that way. Then the whale shot up toward the surface of the water. The whale came down again and dove down, down, down. The squid was still hanging on.

Angela asked, "Will that giant squid kill the whale?"

"I don't think so," the old man said. "If that whale weren't so big, the squid would probably be able to kill it. But I think the whale will get away."

- Read the rest of the story to yourself and be ready to answer some questions. Raise your hand when you're finished.

Suddenly the whale wriggled and turned. Then it shot up toward the surface again. It soon disappeared in the deep blue above Al and the others. In less than half a minute, it returned to the deep water. The squid was no longer hanging on, but Al could see rows of marks on the surface of the whale. These marks hadn't been there before. They must have been made by the cups of the squid's tentacles.

The whale slowly swam next to Al and the others. It was like a huge ship, so big that Al could hardly believe its size. Angela said, "It's hard to believe that there are animals so big."

"Indeed," the old man agreed. "You are looking at the largest animal in the world. It weighs more than ten elephants."

Suddenly the whale stopped, then dove very deep and very fast. Angela said, "I think that whale is afraid of something."

"Look up there and you'll see the animals the whale fears most," the old man said.

Al looked up. He could see something swimming in the dark water. Al said, "I see them. I see four or five big fish. They look black and white."

"They're not fish," the old man said. "They are killer whales. They're not as big as other whales, but they hunt bigger whales and they kill them. No whale can get away from them."

The killer whales suddenly dove down after the blue whale. They moved very fast. They swam past Al, Angela, and the old man. Al could see the sharp teeth of one killer

whale as it swam by. The old man said, "The mouth of that killer whale is so big that Angela could sit inside it."

"No thanks," Angela said. "I don't think I want to get near those fish."

"They are not fish," the old man said. "All whales are warm-blooded animals, just like a dog or a pig or a cat. Fish are cold-blooded."

The killer whales were swimming closer and closer toward the blue whale.

- (After all students have raised their hand:) Everybody, what kind of animals were chasing the blue whale? (Signal.) *Killer whales.* (ND)
- Which whales are bigger? (Signal.) *Blue whales.* (C/C)
- How much did the blue whale weigh? (Signal.) *More than ten elephants.* (ND)
- Imagine that, more than **ten** elephants.
- Why was the blue whale afraid of the killer whales? (Call on a student. Idea: *Because killer whales kill blue whales.*) (DC)
- How big did the old man say the mouth of the killer whale is? (Call on a student. Idea: *Big enough for Angela to sit inside it.*) (ND)
- Everybody, are killer whales **warm-blooded** or **cold-blooded?** (Signal.) *Warm-blooded.* (ND)
- Are fish **warm-blooded** or **cold-blooded?** (Signal.) *Cold-blooded.* (ND)
- Name some other animals that are warm-blooded. (Call on individual students. Ideas: *Humans; dogs; cats; horses; sheep; birds; etc.*) (APK)

EXERCISE 4

Fluency: Rate/Accuracy

Note: There is a fluency checkout in this lesson; therefore, there is no paired practice.

a. Today is a reading checkout day. While you're doing your independent work, I'm going to call on you one at a time to read part of the story from lesson 114.

- Remember, you pass the checkout by reading the passage in less than a minute without making more than 2 mistakes. And when you pass the checkout, you'll color the space for lesson 115 on your thermometer chart.

b. (Call on individual students to read the portion of story 114 with ✿.)

- (Time the student. Note words that are missed and number of words read.)
- (Teacher reference:)

> ✿ The old man said, "There is more to the ocean than pressure. So let's go back down and see some of the other wonders of the ocean. But before we do, I want you to think about what you have just seen. I want you to remember how the balloon [50] changed. And I want you to understand why it changed." The old man stopped talking.
>
> Al thought very hard. He remembered the rule: The deeper [75] something is, the more pressure there is on that thing. He remembered how the balloon got bigger and bigger when there was less pressure on [100] it. After a few moments, Al said, "I'll remember everything."
>
> "Me too," his sister said.
>
> "Good," the old man said. "Now let's go back down ✿ [125] and see some of the wonders of the sea."

- (If the student reads the passage in one minute or less and makes no more than 2 errors, direct the student to color in the space for lesson 115 on the thermometer chart.)

- (If the student makes any mistakes, point to each word that was misread and identify it.)
- (If the student does not meet the rate-error criterion for the passage, direct the student to practice reading the story with the assigned partner.)

End-of-Lesson Activities

INDEPENDENT WORK

Now finish your independent work for lesson 115. Raise your hand when you're finished. (Observe students and give feedback.)

WORKCHECK

a. (Direct students to take out their marking pencils.)
- We're going to check your workbook and textbook items. Remember, if you got an item wrong, make an **X** next to the item.

b. (For each item: Read the item. Call on a student to answer it. If the answer is wrong, say the correct answer. Refer to the Answer Key for the correct answers.)

c. Now use your marking pencil to fix up any items you got wrong. Remember, all mistakes must be fixed up before you hand in your work.

SPELLING

(Present Spelling lesson 115 after completing Reading lesson 115. See *Spelling Presentation Book*.)

> **Note:** A special project occurs after lesson 116. See page 227 for the materials you'll need.

Lessons 116–120 • Planning Page *Looking Ahead*

	Lesson 116	Lesson 117	Lesson 118	Lesson 119	Lesson 120
LESSON EVENTS	Vocabulary Sentences Reading Words Story Reading Paired Practice Independent Work Workcheck Spelling	**Vocabulary Sentence** Vocabulary Sentences Reading Words Story Reading Paired Practice Independent Work Workcheck Spelling	Vocabulary Sentence Reading Words Story Reading Paired Practice Independent Work Workcheck Spelling	Vocabulary Sentences Reading Words Story Reading Paired Practice Independent Work Workcheck Spelling	Fact Game Fluency: Rate/ Accuracy Test Marking the Test Test Remedies Spelling
VOCABULARY SENTENCE	sentence #26 sentence #27 sentence #28	**#29: The <u>triceps</u> <u>muscle</u> is bigger than the <u>biceps</u> <u>muscle</u>.** #28: The <u>squid</u> <u>wriggled</u> its <u>tentacles</u>.	#29: The <u>triceps</u> <u>muscle</u> is bigger than the <u>biceps</u> <u>muscle</u>.	sentence #27 sentence #28 sentence #29	
READING WORDS: WORD TYPES	modeled words multi-syllable words mixed words	words with an ending multi-syllable words	compound words words with an ending	mixed words	
NEW VOCABULARY	intelligent imagination universe balanced		decorated		
STORY BACKGROUND					
STORY	*Al and Angela Go to the Bottom of the Ocean*	*A Test About the Ocean*	*Angela and Al See Our Galaxy*	*Angela and Al Learn About Muscles*	
SKILL ITEMS	Vocabulary sentence Sequencing	Vocabulary sentences	Vocabulary Crossword puzzle	Vocabulary Vocabulary sentence	Test: Vocabulary sentences
SPECIAL MATERIALS	*materials for project				Thermometer charts, dice, Fact Game 120, Fact Game Answer Key, scorecard sheets
SPECIAL PROJECTS/ ACTIVITIES	Project after lesson 116	Activity after lesson 117		Activity for lesson 119–212	

*Reference materials (books on ocean life, encyclopedias, CD-ROMs); poster-making supplies (butcher paper or poster board, markers, crayons, paints, scissors, paste, magazines for pictures).

Comprehension Questions Abbreviations Guide

Access Prior Knowledge = (APK)   Author's Point of View = (APoV)   Author's Purpose = (AP)   Cause/Effect = (C/E)   Charts/Graphs/Diagrams/Visual Aids = (VA)

Classify and Categorize = (C+C)   Compare/Contrast = (C/C)   Determine Character Emotions, Motivation = (DCE)   Drawing Conclusions = (DC)   Drawing Inferences = (DI)

Fact and Opinion = (F/O)   Hypothesizing = (H)   Main Idea = (MI)   Making Connections = (MC)   Making Deductions = (MD)   Making Judgements = (MJ)

Narrative Elements = (NE)   Noting Details = (ND)   Predict = (P)   Reality/Fantasy = (R/F)   Recall Facts/Rules = (RF/R)   Retell = (R)   Sequence = (Seq)

Steps in a Process = (SP)   Story Structure = (SS)   Summarize = (Sum)   Understanding Dialogue = (UD)   Using Context to Confirm Meaning(s) = (UCCM)   Visualize = (V)

EXERCISE 1

Vocabulary Review

a. You learned a sentence that tells about the crystal.
- Everybody, say that sentence. Get ready. (Signal.) *The crystal contained more than a billion molecules.*
- (Repeat until firm.)

b. You learned a sentence that tells about the poem they created.
- Everybody, say that sentence. Get ready. (Signal.) *The poem they created was nonsense.*
- (Repeat until firm.)

c. Here's the last sentence you learned: The squid wriggled its tentacles.
- Everybody, say that sentence. Get ready. (Signal.) *The squid wriggled its tentacles.*
- (Repeat until firm.)

d. What word means **squirmed around in all directions?** (Signal.) *Wriggled.*
- What word names a sea animal? (Signal.) *Squid.*
- What word refers to arms that are like huge snakes? (Signal.) *Tentacles.*
- (Repeat step d until firm.)

e. Once more. Say the sentence that tells what the squid did. Get ready. (Signal.) *The squid wriggled its tentacles.*

EXERCISE 2

Reading Words

Column 1

a. **Find lesson 116 in your textbook.** ✔
- Touch column 1. ✔
- (Teacher reference:)

1. intelligent	4. balanced
2. imagination	5. presented
3. universe	6. biceps

b. Word 1 is **intelligent.** What word? (Signal.) *Intelligent.*
- **Intelligent** is another word for **smart.** Everybody, what's another way of saying **She is a very smart person?** (Signal.) *She is a very intelligent person.*

c. Word 2 is **imagination.** What word? (Signal.) *Imagination.*
- Your imagination is the part of your mind that can think of things that might happen. You can use your imagination to picture a horse that is bright red and yellow. You can use your imagination to picture a baby that is bigger than a building.

d. Word 3 is **universe.** What word? (Signal.) *Universe.*
- Spell **universe.** Get ready. (Tap for each letter.) *U-N-I-V-E-R-S-E.*
- The universe is everything there is—all the galaxies and everything in them. Everybody, what do we call everything there is? (Signal.) *Universe.*

e. Word 4 is **balanced.** What word? (Signal.) *Balanced.*
- Spell **balanced.** Get ready. (Tap for each letter.) *B-A-L-A-N-C-E-D.*
- When things are balanced on a point, they don't tip one way or the other way. Everybody, what do we call things that don't tip one way or the other way? (Signal.) *Balanced.*

f. Word 5 is **presented.** What word? (Signal.) *Presented.*
- Spell **presented.** Get ready. (Tap for each letter.) *P-R-E-S-E-N-T-E-D.*

g. Word 6 is **biceps.** What word? (Signal.) *Biceps.*

h. Let's read those words again.
- Word 1. What word? (Signal.) *Intelligent.*
- (Repeat for words 2–6.)

i. (Repeat step h until firm.)

Column 2

j. Find column 2. ✔
- (Teacher reference:)

1. <u>ex</u>pensive	3. <u>pack</u>age
2. <u>greet</u>ed	4. <u>trans</u>parent

- All these words have more than one syllable. The first syllable of each word is underlined.

k. Word 1. What's the first syllable? (Signal.) *ex.*
- What's the whole word? (Signal.) *Expensive.*

l. Word 2. What's the first syllable? (Signal.) *greet.*
- What's the whole word? (Signal.) *Greeted.*

m. Word 3. What's the first syllable? (Signal.) *pack.*
- What's the whole word? (Signal.) *Package.*

n. Word 4. What's the first syllable? (Signal.) *trans.*
- What's the whole word? (Signal.) *Transparent.*

o. Let's read those words again.
- Word 1. What word? (Signal.) *Expensive.*
- (Repeat for: **2. greeted, 3. package, 4. transparent.**)

p. (Repeat step o until firm.)

Column 3

q. Find column 3. ✔
- (Teacher reference:)

1. couch	3. scratched
2. addressed	4. applauded

r. Word 1. What word? (Signal.) *Couch.*
- (Repeat for words 2–4.)

s. Let's read those words again.
- Word 1. What word? (Signal.) *Couch.*
- (Repeat for words 2–4.)

t. (Repeat step s until firm.)

Individual Turns

(For columns 1–3: Call on individual students, each to read one to three words per turn.)

EXERCISE 3

Story Reading

a. Find part B in your textbook. ✔
- The error limit for group reading is 14 errors. Read carefully.

b. Everybody, touch the title. ✔
- (Call on a student to read the title.) [*Al and Angela Go to the Bottom of the Ocean.*]
- Everybody, what's the title? (Signal.) *Al and Angela Go to the Bottom of the Ocean.* ⓃⒹ
- What's going to happen in this story? (Call on a student. Idea: *Al and Angela will go to the bottom of the ocean.*) Ⓟ
- (Call on individual students to read the story, each student reading two or three sentences at a time. Ask the specified questions as the students read.)

- (**Correct errors:** Tell the word. Direct the student to reread the sentence.)
- (If the group makes more than 14 errors, direct the students to reread the story.)

Al and Angela Go to the Bottom of the Ocean

Al, Angela, and the old man swam after the blue whale. The four killer whales caught up to the blue whale, but just as they were about to sink their huge teeth into the blue whale, the old man made a very funny sound. It was something like a beep, but very high. Suddenly all the killer whales turned around and swam away from the blue whale.

- Why do you think that sound made them swim away? (Call on a student. Ideas: *It scared them; it was a warning sound in "whale talk."*) ⒹⒾ

The old man said, "That sound is part of the language killer whales use. That sound is a warning signal that tells them to swim away fast."

- Everybody, what did the beep tell the killer whales to do? (Signal.) *Swim away fast.* ⓃⒹ

Angela asked, "Do killer whales understand language?"

"Yes," the old man replied. "They use a kind of language."

- Dogs don't really understand language. Everybody, do killer whales understand their own language? (Signal.) *Yes.* ⓃⒹ
- So which are smarter, killer whales or dogs? (Signal.) *Killer whales.* ⒹⒸ

Al watched the killer whales swim out of their sight.

Then the old man said, "We're going to go deeper into the ocean."

Down and down they went, until the water was black. The old man said, "The ocean is over six miles deep in the deepest places. We are going to go down to one of the very deepest places."

- Everybody, about how far will they be from the surface when they get to the bottom? (Signal.) *Six miles.* ⓃⒹ

At last the old man pointed his flashlight down. Al could see the bottom of the ocean. There were no plants on the bottom.

- Why not? (Call on a student. Idea: *Because there's no sunlight.*) (DI)

The old man said, "Plants don't grow this deep in the ocean because there is no sunlight down here."

Suddenly a fish swam by. But it wasn't like any fish that Al had ever seen before. It was very small, and the lights on its side were shining. Then another fish came by—a fat one with great big teeth and a light coming out of its head.

- Everybody, look at the bottom of the page. ✔ (VA)
- You can see some of the fish that Al and the others saw. Can you imagine fish like that?

Al noticed that some other fish were transparent. He could actually see right through them. Suddenly a fish with huge eyes swam into view.

Angela said, "Wow! If I hadn't seen those fish, I never would have believed they were real."

When Al looked around, he was standing next to Angela and the old man in the store.

Angela asked, "What happened?"

Al said, "The trip is over."

The old man said, "Yes, but you must pay for your trip by passing a test on what you saw."

Suddenly, the old man disappeared.

Al opened the door. Ding, ding, the bell went. As they walked outside, Angela's expression was blank. She was staring straight ahead. After they

had walked halfway to the corner of Anywhere Street she said, "Did we really go to the bottom of the ocean? Did it really happen?"

"I don't know," Al said. "Funny things happen when the old man takes you on a trip."

Angela shook her head.

- What kind of expression did Angela have when they left the old man's store? (Call on a student. Idea: *Blank.*) (ND)
- Everybody, show me a blank expression. ✔ (V)

When Al and Angela arrived at home, their mother greeted them. She said, "The strangest thing just happened. The bell rang but when I opened the door, nobody was there. But this package was in front of the door." She held out a flat package that was about the size of a book. She continued, "The package is addressed to both of you."

- Who do you think brought the package to Al and Angela's house? (Call on a student. Idea: *The old man.*) (DI)

Then she handed the package to Angela. Angela quickly tore off the wrapping paper. Inside was a large book. The title was *The Sea*. On the cover was a picture of a giant blue whale fighting with a giant squid.

A little card was sticking out of the book. On the card these words were written: "This book will help you go anywhere and see anything."

- Everybody, who would write a card like that? (Signal.) *The old man.* (DI)
- What picture was on the cover of the book? (Call on a student. Idea: *A blue whale fighting with a squid.*) (ND)
- Everybody, was that picture anything that Al and Angela had seen? (Signal.) *Yes.* (ND)

Al's mother looked puzzled. She said, "Somebody sent you that expensive book. But who would do that?"

"I don't know," Al said.

- Everybody, was he telling the truth? (Signal.) *No.* (MJ)

Al and Angela went into the living room and sat next to each other on the couch as they looked through the book. It showed pictures of the things they had seen in the ocean.

They saw pictures of strange fish with lights on their sides, and they saw killer whales. There were even pictures that showed a balloon getting bigger as it rose from the bottom of the ocean.

For over an hour, Angela and Al looked through the book. Then Al said, "Would you mind if I took the book to school with me tomorrow?"

Angela replied, "Just don't lose it."

"Don't worry," Al said.

- Read the rest of the story to yourself and be ready to answer some questions. Raise your hand when you're finished.

The next day in school, Al asked his science teacher if he could show the book to the other kids in his class. He said, "I think that some of these pictures will help them understand the sea better."

His teacher replied, "Sure. Show some pictures to the class and explain them."

Al hadn't planned on explaining the pictures, and he felt anxious. He said, "I've got a book here that shows some pictures of things in the ocean."

Homer said very loudly, "What's Al doing with a real book?"

Everybody laughed—except Al and the teacher.

The teacher said, "Al has been doing very well in science lately. So let's listen to what he has to say."

Al showed the cover of the book and started to explain. He told about giant squids and blue whales. He told what the blue whale would do to escape from the squid. When he told that the whale would swim very fast to the surface and then dive very quickly, Homer said, "That's impossible. If you go to the surface too fast, you could get the bends and die. So the whale couldn't just zoom up to the surface from 300 feet deep."

"You're wrong, Homer," Al said. "Humans die if they go up too fast, but whales don't. I know."

Before Homer could object, the teacher said, "Al is right. Whales can do that. The great changes in pressure do not seem to bother the whale."

Homer made a sour face, scratched his ear, and mumbled something to himself.

Al went through the part of the book that told about the animals that live in the deepest part of the ocean. After he explained the last picture, he concluded by saying, "Some of the animals that live down there are the most amazing things you've ever seen."

The class applauded. Al's face got hot, and the teacher said, "That was an excellent talk, Al. You told about those things as if you had actually seen them."

Al's face got hotter.

- (After all students have raised their hand:) What did Homer say when Al explained how the blue whale tried to get rid of the squid? (Call on a student. Idea: *That it was impossible for the whale to zoom up to the surface without dying.*) ⓃⒹ
- Everybody, who told Homer that Al was right about what the whales could do? (Signal.) *The teacher.* ⓃⒹ
- How did the students in the class like Al's explanations of the things shown in the book? (Call on a student. Idea: *Very much.*) ⒹⒸ
- How did Al respond when the class applauded? (Call on a student. Idea: *His face got hot.*) ⓃⒹ

Paired Practice

You're going to read aloud to your partner. The **B** members will read first. Then the **A** members will read from the star to the end of the story. (Observe students and give feedback.)

End-of-Lesson Activities

INDEPENDENT WORK

Now finish your independent work for lesson 116. Raise your hand when you're finished. (Observe students and give feedback.)

WORKCHECK

a. (Direct students to take out their marking pencils.)
- We're going to check your workbook and textbook items. Remember, if you got an item wrong, make an **X** next to the item.

b. (For each item: Read the item. Call on a student to answer it. If the answer is wrong, say the correct answer. Refer to the *Answer Key* for the correct answers.)

c. Now use your marking pencil to fix up any items you got wrong. Remember, all mistakes must be fixed up before you hand in your work.

SPELLING

(Present Spelling lesson 116 after completing Reading lesson 116. See *Spelling Presentation Book.*)

Special Project

Note: After completing lesson 116, do this special project with the students. You may do this project during another part of the school day.

Materials: Reference materials (Books on ocean life, encyclopedias, CD-ROMs)

Optional Materials: Poster-making supplies (butcher paper or poster board, markers, crayons, paints, scissors, paste, magazines for pictures)

a. Find page 230 in your textbook. ✔
   - (Call on individual students to read several sentences.)
   - (Teacher reference:)

Special Project

Al and Angela saw incredible animals that live at the bottom of the ocean. You may be able to find pictures of these animals in the encyclopedia or on a CD-ROM. They may have color pictures of the fish that Al and Angela saw. Also look for pictures of fish that live in the deepest parts of the ocean.

b. (Help the students find pictures of deep-sea fish on the computer, in an encyclopedia or in books about fish. This project does not require students to draw the pictures or make a chart; however, you may add this requirement if you wish.)

LESSON 117

EXERCISE 1

Vocabulary

a. **Find page 367 in your textbook.** ✔
- Touch sentence 29. ✔
- This is a new vocabulary sentence. It says: The triceps muscle is bigger than the biceps muscle. Everybody, say that sentence. Get ready. (Signal.) *The triceps muscle is bigger than the biceps muscle.*
- Close your eyes and say the sentence. Get ready. (Signal.) *The triceps muscle is bigger than the biceps muscle.*
- (Repeat until firm.)

b. The sentence refers to the **triceps** and **biceps.** Those are muscles in your upper arm. When you make a muscle, the muscle on the top part of your upper arm is the **biceps.** Everybody, make a muscle and touch your biceps with one finger. (Observe students and give feedback.)
- The back of the upper arm is the **triceps.** Everybody, make a muscle and touch your triceps with one finger. (Observe students and give feedback.)
- When you make a muscle, what's the name of the muscle on top? (Signal.) *Biceps.*
- What's the name of the muscle that covers the rest of the upper arm? (Signal.) *Triceps.*
- Which muscle is bigger, the biceps or the triceps? (Signal.) *Triceps.*

c. The sentence refers to them as **muscles.** In a later lesson, you will see that muscles are attached to bones. Their job is to move those bones so you can walk and jump and do other movements. Everybody, what do we call those body parts that are attached to bones and that move bones? (Signal.) *Muscles.*

d. Listen to the sentence again: The triceps muscle is bigger than the biceps muscle. Everybody, say that sentence. Get ready. (Signal.) *The triceps muscle is bigger than the biceps muscle.*

e. Everybody, what word names the muscle on the back of the upper arm? (Signal.) *Triceps.*
- What word names the muscle on the front of the upper arm? (Signal.) *Biceps.*
- What do we call a part of your body that's attached to bones and that moves bones? (Signal.) *Muscle.*
- (Repeat step e until firm.)

EXERCISE 2

Vocabulary Review

a. You learned a sentence that tells what the squid did.
- Everybody, say that sentence. Get ready. (Signal.) *The squid wriggled its tentacles.*
- (Repeat until firm.)

b. I'll say part of the sentence. When I stop, you say the next word. Listen: The squid . . . Everybody, what's the next word? (Signal.) *Wriggled.*

c. Listen: The . . . Everybody, what's the next word? (Signal.) *Squid.*
- Say the whole sentence. Get ready. (Signal.) *The squid wriggled its tentacles.*

d. Listen: The squid wriggled its . . . Everybody, what's the next word? (Signal.) *Tentacles.*

EXERCISE 3

Reading Words

Column 1

a. Find lesson 117 in your textbook. ✔
- Touch column 1. ✔
- (Teacher reference:)

1. balanced	4. presented
2. flaming	5. muscles
3. silently	

- All these words have an ending.
b. Word 1. What word? (Signal.) *Balanced.*
- Spell **balanced.** Get ready. (Tap for each letter.) *B-A-L-A-N-C-E-D.*
c. Word 2. What word? (Signal.) *Flaming.*
- Spell **flaming.** Get ready. (Tap for each letter.) *F-L-A-M-I-N-G.*

d. Word 3. What word? (Signal.) *Silently.*
- Spell **silently.** Get ready. (Tap for each letter.) *S-I-L-E-N-T-L-Y.*
e. Word 4. What word? (Signal.) *Presented.*
- Spell **presented.** Get ready. (Tap for each letter.) *P-R-E-S-E-N-T-E-D.*
f. Word 5. What word? (Signal.) *Muscles.*
g. Let's read those words again.
- Word 1. What word? (Signal.) *Balanced.*
- (Repeat for: **2. flaming, 3. silently, 4. presented, 5. muscles.**)
h. (Repeat step g until firm.)

Column 2

i. Find column 2. ✔
- (Teacher reference:)

1. <u>in</u>telligent	4. <u>spoon</u>ful
2. <u>tri</u>ceps	5. <u>bi</u>ceps
3. <u>no</u>where	6. <u>un</u>important

- All these words have more than one syllable. The first syllable of each word is underlined.
j. Word 1. What's the first syllable? (Signal.) *in.*
- What's the whole word? (Signal.) *Intelligent.*
k. Word 2. What's the first syllable? (Signal.) *tri.*
- What's the whole word? (Signal.) *Triceps.*
l. Word 3. What's the first syllable? (Signal.) *no.*
- What's the whole word? (Signal.) *Nowhere.*
m. Word 4. What's the first syllable? (Signal.) *spoon.*
- What's the whole word? (Signal.) *Spoonful.*
n. Word 5. What's the first syllable? (Signal.) *bi.*
- What's the whole word? (Signal.) *Biceps.*
o. Word 6. What's the first syllable? (Signal.) *un.*
- What's the whole word? (Signal.) *Unimportant.*
p. Let's read those words again.
- Word 1. What word? (Signal.) *Intelligent.*
- (Repeat for words 2–6.)
q. (Repeat step p until firm.)

Individual Turns
(For columns 1 and 2: Call on individual students, each to read one to three words per turn.)

Story Reading
a. Find part B in your textbook. ✔
- The error limit for group reading is 19 errors. Read carefully.
b. Everybody, touch the title. ✔
- (Call on a student to read the title.) *[A Test About the Ocean.]*
- Everybody, what's the title? (Signal.) *A Test About the Ocean.* (ND)
- (Call on individual students to read the story, each student reading two or three sentences at a time. Ask the specified questions as the students read.)

- (**Correct errors:** Tell the word. Direct the student to reread the sentence.)
- (If the group makes more than 19 errors, direct the students to reread the story.)

A Test About the Ocean
After school, Angela met Al outside. "Come on," she said. "Let's get going."

- Where does she want to go? (Call on a student. Idea: *To the old man's store.*) (DI)
- How do you think she feels about going on trips now? (Call on a student. Ideas: *She likes them; she wants to go on more trips.*) (DCE)

She walked so fast on the way to Anywhere Street that Al had trouble keeping up with her. Al was a little out of breath by the time they reached the store with the familiar sign in the window.

- Why was she walking so fast? (Call on a student. Ideas: *She wanted to get to the store; she wanted to go on another trip.*) (DI)
- Everybody, what did that familiar sign in the window say? (Signal.) *Go Anywhere. See Anything.* (APK)

"Ding, ding."
For a moment, Al and Angela stood silently in the dark store. Then the old man stepped from the darkness. Very loudly he announced, "You may go anywhere and see anything if you pass your test." Without hesitating, he continued. "Angela, here is your first question: How does a squid make itself move?"

- What's the answer? (Call on a student. Idea: *By squirting out water.*) (RF/R)

    Angela cleared her throat and said, "Well, a squid takes in water. Then it blows it out very fast. The water shoots out the back and the squid moves forward—headfirst."

- Everybody, show me how she cleared her throat before she told how the squid moves. ✔ (V)
- Did she give a good explanation of how a squid moves? (Signal.) *Yes.* (DC)

    "Correct," the old man said, and continued without pausing. "Next question, Al. How deep is the deepest part of the ocean?"

- Everybody, what's the answer? (Signal.) *Over six miles deep.* (APK)

    "Over six miles deep," Al replied without hesitating.
    "Next question, Angela. What's the largest animal in the world?"
    "Blue whale," she answered.
    "Next question, Al. How big is the blue whale?"

- How does the blue whale compare with elephants? (Call on a student. Idea: *It weighs more than ten elephants.*) (RF/R)
- How long is it compared to a killer whale? (Call on a student. Idea: *It's much longer than a killer whale.*) (APK)

    Al responded, "The blue whale weighs more than ten elephants and it is much longer than a killer whale."
    Without smiling the old man presented the next question, and others—many others. But Al and Angela answered all of them correctly. Then suddenly, the old man held out his hands and smiled broadly. "You are indeed intelligent students," he said. "Very intelligent. You have passed your test, so where do you want to go and what do you want to see?"
    "I want to see the stars," Angela said.
    "You want a star, you have a star," the old man said.

    Suddenly, Al noticed that there was a hole in the ceiling of the store. Through the hole, Al could see the sun shining brightly.
    "That is a star," the old man announced.
    "But that's just the sun," Angela said.
    "Correct, but the sun is a star."
    Angela said, "I didn't want to see that star. I see it all the time. I wanted to see the other stars."
    "We will visit some of them. But first, let's take a closer look at the sun, so that you have an idea of what it is and how big it is. Look carefully at it."
    Suddenly, the sun seemed to grow larger and larger. Al and Angela were no longer in the store. They were now floating through space, close to the surface of the sun. The surface was not flat. It was made up of flaming gases. One of those flames shot up past Al and the others.
    "That's incredible," Al said.
    "Yes," the old man agreed. "That flame that just shot up is twelve times bigger than Earth."

- Everybody, how big was the flame? (Signal.) *Twelve times bigger than Earth.* (ND)
- Touch Earth in the picture. ✔ (VA)
- Now touch a flame that is twelve times bigger than Earth. ✔ (VA)
- You can see that the flame is very small compared to the sun. So the sun must be many, many times larger than Earth.

    Angela added, "And that flame is nowhere near as big as the sun."
    "Correct," the old man said. Earth is like a tiny dot next to the sun. If we went through the middle of the sun and came out the other side,

we would travel one hundred times as far as we would travel going through ⭐ the middle of the Earth."

- Everybody, if they went through the middle of the sun, how many times farther would they travel than they would travel going through the middle of Earth? (Signal.) *One hundred.* Ⓝ🅓

Al asked, "Do you mean that the sun is a hundred times wider than Earth?"

"Correct," the old man replied.

"Fantastic," Angela exclaimed.

The old man said, "Remember how big the sun is because we're going to look at some other stars."

Everything turned dark for a moment. Then Al noticed that he was approaching another star. It looked small.

The old man said, "We are now very far from Earth. It would take us over five thousand years to get back to Earth if we traveled at the speed of light."

- Everybody, how long would it take them to get back to Earth traveling at the speed of light? (Signal.) *Over five thousand years.* Ⓝ🅓

Then the old man pointed to the star and continued, "That star is very old and very small. At one time that star was as big as our sun. But now it is almost burned out. It is only eight miles through the middle. That's much smaller than Earth. Earth is eight <u>thousand</u> miles through the middle."

- Everybody, how far is it through the middle of the small star? (Signal.) *Eight miles.* Ⓝ🅓
- How far is it through the middle of Earth? (Signal.) *Eight thousand miles.* Ⓝ🅓
- So it's a thousand times farther through the middle of Earth. That star is just a tiny thing.

Angela said, "I had no idea that stars could be so small."

The old man said, "But the most interesting thing about this old star is not how small it is but how much it weighs. It weighs almost as much as it did when it was as large as our sun."

"That's impossible," Al said. "It's not even as big as a moon. It's a tiny little thing."

The old man said, "I will show you how much the matter from this star weighs." The old man suddenly zoomed down to the surface of the star and came back holding a spoonful of bright glowing matter. "Here is one spoonful of matter from the star," he said.

A giant balance scale appeared in the sky. The old man said, "I will put this spoonful of matter on one side of the balance scale. Then we'll see how much weight must go on the other side to make the scale balance."

- Everybody, look at the picture on page 233. ✔ Ⓥ🅐
- You can see the giant balance scale. How much matter from the star is the old man putting on one side of the balance scale? (Signal.) *A spoonful.* Ⓥ🅐
- Then he'll put things on the other side. How will he know when the things on the other side weigh as much as the spoonful of matter? (Call on a student. Idea: *The scale will balance.*) Ⓓ🅘
- Everybody, use your hands to show the pans on the scale after the old man adds the star matter to one side of the scale. ✔ Ⓥ
- Then show what the scale will do when it balances. ✔ Ⓥ

The old man placed the spoonful of matter on one side of the scale. That side went down.

"Angela," the old man said. "Name something that is heavy. I will put it on the other side of the scale and we will see if the scale will balance."

"A big rock," Angela said. A rock appeared on the other side of the scale, but the scale did not move. The side with the spoonful of matter on it stayed down.

- Everybody, which side of the scale was down? (Signal.) *The side with the spoonful of matter.* (ND)
- So which was heavier, the spoonful of matter or the rock? (Signal.) *The spoonful of matter.* (DC)
- Read the rest of the story to yourself and be ready to answer some questions. Raise your hand when you're finished.

"A rock is not heavy enough," the old man said.

"Try a big truck," Al said, and a big truck appeared on the scale. The scale did not move.

"Five more trucks," Angela said. They appeared, but the scale did not move.

"A small mountain," Al said. The trucks disappeared and a mountain appeared. Al waited for the scale to move, but it didn't. Al could not believe it. On one side of the scale was a spoonful of matter. On the other side was a mountain—not a hill, but a mountain. And still the side with the spoonful of matter stayed down.

"A <u>huge</u> mountain," Angela said. One appeared. It was so huge that Al could hardly see the top of it. Slowly, the scale balanced.

"Incredible," Angela said. "One spoonful of matter weighs as much as a huge mountain."

"Yes," the old man said.

- (After all students have raised their hand:) Name some things that did **not** make the scale balance. (Call on a student. Ideas: *A big rock; a big truck; six trucks; a small mountain.*) (ND)

- Everybody, what made the scale finally balance? (Signal.) *A huge mountain.* (ND)
- So how much did the spoonful of matter weigh? (Call on a student. Idea: *The same as a huge mountain.*) (ND)
- That's amazing.

EXERCISE 5

Paired Practice

You're going to read aloud to your partner. The **A** members will read first. Then the **B** members will read from the star to the end of the story. (Observe students and give feedback.)

End-of-Lesson Activities

INDEPENDENT WORK

Now finish your independent work for lesson 117. Raise your hand when you're finished. (Observe students and give feedback.)

WORKCHECK

a. (Direct students to take out their marking pencils.)
- We're going to check your workbook and textbook items. Remember, if you got an item wrong, make an **X** next to the item.
b. (For each item: Read the item. Call on a student to answer it. If the answer is wrong, say the correct answer. Refer to the Answer Key for the correct answers.)
c. Now use your marking pencil to fix up any items you got wrong. Remember, all mistakes must be fixed up before you hand in your work.

SPELLING

(Present Spelling lesson 117 after completing Reading lesson 117. See *Spelling Presentation Book.*)

ACTIVITIES

(Present Activity 23 after completing Reading lesson 117. See *Activities across the Curriculum.*)

EXERCISE 1

Vocabulary Review

a. Here's the new vocabulary sentence: The triceps muscle is bigger than the biceps muscle.
- Everybody, say that sentence. Get ready. (Signal.) *The triceps muscle is bigger than the biceps muscle.*
- (Repeat until firm.)

b. Everybody, what do we call a part of your body that's attached to bones and that moves bones? (Signal.) *Muscle.*
- What word names the muscle on the front of the upper arm? (Signal.) *Biceps.*
- What word names the muscle on the back of the upper arm? (Signal.) *Triceps.*
- (Repeat step b until firm.)

EXERCISE 2

Reading Words

Column 1

a. **Find lesson 118 in your textbook.** ✔
- Touch column 1. ✔
- (Teacher reference:)

1. <u>pin</u>wheel	3. <u>no</u>where
2. <u>snow</u>flake	4. <u>head</u>first

- All these words are compound words. The first part of each word is underlined.

b. Word 1. What's the underlined part? (Signal.) *pin.*
- What's the whole word? (Signal.) *Pinwheel.*

c. Word 2. What's the underlined part? (Signal.) *snow.*
- What's the whole word? (Signal.) *Snowflake.*

d. Word 3. What's the underlined part? (Signal.) *no.*
- What's the whole word? (Signal.) *Nowhere.*

e. Word 4. What's the underlined part? (Signal.) *head.*
- What's the whole word? (Signal.) *Headfirst.*

f. Let's read those words again.
- Word 1. What word? (Signal.) *Pinwheel.*
- (Repeat for words 2–4.)

g. (Repeat step f until firm.)

Column 2

h. Find column 2. ✔
- (Teacher reference:)

1. decorated	3. prettiest
2. brightest	4. zoomed

- All these words have an ending.

i. Word 1 is **decorated.** What word? (Signal.) *Decorated.*
- When you decorate something, you add things to make it look prettier. If you decorate a cake, you could add colored frosting, candies, and other pretty things. Everybody, what are you doing when you add things to make something look prettier? (Signal.) *Decorating.*

j. Word 2. What word? (Signal.) *Brightest.*
- (Repeat for words 3 and 4.)

k. Let's read those words again.
- Word 1. What word? (Signal.) *Decorated.*
- (Repeat for words 2–4.)

l. (Repeat step k until firm.)

Column 3

m. Find column 3. ✔
- (Teacher reference:)

1. Milky Way	3. imagination
2. unimportant	4. universe

n. Number 1. What words? (Signal.) *Milky Way.*

o. Word 2. What word? (Signal.) *Unimportant.*
- (Repeat for words 3 and 4.)

p. Let's read those words again.
- Number 1. What words? (Signal.) *Milky Way.*
- Word 2. What word? (Signal.) *Unimportant.*
- (Repeat for words 3 and 4.)

q. (Repeat step p until firm.)

Individual Turns

(For columns 1–3: Call on individual students, each to read one to three words per turn.)

Story Reading

a. Find part B in your textbook. ✔
- The error limit for group reading is 15 errors. Read carefully.

b. Everybody, touch the title. ✔
- (Call on a student to read the title.) *[Angela and Al See Our Galaxy.]*
- Everybody, what's the title? (Signal.) *Angela and Al See Our Galaxy.* ⓃⒹ
- What's going to happen in this story? (Call on a student. Idea: *Angela and Al will see our galaxy.*) Ⓟ
- (Call on individual students to read the story, each student reading two or three sentences at a time. Ask the specified questions as the students read.)

> - (**Correct errors:** Tell the word. Direct the student to reread the sentence.)
> - (If the group makes more than 15 errors, direct the students to reread the story.)

Angela and Al See Our Galaxy

Al, Angela and the old man were looking at a star that was much, much smaller than the sun. The old man had just shown how much a spoonful of matter from that star weighs.

- How much did it weigh? (Call on a student. Idea: *As much as a huge mountain.*) ⒶⓅⓀ

The old man said, "There are millions of very old stars like this one. They are very small. But there are also very large stars."
"Like our sun," Al said.
"No," the old man said. "Very large."

- Everybody, does the old man agree that the sun is very large? (Signal.) *No.* ⓃⒹ

Suddenly Al noticed that he was moving very fast. He was passing up many stars. Then he seemed to stop. In front of him were two stars. One looked like a tiny speck next to the other.

Angela asked, "Is that small star another tiny star?"
"No," the old man replied. "The very tiny star is the same size as our sun."

- How big was the tiny star? (Call on a student. Idea: *The same size as our sun.*) ⓃⒹ
- So what do you know about the other star? (Call on a student. Idea: *It's huge.*) ⒹⒸ

Al compared the size of the two stars. The star that was as big as the sun looked hundreds of times smaller than the other star. Al was trying to imagine just how big that huge star was. But his mind couldn't get used to the idea that the tiny star was the size of the sun.
The old man pointed to the huge star. He said, "If that star were in the center of our solar system, it would be so big that Mercury would be inside the star."

- Everybody, what would be inside the star? (Signal.) *Mercury.* ⓃⒹ

"Incredible," Angela exclaimed.
The old man continued, "But Mercury would not be the only planet inside the star. Venus, Earth, Mars, and even Jupiter would be inside the star."

- Everybody, name **all** the planets that would be inside the huge star. Get ready. (Signal.) *Mercury, Venus, Earth, Mars, Jupiter.* ⓃⒹ

The old man continued, "That star is so huge that it would take light over 45 minutes to travel from one side of the star to the other side."

- Everybody, how long would it take light to travel from one side of that star to the other side? (Signal.) *Over 45 minutes.* ⓃⒹ
- And about how long does it take light to travel from our sun to Earth? (Signal.) *Eight minutes.* ⓃⒹ
- So that star is so big that our Earth would be far inside it.

Al shook his head. He still couldn't imagine anything so big. "That's the biggest thing I can imagine," Al said.

"Big?" the old man said. "That star is nothing but a speck compared to a galaxy."

- Everybody, what is much bigger than the star? (Signal.) *A galaxy.* (ND)
- How big is the star compared to a galaxy? (Call on a student. Ideas: *Very small; nothing but a speck.*) (ND)
- What is a galaxy? (Call on a student. Idea: *A cloud of stars.*) (APK)

Before Al could say anything, he noticed that he and the others were again speeding through space. They were moving toward a star. But as they zoomed closer and closer, Al observed that it was not a star. It was a cloud of stars. The cloud became larger and larger, until it seemed to fill the whole sky. It was incredible. Some of the stars were shining with all the colors of the rainbow. And the galaxy was shaped like a giant pinwheel. It was the brightest, biggest, most beautiful thing that Al had ever seen in his life. There were so many stars in the galaxy that Al couldn't even begin to count them.

Al and Angela didn't say anything for a long time. They simply looked at the incredible sight. At last Al said, "How many stars are in that galaxy? Are there more than a million?"

"Oh, yes," the old man replied. "Think of a thousand million. That's a billion. Then think of a hundred billion. One hundred billion. That's how many stars are in this galaxy."

- Everybody, how many stars are in the galaxy? (Signal.) *100 billion.* (ND)
- Is that more than a million? (Signal.) *Yes.* (DC)

Al tried to think of a billion and then think of a hundred billion, but the number was too big for his imagination.

The old ☆ man said, "It takes light 100 thousand years to travel from one side of that galaxy to the other side."

- Everybody, how long does it take light to go across that galaxy? (Signal.) *100 thousand years.* (ND)

Al asked, "Are there other galaxies like this one?"

The old man replied, "There are millions of galaxies in the universe, but the one you're looking at is the biggest and prettiest one we know about." Then the old man asked, "Does it look familiar to you?"

"No," Al and Angela said.

"Look carefully," the old man said. "One of the stars is flashing very brightly so that you can see it."

"I see it," Angela said, pointing to one side of the galaxy.

Suddenly Al realized that he was moving toward that star. Al and the others were going through the galaxy now. There were stars all around them.

The old man pointed to the star that had been flashing. "That star is very, very special," the old man said.

"What's so special about it?" Angela asked. "It's just a little star."

The old man said, "The galaxy we're going through is called the Milky Way. And there is a star inside the Milky Way that is called the sun. That star you are moving toward is the sun. Now you know why it is special."

- Everybody, what's the name of the galaxy they are moving through? (Signal.) *The Milky Way.* (ND)
- What's the name of the special star in that galaxy? (Signal.) *The sun.* (ND)
- Read the rest of the story to yourself and be ready to answer some questions. Raise your hand when you're finished.

Al looked at the billions of stars in the Milky Way and noticed how small and unimportant the sun looked. The old man said, "Our sun is small when you think about the size of the universe. Just think—there are stars that are almost eight hundred times bigger than our sun. And there are galaxies that have billions and billions of stars."

Al tried to think about the size of the things he had seen. The sun had flames that were twelve times bigger than Earth. But there were stars that were hundreds of times bigger than the sun. And there were galaxies hundreds and hundreds and hundreds and hundreds and hundreds . . .

"What?" Al said out loud. He was startled for a moment when he realized that he was no longer floating through space. He was standing in the dark store.

The old man said, "Before you leave, I want you to take one more look at the Milky Way. Look up."

Suddenly Al realized that there was no ceiling in the store and that he could see a sky above him, covered with a cloud of stars. The old man explained, "That's how the Milky Way looks from Earth on a summer night. You are looking at it from the side, but it is still beautiful."

Al stared at the sky for a few minutes. Then the sky seemed to fade. Al and Angela were standing alone in the dark store. From somewhere a voice announced, "Pass a test on what you've seen and you can go anywhere and see anything."

"Ding, ding."

The air was cold outside the store. The sky was cloudy and a few snowflakes were starting to fall. Al said, "When I close my eyes, I can still see how the Milky Way looked when we were close to it. I'll never forget that sight as long as I live."

"Me neither," Angela said.

- (After all students have raised their hand:) What was Al thinking about just before he realized that he was back inside the store? (Call on a student. Idea: *The size of the things he had seen.*) (ND)
- The old man removed the ceiling from the store to show Al and Angela how the Milky Way would look on a summer night. Everybody, was it really summer outside the store? (Signal.) *No.* (ND)

- What was the sky like when Al and Angela went outside? (Call on a student. Ideas: *Cloudy; snowy.*) (ND)
- What could Al see when he closed his eyes? (Call on a student. Idea: *How the Milky Way looked.*) (ND)
- Have any of you ever seen the Milky Way? (MC)

Paired Practice

You're going to read aloud to your partner. The **B** members will read first. Then the **A** members will read from the star to the end of the story. (Observe students and give feedback.)

End-of-Lesson Activities

INDEPENDENT WORK

Now finish your independent work for lesson 118. Raise your hand when you're finished. (Observe students and give feedback.)

WORKCHECK

a. (Direct students to take out their marking pencils.)
- We're going to check your workbook and textbook items. Remember, if you got an item wrong, make an **X** next to the item.
b. (For each item: Read the item. Call on a student to answer it. If the answer is wrong, say the correct answer. Refer to the Answer Key for the correct answers.)
c. Now use your marking pencil to fix up any items you got wrong. Remember, all mistakes must be fixed up before you hand in your work.

SPELLING

(Present Spelling lesson 118 after completing Reading lesson 118. See *Spelling Presentation Book.*)

EXERCISE 1

Vocabulary Review

a. You learned a sentence that tells about the poem they created.

- Everybody, say that sentence. Get ready. (Signal.) *The poem they created was nonsense.*
- (Repeat until firm.)

b. You learned a sentence that tells what the squid did.

- Everybody, say that sentence. Get ready. (Signal.) *The squid wriggled its tentacles.*
- (Repeat until firm.)

c. Here's the last sentence you learned: The triceps muscle is bigger than the biceps muscle.

- Everybody, say that sentence. Get ready. (Signal.) *The triceps muscle is bigger than the biceps muscle.*
- (Repeat until firm.)

d. What word names the muscle on the front of the upper arm? (Signal.) *Biceps.*

- What do we call a part of your body that is attached to bones and that moves bones? (Signal.) *Muscle.*
- What word names the muscle on the back of the upper arm? (Signal.) *Triceps.*
- (Repeat step d until firm.)

e. Once more. Say the sentence that tells about the triceps muscle. Get ready. (Signal.) *The triceps muscle is bigger than the biceps muscle.*

EXERCISE 2

Reading Words

a. **Find lesson 119 in your textbook.** ✔

- Touch word 1. ✔
- (Teacher reference:)

1. protect	4. choose
2. thicker	5. difference
3. fired	6. decorated

b. Word 1. What word? (Signal.) *Protect.*

- Spell **protect.** Get ready. (Tap for each letter.) *P-R-O-T-E-C-T.*

c. Word 2. What word? (Signal.) *Thicker.*

- Spell **thicker.** Get ready. (Tap for each letter.) *T-H-I-C-K-E-R.*

d. Word 3. What word? (Signal.) *Fired.*

- Spell **fired.** Get ready. (Tap for each letter.) *F-I-R-E-D.*

e. Word 4. What word? (Signal.) *Choose.*

- Spell **choose.** Get ready. (Tap for each letter.) *C-H-O-O-S-E.*

f. Word 5. What word? (Signal.) *Difference.*

- (Repeat for word 6.)

g. Let's read those words again.

- Word 1. What word? (Signal.) *Protect.*
- (Repeat for words 2–6.)

h. (Repeat step g until firm.)

EXERCISE 3

Story Reading

a. Find part B in your textbook. ✔

- The error limit for group reading is 17 errors. Read carefully.

b. Everybody, touch the title. ✔

- (Call on a student to read the title.) *[Angela and Al Learn About Muscles.]*
- Everybody, what's the title? (Signal.) *Angela and Al Learn About Muscles.* Ⓝ🄳
- (Call on individual students to read the story, each student reading two or three sentences at a time. Ask the specified questions as the students read.)

- (**Correct errors:** Tell the word. Direct the student to reread the sentence.)
- (If the group makes more than 17 errors, direct the students to reread the story.)

Angela and Al Learn About Muscles

The stores were decorated for Christmas. Displays in the windows showed many wonderful presents. But Al tried not to look at them as he walked to school. He didn't have any money, and he didn't know how he was going to buy presents. He paused in front of one store and felt very sad for a moment as he thought about how nice it would be to give his mother a real Christmas gift, something she really wanted, like a toaster. But then he told himself not to think about it. "Come on," Angela said, "or we'll be late for school."

- Why did Al feel sad when he looked at the Christmas displays? (Call on a student. Idea: *Because he didn't have enough money for presents.*) ND
- Everybody, what present did he want to buy his mother? (Signal.) *A toaster.* ND
- What did he tell himself when he started to feel sad about not being able to buy it? (Call on a student. Idea: *Don't think about it.*) ND

❀ Al's mind felt heavy in school that day. It was too filled with facts and thoughts about the things the old man had shown him.

- Why did his mind feel heavy? (Call on a student. Idea: *Because it was so filled with facts and thoughts about what he'd seen on his trip.*) ND

His mind was so filled with information that he didn't feel as if he was ready to learn more. In fact, he said, "Oh, no," to himself when his teacher announced that on Monday the class would have a test on the human body.

- Everybody, what was the test going to be on? (Signal.) *The human body.* ND

Al didn't know much about the human body, and he really didn't want to learn about it. And, he kept thinking about Christmas.

After school, he walked with Angela to Anywhere Street. They walked down the street until they came to the store with the familiar sign in the window. As soon as they entered, the ❀ old man stepped out of the darkness. "Pay for your trip by passing a test," he said in a serious voice. He fired questions at Al and Angela but they knew the answers.

- What does that mean, he fired questions? (Call on a student. Idea: *He asked one after another very fast.*) UCCM

They told him how big the large flames from the sun were.

- How big? (Call on a student. Idea: *Twelve times bigger than Earth.*) APK

They told him how much a spoonful of matter from the very old star weighed.

- How much did it weigh? (Call on a student. Idea: *As much as a huge mountain.*) RF/R

They told him how big the huge star was and how many stars are in the Milky Way.

- Name how much of our solar system would fit inside that star. (Call on a student. Idea: *From the sun through Jupiter.*) APK
- Everybody, how many stars are in the Milky Way? (Signal.) *One hundred billion.* RF/R

Then without smiling, the old man said, "I will choose the trip this time. It is an incredible trip."

"Where are we going?" Angela asked.

"Inside the human body."

"The human body?" Al asked. "That doesn't sound very interesting."

"Let's see how interesting it is," the old man said. As soon as he had spoken those words, then something appeared in the room and the room became light. The form that had appeared looked exactly like a man, but Al could see that it wasn't actually a living person. The man had large muscles and was wearing only swimming trunks.

"He looks very strong," Angela said.

"Correct," the old man replied. "And the first thing we will do is look more carefully at those muscles."

The old man continued, "The body has many parts, and every part has a job to do."

The old man walked up to the model of the man and pointed to one of his arms. "That is how an arm looks to you. But you cannot see all of the parts in the arm because they are under the skin."

Then the arm of the man seemed to change. The skin disappeared and Al could see all the muscles in the arm.

The old man pointed to the muscle on the front of the upper arm. He said, "The name of this muscle is the biceps."

- Everybody, what's the name of the muscle on the front of the upper arm? (Signal.) *Biceps.* ⓃⒹ

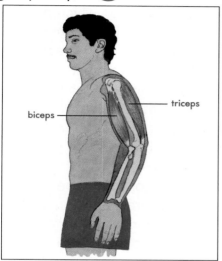

biceps — triceps

- Touch the biceps muscle in the picture. ✔ ⓋⒶ
- Put one arm at your side and touch the muscle on the front of your upper arm. ✔
- Everybody, what's the name of that muscle? (Signal.) *Biceps.* ⓃⒹ

Then the old man pointed to the muscle on the back of the upper arm and said, "This muscle is the triceps."

- Everybody, what's the muscle on the back of the upper arm? (Signal.) *Triceps.* ⓃⒹ
- Put your arm at your side and touch the muscle on the back of your upper arm. ✔
- Everybody, what's the name of that muscle? (Signal.) *Triceps.* ⓃⒹ

The old man said, "If you know the ✮ rule about how muscles work, you can figure out which job each muscle does. When a muscle works, it pulls and gets shorter."

- Everybody, what does a muscle do when it works? (Signal.) *Pulls and gets shorter.* ⓃⒹ
- (Repeat until firm.)

The old man continued, "Watch the man lift a weight. See which muscle is getting shorter and thicker. That's the muscle that is working to lift the weight."

Suddenly a weight appeared in the man's hand. Then the arm started to bend and lift the weight.

The muscle on the front of the arm got shorter and thicker as the weight moved up.

- Everybody, what's the **name** of the muscle that got shorter and thicker? (Signal.) *Biceps.* ⓃⒹ

"Which muscle works to bend the arm?" the old man asked.

Together Al and Angela said, "The biceps."

"Correct," the old man said. "Now the arm will straighten. Watch which muscle straightens the arm."

The arm pushed the weight overhead. As the weight moved overhead, the muscle on the back of the arm became thicker and shorter.

The old man said, "Tell me the name of the muscle that straightens the arm."

- Everybody, what did they say? (Signal.) *Triceps.* ⒹⒸ

"The triceps," Al and Angela answered together.

"How do you know that the triceps straightens the arm?" the old man asked.

Before Al could respond, Angela said, "Because it gets shorter and thicker when the arm straightens."

"Remember the rule," the old man said. "Muscles do only one thing when they work. Muscles pull. And when they pull, they get shorter and thicker. The muscle that is working is the muscle that is getting shorter and thicker."

- Everybody, name the muscle that bends the arm. Get ready. (Signal.) *Biceps.* ⓇⒻ/Ⓡ
- Where is that muscle? (Signal.) *On the front of the upper arm.* ⓇⒻ/Ⓡ
- Name the muscle that straightens the arm. Get ready. (Signal.) *Triceps.* ⓇⒻ/Ⓡ

- Where is that muscle? (Signal.) *On the back of the upper arm.* (RF/R)

> Suddenly the skin disappeared from the rest of the man's body. Al could see every muscle. He could see muscles in the chest, muscles in the legs and muscles of the neck.

- Read the rest of the story to yourself and be ready to answer some questions. Raise your hand when you're finished.

> "Wow!" Angela exclaimed. "I never knew there were so many muscles in the body."
> "Yes," the old man said. "And every muscle has one job. Every muscle helps the man move one part of his body one way. Watch the man move. See if you can figure out which muscle is working."
> The man's leg started to bend back. Angela pointed to the muscle on the back of the upper leg. "There's a muscle getting shorter and thicker."
> The old man said, "That's right. The only muscle that can bend the man's leg is the muscle on the back of the upper leg. It pulls and gets shorter to bend the leg back."
> Now the man's head started to move back and Al could see that the muscles at the back of the neck were getting shorter and thicker. He pointed to them and told the old man that they were the muscles that moved the head back.
> As the man's head started to move forward, Al could see the muscles in the front of the neck getting shorter and thicker. They were moving the head forward.
> Angela observed, "The muscles work in pairs. One muscle moves a part of the body one way. The muscle on the other side of the part moves that part the other way."
> "Correct," the old man replied. "And if one of those muscles is cut,

> the part cannot move. Watch what happens when the muscle in the back of the upper leg is cut." The man's leg started to bend back. Suddenly, it stopped and came forward. The old man explained, "The muscle in the back of the upper leg is cut now, so the man cannot bend the leg back. There is only one muscle that can do that job, and that muscle is not working."
> "That's amazing," Angela said.

- (After all students have raised their hand:) Everybody, on which part of your neck are the muscles that move your head back? (Signal.) *The back.* (ND)
- On which part of your neck are the muscles that move your head forward? (Signal.) *The front.* (ND)
- On which part of your upper leg are the muscles that bend the leg back? (Signal.) *The back.* (ND)
- On which part of your upper leg are the muscles that straighten your leg? (Signal.) *The front.* (ND)
- What did the old man do to one of the muscles? (Call on a student. Idea: *He cut it.*) (ND)
- Where was that muscle? (Call on a student. Idea: *On the back of the upper leg.*) (ND)
- What happened when the muscle was cut? (Call on a student. Ideas: *The leg fell forward; the leg could not bend back.*) (ND)
- Remember, each muscle can do only one job. If the muscle on the back of the upper leg is not working, the body cannot bend the leg.

EXERCISE 4

Paired Practice

You're going to read aloud to your partner. The **A** members will read first. Then the **B** members will read from the star to the end of the story. (Observe students and give feedback.)

End-of-Lesson Activities

Now finish your independent work for lesson 119. Raise your hand when you're finished. (Observe students and give feedback.)

a. (Direct students to take out their marking pencils.)
- We're going to check your workbook and textbook items. Remember, if you got an item wrong, make an **X** next to the item.

b. (For each item: Read the item. Call on a student to answer it. If the answer is wrong, say the correct answer. Refer to the Answer Key for the correct answers.)

c. Now use your marking pencil to fix up any items you got wrong. Remember, all mistakes must be fixed up before you hand in your work.

(Present Spelling lesson 119 after completing Reading lesson 119. See *Spelling Presentation Book.*)

> ***Note:*** You will need to reproduce blackline masters for the Fact Game in lesson 120 (Appendix G in the *Teacher's Guide*).

(Present Activity 24 after completing Reading lessons 119–121. See *Activities across the Curriculum.*)

LESSON 120

Materials for Lesson 120

Fact Game

For each team (4 or 5 students):

- pair of number cubes (or dice)
- copy of Fact Game 120
  (Reproducible blackline masters are in Appendix G at the back of the *Teacher's Guide*.)

For each student:

- a copy of the scorecard sheet (at end of workbook B)

For each monitor:

- a pencil
- Fact Game 120 answer key (at end of textbook B)

Fluency: Rate/Accuracy

Each student needs a thermometer chart.

EXERCISE 1

Fact Game

a. (Divide students into groups of four or five. Assign monitors.)

b. You'll play the game for 10 minutes. (Circulate as students play the game. Comment on groups that are playing well.)

c. (At the end of 10 minutes, have all students who earned more than 10 points stand up.)

- (Tell the monitor of each game that ran smoothly:) Your group did a good job.

EXERCISE 2

Fluency: Rate/Accuracy

a. Today is a test day and a reading checkout day. While you're writing answers, I'm going to call on you one at a time to read part of the story we read in lesson 119.

- Remember, you pass the checkout by reading the passage in less than a minute without making more than 2 mistakes. And when you pass the checkout, you color the space for lesson 120 on your thermometer chart.

Test 12

b. (Call on individual students to read the portion of story 119 marked with ❀.)

- (Time the student. Note words that are missed and number of words read.)
- (Teacher reference:)

❀ Al's mind felt heavy in school that day. It was too filled with facts and thoughts about the things the old man had shown him. His mind was so filled with information that he didn't feel as if he was ready to learn more. In fact, he said, "Oh no," [50] to himself when his teacher announced that on Monday the class would have a test on the human body.

Al didn't know much about the [75] human body, and he really didn't want to learn about it. And, he kept thinking about Christmas.

After school, he walked with Angela to Anywhere [100] Street. They walked down the street until they came to the store with the familiar sign in the window. As soon as they entered, the ❀ [125] old man stepped out of the darkness.

- (If the student reads the passage in one minute or less and makes no more than 2 errors, direct the student to color in the space for lesson 120 on the thermometer chart.)

- (If the student makes any mistakes, point to each word that was misread and identify it.)
- (If the student does not meet the rate-error criterion for the passage, direct the student to practice reading the story with the assigned partner.)

EXERCISE 3

Test

a. **Find page 249 in your textbook.** ✔

- This is a test. You'll work items you've done before.

b. Work carefully. Raise your hand when you've completed all the items. (Observe students but do not give feedback on errors.)

Marking the Test

a. (Check students' work before beginning lesson 121. Refer to the Answer Key for the correct answers.)

b. (Record all test 12 results on the Test Summary Sheet and the Group Summary Sheet. Reproducible Summary Sheets are at the back of the *Teacher's Guide*.)

SPELLING

(Present Spelling lesson 120 after completing Reading lesson 120. See *Spelling Presentation Book*.)

EXERCISE 5

Test Remedies

(Provide any necessary remedies for test 12 before presenting lesson 121. Test remedies are discussed in the *Teacher's Guide*.)

Test 12 Firming Table

Test Item	Introduced in lesson	Test Item	Introduced in lesson	Test Item	Introduced in lesson
1	111	11	118	21	114
2	111	12	119	22	114
3	111	13	119	23	114
4	111	14	119	24	117
5	111	15	119	25	114
6	115	16	119	26	117
7	115	17	119	27	111
8	115	18	114	28	111
9	116	19	114	29	117
10	116	20	114	30	114

	Lesson 121	Lesson 122	Lesson 123	Lesson 124	Lesson 125
LESSON EVENTS	Vocabulary Sentence Reading Words Fact Review Story Reading Paired Practice Independent Work Workcheck Spelling	**Vocabulary Sentence** Reading Words Story Reading Paired Practice Independent Work Workcheck Spelling	Vocabulary Sentence Reading Words Story Reading Paired Practice Fact Review Independent Work Workcheck Spelling	Vocabulary Sentence Reading Words Story Reading Paired Practice Independent Work Workcheck Spelling	Vocabulary Sentence Reading Words Story Background Story Reading Fluency: Rate/Accuracy Independent Work Workcheck Spelling
VOCABULARY SENTENCE	#29: The triceps <u>muscle</u> is bigger than the biceps <u>muscle</u>.	**#30: The <u>injury</u> to his <u>spinal</u> <u>cord</u> <u>paralyzed</u> him.**	#30: The <u>injury</u> to his <u>spinal</u> <u>cord</u> <u>paralyzed</u> him.	sentence #28 sentence #29 sentence #30	#30: The <u>injury</u> to his <u>spinal</u> <u>cord</u> <u>paralyzed</u> him.
READING WORDS: WORD TYPES	modeled words multi-syllable words mixed words	modeled words	modeled words words with an ending	2-syllable words mixed words	modeled words 2-syllable words multi-syllable words
NEW VOCABULARY	blood vessel chamber skull lungs permit protect	cell	cerebrum magnifying image	forearm pulse nerve	retina spiral backbone
STORY BACKGROUND					*Making Pictures With a Magnifying Glass*
STORY	*Al and Angela Learn About Bones*	*Angela and Al Learn About the Heart*	*Al and Angela Follow Blood Through the Body*	*Angela and Al Learn About Nerves*	*Al and Angela Learn About the Brain*
SKILL ITEMS	Vocabulary sentences	Sequencing	Vocabulary	Vocabulary sentence Crossword puzzle	Vocabulary Vocabulary sentences
SPECIAL MATERIALS					Thermometer charts
SPECIAL PROJECTS/ ACTIVITIES		Activity for lessons 122–123	Activity for lesson 123	Activity for lessons 124–125	

Comprehension Questions Abbreviations Guide

Access Prior Knowledge = (APK)   Author's Point of View = (APoV)   Author's Purpose = (AP)   Cause/Effect = (C/E)   Charts/Graphs/Diagrams/Visual Aids = (VA)

Classify and Categorize = (C+C)   Compare/Contrast = (C/C)   Determine Character Emotions, Motivation = (DCE)   Drawing Conclusions = (DC)   Drawing Inferences = (DI)

Fact and Opinion = (F/O)   Hypothesizing = (H)   Main Idea = (MI)   Making Connections = (MC)   Making Deductions = (MD)   Making Judgements = (MJ)

Narrative Elements = (NE)   Noting Details = (ND)   Predict = (P)   Reality/Fantasy = (R/F)   Recall Facts/Rules = (RF/R)   Retell = (R)   Sequence = (Seq)

Steps in a Process = (SP)   Story Structure = (SS)   Summarize = (Sum)   Understanding Dialogue = (UD)   Using Context to Confirm Meaning(s) = (UCCM)   Visualize = (V)

EXERCISE 1

Vocabulary Review

a. You learned a sentence that tells about the triceps muscle.

- Everybody, say that sentence. Get ready. (Signal.) *The triceps muscle is bigger than the biceps muscle.*
- (Repeat until firm.)

b. I'll say part of the sentence. When I stop, you say the next word. Listen: The triceps muscle is bigger than the . . . Everybody, what's the next word? (Signal.) *Biceps.*

- Say the whole sentence. Get ready. (Signal.) *The triceps muscle is bigger than the biceps muscle.*

c. Listen: The triceps . . . Everybody, what's the next word? (Signal.) *Muscle.*

d. Listen: The . . . Everybody, what's the next word? (Signal.) *Triceps.*

- Say the whole sentence. Get ready. (Signal.) *The triceps muscle is bigger than the biceps muscle.*

EXERCISE 2

Reading Words

Column 1

a. **Find lesson 121 in your textbook.** ✔

- Touch column 1. ✔
- (Teacher reference:)

1. blood vessel	4. paralyzed
2. heart	5. skull
3. chamber	6. lungs

b. Number 1 is **blood vessel.** What words? (Signal.) *Blood vessel.*

- A blood vessel is a tube that carries blood through the body. Everybody, what do we call tubes that carry blood? (Signal.) *Blood vessels.*

c. Word 2 is **heart.** What word? (Signal.) *Heart.*

- Spell **heart.** Get ready. (Tap for each letter.) *H-E-A-R-T.*

d. Word 3 is **chamber.** What word? (Signal.) *Chamber.*

- Spell **chamber.** Get ready. (Tap for each letter.) *C-H-A-M-B-E-R.*

- Special rooms are called chambers. Everybody, what's another word for **a special room?** (Signal.) *Chamber.*

e. Word 4 is **paralyzed.** What word? (Signal.) *Paralyzed.*

f. Word 5. What word? (Signal.) *Skull.*

- Spell **skull.** Get ready. (Tap for each letter.) *S-K-U-L-L.*

- Your skull is the bone that covers the top of your head. Everybody, touch your skull. ✔

g. Word 6. What word? (Signal.) *Lungs.*

- Spell **lungs.** Get ready. (Tap for each letter.) *L-U-N-G-S.*

- When you breathe, you use your lungs. They are large organs that are in your chest. They take air in and let air out. Everybody, what are the large organs in your chest that you use when you breathe? (Signal.) *Lungs.*

h. Let's read those words again.

- Number 1. What words? (Signal.) *Blood vessel.*

- Word 2. What word? (Signal.) *Heart.*
- (Repeat for words 3–6.)

i. (Repeat step h until firm.)

Column 2

j. Find column 2. ✔

- (Teacher reference:)

1. <u>per</u>mit	3. <u>dif</u>ference
2. <u>pro</u>tect	4. <u>de</u>monstrating

- All these words have more than one syllable. The first syllable of each word is underlined.

k. Word 1. What's the first syllable? (Signal.) *per.*

- What's the whole word? (Signal.) *Permit.*

- When you let something happen, you **permit** it to happen. Everybody, what are you doing when you let something happen? (Signal.) *Permitting it to happen.*

l. Word 2. What's the first syllable? (Signal.) *pro.*

- What's the whole word? (Signal.) *Protect.*

- When you protect something, you don't let anything hurt it. Everybody, what are you doing when you don't let anything hurt a baby? (Signal.) *Protecting the baby.*
- What are you doing when you don't let anything hurt a puppy? (Signal.) *Protecting the puppy.*

m. Word 3. What's the first syllable? (Signal.) *diff.*
- What's the whole word? (Signal.) *Difference.*

n. Word 4. What's the first syllable? (Signal.) *dem.*
- What's the whole word? (Signal.) *Demonstrating.*

o. Let's read those words again.
- Word 1. What word? (Signal.) *Permit.*
- (Repeat for: **2. protect, 3. difference, 4. demonstrating.**)

p. (Repeat step o until firm.)

Column 3

q. Find column 3. ✔
- (Teacher reference:)

1. Halloween	4. tube
2. ugh	5. injury
3. pink	6. spinal

r. Word 1. What word? (Signal.) *Halloween.*
- (Repeat for words 2–6.)

s. Let's read those words again.
- Word 1. What word? (Signal.) *Halloween.*
- (Repeat for words 2–6.)

t. (Repeat step s until firm.)

Individual Turns

(For columns 1–3: Call on individual students, each to read one to three words per turn.)

EXERCISE 3

Fact Review

a. Let's review some facts you have learned. First we'll go over the facts together. Then I'll call on individual students to do some facts.

b. Everybody, tell me how many jobs each muscle has. (Pause.) Get ready. (Signal.) *One.* APK
- When muscles work, they change in two ways. Tell me if they get **longer** or **shorter**. (Pause.) Get ready. (Signal.) *Shorter.* RF/R
- Tell me if they get **thicker** or **thinner**. (Pause.) Get ready. (Signal.) *Thicker.* APK
- (Repeat step b until firm.) RF/R

c. Does the same muscle bend the arm and straighten the arm? (Signal.) *No.* APK
- Does the same muscle bend the leg and straighten the leg? (Signal.) *No.* RF/R
- Muscles work in pairs. Name the muscle that bends the arm. (Pause.) Get ready. (Signal.) *Biceps.* APK
- Name the muscle that straightens the arm. (Pause.) Get ready. (Signal.) *Triceps.* RF/R
- (Repeat step c until firm.)

d. Name the muscle on the front of the upper arm. (Pause.) Get ready. (Signal.) *Biceps.* APK
- Name the muscle on the back of the upper arm. (Pause.) Get ready. (Signal.) *Triceps.* RF/R
- One muscle moves your head forward. Tell me if that muscle is on the **front** of your neck or the **back** of your neck. (Pause.) Get ready. (Signal.) *Front.* APK
- One muscle moves the head backward. Tell me where that muscle is. (Pause.) Get ready. (Signal.) *Back of the neck.* RF/R
- (Repeat step d until firm.)

Individual Turns
- Now I'm going to call on individual students to do some facts.
- (Call on individual students to do the set of facts in step b, c, or d.)

EXERCISE 4

Story Reading

a. Find part B in your textbook. ✔
- The error limit for group reading is 13 errors. Read carefully.

b. Everybody, touch the title. ✔
- (Call on a student to read the title.) *[Al and Angela Learn About Bones.]*
- Everybody, what's the title? (Signal.) *Al and Angela Learn About Bones.* ND
- What's going to happen in this story? (Call on a student. Idea: *Al and Angela will learn about bones.*) P

- (Call on individual students to read the story, each student reading two or three sentences at a time. Ask the specified questions as the students read.)

- (**Correct errors:** Tell the word. Direct the student to reread the sentence.)
- (If the group makes more than 13 errors, direct the students to reread the story.)

Al and Angela Learn About Bones

Al and Angela were looking at a model of the human body. The model was demonstrating how the muscles worked. The old man had just shown Al and Angela what happens if one of the muscles is cut.

- Which muscle had been cut? (Call on a student. Idea: *The one on the back of the upper leg.*) APK
- So what couldn't the man do? (Call on a student. Idea: *Bend his leg back.*) DC

Now the old man pointed to the model and continued, "The muscles permit the body to move. But the muscles don't work alone. Most of them are attached to bones and the muscles move the bones."

- What do most muscles do? (Call on a student. Idea: *Move bones.*) ND

The old man continued, "I'll show you how important the bones are. First I'll fix up the muscle in the man's leg so that it works again. And then, I'll remove the bones from the legs. Watch what happens."

The man's legs suddenly bent and the man fell over. Angela said, "He can't stand up without bones in his legs."

"Correct," the old man said.

Al added, "So the leg bones help make the legs strong."

- What do the leg bones do? (Call on a student. Idea: *Make the legs strong.*) ND

The old man said, "Yes, some bones help make the body strong. Other bones protect parts of the body that are very important to the body."

- What do other bones do? (Call on a student. Idea: *Protect parts of the body.*) ND

The old man waved his arm. "Look at the bones that are beneath the muscles."

Suddenly the muscles on the man's body disappeared. The man was now nothing but a skeleton. "Ugh," Angela said. "That looks creepy, like an outfit that people wear on Halloween."

"No," the old man said. "The skeleton is not creepy. It does jobs that are very important to the body. Remember, if you didn't have a skeleton, you couldn't stand up, or run, or hold things in your hand."

- Name some things you couldn't do if you didn't have a skeleton. (Call on a student. Ideas: *Stand up; run; hold things; throw a ball; walk; etc.*) ND

The old man walked over to the skeleton and said, "Here are some facts about the skeleton. Listen carefully. There are 206 bones in the body."

- Everybody, say that fact. Get ready. (Signal.) *There are 206 bones in the body.* RF/R
- (Repeat until firm.)
- That's a lot of bones.

The old man continued, "Some bones are very small and some are very big."

The old man touched the hip bone. "Here is a big bone."

- Everybody, touch the hip bone on the skeleton. ✔ VA
- Touch your hip bone. ✔
- That bone is very large.

The old man touched the skull. "Here is another big bone."

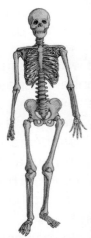

- Everybody, touch the skull on the skeleton. ✔ (VA)
- Touch your skull. ✔
- That bone is **much** bigger than the bones in your fingers.

The old man pointed to the skull. "The skull bone has a special job," he said. "Do you know what is inside the skull?"

"The brain," Al said.

"Correct," the old man replied. Then he said, "Watch." The skull bone disappeared. Al could see the man's brain. It looked very soft. The old man pointed to the back of the brain. "If something hit the brain here, the man would never see again."

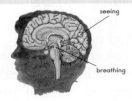

- Everybody, look at the picture of the head and touch the part of the brain that controls seeing. ✔ (VA)
- What would happen if something hit that part of the brain? (Call on a student. Idea: *The person would be blind.*) (ND)
- Everybody, what keeps things from hitting that part of the brain? (Signal.) *The skull.* (DC)

Then the old man touched a lower part of the brain. He said, "And if something hit the brain here, the man would never breathe again."

Angela said, "So the skull protects the brain. Nothing can hit the brain ⭐ because the skull covers the brain."

The old man said, "Correct." Then he pointed to the ribs and continued, "These bones protect other important parts of the body. Watch."

A heart appeared inside the man's chest. The heart was beating. It was much bigger than Al thought it would be.

The old man said, "Your heart is about as big as your fist. And it works all of the time. If it stops beating, you stop living. The ribs protect the heart."

- Everybody, which bones protect the heart? (Signal.) *Ribs.* (ND)
- Touch your ribs. ✔

Something else appeared inside the man's chest—two great big pink lungs. They looked very soft.

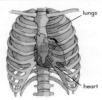

- Everybody, touch the lungs in the picture. ✔ (VA)
- Touch the heart in the picture. ✔ (VA)
- What do you think would happen to the person if something hit those soft lungs? (Call on a student. Ideas: *The person wouldn't be able to breathe; the person would die.*) (DI)
- Everybody, which bones protect the lungs? (Signal.) *Ribs.* (ND)

"What do the lungs do?" Angela asked.

"Lungs take in the air when you breathe," the old man said. "Look at how soft they are. If they are hurt, the man will not be able to breathe. And if he cannot breathe, he will die."

The old man said, "Remember— bones do two things. What are those two things?"

Al answered the question.

- What are the two things that Al said bones do? (Call on a student. Ideas: *Make the body strong and protect body parts.*) (RF/R)

> The old man said, "If you think you can remember everything you have seen, we can learn more about the body. Or would you rather stop the trip now?"
>
> "Let's learn more," Al said. He had almost forgotten that he hadn't wanted to learn about the body. Al said, "Seeing a real body in action is much better than reading about it in a book."

- Read the rest of the story to yourself and be ready to answer some questions. Raise your hand when you're finished.

> The old man smiled and bent down so that his face was very close to Al's. Very softly, the old man said, "It's much better to see a body in action unless you know how to read a book carefully." For a very long moment, the old man stood very close to Al. Then he stood up, waved his arm and said, "Let's continue on our trip. For this part, we're going to go inside the body."
>
> The muscles appeared over the bones of the man's body. Then skin covered the muscles. The man once more looked just like a real person. The only difference about him was that he seemed very big and he seemed to be growing and growing and growing. Soon he was the size of a giant.
>
> "Wow," Angela exclaimed.
>
> Al said, "This is just the way I felt when I went inside a grain of sand."
>
> When the man's body was so huge that Al couldn't see above the man's knee, everything started to become dark. Then Al noticed that he seemed to be floating. He was inside a very large tube that was filled with liquid.
>
> The old man said, "We are now inside the body and we are no bigger than a speck compared to the body."

- (After all students have raised their hand:) What did the old man say they

would do for the next part of the trip? (Call on a student. Idea: *Go in the body.*) (ND)
- What did the model of the man start to do? (Call on a student. Idea: *Get bigger.*) (ND)
- After things went dark, what were Al and Angela inside? (Call on a student. Idea: *A very large tube.*) (ND)
- Everybody, what was the tube filled with? (Signal.) *Liquid.* (ND)
- What do you think that liquid is? (Call on a student. Student preference.) (DI)
- What do you think that tube is? (Call on a student. Student preference.) (DI)
- How big were Al and Angela compared to the body? (Call on a student. Idea: *No bigger than a speck.*) (ND)

EXERCISE 5

Paired Practice

You're going to read aloud to your partner. The **B** members will read first. Then the **A** members will read from the star to the end of the story. (Observe students and give feedback.)

End-of-Lesson Activities

INDEPENDENT WORK

Now finish your independent work for lesson 121. Raise your hand when you're finished. (Observe students and give feedback.)

WORKCHECK

a. (Direct students to take out their marking pencils.)
- We're going to check your workbook and textbook items. Remember, if you got an item wrong, make an **X** next to the item.
b. (For each item: Read the item. Call on a student to answer it. If the answer is wrong, say the correct answer. Refer to the Answer Key for the correct answers.)
c. Now use your marking pencil to fix up any items you got wrong. Remember, all mistakes must be fixed up before you hand in your work.

SPELLING

(Present Spelling lesson 121 after completing Reading lesson 121. See *Spelling Presentation Book.*)

EXERCISE 1

Vocabulary

a. **Find page 367 in your textbook.** ✔
- Touch sentence 30. ✔
- This is a new vocabulary sentence. It says: The injury to his spinal cord paralyzed him. Everybody, say that sentence. Get ready. (Signal.) *The injury to his spinal cord paralyzed him.*
- Close your eyes and say the sentence. Get ready. (Signal.) *The injury to his spinal cord paralyzed him.*
- (Repeat until firm.)

b. The sentence indicates that he had an **injury**. That means he was seriously hurt. Everybody, what word means a **serious hurt?** (Signal.) *Injury.*

c. The injury was to his **spinal cord.** The spinal cord is a bundle of nerves that goes down the middle of your backbone. Everybody, touch your backbone. ✔
- The spinal cord goes all the way from the bottom of your backbone up past your neck into your skull. What do we call the nerves that run up and down inside your backbone? (Signal.) *Spinal cord.*

d. The sentence says that the injury **paralyzed** him. If he is paralyzed, he can't move. His muscles do not obey him when he tells them to move. Spinal cord injuries can make parts of the body paralyzed. Remember, if it can't move, it is paralyzed. Everybody, what word means **it can't move?** (Signal.) *Paralyzed.*

e. Listen to the sentence again: The injury to his spinal cord paralyzed him. Everybody, say that sentence. Get ready. (Signal.) *The injury to his spinal cord paralyzed him.*

f. Everybody, what part names the bundle of nerves that are inside the backbone? (Signal.) *Spinal cord.*
- What word means **a serious hurt?** (Signal.) *Injury.*
- What word describes a part of the body that can't move? (Signal.) *Paralyzed.*
- (Repeat step f until firm.)

EXERCISE 2

Reading Words

Column 1

a. **Find lesson 122 in your textbook.** ✔
- Touch column 1. ✔
- (Teacher reference:)

1. cell	4. chamber
2. blood vessel	5. jerk
3. heart	6. differently

b. Word 1 is **cell.** What word? (Signal.) *Cell.*
- Spell **cell.** Get ready. (Tap for each letter.) *C-E-L-L.*
- Cells are the smallest parts of your body. The smallest part of a bone is a bone cell. Everybody, what's the smallest part of a muscle? (Signal.) *A muscle cell.*
- What's the smallest part of a hair? (Signal.) *A hair cell.*

c. Number 2. What words? (Signal.) *Blood vessel.*

d. Word 3. What word? (Signal.) *Heart.*
- Spell **heart.** Get ready. (Tap for each letter.) *H-E-A-R-T.*

e. Word 4. What word? (Signal.) *Chamber.*
- Spell **chamber.** Get ready. (Tap for each letter.) *C-H-A-M-B-E-R.*

f. Word 5. What word? (Signal.) *Jerk.*
- Spell **jerk.** Get ready. (Tap for each letter.) *J-E-R-K.*

g. Word 6. What word? (Signal.) *Differently.*

h. Let's read those words again.
- Word 1. What word? (Signal.) *Cell.*
- Number 2. What words? (Signal.) *Blood vessel.*
- Word 3. What word? (Signal.) *Heart.*
- (Repeat for words 4–6.)

i. (Repeat step h until firm.)

Column 2

j. Find column 2. ✔
- (Teacher reference:)

1. spinal cord	3. thumb
2. paralyzed	4. injury

k. Number 1. What words? (Signal.) *Spinal cord.*
- Word 2. What word? (Signal.) *Paralyzed.*
- (Repeat for words 3 and 4.)

l. Let's read those words again.
- Number 1. What words? (Signal.) *Spinal cord.*
- Word 2. What word? (Signal.) *Paralyzed.*
- (Repeat for: **3. thumb, 4. injury.**)

m. (Repeat step l until firm.)

Individual Turns

(For columns 1 and 2: Call on individual students, each to read one to three words.)

EXERCISE 3

Story Reading

a. Find part B in your textbook. ✔
- The error limit for group reading is 16 errors. Read carefully.

b. Everybody, touch the title. ✔
- (Call on a student to read the title.) *[Angela and Al Learn About the Heart.]*
- Everybody, what's the title? (Signal.) *Angela and Al Learn About the Heart.* ⓃⒹ
- (Call on individual students to read the story, each student reading two or three sentences at a time. Ask the specified questions as the students read.)

> - (**Correct errors:** Tell the word. Direct the student to reread the sentence.)
> - (If the group makes more than 16 errors, direct the students to reread the story.)

Angela and Al Learn About the Heart

The old man was taking Al and Angela through a tube inside the body. The tube was filled with liquid.

"What's the liquid inside this tube?" Angela asked.

"Blood," the old man replied.

"Ugh," Al said. "I don't like blood."

"Blood is very important to your body," the old man said. "And that blood moves through tubes called blood vessels. We are inside a blood vessel."

- Everybody, what are they inside of? (Signal.) *A blood vessel.* ⓃⒹ
- What does a blood vessel carry? (Signal.) *Blood.* ⓃⒹ

Suddenly Al noticed a great pounding sound—"Cu-boom—cu-boom—cu-boom." The sound was very loud.

"What's that sound?" Angela yelled.

- Why did she yell? (Call on a student. Idea: *Because the pounding sound was so loud.*) ⒹⒾ
- What do you think is making that cu-boom sound? (Call on a student. Idea: *The heart.*) ⒹⒾ

The old man replied, "That's the man's heart."

The old man turned on a flashlight. Al could see the blood vessel and the dark liquid inside it.

Angela said, "That liquid is almost black, but blood is red."

The old man said, "Blood is not always red. We will follow the blood through the body. You will see what happens to it."

"Cu-boom—cu-boom." The sound of the heart was getting louder and louder. Now Al noticed that the liquid inside the tube was moving.

"The heart is like a great pump," the old man explained. "The heart pumps blood through the body night and day. When the heart pumps, the blood in the blood vessels moves."

- Everybody, what part of the body pumps blood? (Signal.) *The heart.* ⓃⒹ
- What happens to the blood in the blood vessels when the heart pounds? (Call on a student. Idea: *It moves.*) ⓃⒹ
- Everybody, what color is the blood inside the vessel that Al and Angela are in? (Signal.) *Almost black.* ⓃⒹ

"Cu-boom—cu-boom." The sound of the heart was so loud Al could hardly stand it.

The old man yelled, "We're going into the heart soon."

The old man's light was shining on something that looked like a strange door in the blood vessel ahead of them. The door was made of muscle. The door kept opening and then closing.

Al and the others were moving toward the door along with everything in the blood vessel. When they were directly in front of the door, Al noticed that he and the others were in a small chamber. The chamber was wider than the rest of the blood vessel. "We are in one chamber of the heart," the old man said.

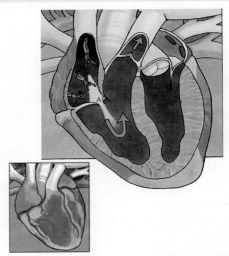

- Where are they now? (Call on a student. Idea: *In a chamber of the heart.*) ⓃⒹ
- The little picture shows how the heart would look to you from the outside. The big picture shows how the heart would look if part of it was cut away and you could see inside it.
- Everybody, touch the small chamber they're in. ✔ ⓋⒶ
- Touch the door that's directly in front of Al. ✔ ⓋⒶ

Suddenly the walls of the chamber changed shape, as if the chamber was suddenly squeezed. At the same time, the heart made a terrible cu-boom sound. Al could feel great pressure. In an instant, the door in the bottom of the chamber opened. Al and the others rushed through the door.

Al felt dizzy. He looked around and observed that he was now in a much larger chamber. Al noticed that the chamber had two doors in the ceiling—the one he had just been pushed through and another one.

The old man said, "The heart is going to pump again. This time we will shoot out of that other door."

Suddenly the walls of the large chamber seemed to be squeezed together. There was great pressure and a great cu-boom sound. At the same time, the second door in the ceiling opened. Al and the others shot up through the door and into a tube.

- Everybody, listen to that part again. We'll go back to when Al and the others were in the first chamber.

Suddenly, the walls of the chamber changed shape, as if the chamber was suddenly squeezed. At the same time, the heart made a terrible cu-boom sound. Al could feel great pressure. In an instant, the door in the bottom of the chamber opened. Al and the others rushed through the door.
- What happened to the walls of the first chamber? (Call on a student. Ideas: *They changed shape; they squeezed together.*) ⓃⒹ
- Where was the door that opened in the first chamber when the heart seemed to squeeze together? (Call on a student. Idea: *At the bottom of the chamber.*) ⓃⒹ
- Touch **A** in the picture. That shows the first door. ✔ ⓋⒶ
- Listen to the next part.

Al felt dizzy. He looked around and observed that he was now in a much larger chamber.
- Everybody, touch that larger chamber. It has an arrow shaped like a U in it. ✔ ⓋⒶ
- Here's the next part.

Al noticed that the chamber had two doors in the ceiling—the one he had just been pushed through and another one.
- Everybody, what's the letter of the door they had just come through? (Signal.) *A.* ⒹⒸ
- What's the letter of the other door? (Signal.) *B.* ⓋⒶ
- Here's the next part.

The old man said, "The heart is going to pump again. This time we will shoot out of that other door."
- Everybody, what's the letter of that door? (Signal.) *B.* ⒹⒸ
- Here's the next part.

Suddenly the walls of the large chamber seemed to be squeezed together. There was great pressure and a great cu-boom sound. At the same time, the second door in the ceiling opened. Al and the others shot up through the door and into a tube.
- Where did Al and the others go after leaving the first chamber? (Call on a student. Idea: *Into another chamber.*) ⓃⒹ
- Which chamber was bigger? (Call on a student. Idea: *The second.*) ⓃⒹ
- Everybody, how many doors were in this chamber? (Signal.) *Two.* ⓃⒹ

- When they were in the big chamber, the heart beat again. What happened this time? (Call on a student. Idea: *They shot through a door in the ceiling and into a tube.*) ⓝ ⓓ
- Everybody, touch the picture and show the path they took when they left the large chamber. ✔ ⓥ ⓐ

When they slowed down, the old man said, "You can hear ✸ two sounds in the heart. The first is the little sound, cu. The other is the big sound, boom. Each time you hear the little sound, blood goes from the first chamber into the second chamber. Each time you hear the boom sound, the blood goes from the second chamber and leaves the heart."

- What happens when the little sound is made? (Call on a student. Idea: *The blood goes from the first chamber into the second chamber.*) ⓝ ⓓ
- What happens when the big boom sound is made? (Call on a student. Idea: *The blood leaves the heart.*) ⓝ ⓓ

Angela said, "Let's see if I understand. The blood makes the little sound when it leaves the little chamber, and makes the big sound when it leaves the big chamber."

"Correct," the old man said.

Al noticed that he and the others were in a tube like the one that they had been in before they entered the heart. But the liquid in this tube moved differently. Each time the heart made the boom sound, everything in the tube moved forward with a great jerk. Then it stopped until the heart boomed again.

- What happened to the things in this tube each time the heart made the boom sound? (Call on a student. Idea: *They jerked forward.*) ⓝ ⓓ
- Then what would the things in the tube do? (Call on a student. Idea: *Stop.*) ⓝ ⓓ

"The heart is pushing blood into this tube," the old man said. "Each time new blood is pushed into the tube, all the other blood in the tube must move forward to make room for the new blood."

"This is a rough ride," Al said. "Where does this tube go now?"

The old man said, "To the lungs."

- Everybody, where is the blood going after it leaves the heart? (Signal.) *To the lungs.* ⓝ ⓓ

Angela said, "Why does this blood vessel go to the lungs?"

The old man said, "The body is burning all the time. That's why it's warm. Remember that—the body is burning all the time. But things can't burn without oxygen."

"What's oxygen?" Al asked.

The old man explained, "Oxygen is part of the air you breathe. The body needs this oxygen if the body is to keep working. The blood in this blood vessel has no more oxygen in it. That is why this blood is black, not red."

- Everybody, what color is the blood in the tube they are in? (Signal.) *Black.* ⓝ ⓓ
- Why is the blood black? (Call on a student. Idea: *Because there's no more oxygen in it.*) ⓝ ⓓ
- Everybody, what color would it be if it had oxygen? (Signal.) *Red.* ⓓ ⓒ

The old man continued, "The only way this blood can get oxygen is to go to the lungs."

- Everybody, where does the blood have to go to get oxygen? (Signal.) *To the lungs.* ⓝ ⓓ
- Read the rest of the story to yourself and be ready to answer some questions. Raise your hand when you're finished.

Angela said, "I just hope I can remember all this. The blood is black because it doesn't have oxygen. So it must go from the heart to the lungs and get oxygen."

The old man said, "And you will have no trouble seeing when the oxygen gets into the blood."

Al noticed that the blood vessel was getting smaller and smaller. It was becoming so small that Al could hardly squeeze through it. Also, the walls of the blood vessel were getting very thin and transparent.

> In the narrow blood vessel, Al could see that the blood was filled with little parts. Some of them were like disks. All the disks were black. Then suddenly he could see the disks change. They were changing color and becoming bright, bright red.
>
> "This is amazing," he shouted to Angela.
>
> The old man said, "The red blood is now full of oxygen. It picked up the oxygen from the lungs. Could you tell when the oxygen entered the blood?" Al said, "When the oxygen entered the blood, the blood became bright red."
>
> "Correct," the old man said.

- (After all students have raised their hand:) Everybody, what color was the blood before it reached the lungs? (Signal.) *Black.* (ND)
- What happened to the size of the blood vessel that Al and the others were in? (Call on a student. Idea: *It got smaller and smaller.*) (ND)
- Al noticed that there were disks in the blood. Everybody, what color were those disks before they got oxygen from the blood? (Signal.) *Black.* (ND)
- What color did the disks change to when they picked up oxygen from the lungs? (Signal.) *Red.* (ND)

EXERCISE 4

Paired Practice

You're going to read aloud to your partner. The **A** members will read first. Then the **B** members will read from the star to the end of the story. (Observe students and give feedback.)

End-of-Lesson Activities

INDEPENDENT WORK

Now finish your independent work for lesson 122. Raise your hand when you're finished. (Observe students and give feedback.)

WORKCHECK

a. (Direct students to take out their marking pencils.)
- We're going to check your workbook and textbook items. Remember, if you got an item wrong, make an **X** next to the item.
b. (For each item: Read the item. Call on a student to answer it. If the answer is wrong, say the correct answer. Refer to the Answer Key for the correct answers.)
c. Now use your marking pencil to fix up any items you got wrong. Remember, all mistakes must be fixed up before you hand in your work.

SPELLING

(Present Spelling lesson 122 after completing Reading lesson 122. See *Spelling Presentation Book.*)

ACTIVITIES

(Present Activity 25 after completing Reading lessons 122–123. See *Activities across the Curriculum.*)

EXERCISE 1

Vocabulary Review

a. Here's the new vocabulary sentence: The injury to his spinal cord paralyzed him.
- Everybody, say that sentence. Get ready. (Signal.) *The injury to his spinal cord paralyzed him.*
- (Repeat until firm.)

b. Everybody, what word describes a part of the body that can't move? (Signal.) *Paralyzed.*
- What part names the bundle of nerves that are inside the backbone? (Signal.) *Spinal cord.*
- What word means **a serious hurt?** (Signal.) *Injury.*
- (Repeat step b until firm.)

EXERCISE 2

Reading Words

Column 1

a. **Find lesson 123 in your textbook.** ✔
- Touch column 1. ✔
- (Teacher reference:)

1. cerebrum	4. boat-shaped
2. magnifying	5. thumb
3. image	6. cell

b. Word 1 is **cerebrum.** What word? (Signal.) *Cerebrum.*
- Spell **cerebrum.** Get ready. (Tap for each letter.) *C-E-R-E-B-R-U-M.*
- The part of the brain that lets you think is called the cerebrum. Everybody, what's the part of the brain that lets you think? (Signal.) *Cerebrum.*

c. Word 2 is **magnifying.** What word? (Signal.) *Magnifying.*
- Something that is magnified is made larger. If a picture is magnified, the picture is made larger. Everybody, what's another word for **made larger?** (Signal.) *Magnified.*

d. Word 3 is **image.** What word? (Signal.) *Image.*

- An image is a picture. If you have an image in your mind, you have a picture in your mind.

e. Word 4. What word? (Signal.) *Boat-shaped.*
- (Repeat for words 5 and 6.)

f. Let's read those words again.
- Word 1. What word? (Signal.) *Cerebrum.*
- (Repeat for words 2–6.)

g. (Repeat step f until firm.)

Column 2

h. Find column 2. ✔
- (Teacher reference:)

1. mixed	3. leads
2. joining	4. branched

- All these words have an ending.

i. Word 1. What word? (Signal.) *Mixed.*
- (Repeat for words 2–4.)

j. Let's read those words again.
- Word 1. What word? (Signal.) *Mixed.*
- (Repeat for words 2–4.)

k. (Repeat step j until firm.)

Individual Turns

(For columns 1 and 2: Call on individual students, each to read one to three words per turn.)

EXERCISE 3

Story Reading

a. Find part B in your textbook. ✔
- The error limit for group reading is 18 errors. Read carefully.

b. Everybody, touch the title. ✔
- (Call on a student to read the title.) *[Al and Angela Follow Blood Through the Body.]*
- Everybody, what's the title? (Signal.) *Al and Angela Follow Blood Through the Body.* (ND)
- (Call on individual students to read the story, each student reading two or three sentences at a time. Ask the specified questions as the students read.)

Al and Angela Follow Blood Through the Body

Al and Angela were inside a blood vessel filled with oxygen blood.

- Everybody, what color is that blood? (Signal.) *Red.* (APK)
- Where did it become red? (Signal.) *In the lungs.* (RF/R)
- What color was it before it reached the lungs? (Signal.) *Black.* (APK)

They had gone through two chambers of the heart. They had gone to the lungs where the blood changed color. Now Angela observed, "The blood vessel is getting bigger." Al noticed that many smaller blood vessels were joining the vessel they were in.

The old man said, "We are leaving the lungs now."

"Where are we going?" Angela asked.

"Back to the heart," the old man said.

"Oh, no!" Angela said. "Not again. Why does the blood have to go back to the heart?"

The old man said, "The blood in this vessel has fresh oxygen, but it must get to the parts of the body that need oxygen. So the heart has to pump this blood to the arms, legs, head and other parts of the body."

- What does the heart have to do with the oxygen blood? (Call on a student. Idea: *Pump it all over the body.*) (ND)

They were getting closer to the heart, and Al could hear it going "cu-boom." The old man said, "This time we're going to go through two new chambers. The second chamber pumps very hard because it must start the blood moving to all parts of the body."

- Everybody, are they going to go through the same two chambers they went through before? (Signal.) *No.* (ND)
- Why does the second chamber they will go through now have to pump so hard? (Call on a student. Idea: *Because it has to start the blood moving to all parts of the body.*) (ND)

They approached a chamber. When they were inside the chamber, the walls of the chamber squeezed together. Everything shot through the door in the floor and they were squeezed into a second chamber. They were in that chamber for only a moment when "BOOOOOMMMMM." The walls of the chamber came together and a door in the chamber opened.

"Whoooosh." Everything in the chamber went flying up into another blood vessel. It felt as if they were moving four hundred miles an hour.

After they had slowed down, Angela said, "Wow! I'm dizzy."

"Me too," Al said.

Angela said, "And I'm all mixed up. First we came into the heart. Then we went out of the heart. Then we came back to the heart."

- That sounds very complicated. Everybody, how many chambers of the heart did they go through **before** they went to the lungs? (Signal.) *2.* (ND)
- How many chambers of the heart did they go through **after** they **left** the lungs? (Signal.) *2.* (ND)
- So how many chambers does the heart have? (Signal.) *4.* (DC)

The old man said, "Just remember this: The blood needs oxygen. Black blood comes to the heart, and the heart pumps the blood to the lungs. That's where the blood gets fresh oxygen and turns bright red. Now the fresh blood goes back to the heart so that it can be pumped to all the parts of the body that need fresh oxygen."

- Everybody, listen to that part again.

  The old man said, "Just remember this: The blood needs oxygen. Black blood comes to the heart, and the heart pumps the blood to the lungs. That's where the blood gets fresh oxygen and turns bright red. Now the fresh blood goes back to the heart so that it can be pumped to all the parts of the body that need fresh oxygen."
- Where does black blood go after leaving the heart? (Signal.) *The lungs.* (ND)
- What happens in the lungs? (Call on a student. Idea: *The blood gets fresh oxygen and turns red.*) (ND)
- Everybody, then where does the blood go? (Signal.) *To the heart.* (ND)
- Where does it go after leaving the heart? (Call on a student. Idea: *To all parts of the body.*) (ND)
- That's where Angela and Al are now, in a tube that goes to some part of the body.

Everything in the blood vessel moved along in jerks. Every time the heart pounded, the blood jerked ahead. Then it would stop. Then the heart would pound again, and everything would jerk ahead.

Angela asked, "Are we going to keep jerking along like this until we reach a part of the body that needs oxygen?"

"Correct," the old man replied. "We are going to a muscle in the hand, and we will continue to jerk along until we get there."

The old man continued, "The blood vessel we are in goes along the inside of the wrist. If you want to feel that, hold your hand so that your palm is facing up."

- Everybody, do that. ✔

"Then feel along your wrist on the side where your thumb is. You will feel a tube that is pounding each time the heart pounds. That is the tube that we are in."

- Hold your hand so your palm is facing up. Find that pounding tube on the thumb side of your wrist. Don't press too hard. (Observe students and give feedback.)
- Hands down.

Angela had trouble finding the blood vessel in her wrist, so the old man ★ helped her.

The old man said, "After we reach the muscles in the man's hand, we will go back in a blood vessel that does not jerk along."

- Everybody, does the vessel they are in now jerk along? (Signal.) *Yes.* (ND)
- When they go back from the hand, will they be in a tube that jerks along? (Signal.) *No.* (ND)

Al noticed that the blood vessel they were in was getting very small. Every now and then the blood vessel branched. And every time the blood vessel branched, it got smaller.

The old man said, "We are now in a muscle. That muscle is in the man's hand."

The blood vessel was now as small as the blood vessels in the lungs, and it was transparent. Al could see rows and rows of boat-shaped forms outside the blood vessel. "What are those things?" he asked.

"Muscle cells," the old man said.

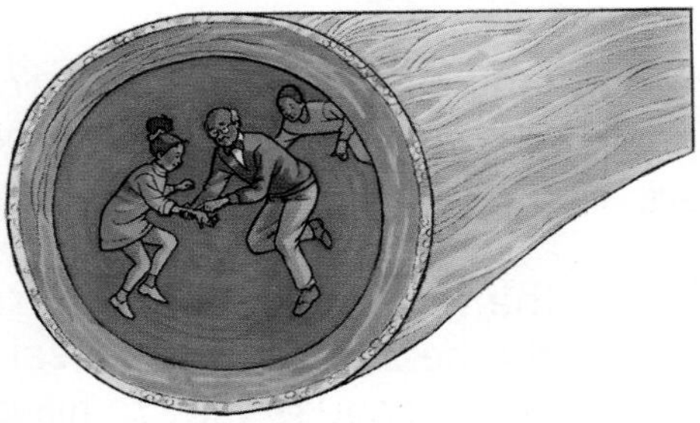

- Everybody, look at the picture on page 262. What are those boat-shaped things on the outside of the blood vessel? (Signal.) *Muscle cells.* (DC)

The old man continued, "Muscles are made up of tiny cells. And each cell needs oxygen as it works. Right now, the oxygen is leaving the blood and going into the muscles."

Angela said, "The blood is changing color. It's getting darker and darker."

- Why is the blood getting darker again? (Call on a student. Idea: *Because the oxygen is leaving it.*) (DI)

The old man said, "The blood has done its job. Now it must go back to the heart and back to the lungs so that it can get fresh oxygen."

The old man pointed to a blue blood vessel on the inside of Angela's wrist. "That's like the one we will go back in. It's blue because it's filled with dark blood."

- Everybody, show me a blue blood vessel on the inside of your wrist. ✔
- Now feel that blood vessel and see if it pounds. ✔

Angela put her fingers on that blue blood vessel. She observed, "It doesn't pound when the heart beats."

"Correct," the old man said. "Remember, the blood vessels that pound go from the heart to different parts of the body. The blood vessels that do not pound are not going from the heart. They are going back to the heart."

- Remember, the blood vessels that pound go **from** the heart. The blood vessels that do not pound go **back** to the heart. Everybody, which blood vessels pound? (Signal.) *The ones that go from the heart.* (RF/R)
- Which blood vessels do not pound? (Signal.) *The ones that go back to the heart.* (RF/R)

"And the vessels that are returning blood to the heart are blue," Al said. "I'll bet that's because they're filled with dark blood."

"Correct," the old man said.

- Why are they blue? (Call on a student. Ideas: *Because they are filled with dark blood; they are filled with blood that has no oxygen.*) (DC)

The old man continued, "If the blood vessel is blue, it is filled with dark blood and it is going back to the heart so the heart can pump the dark blood to the lungs."

- Read the rest of the story to yourself and be ready to answer some questions. Raise your hand when you're finished.

Angela said, "Tell me if I've got this straight. Blood vessels that go from the heart pound every time the heart beats. Blood vessels that are taking dark blood back to the heart do not pound and they are blue. The blood around us is dark so we are now in a tiny blue blood vessel that leads back to the heart."

"Right," the old man said. "You are really thinking now."

Then the old man continued, "If you wish, we can take that trip around the body one more time. We'll first go back to the heart, then to the lungs . . ."

"No," Angela said. "I remember how it works. I don't want to go through the heart again."

"All right," the old man said. "Let's stay in the man's hand and look at another part of the body."

In an instant, Al and the others were no longer inside a blood vessel. They were floating next to something that looked like a huge white rope that stretched as far as Al could see. The rope had many branches coming from it.

- (After all students have raised their hand:) Everybody, what was the color of the tiny blood vessel they were in? (Signal.) *Blue.* (ND)
- What color is the blood inside that blood vessel? (Signal.) *Black.* (ND)
- Where does the blood vessel lead? (Call on a student. Idea: *Back to the heart.*) (ND)
- Everybody, did Angela want to take the trip through the body one more time? (Signal.) *No.* (ND)
- Why not? (Call on a student. Idea: *Because she didn't want to go through the heart again.*) (ND)
- Everybody, in which part of the man's body did they stay? (Signal.) *The hand.* (ND)
- What did Al see when he left the blood vessel? (Call on a student. Idea: *Something that looked like a huge white rope.*) (ND)
- Do you have any idea what the rope with all the branches could be? (Call on individual students. Student preference.) (P)

EXERCISE 4

Paired Practice

You're going to read aloud to your partner. The **B** members will read first. Then the **A** members will read from the star to the end of the story. (Observe students and give feedback.)

EXERCISE 5

Fact Review

a. Let's review the trip Al and Angela just took through the body.

b. Al and Angela went through the heart. How many chambers are in the heart? (Signal.) *4.* (RF/R)

- When they started out, they were moving toward the heart in a blood vessel that had dark blood in it. The blood was dark because it didn't have something. What was that? (Signal.) *Oxygen.* (RF/R)

- The heart pumped that blood through two chambers. Where did the dark blood go after it left the heart? (Signal.) *To the lungs.* (RF/R)

- Did the blood vessel from the heart to the lungs move things at a **steady speed** or did things **stop and start?** (Signal.) *Stop and start.* (RF/R)

- (Repeat step b until firm.)

c. When the blood was in the lungs, it changed color. What color did it become? (Signal.) *Red.* (RF/R)

- It became red because it picked up . . . Get ready. (Signal.) *Oxygen.* (RF/R)

- Where did the red blood go after it left the lungs? (Signal.) *To the heart.* (RF/R)

- And it went through two different chambers.

- After the red blood left the heart this time, where did it go? (Signal.) *To the body.* (RF/R)

- When the blood reached the muscle cells, what happened to the color of the blood? (Signal.) *It got dark.* (RF/R)

- Where does dark blood go after it leaves muscle cells? (Signal.) *To the heart.* (RF/R)

- (Repeat step c until firm.)

End-of-Lesson Activities

INDEPENDENT WORK

Now finish your independent work for lesson 123. Raise your hand when you're finished. (Observe students and give feedback.)

WORKCHECK

a. (Direct students to take out their marking pencils.)

- We're going to check your workbook and textbook items. Remember, if you got an item wrong, make an **X** next to the item.

b. (For each item: Read the item. Call on a student to answer it. If the answer is wrong, say the correct answer. Refer to the Answer Key for the correct answers.)

c. Now use your marking pencil to fix up any items you got wrong. Remember, all mistakes must be fixed up before you hand in your work.

SPELLING

(Present Spelling lesson 123 after completing Reading lesson 123. See *Spelling Presentation Book*.)

ACTIVITIES

(Present Activity 26 after completing Reading lesson 123. See *Activities across the Curriculum*.)

LESSON 124

EXERCISE 1

Vocabulary Review

a. You learned a sentence that tells what the squid did.
- Everybody, say that sentence. Get ready. (Signal.) *The squid wriggled its tentacles.*
- (Repeat until firm.)

b. You learned a sentence that tells about the triceps muscle.
- Everybody, say that sentence. Get ready. (Signal.) *The triceps muscle is bigger than the biceps muscle.*

c. Here's the last sentence you learned: The injury to his spinal cord paralyzed him.
- Everybody, say that sentence. Get ready. (Signal.) *The injury to his spinal cord paralyzed him.*
- (Repeat until firm.)

d. What word means **a serious hurt?** (Signal.) *Injury.*
- What word describes a part of the body that can't move? (Signal.) *Paralyzed.*
- What part names the bundle of nerves that are inside the backbone? (Signal.) *Spinal cord.*
- (Repeat step d until firm.)

e. Once more. Say the sentence that tells what the injury to his spinal cord did. Get ready. (Signal.) *The injury to his spinal cord paralyzed him.*

EXERCISE 2

Reading Words

Column 1

a. **Find lesson 124 in your textbook.** ✔
- Touch column 1. ✔
- (Teacher reference:)

1. **forearm**	3. **trickles**
2. **shoelace**	4. **hollow**

- All these words have more than one syllable. The first syllable of each word is underlined.
b. Word 1. What's the first syllable? (Signal.) *fore.*

- What's the whole word? (Signal.) *Forearm.*
- The forearm is the part of the arm that goes from the elbow to the wrist.
- Everybody, touch your forearm. ✔
c. Word 2. What's the first syllable? (Signal.) *shoe.*
- What's the whole word? (Signal.) *Shoelace.*
d. Word 3. What's the first syllable? (Signal.) *trick.*
- What's the whole word? (Signal.) *Trickles.*
e. Word 4. What's the first syllable? (Signal.) *holl.*
- What's the whole word? (Signal.) *Hollow.*
f. Let's read those words again.
- Word 1. What word? (Signal.) *Forearm.*
- (Repeat for words 2–4.)
g. (Repeat step f until firm.)

Column 2

h. Find column 2. ✔
- (Teacher reference:)

1. **pulse**	3. **shocks**
2. **nerve**	4. **stings**

i. Word 1. What word? (Signal.) *Pulse.*
- Spell **pulse.** Get ready. (Tap for each letter.) *P-U-L-S-E.*
- When something pulses, it beats. When you feel your heart beating through your chest, you are feeling pulses. Everybody, what's another way of saying **a beat?** (Signal.) *A pulse.*
j. Word 2. What word? (Signal.) *Nerve.*
- Spell **nerve.** Get ready. (Tap for each letter.) *N-E-R-V-E.*
- Nerves are like wires that are inside the body. Some nerves deliver messages from the brain to the muscles and tell the muscles how to move. Everybody, what's the name of the wires that tell muscles how to move? (Signal.) *Nerves.*
k. Word 3. What word? (Signal.) *Shocks.*
- Spell **shocks.** Get ready. (Tap for each letter.) *S-H-O-C-K-S.*
l. Word 4. What word? (Signal.) *Stings.*
- Spell **stings.** Get ready. (Tap for each letter.) *S-T-I-N-G-S.*

m. Let's read those words again.
- Word 1. What word? (Signal.) *Pulse.*
- (Repeat for: **2. nerve, 3. shocks, 4. stings.**)

n. (Repeat step m until firm.)

Individual Turns

(For columns 1 and 2: Call on individual students, each to read one to three words per turn.)

EXERCISE 3

Story Reading

a. Find part B in your textbook. ✔
- The error limit for group reading is 15 errors. Read carefully.

b. Everybody, touch the title. ✔
- (Call on a student to read the title.) *[Angela and Al Learn About Nerves.]*
- Everybody, what's the title? (Signal.) *Angela and Al Learn About Nerves.* ⓃⒹ
- What's going to happen in this story? (Call on a student. Idea: *Angela and Al will learn about nerves.*) Ⓟ
- (Call on individual students to read the story, each student reading two or three sentences at a time. Ask the specified questions as the students read.)

- (**Correct errors:** Tell the word. Direct the student to reread the sentence.)
- (If the group makes more than 15 errors, direct the students to reread the story.)

Angela and Al Learn About Nerves

Al studied the white, branching rope for a few moments, trying to figure out what it was. He knew that it was part of the man's hand, but he couldn't imagine what it was. It wasn't a blood vessel; it wasn't a muscle; and it wasn't a bone. At last he asked, "What is that thing that looks like a rope?"

The old man said, "This is a nerve in the man's hand. There are nerves like this one in every part of the body."

Al looked at the long white rope. Then he asked, "What do nerves do?"

✿ The old man said, "A nerve is like an electric wire. It carries messages. This nerve goes from the hand to the man's brain. It carries messages from

- What do nerves do? (Call on a student. Idea: *Carry messages.*) ⓃⒹ
- Everybody, in which part of the man's body was the nerve that Al was looking at? (Signal.) *The hand.* ⓃⒹ
- And that nerve goes from the hand to where? (Call on a student. Idea: *To the man's brain.*) ⓃⒹ

The old man continued, "Hold onto the nerve. You will see what kind of messages they are."

Al and Angela touched the nerve. They could feel little pulses that felt like tiny electric shocks. Pulse, pulse, pulse, the nerve went.

- What did the little pulses feel like? (Call on a student. Idea: *Tiny electric shocks.*) ⓃⒹ

The pulses weren't strong enough to hurt. They felt like little trickles of electricity.

The old man said, "You are feeling the messages that are coming from the man's hand right now. Watch what happens when the man starts to tie his shoe."

Suddenly, the pulses started to go faster and faster.

- Everybody, what happened to the pulses when the man started to tie his shoe? (Signal.) *They went faster.* ⓃⒹ
- So now the nerve was sending **more** messages to the brain.

The old man ✿ said, "The man is feeling things. He is feeling the shoelace. He is feeling how his fingers move. And everything that he feels sends a message to the brain."

- What does the nerve do with everything the man feels? (Call on a student. Idea: *Sends a message to the brain.*) ⓃⒹ

The old man continued, "Those fast pulses are messages about everything the hand feels."

- Everybody, if the hand is feeling a lot of things, would there be **more messages** or **fewer messages?** (Signal.) *More messages.* ⒹⒸ

Lesson 124 **261**

- There are more messages now than there were before, so what do you know about how much the hand is feeling? (Call on a student. Idea: *It's feeling more.*) (DC)

> The old man said, "I'm going to cut the nerve that leads from his hand. No messages will go past the place that is cut. Watch."
>
> Al watched the old man cut the nerve. Suddenly Al could not feel any more pulses in the nerve.
>
> The old man said, "You can follow that nerve all the way to the man's brain and you will find that it does not carry any messages now. The nerve cannot carry messages from the hand because it is no longer connected to the hand."

- Why can't the nerve carry messages from the hand? (Call on a student. Idea: *Because the nerve is cut.*) (ND)

> Angela and Al moved along the nerve, up the man's forearm. The nerve was not pulsing. They returned to where the old man was.

- Where was that? (Call on a student. Idea: *Near the man's hand.*) (ND)

> The old man said, "Remember, if this nerve is cut, the brain doesn't get any messages from the hand. The brain doesn't know what the hand is feeling. So the man could hit his hand with a hammer and he would not feel a thing because the message from his hand can't get to the brain."

- Everybody, where does the nerve lead? (Signal.) *To the brain.* (ND)
- So if it's cut, can the brain know what the hand is feeling? (Signal.) *No.* (ND)

> The old man snapped his fingers. Once again Al could feel the pulses coming through the nerve. "The nerve is no longer cut," the old man said. "So the man can feel things in his hand again."
>
> The old man said, "This nerve goes from the hand to the brain. It tells the brain what the hand feels."

> The old man pointed ✦ to another nerve. "This nerve goes the other way," he said. "It carries messages from the brain to the hand. These messages tell the hand what to do. If the man tells his hand to make a fist, the message comes through that nerve."

- Some nerves go from the hand to the brain. What do they tell the brain? (Call on a student. Idea: *What the hand is feeling.*) (ND)
- The hand needs other nerves. Everybody, where do these nerves go **from?** (Signal.) *The brain.* (ND)
- Where do they go **to?** (Signal.) *The hand.* (ND)
- What do they tell the hand? (Call on a student. Ideas: *What to do; how to move.*) (ND)

> The old man told Al, "Grab both nerves."
>
> Al could feel pulses in both nerves. The old man said, "The nerve that goes <u>from the hand</u> is telling the brain what the hand is <u>feeling</u>. The message <u>from the brain</u> is telling the hand <u>how to move</u> to tie the shoe."

- The message from the brain is telling the hand something. What's that? (Call on a student. Ideas: *How to move; to tie the shoe.*) (ND)

> Al said, "What would happen if you cut the nerve that goes to the man's hand?"
>
> The old man said, "Good question. Let's cut that nerve and find out."
>
> The old man cut the nerve. The pulses going <u>to</u> the hand stopped. But the nerve <u>from</u> the hand continued to pulse.
>
> The old man said, "Watch what happens when a bee stings the man's finger." The nerve leading from the man's hand began to pulse very rapidly.

- What does that mean? (Call on a student. Ideas: *The hand was feeling a lot; the hand was sending messages to the brain.*) (DC)

But there was no pulsing in the nerve that went to the man's hand.

- What does that mean? (Call on a student. Idea: *The brain wasn't sending any messages to the hand.*) (DC)

The old man explained, "The man can feel the pain in his hand, but he can't do anything about it. He can't move that hand. That hand is paralyzed. That means the hand cannot move, no matter how hard the man tells himself that he wants to move it."

- Everybody, can the man feel things in the hand? (Signal.) *Yes.* (DC)
- Can the man move the hand? (Signal.) *No.* (DC)
- So the hand is paralyzed.
- Read the rest of the story to yourself and be ready to answer some questions. Raise your hand when you're finished.

Angela said, "Let me make sure that I have everything straight. The nerves that go from the hand to the brain tell the brain everything that the hand feels. The nerves that go from the brain to the hand tell the hand how to move. And the hand can't move without the message from the brain."

"Correct," the old man said. "There is an easy way to show how the nerves work. Close your eyes, Angela."

Angela closed her eyes. Then the old man said, "Hold your hand up in the air. Hold it up as far as it can go."

Angela kept her eyes closed and held up her hand. The old man said, "How did your muscles know what to do? Do your muscles have ears?"

Angela smiled. "No," she said. "I told my muscles what to do."

"Correct," the old man said and continued. "Nerves took the message from your brain and told your arm what to do. But how do you know that your hand is over your head? You can't see your hand because

your eyes are closed. So how do you know that your hand isn't in your pocket?"

Angela said, "Well, I can feel my hand. I can feel that it's over my head."

The old man said, "You can feel your hand because your brain is getting messages from your hand. You know that your hand is over your head because your hand is sending messages to your brain."

Angela opened her eyes. "Wow!" she said. "The body is really something."

- (After all students have raised their hand:) To show Angela how nerves work, the old man had her do something. What was that? (Call on a student. Idea: *Close her eyes and hold her hand high up in the air.*) (ND)
- How did her muscles know what to do when she moved her hand over her head? (Call on a student. Ideas: *Her brain told them what to do; they received messages.*) (ND)
- How did she know that her hand was over her head and not in her pocket? (Call on a student. Ideas: *Her brain got messages from her hand; she could feel her hand over her head.*) (ND)
- Everybody, which nerves told her that her hand was over her head, the nerves that go **to** the brain or the nerves that go **from** the brain? (Signal.) *The nerves that go to the brain.* (ND)
- Which nerves told her arm how to move when she held her hand over her head? (Signal.) *The nerves that go from the brain.* (ND)

EXERCISE 4

Paired Practice

You're going to read aloud to your partner. The **A** members will read first. Then the **B** members will read from the star to the end of the story. (Observe students and give feedback.)

End-of-Lesson Activities

INDEPENDENT WORK

Now finish your independent work for lesson 124. Raise your hand when you're finished. (Observe students and give feedback.)

WORKCHECK

a. (Direct students to take out their marking pencils.)

- We're going to check your workbook and textbook items. Remember, if you got an item wrong, make an **X** next to the item.

b. (For each item: Read the item. Call on a student to answer it. If the answer is wrong, say the correct answer. Refer to the Answer Key for the correct answers.)

c. Now use your marking pencil to fix up any items you got wrong. Remember, all mistakes must be fixed up before you hand in your work.

SPELLING

(Present Spelling lesson 124 after completing Reading lesson 124. See *Spelling Presentation Book.*)

ACTIVITIES

(Present Activity 27 after completing Reading lessons 124–125. See *Activities across the Curriculum.*)

EXERCISE 1

Vocabulary Review

a. You learned a sentence that tells what the injury to his spinal cord did.
  • Everybody, say that sentence. Get ready. (Signal.) *The injury to his spinal cord paralyzed him.*
  • (Repeat until firm.)
b. I'll say part of the sentence. When I stop, you say the next word. Listen: The . . . Everybody, what's the next word? (Signal.) *Injury.*
c. Listen: The injury to his . . . Everybody, what's the next part? (Signal.) *Spinal cord.*
  • Say the whole sentence. Get ready. (Signal.) *The injury to his spinal cord paralyzed him.*
d. Listen: The injury to his spinal cord . . . Everybody, what's the next word? (Signal.) *Paralyzed.*

EXERCISE 2

Reading Words

Column 1

a. **Find lesson 125 in your textbook.** ✔
  • Touch column 1. ✔
  • (Teacher reference:)

1. retina	3. shovel
2. spiral	4. collect

b. Word 1 is **retina.** What word? (Signal.) *Retina.*
  • Spell **retina.** Get ready. (Tap for each letter.) *R-E-T-I-N-A.*
  • The retina is part of the eye. You'll read more about it.
c. Word 2 is **spiral.** What word? (Signal.) *Spiral.*
  • Spell **spiral.** Get ready. (Tap for each letter.) *S-P-I-R-A-L.*
  • A spiral is a circle that keeps getting bigger. Everybody, what do we call a circle that keeps getting bigger? (Signal.) *Spiral.*
d. Word 3 is **shovel.** What word? (Signal.) *Shovel.*
  • Spell **shovel.** Get ready. (Tap for each letter.) *S-H-O-V-E-L.*
e. Word 4 is **collect.** What word? (Signal.) *Collect.*
  • Spell **collect.** Get ready. (Tap for each letter.) *C-O-L-L-E-C-T.*
f. Let's read those words again.
  • Word 1. What word? (Signal.) *Retina.*
  • (Repeat for words 2–4.)
g. (Repeat step f until firm.)

Column 2

h. Find column 2. ✔
  • (Teacher reference:)

1. <u>back</u>bone	3. <u>mass</u>es
2. <u>bun</u>dle	4. <u>im</u>age

  • All these words have more than one syllable. The first syllable of each word is underlined.
i. Word 1. What's the first syllable? (Signal.) *back.*
  • What's the whole word? (Signal.) *Backbone.*
  • The bones that run from your skull down the middle of your back are called the backbone.
j. Word 2. What's the first syllable? (Signal.) *bun.*
  • What's the whole word? (Signal.) *Bundle.*
k. Word 3. What's the first syllable? (Signal.) *mass.*
  • What's the whole word? (Signal.) *Masses.*
l. Word 4. What's the first syllable? (Signal.) *im.*
  • What's the whole word? (Signal.) *Image.*
m. Let's read those words again.
  • Word 1. What word? (Signal.) *Backbone.*
  • (Repeat for words 2–4.)
n. (Repeat step m until firm.)

Column 3

o. Find column 3. ✔
  • (Teacher reference:)

1. cerebrum	3. hollow
2. blind	4. magnifying

p. Word 1. What word? (Signal.) *Cerebrum.*
  • (Repeat for words 2–4.)

q. Let's read those words again.
- Word 1. What word? (Signal.) *Cerebrum.*
- (Repeat for: **2. blind, 3. hollow, 4. magnifying.**)
r. (Repeat step q until firm.)

Individual Turns

(For columns 1–3: Call on individual students, each to read one to three words per turn.)

EXERCISE 3

Story Background

a. Find part B in your textbook. ✔
- You're going to read the next story about Al and Angela. First you'll read the information passage. It gives some facts about using a magnifying glass.
b. Everybody, touch the title. ✔
- (Call on a student to read the title.) *[Making Pictures With a Magnifying Glass.]*
- Everybody, what's the title? (Signal.) *Making Pictures With a Magnifying Glass.* (ND)
c. (Call on individual students to read the passage, each student reading two or three sentences at a time. Ask the specified questions as the students read.)

> ### Making Pictures With a Magnifying Glass
>
> You can make pictures in a dark room by using a magnifying glass. Picture A shows a magnifying glass that is near a flower. The picture of the flower is on the dark wall. The picture is upside down.

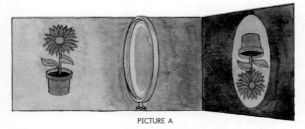

PICTURE A

- Everybody, touch the actual flower in picture A. That flower is in bright light. ✔ (VA)
- Touch the magnifying glass. ✔ (VA)
- The light from the flower passes through the lens.
- Touch the flower that's upside down in picture A. ✔ (VA)
- That's the picture of the flower after the light goes through the lens.

> Picture B shows how the picture got on the wall. The light that enters the magnifying glass bends. When it hits the wall, the light from the top of the flower is on the bottom of the picture. The light from the bottom of the flower pot is on the top of the picture.

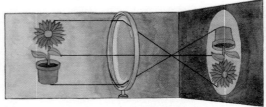

PICTURE B

- Everybody, look at picture B. Touch the line that goes from the top of the flower. Follow it through the lens of the magnifying glass to the picture. ✔ (VA)
- That light bends when it passes through the lens. The same thing happens with the light from the bottom of the flower pot. Does that light end up at the **top** of the picture or the **bottom** of the picture? (Signal.) *Top.* (DC)
- The next part tells how the human eye works. Picture C shows two pictures of an eye. The picture in the small box shows what the eye looks like if no part is cut away.
- Touch that picture. ✔ (VA)
- The big picture shows what the eye would look like if half of it was cut away and you could see inside it. Touch the cut-away eye. ✔ (VA)

> The human eye works just like a magnifying glass in a dark room. The light enters a hole in the front of the eye. The light bends, and the picture is on the back of the eye. Notice that the picture is upside down. This is the image the person sees.

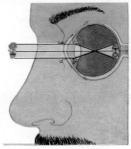

PICTURE C

- Everybody, does the light enter from the **front** of the eyeball or the **back** of the eyeball? (Signal.) *Front.* (ND)
- Where does the picture form, at the **front** or at the **back** of the eyeball? (Signal.) *Back.* (ND)
- The light enters the hole in the front of the eye. That looks like a black circle on the eye in the box. Touch that circle. ✔ (VA)
- Everybody, look at the cut-away view of an eye. Part of the eye bends the light. Everybody, touch that part. ✔ (VA)
- That part is called a lens, and it works just like the lens of a magnifying glass.

EXERCISE 4

Story Reading

a. Find part C in your textbook. ✔
- The error limit for group reading is 9 errors. Read carefully.
b. Everybody, touch the title. ✔
- (Call on a student to read the title.) [*Al and Angela Learn About the Brain.*]
- Everybody, what's the title? (Signal.) *Al and Angela Learn About the Brain.* (ND)
- (Call on individual students to read the story, each student reading two or three sentences at a time. Ask the specified questions as the students read.

- (**Correct errors:** Tell the word. Direct the student to reread the sentence.)
- (If the group makes more than 9 errors, direct the students to reread the story.)

Al and Angela Learn About the Brain

Al, Angela and the old man were in the human body looking at nerves. The old man was saying, "Remember—every part of the body must have two kinds of nerves."

- One type of nerve carries messages from the **body part.** Everybody, where does that nerve lead? (Signal.) *To the brain.* (APK)
- One type of nerve carries messages from the **brain.** Where does that nerve lead? (Call on a student. Idea: *To the body part.*) (RF/R)
- What do nerves that lead to a body part tell the part? (Call on a student. Ideas: *How to move; what to do.*) (APK)
- What do nerves that lead from a body part to the brain tell the brain? (Call on a student. Idea: *What the part feels.*) (RF/R)

Angela said, "One kind of nerve sends the messages to the brain and the other kind of nerve sends messages from the brain to the body."

"Correct," the old man replied. "Now let's follow this nerve and see how it gets to the brain. We are moving up the arm toward the shoulder."

As they moved along, Al noticed that other nerves joined the nerve they were following and that the nerve they were following became thicker and thicker.

The old man said, "We are at the shoulder now and we are moving toward the spinal cord."

- Everybody, touch the part of your body to show me where Al and Angela are now. ✔
- Tell me where they are going. (Signal.) *To the spinal cord.* (ND)
- That's where your backbone is. Everybody, move along your shoulder until you come to your backbone. ✔
- That's where Al and Angela are going.

"What's the spinal cord?" Angela asked.

The old man said, "Do you know where your backbone is?"

Angela said, "Sure. It goes up and down the middle of my back."

The old man touched his backbone. Then he said, "The nerves that go to the brain go up through the backbone. There is a great bundle of nerves that goes right through the middle of the backbone. The nerves form a great cord, or rope. That cord is called the spinal cord."

- Where is the spinal cord? (Call on a student. Idea: *In the middle of the backbone.*) (ND)

"Wow!" Angela exclaimed. Then she repeated "spinal cord" to herself four times.

- Why do you think she did that? (Call on a student. Idea: *So she'd remember the name.*) (DI)

Al could now see the backbone directly ahead of them. It was made up of little bones, one bone on top of the other. The nerve that they were following went right into the backbone along with some nerves from other parts of the body. Some of these nerves were thick and some were thin.

Angela said, "There must be hundreds of nerves in the body."

"Correct," the old man said. "Just remember—every part of the body must have two types of nerves. And all those nerves go through the spinal cord."

Al, Angela and the old man continued to follow the nerve into the backbone. Al could now see that each bone in the backbone was hollow.

A very thick bundle of nerves was running up and down through the middle of the hollow bones. There were so many nerves that Al could hardly keep track of the nerve they had been following.

- What is strange about the bones in the backbone? (Call on a student. Idea: *They're hollow.*) (ND)
- Everybody, what do we call the bundle of nerves that goes up and down through the middle of the backbone? (Signal.) *The spinal cord.* (ND)

Al could feel all kinds of messages in the nerves.

The old man said, "When we reach the top of the spinal cord, we'll ⭐ go into the brain. We don't have very far to go, because we entered the spinal cord at the man's shoulder."

- Everybody, touch your backbone between your shoulders. ✔
- Now move up until you can feel your skull. ✔
- That's where Al and Angela are going now. They're moving right through the middle of the backbone.
- Read the rest of the story to yourself and be ready to answer some questions. Raise your hand when you're finished.

As Al looked down the spinal cord, he could see that some bundles of nerves entered down at the bottom of the man's backbone. Just then the old man said, "We are getting ready to enter the brain."

Al looked at the great masses of nerves at the top of the spinal cord. "Wow!" he said. "Look at all the nerves that go to the brain."

"No," the old man said. "Remember—many of these nerves are coming <u>from</u> the brain."

"I keep forgetting," Al said.

Now Angela, Al and the old man moved into the brain. Millions of small nerves went this way and that way. Some of these nerves were very short. As Al moved through this mass of nerves, he could feel that they were pulsing all the time. Some of the pulses were strong, and some were weak.

The old man said, "We are in the section of the brain that controls things you don't have to think about. You don't have to tell yourself to sweat when your body gets hot. You don't have to tell your heart to pound hard when you're running and your body needs more oxygen. You don't have to tell your body to breathe when you're asleep. All of the things that you don't think about take place in this part of the brain."

As Al, Angela and the old man kept moving up through the brain, Al noticed that the brain was starting to look different. There were even more nerves than there were in the lower part of the brain. The old man said, "Now we are going into the part of the brain that does the thinking. This part is called the cerebrum. When you tell your hand to make a fist, this is the part of the brain that is working. When you think about something that you see, this is the part that does the thinking. When you think about what somebody says to you, you are using this part."

Angela asked, "What did you say this part of the brain is called?"

Al told her.

"Correct," the old man said. "The thinking part of the brain is the cerebrum."

Angela and Al looked at the nerves that tangled this way and that way through the cerebrum. "Wow!" Angela exclaimed.

- (After all students have raised their hand:) When Al and Angela first entered the brain, they were in the part that controls some things the body does. What things are those? (Call on a student. Ideas: *Things you don't have to think about; things like sweating; breathing.*) (ND)
- When they moved up through the brain they came to another part. Everybody, did that part have **more nerves** or **fewer nerves?** (Signal.) *More nerves.* (ND)
- What is the name of that part? (Signal.) *Cerebrum.* (ND)
- What does the cerebrum do? (Call on a student. Idea: *It does the thinking.*) (ND)

<hr>

EXERCISE 5

Fluency: Rate/Accuracy

> *Note:* There is a fluency checkout in this lesson; therefore, there is no paired practice.

a. Today is a reading checkout day. While you're doing your independent work, I'm going to call on you one at a time to read part of the story from lesson 124.
- Remember, you pass the checkout by reading the passage in less than a minute without making more than 2 mistakes. And when you pass the checkout, you'll color the space for lesson 125 on your thermometer chart.
b. (Call on individual students to read the portion of story 124 with ❀.)
- (Time the student. Note words that are missed and number of words read.)
- (Teacher reference:)

> ❀ The old man said, "A nerve is like an electric wire. It carries messages. This nerve goes from the hand to the man's brain. It carries messages from the hand."
> The old man continued, "Hold onto the nerve. You will see what kind of messages they are."
> Al and Angela [50] touched the nerve. They could feel little pulses that felt like tiny electric shocks.

> Pulse, pulse, pulse, the nerve went. The pulses weren't strong enough [75] to hurt. They felt like little trickles of electricity.
> The old man said, "You are feeling the messages that are coming from the man's hand [100] right now. Watch what happens when the man starts to tie his shoe."
> Suddenly, the pulses started to go faster and faster.
> The old man ❀ [125] said, "The man is feeling things."

- (If the student reads the passage in one minute or less and makes no more than 2 errors, direct the student to color in the space for lesson 125 on the thermometer chart.)

> - (If the student makes any mistakes, point to each word that was misread and identify it.)
> - (If the student does not meet the rate-error criterion for the passage, direct the student to practice reading the story with the assigned partner.)

End-of-Lesson Activities

INDEPENDENT WORK

Now finish your independent work for lesson 125. Raise your hand when you're finished. (Observe students and give feedback.)

WORKCHECK

a. (Direct students to take out their marking pencils.)
- We're going to check your workbook and textbook items. Remember, if you got an item wrong, make an **X** next to the item.
b. (For each item: Read the item. Call on a student to answer it. If the answer is wrong, say the correct answer. Refer to the Answer Key for the correct answers.)
c. Now use your marking pencil to fix up any items you got wrong. Remember, all mistakes must be fixed up before you hand in your work.

SPELLING

(Present Spelling lesson 125 after completing Reading lesson 125. See *Spelling Presentation Book.*)

Lessons 126–130 • Planning Page   *Looking Ahead*

	Lesson 126	Lesson 127	Lesson 128	Lesson 129	Lesson 130
LESSON EVENTS	Reading Words Story Background Story Reading Paired Practice Independent Work Workcheck Spelling	**Vocabulary Sentence** Reading Words Vocabulary Sentence Story Reading Paired Practice Independent Work Workcheck Spelling	Vocabulary Sentence Reading Words Story Reading Paired Practice Independent Work Workcheck Spelling	Vocabulary Sentences Reading Words Story Background Story Reading Paired Practice Independent Work Workcheck Spelling	Fact Game Fluency: Rate/ Accuracy Test Marking the Test Test Remedies Spelling
VOCABULARY SENTENCE		**#31: A <u>single</u> star was <u>near</u> the <u>horizon</u>.**	#31: A <u>single</u> star was <u>near</u> the <u>horizon</u>.	sentence #29 sentence #30 sentence #31	
READING WORDS: WORD TYPES	mixed words compound words	mixed words	2-syllable words	modeled words multi-syllable words words with an ending	
NEW VOCABULARY				absolutely suspended briskly	
STORY BACKGROUND	*How the Eye Works*			*The Earth and the Sun*	
STORY	*Angela and Al Learn About the Eye*	*Al and Angela Learn About the Ear*	*Angela and Al Study for a Test*	*Angela and Al Take a Test on the Human Body*	
SKILL ITEMS	Vocabulary	Sequencing	Crossword puzzle	Vocabulary sentence	Test: Vocabulary sentences
SPECIAL MATERIALS					Thermometer charts, dice, Fact Game 130, Fact Game Answer Key, scorecard sheets
SPECIAL PROJECTS/ ACTIVITIES	Activity after lessons 126–127			Activity after lesson 129	

Comprehension Questions Abbreviations Guide

Access Prior Knowledge = (APK)   Author's Point of View = (APoV)   Author's Purpose = (AP)   Cause/Effect = (C/E)   Charts/Graphs/Diagrams/Visual Aids = (VA)

Classify and Categorize = (C+C)   Compare/Contrast = (C/C)   Determine Character Emotions, Motivation = (DCE)   Drawing Conclusions = (DC)   Drawing Inferences = (DI)

Fact and Opinion = (F/O)   Hypothesizing = (H)   Main Idea = (MI)   Making Connections = (MC)   Making Deductions = (MD)   Making Judgements = (MJ)

Narrative Elements = (NE)   Noting Details = (ND)   Predict = (P)   Reality/Fantasy = (R/F)   Recall Facts/Rules = (RF/R)   Retell = (R)   Sequence = (Seq)

Steps in a Process = (SP)   Story Structure = (SS)   Summarize = (Sum)   Understanding Dialogue = (UD)   Using Context to Confirm Meaning(s) = (UCCM)   Visualize = (V)

EXERCISE 1

Reading Words

Column 1

a. **Find lesson 126 in your textbook.**
- Touch column 1. ✔
- (Teacher reference:)

1. horizon	5. tying
2. lens	6. backbone
3. pupil	7. single
4. retina	

b. Word 1. What word? (Signal.) *Horizon.*
- (Repeat for words 2–7.)
c. Let's read those words again.
- Word 1. What word? (Signal.) *Horizon.*
- (Repeat for words 2–7.)
d. (Repeat step c until firm.)

Column 2

e. Find column 2. ✔
- (Teacher reference:)

1. bedroom	4. maybe
2. eyeball	5. forearm
3. mailman	6. shoelace

- All these words are compound words. The first part of each word is underlined.
f. Word 1. What's the underlined part? (Signal.) *bed.*
- What's the whole word? (Signal.) *Bedroom.*
- Spell **bedroom.** Get ready. (Tap for each letter.) *B-E-D-R-O-O-M.*
g. Word 2. What's the underlined part? (Signal.) *eye.*
- What's the whole word? (Signal.) *Eyeball.*
- Spell **eyeball.** Get ready. (Tap for each letter.) *E-Y-E-B-A-L-L.*
h. Word 3. What's the underlined part? (Signal.) *mail.*
- What's the whole word? (Signal.) *Mailman.*
- Spell **mailman.** Get ready. (Tap for each letter.) *M-A-I-L-M-A-N.*
i. Word 4. What's the underlined part? (Signal.) *may.*

- What's the whole word? (Signal.) *Maybe.*
- Spell **maybe.** Get ready. (Tap for each letter.) *M-A-Y-B-E.*
j. Word 5. What's the underlined part? (Signal.) *fore.*
- What's the whole word? (Signal.) *Forearm.*
k. Word 6. What's the underlined part? (Signal.) *shoe.*
- What's the whole word? (Signal.) *Shoelace.*
l. Let's read those words again.
- Word 1. What word? (Signal.) *Bedroom.*
- (Repeat for words 2–6.)
m. (Repeat step l until firm.)

Individual Turns

(For columns 1 and 2: Call on individual students, each to read one to three words per turn.)

EXERCISE 2

Story Background

a. Find part B in your textbook. ✔
- You're going to read the next story about Al and Angela. First you'll read the information passage. It gives some facts about the eye.
b. Everybody, touch the title. ✔
- (Call on a student to read the title.) *[How the Eye Works.]*
- Everybody, what's the title? (Signal.) *How the Eye Works.* ⓃⒹ
c. (Call on individual students to read the passage, each student reading two or three sentences at a time. Ask the specified questions as the students read.)

How the Eye Works

The eye works just like a magnifying glass. The eye bends the light. The light forms a picture on the back of the eyeball. That's the image the person sees.

- Everybody, does the picture form on the **front** of the eyeball or the **back** of the eyeball? (Signal.) *Back.* ⓇⒻ/Ⓡ

- Is that picture right side up or upside down? (Signal.) *Upside down.* (RF/R)

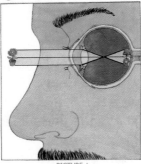
PICTURE 1

- Picture 1 shows the image that is formed on the back of the eye. Touch the top part of the flower on the back of the eye. ✔ (VA)
- Touch the bottom part of the flower pot on the back of the eye. ✔ (VA)

If you look at the eye from the front, you can see the hole that light enters. It's called the pupil. The pupil looks like a round black disk in the middle of the eye.

Remember, the pupil is a hole. It's black because the inside of the eyeball is dark. Behind the pupil is a lens. That's the part that bends the light.

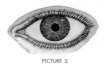
PICTURE 2

- Everybody, what do we call the hole in the front of the eye? (Signal.) *Pupil.* (RF/R)
- What color is the pupil? (Signal.) *Black.* (RF/R)
- Why does it look black? (Call on a student. Idea: *Because the inside of the eyeball is dark.*) (RF/R)
- Touch the pupil in picture 2. ✔ (VA)
- Everybody, what part is behind the pupil? (Signal.) *Lens.* (RF/R)
- What does the lens do? (Call on a student. Idea: *Bends the light.*) (RF/R)

EXERCISE 3

Story Reading

a. Find part C in your textbook. ✔
- The error limit for group reading is 14 errors. Read carefully.
b. Everybody, touch the title. ✔

- (Call on a student to read the title.) [*Al and Angela Learn About the Eye.*]
- Everybody, what's the title? (Signal.) *Al and Angela Learn About the Eye.* (ND)
- (Call on individual students to read the story, each student reading two or three sentences at a time. Ask the specified questions as the students read.)

- (**Correct errors:** Tell the word. Direct the student to reread the sentence.)
- (If the group makes more than 14 errors, direct the students to reread the story.)

Al and Angela Learn About the Eye

"Wow!" Al said as he observed the thinking part of the human brain.

- Everybody, what's the name of that part? (Signal.) *Cerebrum.* (APK)

There were millions and millions of nerves inside the cerebrum.

The old man said, "Observe what the brain does when the man does different things. The man is sitting in his bedroom. He just finished tying his shoe. The man just woke up, so he is still a little sleepy. Watch what happens to his brain when a lion walks into his bedroom."

Suddenly the nerves behind Al started to pulse rapidly. An instant later, every nerve in the brain seemed to be pulsing. Nerves were firing all around Al.

Angela said, "This man's brain is going wild."

The old man snapped his fingers and said, "The lion is gone now." The pulsing in the brain started to slow down again.

"Here's what happened," the old man said. "The man looked at the lion. When the brain realized what he was looking at, part of the brain started to work very hard. The man became frightened. So every part of his brain tried to work at the same time. Then the lion disappeared and the man's brain started to slow down. The man started to wonder how a lion got into his bedroom. He started thinking that maybe he was just having a bad dream."

"Poor man," Al said. Then he laughed. "That was a dirty trick to play on him."

The old man said, "Yes, it was. But it really showed us how his brain works."

Angela, Al and the old man moved to the left side of the brain. Al could now see a great thick bundle of nerves leading to the back of the brain. "What is that?" he asked.

The old man explained, "Those are the nerves that come from his left eye. Each eye has a great bundle of nerves that goes to the brain. The pulses from those nerves go to the back of the brain."

- Everybody, where did the bundle of nerves they were looking at come from? (Signal.) *The left eye.* (ND)
- To which part of the brain did the huge bundle of nerves lead? (Signal.) *The back.* (ND)

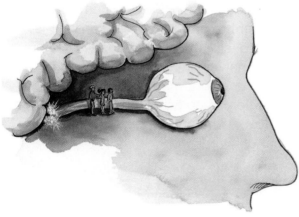

- Everybody, look at the picture. Are Al and the others facing the **front** or the **back** of the man's head? (Signal.) *Front.* (DC)
- The eyeball is in front of them. Touch the eyeball. ✔ (VA)
- They are standing next to a great bundle of nerves. It goes from the eyeball to the brain. Touch the bundle. ✔ (VA)
- Behind them is the part of the brain the bundle leads to. You can see the sparks where the nerves are firing. Touch that part of the brain. ✔ (VA)

The old man continued, "Right now the man is looking out the window. He is watching the mailman walk down the street and his brain is paying attention to the mailman."

The old man said, "If you want to see the things the man is looking at, just follow this bundle of nerves to the eye."

Angela, Al and the old man moved along the big nerve to the eye. Then they went inside the big nerve. When they came ⭐ out, they were inside the eye. It was a great round chamber that seemed bigger than a big building.

On the other side of the chamber was a big round window. Light was coming through the window. The rest of the chamber was very dark.

- Part of the eye was dark and part had a round window in it. The big round window is the pupil. Everybody, what's just **behind** the pupil? (Signal.) *Lens.* (APK)

The old man said, "We are inside the eyeball, near the back of it. You can't see this part of the eye when you look at somebody. You can see only the front of the eye." The old man pointed to the round window on the front of the eyeball. "That is the part that lets light into the eye."

- Everybody, what's the name of that part? (Signal.) *Pupil.* (RF/R)

Then the old man said, "Turn around. Look at the back of the eyeball. It is called the retina. On the retina you will see what the man is looking at."

- What's the part of the eyeball where the image is formed? (Signal.) *Retina.* (APK)
- Read the rest of the story to yourself and be ready to answer some questions. Raise your hand when you're finished.

As the old man talked, Al turned around and looked at the retina. At first he could not believe what he saw. There was a great big picture on the back of the eyeball. The picture went from the top of the eyeball to the bottom of the eyeball. And it went from one side all the way to the other side. Al studied the picture. He could see things in the picture and he could see the colors. He could see a mailman walking, a tree, a sidewalk and a little dog. He could see houses. But everything he saw was upside down.

Angela was looking at the picture too. She said, "I don't believe it. This is like being at a movie with everything upside down."

"Correct," the old man said. "And everything is in color."

"Wow!" Angela said. "I still don't believe it."

The old man said, "In a moment the man will look down to see if his shoes are tied. Watch the picture."

Suddenly, the picture changed. Al could see two shoes in the picture. He could also see part of the man's legs. One of the shoes was not tied. The shoe started to get bigger and bigger.

The old man said, "The man is bending down now. He's getting closer to his shoes. That's why they look bigger."

The man's hands came into the picture. They started to tie the shoe.

Al said, "This is amazing. We can observe everything the man sees by looking at the man's retina."

Angela added, "And each picture goes to the brain through a huge nerve."

"You are both correct," the old man said.

- (After all students have raised their hand:) As Angela and Al watched what the man was looking at, the man did something. What was that? (Call on a student. Ideas: *Looked down at his shoes; bent over to tie his shoe.*) (ND)
- His shoes got bigger. Why? (Call on a student. Idea: *Because the man's eyes were moving closer to the shoes.*) (ND)
- Everybody, what part of the eye could Al and Angela look at to see everything the man saw? (Signal.) *Retina.* (ND)

Paired Practice

You're going to read aloud to your partner. The **B** members will read first. Then the **A** members will read from the star to the end of the story. (Observe students and give feedback.)

End-of-Lesson Activities

INDEPENDENT WORK

Now finish your independent work for lesson 126. Raise your hand when you're finished. (Observe students and give feedback.)

WORKCHECK

a. (Direct students to take out their marking pencils.)
- We're going to check your workbook and textbook items. Remember, if you got an item wrong, make an **X** next to the item.
b. (For each item: Read the item. Call on a student to answer it. If the answer is wrong, say the correct answer. Refer to the Answer Key for the correct answers.)
c. Now use your marking pencil to fix up any items you got wrong. Remember, all mistakes must be fixed up before you hand in your work.

SPELLING

(Present Spelling lesson 126 after completing Reading lesson 126. See *Spelling Presentation Book*.)

ACTIVITIES

(Present Activity 28 after completing Reading lessons 126–127. See *Activities across the Curriculum*.)

EXERCISE 1

Vocabulary

a. **Find the vocabulary sentences at the back of your textbook.** ✔
- Touch sentence 31. ✔
- This is a new vocabulary sentence. It says: A single star was near the horizon. Everybody, say that sentence. Get ready. (Signal.) *A single star was near the horizon.*
- Close your eyes and say the sentence. Get ready. (Signal.) *A single star was near the horizon.*
- (Repeat until firm.)

b. The sentence refers to a **single** star. **Single** means **one.** If there is a single star, there is just one star. How would you refer to **one tree?** (Signal.) *A single tree.*

c. The single star was near the **horizon.** The horizon is the line where the earth ends and the sky begins. It's called the horizon because the line between the earth and the sky is usually horizontal. Everybody, what do we call the line between the earth and the sky? (Signal.) *Horizon.*

d. Listen to the sentence again: A single star was near the horizon. Everybody, say that sentence. Get ready. (Signal.) *A single star was near the horizon.*

e. Everybody, what word names the line between the earth and the sky? (Signal.) *Horizon.*
- What word means **one?** (Signal.) *Single.*

EXERCISE 2

Reading Words

Column 1

a. **Find lesson 127 in your textbook.** ✔
- Touch column 1. ✔
- (Teacher reference:)

1. collects	5. blind
2. horizon	6. spiral
3. discussed	7. explained
4. single	

b. Word 1. What word? (Signal.) *Collects.*
- Spell **collects.** Get ready. (Tap for each letter.) *C-O-L-L-E-C-T-S.*

c. Word 2. What word? (Signal.) *Horizon.*
- Spell **horizon.** Get ready. (Tap for each letter.) *H-O-R-I-Z-O-N.*

d. Word 3. What word? (Signal.) *Discussed.*
- Spell **discussed.** Get ready. (Tap for each letter.) *D-I-S-C-U-S-S-E-D.*

e. Word 4. What word? (Signal.) *Single.*
- Spell **single.** Get ready. (Tap for each letter.) *S-I-N-G-L-E.*

f. Word 5. What word? (Signal.) *Blind.*
- (Repeat for words 6 and 7.)

g. Let's read those words again.
- Word 1. What word? (Signal.) *Collects.*
- (Repeat for words 2–7.)

h. (Repeat step g until firm.)

EXERCISE 3

Story Reading

a. Find part B in your textbook. ✔
- The error limit for group reading is 17 errors. Read carefully.

b. Everybody, touch the title. ✔
- (Call on a student to read the title.) *[Al and Angela Learn About the Ear.]*
- Everybody, what's the title? (Signal.) *Al and Angela Learn About the Ear.* (ND)
- (Call on individual students to read the story, each student reading two or three sentences at a time. Ask the specified questions as the students read.)

- (**Correct errors:** Tell the word. Direct the student to reread the sentence.)
- (If the group makes more than 17 errors, direct the students to reread the story.)

Al and Angela Learn About the Ear

Angela, Al and the old man were inside a man's eye. By looking at the image on the retina, they could see a picture of everything the man saw.

Angela said, "I don't understand how the picture from the eye gets into that nerve that goes to the brain."

"I will explain," the old man said, pointing to the retina. "The retina can feel light. There are thousands of nerves in the retina. Each nerve can feel if light hits it. All the nerves that feel light send a message. These messages go down that big bundle of nerves to the back of the brain."

- Everybody, what is the retina covered with? (Signal.) *Nerves.* (ND)
- What does each of those nerves feel? (Signal.) *Light.* (ND)
- Those feelings go into the big bundle of nerves. Where does the big bundle of nerves go? (Signal.) *To the back of the brain.* (ND)

Al thought for a moment. Then he said, "What if that big nerve from the eye to the brain was cut? Would the man be able to see anything?"

- Everybody, what's the answer? (Signal.) *No.* (DI)

The old man said, "The man would be blind in that eye if the nerve was cut."

The old man pointed to the window in the front of the eye. He said, "Right behind the pupil is a very important part of the eye. Do you know the name of that part?"

- Everybody, what's the answer? (Signal.) *The lens.* (APK)

Angela said, "I remember that. That's the lens. The lens bends the light that comes into the eye."

Al said, "Bends the light? What do you mean?"

Angela said, "Look at the picture on the back of the eye. That picture is upside down. How did it get upside down?"

Al said, "I don't know."

Angela explained, "The lens in the eye bent the light so that it would form a picture on the retina. After the light is bent, the picture is upside down."

Al and Angela watched the pictures on the retina for a few minutes. During this time, Al kept thinking about where he had been. He had thought that a trip inside the body would be boring.

- Everybody, was he finding it boring? (Signal.) *No.* (MJ)

Suddenly the old man said, "Let's go to the ear." Slowly Angela, Al, and the old man went back down the nerve from the eye and back into the brain. They moved to the side of the brain, where they came to a strange chamber that was shaped like a spiral. They entered at the small end of the chamber. And then they started to follow it as it spiraled around and around, becoming larger and larger.

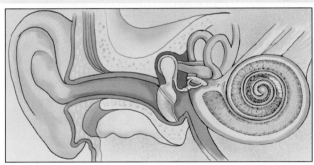

- Everybody, touch the picture. ✔ (VA)
- That picture shows Al and the others entering the part of the ear that is next to the brain. Everybody, what shape is that chamber? (Signal.) *Spiral.* (ND)
- Are Al and the others entering at the **big end** or the **small end** of the spiral? (Signal.) *The small end.* (ND)
- Touch the place where they entered the spiral and follow the spiral all the way around to the big end. ✔ (VA)

"Is this what the inside of my ear looks like?" Angela asked.

"Yes," the old man said. "When you look at a person's ear, you see only the outside part of the ear. The part you see works like a funnel. It collects the sound and directs it into the inner ear. That's where we are now. But you can't see the inner ear from the outside."

- Touch the part of the ear you can see from the outside. ✔ (DC)
- Touch the spiral part that is on the inside. ✔ (VA)
- The outer part collects the sound like a funnel does. Then the sound goes into the spiral part.
- Everybody, are Al and the others in the part of the ear that is on the outside of the skull? (Signal.) *No.* (ND)
- What part are they in? (Signal.) *The inner ear.* (ND)
- The outer part of the ear works like a funnel for sound. What does that mean? (Call on a student. Idea: *It collects the sound and directs it into the inner ear.*) (DC)
- If you make the funnel bigger, you can hear more. Everybody, cup your hand behind your ear and bend your ear until it is sticking straight out with your cupped hand behind it. ✔
- Notice how much more you can hear now because the funnel is bigger.

The old man explained, "We're way inside the ear, at the place it joins the brain."

Rows of hairs lined the inside of the chamber. The old man pointed to a hair. He said, "There is a nerve that goes to the brain from every hair in the ear. And when the hair vibrates, the nerve pulses. The more the hair vibrates, the harder the nerve pulses."

- Everybody, what was lining the whole chamber? (Signal.) *Hairs.* (ND)
- What is each hair connected to? (Signal.) *A nerve.* (ND)
- What happens when the hair moves? (Call on a student. Idea: *The nerve pulses.*) (ND)
- What happens if the hair vibrates very hard? (Call on a student. Idea: *The nerve pulses harder.*) (ND)

"Wow!" Angela exclaimed. "Look at all the hairs inside this ear. And every hair can make a nerve pulse."

Al, Angela and the old man went down and around the spiral. The chamber got bigger and bigger as they moved through it.

The old man said, "In a moment the man will hear a church bell. It is a very big bell and it makes a very deep sound."

Al wasn't sure what to expect. Then suddenly—"BONNNNNG, BONNNNNNG"—the chamber seemed to tremble. The sound was very, very loud.

- Make a deep sound like that church bell. (Call on a student.) (V)

Al looked around at the hairs inside the chamber. "Look," he said, and pointed to the largest part of the chamber. Every hair in that part of the chamber was vibrating. But no hairs in the other parts of the chamber were vibrating.

- Everybody, in which part of the chamber were the hairs vibrating? (Signal.) *The largest part.* (ND)
- Touch that part of the chamber in the picture. ✔ (VA)
- What about the hairs in the other parts of the chamber? (Call on a student. Idea: *They weren't vibrating.*) (ND)

"Some of those hairs aren't working," Al said. "When the bell sounded, only some of them vibrated."

The bell sounded again. "BONNNNG, BONNNNG." Again, the hairs in only one part of the chamber vibrated.

- Everybody, which part is that? (Signal.) *The largest part.* (ND)

"Al is right," Angela said. "Only the hairs in one part of this chamber are working."

The old man said, "Watch what happens when the man listens to a different bell. In a moment he will hear a telephone ring. Watch."

Al watched. "Rrrrrring . . . Rrrrring . . . Rrrrring."

- Make the sound of a telephone bell. (Call on a student.) (V)

- Do you think that sound will make the hairs at the big end of the chamber vibrate? (Call on a student. Idea: *No.*) Ⓓ
- In which part of the chamber do you think hairs will vibrate? (Call on a student. Ideas: *The middle part; the small part.*) Ⓟ

> As soon as the telephone started to ring, the hairs in the middle part of the chamber began vibrating but the hairs at the large end of the chamber did not vibrate.

- Everybody, in which part of the chamber were the hairs that vibrated? (Signal.) *The middle part.* ⓃⒹ
- What did the hairs at the big end of the chamber do? (Call on a student. Ideas: *Nothing; they didn't move.*) ⓃⒹ

> Angela pointed to the vibrating hairs and said, "The hairs in that part of the ear didn't work when the church bell rang. But look at them now. They vibrate when the telephone rings."
> The old man smiled and said, "I want both of you to think. The man is now going to hear a very high whistle. It is much higher than a telephone ring. Can you tell me where the hair will vibrate when the man hears the whistle?"

- Who can make a high whistling sound? (Call on a student.) Ⓥ
- Everybody, in which part of the chamber did the hairs vibrate when the **deep** bell sounded? (Signal.) *The largest part.* ⓃⒹ
- In which part of the chamber did the hairs vibrate when the **telephone** bell sounded? (Signal.) *The middle part.* ⓃⒹ
- In which part of the chamber do you think hairs will vibrate when the whistle sounds? (Call on a student. Idea: *The smallest part.*) Ⓓ
- Read the rest of the story to yourself and be ready to answer some questions. Raise your hand when you're finished.

> Al started thinking. The church bell was very deep, very low. The hairs that vibrated when this bell sounded were in the large end of the chamber. The ring of the telephone was a

> higher ring. The hairs that moved when the telephone rang were in the middle of the chamber. Al said to himself, "If the whistle is higher than the telephone, it would vibrate the hairs at the small end of the chamber."
> Al pointed to the small end of the chamber. Angela also pointed to that part at the same time. Al said, "The hairs will move in that part of the ear."
> The old man clapped his hands, smiled, and then he put his arms around Al and Angela. "You are both smart and I am proud of you."
> Al smiled. Angela smiled. The old man smiled. Then, "tweeeeet." The hairs near the small end of the chamber started to vibrate. The old man said, "That's all there is to the inner ear. High sounds are picked up at the small end of the chamber. Lower sounds are picked up in the middle of the chamber. And the lowest sounds are picked up where the chamber is the largest."
> Al looked at the hairs inside the ear. He didn't say anything. He just observed them and thought.

- (After all students have raised their hand:) Everybody, did Al figure out where the hairs would move when the whistle sounded? (Signal.) *Yes.* ⓃⒹ
- In which part of the ear did the hairs vibrate for that sound? (Signal.) *The smallest part.* ⓃⒹ
- Where is the chamber the biggest, near the outside or near the inside? (Signal.) *Near the outside.* ⓃⒹ
- Are low sounds picked up in the big part or the small part? (Signal.) *Big part.* ⓃⒹ
- Are the very highest sounds picked up in the big part or the small part? (Signal.) *Small part.* ⓃⒹ
- That's all there is to the inner ear.

EXERCISE 4

Paired Practice

You're going to read aloud to your partner. The **A** members will read first. Then the **B** members will read from the star to the end of the story. (Observe students and give feedback.)

End-of-Lesson Activities

INDEPENDENT WORK

Now finish your independent work for lesson 127. Raise your hand when you're finished. (Observe students and give feedback.)

WORKCHECK

a. (Direct students to take out their marking pencils.)

- We're going to check your workbook and textbook items. Remember, if you got an item wrong, make an **X** next to the item.

b. (For each item: Read the item. Call on a student to answer it. If the answer is wrong, say the correct answer. Refer to the Answer Key for the correct answers.)

c. Now use your marking pencil to fix up any items you got wrong. Remember, all mistakes must be fixed up before you hand in your work.

SPELLING

(Present Spelling lesson 127 after completing Reading lesson 127. See *Spelling Presentation Book.*)

LESSON 128

EXERCISE 1

Vocabulary Review

a. Here's the new vocabulary sentence: A single star was near the horizon.

- Everybody, say that sentence. Get ready. (Signal.) *A single star was near the horizon.*
- (Repeat until firm.)

b. Everybody, what word means **one**? (Signal.) *Single.*

- What word names the line between the earth and the sky? (Signal.) *Horizon.*

EXERCISE 2

Reading Words

a. **Find lesson 128 in your textbook.** ✔

- Touch word 1. ✔
- (Teacher reference:)

1. **briskly**	4. **snowball**
2. **shovel**	5. **discussed**
3. **dressing**	

b. Word 1. What word? (Signal.) *Briskly.*

- Spell **briskly.** Get ready. (Tap for each letter.) *B-R-I-S-K-L-Y.*

c. Word 2. What word? (Signal.) *Shovel.*

- Spell **shovel.** Get ready. (Tap for each letter.) *S-H-O-V-E-L.*

d. Word 3. What word? (Signal.) *Dressing.*

- Spell **dressing.** Get ready. (Tap for each letter.) *D-R-E-S-S-I-N-G.*

e. Word 4. What word? (Signal.) *Snowball.*

- Spell **snowball.** Get ready. (Tap for each letter.) *S-N-O-W-B-A-L-L.*

f. Word 5. What word? (Signal.) *Discussed.*

g. Let's read those words again.

- Word 1. What word? (Signal.) *Briskly.*
- (Repeat for words 2–5.)

h. (Repeat step g until firm.)

EXERCISE 3

Story Reading

a. Find part B in your textbook. ✔

- The error limit for group reading is 13 errors. Read carefully.

b. Everybody, touch the title. ✔

- (Call on a student to read the title.) *[Angela and Al Study for a Test.]*
- Everybody, what's the title? (Signal.) *Angela and Al Study for a Test.* (ND)
- (Call on individual students to read the story, each student reading two or three sentences at a time. Ask the specified questions as the students read.)

- (**Correct errors:** Tell the word. Direct the student to reread the sentence.)
- (If the group makes more than 13 errors, direct the students to reread the story.)

Angela and Al Study for a Test

Al and Angela were inside the human body. They had just learned about the parts of the ear that vibrate when different sounds enter the ear. They had learned where the hairs are that vibrate for low sounds and for high sounds.

- Everybody, where are the hairs that pick up low sounds, at the **big end** of the chamber or at the **small end**? (Signal.) *At the big end.* (APK)
- Where are the hairs that pick up very high sounds? (Signal.) *At the small end.* (RF/R)

The old man said, "The human body is amazing, and we could continue this trip through the body for hours without seeing everything. But we have seen enough for one trip. So remember the things you have seen. Remember the muscles, the bones, the nerves, the heart, the blood, the brain, the eye and the ear. Remember everything."

The old man's voice seemed to change and Al felt as if he was moving through space. Suddenly he realized that he was once more standing inside the dark store.

The old man said, "Go anywhere. See anything. And pay for your trip by passing a test on what you see."

Angela said, "I just hope that I can remember everything we saw. We saw so much. I don't know that I can remember everything."

The old man handed a book to Angela and Al. Al moved the book close to his face so that he could read the title, *The Human Body.*

- Why did he have to move it close to his face? (Call on a student. Idea: *Because it was dark in the store.*) (DI)

The old man said, "That book will help you study for your test. Tomorrow is Saturday, and my store will be closed. So come back Monday."

"Thank you for the book," Al said. "We'll return it on Monday."

The old man said, "Nobody brings things back to this store. If you get something, it's yours."

- Everybody, does the old man want the book back? (Signal.) *No.* (DC)
- That's a nice gift.

Suddenly the room became very quiet. Angela and Al waited for a few moments before Al said, "Let's go."

Angela and Al went outside, where it was starting to snow. A layer of snow a few inches thick was on the sidewalk.

- Everybody, show me how deep that snow was. ✔ (V)

After Angela and Al had walked to the corner of Anywhere Street, Al turned around. The only footprints in the snow were his and Angela's.

The street around the corner of Anywhere Street was crowded with people, and Al could hear Christmas music.

Angela said, "Next week is Christmas. Look at all the people out shopping for presents."

As Al looked, he remembered that he didn't have any money to buy Christmas presents.

- How did that make him feel? (Call on a student. Idea: *Sad.*) (DCE)

He said, "I guess Christmas is fun if you have money to buy presents for people."

Angela agreed. Then she added, "Christmas makes me feel sad. I just wish . . ."

- What do you think she was going to say? (Call on individual students. Accept reasonable responses.) (MJ)

"Let's not think about that," Al said. "Let's figure out how we're going to study for that test on Monday."

"Well," Angela said, "tomorrow morning we'll get together and go through that book until we get tired."

Al and Angela didn't say much more as they walked home. The snow was falling gently. In the distance were sounds of Christmas music. The air seemed almost too warm for snow to be falling.

• • •

Al's mother said, "Before you do anything else this morning, I want you to shovel the sidewalk."

- During what part of the day is this part of the story taking place? (Call on a student. Idea: *In the morning.*) (DI)
- What does Al's mother want Al to do? (Call on a student. Idea: *Shovel the snow off the sidewalk.*) (ND)
- Everybody, show me how much snow had been on the sidewalk when we left Al and Angela. ✔ (V)

Al was in his bedroom, just finishing dressing. "Oh, Mom," he said. "That snow must be almost a yard deep."

- Everybody, how deep is the snow now? (Signal.) *Almost a yard deep.* (ND)
- So what must have happened during the night? (Call on a student. Idea: *It snowed a lot.*) (DI)

His mother said, "Just go down and eat breakfast, then shovel that walk."

Al sighed and said, "Oh, all right." ★

Al ate breakfast quickly. Then he put on his jacket and his gloves. Angela was waiting for him at the door. She was wearing a warm coat and earmuffs. She said, "You shovel for a while and then I'll shovel for a while."

"Yeah," Al said. "Let's get it finished as fast as we can."

Al got the shovel and started to work. He shoveled and shoveled until his back started to hurt from bending over, and he started to sweat. Just as he straightened up and was ready to tell Angela that it was her turn to shovel, wham. Something hit him in the middle of his back. Al turned around and noticed Angela hiding behind a tree. She was holding a snowball and smiling.

- Do you think she had anything to do with Al getting hit with something? (Call on a student. Idea: *Yes.*) (DI)
- What do you think she did? (Call on a student. Idea: *Threw a snowball at him.*) (DC)
- Read the rest of the story to yourself and be ready to answer some questions. Raise your hand when you're finished.

As Al bent down to make a snowball, she threw another snowball. Whizzz, it flew over Al's head. Al stood up and was ready to throw his snowball when—wham. Right in the middle of his chest. "Is that all the harder you can throw?" he shouted and sent his snowball whizzing toward Angela. She ducked behind the tree and the snowball sailed by her.

Whiiizzzz. Angela threw a snowball that missed Al.

Whiiizzzz. Al threw a snowball that missed Angela.

Wham. Al hit Angela in the shoulder.

Whiiizzzz. Angela missed.

"What's going on out there?" Al's mother was standing on the front steps with her hands on her hips. "You can play with snowballs <u>after</u> you shovel the walk."

Angela shoveled until she was tired. Then she rested while Al shoveled. Soon the walk was clear of snow.

Then Angela said, "Let's study. Maybe we can throw snowballs when we're through."

They went inside where it felt very warm. Angela got the book and opened it. The first part told about muscles. The pictures looked just like things that Al and Angela had seen on their trip.

The next part of the book told about the bones. This part also showed things they had seen, like a man with no bones in his legs.

Angela read parts of the book aloud. When she came to a sentence that said, "Bones do two things," Al said, "I know what those things are." He explained them.

For over four hours, Angela and Al went through the book and talked about the things they read. They discussed the heart and the blood. They talked about the two kinds of nerves that are in the body. They discussed the brain, the eye and the ear. When they were finished with the book, it was getting dark in the room.

"Hey, Mom," Al called. "What time is it?"

"Four o'clock," she called from the other room.

Al said, "I've had enough studying for a while. Let's go outside and I'll give you a lesson in throwing snowballs."

Angela said, "How can you give lessons in something you don't know how to do?"

They went outside, where the snow was still falling. The walk that they had shoveled earlier was covered with about three inches of snow. Al ran behind a tree, made a large wet snowball, stood up and said, "Here's how to . . ." Splat. Right in his chest.

- (After all students have raised their hand:) Everybody, what did the first part of the book tell about? (Signal.) *Muscles.* (ND)
- Where had Angela seen some of the things the book showed? (Call on a student. Idea: *On her trip to the human body.*) (APK)

- Al knew the two things that bones do. What are those things? (Call on a student. Idea: *Make the body strong and protect parts of the body.*) (APK)
- Everybody, how long did Al and Angela read the book? (Signal.) *Over four hours.* (ND)
- What time was it when they finished reading the book? (Signal.) *4 o'clock.* (ND)
- That must have been a very interesting book.
- What did Al and Angela do after they finished with the book? (Call on a student. Idea: *Went outside to throw snowballs.*) (ND)
- What happened when Al was going to demonstrate snowball throwing to Angela? (Call on a student. Idea: *She hit him in the chest with a snowball.*) (ND)

EXERCISE 4

Paired Practice

You're going to read aloud to your partner. The **B** members will read first. Then the **A** members will read from the star to the end of the story. (Observe students and give feedback.)

End-of-Lesson Activities

INDEPENDENT WORK

Now finish your independent work for lesson 128. Raise your hand when you're finished. (Observe students and give feedback.)

WORKCHECK

a. (Direct students to take out their marking pencils.)
- We're going to check your workbook and textbook items. Remember, if you got an item wrong, make an **X** next to the item.
b. (For each item: Read the item. Call on a student to answer it. If the answer is wrong, say the correct answer. Refer to the Answer Key for the correct answers.)
c. Now use your marking pencil to fix up any items you got wrong. Remember, all mistakes must be fixed up before you hand in your work.

SPELLING

(Present Spelling lesson 128 after completing Reading lesson 128. See *Spelling Presentation Book.*)

EXERCISE 1

Vocabulary Review

a. You learned a sentence that tells about the triceps muscle.

- Everybody, say that sentence. Get ready. (Signal.) *The triceps muscle is bigger than the biceps muscle.*
- (Repeat until firm.)

b. You learned a sentence that tells what the injury to his spinal cord did.

- Everybody, say that sentence. Get ready. (Signal.) *The injury to his spinal cord paralyzed him.*
- (Repeat until firm.)

c. Here's the last sentence you learned: A single star was near the horizon.

- Everybody, say that sentence. Get ready. (Signal.) *A single star was near the horizon.*
- (Repeat until firm.)

d. What word names the line between the earth and the sky? (Signal.) *Horizon.*

- What word means **one?** (Signal.) *Single.*

e. Once more. Say the sentence that tells where a single star was. Get ready. (Signal.) *A single star was near the horizon.*

EXERCISE 2

Reading Words

Column 1

a. **Find lesson 129 in your textbook.** ✔

- Touch column 1. ✔
- (Teacher reference:)

1. absolutely	4. flunk
2. thermometer	5. grade
3. suspended	

b. Word 1 is **absolutely.** What word? (Signal.) *Absolutely.*

- **Absolutely** is another word for **totally** or **completely.** Everybody, what's another way of saying **They were completely wrong?** (Signal.) *They were absolutely wrong.*

- What's another way of saying **They were totally poor?** (Signal.) *They were absolutely poor.*

c. Word 2 is **thermometer.** What word? (Signal.) *Thermometer.*

d. Word 3 is **suspended.** What word? (Signal.) *Suspended.*

- Things that are suspended are hung in space. Everybody, what word means **hung in space?** (Signal.) *Suspended.*

e. Word 4. What word? (Signal.) *Flunk.*

- Word 5. What word? (Signal.) *Grade.*

f. Let's read those words again.

- Word 1. What word? (Signal.) *Absolutely.*
- (Repeat for words 2–5.)

g. (Repeat step f until firm.)

Column 2

h. Find column 2. ✔

- (Teacher reference:)

1. correct	4. nighttime
2. throughout	5. closest
3. everybody	

- All these words have more than one syllable. The first part of each word is underlined.

i. Word 1. What's the underlined part? (Signal.) *corr.*

- What's the whole word? (Signal.) *Correct.*

j. Word 2. What's the underlined part? (Signal.) *through.*

- What's the whole word? (Signal.) *Throughout.*

k. Word 3. What's the underlined part? (Signal.) *every.*

- What's the whole word? (Signal.) *Everybody.*

l. Word 4. What's the underlined part? (Signal.) *night.*

- What's the whole word? (Signal.) *Nighttime.*

m. Word 5. What's the underlined part? (Signal.) *Close.*

- What's the whole word? (Signal.) *Closest.*

n. Let's read those words again.
- Word 1. What word? (Signal.) *Correct.*
- (Repeat for: **2. throughout, 3. everybody, 4. nighttime, 5. closest.**)
o. (Repeat step n until firm.)

Column 3

p. Find column 3. ✔
- (Teacher reference:)

1. **briskly**	4. **mistakes**
2. **flipped**	5. **nodding**
3. **erasing**	6. **darkness**

- All these words have an ending.
q. Word 1. What word? (Signal.) *Briskly.*
- **Briskly** means **fast** and **peppy.** Everybody, what's another way of saying **She walked fast?** (Signal.) *She walked briskly.*
- What's another way of saying **The wind blew fast?** (Signal.) *The wind blew briskly.*
r. Word 2. What word? (Signal.) *Flipped.*
- (Repeat for words 3–6.)
s. Let's read those words again.
- Word 1. What word? (Signal.) *Briskly.*
- (Repeat for words 2–6.)
t. (Repeat step s until firm.)

Individual Turns

(For columns 1–3: Call on individual students, each to read one to three words per turn.)

EXERCISE 3

Story Background

a. Find part B in your textbook. ✔
- You're going to read the next story about Al and Angela. First you'll read the information passage. It gives some facts about the earth.
b. Everybody, touch the title. ✔
- (Call on a student to read the title.) *[The Earth and the Sun.]*
- Everybody, what's the title? (Signal.) *The Earth and the Sun.* ⓃⒹ
c. (Call on individual students to read the passage, each student reading two or three sentences at a time. Ask specified questions as the students read.)

The Earth and the Sun

You've learned that the earth tilts. During our summertime, does the North Pole tilt toward the sun or away from the sun?

- Everybody, what's the answer? (Signal.) *Toward the sun.* ⒶⓅⓀ

During our wintertime, does the North Pole tilt toward the sun or away from the sun?

- Everybody, what's the answer? (Signal.) *Away from the sun.* ⓇⒻ/Ⓡ

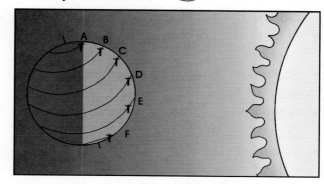

Look at picture 1. You can figure out which half of the earth is closest to the sun. That's the half that is bright.

- Everybody, touch the half of the earth that is closest to the sun in picture 1. You should be touching the right half. ✔ ⓋⒶ
- Look at the North Pole in that picture. Is that pole tilting toward the sun or away from the sun? (Signal.) *Away from the sun.* ⒹⒸ
- In which of our seasons does the North Pole tilt away from the sun? (Signal.) *Winter.* ⓇⒻ/Ⓡ

What season is it in picture 1?

- Everybody, what's the answer? (Signal.) *Winter.* ⒶⓅⓀ
- How do you know it's winter? (Call on a student. Idea: *Because the North Pole is tilting away from the sun.*) ⒹⒸ

The earth turns around one time every 24 hours.

- Everybody, say that rule. Get ready. (Signal.) *The earth turns around one time every 24 hours.* ⓇⒻ/Ⓡ

Every time the earth turns around one time, most places on the earth have night and day. But it's different at the poles. The lines on the earth show how far people in different parts of the earth move every time the earth turns around. Touch person A.

- Everybody, do it. ✔ (VA)

In 24 hours, that person follows the line around the earth and goes all the way back to point A.

- Everybody, touch the person at **A** in picture 1. ✔ (VA)
- Is that person in daylight or in darkness? (Signal.) *In darkness.* (DC)
- Start at **A** and follow the path to the other side. ✔ (VA)
- Is the person in daylight or in darkness? (Signal.) *In darkness.* (DC)
- When the person goes around the other side of the earth back to the letter **A,** will the person be in daylight or in darkness? (Signal.) *In darkness.* (VA)
- So is person A ever in daylight? (Signal.) *No.* (DC)
- Remember that during winter there is no daylight at the North Pole.

Which person goes farther in 24 hours, person A or person D?

- Everybody, which line is longer, the line for A or the line for D? (Signal.) *The line for D.* (VA)
- So who goes farther, person A or person D? (Signal.) *Person D.* (DC)
- When the earth turns around, is person D ever in daylight? (Signal.) *Yes.* (DC)

When the earth goes around, person A is in darkness all the time. Person D is in daylight part of the time and in darkness part of the time. Person F is in daylight all the time.

- Everybody, touch person F. ✔ (VA)
- Does that person start out in daylight? (Signal.) *Yes.* (DC)

- Remember—during our winter, there is only daylight all the time at the South Pole. And there is only darkness all the time at the North Pole.

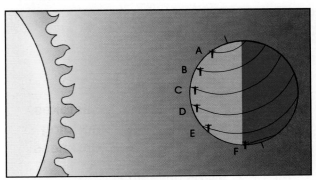

Look at picture 2. It shows the same people in the same places. But it shows our summer, not winter. During summer, person A is always in sunlight as the earth turns around. And person F is always in darkness as the earth turns around.

- Look at picture 2. Does that picture show our summer or our winter? (Signal.) *Our summer.* (ND)
- Touch person A. ✔ (VA)
- Does that person start in daylight or darkness? (Signal.) *In daylight.* (DC)
- Does that person ever go into darkness? (Signal.) *No.* (DC)
- Touch person F. ✔ (VA)
- Does that person start out in daylight or darkness? (Signal.) *In darkness.* (DC)
- Does that person ever go into daylight? (Signal.) *No.* (DC)

EXERCISE 4

Story Reading

a. Find part C in your textbook. ✔
- The error limit for group reading is 13 errors. Read carefully.
b. Everybody, touch the title. ✔
- (Call on a student to read the title.) *[Angela and Al Take a Test on the Human Body.]*
- Everybody, what's the title? (Signal.) *Angela and Al Take a Test on the Human Body.* (ND)

- (Call on individual students to read the story, each student reading two or three sentences at a time. Ask the specified questions as the students read.)

- (**Correct errors:** Tell the word. Direct the student to reread the sentence.)
- (If the group makes more than 13 errors, direct the students to reread the story.)

Angela and Al Take a Test on the Human Body

"I know you have been looking forward to this Monday morning," Al's teacher said to the class. "Today we are going to have our test in science."

- Everybody, is she serious about the kids looking forward to taking the test? (Signal.) *No.* DI

Some of the kids said, "Oh, no!" Al didn't say anything.

- Why do you think Al didn't say "Oh no"? (Call on a student. Idea: *Because he was ready for the test.*) DI

Homer asked, "Are some people going to flunk this test?"
The teacher said, "If they don't get enough correct answers, they will fail the test."
Homer turned to Al and said, "Did you hear that? You're going to flunk the test."

- Why do you think he's talking mean like that to Al? (Call on a student. Ideas: *To make Al mad; because he's not a nice person.*) MJ

Some of the kids laughed.
Al said, "Oh yeah? I'll get more answers . . ."

- What do you think he was going to say? (Call on a student. Idea: *I'll get more answers right than you will.*) P

"Both of you, stop that," the teacher said. Then she said to Homer, "I don't know what's going on between you and Al, but I don't want that kind of talk in this classroom.

Al has been doing a very good job in science these past two weeks. In fact, I don't know a student who is doing better."
Some of the kids laughed and Homer looked down. The teacher passed out the test. There were forty questions on the test. Most were about the body.
Al knew the answer to every single question. He wrote down the answers and then read his test over to make sure that there were no mistakes. He took his paper up to the teacher's desk.
As he walked past Homer's desk, he noticed that Homer was still working on the fifteenth question. Homer was erasing something that he had written.

- Everybody, which question was Homer working on? (Signal.) *The fifteenth.* ND
- How many questions were on the test? (Signal.) *Forty.* ND
- So was Homer nearly finished with the test? (Signal.) *No.* DC
- Do you think that he'll do as well on that test as Al? (Call on a student. Idea: *No.*) MJ

The teacher looked at Al and asked, "Did you finish the test already?"
Al responded by nodding his head yes. He went back to his desk, took out the book on the human body and started to read it again.
As he was reading about the cerebrum, he noticed that the teacher was standing next to his desk. She said, "Al, here is your test. You got everything right. I have given that test for years and I don't remember anybody getting everything right before."

- How do you think Al felt about that? (Call on a student. Ideas: *Proud; smart.*) DCE

The teacher told everybody their grades before school was out. Al got an A plus, the highest grade possible. Homer got a B.

- How do you think Homer feels now? (Call on a student. Ideas: *Not so smart; embarrassed.*) (DCE)

Al met Angela outside school, where he told her about the test. "I got every single answer correct," he said. "Imagine that. I never thought I would be smart in ✿ school, but I am smart."

She said, "Oh, it was probably a very easy test."

"No way," he said. "It was the hardest test you'll ever see."

Then he continued, ✦ "Wait a minute. I have that test in my notebook. I'll bet you can't answer every question correctly."

They stopped while Al flipped through his notebook until he found the test. Al pulled it out and said, "I'll read the questions. You tell me the answers."

The wind blew briskly, carrying small flakes of snow. Al had trouble holding the test up so that he could read the items. He read them, and Angela answered every item correctly. After she had finished, she looked at Al and smiled. "I told you it was an easy test," she said.

He shook his head and put the test back in his notebook. Then he announced, "But you wouldn't have been able to answer the questions if you hadn't gone on the trip through the human body. And you wouldn't have gone on the trip through the human body if I hadn't made you go. So, I'm the one you can thank for knowing all those answers."

She shook her head. "Yes, you are the greatest," she said smiling. "Without you, I wouldn't know anything. You're the smartest person in the world."

- Everybody, is she **serious** or **just trying to get Al mad?** (Signal.) *Just trying to get Al mad.* (DI)

She began to laugh and Al could feel himself becoming angry.

Then suddenly, her expression changed and became serious. She put her arm around him and said, "I'm really glad you talked me into going on that trip. It was the most amazing thing I've ever seen."

Al looked down and smiled. He was no longer angry.

- Read the rest of the story to yourself and be ready to answer some questions. Raise your hand when you're finished.

As soon as Al and Angela turned the corner at Anywhere Street, they could no longer hear the cars and the people or the sound of Christmas songs. They walked up to the store. The sign was still in the window: GO ANYWHERE. SEE ANYTHING.

As they went into the store, the bell went ding, ding. Inside, they waited.

Suddenly the old man was standing in front of them. He said, "There will be no test for you today."

Al looked at Angela. Then he looked back at the old man. Al asked, "But we're ready for the test. Why can't we take it now?"

The old man smiled. He said, "You can't take it because you have already taken it. I happen to know that both of you correctly answered all the questions on a science test. So why should I waste time giving you another test? Simply tell me where you want to go and what you want to see and we will go on another trip together."

- (After all students have raised their hands:) Everybody, did the old man give Angela and Al a test? (Signal.) *No.* (ND)
- Why not? (Call on a student. Idea: *Because they had already passed a test.*) (ND)

Paired Practice

You're going to read aloud to your partner. The **A** members will read first. Then the **B** members will read from the star to the end of the story. (Observe students and give feedback.)

End-of-Lesson Activities

INDEPENDENT WORK

Now finish your independent work for lesson 129. Raise your hand when you're finished. (Observe students and give feedback.)

WORKCHECK

a. (Direct students to take out their marking pencils.)

- We're going to check your workbook and textbook items. Remember, if you got an item wrong, make an **X** next to the item.

b. (For each item: Read the item. Call on a student to answer it. If the answer is wrong, say the correct answer. Refer to the Answer Key for the correct answers.)

c. Now use your marking pencil to fix up any items you got wrong. Remember, all mistakes must be fixed up before you hand in your work.

SPELLING

(Present Spelling lesson 129 after completing Reading lesson 129. See *Spelling Presentation Book.*)

ACTIVITIES

(Present Activity 29 after completing Reading lesson 129. See *Activities across the Curriculum.*)

Note: You will need to reproduce blackline masters for the Fact Game in lesson 130 (Appendix G in the *Teacher's Guide*).

LESSON 130

Test 13

Materials for Lesson 130
Fact Game
For each team (4 or 5 students):
- pair of number cubes (or dice)
- copy of Fact Game 130
  (Reproducible blackline masters are
  in Appendix G of the *Teacher's Guide*.)
For each student:
- their copy of the scorecard sheet (at
  end of workbook B)
For each monitor:
- a pencil
- Fact Game 130 answer key (at end
  of textbook B)
Fluency: Rate/Accuracy
Each student needs their thermometer chart.

EXERCISE 1

Fact Game

a. (Divide students into groups of four or
   five. Assign monitors.)

b. You'll play the fact game for 10 minutes.

- (Circulate as students play the game.
  Comment on groups that are playing
  well.)

c. (At the end of 10 minutes, have all
   students who earned more than 10
   points stand up.)

- (Tell the monitor of each game that ran
  smoothly:) Your group did a good job.

EXERCISE 2

Fluency: Rate/Accuracy

a. Today is a test day and a reading
   checkout day. While you're writing
   answers, I'm going to call on you one at
   a time to read part of the story we read
   in lesson 129.

- Remember, you pass the checkout by
  reading the passage in less than a
  minute without making more than 2
  mistakes. And when you pass the
  checkout, you color the space for lesson
  130 on your thermometer chart.

b. (Call on individual students to read the
   portion of story 129 marked with ✿.)

- (Time the student. Note words that are
  missed and number of words read.)

- (Teacher reference:)

> ✿ Al responded by nodding his head
> yes. He went back to his desk, took
> out the book on the human body and
> started to read it again.
>   As he was reading about the
> cerebrum, he noticed that the teacher
> was standing next to his desk. She
> said, "Al, here is [50] your test. You
> got everything right. I have given that
> test for years and I don't remember
> anybody getting everything right
> before."
>   The teacher told [75] everybody
> their grades before school was out.
> Al got an A plus, the highest grade
> possible. Homer got a B.
>   Al met Angela outside school,
> [100] where he told her about the
> test. "I got every single answer
> correct," he said. "Imagine that. I
> never thought I would be smart in
> ✿ [125] school, but I am smart."

- (If the student reads the passage in one
  minute or less and makes no more than
  2 errors, direct the student to color in the
  space for lesson 130 on the thermometer
  chart.)

- (If the student makes any mistakes, point
  to each word that was misread and
  identify it.)

- (If the student does not meet the rate-
  error criterion for the passage, direct the
  student to practice reading the story with
  the assigned partner.)

Test

a. **Find page 301 in your textbook.** ✔
- This is a test. You'll work items you've done before.
b. Work carefully. Raise your hand when you've completed all the items. (Observe students but do not give feedback on errors.)

EXERCISE 4

Marking The Test

a. (Check students' work before beginning lesson 131. Refer to the Answer Key for the correct answers.)
b. (Record all test 13 results on the Test Summary Sheet and the Group Summary Sheet. Reproducible Summary Sheets are at the back of the *Teacher's Guide*.)

EXERCISE 5

Test Remedies

(Provide any necessary remedies for test 13 before presenting lesson 131. Test remedies are discussed in the *Teacher's Guide*.)

Test 12 Firming Table

Test Item	Introduced in lesson	Test Item	Introduced in lesson	Test Item	Introduced in lesson
1	121	11	123	21	127
2	121	12	123	22	127
3	122	13	124	23	126
4	122	14	124	24	122
5	122	15	125	25	127
6	122	16	125	26	122
7	123	17	125	27	127
8	123	18	126	28	122
9	123	19	127		
10	123	20	127		

SPELLING

(Present Spelling lesson 130 after completing Reading lesson 130. See *Spelling Presentation Book*.)

Lessons 131–135 • Planning Page   *Looking Ahead*

	Lesson 131	Lesson 132	Lesson 133	Lesson 134	Lesson 135
LESSON EVENTS	Vocabulary Sentence Reading Words Story Reading Paired Practice Independent Work Workcheck Spelling	**Vocabulary Sentence** Reading Words Story Reading Paired Practice Independent Work Workcheck Spelling	Vocabulary Sentence Reading Words Story Background Story Reading Paired Practice Independent Work Workcheck Spelling	Vocabulary Sentences Reading Words Story Reading Paired Practice Independent Work Workcheck Spelling	Vocabulary Sentence Reading Words Story Background Story Reading Fluency: Rate/Accuracy Independent Work Workcheck Spelling
VOCABULARY SENTENCE	#31: A single star was near the horizon.	**#32: Troops of baboons moved across the veld.**	#32: Troops of baboons moved across the veld.	sentence #30 sentence #31 sentence #32	#32: Troops of baboons moved across the veld.
READING WORDS: WORD TYPES	modeled words compound words multi-syllable words	modeled words mixed words	mixed words multi-syllable words	modeled words mixed words	2-syllable words mixed words
NEW VOCABULARY	attractive comment	prevent regular	Endurance iris	gorilla leopard porpoise	sabers
STORY BACKGROUND			*The Camera and the Eye*		*Animals*
STORY	*Winter at the North Pole*	*Angela and Al Learn About Snowflakes*	*A Trip to the South Pole*	*A Book about the Poles*	*Angela and Al Buy Christmas Presents*
SKILL ITEMS	Vocabulary sentences		Vocabulary	Sequencing Vocabulary sentence	Vocabulary sentences
SPECIAL MATERIALS					Thermometer charts
SPECIAL PROJECTS/ ACTIVITIES		Activity after lesson 132	Activity after lesson 133		

Comprehension Questions Abbreviations Guide

Access Prior Knowledge = (APK)   Author's Point of View = (APoV)   Author's Purpose = (AP)   Cause/Effect = (C/E)   Charts/Graphs/Diagrams/Visual Aids = (VA)

Classify and Categorize = (C+C)   Compare/Contrast = (C/C)   Determine Character Emotions, Motivation = (DCE)   Drawing Conclusions = (DC)   Drawing Inferences = (DI)

Fact and Opinion = (F/O)   Hypothesizing = (H)   Main Idea = (MI)   Making Connections = (MC)   Making Deductions = (MD)   Making Judgements = (MJ)

Narrative Elements = (NE)   Noting Details = (ND)   Predict = (P)   Reality/Fantasy = (R/F)   Recall Facts/Rules = (RF/R)   Retell = (R)   Sequence = (Seq)

Steps in a Process = (SP)   Story Structure = (SS)   Summarize = (Sum)   Understanding Dialogue = (UD)   Using Context to Confirm Meaning(s) = (UCCM)   Visualize = (V)

EXERCISE 1

Vocabulary Review

a. You learned a sentence that tells where a single star was.

- Everybody, say that sentence. Get ready. (Signal.) *A single star was near the horizon.*
- (Repeat until firm.)

b. I'll say part of the sentence. When I stop, you say the next word. Listen: A . . . Everybody, what's the next word? (Signal.) *Single.*

c. Listen: A single star was near the . . . Everybody, what's the next word? (Signal.) *Horizon.*

- Say the whole sentence. Get ready. (Signal.) *A single star was near the horizon.*

EXERCISE 2

Reading Words

Column 1

a. **Find lesson 131 in your textbook.** ✔

- Touch column 1. ✔
- (Teacher reference:)

1. **attractive**	4. **troops**
2. **veld**	5. **baboon**
3. **comment**	

b. Word 1 is **attractive.** What word? (Signal.) *Attractive.*

- **Attractive** is another word for **pretty.** Everybody, what's another way of saying **They have a pretty yard?** (Signal.) *They have an attractive yard.*
- What's another way of saying **She is very pretty?** (Signal.) *She is very attractive.*

c. Word 2 is **veld.** What word? (Signal.) *Veld.*

- Spell **veld.** Get ready. (Tap for each letter.) *V-E-L-D.*
- You'll find out what a veld is in the next lesson.

d. Word 3. What word? (Signal.) *Comment.*

- When you comment about something, you tell about that thing. If you comment about a meal, you tell about the meal. Everybody, what are you doing if you tell about a vacation? (Signal.) *Commenting about the vacation.*

e. Word 4. What word? (Signal.) *Troops.*

- Word 5. What word? (Signal.) *Baboon.*

f. Let's read those words again, the fast way.

- Word 1. What word? (Signal.) *Attractive.*
- (Repeat for words 2–5.)

g. (Repeat step f until firm.)

Column 2

h. Find column 2. ✔

- (Teacher reference:)

1. **throughout**	3. **everybody**
2. **summertime**	4. **nighttime**

- All these words are compound words. The first part of each word is underlined.

i. Word 1. What's the underlined part? (Signal.) *through.*

- What's the whole word? (Signal.) *Throughout.*

j. Word 2. What's the underlined part? (Signal.) *summer.*

- What's the whole word? (Signal.) *Summertime.*

k. Word 3. What's the underlined part? (Signal.) *every.*

- What's the whole word? (Signal.) *Everybody.*

l. Word 4. What's the underlined part? (Signal.) *night.*

- What's the whole word? (Signal.) *Nighttime.*

m. Let's read those words again.

- Word 1. What word? (Signal.) *Throughout.*
- (Repeat for words 2–4.)

n. (Repeat step m until firm.)

Column 3

o. Find column 3. ✔
•   (Teacher reference:)

1. lighting	4. suspended
2. strongest	5. thermometer
3. mitten	6. absolutely

p. Word 1. What word? (Signal.) *Lighting.*
•   Spell **lighting.** Get ready. (Tap for each letter.) *L-I-G-H-T-I-N-G.*
q. Word 2. What word? (Signal.) *Strongest.*
•   Spell **strongest.** Get ready. (Tap for each letter.) *S-T-R-O-N-G-E-S-T.*
r. Word 3. What word? (Signal.) *Mitten.*
•   Spell **mitten.** Get ready. (Tap for each letter.) *M-I-T-T-E-N.*
s. Word 4. What word? (Signal.) *Suspended.*
t. Word 5. What word? (Signal.) *Thermometer.*
u. Word 6. What word? (Signal.) *Absolutely.*
v. Let's read those words again.
•   Word 1. What word? (Signal.) *Lighting.*
•   (Repeat for words 2–6.)
w. (Repeat step v until firm.)

Individual Turns

(For columns 1–3: Call on individual students, each to read one to three words per turn.)

EXERCISE 3

Story Reading

a. Find part B in your textbook. ✔
•   The error limit for group reading is 14 errors. Read carefully.
b. Everybody, touch the title. ✔
•   (Call on a student to read the title.) *[Winter at the North Pole.]*
•   Everybody, what's the title? (Signal.) *Winter at the North Pole.* ⓃⒹ
•   (Call on individual students to read the story, each student reading two or three sentences at a time. Ask the specified questions as the students read.)

•   (**Correct errors:** Tell the word. Direct the student to reread the sentence.)
•   (If the group makes more than 14 errors, direct the students to reread the story.)

Winter at the North Pole

Al and Angela were in the old man's store getting ready for another trip.

Angela said, "I don't care where we go. I'll go anywhere."

"Good," the old man said. "We will go to the poles of the earth."

"What are those?" Al asked.

The old man explained.

•   Name the two poles of the earth. (Call on a student.) *[The North Pole and the South Pole.]* ⒶⓅⓀ
•   What is the weather like at the poles? *(Call on a student. Idea: Very cold.)* ⒶⓅⓀ

The air suddenly became very cold. The cold was so bitter that Al could hardly breathe. He closed his eyes for a moment. When he opened them, they started to burn from the cold. Al now realized that he was wearing a great coat with a big hood, and a thick mitten on each hand. But he was still cold.

"Where are we?" Al asked.

"At the North Pole," the old man responded.

Al looked up. There were stars in the sky, but the sky was black.

Angela said, "Why is it so dark here?"

"Because it is winter at the North Pole," the old man replied. "The sun doesn't shine all winter long at the North Pole."

•   Why was it dark at the North Pole? (Call on a student. Ideas: *Because it was winter; because the North Pole was tilting away from the sun.*) ⓃⒹ
•   How long does it stay dark at the North Pole? (Call on a student. Idea: *All winter.*) ⓃⒹ

Al started to cough. He coughed and coughed. The more he coughed, the more the cold hurt his lungs. The old man snapped his fingers, and suddenly Al didn't feel cold anymore.

"Wow!" Al said. "That cold air really hurts."

"Correct," the old man said. "If you lived near the North Pole, you would have to be very careful during the cold weather. If you start breathing too hard, the cold air will freeze your lungs. It will also freeze the inside of your nose and the inside of your mouth."

- What did the cold air make Al start to do? (Call on a student.) *[Cough.]* ⓃⒹ
- What body parts can freeze at the North Pole if you're not careful? (Call on a student. Ideas: *Lungs; the inside of your nose; the inside of your mouth.*) ⓃⒹ

Al said, "How cold is it here?"
The old man held up a thermometer. He turned a light on the thermometer and said, "Read it."
Al read the thermometer. The red line was at sixty below zero.
Angela said, "<u>That</u> is cold."

- Everybody, how cold was it at the North Pole? (Signal.) *60 below zero.* ⓃⒹ
- Can you imagine anything that cold? (Call on individual students. Student preference.) ⓂⒸ

She was quiet for a moment and then she said, "I still don't understand why it's dark here in the wintertime."
The old man said, "I will show you."
The old man snapped his fingers, and models of the sun and the earth appeared in front of Al and Angela. Both the earth and the sun were suspended in the air. The sun was shining brightly, lighting up everything around it. The old man pointed to the model of the earth, which was slowly turning as it hung in the air.
"You know that the earth is tilted," the old man said, pointing to the model of the earth.
"Yes," Al said. "And I can tell what season it is by looking at which way the North Pole is tilting."

- Everybody, when the North Pole tilts **toward** the sun, what season do we have? (Signal.) *Summer.* ⒶⓅⓀ
- When the North Pole tilts **away from** the sun, what season do we have? (Signal.) *Winter.* ⒶⓅⓀ
- What season is it in the story? (Signal.) *Winter.* ⒶⓅⓀ

- So which way is the North Pole tilting? (Signal.) *Away from the sun.* ⒹⒸ

- Touch the North Pole of the model earth in the picture. ✔ Ⓥ Ⓐ
- Which way is it tilting? (Signal.) *Away from the sun.* ⓋⒶ
- So what season is it for the model earth? (Signal.) *Winter.* ⒹⒸ
- You can see that everything around the North Pole is in a shadow. The shadow is darkness.

The old man asked, "What season is it at the North Pole of this earth?"
"Winter," Al said.
"And how do you know that it is winter?"
Angela explained.

- What did she say? (Call on a student. Idea: *Because the North Pole was tilting away from the sun.*) ⒹⒾ

"Correct," the old man said and then pointed to the earth. "Can you show where we are on this model?"
"Yes," Angela said. She walked over to the model and pointed to the part where she and the others were.

- Everybody, touch that part. ✔ ⓋⒶ
- You should be touching the North Pole.

The old man said, "Let's put models of us on that globe so that we can see what happens as the earth turns around." The old man snapped his fingers. Suddenly, three tiny forms appeared at the North Pole of the globe. Al looked at Angela and smiled.

"Observe the earth as it turns around," the old man said.

The model began spinning around faster and faster as Al and Angela studied it. Suddenly Angela said, "I get it. I know why it's dark here all winter."

"Explain," the old man said.

Angela said, "Half the globe is dark. The North Pole tilts away from the sun. So as long as the North Pole tilts this way, it is on the half of the earth that is dark all the time. The earth turns around and around, but the North Pole always stays on the dark side."

"A very good explanation," the old man said to Angela. Then he asked, "Can you figure out what the days and nights would be like during the summertime at the North Pole?"

- Read the rest of the story to yourself and be ready to answer some questions. Raise your hand when you're finished.

Al and Angela looked at the globe. Al tried to figure out the answer but he was having trouble.

The old man said, "If you use the facts you know, you can figure out the answer. Tell me how the North Pole tilts during the summertime."

"Toward the sun," Al said.

As soon as he had spoken, the model of the earth moved so that the North Pole was tilting toward the sun. "There," the old man said. "Now you see us at the North Pole during summertime."

Al watched the earth spin around one time, two times, three times. Then he pointed to the little people who were at the North Pole. He said, "Now the North Pole is always on the half of the earth that is lit up by the sun. The earth turns around and around but the North Pole is always in the sun."

The old man added, "That means the sun shines all the time during summer at the North Pole. There is no time when the sun sets. You can see the sun all day and all night."

The old man snapped his fingers and the models of the sun and the earth disappeared. It was now so dark that Al couldn't see anything except spots in front of his eyes. He rubbed his eyes as he listened to what Angela was saying. "So it is dark at the North Pole throughout the whole winter," she said. "The sun never shines because the North Pole tilts away from the sun and is on the half of the earth that is always dark."

"That is absolutely right," the old man responded.

Then the old man said, "I want you to feel winter at the North Pole for a few minutes. Think about what it would be like to live here."

The wind howled and Al felt it blowing snow in swirls around him. He could feel how cold it was. He wondered how anything could grow here or live here. What would they eat? How would they stay warm? How would they keep from going crazy even if they could stay alive? The strongest feeling that Al had was that he wanted to get out of this terrible place.

- (After all students have raised their hand:) How long does the sun shine on the North Pole during summer? (Call on a student. Idea: *All the time.*) ⓝⓓ
- What did the old man want Angela and Al to feel for a few minutes? (Call on a student. Idea: *Winter at the North Pole.*) ⓝⓓ
- What were some of the questions Al had about living at the North Pole? (Call on individual students. Ideas: *How could anything grow there? How could anything live there? What would they eat? How would they stay warm? How would they keep from going crazy even if they could stay alive?*) ⓝⓓ
- What did Al want to do? (Call on a student. Idea: *Leave the North Pole.*) ⓝⓓ

Paired Practice

You're going to read aloud to your partner. The **B** members will read first. Then the **A** members will read from the star to the end of the story.

(Observe students and give feedback.)

End-of-Lesson Activities

Now finish your independent work for lesson 131. Raise your hand when you're finished. (Observe students and give feedback.)

a. (Direct students to take out their marking pencils.)

• We're going to check your workbook and textbook items. Remember, if you got an item wrong, make an **X** next to the item.

b. (For each item: Read the item. Call on a student to answer it. If the answer is wrong, say the correct answer. Refer to the Answer Key for the correct answers.)

c. Now use your marking pencil to fix up any items you got wrong. Remember, all mistakes must be fixed up before you hand in your work.

(Present Spelling lesson 131 after completing Reading lesson 131. See *Spelling Presentation Book*.)

LESSON 132

EXERCISE 1

Vocabulary

a. **Find page 367 in your textbook.** ✔
- Touch sentence 32. ✔
- This is a new vocabulary sentence. It says: Troops of baboons moved across the veld. Everybody, say that sentence. Get ready. (Signal.) *Troops of baboons moved across the veld.*
- Close your eyes and say the sentence. Get ready. (Signal.) *Troops of baboons moved across the veld.*
- (Repeat until firm.)

b. Baboons are a kind of monkey. They are big and they are smart. Everybody, what's the name of a big member of the monkey family? (Signal.) *Baboon.*

c. The sentence refers to **troops** of baboons. A troop is a group of baboons that are related. Everybody, what do we call a group of related baboons? (Signal.) *Troop.*

d. The sentence says that troops of baboons moved across the **veld.** The veld is a large open plain or field in Africa that goes for miles and miles. What do we call a large field in Africa? (Signal.) *Veld.*

e. Listen to the sentence again: Troops of baboons moved across the veld. Everybody, say that sentence. Get ready. (Signal.) *Troops of baboons moved across the veld.*

f. Everybody, what word refers to a large field in Africa? (Signal.) *Veld.*
- What word names a large member of the monkey family? (Signal.) *Baboon.*
- What word refers to **groups** of baboons? (Signal.) *Troops.*
- (Repeat step f until firm.)

EXERCISE 2

Reading Words

Column 1

a. Find lesson 132 in your textbook. ✔
- Touch column 1. ✔

- (Teacher reference:)

1. prevent	3. curvy
2. regular	4. camera

b. Word 1 is prevent. What word? (Signal.) *Prevent.*
- Spell **prevent.** Get ready. (Tap for each letter.) *P-R-E-V-E-N-T.*
- When you prevent something, you make sure it doesn't happen. When you make sure that a fire can't start, you prevent the fire. Everybody, what word means **make sure something doesn't happen?** (Signal.) *Prevent.*

c. Word 2 is **regular.** What word? (Signal.) *Regular.*
- Spell **regular.** Get ready. (Tap for each letter.) *R-E-G-U-L-A-R.*
- **Regular** is another word for **usual** or **ordinary.** If the usual time for lunch is 11:30, that's the regular time for lunch. Everybody, what's another word for **usual** or **ordinary?** (Signal.) *Regular.*

d. Word 3 is **curvy.** What word? (Signal.) *Curvy.*
- Spell **curvy.** Get ready. (Tap for each letter.) *C-U-R-V-Y.*

e. Word 4 is **camera.** What word? (Signal.) *Camera.*
- Spell **camera.** Get ready. (Tap for each letter.) *C-A-M-E-R-A.*

f. Let's read those words again.
- Word 1. What word? (Signal.) *Prevent.*
- (Repeat for words 2–4.)

g. (Repeat step f until firm.)

Column 2

h. Find column 2. ✔
- (Teacher reference:)

1. attractive	4. decorations
2. commented	5. scooped
3. examined	

- All these words have an ending.
i. Word 1. What word? (Signal.) *Attractive.*
- (Repeat for words 2–5.)

j. Let's read those words again.
- Word 1. What word? (Signal.) *Attractive.*
- (Repeat for: **2. commented,
  3. examined, 4. decorations,
  5. scooped.**)
k. (Repeat step j until firm.)

Column 3

l. Find column 3. ✔
- (Teacher reference:)

1. veld	**4. iris**
2. aha	**5. square**
3. baboon	

m. Word 1. What word? (Signal.) *Veld.*
- (Repeat for words 2–5.)
n. Let's read those words again.
- Word 1. What word? (Signal.) *Veld.*
- (Repeat for words 2–5.)
o. (Repeat step n until firm.)

Individual Turns

(For columns 1–3: Call on individual students, each to read one to three words per turn.)

EXERCISE 3

Story Reading

a. Find part B in your textbook. ✔
- The error limit for group reading is 17. Read carefully.
b. Everybody, touch the title. ✔
- (Call on a student to read the title.) *[Angela and Al Learn About Snowflakes.]*
- Everybody, what's the title? (Signal.) *Angela and Al Learn About Snowflakes.* ⓃⒹ
- (Call on individual students to read the story, each student reading two or three sentences at a time. Ask the specified questions as the students read.)

- (**Correct errors:** Tell the word. Direct the student to reread the sentence.)
- (If the group makes more than 17 errors, direct the students to reread the story.)

Angela and Al Learn About Snowflakes

After standing quietly for a couple of minutes, Al said, "Could we leave this place? There doesn't seem to be anything interesting to see here." The old man snapped his fingers. Suddenly Al no longer felt cold.

- Everybody, where are Al, Angela, and the old man? (Signal.) *North Pole.* ⒶⓅⓀ

Angela laughed and said, "Yes, the only thing around us is wind and snow."

"Snow," the old man repeated. "Perhaps you would like to take a closer look at snow."

Al said, "I've seen a lot of snow. In fact, I've shoveled a lot of it."

The old man turned on a flashlight and directed the beam into a swirling mass of snow that was blowing in the wind. "Observe," he said. Suddenly, one of the snowflakes in the beam of light started to grow. Al watched it as it grew in size until it was as large as a basketball.

- Everybody, show me how large it became. ✔ Ⓥ

The snowflake was beautiful. It was very flat and it looked like a very fancy wheel with six spokes that came out from the center.

- Everybody, how many spokes did it have? (Signal.) *Six.* ⓃⒹ

Each spoke was covered with fancy decorations, and each spoke looked just like the others.

The old man said, "You are looking at an ordinary snowflake. Do you think it is attractive?"

"It's beautiful," Angela exclaimed.

The old man said, "Well, look around you at the millions and millions of snowflakes. And as you look at them, think about this fact: No two snowflakes look the same."

- Do any two snowflakes look the same? (Call on a student. Idea: *No.*) ⓃⒹ

"That's incredible," Angela exclaimed.

The old man said, "Don't take my word for it. Pick out any snowflake you wish. I will make it big so that you can see if it's the same as the one we already have."

Angela pointed to a snowflake that landed on her mitten. "Make that snowflake big," she said.

The snowflake floated into the air and then it started to grow. Soon it was as large as the first snowflake.

- Everybody, show me how big it became. ✔ Ⓥ

It was shaped like a fancy wheel with spokes. But it didn't look anything like the first snowflake.

Al and Angela looked at the two snowflakes. "Wow!" Angela said. "I never knew snowflakes were so pretty."

Al scooped up a handful of snow. "Could you make all of these snowflakes big?" he asked.

The old man snapped his fingers. The snowflakes became suspended in the air and started to grow. Soon every one of them was as big as a basketball. Hundreds of huge snowflakes surrounded Al and Angela.

Al examined them. Every snowflake had spokes, but no two snowflakes looked exactly the same.

- Everybody, look at the picture of the snowflakes. You can see that no two snowflakes look exactly the same.

Angela and Al looked at the snowflakes for about a minute. Finally the old man said, "Each snowflake is different, but there is something the same about all of them. Study the snowflakes and see if you can figure out what is the same."

- Everybody, do it. Look at the picture and see if you can figure out what is the same about all the snowflakes but don't say anything yet. (Wait.)

Al looked at the different snowflakes. Some had thin spokes that were decorated. Some had fat spokes that came to a sharp point. Some had shorter spokes, and some had longer spokes.

"They all have spokes," Al said.

"Correct," the old man replied. "Can you tell me what is the same about all the spokes?"

Al counted the spokes of a very fancy snowflake with a large center part and short spokes. "Six spokes," he said to himself. He ✦ looked at another and counted the spokes. "Six spokes," he repeated to himself.

Just then Angela said, "They all have six spokes."

"I was just going to say that," Al said. Angela looked at Al and made a face.

- Everybody, how are all the snowflakes the same? (Signal.) *They all have six spokes.* ⓃⒹ
- Raise your hand if you figured that out before Angela did.
- Count the spokes and see if there are six on each snowflake. ✔ Ⓥ🅐

"Very good," the old man commented. "Now you know something about snowflakes that you didn't know before. Are you ready to learn more about the snow at the North Pole?"

"How much more is there?" Al asked. Before he completed the question, he noticed that he was starting to sink into the snow, straight down inside a hole that was forming.

The old man said, "We are now 10 feet below the surface of the snow. And we are a long way from the bottom of the snow."

- Everybody, how deep were they below the surface of the snow? (Signal.) *10 feet.* ⓃⒹ
- The ceiling in most rooms is only 8 feet high, so they were already down pretty far.

The old man continued, "Let's go down another 10 feet and see what is down there."

- Do you think they'll reach the bottom of the snow? (Call on individual students. Student preference.) ⓟ

Angela, Al and the old man sank deeper into the snow. They were still not at the bottom of the snow.
Angela said, "Wow! We're down 20 feet and we're still in the snow."
"Correct," the old man said.
Al felt the sides of the hole. The snow was hard, almost like ice. He asked, "And why is the snow so hard? It's almost like ice."
The old man said, "I will show you why the snow is hard."
The old man pulled a small block of snow from the wall of the hole and handed it to Angela. The block was about as big as the blocks that children play with.

- Everybody, show me how big that is. ✔ ⓥ

Then the old man put another small block on top of the first block. Then the old man added more blocks to the pile. Angela said, "Stop. This pile is getting too heavy to hold."
"Aha," the old man said. "The pile of blocks you are holding is only three feet high. And it is getting too heavy to hold. Think how heavy the pile would be when it is 20 feet high."

- Everybody, how high was the pile of blocks that Angela was holding? (Signal.) *3 feet.* ⓝⓓ
- How deep was the hole? (Signal.) *20 feet.* ⓝⓓ
- So how many feet of snow would be pushing down on the snow at the bottom of the hole? (Signal.) *20.* ⓝⓓ
- That's a lot of weight. No wonder the snow was like ice. It's squashed together.
- Read the rest of the story to yourself and be ready to answer some questions. Raise your hand when you're finished.

The old man snapped his fingers and the pile of snow blocks disappeared.

Angela said, "I get it. Snow is heavy. It pushes down with so much pressure that it packs the snow together. That's why the snow down here is almost like ice."
"Correct," the old man said. "Let's go down to the bottom."
The hole got deeper. Angela, Al and the old man went down another 10 feet and stopped. They did the same thing again and again. Still, they had not reached the bottom of the snow.
"We are now 70 feet below the surface of the snow," the old man said. "Get ready for a surprise. We are going to see what is at the bottom of the snow."
The hole got a little deeper. Suddenly Angela, Al and the old man were no longer in the snow and ice. They were underwater.
The old man said, "There is no land at the North Pole. There is just snow and ice. The snow and ice float in water."
"No land?" Angela asked.
"That's right," the old man replied. "The North Pole is bigger than any state in the United States. But it is nothing but ice and snow floating in the ocean."
"Wow!" Angela exclaimed.
"Wow!" Al exclaimed.

- (After all students have raised their hand:) Everybody, what was beneath all the snow? (Signal.) *Water.* ⓝⓓ
- About how deep was the snow? (Call on a student. Idea: *Over 70 feet deep.*) ⓝⓓ
- Everybody, are there any states in the United States as big as the mass of snow at the North Pole? (Signal.) *No.* ⓝⓓ

EXERCISE 4

Paired Practice

You're going to read aloud to your partner. The **A** members will read first. Then the **B** members will read from the star to the end of the story.

(Observe students and give feedback.)

End-of-Lesson Activities

INDEPENDENT WORK

Now finish your independent work for lesson 132. Raise your hand when you're finished. (Observe students and give feedback.)

WORKCHECK

a. (Direct students to take out their marking pencils.)

- We're going to check your workbook and textbook items. Remember, if you got an item wrong, make an **X** next to the item.

b. (For each item: Read the item. Call on a student to answer it. If the answer is wrong, say the correct answer. Refer to the Answer Key for the correct answers.)

c. Now use your marking pencil to fix up any items you got wrong. Remember, all mistakes must be fixed up before you hand in your work.

SPELLING

(Present Spelling lesson 132 after completing Reading lesson 132. See *Spelling Presentation Book.*)

ACTIVITIES

(Present Activity 30 after completing Reading lesson 132. See *Activities across the Curriculum*.)

EXERCISE 1

Vocabulary Review

a. Here's the new vocabulary sentence: Troops of baboons moved across the veld.
- Everybody, say that sentence. Get ready. (Signal.) *Troops of baboons moved across the veld.*
- (Repeat until firm.)

b. Everybody, what word refers to a large field in Africa? (Signal.) *Veld.*
- What word refers to **groups** of baboons? (Signal.) *Troops.*
- What word names a large member of the monkey family? (Signal.) *Baboons.*

EXERCISE 2

Reading Words

Column 1

a. **Find lesson 133 in your textbook.** ✔
- Touch column 1. ✔
- (Teacher reference:)

1. **Endurance**	3. **square**
2. **iris**	4. **curved**

b. Word 1. What word? (Signal.) *Endurance.*
- Spell **Endurance**. Get ready. (Tap for each letter.) *E-N-D-U-R-A-N-C-E.*
- Endurance is the name of a ship you will read about.

c. Word 2. What word? (Signal.) *Iris.*
- Spell **iris.** Get ready. (Tap for each letter.) *I-R-I-S.*
- The iris of the eye is the part that is colored. Some irises are blue or green. Some are brown or almost black.

d. Word 3. What word? (Signal.) *Square.*
- Spell **square.** Get ready. (Tap for each letter.) *S-Q-U-A-R-E.*

e. Word 4. What word? (Signal.) *Curved.*

f. Let's read those words again.
- Word 1. What word? (Signal.) *Endurance.*
- (Repeat for words 2–4.)

g. (Repeat step f until firm.)

Column 2

h. Find column 2. ✔
- (Teacher reference:)

1. **titled**	3. **camera**
2. **prevents**	4. **retina**

i. Word 1. What word? (Signal.) *Titled.*
- (Repeat for words 2–4.)

j. Let's read those words again.
- Word 1. What word? (Signal.) *Titled.*
- (Repeat for words 2–4.)

k. (Repeat step j until firm.)

Individual Turns

(For columns 1 and 2: Call on individual students, each to read one to three words per turn.)

EXERCISE 3

Story Background

a. Find part B in your textbook. ✔
- You're going to read the next story about Al and Angela. First you'll read the information passage. It gives some facts about eyes and cameras.

b. Everybody, touch the title. ✔
- (Call on a student to read the title.) *[The Camera and the Eye.]*
- Everybody, what's the title? (Signal.) *The Camera and the Eye.* ⓝⓓ

c. (Call on individual students to read the passage, each student reading two or three sentences at a time. Ask the specified questions as the students read.)

The Camera and the Eye

A camera may not look like an eye, but it works a lot like an eye. Here is a camera.

Here's how it looks if we cut the camera in half and look at it from the side.

The inside of a camera is dark like the inside of the eye. There is a piece of curved glass at the front of the camera. That's the lens.

- Everybody, look at picture 2. Touch the curved glass in front of the camera. ✔ (VA)
- What is that part called? (Signal.) *The lens.* (RF/R)
- It looks like the lens in the eye and it has the same name.

The camera lens works like the lens of an eye. The lens is transparent so that light can pass through it. The only way that light can get inside the camera is to pass through the lens. The lens bends the light. The paths of light cross after they go through the lens and then they form an image at the back of the camera. That image is upside down.

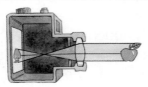

- Everybody, touch the lens in picture 3. ✔ (VA)
- The paths of light cross. Touch the point where the paths cross. ✔ (VA)
- Then the paths go to the back of the camera. Touch the image at the back of the camera. ✔ (VA)
- Is that image **upside down** or **right side up?** (Signal.) *Upside down.* (DC)
- That's just how the eye works.

The camera doesn't have a retina to feel the light, but it has film stretched out across the back of the camera. The picture is formed on the film, and the film feels the light.

- Everybody, does the camera have a retina? (Signal.) *No.* (ND)

- What part of the camera is like a retina? (Signal.) *The film.* (RF/R)
- The film feels light just the way the retina does.

Both the camera and the eye have an iris.

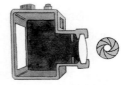

- Everybody, what's another part that the camera and the eye have? (Signal.) *An iris.* (RF/R)
- Touch the iris in picture 4. ✔ (VA)

When you're taking a picture in a dark place, a larger hole lets in enough light for a good picture. The iris can open up and make a large hole like this.

- Picture 5 shows the front of a camera. The iris is that part that is just around the hole. Touch the iris in picture 5. ✔
- That shows what the hole looks like when the iris is open. The hole is large. Would you want the large hole when you're taking pictures in **a bright place** or **a dark place?** (Signal.) *A dark place.* (DC)
- Remember, if there's not much light outside, the hole has to be big or there won't be enough light on the film to make a good picture.

When you're taking a picture in a very bright place, the iris can close down and make a very small hole like this.

- Touch the iris in picture 6. ✔ (VA)

- The iris is closed down so the hole is very small. Would the iris look like this when it's **very bright** out or **dark?** (Signal.) *Very bright.* (RF/R)

  The small hole doesn't let too much light reach the film.

- Remember, if it's bright out, the hole has to be very small or too much light will reach the film.

  The eye works the same way. When it's dark out, the iris makes the pupil larger. That large hole lets in a lot of light.

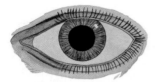

- Everybody, touch picture 7. ✔ (VA)
- Is the pupil **large** or **small?** (Signal.) *Large.* (VA)
- Does the eye look like that in **a bright place** or **a dark place?** (Signal.) *A dark place.* (DC)

  When it's bright out, the iris makes the pupil very small. The small hole prevents too much light from hitting the retina.

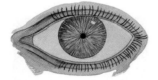

- Everybody, touch picture 8. ✔ (VA)
- Is the pupil **large** or **small?** (Signal.) *Small.* (VA)
- Does the eye look like that in **a bright place** or **a dark place?** (Signal.) *A bright place.* (DC)

  The parts of a camera are easy to remember if you remember the parts of an eye. Both the eye and the camera have a lens. Both the eye and the camera have an iris. Both have a part where the picture forms.

Story Reading

a. Find part C in your textbook. ✔
- The error limit for group reading is 7 errors. Read carefully.

b. Everybody, touch the title. ✔
- (Call on a student to read the title.) [*A Trip to the South Pole.*]
- Everybody, what's the title? (Signal.) *A Trip to the South Pole.* (ND)
- (Call on individual students to read the story, each student reading two or three sentences at a time. Ask the specified questions as the students read.)

- (**Correct errors:** Tell the word. Direct the student to reread the sentence.)
- (If the group makes more than 7 errors, direct the students to reread the story.)

A Trip to the South Pole

  Al, Angela and the old man were in the dark cold water below the North Pole. They had gone down from the surface of the snow until they had reached the water.

- Everybody, about how far had they gone through snow? (Signal.) *70 feet.* (APK)

  The old man said, "We have seen one pole. Now let's go to the other pole. But before we do . . ."
  Al and Angela no longer seemed to be underwater. A model of the sun and the earth appeared in front of them. The old man said, "Look at the globe and tell me what season it is at the North Pole."
  Angela quickly answered.

- How could she tell what season it was? (Call on a student. Idea: *By looking at which way the North Pole was tilting.*) (APK)

The old man pointed to the South Pole. "When the North Pole tilts away from the sun, the South Pole tilts . . ."

"Toward the sun," Al said, pointing to it.

- Everybody, which way is the North Pole tilting? (Signal.) *Away from the sun.* (VA)
- So which way is the **South** Pole tilting? (Signal.) *Toward the sun.* (DC)

Angela said, "That means the South Pole is on the half of the earth that is in sunlight all the time."

"Correct," the old man said. "Look at the model of us standing on the South Pole as the earth turns around and around."

Al and Angela watched. The models of three tiny people were standing on the South Pole. As the globe turned around and around, the three tiny people remained on the half of the globe that was in the sunlight.

- Everybody, touch the people on the South Pole. ✔ (VA)
- Are they on the **daylight side** of the globe or the **dark side** of the globe? (Signal.) *The daylight side.* (DC)
- Will they stay on the daylight side when the earth turns around and around? (Signal.) *Yes.* (DC)
- So how much darkness will there be at the **South** Pole during all of our winter? (Call on a student. Idea: *None.*) (DC)
- And how much daylight will there be at the **North** Pole during all of our winter? (Call on a student. Idea: *None.*) (DC)

The old man said, "Now we will go to the South Pole. But the earth will be spinning around hundreds of times faster than it usually spins."

- The earth turns very slowly, but how fast will it be turning when the old man takes Al and Angela to the South Pole? (Call on a student. Idea: *Hundreds of times faster.*) (ND)

Suddenly, things started to get brighter and brighter. Al could see that he was standing on snow. He could see the sun. It was just above the horizon. The air was very cold.

- Everybody, was the sun high overhead? (Signal.) *No.* (DC)

Al quickly observed that the sun was moving. But it was not coming up and it was not setting. It was just moving in a great circle ✦ along the horizon. Soon it had gone in a full circle and was starting another circle.

The old man said, "Remember, the earth is spinning very fast. If the earth was spinning at its regular speed, it would take 24 hours for the sun to make a full circle. You just saw it make a circle in only a few seconds."

- Everybody, touch the picture on the next page. ✔ (VA)
- It shows the path the sun followed. Follow the arrows around the horizon. ✔ (VA)
- It would normally take one full day for the sun to move all the way around like that. Why were they able to observe that circle in only a few seconds? (Call on a student. Idea: *Because the old man made the earth turn so fast.*) (DC)
- Read the rest of the story to yourself and be ready to answer some questions. Raise your hand when you're finished.

"Amazing," Angela exclaimed. "The sun just moves around and around the horizon."

"Correct," the old man said. "It makes one full circle every 24 hours."

The old man continued, "Do you want to see how deep the snow is at the South Pole?"

"Sure," Angela said. "And I know just what's going to happen. We're going to go down 70 feet. And then we'll be in the ocean, because there is no land under the South Pole."

"Let's see if you are right," the old man said.

Al and the others started sinking down and down into the packed snow—for over a mile.

And then—Al, Angela and the old man were going through rock.

Angela said, "I was wrong. There is land under the South Pole."

"Correct," the old man said. "There is no land under the North Pole, but there is a great mass of land under the South Pole."

"How big is the mass of land under the South Pole?" Angela asked.

The old man replied, "Think of a square that is one mile on each side. That's a large square."

The old man continued. "Now think of a thousand squares that big."

As Al was trying to think about a place that big, the old man continued. "Now think of five million squares that big. That's how big the land under the South Pole is."

Angela said, "Five million square miles. That's incredible."

- (After all students have raised their hand:) Everybody, how far down through the snow did Al and the others go? (Signal.) *Over a mile.* (ND)
- What was under the snow? (Call on a student. Ideas: *Rock; land.*) (ND)
- Everybody, how many square miles is the mass of land under the South Pole? (Signal.) *5 million.* (ND)
- That's a very large place.

- How thick is the snow at the North Pole? (Signal.) *70 feet.* (ND)
- How big is the land mass under the North Pole? (Call on a student. Idea: *There's no land under the North Pole.*) (APK)

EXERCISE 5

Paired Practice

You're going to read aloud to your partner. The **B** members will read first. Then the **A** members will read from the star to the end of the story.
(Observe students and give feedback.)

End-of-Lesson Activities

INDEPENDENT WORK

Now finish your independent work for lesson 133. Raise your hand when you're finished. (Observe students and give feedback.)

WORKCHECK

a. (Direct students to take out their marking pencils.)
- We're going to check your workbook and textbook items. Remember, if you got an item wrong, make an **X** next to the item.
b. (For each item: Read the item. Call on a student to answer it. If the answer is wrong, say the correct answer. Refer to the Answer Key for the correct answers.)
c. Now use your marking pencil to fix up any items you got wrong. Remember, all mistakes must be fixed up before you hand in your work.

SPELLING

(Present Spelling lesson 133 after completing Reading lesson 133. See *Spelling Presentation Book.*)

ACTIVITIES

(Present Activity 31 after completing Reading lesson 133. See *Activities across the Curriculum.*)

EXERCISE 1

Vocabulary Review

a. You learned a sentence that tells what the injury to his spinal cord did.
- Everybody, say that sentence. Get ready. (Signal.) *The injury to his spinal cord paralyzed him.*
- (Repeat until firm.)

b. You learned a sentence that tells where a single star was.
- Everybody, say that sentence. Get ready. (Signal.) *A single star was near the horizon.*
- (Repeat until firm.)

c. Here's the last sentence you learned: Troops of baboons moved across the veld.
- Everybody, say that sentence. Get ready. (Signal.) *Troops of baboons moved across the veld.*
- (Repeat until firm.)

d. What word names a large member of the monkey family? (Signal.) *Baboons.*
- What word refers to a large field in Africa? (Signal.) *Veld.*
- What word refers to **groups** of baboons? (Signal.) *Troops.*
- (Repeat step d until firm.)

e. Once more. Say the sentence that tells what troops of baboons did. Get ready. (Signal.) *Troops of baboons moved across the veld.*

EXERCISE 2

Reading Words

Column 1

a. **Find lesson 134 in your textbook.** ✔
- Touch column 1. ✔
- (Teacher reference:)

1. gorilla	3. porpoise
2. leopard	4. doorbell

b. Word 1 is **gorilla.** What word? (Signal.) *Gorilla.*
- Spell **gorilla.** Get ready. (Tap for each letter.) *G-O-R-I-L-L-A.*

- A gorilla is a huge member of the ape family. A gorilla is much larger and stronger than a man.

c. Word 2 is **leopard.** What word? (Signal.) *Leopard.*
- Spell **leopard.** Get ready. (Tap for each letter.) *L-E-O-P-A-R-D.*
- A leopard is a member of the cat family that lives in Africa. A leopard is smaller than a lion, and it has spots.

d. Word 3 is **porpoise.** What word? (Signal.) *Porpoise.*
- Spell **porpoise.** Get ready. (Tap for each letter.) *P-O-R-P-O-I-S-E.*
- A porpoise is sometimes called a dolphin. It is a small member of the whale family. Everybody, what's the name of a small member of the whale family? (Signal.) *Porpoise.*

e. Word 4. What word? (Signal.) *Doorbell.*
- Spell **doorbell.** Get ready. (Tap for each letter.) *D-O-O-R-B-E-L-L.*

f. Let's read those words again.
- Word 1. What word? (Signal.) *Gorilla.*
- (Repeat for words 2–4.)

g. (Repeat step f until firm.)

Column 2

h. Find column 2. ✔
- (Teacher reference:)

1. sweater	4. Johnson
2. camp	5. spun
3. snowstorm	

i. Word 1. What word? (Signal.) *Sweater.*
- (Repeat for words 2–5.)

j. Let's read those words again.
- Word 1. What word? (Signal.) *Sweater.*
- (Repeat for words 2–5.)

k. (Repeat step j until firm.)

Column 3

l. Find column 3. ✔
- (Teacher reference:)

1. curb	4. titled
2. party	5. crept
3. Scott	

m. Word 1. What word? (Signal.) *Curb.*
- (Repeat for words: **2. party, 3. Scott, 4. titled, 5. crept.**)

n. Let's read those words again.
- Word 1. What word? (Signal.) *Curb.*
- (Repeat for words: **2. party, 3. Scott, 4. titled, 5. crept.**)

o. (Repeat step n until firm.)

Individual Turns

(For columns 1–3: Call on individual students, each to read one to three words per turn.)

Story Reading

a. Find part B in your textbook. ✔
- The error limit for group reading is 16 errors. Read carefully.

b. Everybody, touch the title. ✔
- (Call on a student to read the title.) [A Book About the Poles.]
- Everybody, what's the title? (Signal.) *A Book About the Poles.* (ND)
- (Call on individual students to read the story, each student reading two or three sentences at a time. Ask the specified questions as the students read.)

- **(Correct errors:** Tell the word. Direct the student to reread the sentence.)
- (If the group makes more than 16 errors, direct the students to reread the story.)

A Book About the Poles

The trip to the poles was nearly over and Al was trying to remember everything he had seen. He was thinking about what was under each of the poles.

- Everybody, what was under the North Pole? (Signal.) *Water.* (RF/R)
- What was under the South Pole? (Call on a student. Ideas: *Land; rock.*) (RF/R)

He thought about how deep the snow was at the poles.

- How deep was it at the North Pole? (Signal.) *70 feet.* (RF/R)
- How deep was the snow at the South Pole? (Call on a student. Idea: *Over a mile.*) (RF/R)

He reminded himself about which pole has daylight all the time when the North Pole tilts away from the sun.

- Everybody, which pole has daylight all the time when the North Pole tilts **away from** the sun? (Signal.) *South Pole.* (RF/R)
- Which pole is **completely dark** when the North Pole tilts away from the sun? (Signal.) *North Pole.* (RF/R)
- What **season** are we having when the North Pole tilts away from the sun? (Signal.) *Winter.* (RF/R)

His mind went over the facts that he had learned about snowflakes.

- Name some things he learned about snowflakes. (Call on a student. Ideas: *They're beautiful; no two snowflakes look exactly the same; all snowflakes have six spokes.*) (APK)

Suddenly everything started to grow dark, and Al realized that he was back in the store on Anywhere Street.

Through the darkness the old man said, "Go anywhere. See anything. Pay for your trip by passing a test on what you see."

✿ "We'll be back tomorrow to take the test," Angela said.

"Good," the old man replied.

Then the inside of the store grew very quiet. The old man had disappeared.

"Let's go," Al said.

Angela opened the door. The bell went ding, ding. Outside, the snow was very deep and new snow was starting to fall. The snow on the sidewalk in front of the store was above Al's knees.

Angela said, "It's amazing to look at all this snow and realize that no two snowflakes are exactly the same."

Al and Angela started wading through the snow to the corner of Anywhere Street. And as soon as they went around the corner, Al could hear the sound of Christmas songs and could see people on ✿ the sidewalk. Cars in the street were moving very slowly through the snow.

One car near the curb was stuck in the snow. The driver was trying to move the car. "Wzzzzzz."

- What was making that sound? (Call on a student. Idea: *The tires spinning in the snow.*) (DI)

The tires spun around and around, but the car did not move forward.

The driver rolled down the window and called to Al and his sister, "Can you give me a hand? I'm late and I've got to get home."

"Sure thing," Angela said.

As she and Al got behind the car, she said, "When I count to three, push hard."

Al got set. "One . . . two . . . three." Al pushed as hard as he could. The tires went "wzzzzzz." But Al's feet slipped out from under him and the car did not move.

"Let's try it again," Angela said. "One . . . two . . . three." This time Al's feet did not slip. He pushed. Angela pushed. The car tires went "wzzzzzz," and the car started to move forward.

"Wzzzzzz." Now the car was moving a little faster—three feet, six feet, nine feet. The car crept along, almost stopping. "Wzzzzzz." Push, push! Now the car started moving faster and faster as it got into the tracks that other cars had made.

- Everybody, was the snow in these tracks as deep as the other snow? (Signal.) *No.* (DI)
- So will the car have an easier time moving if it stays in the tracks? (Signal.) *Yes.* (DC)

The driver drove to the next corner, pulled over, and stopped.

"Hey," he called, and motioned to Al and Angela.

They ran over to the car. The driver handed each of them a five-dollar bill. "Thanks a lot," he said. "Today's my wife's birthday and I can't be late for the party."

"Wow!" Angela said. "Thanks a lot."

"Yeah, thanks," Al said.

The car drove away. Al was out of breath. He stood there for a moment breathing hard and trying to catch his breath. Suddenly he felt very strange, almost the way he felt on trips with the old man. People walked by ⋆ on the sidewalk. The sound of Christmas songs came from the stores. Soft snowflakes fell against Al's face and melted. As Al stood there, a new thought came to him. If only he had some more money, he would be able to buy Christmas presents for his sister and his mother.

- Everybody, what did he want to buy for his mother? (Signal.) *Toaster.* (APK)
- How much money do you think he would need to buy a good toaster? (Call on a student. Accept reasonable responses.) (MJ)

"Come on," Angela said. "We'd better get home."

As they walked on the packed snow, Al kept thinking, "If only I had some more money, I would be able to buy Christmas presents."

The snow in front of Al's house was almost two feet deep.

- Everybody, show me how deep that snow was. ✔ (V)
- So a lot of snow has fallen.

It didn't look as if Al and Angela had shoveled the walk the other day. They waded through the snow and went up the front steps. Their mother called from the kitchen. "Take your boots off and leave them in the hall."

- Why did she say that? (Call on a student. Ideas: *So the snow wouldn't melt all over the house; so they wouldn't make a mess.*) (DI)

They took off their boots. Then they brushed the snow from their jackets, hung them up, and walked into the kitchen.

"Where have you been?" their mother asked. "You shouldn't be out in weather like this. They say that this is the worst snowstorm we've had in twenty years."

"It's pretty bad," Al said. "And it's still snowing out there. In fact, it's snowing harder than ever."

"Did you hear what they said about school on the radio?" his mother asked.

"No."

"They said that the schools will be closed tomorrow. And you start your Christmas vacation the day after tomorrow. So it looks as if your vacation has already started."

- When was the vacation supposed to start? (Call on a student. Idea: *The day after tomorrow.*) (ND)
- Why was it starting early? (Call on a student. Ideas: *Because there was so much snow; because school was closed.*) (ND)
- How would you like that if you were Al or Angela? (Call on individual students. Student preference.) (MC)
- Read the rest of the story to yourself and be ready to answer some questions. Raise your hand when you're finished.

Al smiled, but he didn't hate school the way he had hated it before he started going to the old man's store. He had always been glad when the school closed, but he wasn't so glad now. He actually liked going to school. Why not? He was now good at schoolwork.

Al ate supper. Just after he finished eating, the doorbell rang. "I'll get it," Al said, and went to the door.

A mailman was standing in the doorway, covered with snow. "I have a package for Al Johnson and Angela Johnson."

"That's us," Al said.

The man handed Al the package. Al thanked him and closed the door. Then he opened the package. A book titled *The Poles* was inside the package. Al knew who must have sent the book.

He sat down with Angela and started to look through the book. The first part told about people who had tried to reach the poles.

This part of the book told about interesting adventures. The people on a ship named *Endurance* had an incredible adventure trying to get to the South Pole. The ship became trapped in the ice. It drifted over five hundred miles in the ice. For nearly a year, the ship drifted. Finally the ice crushed the ship and the ship sank. But none of the men on the ship died. They all made it home.

The adventure of Robert Scott and four other men did not have a happy ending. They reached the South Pole. Then they started back across the mass of snow. All the men died. Fifty years later Scott's camp looked almost as it did on the day that he had left it. There was food on the tables. And the food was still good after fifty years.

- (After all students have raised their hand:) Everybody, was Al very happy that school was out? (Signal.) *No.* (ND)
- Why not? (Call on a student. Idea: *Because he liked school now.*) (ND)
- What did the mailman deliver after supper? (Call on a student. Ideas: *A package; a book.*) (ND)
- Who do you think sent that package? (Call on a student. Idea: *The old man.*) (DC)
- The book told about adventures that people had trying to reach the poles. What happened to the ship Endurance? (Call on a student. Ideas: *It got trapped in the ice; it drifted in the ice for almost a year; it got crushed by the ice; it sank.*) (ND)
- How many men on that ship died? (Call on a student. Idea: *None.*) (ND)
- What happened to Scott and the men with him? (Call on a student. Idea: *They died.*) (ND)
- What was unusual about Scott's camp when people found it fifty years later? (Call on a student. Ideas: *It looked like it had when Scott left it; the food was still good.*) (ND)

EXERCISE 4

Paired Practice

You're going to read aloud to your partner. The **A** members will read first. Then the **B** members will read from the star to the end of the story.

(Observe students and give feedback.)

End-of-Lesson Activities

Now finish your independent work for lesson 134. Raise your hand when you're finished. (Observe students and give feedback.)

a. (Direct students to take out their marking pencils.)

• We're going to check your workbook and textbook items. Remember, if you got an item wrong, make an **X** next to the item.

b. (For each item: Read the item. Call on a student to answer it. If the answer is wrong, say the correct answer. Refer to the Answer Key for the correct answers.)

c. Now use your marking pencil to fix up any items you got wrong. Remember, all mistakes must be fixed up before you hand in your work.

(Present Spelling lesson 134 after completing Reading lesson 134. See *Spelling Presentation Book.*)

EXERCISE 1

Vocabulary Review

a. You learned a sentence that tells what troops of baboons did.

- Everybody, say that sentence. Get ready. (Signal.) *Troops of baboons moved across the veld.*
- (Repeat until firm.)

b. Everybody, what's the **first** word of the sentence? (Signal.) *Troops.*

c. I'll say part of the sentence. When I stop, you say the next word. Listen: Troops of . . . Everybody, what's the next word? (Signal.) *Baboons.*

- Say the whole sentence. Get ready. (Signal.) *Troops of baboons moved across the veld.*

d. Listen: Troops of baboons moved across the . . . Everybody, what's the next word? (Signal.) *Veld.*

EXERCISE 2

Reading Words

Column 1

a. **Find lesson 135 in your textbook.** ✔

- Touch column 1. ✔
- (Teacher reference:)

1. **gorilla**	3. **wallet**
2. **sweaters**	4. **porpoise**

- All these words have more than one syllable. The first syllable of each word is underlined.

b. Word 1. What's the first syllable? (Signal.) *gor.*

- What's the whole word? (Signal.) *Gorilla.*
- Spell **gorilla.** Get ready. (Tap for each letter.) *G-O-R-I-L-L-A.*

c. Word 2. What's the first syllable? (Signal.) *sweat.*

- What's the whole word? (Signal.) *Sweaters.*
- Spell **sweaters.** Get ready. (Tap for each letter.) *S-W-E-A-T-E-R-S.*

d. Word 3. What's the first syllable? (Signal.) *wall.*

- What's the whole word? (Signal.) *Wallet.*
- Spell **wallet.** Get ready. (Tap for each letter.) *W-A-L-L-E-T.*

e. Word 4. What's the first syllable? (Signal.) *por.*

- What's the whole word? (Signal.) *Porpoise.*
- Spell **porpoise.** Get ready. (Tap for each letter.) *P-O-R-P-O-I-S-E.*

f. Let's read those words again.

- Word 1. What word? (Signal.) *Gorilla.*
- (Repeat for words 2–4.)

g. (Repeat step f until firm.)

Column 2

h. Find column 2. ✔

- (Teacher reference:)

1. **sabers**	4. **quick**
2. **history**	5. **slices**
3. **leopard**	6. **baboon**

i. Word 1. What word? (Signal.) *Sabers.*

- A saber is a kind of sword.

j. Word 2. What word? (Signal.) *History.*

- (Repeat for words 3–6.)

k. Let's read those words again.

- Word 1. What word? (Signal.) *Sabers.*
- (Repeat for words 2–6.)

l. (Repeat step k until firm.)

Individual Turns

(For columns 1 and 2: Call on individual students, each to read one to three words per turn.)

EXERCISE 3

Story Background

a. Find part B in your textbook. ✔

- You're going to read the next story about Al and Angela. First you'll read the information passage. It gives some facts about animals.

b. Everybody, touch the title. ✔

- (Call on a student to read the title.) *[Animals.]*
- Everybody, what's the title? (Signal.) *Animals.* (ND)

c. (Call on individual students to read the passage, each student reading two or three sentences at a time. Ask the specified questions as the students read.)

Animals

Here are some of the animals you are going to read about in later lessons.

- Read the name above each picture. (Call on a student.) *[Baboon, gorilla, saber-toothed tiger, porpoise, leopard.]* (VA)

The baboon is a very smart animal that lives in large groups called <u>troops</u>.

- Everybody, what are groups of baboons called? (Signal.) *Troops.* (RF/R)

A gorilla looks something like a baboon but it is much bigger and stronger and has no tail.

- Everybody, name the animal that looks something like a baboon but is much bigger. Get ready. (Signal.) *Gorilla.* (RF/R)

A leopard is in the same family as lions and tigers. A leopard has spots. It is no bigger than a big dog, but it is very strong and very quick.

- Everybody, name the animal in the cat family that has spots and is the size of a big dog. Get ready. (Signal.) *Leopard.* (RF/R)

A porpoise is in the same family as whales. All the animals in that family are warm-blooded. Some people think that the porpoise is the smartest animal in that family.

- Everybody, name the animal in the whale family that some people think is the smartest animal in that family. Get ready. (Signal.) *Porpoise.* (RF/R)
- Is that animal **warm-blooded** or **cold-blooded?** (Signal.) *Warm-blooded.* (RF/R)

The saber-toothed tiger no longer lives on Earth. It had teeth that stuck out like sabers or swords. It lived on Earth until around 25 thousand years ago.

- Why is it called a saber-toothed tiger? (Call on a student. Idea: *Because it had teeth like sabers.*) (RF/R)
- Everybody, how long ago did it disappear from Earth? (Signal.) *25 thousand years ago.* (RF/R)

EXERCISE 4

Story Reading

a. Find part C in your textbook. ✔
- The error limit for group reading is 9 errors. Read carefully.
b. Everybody, touch the title. ✔
- (Call on a student to read the title.) *[Angela and Al Buy Christmas Presents.]*
- Everybody, what's the title? (Signal.) *Angela and Al Buy Christmas Presents.* (APK)
- How much money did they get for pushing the car out of the snow? (Call on a student. Ideas: *Five dollars each; ten dollars.*) (APK)
- Everybody, is that enough to buy nice presents? (Signal.) *No.* (MJ)
- I wonder if they'll get more money.
- (Call on individual students to read the story, each student reading two or three sentences at a time. Ask the specified questions as the students read.

- (**Correct errors:** Tell the word. Direct the student to reread the sentence.)
- (If the group makes more than 9 errors, direct the students to reread the story.)

Angela and Al Buy Christmas Presents

Al looked out of the window the next morning. He couldn't see anything but snow through the window.

He went into the kitchen. His mother was setting the table. "What are you going to do today?" she asked.

"I don't know," Al said. "I thought I'd go to the library and read another book about the poles."

- Why doesn't he have to go to school? (Call on a student. Ideas: *Because the schools are closed; because there's so much snow on the ground.*) APK

His mother said, "The library is closed. Most of the stores are closed. Almost everything is closed."

- Why is almost everything closed? (Call on a student. Idea: *Because it snowed so much.*) DI

After breakfast Al whispered to Angela, "I wonder whether the old man's store would be open today."

"Let's see," she replied.

They put on their boots and heavy coats. As they were going outside, their mother said, "Come home before lunch time."

"Okay, Mom," they replied as they walked out the door.

Christmas songs still came from some of the stores. But there weren't many people on the streets. Al listened to the songs and started thinking about Christmas again. If only he had a few more dollars . . .

- What did he want to do? (Call on a student. Idea: *Buy Christmas presents.*) APK

Angela and Al turned the corner at Anywhere Street and then they both stopped. The snow had been shoveled in front of all the buildings except one. The only building that had snow in front of it was the old man's store. And the snow in front of the store was over three feet deep.

- Everybody, show me how deep that snow was. ✔
- How would you like to shovel all that snow? (Call on individual students. Student preference.) MC

"That sure is strange," Angela said.

Al and Angela walked through the snow in front of the old man's store. They opened the door. "Ding, ding." Plop—a great pile of snow fell inside. Al looked up and saw the old man standing right in front of them, holding a big snow shovel.

"Go anywhere. See anything. But first shovel my walk. I will pay you."

"You don't have to pay us," Al said.

"If you shovel my walk, I will pay you," the old man replied.

Al shoveled until he was tired. Then Angela shoveled. Then Al shoveled again.

At last the walk was shoveled. Angela and Al went inside. "Ding, ding." The old man was waiting for them. He handed two dollars to Angela and two dollars to Al.

The old man said, "Take the money to the store next door and buy your Christmas presents."

Al said, "I don't have enough money with me. I only have two dollars."

"What do ⭐ you want to buy?" the old man asked.

Al whispered to the old man so that Angela wouldn't hear. "I want to buy a toaster for my mother and a wallet for my sister. But I don't have enough money with me. I only have two dollars."

The old man said, "Take your two dollars to the store next door and buy the gifts. I want Angela to stay with me while you shop."

- Read the rest of the story to yourself and be ready to answer some questions. Raise your hand when you're finished.

Al was puzzled as he went to the store next door. Inside that store, a bell went ding, ding. One wall of the store was filled with wallets. There were wallets of every size and every shape. There were brown wallets and white wallets and pink wallets and black wallets. Al figured that there must have been more than two hundred wallets on that wall.

And the other wall was covered with toasters. There were big toasters and little toasters. There were silver toasters, gold toasters, red toasters. There were toasters for two slices of bread, for three slices of bread, for four slices of bread and even for eight slices of bread.

And that's all there was in the whole store—toasters and wallets.

A little old man came out of the back. "You will find anything you want in this store—as long as you want a toaster or a wallet." The old man laughed so hard that Al thought he would fall over. "What can I sell you? All wallets cost one dollar. All toasters cost one dollar. What do you want to buy?"

Al said, "That's wrong. Toasters cost a lot more than one dollar. So do those wallets."

The old man looked very angry. "This is my store," he said. "Don't tell me how much things should cost in this store."

Al picked out a big toaster and a beautiful pink wallet with many plastic windows and a secret pocket for money.

After Al came back to the old man's store, Angela went to the store next door. While she was gone, Al talked to the old man. When she came back, she said, "That's the strangest store I have ever seen. It had nothing but books and women's sweaters." Al had a pretty good idea of what he was going to get from Angela for Christmas.

- (After all students have raised their hand:) Everybody, what did Al buy for his mother? (Signal.) *A toaster.* (ND)
- What did he buy for his sister? (Signal.) *A wallet.* (ND)
- How much did each present cost? (Signal.) *One dollar.* (ND)
- Did Angela go to the store at the same time Al went there? (Signal.) *No.* (ND)
- What did she say was in the store when she was there? (Call on a student. Idea: *Books and women's sweaters.*) (ND)
- Al could figure out what she had bought for him. Everybody, what was that? (Signal.) *A book.* (DC)
- Who is the woman's sweater for? (Call on a student. Idea: *Their mother.*) (DI)

EXERCISE 5

Fluency: Rate/Accuracy

> *Note:* There is a fluency checkout in this lesson; therefore, there is no paired practice.

a. Today is a reading checkout day. While you're doing your independent work, I'm going to call on you one at a time to read part of the story from lesson 134.
- Remember, you pass the checkout by reading the passage in less than a minute without making more than 2 mistakes. And when you pass the checkout, you'll color the space for lesson 135 on your thermometer chart.
b. (Call on individual students to read the portion of story 134 with ❀.)
- (Time the student. Note words that are missed and number of words read.)

- (Teacher reference:)

> ✿ "We'll be back tomorrow to take the test," Angela said.
>
> "Good," the old man replied.
>
> Then the inside of the store grew very quiet. The old man had disappeared.
>
> "Let's go," Al said.
>
> Angela opened the door. The bell went ding, ding. Outside, the snow was very deep and new [50] snow was starting to fall. The snow on the sidewalk in front of the store was above Al's knees.
>
> Angela said, "It's amazing to look [75] at all this snow and realize that no two snowflakes are exactly the same."
>
> Al and Angela started wading through the snow to the corner [100] of Anywhere Street. And as soon as they went around the corner, Al could hear the sound of Christmas songs and see people on ✿ [125] the sidewalk.

- (If the student reads the passage in one minute or less and makes no more than 2 errors, direct the student to color in the space for lesson 135 on the thermometer chart.)

- (If the student makes any mistakes, point to each word that was misread and identify it.)
- (If the student does not meet the rate-error criterion for the passage, direct the student to practice reading the story with the assigned partner.)

End-of-Lesson Activities

INDEPENDENT WORK

Now finish your independent work for lesson 135. Raise your hand when you're finished. (Observe students and give feedback.)

WORKCHECK

a. (Direct students to take out their marking pencils.)
- We're going to check your workbook and textbook items. Remember, if you got an item wrong, make an **X** next to the item.
b. (For each item: Read the item. Call on a student to answer it. If the answer is wrong, say the correct answer. Refer to the Answer Key for the correct answers.)
c. Now use your marking pencil to fix up any items you got wrong. Remember, all mistakes must be fixed up before you hand in your work.

SPELLING

(Present Spelling lesson 135 after completing Reading lesson 135. See *Spelling Presentation Book*.)

Lessons 136–140 • Planning Page   *Looking Ahead*

	Lesson 136	Lesson 137	Lesson 138	Lesson 139	Lesson 140
LESSON EVENTS	Fact Review Reading Words Story Reading Paired Practice Independent Work Workcheck Spelling	Reading Words Story Reading Paired Practice Independent Work Workcheck Spelling	Reading Words Story Reading Paired Practice Independent Work Workcheck Spelling	Reading Words Story Reading Paired Practice Independent Work Workcheck Spelling	Fact Game Fluency: Rate/ Accuracy Test Marking the Test Test Remedies Spelling
VOCABULARY SENTENCE					
READING WORDS: WORD TYPES	modeled words	–s words multi-syllable words	compound words mixed words	multi-syllable words	
NEW VOCABULARY	Plateosaurus history	extends	dragonflies	terrific	
STORY BACKGROUND					
STORY	*Angela and Al Go to the Library*	*Angela and Al Read About Baboons*	*Angela and Al Finish Their Last Trip*	*Go Anywhere—See Anything With Books*	
SKILL ITEMS		Crossword puzzle	Vocabulary		Test: Vocabulary sentences
SPECIAL MATERIALS					Thermometer charts, dice, Fact Game 140, Fact Game Answer Key, scorecard sheets, *materials for project
SPECIAL PROJECTS/ ACTIVITIES					Project after lesson 140

*Library books, pencils, lined paper.

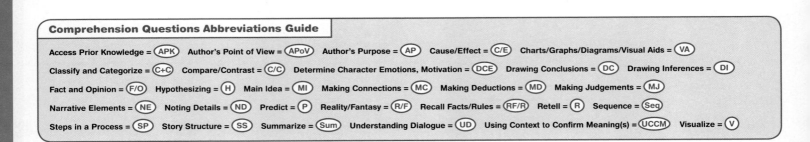

Comprehension Questions Abbreviations Guide

Access Prior Knowledge = (APK)   Author's Point of View = (APoV)   Author's Purpose = (AP)   Cause/Effect = (C/E)   Charts/Graphs/Diagrams/Visual Aids = (VA)

Classify and Categorize = (C+C)   Compare/Contrast = (C/C)   Determine Character Emotions, Motivation = (DCE)   Drawing Conclusions = (DC)   Drawing Inferences = (DI)

Fact and Opinion = (F/O)   Hypothesizing = (H)   Main Idea = (MI)   Making Connections = (MC)   Making Deductions = (MD)   Making Judgements = (MJ)

Narrative Elements = (NE)   Noting Details = (ND)   Predict = (P)   Reality/Fantasy = (R/F)   Recall Facts/Rules = (RF/R)   Retell = (R)   Sequence = (Seq)

Steps in a Process = (SP)   Story Structure = (SS)   Summarize = (Sum)   Understanding Dialogue = (UD)   Using Context to Confirm Meaning(s) = (UCCM)   Visualize = (V)

EXERCISE 1

Fact Review

a. Let's review some facts you have learned. First we'll go over the facts together. Then I'll call on individual students to do some facts.

b. Tell me if the **North** Pole tilts **toward the sun** or **away from the sun** during our winter. (Pause.) Get ready. (Signal.) *Away from the sun.* (RF/R)

• Tell me if the **South** Pole tilts **toward the sun** or **away from the sun** during our winter. (Pause.) Get ready. (Signal.) *Toward the sun.* (RF/R)

• Tell me how many hours it takes the sun to make a full circle around a person who is at the North Pole. (Pause.) Get ready. (Signal.) *24.* (RF/R)

• (Repeat step b until firm.)

c. Tell me if the **North** Pole is always **dark** or **light** during our winter. (Pause.) Get ready. (Signal.) *Dark.* (RF/R)

• Tell me if the **South** Pole is always **dark** or **light** during our winter. (Pause.) Get ready. (Signal.) *Light.* (RF/R)

• Tell me how deep the snow is at the South Pole. (Pause.) Get ready. (Signal.) *Over a mile.* (RF/R)

• Tell me what's under the snow at the North Pole. (Pause.) Get ready. (Signal.) *Water.* (RF/R)

• (Repeat step c until firm.)

Individual Turns

• Now I'm going to call on individual students to do some facts.

• (Call on individual students to do the set of facts in steps b or c.)

EXERCISE 2

Reading Words

Column 1

a. **Find lesson 136 in your textbook.** ✔

• Touch word 1. ✔

• (Teacher reference:)

1. Plateosaurus	5. typed
2. enemies	6. screen
3. extend	7. known
4. history	

b. Word 1 is **Plateosaurus (plate-ē-ō-SAU-rus).** What word? (Signal.) *Plateosaurus.*

• Plateosaurus was the very first dinosaur. You'll read about it.

c. Word 2 is **enemies.** What word? (Signal.) *Enemies.*

• Spell **enemies.** Get ready. (Tap for each letter.) *E-N-E-M-I-E-S.*

d. Word 3. What word? (Signal.) *Extend.*

• Spell **extend.** Get ready. (Tap for each letter.) *E-X-T-E-N-D.*

e. Word 4. What word? (Signal.) *History.*

• History is the study of the past. When we study what happened hundreds or thousands of years ago, we are studying history. Everybody, what's the name of the study of the past? (Signal.) *History.*

f. Word 5. What word? (Signal.) *Typed.*

• (Repeat for words 6 and 7.)

g. Let's read those words again.

• Word 1. What word? (Signal.) *Plateosaurus.*

• (Repeat for words 2–7.)

h. (Repeat step g until firm.)

EXERCISE 3

Story Reading

a. Find part B in your textbook. ✔

• The error limit for group reading is 10 errors. Read carefully.

b. Everybody, touch the title. ✔

• (Call on a student to read the title.) *[Angela and Al Go to the Library.]*

• Everybody, what's the title? (Signal.) *Angela and Al Go to the Library.* (ND)

• (Call on individual students to read the story, each student reading two or three sentences at a time. Ask the specified questions as the students read.)

Angela and Al Go to the Library

Al and Angela were inside the old man's store. Al felt excited about the presents he had bought.

- What were they? (Call on a student.) *[A toaster and a wallet.]* (APK)

He had almost forgotten that he and Angela had to take a test on their last trip.

The old man asked them many questions. Al and Angela answered all of them.

Then the old man said, "You have passed the test. But this is your last trip. I cannot take you on any more trips."

"Why not?" Al asked. "Didn't we do a good job on the tests?"

"You did a wonderful job," the old man said. Then he put his arms around Angela and Al.

The old man continued, "You don't need the trips anymore. When you first came to me, you needed to see things. You needed to learn about the world. And you needed to learn that it is fun to learn. Now you have learned these things, so you no longer need the trips. You have learned how to take a trip by reading books."

- Why did Al need the trips when he first came to the store? (Call on a student. Ideas: *Because he needed to see things; because he needed to learn about the world; because he needed to learn that it's fun to learn.*) (ND)
- Why doesn't he need the trips now? (Call on a student. Ideas: *Because he has learned things; because he can take trips by reading books.*) (ND)
- How do you think he feels about never being able to go on trips with the old man again? (Call on a student. Idea: *Sad.*) (DCE)

The room was silent. Al and Angela stood there looking at the old man. Al didn't know what to say. The trips were the most exciting things in Al's life. But maybe the old man was right. Al had read the book about the poles. He had learned things that he had not seen on his trip to the poles. And when Al had read the book, he had almost felt as if he was on a trip.

- Name some things that Al read about in the book that he didn't see at the South Pole. (Call on a student. Idea: *About the ship Endurance and about Scott and his men.*) (APK)

The old man said, "Since this is our last trip, let me choose where we will go."

"Sure," Angela said. She sounded sad.

The old man said, "Good. We will take a trip into the world of books."

Slowly the room got brighter. The walls seemed to melt. Rows and rows of books started to appear. Al realized that he and Angela were in a library—a very large library.

The old man said, "There are over three million books in this library. Think of it—over three million books. And think of how those books got here. They didn't fall out of the sky like snowflakes. Somebody wrote every book that is here. And many of these books are very, very old. Some were written by people who lived over two thousand years ago."

- Everybody, how many books are in the library? (Signal.) *Over 3 million.* (ND)
- How long ago were some of the books written? (Signal.) *Over 2000 years ago.* (ND)
- That's amazing.

"Think of it," the old man said, waving his arms. "In this building is nearly everything that we have learned about our world and the things in it. The books in this building tell about science. They tell nearly everything that is known about arithmetic, and they tell about history. They tell what is known about every place in the universe from the galaxies to the bottom of the sea. They tell about music and art and about the human brain. They tell how to train your dog or how to build a rocket. And they tell almost every story that people have ever told— good stories, bad stories, old stories, and new stories."

- Read the rest of the story to yourself and be ready to answer some questions. Raise your hand when you're finished.

> As the old man walked across the library, his shoes went "clack, clack, clack" on the floor. The old man walked into a room with rows of computers. The old man said, "And here is the brain of the library. Name anything that you want to read about. Name anything at all."
>
> Angela said, "I like to read about all of the different kinds of animals."
>
> "Animals," the old man said and typed the word <u>animals</u> in the computer.
>
> Some facts appeared on the computer screen. The old man said, "The computer tells us that there are over three thousand books on animals. If you wish, the computer will list all the titles. Or you can give the computer more information about the kinds of animals you are interested in."
>
> Angela said, "Well, I don't really care that much. I like all . . ."
>
> Before she could finish her sentence, the old man said, "I will select some titles for you."
>
> The old man quickly pressed some keys on the computer keyboard. Then he said, "Our books will be here in a moment."
>
> The old man stood up and walked over to a small door in the wall. Suddenly a light over the door went on. The old man opened the door and there was a pile of books inside.
>
> The old man picked them up and carried them over to a table. He picked up a book titled *Animals in Africa* and handed it to Al. The old man said, "Start reading for us and we'll go on a new kind of trip."
>
> Al picked up the book and started to read.

- (After all students have raised their hand:) Everybody, what was the brain of the library? (Signal.) *Computer.* ⓓⒸ
- What did Angela want to read about? (Call on a student.) [*Animals.*] ⓃⒹ
- How many books on animals were in the library? (Signal.) *Over 3,000.* ⓃⒹ
- Did the old man order **one book** or **more than one?** (Signal.) *More than one.* ⓃⒹ
- What was the name of the book the old man selected from the pile? (Signal.) *Animals in Africa.* ⓃⒹ
- Who was going to read first from that book? (Signal.) *Al.* ⓃⒹ
- The old man said they were going on a new kind of trip. How were they going to go on a trip? (Call on a student. Idea: *By reading a book.*) ⓓⒸ

EXERCISE 4

Paired Practice

You're going to read aloud to your partner. The **B** members will read first. Then the **A** members will read from the star to the end of the story.
(Observe students and give feedback.)

End-of-Lesson Activities

INDEPENDENT WORK

Now finish your independent work for lesson 136. Raise your hand when you're finished. (Observe students and give feedback.)

WORKCHECK

a. (Direct students to take out their marking pencils.)
- We're going to check your workbook and textbook items. Remember, if you got an item wrong, make an **X** next to the item.
b. (For each item: Read the item. Call on a student to answer it. If the answer is wrong, say the correct answer. Refer to the Answer Key for the correct answers.)
c. Now use your marking pencil to fix up any items you got wrong. Remember, all mistakes must be fixed up before you hand in your work.

SPELLING

(Present Spelling lesson 136 after completing Reading lesson 136. See *Spelling Presentation Book.*)

EXERCISE 1

Reading Words

Column 1

a. **Find lesson 137 in your textbook.** ✔
- Touch column 1. ✔
- (Teacher reference:)

1. extends	**3. barks**
2. giraffes	**4. enemies**

- All these words end with the letter **S**.
b. Word 1. What word? (Signal.) *Extends.*
- When you extend something, you stretch it out.
c. Word 2. What word? (Signal.) *Giraffes.*
- (Repeat for words 3 and 4.)
d. Let's read those words again.
- Word 1. What word? (Signal.) *Extends.*
- (Repeat for words 2–4.)
e. (Repeat step d until firm.)

Column 2

f. Find column 2. ✔
- (Teacher reference:)

1. era	**4. Plateosaurus**
2. flat-topped	**5. Africa**
3. next-smartest	

g. Word 1. What word? (Signal.) *Era.*
- (Repeat for words 2–5.)
h. Let's read those words again.
- Word 1. What word? (Signal.) *Era.*
- (Repeat for words 2–5.)
i. (Repeat step h until firm.)

Individual Turns

(For columns 1 and 2: Call on individual students, each to read one to three words per turn.)

EXERCISE 2

Story Reading

a. Find part B in your textbook. ✔
- The error limit for group reading is 14 errors. Read carefully.
b. Everybody, touch the title. ✔
- (Call on a student to read the title.) *[Angela and Al Read About Baboons.]*

- Everybody, what's the title? (Signal.) *Angela and Al Read About Baboons.* ⓃⒹ
- (Call on individual students to read the story, each student reading two or three sentences at a time. Ask the specified questions as the students read.)

- (**Correct errors:** Tell the word. Direct the student to reread the sentence.)
- (If the group makes more than 14 errors, direct the students to reread the story.)

Angela and Al Read About Baboons

Al read the first page of the book about animals in Africa.

- All the parts of this story that are in boxes are the pages from the books that they are reading.

Africa has a wet season and a dry season. You are in Africa during the dry season. You are on the veld. The veld is a great field of grass that extends for many miles.

- What is the veld? (Call on a student.) *[A great field of grass.]* ⓃⒹ

The veld is dry and hot and the sun is burning down on you. In the distance you can see bright blue mountains and trees with flat tops. You can also see many animals moving in long lines. They are walking to a water hole. You see a troop of baboons. You see a group of giraffes. You see a group of lions. And you see many other groups of animals.

As Al sat there in the library, he started to feel as if he was going on a trip. He could almost feel the sun and see the flat-topped trees.

- Everybody, close your eyes. Listen to me read that page in the book again and see if you can get the feeling that you are seeing the things the story tells about:

Africa has a wet season and a dry season. You are in Africa during the dry season. You are on the veld. The veld is a great field of grass that extends for many miles. The veld is dry and hot and the sun is burning down on you. In the distance you can see bright blue mountains and trees with flat tops. You can also see many animals moving in long lines. They are walking to a water hole. You see a troop of baboons. You see a group of giraffes. You see a group of lions. And you see many other groups of animals.

Al read the first part of the next page.

Leopards and monkeys drink from the water hole at the same time.

The leopards do not kill the monkeys at the water hole because the animals come to drink, not to fight or kill. So all day long the animals wait their turn at the water hole. They drink and then they slowly walk away across the veld.

Now, Angela read part of the page.

The veld has not changed much in a million years or more, but some of the animals that wait their turn at the water hole have changed. At one time the saber-toothed tiger waited in line.

Suddenly the old man took the book from Angela and said, "Perhaps you will want to come back and read the rest of this book."

Angela said, "Yes, I would like to continue reading this book right now."

The old man said, "Not now. But you can come back to the library sometime. The book is here waiting for you to read it and take you on a trip to Africa. It will teach you about many things you have never seen before."

The old man put the book down on the table and picked up another book from the pile. The title of this book was *How Animals Learn*. The old man opened the book to the first page. He said, "I will read to you." He read:

Everyone agrees that humans are smarter than other animals. Humans can do more than the other animals and humans can learn more. But which animal is the next-smartest? Some people say it is the porpoise.

Others say that it is the gorilla. But I believe the baboon is the next-smartest animal.

Observe a troop of baboons.

The troop is like a large family and it has many enemies—lions and leopards. So the troop has to be very smart and careful. The troop has lookouts who sit on high cliffs and watch for danger.

We see three lookouts. One is on the top of the cliff. The two other lookouts are about halfway down the cliff. There is something moving above one of the lookouts. It is a baby baboon who is sneaking up behind the lookout. The lookout turns and looks at the baby baboon. Then the lookout turns away, pretending that he does not see the baby. The baby baboon stands up on a rock just above the lookout and leaps onto the lookout.

The lookout is strong enough to kill a leopard with his hands. But the lookout falls down.

"Ahhh, ahhh," he cries and pretends that he is hurt.

The baby baboon jumps on the lookout again. "Eeeeee," the baby calls.

"Ahhh," the lookout cries.

The lookout plays with the baby baboon for a few minutes. Then the lookout sits up and barks at the baby. The baby stops playing. The lookout barks again and then slaps the baby on its behind. The baby runs away back to the troop.

"Wow!" Angela said. "That baboon was playing with the baby just like a human plays with a baby."

"Correct," the old man said.

- Everybody, did the lookout see the baby? (Signal.) *Yes.* (ND)
- Why did the lookout pretend **not** to see it? (Call on a student. Idea: *Because it was playing with the baby.*) (DC)
- Everybody, was the lookout really hurt when the baby jumped on him? (Signal.) *No.* (DC)
- But what did the lookout do? (Call on a student. Idea: *Cried out like it was hurt.*) (ND)

- How did the lookout first signal the baby that it was time to stop playing? (Call on a student. Idea: *By barking at the baby.*) (DI)
- Then what did the lookout do? (Call on a student. Idea: *Barked again and slapped the baby on its behind.*) (ND)
- Read the rest of the story to yourself and be ready to answer some questions. Raise your hand when you're finished.

> The old man handed the book to Al. "Why don't you read a little to us?" the old man said.
>
> Al read:
>
> Let's do something to see just how smart baboons are. Let's put some food inside a wooden box that is about a foot wide and a foot high. That box is very strong. We put the box out in the field near the troop.
>
> One of the larger baboons comes up to the box and smells it. Then he calls out. Other baboons come over to the box. One starts biting at a corner of the box.
>
> A second baboon pushes the first baboon away. The second baboon starts biting at a corner of the box.
>
> The biggest baboon says, "Uhhhaaa, raaah." He picks up a large rock. He stands next to the box and holds the rock over his head with both hands.
>
> He throws the rock at the box very hard. The other baboons watch for a moment. Then they pick up rocks and start throwing them at the box. Soon the box starts to break.
>
> One of the baboons reaches inside the box and grabs a small piece of food. He quickly puts the food in his mouth. The biggest baboon hits this baboon. No other baboon tries to eat the food. They carry the food back to the troop.
>
> The baboons used rocks as tools for opening the box. An animal must be very smart to use tools.

> The old man said, "We don't have time to read more from that book."
>
> "Too bad," Al said. "That was interesting. I never thought of a rock as a tool before."
>
> Angela said, "I'd like to read more about baboons."
>
> The old man said, "Come back to the library and read about them. There are a lot of books about baboons."

- (After all students have raised their hand:) What did the people put out in the field to see how smart the baboons were? (Call on a student. Idea: *A box with food in it.*) (ND)
- How did the baboons **first** try to get inside the box? (Call on a student. Idea: *By biting on it.*) (ND)
- What did the biggest baboon do? (Call on a student. Idea: *Threw a big rock at the box.*) (ND)
- Then what did the other baboons do? (Call on a student. Idea: *Threw rocks at the box.*) (ND)
- What happened to the box? (Call on a student. Idea: *It broke.*) (ND)
- Everybody, did the baboons eat all the food inside the box? (Signal.) *No.* (ND)
- What happened? (Call on a student. Idea: *The biggest baboon made them take the food back to the troop.*) (ND)
- Everybody, when you use rocks to help you do a job, what are you using the rocks as? (Signal.) *Tools.* (DC)
- Is an animal that uses tools very smart? (Signal.) *Yes.* (ND)
- How much more of that book did the old man read? (Call on a student. Idea: *No more.*) (ND)
- Do you think you'd ever like to read more about baboons? (Call on a student. Student preference.) (MC)

EXERCISE 3

Paired Practice

You're going to read aloud to your partner. The **A** members will read first. Then the **B** members will read from the star to the end of the story.

(Observe students and give feedback.)

End-of-Lesson Activities

INDEPENDENT WORK

Now finish your independent work for lesson 137. Raise your hand when you're finished. (Observe students and give feedback.)

WORKCHECK

a. (Direct students to take out their marking pencils.)
• We're going to check your workbook and textbook items. Remember, if you got an item wrong, make an **X** next to the item.

b. (For each item: Read the item. Call on a student to answer it. If the answer is wrong, say the correct answer. Refer to the Answer Key for the correct answers.)

c. Now use your marking pencil to fix up any items you got wrong. Remember, all mistakes must be fixed up before you hand in your work.

SPELLING

(Present Spelling lesson 137 after completing Reading lesson 137. See *Spelling Presentation Book.*)

EXERCISE 1

Reading Words

Column 1

a. **Find lesson 138 in your textbook.** ✔
- Touch column 1. ✔
- (Teacher reference:)

1. <u>dragon</u>flies	4. <u>book</u>store
2. <u>space</u>ships	5. <u>cook</u>book
3. <u>any</u>time	

- All these words are compound words. The first part of each word is underlined.
b. Word 1. What's the underlined part? (Signal.) *dragon.*
- What's the whole word? (Signal.) *Dragonflies.*
- Dragonflies are insects with wings that you can see through.
c. Word 2. What's the underlined part? (Signal.) *space.*
- What's the whole word? (Signal.) *Spaceships.*
d. Word 3. What's the underlined part? (Signal.) *any.*
- What's the whole word? (Signal.) *Anytime.*
e. Word 4. What's the underlined part? (Signal.) *book.*
- What's the whole word? (Signal.) *Bookstore.*
f. Word 5. What's the underlined part? (Signal.) *cook.*
- What's the whole word? (Signal.) *Cookbook.*
g. Let's read those words again.
- Word 1. What word? (Signal.) *Dragonflies.*
- (Repeat for words 2–5.)
h. (Repeat step g until firm.)

Column 2

i. Find column 2. ✔
- (Teacher reference:)

1. Plateosaurus	4. stack
2. rabbit	5. packages
3. pages	6. era

j. Word 1. What word? (Signal.) *Plateosaurus.*
k. Word 2. What word? (Signal.) *Rabbit.*
- Spell **rabbit.** Get ready. (Tap for each letter.) *R-A-B-B-I-T.*
l. Word 3. What word? (Signal.) *Pages.*
- Spell **pages.** Get ready. (Tap for each letter.) *P-A-G-E-S.*
m. Word 4. What word? (Signal.) *Stack.*
- Spell **stack.** Get ready. (Tap for each letter.) *S-T-A-C-K.*
n. Word 5. What word? (Signal.) *Packages.*
- Spell **packages.** Get ready. (Tap for each letter.) *P-A-C-K-A-G-E-S.*
o. Word 6. What word? (Signal.) *Era.*
p. Let's read those words again.
- Word 1. What word? (Signal.) *Plateosaurus.*
- (Repeat for words 2–6.)
q. (Repeat step p until firm.)

Individual Turns

(For columns 1 and 2: Call on individual students, each to read one to three words per turn.)

EXERCISE 2

Story Reading

a. Find part B in your textbook. ✔
- The error limit for group reading is 15 errors. Read carefully.
b. Everybody, touch the title. ✔
- (Call on a student to read the title.) *[Angela and Al Finish Their Last Trip.]*
- Everybody, what's the title? (Signal.) *Angela and Al Finish Their Last Trip.* ⓃⒹ
- Where is this trip? (Call on a student. Idea: *In a library.*) ⒶⓅⓀ
- (Call on individual students to read the story, each student reading two or three sentences at a time. Ask the specified questions as the students read.)

- (**Correct errors:** Tell the word. Direct the student to reread the sentence.)
- (If the group makes more than 15 errors, direct the students to reread the story.)

Angela and Al Finish Their Last Trip

Al, Angela, and the old man were in a library that had over three million books. Angela and Al had read the first few pages in two books.

The old man said, "What else do you want to read about? Where do you want to go? What do you want to see? You can go anywhere and see anything in this library."

Al said, "I always wanted to know more about dinosaurs."

So the old man went over to a computer and pressed some keys. A few minutes later the light over the little door went on. The old man opened the door, took out a pile of books and carried them to one of the tables. He announced, "This library has over six hundred books on dinosaurs. I think you'll enjoy the ones I selected."

The book on the top of the pile was *The First Dinosaurs*.

- Everybody, what was the title? (Signal.) *The First Dinosaurs.* ⓃⒹ
- That title tells you that some dinosaurs came before other dinosaurs. This book tells about the **first** ones.

The old man read the first page out loud.

Dinosaurs lived during the Mesozoic era. The Mesozoic era started about 235 million years ago.

- Everybody, which era did dinosaurs live in? (Signal.) *Mesozoic.* ⓃⒹ
- When did the Mesozoic start? (Signal.) *About 235 million years ago.* ⓃⒹ

The Mesozoic era was the time of the dinosaurs. Some dinosaurs were no bigger than a rabbit. Some ate plants. Some ate other animals. Let's go back to the beginning of the Mesozoic and look at dinosaurs that lived before Triceratops and Tyrannosaurus.

- Everybody, were Triceratops and Tyrannosaurus the first dinosaurs? (Signal.) *No.* ⒹⒸ

The old man read about a jungle with very strange plants, about dragonflies bigger than most birds and about bees as big as your fist.

- Name some things that were in the jungle when the first dinosaurs lived. (Call on a student. Ideas: *Strange plants; huge dragonflies; huge bees.*) ⓃⒹ
- Everybody, look at the picture. Touch a dragonfly in that picture. ✔ ⓋⒶ
- Show me how big that dragonfly was. ✔ ⓋⒶ
- Touch a bee in the picture. ✔ ⓋⒶ
- Show me how big that bee was. ✔ ⓋⒶ
- How do you think it would feel to be stung by that bee? (Call on a student. Idea: *It would hurt a lot.*) ⓂⒿ

The jungle was hot and wet and the trees and the grass were strange.

The old man read about one of the first great dinosaurs, Plateosaurus. These dinosaurs were over 20 feet long. The book had a picture of Plateosaurus.

- Everybody, about how long was Plateosaurus? (Signal.) *20 feet long.* ⓃⒹ

Angela and Al took turns reading parts of other books. Every book that they started to read seemed very interesting. But the old man did not let them read very much from each book. He kept telling them, "You can find this book in your library. If you want to read it, it is there. It is waiting to take you on a trip."

After Angela, Al and the old man had looked at books on dinosaurs, Angela said that she wanted to learn more about the planets in the solar system. She said, "I didn't get to go on those trips."

- Why didn't she get to go on the trips to some of the other planets? (Call on a student. Idea: *Because she hadn't started going on trips yet when Al went to the other planets.*) APK
- Everybody, did she get to go anywhere in the universe? (Signal.) *Yes.* APK
- Where did she go? (Call on a student. Idea: *To the sun and to the Milky Way.*) APK

The old man went back to a computer. A few minutes later Angela and Al were looking at books about the solar system. Some books told about spaceships and trips to the moon. Others told about Jupiter and Saturn.

After going through the stack of books on the solar system, the old man stood up and said, "How did you like this trip? Did you like it as much as the trip to the bottom of the ocean?"

"No, I didn't," Al said. Angela agreed.

The old man said, "Did you like this trip as much as the trip to the poles or the human body?"

"No, I didn't," Angela said.

The old man smiled. Then he said, "Taking a trip from a book ⭐ is not as easy as taking a real trip. You have to use your imagination to take a trip from a book. You have to think harder about what you are reading."

- Why is it harder to go on a trip from a book than it is to go on a real trip? (Call on a student. Ideas: *Because you have to use your imagination; you have to think hard about what you're reading.*) ND
- Do you think a trip from a book could be almost as interesting as a real trip? (Call on a student. Idea: *Yes.*) MJ

The old man continued, "You can't go on real trips anymore. But you can still go back to the bottom of the sea with a book. And if you want to visit the other planets, take a trip from a book."

The old man stopped talking. The library was quiet. Al was thinking, "Maybe the trip from a book would not be as good as a real trip, but it would still be a good trip. It would be fun to take a trip to Africa and learn about the baboons. It would be fun to go back to the Mesozoic and read about Plateosaurus."

Slowly the walls of the library started to melt and everything started to become darker and darker. Al realized that he was back in the store.

The old man said, "I would like to shake your hands. I enjoyed the trips that we took together."

As the old man shook Al's hand, Al felt very sad. He wanted to say something to the old man, but he couldn't seem to talk. So he just nodded his head.

- Why couldn't he talk? (Call on a student. Idea: *Because he was so sad.*) DI
- Read the rest of the story to yourself and be ready to answer some questions. Raise your hand when you're finished.

"Angela," the old man said. "I want to shake your hand, too. You're an intelligent girl and a good thinker. Just keep on learning and thinking."

As the old man shook Angela's hand, Angela nodded. Then slowly the old man stepped back into the darkness, and the inside of the store was very quiet. The old man had gone.

"Can we come back to see you sometime?" Angela asked. Her voice was high and it trembled as she talked.

There was no answer.

Angela said, "You don't have to take us on a trip. I just thought we could come back and talk to you sometime." There was no answer.

Angela and Al stood in the dark store for a long moment. Finally Al said, "He's gone."

Angela and Al picked up their packages and went outside. The bell on the door did not go ding, ding when they went outside. Angela said, "Look," and pointed to the window of the store. The sign was gone. The window was empty. Al felt very sad.

They walked past the store where they had bought the presents. "Look," Angela said. The store was empty and dark.

Angela said, "I don't understand this. Sometimes I think that I'm just having a dream. The store had lots of things in it, and now it is empty."

As Angela and Al walked home, they didn't talk very much.

It was starting to snow again. Most of the sidewalks were shoveled, but a thin layer of new snow was forming on them.

Al didn't say anything at dinner. After dinner he wrapped the presents that he had bought at the strange store. Imagine buying a beautiful toaster for only a dollar. It didn't make sense. Nothing made sense to Al on the night before Christmas.

- (After all students have raised their hand:) Name some things that were different when Al and Angela went outside. (Call on a student. Ideas: *The bell didn't ring; the sign in the window was gone; the gift store was empty.*) (ND)
- How much did Al say at dinnertime? (Call on a student. Idea: *Nothing.*) (ND)
- Why didn't he talk? (Call on a student. Ideas: *Because he was confused; sad.*) (DI)

- What did he do after dinner? (Call on a student. Idea: *Wrapped Christmas presents.*) (ND)
- What was special about the next day? (Call on a student. Idea: *The next day was Christmas.*) (DC)

EXERCISE 3

Paired Practice

You're going to read aloud to your partner. The **B** members will read first. Then the **A** members will read from the star to the end of the story.
(Observe students and give feedback.)

End-of-Lesson Activities

INDEPENDENT WORK

Now finish your independent work for lesson 138. Raise your hand when you're finished. (Observe students and give feedback.)

WORKCHECK

a. (Direct students to take out their marking pencils.)
- We're going to check your workbook and textbook items. Remember, if you got an item wrong, make an **X** next to the item.
b. (For each item: Read the item. Call on a student to answer it. If the answer is wrong, say the correct answer. Refer to the Answer Key for the correct answers.)
c. Now use your marking pencil to fix up any items you got wrong. Remember, all mistakes must be fixed up before you hand in your work.

SPELLING

(Present Spelling lesson 138 after completing Reading lesson 138. See *Spelling Presentation Book.*)

Reading Words

a. **Find lesson 139 in your textbook.** ✔
- Touch word 1. ✔
- (Teacher reference:)

1. **terrific**	5. **bookstore**
2. **pancakes**	6. **Anderson**
3. **cookbook**	7. **anytime**
4. **merry**	

b. Word 1. What word? (Signal.) *Terrific.*
- Spell **terrific.** Get ready. (Tap for each letter.) *T-E-R-R-I-F-I-C.*
- **Terrific** is another word for **wonderful.** Everybody, what's another way of saying **They had a wonderful time?** (Signal.) *They had a terrific time.*
c. Word 2. What word? (Signal.) *Pancakes.*
- Spell **pancakes.** Get ready. (Tap for each letter.) *P-A-N-C-A-K-E-S.*
d. Word 3. What word? (Signal.) *Cookbook.*
- Spell **cookbook.** Get ready. (Tap for each letter.) *C-O-O-K-B-O-O-K.*
e. Word 4. What word? (Signal.) *Merry.*
- Spell **merry.** Get ready. (Tap for each letter.) *M-E-R-R-Y.*
- Yes, they felt very **merry.**
f. Word 5. What word? (Signal.) *Bookstore.*
- (Repeat for words 6 and 7.)
g. Let's read those words again.
- Word 1. What word? (Signal.) *Terrific.*
- (Repeat for words 2–7.)
h. (Repeat step g until firm.)

Story Reading

a. **Find part B in your textbook.** ✔
- The error limit for group reading is 14 errors. Read carefully.
b. Everybody, touch the title. ✔
- (Call on a student to read the title.) *[Go Anywhere—See Anything With Books.]*
- Everybody, what's the title? (Signal.) *Go Anywhere—See Anything With Books.* ⓃⒹ
- (Call on individual students to read the story, each student reading two or three sentences at a time. Ask the specified questions as the students read.)

- • (**Correct errors:** Tell the word. Direct the student to reread the sentence.)
- • (If the group makes more than 14 errors, direct the students to reread the story.)

Go Anywhere—See Anything With Books

Al got up early on Christmas morning. He gave the presents to his mother and Angela.

- Everybody, what did he give to his mother? (Signal.) *A toaster.* ⒶⓅⓀ
- What did he give to Angela? (Signal.) *A wallet.* ⒶⓅⓀ

His mother was so happy with the toaster that she started to cry. And Angela really liked the wallet.

Al's mother gave Al a book. She said, "We don't have much money this year, so I couldn't get you anything expensive. I noticed that you've been reading a lot of books lately, so I got you a book. I hope you like it." It was one of the books that Al had seen on his trip to the library. It was all about the animals in Africa.

"Thanks, Mama," Al said. "It's a terrific present."

After everybody had opened the presents, Al's mother fixed a big breakfast of pancakes. Al ate so many that he could hardly stand up. "I'm too full," he said.

"Me too," Angela said.

Their mother said, "I think we should go for a walk and work off our breakfast."

- What does she mean, work off their breakfast? (Call on a student. Idea: *Get some exercise to help digest their food.*) ⒹⒸ

So everybody got dressed and went outside. It was a beautiful day. All the buildings were covered with fresh snow. They seemed to shine in the bright sunlight. Everything looked clean and white.

"Let's go this way," Al said, and pointed in the direction of the old man's store.

Soon they were walking down the street next to Anywhere Street. Angela said, "Why don't we walk down Anywhere Street?"

Al's mother said, "Anywhere Street? There's no street called Anywhere Street around here."

"Sure there is," Angela said. "It's right up there at the corner."

The street sign on the corner was covered with snow. All Al could read was the first letter in the name. It was an A.

Al said, "See—that's an A. It's the first letter in Anywhere."

- Everybody, touch the street sign in the picture. ✔ (VA)
- How would you get the snow off that sign to show what the whole name is? (Call on a student. Ideas: *Throw a snowball at it; hit it with a long stick; etc.*) (DI)

🌸 Angela made a snowball and threw it at the sign. When the snowball hit the sign, the snow dropped off. Now they could read the name on the sign. But the sign did not say ANYWHERE STREET. It said ANDERSON STREET.

"I told you," their mother said. "There's no Anywhere Street in this city."

Al shook his head. He didn't know what to say.

Slowly, Al and the others started to walk down Anderson Street. The street looked a little different. Most of the stores on the street were closed. But the old man's store was open. And so was the store next to it.

Angela and Al stopped in front of the store next to the old man's store. It had many different items 🌸 in the window and on the shelves. And there was a big sign in the window: GIFT SHOP—GIFTS FOR EVERYONE.

Al said, "Wow, that's strange! The other day . . ." Al didn't finish the sentence.

- Why? (Call on a student. Idea: *Because his mother wouldn't believe him.*) (DI)

Angela shrugged and smiled at Al. Then she said, "Look at the old man's store."

Al ran over to the window of the old man's store. There were two big signs in the window. One said GO ANYWHERE. SEE ANYTHING—WITH BOOKS. The other sign said BOOKSTORE.

- Everybody, what did the first sign on the old man's store say? (Signal.) *Go Anywhere. See Anything—With Books.* (ND)
- What did the second sign say? (Signal.) *Bookstore.* (ND)
- What kind of store was the old man's store now? (Signal.) *A bookstore.* (DC)

The inside of the store looked very bright. Al could see shelves filled with books. And there was the old man sitting in a chair, reading a book.

Angela said, "Let's go inside and say hello." Before her mother could object, Angela opened the door. ✦ The bell went ding, ding.

- Name something that is the **same** about the store now. (Call on a student. Ideas: *The bell; the old man.*) (ND)
- Name some things that are **different.** (Call on a student. Idea: *It was bright inside and it was filled with shelves of books.*) (ND)

The old man stood up and walked over to Al and the others. "Hello, hello," he said. "Go anywhere, see anything with a book. I have books that will take you to the moon or to the center of the earth. I have books on birds, books on baboons or books on bottles. Where do you want to go? What do you want to see? I have books that will take you anywhere you want to go."

"We're just looking," Al's mother said. "We don't want to buy anything."

The old man laughed. "Young woman," he said, "you are in luck. Every year I give a book to the first people who come in on Christmas Day. You are the first people here. So I will give you free books."

- Read the rest of the story to yourself and be ready to answer some questions. Raise your hand when you're finished.

The old man ran over to one of the shelves and came back with a thick book. He handed the book to Al's mother. "Here is your book, young woman."

Al's mother said, "I don't read very much."

"But you will like this book."

Al's mother looked at the book.

"Oh," she exclaimed. "This is that cookbook I've been wanting for years. Oh, I can't take that. It's much too expensive."

The old man said to her, "I like to give gifts on Christmas, but I don't have a family. So you would make me very happy if you would keep the book."

Al's mother smiled. "Thank you very much," she said.

Then the old man took a great big book from the shelf. He handed the book to Al and Angela. Al read the title, *Go Anywhere. See Anything.*

The old man said, "You will really like that book. It tells all about the wonders of the world. That book will take you to places most people have never seen. It will take you to a molecule and it will take you inside the human brain. It will take you anywhere."

"Wow!" Al said.

"Thanks a lot," Angela said.

The old man talked to Al and the others for a while. Then Al's mother said, "We'd better get going. I have to cook a big Christmas dinner."

When Angela opened the door, the bell went ding, ding. The old man followed them outside. "Have a merry Christmas," he said.

Al said, "This is the best Christmas I ever had." Al felt very happy and very sad at the same time.

The old man said, "And come back and see me sometime. I have a lot of good books. Come in and read them. You don't have to buy them. Come in anytime."

"We will," Angela said.

Then they all started walking back down Anderson Street. They walked past the gift shop to the corner.

When they reached the corner, Angela turned to Al. "Did this really happen? Did we really go on all those trips? Or was it just some kind of dream?"

"I don't know," Al said. "But it sure was great. It was really great."

Later that day Al's mother fixed the best Christmas dinner Al ever had. And after dinner Angela and Al read from the book *Go Anywhere. See Anything.* It was the best book that Al had ever read. And Al had the best Christmas ever.

- (After all students have raised their hand:) Everybody, what was the title of the book the old man gave to Al and Angela? (Signal.) *Go Anywhere. See Anything.* (ND)

- What did the old man tell Al and Angela when they were outside the bookstore? (Call on a student. Ideas: *To have a merry Christmas; to come back and read some of his books.*) (ND)
- How good was that Christmas for Al? (Call on a student. Ideas: *Very good; best ever.*) (ND)
- Everybody, is the story about Al and Angela fiction or non-fiction? (Signal.) *Fiction.* (R/F)
- Did it tell things that are true even though the story is fiction? (Signal.) *Yes.* (DC)
- Is it really possible for you to go inside the human body or go to Jupiter? (Signal.) *No.* (DC)
- Did the story tell you some way to visit these places? (Signal.) *Yes.* (DC)
- How? (Call on a student. Idea: *By reading books.*) (ND)

<hr>

EXERCISE 3

Paired Practice

You're going to read aloud to your partner. The **A** members will read first. Then the **B** members will read from the star to the end of the story.
(Observe students and give feedback.)

End-of-Lesson Activities

INDEPENDENT WORK

Now finish your independent work for lesson 138. Raise your hand when you're finished. (Observe students and give feedback.)

WORKCHECK

a. (Direct students to take out their marking pencils.)
- We're going to check your workbook and textbook items. Remember, if you got an item wrong, make an **X** next to the item.
b. (For each item: Read the item. Call on a student to answer it. If the answer is wrong, say the correct answer. Refer to the Answer Key for the correct answers.)
c. Now use your marking pencil to fix up any items you got wrong. Remember, all mistakes must be fixed up before you hand in your work.

Note: You will need to reproduce blackline masters for the Fact Game in lesson 140 (Appendix G in the *Teacher's Guide.*)
You will also need materials for a special project that occurs after lesson 140. See page 336 for details.

SPELLING

(Present Spelling lesson 139 after completing Reading lesson 139. See *Spelling Presentation Book.*)

Materials for Lesson 140
Fact Game
For each team (4 or 5 students):
- pair of number cubes (or dice)
- copy of Fact Game 140
  (Reproducible blackline masters are
  in Appendix G of the *Teacher's Guide.*)

For each student:
- their copy of the scorecard sheet (at
  end of workbook B)

For each monitor:
- a pencil
- Fact Game 90 answer key (at end
  of textbook B)

Fluency: Rate/Accuracy
Each student needs their thermometer chart.

EXERCISE 1

Fact Game

a. (Divide students into groups of four or five. Assign monitors.)

b. You'll play the game for 10 minutes. (Circulate as students play the game. Comment on groups that are playing well.)

c. (At the end of 10 minutes, have all students who earned more than 10 points stand up.)

- (Tell the monitor of each game that ran smoothly:) Your group did a good job.

EXERCISE 2

Fluency: Rate/Accuracy

a. Today is a test day and a reading checkout day. While you're writing answers, I'm going to call on you one at a time to read part of the story we read in lesson 139.

- Remember, you pass the checkout by reading the passage in less than a minute without making more than 2 mistakes. And when you pass the checkout, you color the space for lesson 140 on your thermometer chart.

b. (Call on individual students to read the portion of story 139 marked with ✿.)

- (Time the student. Note words that are missed and number of words read.)

- (Teacher reference:)

✿ Angela made a snowball and threw it at the sign. When the snowball hit the sign, the snow dropped off. Now they could read the name on the sign. But the sign did not say ANYWHERE STREET. It said ANDERSON STREET.

"I told you," their mother said. "There's no Anywhere [50] Street in this city."

Al shook his head. He didn't know what to say.

Slowly, Al and the others started to walk down Anderson Street. [75] The street looked a little different. Most of the stores on the street were closed. But the old man's store was open. And so was [100] the store next to it.

Al and Angela stopped in front of the store next to the old man's store. It had many different items ✿ [125] in the window and on the shelves.

- (If the student reads the passage in one minute or less and makes no more than 2 errors, direct the student to color in the space for lesson 140 on the thermometer chart.)

- (If the student makes any mistakes, point to each word that was misread and identify it.)

- (If the student does not meet the rate-error criterion for the passage, direct the student to practice reading the story with the assigned partner.)

EXERCISE 3

Test

a. **Find page 358 in your textbook.** ✔

- This is a test. You'll work items you've done before.

b. Work carefully. Raise your hand when you've completed all the items. (Observe students but do not give feedback on errors.)

EXERCISE 4

Marking The Test

a. (Check students' work. Refer to the Answer Key for the correct answers.)

b. (Record all test 14 results on the Test Summary Sheet and the Group Summary Sheet. Reproducible Summary Sheets are at the back of the *Teacher's Guide.*)

EXERCISE 5

Test Remedies

(Provide any necessary remedies for test 14. Test remedies are discussed in the *Teacher's Guide.*)

Test 14 Firming Table

Test Item	Introduced in lesson	Test Item	Introduced in lesson	Test Item	Introduced in lesson
1	132	13	133	25	137
2	132	14	133	26	137
3	133	15	133	27	138
4	133	16	133	28	138
5	133	17	133	29	138
6	133	18	135	30	138
7	133	19	135	31	152
8	133	20	135	32	147
9	133	21	135	33	152
10	133	22	135	34	147
11	133	23	135	35	152
12	133	24	135		

SPELLING

(Present Spelling lesson 140 after completing Reading lesson 140. See *Spelling Presentation Book.*)

Special Project

Note: After completing lesson 140, do this project with the students. You may do this project during another part of the school day.

Materials: Library books, pencils, and lined paper

a. Everybody, find page 361 in your textbook. ✔
- (Call on individual students to read several sentences.)
- (Teacher reference:)

Special Project

Here are the last places that Al and Angela visited:

- ◆ The human body
- ◆ The poles
- ◆ The Milky Way

Pick one of those three places. Go to the library and find a book that tells about the place and that has good pictures that you could show to the class.

Find a part of the book that is very interesting. Show the class one or two pictures from that part. Tell at least three facts that the book gave about each picture you show.

b. We'll form groups so that we can work together on this project. I'll read the names of the places. Raise your hand if you want to be in the group that finds out more about that place. You can be in only one group.
- The human body. (Write down the names of the students who raise their hand.)
- The poles. (Write down the names of the students who raise their hand.)
- The Milky Way. (Write down the names of the students who raise their hand.)
- (If the groups are greatly unequal in size, ask if any students from the largest group would go into the smallest group.)

c. (Arrange a time when the groups can go to the library and find books.)

d. (Arrange a time when the groups can present, either to your class, to another class, or possibly first to your class and then to another class. Praise groups that show interesting things and give informative presentations.)
- (Each group can show one or two pictures. For each picture shown to the class, the group must tell at least three facts about the picture. Every student in the group must present at least one fact.)

Grade 3 Reading Curriculum Map

	1	2	3	4	5	6
Vocabulary						
Model Vocabulary Sentence			1			
Review				1	1, 6	1
Word Attack/Reading Words						
Decoding and Word Analysis						
Modeled Words	1.1			2.1	2.1	2.1
Words with Endings: –ed, –ly, –er, –y, –ing, –s	1.2	1.1				2.2
Compound Words						
Multi-syllable Words					2.2	
Proper Nouns						
Words with Underlined Parts			2.2		2.2	
Names of the Months						
Mixed Words/Review	1.3, 1.4	1.2	2.1	2.2	2.3	2.3
Informal Assessment	IT	IT	IT	IT	IT	IT2.1
Selection Vocabulary	1.1, 1.4	1.1	2.1, 2.2	2.1	2.1	2.1–2.3
Fluency Read wordlists accurately, fluently	1.1–1.4	1.1, 1.2	2.1, 2.2	2.1, 2.2	2.1–2.3	
Comprehension and Background						
Read Decodable Text	2	2	3	3	3	3
Comprehension						
Recall Facts/Rules	2, 3	2, 3	3, 4	3, 6	3, 6	3, 6
Study Skills						
Interpret Chart/Graph/Visual Aid	2	2, 3	3, 4	3, 6	3	3, 6
Compare/Contrast						
Informal Assessment						
Ongoing Comprehension Check	2, IT	2, IT	3, IT	3, IT	3, IT	3, IT
Story Reading						
Read/Reread Decodable Text	4	4	5	4	4	4
Teacher models fluency/expression		6	4	7		
Comprehension						
Predict/Confirm Prediction	4, 6, IW	4			4, IW	4
Recall Facts/Rules	4, 6, IW	4, 6, IW	5, 7, IW	6	4, 6, IW	6, IW
Note Details	4, 6	4, 6, IW	5, 7, IW	4, 6	4, 6, IW	4, 6, IW
Visualize						
Make Connections	4	4				
Draw Inferences	4			4	4	
Draw Conclusions	4	4	5	4, 6	4	4, 6
Activate Prior Knowledge						6, IW
Determine Character Emotion, Motivation				4		
Compare/Contrast						
Make Judgments				6		
Understanding Dialogue						
Sequencing						
Using Context to Confirm Meaning	6		7			
Study Skills						
Interpret Chart/Graph/Visual Aid				6	6	
Expanded Activity						6, IW
Informal Assessment						
Ongoing Comprehension Check	4, IW	4, IW	5, IW	4, IW	4, IW	4, IW
Ongoing Decoding Accuracy	4, IT	4, IT	5, IT	4, 6, IT	4, 6, IT	4, 5, IT
Poem						
Paired Practice for Fluency						
Ongoing practice to build fluency	5	5	6	5	5	5
Independent Work / Workcheck						
Ongoing Informal Assessment	Workcheck	Workcheck	Workcheck	Workcheck	Workcheck	Workcheck
Special Project						
Fact Game						
Formal Assessment						
Individual Fluency Checkout (name?)						
Mastery Test						
Spelling						
Patterns	1.1	2.1	3.1, 3.2	4.1, 4.2		
Homonyms	1.2	2.2				6.2
Sentence	1.3	2.3	3.3	4.3		6.3
Test					5	
Word Introduction						6.1
Review						
Phonemic Segmentation						

7	8	9	10	11	12	13	14	15
					1			
						1	1, 6	1, 5
		1.1		1.1	2.1	2.1		2.1
1.1				1.4		2.3		2.2, 2.4
				1.2		2.2		
	1.1				2.2			
		1.3						
1.1		1.2			2.2	2.2	2.1	
				1.3				
1.2	1.2			1.5	2.3, 2.4	2.4, 2.5	2.2, 2.3	2.3
IT		IT		IT	IT	IT	IT	
		1.1		1.1	2.1, 2.2	2.1, 2.2, 2.3, 2.5	2.1, 2.2	2.1, 2.2, 2.4
1.1, 1.2	1.1, 1.2	1.1–1.3		1.1–1.5	2.1–2.4	2.1–2.5	2.1–2.3	2.1–2.4
2	2	2		2	3	3	3	3
2, 5	2, 5	2, 5		2, 5	3, 6	6	3, 6	3, IW
2, 5	2, 5	2, 5		2	3	3	3	3, IW
	5					3		
2, IT	2, IT	2, IT		2, IT	3, IT	3, IT	3, IT	3, IT
3	3	3		3	4	4	4	4
3	3	3, 5						4
3, IW	3, IW	5, IW		3, 5, IW	3, 4, IW	4, 6, IW	4, 6, IW	4, 6, IW
3, 5, IW	3, 5	3, 5, IW		3, 5	4, 6, IW	4, 6	4, IW	4, 6
							4	4
5	3			3				
3					4		4	4
3, IW	3, IW	3		3, IW	3, 4, 6, IW	4, 6	4, 6, IW	4, IW
3, IW	3, IW	IW		3, 5, IW		IW	4, IW	4, IW
3		5, IW				4		4
5, IW	5, IW	3, IW		3	IW	4, 6		4
3					4	6	4	
5	3, IW			3				
								5
								5
3, 5, IW	5, IW	3, 5, IW		3, 5 IW	IW	4, 6, IW	IW	IW
3, IW	3, IW	3, IW		3, IW	4, IW	4, IW	4, IW	4, IW
3, 5, IT	3, 5, IT	3, 5, IT		3, 5, IT	4, 6, IT	4, IT	4, IT	4, 5, IT
4	4	4		4	5	5	5	
Workcheck	Workcheck	Workcheck		Workcheck	Workcheck	Workcheck	Workcheck, Activity	Workcheck
			after Lesson 10		after Lesson 12			
			1					
			2					5
			3					
7.1	8.2	9.1, 9.2		11.1	12.1	13.1, 13.2	14.1	
7.2								
7.3	8.3			11.2				
			10					15
	8.1							
		9.3		11.3	12.3	13.3	14.3	
					12.2		14.2	

	16	17	18	19	20	21
Vocabulary						
Model Vocabulary Sentence	1					1
Review		1	1, 6	1, 5		
Word Attack/Reading Words						
Decoding and Word Analysis						
Modeled Words	2.1	2.1				2.1
Words with Endings: –ed, –ly, –er, –y, –ing, –s	2.2, 2.3					2.2
Compound Words						
Multi-syllable Words						
Proper Nouns						
Words with Underlined Parts				2.1		
Mixed Words/Review	2.4	2.2	2.1	2.2		2.3
Informal Assessment	IT	IT		IT		IT
Selection Vocabulary	2.1, 2.2	2.1		2.1		2.1–2.3
Fluency Read wordlists accurately, fluently	2.1–2.4	2.1, 2.2	2.1	2.1, 2.2		2.1–2.3
Comprehension and Background						
Read Decodable Text	3		3			3
Comprehension						
Recall Facts/Rules	3, IW		3, IW			3, IW
Make Inferences						
Study Skills						
Interpret Chart/Graph/Visual Aid			3, IW			3, IW
Compare/Contrast	IW					
Informal Assessment						
Ongoing Comprehension Check	3, IT		3, IT			3, IT
Story Reading						
Read/Reread Decodable Text	4	3	4	3		4
Teacher models fluency/expression		3	4	3		
Comprehension						
Predict/Confirm Prediction		3		3		4
Recall Facts/Rules	4, IW	3, IW	4, IW	IW		4, IW
Note Details	4, 6	3, IW	4, IW	3, IW		4, IW
Visualize		3	4	3		
Make Connections		3	4			
Draw Inferences	4	3	4	3		4
Draw Conclusions	4, IW	3, IW	3, IW	3, IW		4, IW
Activate Prior Knowledge	IW	3, IW	4, IW	3, IW		4, IW
Identify Cause/Effect						IW
Determine Character Emotion, Motivation	4		4	3		4
Compare/Contrast	IW	IW	4	3		
Make Judgments			4			
Understanding Dialogue						
Sequencing	6	5	IW	3, IW		
Story Structure						
Using Context to Confirm Meaning			4	3		
Study Skills						
Interpret Chart/Graph/Visual Aid	4, IW	3, IW	4, IW	3, IW		4, IW
Informal Assessment						
Ongoing Comprehension Check	4, IW	3, IW	4, IW	3, IW		4, IW
Ongoing Decoding Accuracy	4, IT	3, IT	4, IT	3, IT		4, IT
Poem						
Paired Practice for Fluency						
Ongoing practice to build fluency	5	4	5	4		5
Independent Work / Workcheck						
Ongoing Informal Assessment	Workcheck	Workcheck	Workcheck	Workcheck		Workcheck, Activity
Special Project						
Fact Game					1	
Formal Assessment						
Individual Fluency Checkout					2	
Mastery Test					3	
Out-of-Program Mastery Test						
Spelling						
Patterns	16.1	17.1	18.2	19.2		21.1
Homonyms		17.2				21.2
Sentence	16.2					
Test					20	
Word Introduction						
Review	16.3	17.3	18.3	19.3		21.3
Phonemic Segmentation						
Affixes			18.1	19.1		

   Key: (for Teachers)   Ex 2.1 = Exercise 2, Column 1   IT = Individual Turns   IW = Independent Work

22	23	24	25	26	27	28	29	30
			1				1	
1	1	1		1	1	1		
2.1	2.1		2.1	2.1			2.1	
2.2			2.4	2.4				
			2.5			2.1		
		2.1		2.2, 2.3	2.1	2.2		
		2.2						
2.3	1.1, 2.3	2.3	2.2, 2.3		2.2	2.3	2.2–2.4	
IT	IT	IT	IT	IT	IT	IT	IT	
2.1	2.1, 2.2	2.2	2.1, 2.3, IW	2.1	2.2, IW	2.2, 2.3, IW	2.1, 2.2, 2.3	
2.1–2.3	2.1–2.3	2.1–2.3	2.1–2.5	2.1–2.4	2.1, 2.2	2.1–2.3	2.1–2.4	
3		3			3			
					3, IW			
3, IW		3, IW						
					3			
3, IW		3, IW						
3, IT		3, IT			3, IT			
4	3	4	3	3	4	3	3	
4								
4	4		3	3		3	3	
4, IW	3, IW	4, IW	IW	3, IW	4, IW	3, IW	IW	
4, IW	3, IW	4, IW	3, IW	3, IW	4, IW	3, IW	3, IW	
		4	3		4	3		
4			3	3	4	3	3	
4, IW	3, IW	4	3	3, IW	4	3, IW	3, IW	
4, IW	3, IW	IW	3, IW	3, IW	IW	IW	IW	
	IW		IW		IW		IW	
4		4		3			3, IW	
4	3	IW				3		
		4	3					
		IW	3, IW	IW		IW	IW	
4		4				3		
4		4		3			3	
4, IW	3, IW	4, IW	3, IW	3, IW	4, IW	IW	3, IW	
4, IW	3, IT	4, IW	3, IW	3, IW	4, IW	3, IW	3, IW	
4, IT	3, IT	4, IT	3, IT	3, IT	4, IT	3, IT	3, IT	
5	4	5		4	5	4	4	
Workcheck, Activity	Workcheck, Activity	Workcheck, Activity	Workcheck, Activity	Workcheck	Workcheck	Workcheck	Workcheck	
after Lesson 22								
								1
			4					
								2
								3
22.1, 22.2	23.1, 23.2	24.1, 24.2		26.1, 26.2	27.1, 27.2	28.1	29.1, 29.2	
			25					30
22.3	23.3	24.3		26.3	27.3	28.3	29.3	
						28.2		

	31	32	33	34	35	36
Vocabulary						
Model Vocabulary Sentence			2			1
Review	1	1	1	1	1	2
Word Attack/Reading Words						
Decoding and Word Analysis						
Modeled Words		2.1		2.1	2.1	3.1
Words with Endings: –ed, –ly, –er, –y, –ing, –s	2.2				2.3	
Compound Words					2.2	
Multi-syllable Words	2.1		3.1	2.2		3.2
Words with Underlined Parts						
Mixed Words/Review	2.3	2.2–2.4	3.2, 3.3	2.3	2.4	3.3, 3.4
Informal Assessment	IT	IT	IT	IT	IT	IT
Selection Vocabulary		2.1, 2.2	3.1–3.3	2.1–2.3	2.1, 2.3	3.1, 3.2
Fluency Read wordlists accurately, fluently	2.1–2.3	2.1–2.4	3.1–3.3	2.1–2.3	2.1–2.4	3.1–3.4
Comprehension and Background						
Read Decodable Text			4	3		4
Comprehension						
Recall Facts/Rules			4, IW	3		4, IW
Study Skills						
Interpret Chart/Graph/Visual Aid			4, IW			
Informal Assessment						
Ongoing Comprehension Check			4, IT	3, IT		4, it
Story Reading						
Read/Reread Decodable Text	3	3	5	4	3	5
Teacher models fluency/expression	3		5	3, 4		
Comprehension						
Predict/Confirm Prediction	3	3			3	5
Recall Facts/Rules	IW	IW	5, IW	4, IW	IW	5, IW
Note Details	3, IW	3, IW	5, IW	4, IW	3, IW	5, IW
Visualize	3		5			5
Make Connections	3					
Draw Inferences		3	5	4	3	5
Draw Conclusions	3, IW	3, IW	5, IW	4, IW	3, IW	5, IW
Activate Prior Knowledge	3, IW	IW	5, IW	4, IW	3, IW	5, IW
Identify Cause/Effect	IW			IW	IW	
Determine Character Emotion, Motivation	3	3	5		3	
Compare/Contrast						
Make Judgments	3	3			3	
Understanding Dialogue				4	3	5
Sequencing	IW		IW		IW	
Story Structure				4	3	
Using Context to Confirm Meaning		3	5			5
Study Skills						
Interpret Chart/Graph/Visual Aid	3, IW	3, IW	5, IW	IW	3, IW	5, IW
Study Item						
Informal Assessment						
Ongoing Comprehension Check	3, IW	3, IW	5, IW	4, IW	3, IW	5, IW
Ongoing Decoding Accuracy	3, IT	3, IT	5, IT	4, IT	3, 4, IT	5, IT
Poem						
Paired Practice for Fluency						
Ongoing practice to build fluency	4	4	6	5		6
Independent Work / Workcheck						
Ongoing Informal Assessment	Workcheck	Workcheck	Workcheck, Activity	Workcheck	Workcheck	Workcheck, Activity
Special Project					after Lesson 35	
Fact Game						
Formal Assessment						
Individual Fluency Checkout					4	
Mastery Test						
Spelling						
Patterns	31.1, 31.2	32.1, 32.2	33.1, 33.2	34.1		
Sentence						36.1
Test					35	
Review	31.3	32.3	33.3	34.3		36.3
Reading Vocabulary						
Affixes						
Spelling Rules				34.2		36.2

37	38	39	40	41	42	43	44	45
		1				1		
1	1	2		1	1, IW	2, IW	1, IW	1, IW
	2.1	3.1		2.1			2.3	2.1
2.3				2.3, 2.4	2.3		2.2	
2.2				2.2			2.1	
2.1		3.2			2.1, 2.2	3.1		
					2.1, 2.2	3.1	2.1	
2.4	2.2	3.3		2.5	2.4	3.2, 3.3		2.2, 2.3
IT	IT	IT		IT	IT	IT	IT	IT
2.1, 2.3	2.1	3.1, 3.2		2.1, 2.4	2.1, 2.2, 2.3	3.1	2.3	2.1
2.1–2.4	2.1, 2.2	2.1–2.3		2.1–2.5	2.1–2.4	3.1–3.3	2.1–2.3	2.1–2.3
3	3	4		3	3	4	3	3
					3	4	3	
				3		4		3
3, IW	3, IW	4, IW		3, IW	3, IW	4	IW	3, IW
3, IW	3, IW	4, IW		3, IW	3, IW	4, IW	3, IW	3, IW
	3							3
3				3	3	4	3	
3		4		3	3	4	3	
3, IW	3, IW	4, IW		3, IW	3, IW	4, IW	3, IW	3, IW
3, IW	IW	IW		IW	3, IW	4, IW	3, IW	3, IW
IW	IW	IW		IW	3	4	IW	3, IW
		4			3	4		3
					3		3, IW	
3	3	4		3		4	3	
					3	4		3
3	IW	IW		IW		4, IW	3, IW	IW
	3	4		3				
IW	IW	IW		IW	3, IW	4, IW	3, IW	3, IW
5, IW	5, IW						5, IW	
3, IW	3, IW	4, IT		3, IW	3, IW	4, IW	3, IW	3, IW
				3, IT	3, IT	4, IT	3, IT	3, IT
4	4	5		4	4	5	4	
Workcheck	Workcheck	Workcheck		Workcheck, Activity	Workcheck	Workcheck	Workcheck	Workcheck, Activity
			1					
			2					4
			3					
37.1	38.1, 38.2	39.1		41.1	42.1	43.1		
			40					45
37.3	38.3	39.3			42.3	43.3	44.3	
				41.3				
		39.2		41.2	42.2	43.2	44.1, 44.2	
37.2								

	46	47	48	49	50	51
Vocabulary						
Model Vocabulary Sentence	1			1		
Review	2, IW	1, IW	1, IW	2, IW		1, IW
Word Attack/Reading Words						
Decoding and Word Analysis						
Modeled Words	3.1	2.3	2.1			2.1
Words with Endings: –ed, –ly, –er, –y, –ing, –s	3.3	2.2		3.2		2.3
Compound Words		2.1				
Multi-syllable Words	3.2			3.1		2.2
Words with Underlined Parts		2.1		3.1		2.2
Planet Names						
Numbers						
Mixed Words/Review	3.4		2.2	3.3, 3.4		2.4
Informal Assessment	IT	IT	IT	IT		IT
Selection Vocabulary	3.1	2.3	2.1	3.2		2.1
Fluency Read wordlists accurately, fluently	3.1–3.4	2.1–2.3	2.1, 2.2	3.1–3.4		2.1–2.4
Comprehension and Background						
Read Decodable Text						
Comprehension						
Recall Facts/Rules						
Make Inferences						
Study Skills						
Interpret Chart/Graph/Visual Aid						
Compare/Contrast						
Globe						
Fact Review						
Informal Assessment						
Ongoing Comprehension Check						
Story Reading						
Read/Reread Decodable Text	4	3	3	4		3
Teacher models fluency/expression	4	3		4		
Comprehension						
Predict/Confirm Prediction	4			4		3
Recall Facts/Rules	4, IW	IW	3, IW	4, IW		IW
Note Details	4, IW	3, IW	3, IW	4, IW		3, IW
Visualize		3		4		
Make Connections	4					
Draw Inferences		3	3, IW	4		3
Draw Conclusions	4, IW	3, IW	3, IW	4, IW		3, IW
Activate Prior Knowledge	4, IW	IW	3, IW	4, IW		
Identify Cause/Effect		IW	IW	IW		
Determine Character Emotion, Motivation			3			
Compare/Contrast			IW	IW		IW
Make Judgments		3		4		3
Understanding Dialogue	4			4		
Reality/Fantasy						
Sequencing		3, IW	3	IW		IW
Story Structure		3				
Using Context to Confirm Meaning	4		3			
Study Skills						
Interpret Chart/Graph/Visual Aid	4, IW	3, IW	3, IW	IW		IW
Study Item						5, IW
Informal Assessment						
Ongoing Comprehension Check	4, IW	3, IW	3, IW	4, IW		3, IW
Ongoing Decoding Accuracy	4, IT	3, IT	3, IT	4, IT		3, IT
Poem						
Paired Practice for Fluency						
Ongoing practice to build fluency	5	4	4	5		4
Independent Work / Workcheck						
Ongoing Informal Assessment	Workcheck	Workcheck	Workcheck	Workcheck		Workcheck
Special Project						
Fact Game					1	
Formal Assessment						
Individual Fluency Checkout					2	
Mastery Test					3	
Spelling						
Patterns						
Sentence	46.1	47.1, 47.2	48.1	49.1		
Test					50	
Word Introduction						
Review	46.3	47.3	48.3	49.3		51.3
Affixes	46.2			49.2		51.2
Word Parts						51.1
Spelling Rules		48.2				

   Key: (for Teachers)   Ex 2.1 = Exercise 2, Column 1   IT = Individual Turns   IW = Independent Work

52	53	54	55	56	57	58	59	60
	1			1			1	
1, IW	2, IW	1, IW	1, IW	2, IW	1, IW	1, IW	2, IW	
2.1	3.1	2.1	2.1		2.2	2.1	3.1	
	3.2		2.3	3.2, 3.3	2.3	2.2	3.2, 3.3	
						2.1		
2.3		2.5	2.2	3.1	2.2			
2.3				3.1	2.2			
	3.3							
		2.2						
2.2, 2.4	3.4	2.3, 2.4		3.4	2.1, 2.4, 2.5	2.3	3.4, 3.5	
IT	IT	IT	IT	IT	IT	IT	IT	
2.1, 2.3	3.1, 3.2	2.3	2.1	IW	2.2	2.1, 2.2	3.1	
2.1–2.4	3.1–3.4	2.1–2.5	2.1–2.3	3.1–3.4	2.1–2.4	2.1–2.4	3.1–3.5	
3	4	3		4		3		
3, IW	4, IW	3, IW		4, IW		3, IW		
						3		
3, IW	4, IW	3, IW		4, IW				
3, IW								
			3	5				
				7				
3, IT	4, IT	3, IT	3, IT	4, IT		3, IT		
4	5	4	4	6	3	4	4	
					3			
					3	4		
IW	5, IW	4, IW	4, IW	IW	3, IW	4, IW	4, IW	
4, IW	5, IW	4, IW	4, IW	6, IW	3, IW	4, IW	4, IW	
					3		4, IW	
4					3			
4			4	6	3	4		
IW	IW	4, IW	4, IW	6, IW	3, IW	4, IW	4, IW	
4, IW	5, IW	4	4, IW	6, IW	3, IW	IW	4, IW	
				IW				
	5							
IW		4, IW	4, IW			IW	IW	
4					3			
	5							
	5		4					
IW			4					
			4					
			4		3		4	
				IW	3, IW	4, IW	4, IW	
4, IW	5, IW	4, IW						
4, IW	5, IW	4, IW	4, IW	6, IW	3, IW	4, IW	4, IW	
4, IT	5, IT	4, IT	4, 5, IT	6, IT	3, IT	4, IT	4, IT	
5	6	5		8	4	5	5	
Workcheck	Workcheck, Activity	Workcheck	Workcheck	Workcheck, Activity	Workcheck	Workcheck	Workcheck	
after Lesson 52								
								1
			5					2
								3
				56.1	57.1	58.1		
			55					60
							59.1	
52.3	53.3	54.3		56.3	57.3	58.3	59.3	
51.2	52.2	53.2	54.2					
51.1	52.1	53.1	54.1	56.2	57.2	58.2	59.2	

	61	62	63	64	65	66
Vocabulary						
Model Vocabulary Sentence				1		
Review	2, IW	1, IW	1, IW		1	1, IW
Word Attack/Reading Words						
Decoding and Word Analysis						
Sounds/Sound Combinations						2.2
Modeled Words	3.1	2.1	2.1	2.2	2.1	2.1
Words with Endings: –ed, –ly, –er, –y, –ing, –s	3.2	2.2		2.3		
Compound Words			2.2			
Multi-syllable Words		2.1		2.1		
Words with Underlined Parts			2.2			
Mixed Words/Review	3.3	2.3, 2.4	2.3			2.3, 2.4
Informal Assessment	IT	IT	IT	IT		IT
Selection Vocabulary	3.1, 3.2	2.1	2.1	2.2	2.1	2.1
Fluency Read wordlists accurately, fluently	3.1–3.3	2.1–2.4	2.1–2.3	2.1–2.3	2.1	2.1–2.4
Comprehension and Background						
Read Decodable Text		3				
Comprehension						
Recall Facts/Rules		3, IW				
Study Skills						
Interpret Chart/Graph/Visual Aid						
Fact Review	1, IT			3, IT		
Informal Assessment						
Ongoing Comprehension Check		3, IT				
Story Reading						
Read/Reread Decodable Text	4	4	3	4	3	3
Teacher models fluency/expression				4	5	3
Comprehension						
Predict/Confirm Prediction					4	
Recall Facts/Rules	4, IW	4, IW	IW	IW	3, IW	
Note Details	4, IW	4, IW	3, IW	4, IW	3, IW	3, IW
Visualize	4	4				
Make Connections		4	3			3
Draw Inferences	4	4	3	4		3
Draw Conclusions	4, IW	IW	3, IW	4, IW	3, IW	3, IW
Activate Prior Knowledge	4, IW	4, IW	IW	4, IW	3, IW	3, IW
Identify Cause/Effect	IW	IW		IW		
Determine Character Emotion, Motivation					3	3
Compare/Contrast	IW	IW	IW	IW	3	IW
Make Judgments		4		4		
Understanding Dialogue						3
Sequencing		IW	IW		IW	
Story Structure						3
Using Context to Confirm Meaning						3
Study Skills						
Interpret Chart/Graph/Visual Aid	4, IW	IW	3, IW	IW	3, IW	
Expanded Activity					5, IW	
Informal Assessment						
Ongoing Comprehension Check	4, IW	4, IW	3, IW	4, IW	3, IW	3, IW
Ongoing Decoding Accuracy	4, IT	4, IT	3, IT	4, IT	3, 4, IT	3, IT
Poem						
Paired Practice for Fluency						
Ongoing practice to build fluency	5	5	4	5		4
Independent Work / Workcheck						
Ongoing Informal Assessment	Workcheck, Activity	Workcheck	Workcheck	Workcheck, Activity	Workcheck	Workcheck
Special Project						after Lesson 66
Formal Assessment						
Individual Fluency Checkout					4	
Mastery Test						
Spelling						
Patterns						66.1
Sentence	61.1	62.1	63.1	64.1		
Test					65	
Review		62.3	63.3	64.3		66.3
Reading Vocabulary	61.3					
Affixes		62.2				66.2
Word Parts	61.2		63.2	64.2		
Vowels and Consonants						
Spelling Rules						

   Key: (for Teachers)   Ex 2.1 = Exercise 2, Column 1   IT = Individual Turns   IW = Independent Work

67	68	69	70
2			
1, IW	1, IW	1, IW	
3.1	2.1		
3.2		2.1	
		2.2	
		2.2	
3.3, 3.4	2.2	2.3	
IT	IT	IT	
3.1	2.1		
3.1–3.4	2.1, 2.2	2.1–2.3	
5		3	
IW		3, IW	
5, IW			
4			
5, IT		3, IT	
6	3	4	
	3	4	
6	3		
6, IW	3, IW	4, IW	
6	3		
6	3	4	
6, IW	3, IW	4, IW	
IW		4, IW	
	3	4	
6	3	4	
IW	IW		
		4	
	3		
		4	
6		4	
6, IW		4	
6, IW	3, IW	4, IW	
6, IT	3, IT	4, IT	
7	4	5	
Workcheck	Workcheck	Workcheck, Activity	
			1
			20
67.1			
			70
66.3	67.3	68.3	69.3
66.2	67.2	68.2	
			69.2
		68.1	69.1

	71	72	73	74	75	76
Vocabulary						
Model Vocabulary Sentence	2			2		
Review	1, IW	1, IW	1, IW	1, IW	1, IW	1, IW
Word Attack/Reading Words						
Decoding and Word Analysis						
Sounds/Sound Combinations						
Modeled Words	3.1	2.1	2.1			2.1
Compound Words						
Multi-syllable Words		2.2				
Words with Underlined Parts		2.2		3.2		
Mixed Words/Review	3.2	2.3	2.2	3.1, 3.3		
Informal Assessment	IT	IT	IT	IT		IT
Selection Vocabulary	3.1	2.1–2.3	2.1, 2.2	3.1	2.1	2.1
Fluency Read wordlists accurately, fluently	3.1, 3.2	2.1–2.3	2.1, 2.2	3.1–2.3	2.1	2.1
Comprehension and Background						
Read Decodable Text	4					
Comprehension						
Recall Facts/Rules	4, IW					
Study Skills						
Interpret Chart/Graph/Visual Aid	4					
Compare/Contrast						
Fact Review		3, IT				
Informal Assessment						
Ongoing Comprehension Check	4, IT					
Story Reading						
Read/Reread Decodable Text	5	4	3	4	3	3
Teacher models fluency/expression				4	3	
Comprehension						
Predict/Confirm Prediction	5	4	3	4	3	
Recall Facts/Rules	IW	IW	3, IW	4, IW	3, IW	
Note Details	5, IW	4, IW	3, IW	4, IW	3, IW	3, IW
Visualize	5	4	3			
Make Connections		4	3	4		3
Draw Inferences	5	4	3	4	3	3, 1W
Draw Conclusions	5, IW	4, IW	3, IW	4, IW	3, IW	3, IW
Activate Prior Knowledge	IW	4, IW	3, IW	IW	3	3, 1W
Identify Cause/Effect			3, IW	IW		
Determine Character Emotion, Motivation		IW			3	3
Compare/Contrast			3			
Make Judgments	5		3	4	3	
Understanding Dialogue	5	4				
Reality/Fantasy	5	IW	3, IW		IW	1W
Sequencing				4		
Story Structure	5	4	3	4	3	
Using Context to Confirm Meaning						
Study Skills						
Interpret Chart/Graph/Visual Aid	5, IW		3, IW	4, IW	3, IW	1W
Study Item				6		
Crossword puzzle					4	5
Informal Assessment						
Ongoing Comprehension Check	5, IW	4, IW	3, IW	4, IW	3, IW	3, 1W
Ongoing Decoding Accuracy	5, IT	4, IT	3, IT	4, IT	3, 5, IT	3, IT
Poem						
Paired Practice for Fluency						
Ongoing practice to build fluency	6	5	4	5		4
Independent Work / Workcheck						
Ongoing Informal Assessment	Workcheck	Workcheck	Workcheck	Workcheck, Activity	Workcheck	Workcheck
Special Project						
Fact Game						
Formal Assessment						
Individual Fluency Checkout					5	
Mastery Test						
Spelling						
Patterns		72.2				
Sentence						
Test					75	
Word Introduction						
Review	71.3	72.3	73.3			76.3
Reading Vocabulary						
Affixes	71.2			74.2		
Word Parts			73.2			76.2
Vowels and Consonants						
Spelling Rules	71.1	72.1	73.1	74.1		76.1

| Key: (for Teachers)   Ex 2.1 = Exercise 2, Column 1   IT = Individual Turns   IW = Independent Work

77	78	79	80	81	82	83	84	85
	1					1		
1, IW		1, IW		1, IW	1, IW		1, IW	1, IW
	2.1							
2.1				2.1	2.1		2.1	2.1
					2.1			
2.1				2.2	2.2	2.1	2.2	
2.2	2.2	2.1			2.3	2.2		2.2, 2.3
IT	IT			IT	IT	IT	IT	IT
2.1, 2.2	2.1, 2.2	2.1		2.1, 2.2	2.1, 2.2		2.1, 2.2	2.1, 2.2
				2.1, 2.2	2.1–2.3	2.1, 2.2	2.1, 2.2	2.1–2.3
		3					3	
		3, IW						
		3					3, 1W	
		3, IW						
							3, 1W	
						3		
		3, IT				3, IT	3, IT	
3	3	4		3	3	4	4	3
				3		4		
3	3				3	4	4	3
3, IW	3, IW	IW		3, IW	3, IW	4, IW	4, IW	3, IW
3, IW	3, IW	4, IW		3, IW	3, IW	4, IW	4, IW	3, IW
	3	4		3	3		4	3
	3			3		4		3
3, IW	3, IW	4, IW		3	3	4	4	3
3, IW	3, IW	4, IW		3, IW	3, IW	4, IW	4, IW	3, IW
3, IW	3	4		3, IW	3, IW	4, IW	IW	
		IW			IW	IW	IW	IW
	3			3, IW	3		4	
					IW	IW	IW	IW
3	3	4			3	4		3
3	3			3				
	3	4, IW			IW		IW	
		4		3				
				3	3			3
	3, IW			IW	3, IW	4, IW	IW	IW
5								
3, IW	3, IW	4, IW		3, IW	3, IW	4, IW	4, IW	3, IW
3, IT	3, IT	4, IT	2	3, IT	3, IT	4, IT	4, IT	3, 4, IT
4	4	5		4	4	5	5	
Workcheck	Workcheck	Workcheck		Workcheck	Workcheck, Activity	Workcheck	Workcheck	Workcheck
							after Lesson 84	
			1					
			2					4
			3					
				81.1	82.1	83.1	84.1	
			80					85
77.2								
77.3	78.3	79.3			82.3	83.3		
				81.3				
	78.2	79.2				83.2	84.2	
				81.2	82.2			
77.1	78.1	79.1						

	86	87	88	89	90	91
Vocabulary						
Model Vocabulary Sentence	2					1
Review	1, IW	1, IW	1, IW	1, IW		
Word Attack/Reading Words						
Decoding and Word Analysis						
Modeled Words	3.1	2.1	2.1	2.1		2.1
Words with Endings: –ed, –ly, –er, –y, –ing, –s		2.2		2.2		2.2
Compound Words						
Multi-syllable Words						
Words with Underlined Parts	3.2			2.3		
Mixed Words/Review	3.3	2.3, 2.4	2.2	2.4		2.3, 2.4
Informal Assessment	IT	IT	IT	IT		IT
Selection Vocabulary	3.1, 3.2	2.1, 2.2	2.1, 2.2	2.1		2.1, 2.4
Fluency Read wordlists accurately, fluently	3.1–3.3	2.1–2.4	2.1, 2.2	2.1–2.4		2.1–2.4
Comprehension and Background						
Read Decodable Text	4			4		3
Comprehension						
Recall Facts/Rules	4, IW			4, IW		3, IW
Study Skills						
Interpret Chart/Graph/Visual Aid	4, IW			4		3, IW
Compare/Contrast	4, IW					
Fact Review		3		3, IT		
Informal Assessment						
Ongoing Comprehension Check	4, IT	3, IT		3, 4, IT		3, IT
Story Reading						
Read/Reread Decodable Text	5	4	3	5		4
Teacher models fluency/expression	5	4				
Comprehension						
Predict/Confirm Prediction	5			5		4
Recall Facts/Rules	5, IW	4, IW	IW	5, IW		4, IW
Note Details	5, IW	4, IW	3, IW	5, IW		4, IW
Visualize		4				
Make Connections			3			
Draw Inferences	5	4	3	5		4
Draw Conclusions	5, IW	4, IW	3	5, IW		
Activate Prior Knowledge	5, IW	IW	3, IW	5, IW		IW
Identify Cause/Effect						
Determine Character Emotion, Motivation	5, IW	4		5		
Compare/Contrast	IW	4	3, IW	5, IW		4
Make Judgments			3			
Understanding Dialogue						
Sequencing			IW	5		
Story Structure				5		
Using Context to Confirm Meaning	5	4	3			
Study Skills						
Interpret Chart/Graph/Visual Aid	IW	4, IW	3, IW	IW		4, IW
Informal Assessment						
Ongoing Comprehension Check	5, IW	4, IW	3, IW	5, IW		4, IW
Ongoing Decoding Accuracy	5, IT	4, IT	3, IT	5, IT	2	4, IT
Poem						
Paired Practice for Fluency						
Ongoing practice to build fluency	6	5	4	6		5
Independent Work / Workcheck						
Ongoing Informal Assessment	Workcheck, Activity	Workcheck, Activity	Workcheck, Activity	Workcheck, Activity		Workcheck
Special Project						
Fact Game					1	
Formal Assessment						
Individual Fluency Checkout					2	
Mastery Test					3	
Spelling						
Sentence			88.1			91.2
Test					90	
Word Introduction		87.1				
Review	86.3	87.3	88.3	89.3		91.3
Phonemic Segmentation						
Affixes			88.2			
Word Parts	86.1	87.2		89.1		
Vowels and Consonants	86.2			89.2		
Spelling Rules						91.1

Key: (for Teachers)   Ex 2.1 = Exercise 2, Column 1   IT = Individual Turns   IW = Independent Work

92	93	94	95	96	97	98	99	100
			1					
1	1, IW	1, IW		1	1, IW	1, IW		
2.1	2.1	2.1	2.1	2.1		2.1	1.1	
2.2		2.2	2.2	2.2		2.2		
		2.3			2.1			
	2.2						1.2	
2.3	2.3	2.4	2.3	2.3, 2.41	2.2, 2.3		1.3	
IT	IT	IT	IT	IT	IT	IT	IT	
2.1	2.1–2.3	2.1	2.1	2.1	2.2, 2.3	2.1, 2.2	1.1–1.3	
2.1–2.3	2.1–2.3	2.1–2.4	2.1–2.4	2.1–2.4	2.1–2.3	2.1, 2.2	1.1–1.3	
3			3	3		3		
3, IW			3, IW	3, IW		3, IW		
3, IW								
3, IT			3, IT	3, IT		3, IT		
4	3	3	4	4	3	4	2	
					3			
4	3	3		4	3		2	
4	3	3, IW	IW	4, IW	3, IW	4, IW	2, IW	
4, IW	3, IW	3, IW	4, IW	4, IW	3, IW	4, IW	2, IW	
		3		4, IW	3	4		
IW	3, IW	3, IW	4, IW	4, IW	3, IW	4, IW	2, IW	
4, IW	IW	3, IW	4, IW	IW	IW	4	2, IW	
						IW		
		IW		4				
		3						
4	3	3		4	3		2	
							2	
		3		4		4		
				4				
4, IW	3, IW	3, IW	4, IW	4, IW	3, IW	4, IW	IW	
4, IW	3, IW	3, IW	4, IW	4, IW	3, IW	4, IW	2, IW	
4, IT	3, IT	3, IT	4, 5, IT	4, IT	3, IT	4, IT	2, IT	2
5	4	4		5	4	5	3	
Workcheck	Workcheck	Workcheck, Activity	Workcheck	WorkchecK	WorkchecK	WorkchecK	WorkchecK	
								after Lesson 100
								1
			5					2
								3
				96.2				
			95					100
92.3	93.3	94.3		96.3	97.3		99.3	
						98.2		
92.2	93.2	94.2			97.2		99.2	
92.1	93.1	94.1		96.1	97.1	98.1	99.1	

	101	102	103	104	105	106
Vocabulary						
Model Vocabulary Sentence		1				1
Review			1	2, IW	1, IW	
Word Attack/Reading Words						
Decoding and Word Analysis						
Modeled Words	1.1	2.1	2.1	3.1	2.1	2.1
Words with Endings: –ed, –ly, –er, –y, –ing, –s	1.2					
Multi-syllable Words		2.2				
Words with Underlined Parts	1.3					
Mixed Words/Review						
Informal Assessment	IT	IT				
Selection Vocabulary	1.1	2.1, 2.2	2.1	3.1	2.1	2.1
Fluency Read wordlists accurately, fluently	1.1–1.3	2.1, 2.2	2.1	3.1	2.1	2.1
Comprehension and Background						
Read Decodable Text		4				
Comprehension						
Recall Facts/Rules		4, IW				
Fact Review		3		1, IT	4, IT	
Informal Assessment						
Ongoing Comprehension Check		4, IT				
Story Reading						
Read/Reread Decodable Text	2	5	3	4	3	3
Teacher models fluency/expression			3			
Comprehension						
Predict/Confirm Prediction		5	3		3	
Recall Facts/Rules	2, IW	5, IW	3, IW	4, IW	3, IW	3, IW
Note Details	2, IW	5, IW	3, IW	4, IW	3, IW	3, IW
Visualize						
Make Connections	2			4, IW		
Draw Inferences			3	4	3	
Draw Conclusions	2, IW	5, IW	3, IW		3, IW	3, IW
Activate Prior Knowledge	2, IW	5, IW	3, IW	4, IW	3, IW	3, IW
Identify Cause/Effect				4, IW		
Determine Character Emotion, Motivation	2	5		4		3
Compare/Contrast	2, IW	5	3, IW			
Make Judgments	2		3	4		
Understanding Dialogue			3	4		
Sequencing					3	3, IW
Using Context to Confirm Meaning						
Study Skills						
Interpret Chart/Graph/Visual Aid		5				
Informal Assessment						
Ongoing Comprehension Check	2, IW	5, IW	3, IW	4, IW	3, IW	3, IW
Ongoing Decoding Accuracy	2, IT	5, IT	3, IT	4, IT	3, 5, IT	3, IT
Poem						
Paired Practice for Fluency						
Ongoing practice to build fluency	3	6	4	5		4
Independent Work / Workcheck						
Ongoing Informal Assessment	Workcheck	Workcheck	Workcheck	Workcheck	Workcheck, Activity	Workcheck
Special Project						after Lesson 106
Fact Game						
Formal Assessment						
Individual Fluency Checkout					5	
Mastery Test						
Spelling						
Sentence			103.2	104.2		106.2
Test					105	
Word Introduction						
Review		102.3	103.3	104.3		106.3
Reading Vocabulary	101.3					
Affixes						
Word Parts	101.2	102.2				
Spelling Rules	101.1	102.1	103.1	104.1		106.1

| Key: (for Teachers)   Ex 2.1 = Exercise 2, Column 1   IT = Individual Turns   IW = Independent Work

107	108	109	110	111	112	113	114	115
				1			1	
2, IW	1, IW	1, IW			1, IW	2, IW	2, IW	1, IW
	2.1	2.1		2.1	2.1	3.1		2.1
				2.2				
3.1							3.1	2.2
							3.1	
					2.2		3.2	
				IT	IT		IT	IT
3.1		2.1		2.1	2.1	3.1	3.2	2.1, 2.2
3.1	2.1	2.1		2.1, 2.2	2.1, 2.2	3.1	3.1, 3.2	2.1, 2.2
1, IT						1, IT		
4	3	3		3	3	4	4	3
		3		3				
4	3	3		3	3		4	
4, IW	3, IW	3, IW		3, IW	3, IW		4, IW	3, IW
4, IW	3, IW	3, IW		3, IW	3, IW	4, IW	4, IW	3, IW
		3				4	4	
					3			
4	3	3		3		4		
4, IW	3, IW	3, IW		3, IW	3, IW	4, IW	4, IW	3, IW
4, IW	3, IW	3, IW			3, IW	4, IW		3, IW
				3, IW	IW	IW		3, IW
						4, IW		
		3		3, IW			4, IW	3, IW
4	4	3			3		4	
		3			3	4		3
				3				
				3, IW				3, IW
4, IW	3, IW	3, IW		3, IW	3, IW	4, IW	4, IW	3, IW
4, IT	3, IT	3, IT	2	3, IT	3, IT	4, IT	4, IT	3, 4, IT
5	4	4		4	4	5	5	
Workcheck	Workcheck	Workcheck		Workcheck	Workcheck	Workcheck	Workcheck	Workcheck
				after Lesson 111				
			1					
			2					4
			3					
107.2		109.1			112.2		114.2	
			110					115
	108.1					113.1		
107.3	108.3	109.3		111.3	112.3	113.3	114.3	
		109.2		111.1	112.1			
	108.2			111.2		113.2		
107.1							114.1	

	116	117	118	119	120	121
Vocabulary						
Model Vocabulary Sentence		1				
Review	1, IW	2, IW	1, IW	1, IW		1, IW
Word Attack/Reading Words						
Decoding and Word Analysis						
Modeled Words	2.1	3.1		2.1		2.1
Words with Endings: –ed, –ly, –er, –y, –ing, –s			2.2			
Compound Words			2.1			
Multi-syllable Words	2.2	3.2				2.2
Words with Underlined Parts			2.1			2.2
Mixed Words/Review	2.3		2.3			2.3
Informal Assessment	IT	IT	IT			IT
Selection Vocabulary	2.1	3.1	2.2	2.1		2.1
Fluency Read wordlists accurately, fluently	2.1–2.3	3.1, 3.2	2.1–2.3	2.1		2.1–2.3
Comprehension and Background						
Read Decodable Text						
Comprehension						
Recall Facts/Rules						
Study Skills						
Interpret Chart/Graph/Visual Aid						
Fact Review						3
Informal Assessment						
Ongoing Comprehension Check						
Story Reading						
Read/Reread Decodable Text	3	4	3	3		4
Teacher models fluency/expression						
Comprehension						
Predict/Confirm Prediction	3		3			4
Recall Facts/Rules	3, IW	4, IW	3, IW	3, IW		4, IW
Note Details	3, IW	4, IW	3, IW	3, IW		4, IW
Visualize	3	4				
Make Connections			3			
Draw Inferences	3	4				4
Draw Conclusions	3, IW	4, IW	3, IW	3, IW		4, IW
Activate Prior Knowledge		4, IW	3, IW	3, IW		4, IW
Identify Cause/Effect		IW	IW	IW		
Determine Character Emotion, Motivation		4				
Compare/Contrast		IW	IW	IW		
Make Judgments	3					4
Understanding Dialogue	3					
Sequencing						
Using Context to Confirm Meaning				3		
Study Skills						
Interpret Chart/Graph/Visual Aid	3, IW	4, IW	IW	3, IW		4
Informal Assessment						
Ongoing Comprehension Check	3, IW	4, IW	3, IW	3, IW		4, IW
Ongoing Decoding Accuracy	3, IT	4, IT	3, IT	3, IT		4, IT
Poem						
Paired Practice for Fluency						
Ongoing practice to build fluency	4	5	4	4		5
Independent Work / Workcheck						
Ongoing Informal Assessment	Workcheck	Workcheck, Activity	Workcheck	Workcheck, Activity		Workcheck
Special Project	after Lesson 116					
Fact Game					1	
Formal Assessment						
Individual Fluency Checkout					2	
Out-of-Program Mastery Test					3	
Spelling						
Sentence	116.2	117.2	118.2	119.2		121.2
Test					120	
Word Introduction						
Review		117.3	118.3	119.3		121.3
Reading Vocabulary	116.3					
Word Parts				119.1		
Compounds						121.2
Spelling Rules	116.1	117.1	118.1			

122	123	124	125	126	127	128	129	130
1					1			
	1, IW	1, IW	1, IW			1, IW	1, IW	
2.1	2.1	2.2	2.1	1.2	2.1		2.1	
	2.2						2.3	
		2.1	2.2			2.1	2.2	
							2.2	
2.2			2.3	1.1				
IT	IT	IT	IT	IT			IT	
2.1	2.1	2.2	2.1	1.2	2.1	2.1	2.1	
2.1, 2.2	2.1, 2.2	2.1, 2.2	2.1–2.3	1.1, 1.2	2.1	2.1	2.1–2.3	
			3	2			3	
			IW	2			3, IW	
			3	2			3, IW	
	5							
			3, IT	2, IT			3, IT	
3	3	3	4	3	3	3	4	
3	3							
	3	3			3	3	4	
3, IW	3, IW	3, IW	4, IW	3, IW	3, IW	3, IW	IW	
3, IW	3, IW	3, IW	4, IW	3, IW	3, IW	3, IW	4, IW	
	3	3	4		3	3		
3	3		4, IW		3	3	4	
3, IW	3, IW	3, IW	4, IW	3, IW	3, IW	3, IW	4, IW	
3, IW	3, IW	IW	4, IW	3, IW	3, IW	3, IW		
3		3	4		3, IW			
						3	4	
3	3		4			3	3	
3					3	3	4	
3							4	
						3		
		3						
3, IW	3, IW	3, IW	4, IW	3, IW	3, IW			
3, IW	3, IW	3, IW	4, IW	3, IW	3, IW	3, IW	4, IW	
3, IT	3, IT	3, IT	4, 5, IT	3, IT	3, IT	3, IT	4, IT	2
4	4	4		4	4	4	5	
Workcheck, Activity	Workcheck, Activity	Workcheck, Activity	Workcheck	Workcheck, Activity	Workcheck	Workcheck	Workcheck, Activity	
								1
			5					2
								3
			125					130
							129.1	
122.3	123	124.3		126.3	127.3	128	129.3	
122.1				126.1	127.1		129.2	
122.2		124.2		126.2	127.2			
		124.1						

	131	132	133	134	135	136
Vocabulary						
Model Vocabulary Sentence		1				
Review	1, IW		1, IW	1, IW	1, IW	
Word Attack/Reading Words						
Decoding and Word Analysis						
Modeled Words	2.1	2.1	2.1	2.1	2.1	2.1
Words with Endings: –ed, –ly, –er, –y, –ing, –s		2.2				
Compound Words	2.2					
Words with Underlined Parts	2.2					
Mixed Words/Review	2.3	2.3	2.2	2.2, 2.3	2.2	
Informal Assessment	IT	IT	IT	IT	IT	
Selection Vocabulary	2.1	2.1	2.1	2.1	2.1	2.1
Fluency Read wordlists accurately, fluently	2.1–2.3	2.1–2.3	2.1, 2.2	2.1–2.3	2.1, 2.2	2.1
Comprehension and Background						
Read Decodable Text			3		3	
Comprehension						
Recall Facts/Rules				3, IW	3, IW	
Study Skills						
Interpret Chart/Graph/Visual Aid				3, IW	3, IW	
Fact Review						1, IT
Informal Assessment						
Ongoing Comprehension Check				3, IT	3, IT	
Story Reading						
Read/Reread Decodable Text	3	3	4	3	4	3
Teacher models fluency/expression						
Comprehension						
Predict/Confirm Prediction		3		3		
Recall Facts/Rules	3, IW	3, IW	4, IW	3, IW	4, IW	
Note Details	3, IW	3, IW	4, IW	3, IW	4, IW	3, IW
Visualize		3		3	4, IW	
Make Connections	3		4	3	4, IW	
Draw Inferences	3			3	4, IW	
Draw Conclusions	3, IW	IW	4, IW	3	4, IW	3
Activate Prior Knowledge	3, IW	3, IW	4, IW	3, IW	4, IW	3, IW
Identify Cause/Effect	3, IW	3, IW	4, IW	3	4, IW	
Determine Character Emotion, Motivation					4	3
Compare/Contrast	3, IW	3, IW	4, IW	3, IW		
Make Judgments		3		3	4	
Understanding Dialogue						
Reality/Fantasy						
Story Structure						
Using Context to Confirm Meaning						
Study Skills						
Interpret Chart/Graph/Visual Aid	3, IW	3, IW	4, IW	3, IW	IW	
Informal Assessment						
Ongoing Comprehension Check	3, IW	3, IW	4, IW	3, IW	4, IW	3, IW
Ongoing Decoding Accuracy	3, IT	3, IT	4, IT	3, IT	4, 5, IT	3, IT
Poem						
Paired Practice for Fluency						
Ongoing practice to build fluency	4	4	5	4		4
Independent Work / Workcheck						
Ongoing Informal Assessment	Workcheck	Workcheck, Activity	Workcheck, Activity	Workcheck	Workcheck	Workcheck
Special Project						
Fact Game						
Formal Assessment						
Individual Fluency Checkout					5	
Mastery Test						
Spelling						
Sentence						
Test					135	
Review	131.3	132.3	133	134.3		136.3
Word Parts	131.1	132.2		134.1, 134.2		136.1, 136.2
Compounds	131.2	132.2				

| Key: (for Teachers)   Ex 2.1 = Exercise 2, Column 1   IT = Individual Turns   IW = Independent Work

137	138	139	140
	1.2	1.1	
1.1			
	1.1		
	1.1		
1.2			
IT	IT		
	1.2	1.1	
1.1, 1.2	1.1, 1.2	1.1	
2	2	2	
2			
	2, IW	2, IW	
2, IW	2, IW	2, IW	
2	2	2	
2	2		
2	2	2	
2, IW	2, IW	2, IW	
	2, IW	2, IW	
	2, IW		
	2		
	2, IW	2, IW	
	2		
		2	
2	2	2	
		2	
	2, IW	2, IW	
2, IW	2, IW	2, IW	
2, IT	2, IT	2, IT	2
3	3	3	
Workcheck	Workcheck	Workcheck	
			after Lesson 140
			1
			2
			3
137.1		139.1	
			140
137.3	138	139.3	
137.2		139.2	